# IN THE PUBLIC INTEREST—III

**A REPORT BY
THE NATIONAL NEWS COUNCIL
1979 - 1983**

Additional copies of In the Public Interest—III are available at $10.00 each to cover the cost of production, mailing and handling.
Additional copies may be obtained by sending your check or money order to

The National News Council
805 Third Avenue
New York, NY 10022

The National News Council is a not-for-profit organization. Contributions may be sent to the above address.

---

Other Council publications:

In the Public Interest—I
    A Report by The National News Council-1973-75      $2.50
In the Public Interest—II
    A Report by The National News Council—1975-78      6.00
Protecting Two Vital Freedoms:
    Fair Trial and Free Press—1980      2.50
Covering Crime:
    How Much Press-Police Cooperation? How Little?—1981      2.50
After 'Jimmy's World':
    Tightening Up In Editing-1981      5.00
Who Said That?
    A Report on the Use of Unidentified Sources—1983      3.00

Single copies of Volumes I, II and III of In the Public Interest are available as a group at a special rate of $16.00.
Prices quoted for the prior Council publications listed reflect higher costs of mailing since original publication. For copies of the above reports, send check or money order to:

The National News Council
805 Third Avenue
New York, NY 10022

# IN THE PUBLIC INTEREST—III

## A Report By
## THE NATIONAL NEWS COUNCIL
## 1979 - 1983

## With an Index
## of Complaints
## 1973 - 1983

Published by **The National News Council, Inc.**
805 Third Avenue, New York, N.Y. 10022
© 1984 **The National News Council, Inc.**
This report covers the period January 1, 1979, through July 31, 1983.

**Library of Congress Cataloging In Publication Data**

National News Council (U.S.)
        In the public interest—III
           "This report covers the period January 1, 1979 through July 31, 1983."
        Includes index.
           1. Journalistic ethics—United States. 2. Journalism—Social aspects—United States. 3. Liberty of the press—United States. 4. National News Council (U.S.)
1. Title
PN4888.E8N37    1983    174'.9097    83-61764
ISBN 0-914371-00-2

This publication made possible in part
by grants from the
W. H. Brady Foundation
and
The Chicago Sun-Times
Charities Fund

# Contents

# IN THE PUBLIC INTEREST—III

PAGE

President's Foreword—A Personal View . . . . . . . . . . . . . . . . . . . . . . xiii
Complaints Handled by the Council. . . . . . . . . . . . . . . . . . . . . . . . . . 1
Defending Press Freedom . . . . . . . . . . . . . . . . . . . . . . . . . . . . . . . . 500
Contributors to the Council . . . . . . . . . . . . . . . . . . . . . . . . . . . . . . 564
The Council's Rules of Procedure . . . . . . . . . . . . . . . . . . . . . . . . . . 567
The Council's By-Laws . . . . . . . . . . . . . . . . . . . . . . . . . . . . . . . . . . 571
How to Complain to the Council . . . . . . . . . . . . . . . . . . . . . . . . . . . 580
Index of Complaints—1973–1983 . . . . . . . . . . . . . . . . . . . . . . . . . . 581

# The Council

# Its Members, Advisers, Staff

## MEMBERS

| | |
|---|---|
| Lucy Wilson Benson | Chairman. Former Under Secretary of State; former President, League of Women Voters of the U.S. |
| Richard S. Salant | President and Chief Executive Officer. Former President, CBS News; former Vice Chairman, NBC. |
| Elie Abel | Vice-Chairman. Harry and Norman Chandler Professor of Journalism, Stanford University. |
| S. William Scott | Treasurer. President and Chief Operating Officer, Satellite News Channels. |
| H. Brandt Ayers | Editor and Publisher, *The Anniston Star.* |
| Edward W. Barrett | Founder and former Publisher, *Columbia Journalism Review*; former Dean, Graduate School of Journalism, Columbia University. |
| Derrick A. Bell, Jr. | Dean, School of Law, University of Oregon. |
| Midge Decter | Author; Executive Director, Committee for the Free World. |
| William H. Hornby | Senior Editor, *The Denver Post;* former President, American Society of Newspaper Editors. |

| Barry Bing-<br>ham, Sr. | Chairman of the Board, Courier-Journal & Louisville<br>Times Co. |
|---|---|
| William H.<br>Brady, Jr. | Chairman, W.H. Brady Co., Milwaukee. |
| Joan Ganz<br>Cooney | President, Children's Television Workshop, New<br>York. |
| Julian<br>Goodman | Former Chairman, NBC. |
| Norman E.<br>Isaacs | Educator; former President, American Society of<br>Newspaper Editors. |
| Robert B.<br>McKay | Director, Aspen Institute Program on Justice, Society<br>and the Individual. |
| William A.<br>Rusher | Publisher, *National Review*. |

## FORMER MEMBERS

The following former members served on the Council during parts of the 1979-1983 period covered by this report. They are identified according to their affiliations at the time of Council service.

| Jeffrey Bell | Consultant; Visiting Professor of Politics, Eagleton<br>Institute, Rutgers University. |
|---|---|
| William H.<br>Brady, Jr. | Chairman, William H. Brady Co., Milwaukee. |
| Joan Ganz<br>Cooney | President, Children's Television Workshop. |
| Irving<br>Dillard | Formerly Editorial Page Editor, *St. Louis Post-<br>Dispatch*. |

| | |
|---|---|
| Albert Gore | Former U.S. Senator from Tennessee; Chairman of the Board, Island Creek Coal Company, Lexington, Kentucky. |
| Edith Green | Former Congresswoman from Oregon. |
| Dorothy R. Height | President, National Council of Negro Women. |
| Molly Ivins | Co-Editor, *Texas Observer*. |
| Henry L. Lacayo | Assistant to the President, United Automobile Workers. |
| Walter J. Leonard | President, Fisk University. |
| R. Peter Straus | President, Straus Communications, Inc., New York. |
| Roger J. Traynor | First Chairman of the Council; former Chief Justice, California Supreme Court. |

## STAFF

| | |
|---|---|
| William B. Arthur | Executive Director. Former President, Society of Professional Journalists, Sigma Delta Chi; former Chairman, American Society of Magazine Editors. |
| Richard P. Cunningham | Associate Director, Secretary to the Council. Former Reader's Representative, the *Minneapolis Tribune*. |
| A. H. Raskin | Associate Director. Former Assistant Editorial Page Editor, *The New York Times*. |
| Clifford Chase | Editorial Assistant. |

# President's Foreword

# A Personal View

This volume, embodying all formal decisions and actions of The National News Council from 1979 to July 31, 1983, is the third in the continuing series. *In the Public Interest* covered August 1, 1973 to July 31, 1975. *In The Public Interest—II* covered August 1, 1975 through 1978. This report, thus, completes the record of the first decade of the Council's life.

While the Council's decisions and actions reported in these three volumes speak for themselves, and permit the reader to reach his or her own conclusions on what the Council has done and whether or not it has acted wisely, it is an appropriate time for me to take stock in this Foreword. In so doing, I note my various angles of vision during the relevant period: I was a member of The Twentieth Century Fund Task Force which in 1973 recommended the creation of The National News Council. From mid-1976 to September 1980, I was a member of the Council. For the remaining periods of the past decade, I was something of a defendant before the Council since I was, until 1979, President of CBS News, and thus had responsibility for some of the broadcasts about which fairness and accuracy complaints were decided by Council, some finding the complaints warranted, and some not. And for a short time—only since May 1, 1983—I have been President and Chief Executive Officer of the Council.

The Twentieth Century Task Force Report stated that the core of the Council idea was "to make press freedom more secure by providing an independent forum for debate about media responsibility and performance, so that such debate need not take place in government hearing rooms or on the political campaign trail." The report recognized that the Council was "not a panacea for the ills of the press." It warned that the proposed group "will not resolve all the problems facing the print and broadcast media, nor will it answer all the criticisms voiced by the public and the politicians." Ten years of the Council's life establish the accuracy of these warnings, of the reality of the need for patience and of modest expectations.

In 1975, the foundations which largely funded the early years of the Council's life set up an Evaluation Committee to appraise the first two years' work "to determine if the experiment was worth continuing." The Evaluation Committee concluded that the Council's "importance to the national body politic is such that every effort should be made not only to continue The Council, but actively to seek, deepen and broaden the opening pathway which it has hewed out." At the same time, the Committee reported that "a period of ten years will be required before a sound evaluation of the permanent usefulness of The Council can be made."

Four years later, in 1979, in the Foreword to Part II of this series, Norman Isaacs, then the Chairman and Chief Executive Officer of the Council, to whom the Council owes so much, wrote that "On the basis of where we now stand, we find much hope for the belief that four years hence the record of the decade's work will be such that both public and press will be united in the conviction that The National News Council has proved itself to be an essential part of the communications fabric of the United States."

Those four years are now up: The decade has been completed. These have been neither the best nor the worst of years. But Norman Isaacs' hope has surely fallen short of realization. An assessment of the ten years which the Evaluation Committee called for compels my personal conclusion that the Council's "importance to the national body politic," however clear conceptually, as I believe it is, has not been established as a reality.

Most, but not all, of the obstacles to the Council's greater success have been external. Important elements of the press—and most notably the *New York Times*, which often serves as a bellwether—have been hostile, looking on the Council as superfluous at best, and as a threat to press freedom at worst. An even larger segment of the press has been indifferent, and has ignored the Council. Yet, unless the Council can earn the respect of the press—or most of it—through recognition of the contribution that the existence of such an independent review body makes to media credibility, its purposes are defeated at the threshold.

This is so for a number of reasons. First, the Council can, and should, have no sanctions other than the persuasiveness and good sense of its actions. In contrast to all other nations where press councils of one kind or another have been established—with varying degrees of success—in the United States, there is only the carrot, and never—happily—the stick of government legislation or other intrusion by force as the alternative to self-regulation. It is for this basic, and fortunate, reason that our News Council must make it on its own, with no threat of Government alternative.

Second, the "public" is too amorphous a target, and the Council's resources necessarily are too limited, to depend only on public demand to assure the Council's success or to force—or shame—the press to accept the Council's actions and decisions. For one important and unavoidable reason, as a practical matter the public cannot know about the Council *except through the press*. Without press acceptance through the press' own conviction that the Council is serving the cause of freedom and journalistic excellence, the Council is cut off at the pass. And so the most direct, the most effective, the surest, the quickest road to a higher level of press performance is the press' own road.

I am not sure that these truths, as I see them now, were fully recognized by the Task Force or the Council at the beginning of the Council's life. Rather, it was thought that by establishing the Council as a place for the public to go for a second look when any member of the public felt that a news story was unfair or inaccurate, the crisis of public confidence in the press could be ameliorated. At least some of the hostility and distrust of the public toward the press arise out of the public's frustration that it must, except for the doubtful remedy of libel cases, take its complaints of unfairness and inaccuracy to the very entity which the member of the public is accusing—and more often than not is turned away with no answer or with nothing more thoughtful than "we stand by our story." The Council's consideration of the public's complaints of unfairness and inaccuracy would, it was thought, serve not only to relieve those frustrations and bitterness by providing a place for the public to go, but could also serve to explain to the public the workings of the press and to provide an objective examination of the issues involved in each case. These examinations might be of benefit not only to the particular news organization involved but to other news organizations.

But the Council's ten years of activities have not created a public constituency which can demand acceptance of the Council by the press. While over the ten years of its life, the Council recorded 1,045 formal complaints, of which 217 qualified under its purview and were acted upon, given the reach of print and broadcast news and the 200 million-plus population of the United States, these are unimpressive figures. But they are not surprising, since even voracious consumers of news—print and broadcast—have never heard of the Council.

And so the Council has been faced with problems. It has lacked visibility; it has been hobbled by lack of funds and far too small a staff assigned to do too much.*

It is not suprising, then—indeed it is inevitable—that these have not been the best of years. But it is too soon to sink in the slough of despond. For it is equally true that these have not been the worst of years. A national news council, for this country, was a novel concept which by any realistic analysis could not have expected quick press acceptance. Nothing is more traditional—and properly so—for the American press, which alone among all American free enterprises, has a special Constitutional protection against government intrusion, to look with suspicion at any proposal which seems to threaten, however remotely, intrusion by any outsiders into the reporting and editing process. Historically, the American press has initially and violently reacted against the notion of anybody's looking over its shoulder.

But I believe that sober second thoughts, and ten years is not too short a time for such thoughts, should, and, if we do our job properly, will persuade conscientious, thoughtful and open-minded editors that an objective, expert body, without sanctions, whose functions are to examine complaints, to speak out on press freedom issues, and to analyze recurring problems of journalistic ethics is a protection, not a derogation, of press freedom. It is encouraging then, and cause for hope, that the ten years have seen concrete signs of increased press support. During the first three years of the Council's life, only one news organization, The Minneapolis Star and Tribune Company, contributed to the funding of the Council. Today, 41 news organizations contribute.

But above all, I remain as persuaded now as I was ten years ago when I enthusiastically joined in the recommendation of the Task Force that the Council be created, that the Council represents a sound, important and viable concept. Despite the inherent obstacles; despite the fact that the very notion of the Council ran so deeply contrary to the automatic instincts of the press; despite the shortfall in funds and in staff, the Council has accomplished something very significant: It has survived. And it has the enormous advantage of a foundation of hands-on experi-

*The British Press Council, which has been severely criticized for being understaffed and underfinanced, has a budget almost twice The National News Council's and a staff 50 percent larger than ours. Yet the British Press Council serves a population less than one-fourth the American population, and it deals only with hundreds of newspapers—daily and weekly—while there are over 1,700 daily newspapers in this country, about a thousand television stations and 10,000 radio stations.

ence on which it can build: It has the invaluable benefit of ten years of trial and error, and of experience from which it has learned.

Over the first ten years, the Council has produced a body of sound case findings and a collection of useful studies of journalistic issues. It has provided cases for the study of ethics in journalism schools, and as a result a decade's worth of journalism students have started their careers aware, and perhaps more accepting than their forbears, of news councils and other mechanisms designed to promote accountability in the news media. At the same time, the Council's activities have not borne out the fears of some editors that it would design and impose a code of journalistic practice; that it would detract attention from threats to the freedom of the press; or that it would foster a public attitude that was receptive to governmental interference in the press.

I refuse to believe that a concept so important and so sound as that which gave birth to the News Council cannot be brought to reality on the basis of its ten years of experience.

I am persuaded, therefore, that in the period that lies ahead, the Council can indeed, and will, find ways to translate the vital and valid concept which underlies its creation into the reality of its "importance to the national body politic"—and to press freedom and responsibility. It is imperative that the effort be renewed and continued.

Richard S. Salant

# Part 1

# Complaints Handled By The Council

"You *can* fight city hall. Even when it's a newspaper," the headline said over an article in the July, 1980, issue of the magazine, *medical economics*. The sub-title read: "When this doctor's fees were erroneously inflated in a news story, his demands for retraction were ignored. But a watchdog agency got him even more."

The article was by-lined by Dr. Gary A. Hogge of Louisville, Kentucky, a general practitioner. On October 14, 1979, Dr. Hogge read a front-page report in that day's *Courier-Journal* on fees charged by various medical specialists in the Louisville area, and at the top of a listing of fees paid to general practitioners he saw his name. His fee was given as $35.00 for an initial office visit. Two other doctors were listed at the same figure.

"I didn't know whether the other guys actually charged $35 for an initial office OV," Dr. Hogge wrote, "but I sure knew I didn't. At the time, I was charging $15 for an initial OV and $12 for any future visits of reasonable length, with a slight additional charge for longer visits."

"My first thought was concern for the impact the article might have on my patients," the doctor wrote. "I really didn't think it would cause me any material loss, but I could see them saying to themselves (and others), 'That greedy s.o.b.' Indeed, that same morning several nurses and technicians—some of whom were my patients and should have known better—made supposedly kidding remarks such as, 'You're really gouging 'em, ain'tcha, Doc?' They left no doubt in my mind that they believed what they had read; after all, hadn't it been printed in the *newspaper*?"

What followed in Dr. Hogge's search for redress is reported in the pages that follow under Complaint No. 173: Dr. Gary A. Hogge against *The Courier-Journal* (Page 113).

Complaint No. 173 is one of 217 complaints which have gone through

1

full processing by The National News Council. It was found warranted, and *The Courier-Journal*, a newspaper with a national reputation for accountability to the public which it serves, reported the Council's finding in a Page 1 story. This was followed later by a column written by the paper's executive editor in which he said ". . . I accept the Council's decision without quibble. I apologize to Dr. Hogge for the error, which was a collective one and shouldn't be ascribed to a single individual."

"Being, by nature, somewhat cynical, I was surprised to get anything near this much redress of injustice," Dr. Hogge wrote. "It shows that if you're right—and willing—you can fight 'bad press'—and even win."

Shortly before the Council began its operations in 1973, its first chairman, the late Roger J. Traynor, former Chief Justice of the California Supreme Court, declared in an interview "If the media have been inaccurate or unfair, why should they be immune from criticism? If a person has been aggrieved why should his grievance not be exposed and redressed at least to the extent that the findings of an impartial and reputable body such as a press council, dedicated to fairness and objectivity, are given publicity? Why should the media not be vindicated when they are unfairly attacked?" In the ten years that have elapsed since Justice Traynor posed these questions, the Council has found 33 percent of the complaints that have been brought before it warranted—as occurred in Complaint No. 173—or partially warranted. Fifty percent, however, have been found unwarranted, and 17 percent were either dismissed or withdrawn. Of the complaints reported in this volume, from 1979 to the present, 59 percent were found warranted in whole or in part, 33 percent unwarranted, and 8 percent dismissed. These latter percentages represent a significant change from the earlier patterns, principally attributable to the increased clarity that developed over the years in the purview of the Council. This enabled the Council's staff to focus its analysis on cases that raised issues of national importance to journalism and also to assist complainants in obtaining corrective action from news organizations without the necessity for formal proceedings before the Council.

Perhaps the most challenging complaint ever presented to the Council involved a threshold question that was at least as difficult for the Council and the news organization affected as any of the tangled issues in the case itself. This was the complaint brought by ten members of the journalism faculty at Howard University against *The Washington Post* (Complaint No. 188, Page 244) in 1980 in connection with its publication of a

2

fabricated story entitled "Jimmy's World" that had been awarded a Pulitzer Prize.

Whether to accept the complaint at all constituted a problem for the Council because of its deeply held conviction that its monitorial role should be confined to situations in which a news organization has failed to take any independent corrective action when its attention is called to instances of possible unfairness or inaccuracy. In this case, on discovering belatedly that it had been hoodwinked by one of its reporters, *The Post* not only insisted on the reporter's resignation and on return of the Pulitzer Prize, but instructed its own ombudsman to undertake an investigation intended to give its readers the fullest possible information about everything that had contributed to the hoax. The 18,000-word self-indictment that appeared in *The Post* as a result of this inquiry was a remarkably candid and comprehensive assertion by a major newspaper of its duty to be accountable to the community. It was accompanied by an editorial apology for the many lapses from *The Post's* own standards that had gone into the episode.

Nevertheless, the Council agreed with the filers of the complaint that the miscarriages were of such dimensions in their implications for all journalism that no self-examination could be considered adequate. The publishers of *The Post*, to their credit, concurred in the judgment that an impartial outside investigation was in order and the Council received total cooperation at all levels of the newspaper, despite many features of the complaint which *The Post* considered overdrawn. The Council applauded the basic report by the ombudsman as a model attempt at total disclosure, but found that *The Post* had been derelict in ways not considered in the report, notably the lack of human concern for the fate of the 8-year-old boy whom it believed to be a narcotics addict mortally endangered. On the basis of the Council's own assessment, plus opinions it obtained from thirty of the country's foremost editors, the Council's decision went beyond the specifics of the complaint to enumerate twelve editorial practices in need of more rigorous observance by all news organizations for better journalistic performance. Later, the Council issued a white paper entitled "After 'Jimmy's World': Tightening Up In Editing" that contained, in addition to Complaint No. 188, investigative reports by Council staff on journalistic hoaxes in general, on the defects the case indicated in Pulitzer Prize procedures and on the functioning of ombudsmen as readers' representatives in the operation of their news organizations.

Through its publication of widely circulated white papers, such as

"After 'Jimmy's World,'" dealing with commonly recurring and important issues of press ethics and journalistic policies, the Council has begun to assume a much more extensive clearing-house function for publishers, editors, broadcasters and schools of journalism on matters of moment to them and the community. Subjects dealt with have included the relations between the media and law-enforcement agencies, the use of unidentifed sources and the disagreements which occur between the bar and the press in criminal trial procedures. The Council intends to broaden its program for such white papers in the future. At the time this volume of "In the Public Interest" was in preparation, white papers were being prepared on the identification of victims of crime and on ethical issues involved in outside activities by journalists. Others were under consideration.

In 1981, the Council began publication of a monthly newsletter entitled "Excerpts," which culls highlights from columns written by the 31 ombudsmen, or reader/viewer representatives throughout the nation and in Canada who are charged with the responsibility of considering complaints from those seeking redress for alleged inaccuracies or unfairness in news reports. "Excerpts" is edited and published by the Council on behalf of the Organization of News Ombudsmen, and is distributed not only to that organization's members, but also to journalism schools and others who have expressed an interest.

In order to provide prompt comment on fast-breaking journalistic issues between News Council meetings, the Council authorized its president, Richard S. Salant, to issue statements as the need arose over his own name. Under that mandate in his first months as president, Mr. Salant issued press statements:

● Criticizing the National Highway Traffic Safety Administration for tampering with a car to produce accident film, and criticizing television news people for failing to ask the questions that would have revealed that the car was tampered with.

● Warning that news organizations might become reluctant to conduct self-examinations of news practices if the courts decreed that the results of such examinations must be made available to plaintiffs in libel suits.

● Criticizing a federal appellate judge's decision that opinion is not immune from libel unless it is accompanied by a full and accurate account of the material background facts.

● Criticizing as violation of the First Amendment a Massachusetts judge's order prohibiting the New Bedford *Standard-Times* from publishing an interview with a rape suspect.

● Supporting the Akron, Ohio, *Beacon Journal* in its challenge to the

constitutionality of an Ohio law allowing anyone claiming injury resulting from an erroneous news story to write a retraction which the newspaper must publish unedited in the same type and position as the original
report.

The following is a tabulation of complaints handled by the full Council from August 1, 1973 through July 31, 1983.

| | Total Complaints | Complaints Found Unwarranted | Complaints Found Warranted | Complaints Partially Warranted (category new; begun 6/13/80) | Complaints Dismissed | Complaints Withdrawn |
|---|---|---|---|---|---|---|
| Wire Services | 19 | 12 | 4 | | 3 | |
| TV Networks | 76 | 49 | 15 | 4 | 7 | 1 |
| TV Stations | 8 | 5 | 1 | 1 | 1 | |
| Radio Networks | 3 | 2 | | | 1 | |
| Magazines | 29 | 8 | 14 | 3 | 4 | |
| Newspapers | 61 | 27 | 18 | 9 | 6 | 1 |
| News Services, Syndicates | 27 | 11 | 5 | 1 | 10 | |
| Columnists, Self-Syndicated | 1 | | 1 | | | |
| Other* | 8 | 2 | 1 | | 5 | |
| Total | 232** | 116 | 59 | 18 | 37 | 2 |

\* Different types of news organizations cited with the same complaint.

\** Includes 7 complaints involving 2 separate decisions and 1 involving 3 separate decisions.

This listing includes all complaints handled by the full Council from August 1, 1973, through July 31, 1983. The complete texts of complaints handled from August 1, 1973, through July 31, 1975 (Complaints No. 1 through 61), were included in a Council report— "In The Public Interest" covering that period of the Council's history. The complete texts of complaints handled from August 1, 1975, through December 31, 1978 (Complaints No. 62 through 153) were included in the Council's report "In The Public Interest—II." The complete texts of complaints handled from January 1, 1979, through July 31, 1983 (Complaints No. 154 through 217) are included in this report— "In The Public Interest—III."

## NATIONAL NEWS COUNCIL COMPLAINTS

| COMPLAINT NO. | COMPLAINANT | IDENTIFICATION NO. | SUBJECT AND NEWS ORGANIZATION | DATE FILED | ACTION |
|---|---|---|---|---|---|
| 1 | Mrs. Thomas Donovan | 74-73 | Copley News Service (abortion coverage) | 12/20/73 | Unwarranted (1/28/74) |
| 2 | Howard Snow | 22-74 | The Charlotte News (Letters to the Editor) | 2/12/74 | Dismissed (1/28/74) |
| 3 | Virginia Van Liew | 63-73 | NBC-TV (Agnew's life style) | 12/10/73 | Unwarranted (3/24/74) |
| 4 | Tom G. Cote | 65-73 | Tom Braden (firing of Nixon critics) | 12/11/73 | Unwarranted (5/10/74 |

| COMPLAINT NO. | COMPLAINANT | IDENTIFICATION NO. | SUBJECT AND NEWS ORGANIZATION | DATE FILED | ACTION |
|---|---|---|---|---|---|
| 5 | Tom G. Cote | 66-73 | Charles Bartlett (Agnew investigation leaks) | 12/11/73 | Unwarranted (3/24/74) |
| 6 | Horace P. Rowley | 57-73 | Corporation for Public Broadcasting (Kawaida Towers) | 11/20/73 | Unwarranted (6/25/73) |
| 7 | Accuracy In Media | 58-73 | Newsweek (Slaughterhouse in Santiago) | 12/1/73 | Upheld (3/25/74) |
| 8 | Carl E. Anderson | 70-73 | ABC, et al. (election projections) | 12/14/73 | Dismissed (1/28/78) |
| 9 | Warren F. Kelley | 71-73 | The Press (mental patients) | 12/16/73 | Dismissed (1/28/74) |
| 10 | A. Wood Hardin | 73-73 | CBS-TV (military alert) | 12/19/73 | Unwarranted (1/28/74) |
| 11 | M.B. Schnapper | 2-74 | The Press (officials' gifts) | 1/3/74 | Unwarranted (3/25/74) |
| 12 | Robert A. Edwards | 8-74 | Mutual Broadcasting System (news directive) | 1/22/74 | Unwarranted (9/24/74) |
| 13 | Richard N. Thayer | 25-74 | CBS-TV (militant Indians) | 2/16/74 | Unwarranted (3/24/74) |
| 14 | Mary Gaumond | 29-74 | Washington Star-News (anti-administration bias) | 2/18/74 | Dismissed (3/24/74) |
| 15 | William G. Howe | 24-74 | NBC-TV (abortion rallies) | 2/15/74 | Unwarranted (3/25/74) |

| | | | | |
|---|---|---|---|---|
| 16 | Andrew Aguilar | *The New York Times* (Mexican Americans—ad) | 3/7/74 | Dismissed (3/24/74) |
| 17 | Gene De Vaux | *The New York Times* (Anthony Lewis columns) | 2/19/74 | Dismissed (3/24/74) |
| 18 | Kenneth L. Rossman | NBC-TV (Huntsville holiday) | 2/19/74 | Upheld (5/10/74) |
| 19 | Alphonse E. Champagne | NBC-TV, et al. (Nixon/Agnew commentary) | 2/20/74 | Unwarranted (3/24/74) |
| 20 | Elizabeth Teter | ABC-TV, et al. (instant analysis) | 2/25/74 | Dismissed (5/10/74) |
| 21 | Accuracy In Media, ex rel. Lang | *The New York Times* (herbicides study) | 3/3/74 | Upheld (6/25/74) |
| 22 | C.T. Budny | *The Philadelphia Inquirer* (carrot juice) | 2/18/74 | Dismissed (3/24/74) |
| 23 | Theodore W. Johnson | Capitol Hill News Service (Sen. Gravel rating) | 1/22/74 | Dismissed (9/24/74) |
| 24 | Joseph Behr | NBC-TV (Kissinger quote) | 1/30/74 | Unwarranted (5/10/74) |
| 25 | Mobil Oil Corporation | ABC-TV (oil documentary—Mobil) | 3/22/74 | Unwarranted (5/10/74) |
| 26 | John M. Ashbrook, ex rel. Martin | *The New York Times* (Ambassador Martin cablegram) | 3/20/74 | Unwarranted (9/24/74) |
| 27 | Walter De Vault | Copley News Service (canning industry) | 4/2/74 | Resolved (5/2/74) |

| COMPLAINT NO. | COMPLAINANT | IDENTIFICATION NO. | SUBJECT AND NEWS ORGANIZATION | DATE FILED | ACTION |
|---|---|---|---|---|---|
| 28 | John F. Carter | 66-74 | *The Wall Street Journal* (Brokers Diversified, Inc.) | 4/4/74 | Unwarranted (12/10/74) |
| 29 | Roy Traband | 62-74 | CBS-TV (firearms legislation) | 3/29/74 | Dismissed (6/25/74) |
| 30 | Dr. Hettie H. Fisher | 69-74 | Associated Press (Harris poll) | 4/11/74 | Unwarranted (9/24/74) |
| 31 | Lawrence V. Cott | 72-74 | *Time* (Chilean Junta) | 4/21/74 | Dismissed (6/25/74) |
| 32 | Dr. Ellie Shneour | 83-74 | Griffin Productions (Merv Griffin Show) | 5/2/74 | Dismissed (6/24/74) |
| 33 | Dr. Abraham B. Bergman | 90-74 | Knight News Service (SIDS) | 5/20/74 | Upheld (9/24/74) |
| 34 | Roger Pilan, et al. | 86-74 | CBS-TV (The Mysterious Alert) | 5/7/74 | Unwarranted (6/25/74) |
| 35 | William Holt | 96-74 | CBS-TV (millionaire friends) | 5/28/74 | Unwarranted (6/25/74) |
| 36 | William Holt | 100-74 | CBS-TV (milk fund deal) | 6/5/74 | Unwarranted (6/25/74) |
| 37 | William Holt | 101-74 | CBS-TV (Santarelli resignation) | 6/5/74 | Unwarranted (9/24/74) |
| 38 | Kenneth L. Rossman | 103-74 | *The Huntsville Times* (editorial cartoons) | 6/13/74 | Dismissed (6/25/74) |

| # | Name | No. | Source | Date | Decision |
|---|------|-----|--------|------|----------|
| 39 | Carter W. Kirk | 81-74 | Associated Press (Western land developer) | 5/2/74 | Dismissed (6/25/74) |
| 40 | G.R. Brainard | 106-74 | Associated Press (Douglas speech) | 6/26/74 | Dismissed (9/24/74) |
| 41 | William Zevenbergen | 107-74 | Associated Press (federal wages) | 6/26/74 | Unwarranted (9/24/74) |
| 42 | Thomas Noreuil | 109-74 | Associated Press (Sir Henniker-Heaton) | 6/30/74 | Dismissed (9/24/74) |
| 43 | Mrs. Robert H. Smith | 114-74 | ABC-TV (Billy Graham statement) | 7/17/74 | Unwarranted (9/24/74) |
| 44 | William F. Gavin | 120-74 | *The New York Times* (Roman Catholics) | 8/1/74 | Unwarranted (12/10/74) |
| 45 | John F. Carter | 125-74 | *The Wall Street Journal* (Brokers Diversified, Inc.) | 8/13/74 | Unwarranted (12/10/74) |
| 46 | Accuracy In Media | 129-74 | Jack Anderson (Police Academy) | 9/7/74 | Upheld (2/4/75) |
| 47 | John Haydon | 138-74 | NBC-TV (American Samoa) | 11/11/74 | Upheld (4/8/75) |
| 48 | James Swift | 135-74 | *The New York Times* (supertankers) | 10/29/74 | Dismissed (6/17/75) |
| 49 | Sue Porter, et al. | 136-74 | Associated Press, et al. (pesticide ban) | 10/29/74 | Unwarranted (12/10/74) |
| 50 | Earle A. Giddens, ex rel. Institute for American Strategy | 142-74 | CBS-TV (IAS study) | 12/2/74 | Dismissed (4/8/75) |

| COMPLAINT NO. | COMPLAINANT | IDENTIFICATION NO. | SUBJECT AND NEWS ORGANIZATION | DATE FILED | ACTION |
|---|---|---|---|---|---|
| 51 | Guy Gran (Indochina Resource Center) | 2-75 | Evans and Novak (Vietnam aid) | 1/6/75 | Dismissed (6/17/75) |
| 52 | Washington Observer Newsletter | 144-74 | Associated Press, et al. (Soviet territorial demands) | 12/7/74 | Unwarranted (4/7/75) |
| 53 | Liberty Lobby | 143-74 | Associated Press, et al. (Bilderberg Conference) | 12/2/74 | Unwarranted (2/4/75) |
| 54 | Roger Pilon, et al. | 147-74 | CBS-TV (busing demonstrations) | 12/15/74 | Unwarranted (2/4/75) |
| 55 | The Village Voice | 5-75 | The New York Times (attribution) | 1/23/75 | Unwarranted (2/4/75) |
| 56 | Maurice B. Frank | 147-74 | Newhouse News Service (Mansion House) | 12/20/74 | Upheld (11/11/75) |
| 57 | Harry Connor, ex rel. Sheridan | 9-75 | The Washington Post (U.S.S. Monitor) | 2/27/75 | Unwarranted (6/17/75) |
| 58 | William Holt | 15-75 | ABC-TV, CBS-TV (President's speech follow-up) | 4/10/75 | Unwarranted (6/17/75) |
| 59 | Accuracy In Media | 22-75 | The New York Times (bloodbath allegations) | 4/27/75 | Unwarranted (6/17/75) |
| 60 | Dr. William G. Howe | 24-75 | CBS-TV (The IQ Myth) | 4/29/75 | Unwarranted (6/17/75) |
| 61 | American Jewish Congress | 33-75 | CBS-TV (60 Minutes) | 5/28/75 | Withdrawn (2/10/76) |

| No. | Complainant | Case | Media (Subject) | Date | Ruling |
|---|---|---|---|---|---|
| 62 | Dr. Abraham Bergman | 26-75 | Associated Press, et al. (SIDS) | 5/5/75 | Unwarranted (9/16/75) |
| 63 | Gareth Porter (IRC) | 37-75 | ABC-TV (Howard K. Smith) | 6/6/75 | Unwarranted (9/16/75) |
| 64 | Accuracy In Media | 39-75 | CBS-TV (Castro, Cuba and the U.S.A.) | 6/12/75 | Unwarranted (9/16/75) |
| 65 | Consul of Monaco | 40-75 | National Star (Grace-Rainier Split) | 6/13/75 | Upheld (9/17/75) |
| 66 | Pennsylvania Program for Women and Girl Offenders, Inc. | 16-75 | The National Observer (female crime rate) | 4/11/75 | Upheld (9/17/75) |
| 67 | Gareth Porter (IRC) | 36-75 | CBS-TV (bloodbath allegations) | 6/6/75 | Unwarranted (9/17/75) |
| 68 | The Wolper Organization, Inc. | 34-75 | The New York Times (O'Connor review (Wolper)) | 6/26/75 | Unwarranted (11/11/75) |
| 69 | Dr. Stephen Barrett | 67-75 | Chicago Sun-Times–Chicago Daily News News Service (chiropractic) | 10/14/75 | Unwarranted (11/11/75) |
| 70 | Judy Clark | 69-75 | CBS-TV (racism/busing) | 11/3/75 | Unwarranted (11/11/75) |
| 71 | Roger Pilon | 55-75 | CBS-TV (Panama Canal) | 8/10/75 | Unwarranted (1/20/76) |
| 72 | Dr. Henry Fetterman | 73-75 | Associated Press (malpractice suit) | 11/19/75 | Unwarranted (1/20/76) |

| COMPLAINT NO. | COMPLAINANT | IDENTIFICATION NO. | SUBJECT AND NEWS ORGANIZATION | DATE FILED | ACTION |
| --- | --- | --- | --- | --- | --- |
| 73 | Audrey Miles | 68A-75 | Reuters (weapons theft) | 10/30/75 | Unwarranted (3/30/76) |
| 74 | Roy E. Traband | 79-75 | CBS-TV (bonus marchers) | 12/28/75 | Upheld (3/30/76) |
| 75 | Judith Moyers, et al. | 1A-76 | *The Washington Post* (Reid speech) | 1/6/76 | Upheld (3/30/76) |
| 76 | Thomas Duffy | 5-76 | ABC-TV (IRA denial) | 2/5/76 | Unwarranted (3/30/76) |
| 77 | Dr. Stephen Barrett | 70-75 | De Toledano/Copley News Service (fluoridation) | 11/5/75 | Dismissed (3/30/76) |
| 78 | Henry J. Bender | 12-76 | Associated Press/ *St. Paul Pioneer Press* (elderly budget cuts) | 2/27/76 | Unwarranted (AP) (3/30/76) Upheld (St. Paul) (3/30/76) |
| 79 | Donald L. Nordeen | 27-76 | CBS-TV (auto repair costs) | 3/15/76 | Unwarranted (6/15/76) |
| 80 | National Council of Irish Americans | 11-76 | *The New York Times* (Irish relief funds (Swartz)) | 2/9/76 | Unwarranted (6/15/76) |
| 81 | Fran Lee | 30-76 | Cleveland Amory (veterinarian (Amory)) | 3/7/76 | Dismissed (6/15/76) |
| 82 | Morris H. Kramer | 32-76 | *The New York Times* | 3/25/76 | Unwarranted |

| No. | Complainant | Case No. | Media (Subject) | Date | Decision |
|---|---|---|---|---|---|
| | | | (OP-ED page ads) | | (6/15/76) |
| 83 | Earl R. Blair | 37-76 | The Chicago Tribune/WGN-TV (Reagan speech) | 4/1/76 | Unwarranted (6/15/76) |
| 84 | Carolyn Neustadt | 42-76 | CBS-TV (Israeli Arabs) | 4/12/76 | Unwarranted (6/15/76) |
| 85 | Dr. Stephen Barrett | 14-76 | Kilpatrick/Washington Star Syndicate, Inc. (Laetrile (Kilpatrick)) | 4/6/76 | Unwarranted/ Dismissed (6/15/76) |
| 86 | Committee For Rescue of Syrian Jewry | 29-76 | CBS-TV (Syrian Jewry—Update) | 3/29/76 | Unwarranted (6/15/76) |
| 87 | Nicaragua Government Information Service | 40-76 | Jack Anderson (President Somoza (Anderson)) | 4/19/76 | Upheld/ Dismissed (9/21/76) |
| 88 | American Dental Assn. | 4-76 | Reader's Digest (American Dental Assn.) | 3/12/76 | Upheld/ Dismissed (9/21/76) |
| 89 | James A. Khatami | 55-76 | The New York Times (CIA involvement in Angola) | 6/13/76 | Unwarranted (9/21/76) |
| 90 | Edward S. Slagle | 63A-76 | NBC News (Kiker interview) | 8/15/76 | Unwarranted (9/21/76) |
| 91 | Audrey Miles | 68B-75 | The San Francisco Chronicle (weapons thefts (S.F. Chronicle)) | 10/30/75 | Unwarranted (9/21/76) |

| COMPLAINT NO. | COMPLAINANT | IDENTIFICATION NO. | SUBJECT AND NEWS ORGANIZATION | DATE FILED | ACTION |
|---|---|---|---|---|---|
| 92 | Thomas C. Maloney | 68-76 | News Journal Company (press conference (Maloney)) | 8/27/76 | Unwarranted (9/21/76) |
| 93 | Edward S. Slagle | 63B-76 | NBC News (Pettit interview) | 8/15/76 | Unwarranted (11/16/76) |
| 94 | National Council of Irish Americans | 59-76 | Associated Press (religious identification (Swartz)) | 7/12/76 | Unwarranted (11/16/76) |
| 95 | D.C. Duggan | 73-76 | Associated Press (Carter foreword) | 9/18/76 | Unwarranted (11/16/76) |
| 96 | International Chiropractors Assn. | 60-76 | Consumer Reports (chiropractic (Consumer Reports)) | 7/19/76 | Unwarranted (11/16/76) |
| 97 | Peter Reichenberg | 64-76 | CBS News (women's peace movement/ Northern Ireland) | 8/23/76 | Unwarranted (11/16/76) |
| 98 | Edmund P. Hennelly | 76-76 | WABC-TV News (oil teaser) | 10/13/76 | Upheld (1/18/77) |
| 99 | Richard K. Cook | 81-76 | NBC News (Dean interview) | 12/7/76 | Unwarranted (1/18/77) |
| 100 | A.J. Montanari | 84-76 | CBS News (Montanari school) | 12/7/76 | Unwarranted/ Upheld (1/18/77) |

| No. | Complainant | Respondent | Case No. | Date Filed | Disposition (Date) |
|---|---|---|---|---|---|
| 101 | Nicaragua Government Information Service | Jack Anderson/ United Feature Syndicate (Anderson retraction) | 6-77 | 1/20/77 | Upheld (3/22/77) |
| 102 | Standard Oil Company of California | ABC News (oil industry legislation) | 22-77 | 2/28/77 | Unwarranted (3/22/77) |
| 103 | Mrs. Paul Maloney | CBS News (Larry Flynt jury) | 21-77 | 2/18/77 | Unwarranted (3/22/77) |
| 104 | Florida Real Estate Commission | CBS News (Florida Real Estate) | 16-77 | 2/11/77 | Unwarranted (3/22/77) |
| 105 | State Medical Society of Wisconsin | The Milwaukee Journal (Medicaid fraud) | 47-77 | 5/3/77 | Unwarranted (6/21/77) |
| 106 | Mary E. Juergens | Chicago Tribune— New York News Syndicate, Inc. (right-to-die poll) | 34-77 | 3/31/77 | No action taken (6/21/77) |
| 107 | Nicaragua Government Information Service | Time (oppression allegations) | 37-77 | 4/15/77 | Warranted/ Unwarranted (6/21/77) |
| 108 | Novotny Furs, Inc. | Bill Mauldin (Field Newspaper Syndicate) (anti-furrier cartoon) | 36-77 | 4/7/77 | Unwarranted (6/21/77) |
| 109 | VIVA (Voice For Innocent Victims of Abortion) | The New York Times (abortion coverage) | 20-77 | 2/14/77 | Dismissed (6/21/77) |
| 110 | Iowans For Life, Inc. | Des Moines Register & Tribune (abortion coverage) | 28-77 | 3/22/77 | Unwarranted (6/21/77) |

| COMPLAINT NO. | COMPLAINANT | IDENTIFICATION NO. | SUBJECT AND NEWS ORGANIZATION | DATE FILED | ACTION |
|---|---|---|---|---|---|
| 111 | Elmer Kral, et al. | 19-77 | The National Enquirer (UFO stories) | 2/12/77 | Warranted (6/21/77) |
| 112 | Marshall E. Baker | 23-77 | Forbes Magazine (Deltona financial condition) | 2/28/77 | Warranted (6/21/77) |
| 113 | Stephen Barrett | 26-77 | Parade magazine (J. Anthony Morris dismissal by FDA) | 3/17/77 | Warranted (9/20/77) |
| 114 | Alan Blum | 63-77 | Miami Herald (cigarette advertising) | 7/5/77 | Unwarranted (9/20/77) |
| 115 | Arthur Krause & Lesley Wischmann | 65-77 66-77 | Associated Press & United Press International (Kent State misidentifications) | 7/13/77 7/16/77 | Warranted (AP) Unwarranted (UPI) (9/20/77) |
| 116 | Syntex Corporation | 41-77 | United Press International (Senate drug hearing) | 5/1/77 | Warranted (9/20/77) |
| 117 | Bernard Cohen, et al. | 17-77 | NBC News (Radioactive waste) | 2/23/77 | Warranted (11/15/77) |
| 118 | Fund For Animals | 39-77 | NBC-TV/Survival Anglia, Ltd. (Kangaroos) | 4/21/77 | held in abeyance (11/15/77) |
| 119 | Joel M. Boriskin | 58-77 | National Enquirer (fluoridation coverage) | 6/24/77 | Unwarranted (11/15/77) |
| 120 | John Yiamouyiannis | 72a-77 | The Shreveport Times (fluoridation coverage) | 8/11/77 | Unwarranted (11/15/77) |

| | | | | |
|---|---|---|---|---|
| 121 | John Yiamouyiannis | 72b-77 | KSLA-TV, Shreveport, La. (fluoridation coverage) | 8/11/77 | Unwarranted (11/15/77) |
| 122 | Cape Cod Chamber of Commerce | 70a-77 | *Country Journal* (Cape water supply) | 8/8/77 | Warranted (11/15/77) |
| 123 | Cape Cod Chamber of Commerce | 70b-77 | *The Boston Herald American* (Cape water supply) | 8/8/77 | Unwarranted (11/15/77) |
| 124 | Novotny Furs, Inc. | 79-77 | Gene Basset (United Features Syndicate) (Canadian seal hunt cartoon) | 7/14/77 | Unwarranted (11/15/77) |
| 125 | American Postal Workers Union | 69-77 | Bryce Anderson (self-syndicated columnist) (union lobbying expenditures) | 8/10/77 | Warranted (11/15/77) |
| 126 | Central States, Southeast and Southwest Areas Health and Welfare Pension Funds | 68-77 | *Time* magazine (Teamster fund management) | 8/4/77 | Warranted (1/31/78) |
| 127 | Robert Sheaffer | 46-77 | NBC-TV (owned and operated stations division) & Landsburg Productions (Bermuda Triangle) | 5/5/77 | Warranted (1/31/78) |
| 128 | Stephen Barrett | 91-77 | *The New York Times Magazine* (J. Anthony Morris dismissal by FDA) | 12/6/77 | Warranted (1/31/78) |
| 129 | Samuel Taylor | 85-77 | WBBM-TV (Chicago) (Laetrile coverage) | 10/17/77 | Unwarranted (1/31/78) |

| COMPLAINT NO. | COMPLAINANT | IDENTIFICATION NO. | SUBJECT AND NEWS ORGANIZATION | DATE FILED | ACTION |
|---|---|---|---|---|---|
| 130 | Vincent Dole / Lee Koenigsberg | 97-77 | New York magazine (methadone story) | 12/5/77 | Unwarranted (1/31/78 and (4/25/78) |
| 131 | Paul Driscoll | 96a-77 | CBS News (abortion coverage) | 12/12/77 | Warranted (4/25/78) |
| 132 | Paul Driscoll | 96b-77 | The New York Times (abortion coverage) | 12/12/77 | Warranted (4/25/78) |
| 133 | South Dakota Right to Life Corporation | 15-78 | CBS News (abortion coverage) | 2/1/78 | Unwarranted (4/25/78) |
| 134 | William Gavin | 18-78 | The New York Times (abortion coverage) | 2/2/78 | Warranted (4/25/78) |
| 135 | Right to Life of Longview (Texas) | 21-78 | CBS News, NBC News (abortion coverage) | 2/14/78 | Unwarranted (4/25/78) |
| 136 | Prince Georges (Md.) Right to Life | 92-77 | WJLA-TV (Washington, D.C.) (abortion coverage) | 12/8/77 | Unwarranted (4/25/78) |
| 137 | Michael Ryan | 27-78 | United Press International (coal strike coverage) | 2/28/78 | Unwarranted (4/25/78) |
| 138 | Karl Meyer | 8-78 | WABC-TV (New York City) (Uganda program) | 1/18/78 | Resolved (4/25/78) |
| 139 | Media Alliance (San Francisco) | 1-78 | New Times (Chinatown article) | 12/8/77 | Resolved (4/25/78) |
| 140 | Joseph Belden | 6-78 | Conservative Digest | 1/11/78 | Warranted |

| No. | Complainant | Media (subject) | Docket | Date Filed | Decision (Date) |
|---|---|---|---|---|---|
|  |  | (Saigon photograph) |  |  | (4/25/78) |
| 141 | Michael Halberstam | CBS News (60 Minutes) (treatment for heart disease) | 10-78 | 1/23/78 | Unwarranted (4/25/78) |
| 142 | AFL-CIO Task Force on Labor Law Reform | The Woonsocket (R.I. Call (opinion advertisement) | 37-78 | 3/31/78 | Withdrawn (6/27/78) |
| 143 | Billie M. Howes | Daily Hampshire Gazette (anonymous letters) | 44-78 | 5/10/78 | Warranted (6/27/78) |
| 144 | Public Employee Dept. AFL-CIO | Time (Civil Service article) | 48-78 | 5/1/78 | Unwarranted (6/27/78) |
| 145 | Stephen Kohn (bu exposure) | The Boston Globe (B.U. coverage) | 60-78 | 6/6/78 | Unwarranted (6/27/78) |
| 146 | Julie Blonigen | ABC-TV (pro-life convention) | 76-78 | 7/20/78 | Unwarranted (9/12/78) |
| 147 | Hospital Physician | New Times (survey interpretation) | 65-78 | 6/13/78 | Unwarranted (9/12/78) |
| 148 | John P. Scanlon | NBC-TV (prosecution witness) | 73-78 | 7/11/78 | Unwarranted (9/12/78) |
| 149 | Bill Holt | CBS-TV (traveling salesmen) | 80-78 | 7/26/78 | Warranted (9/12/78) |
| 150 | Barbara Boxer | NBC News (Marin County lifestyle) | 83-78 | 8/1/78 | Warranted (12/6/78) |
| 151 | Catholic Defense League | New York Times (abortion articles) | 72-78 | 7/11/78 | Warranted/Unwarranted (12/6/78) |

| COMPLAINT NO. | COMPLAINANT | IDENTIFICATION NO. | SUBJECT AND NEWS ORGANIZATION | DATE FILED | ACTION |
|---|---|---|---|---|---|
| 152 | William F. Gavin | 100-78 | *New York Times* (abortion; labelling) | 6/20/78 | Warranted (12/6/78) |
| 153 | Catholic Defense League | 72-78 | WCBS-TV (crowd estimate) | 7/11/78 | Unwarranted (12/6/78) |
| 154 | *Vegetarian Times* | 89-78 | CBS-TV (breastfeeding data) | 8/19/78 | Resolved (12/6/78) |
| 155 | Rabbi Joseph B. Glaser (Central Conference of American Rabbis) | 5-79 | ABC-TV (Palestinian viewpoint) | 1/12/79 | Unwarranted (3/9/79) |
| 156 | Ira Glasser (American Civil Liberties Union) | 6-79 | WCBS Newsradio (Judge Taylor editorial) | 1/3/79 | Resolved (3/9/79) |
| 157 | Eleanor M. Fala | 115-78 | *Philadelphia Bulletin* (nutrition articles) | 12/14/78 | Unwarranted (3/9/79) |
| 158 | Theodore Kheel | 116-78 | *New York* magazine ("malicious" publication) | 12/19/78 | Partially Upheld Partially Unwarranted (3/9/79) |
| 159 | Bernard L. Cohen | 74-78 | ABC-TV (low-level radiation) | 7/21/78 | Unwarranted (3/9/79) |
| 160 | Jane Newton (Oregon Women for Timber) | 85-78 | ABC-TV (herbicide report) | 8/8/78 | Unwarranted (3/9/79) |

| No. | Complainant | Subject | Case No. | Date | Outcome |
|---|---|---|---|---|---|
| 161 | Leo T. Loera | CBS-TV (officer survival program in Riverside, CA.) | 14-79 | 2/5/79 | Warranted (3/9/79) |
| (161) | Reconsideration—requested by CBS | | | 3/14/79 | Finding Partially Upheld; Partially Withdrawn (6/11/79) |
| 162 | Maurice Stans | NEWSPAPER ENTERPRISE ASSN. (Angle-Walters column) | 99-78 | 9/26/78 | Neither Upheld nor found unwarranted (6/11/79) |
| 163 | Eliot Janeway | ESQUIRE (Janeway profile) | 18-79 | 2/27/79 | Warranted (6/11/79) |
| 164 | Pharmaceutical Mfg. Assn. | ABC News (prescription drugs) | 118-78 | 12/29/78 | Unwarranted (6/11/79) |
| 165 | Martin Ilivicky (Bryant High School) | WNET/Thirteen (high school truancy) | 103-78 | Notification (11/3/78) Filed (2/12/79) | Warranted (6/11/79) |
| 166 | Roslyn M. Litman | KDKA-TV (federal judgeship) | 17-79 | 2/20/79 | Unwarranted (9/20/79) |
| 167 | Joseph Gavrin (NY State Council of Voluntary Child Care Agencies) | New York magazine (child-care expose) | 19-79 | (3/1/79) | Unwarranted (9/21/79) |

| COMPLAINT NO. | COMPLAINANT | IDENTIFICATION NO. | SUBJECT AND NEWS ORGANIZATION | DATE FILED | ACTION |
|---|---|---|---|---|---|
| 168 | Robert B. Hayes/ Boise Cascade | 54-79 | United Press Int'l (1972 annual report) | (8/17/79) | Warranted (9/21/79) |
| 169 | Shell Oil Company | 63-79 | NBC News ("Fly Now, Freeze Later" first of a five-part series on the oil companies) | 10/24/79 | Warranted (11/30/79) |
| 170 | Chris Beaudin | 65-79 | The Bay City Times (letters to the editor) | 11/2/79 | Dismissed (11/30/79—lack of purview) |
| 171 | Debra Ryba | 62-79 | New York Post ("provocative & biased" front page headlines) | 10/19/79 | Dismissed (11/30/79—lack of purview) |
| 172 | Exxon Corp. | 67-79 | NBC News ("Dirty Oil and Dirty Air" second of five-part series on the oil companies) | 11/16/79 | Warranted (3/6/80) |
| 173 | Dr. Gary A. Hogge | 70-79 | The Courier-Journal (article on doctors' fees) | 11/26/79 | Warranted (3/6/80) |
| 174 | American-Arab Relations Comm. | 28-80 | CBS News, Radio (attribution-Palestinian raid) | 4/22/80 | Unwarranted (6/13/80) |
| 175 | Catholic League for | 32-80 | Camden Courier-Post | 5/1/80 | Unwarranted |

| No. | Complainant | Ref. | Media (Subject) | Date | Determination |
|---|---|---|---|---|---|
|  | Religious & Civil Rights |  | (Gannett News Service stories on Pauline Fathers) |  | (6/13/80) |
| 176 | Enrique Durand | 12-80 | *Columbia Journalism Review* (UPI's Latin-American desk) |  | Warranted (6/13/80) |
| 177 | San Francisco Board of Supervisors, S.F. Human Rights Commission, National Gay Task Force, Randy Alfred, et al. | 71-80 | CBS News (Documentary, "Gay Power Gay Politics," on S.F. homosexual community.) | 7/10/80 | Partially upheld Partially unwarranted (9/18/80) |
| 178 | Veterans Administration Department of Medicine and Surgery | 41-80 | *National Enquirer* (crime in VA hospitals) | 5/23/80 | Warranted (9/18/80) |
| 179 | Dr. Robert W. Miller | 75-80 | CBS News ("60 Minutes" segment on Love Canal hazards) | 7/23/80 | Unwarranted (9/19/80) |
| 180 | Drs. Stephen Barrett and Victor Herbert | 73-80 | *US* magazine (article on Kurt Donsbach's University of Nutrition) | 7/18/80 | Warranted (9/19/80) |
| 181 | Doctors Ought to Care (DOC) | 42-80 | NBC News ("Prime Time Saturday" furniture made with polyurethane padding) | 5/9/80 | Unwarranted (9/19/80) |
| 182 | Rev. Lynn Bergfalk | 40-80 | *New Yorker* magazine (article by Trillin on refugees in Fairfield, Iowa.) | 5/21/80 | Warranted (12/5/80) |

| COMPLAINT NO. | COMPLAINANT | IDENTIFICATION NO. | SUBJECT AND NEWS ORGANIZATION | DATE FILED | ACTION |
|---|---|---|---|---|---|
| 183 | Howard Ruff | 74-80 | Chicago Tribune-New York news Syndicate (column by Dan Dorfman about Ruff and his vendors) | 7/4/80 | Partially upheld, Partially unwarranted (12/5/80) |
| 184 | The Association of American Railroads | 102-80 | ABC News ("20/20" segment "Working on the Railroad") | 7/7/80 (Initiated) 11-18-80 | Partially warranted (3/6/81) (formally filed) |
| 185 | Dr. Victor Herbert | 5-81 | People magazine (mega-vitamin article 12/15/80) | 1/9/81 | Warranted (3/6/81) |
| 186 | Rupert Allan | 10-81 | Los Angeles Herald Examiner | 1/26/81 | Partially warranted (3/6/81) |
| 187 | Charles Mohr, Nan Robertson and James Wooten | 11-81 | LIFE magazine "The Ghost Burglar and the Good Doctor") | 2/6/81 | Partially warranted (3/6/81) |
| 188 | Howard University Journalism Faculty | 23-81 | Washington Post ("Jimmy's World" hoax and ombudsman's report) | 4/24/81 | Partially warranted (6/12/81) |
| 189 | Larry Lowenstein and | 24-81 | Teresa Carpenter and | 5/11/81 | Warranted |

| No. | Complainant | Date | Subject | Determination |
| --- | --- | --- | --- | --- |
|  | James Wechsler |  | Village Voice ("From Herosim to Madness," Pulitzer Prize-winner) | (6/11/81) |
| 190 | Barrett (Lehigh Valley Committee Against Health Fraud) | 5/11/81 | Parade magazine and Jack Anderson (4/26/81 column: portion on firing of Dr. J. Anthony Morris) | Unwarranted (9/24/81) |
| 191 | Barrett (LVCAHF) | 5/28/81 | Los Angeles Times Syndicate ("Bathing Suit Diet") | Unwarranted (9/24/81) |
| 192 | Sunkist Growers, Inc. | 7/21/81 | The New York Times and Time (articles on Federal Marketing order for oranges: misidentification of photo) | Unwarranted (9/24/81) |
| 193 | American-Arab Anti-Discrimination Committee (Zogby | 7/30/81 | ABC News ("Nightline" coverage, 7/22/81, of Israeli-Palestinian conflict) | Unwarranted (9/24/81) |
| 194 | Robert Gulack | 9/14/81 | New York Daily News (9/14/81 story on "germ warfare") | Warranted (12/3/81) |
| 195 | Jan Reynolds and Judy Gibson | 9/22/81 | Winfield (KS) Daily Courier (8/27/81 handling of rape hearing) | Unwarranted (12/3/81) |
| 196 | Larry L. Constantine | 10/5/81 | Time (Child-adult sex) | Warranted (4/22/82) |

| COMPLAINT NO. | COMPLAINANT | IDENTIFICATION NO. | SUBJECT AND NEWS ORGANIZATION | DATE FILED | ACTION |
|---|---|---|---|---|---|
| 197 | Bruce Cameron and Leonel Gomez | 55-81 | *The Wall Street Journal* (El Salvador editorial) | 10/24/81 | Unwarranted (4/22/82) |
| 198 | Herbert D. Kerman | 59-81 | *The Washington Post*, ABC NEWS "20/20", and *Mother Jones* (War on Cancer) | 11/3/81 | Partially warranted (4/23/82) |
| 199 | Albert G. Daniels | 66-81 | *Reader's Digest* (Three Mile Island) | 11/25/81 | Partially warranted (4/22/82) |
| 200 | Lyle M. Nelson | 18-82 | ABC News "20/20" ("A Target for Spies") | 3/15/82 | Partially warranted (4/23/82) |
| 201 | Public Affairs Council | 21-82 | CBS News (Moyers report on political action committees) | 3/22/82 | Unwarranted (4/23/82) |
| 202 | William Kalis (Bahamas News Bureau) | 3-81 | WTVJ-TV Miami (Haitian refugees on Cay Lobos) | 1/5/81 | Partially warranted (9/23/82) |
| 203 | American Irish Unity Committee | 24-82 | *The New York Times* (Irish prime-minister misquote) | 4/14/82 | Partially warranted 9/23/82 |
| 204 | Charles Mendelson | 25-82 | *New York Post* (identification of | 4/27/82 | Partially warranted |

| No. | Complainant | Case No. | Respondent | Date | Finding |
|---|---|---|---|---|---|
| | | | teenaged rape victim) | | (9/24/82) |
| 205 | American Electric Power Service Corporation, Columbus, OH | 40-82 | Chicago-Tribune-New York News Syndicate (Dorfman column on investment in utilities) | 7/27/82 | Unwarranted 9/23/82 |
| 206 | Jim Bouman | 44-82 | The Milwaukee Journal and The Milwaukee Sentinel (conflict of interest) | 8/9/82 | Partially warranted 9/23/82 |
| 207 | Peter Zeisler (Theater Communications Group) | 45-82 | The Morning News Wilmington, DE (column on theater conference) | 8/24/82 | Dismissed 9/23/82 |
| 208 | Coalition for Environ-mental-Energy Balance | 38-82 | CBS News (acid rain) | 7/21/82 | "Deficient" but not unfair 12/3/82 |
| 209 | Coalition for Environ-mental-Energy Balance | 53-82 | Corporation for Public Broadcasting and Robert Richter Productions (acid rain) | 8/19/82 | "Deficient" but not unfair 12/3/82 |
| 210 | Arizonans for a Bilateral Nuclear Weapons Freeze | 60-82 | The Wall Street Journal (Journal-Gallup Survey on unilateral freeze) | 10/26/82 | Warranted 12/2/82 |
| 211 | Dr. Robert M. Kohn, M.D. | 19-82 | Dr. Robert Mendelsohn and Columbia Features Syndicate | 3/15/82 | Partially warranted 3/31/83 |

| COMPLAINT NO. | COMPLAINANT | IDENTIFICATION NO. | SUBJECT AND NEWS ORGANIZATION | DATE FILED | ACTION |
|---|---|---|---|---|---|
| 212 | AFL-CIO | 63-82 | Forbes Magazine | 12/18/82 | Partially warranted 3/31/83 |
| 213 | Atomic Industrial Forum | 64-82 | The Washington Post | 12/14/82 | Partially warranted 4/1/83 |
| 214 | Robert M. Shubow | 1-83 | *San Francisco Chronicle* (Patel clan coverage) | 12/27/82 | Warranted 6/20/83 |
| 215 | American Irish Unity Committee | 6-83 | The *New York Times* (IRA trial coverage) | 1/13/83 | Partially warranted 6/20/83 |
| 216 | American Irish Unity Committee | 17-83 | NBC News | 3/21/83 | Dismissed with comments 6/20/83 |
| 217 | American Irish Unity Committee | 27-83 | New York *Daily News* | 6/3/83 | Unwarranted 6/20/83 |

## COMPLAINT NO. 155     (Filed Jan. 12, 1979)
### GLASER (Central Conference of American Rabbis)
### against
### ABC-TV NEWS

**Complaint:** Rabbi Joseph B. Glaser, executive vice president of the Central Conference of American Rabbis, complained that an ABC-TV News documentary, "Terror in the Promised Land" (October 30, 1978) constituted a "propagandistic apologia for the terrorist activities of the Palestine Liberation Organization." Fourteen charges were included in the complaint.

The program offered what was described as a "Palestinian perception of right and wrong." Citing this point, the complainant asked:

> . . . is the public's understanding of the 'Palestinian role in the Mideast' advanced by a program which offers admitted terrorists — killers of innocent women and children — every opportunity to justify their crimes while the ABC interviewer fails to pose a single critical question to them?

Rabbi Glaser said that it was "an egregious falsification" to identify one sequence in which stock footage was used as depicting "Jews driving the Arabs out of Jerusalem" in 1948. He charged that the film came from Movietone stock footage which "is clearly and correctly labeled in Movietone's catalogue as 'Arabs driving Jews out of Jerusalem'."

Rabbi Glaser also contended that: "The 'Palestinian tragedy' is described as an extension of the Holocaust, 'thereby implying an equation of the two tragedies,' although the Holocaust cost the lives of six million Jews while there has been no breath of genocide in the Palestinian situation."

Other points include a complaint that Raanan Weitz, who was interviewed in the broadcast, was incorrectly identified as the "director of the Jewish National Fund." The complainant said Mr. Weitz had no connection with the Fund.

The complainant further contended that the language of the broadcast was manipulated. He objected also to the manner of describing PLO members who were seen on the program, and said that there were distortions in the description of the origins of the Palestinian problems and in a scene that referred to the Maalot raid and massacre of Jews in that community.

**Response:** Richard C. Wald, senior vice president of ABC News, in a February 27 letter to the Council enclosed copies of correspondence which he had with the Anti-Defamation League about the program, as well as a general reply ABC News had prepared in response to criticisms of the program. ABC News also provided the Council with a videotape and transcript of the broadcast.

The general reply said that the program did not condone terrorist activity and that it was not about right and wrong but "about the view of right and wrong held by certain Palestinians."

**Council finding:** The complainant has asked the Council to determine whether "Terror in the Promised Land" meets responsible standards of journalism. The Council believes that it does.

In an area where tensions are as great as they are in the Middle East, the program provided insights into the people who make up the Palestine Liberation Organization. ABC News did not attempt to glorify the deeds of the PLO terrorists. Rather, it examined the reasons for the fanaticism of the terrorists.

The program was carefully introduced by Frank Reynolds as an attempt to understand:

> Why people choose to kill innocent men, women, and children even if they are likely to die at the same time. . . . This is not a program about right and wrong. It is about a certain Palestinian perception of right and wrong. Whatever may be thought of them, they exist and they cannot be ignored by those who work for peace. We know that some of you will be outraged and many will be disturbed. But we believe that one hour from now you will be better informed. And that is our reason for presenting this broadcast.

And at the close, Reynolds added:

> To refuse to listen is to strengthen their argument that violence is their only recourse. I believe everything possible must be done to persuade them they are wrong about that . . . to encourage them to turn away from terror toward peace.

Clearly, such expressions do not constitute an assessment of right and wrong. Rather, they emphasize the journalistic function of providing information.

Much of what the complainant cites in the 14-point complaint as specific examples of bias and distortion concerns the manner in which ABC chose to present the documentary. This includes the use of music in certain portions of the program, a practice the Council believes is of dubious journalistic value.

Rabbi Glaser said, "Language is carefully manipulated, in Orwellian fashion so that . . . the victims of the terrorist raid at Maalot are not women and children but 'people' . . . murderers are 'commandos' . . . terrorists about to depart on missions of slaughter of innocent civilians are 'martyrs'."

The Council can only observe that these are Palestinian perception of the situations described and they were properly identified as such.

Referring to the extermination of Jews in Germany and German-controlled territories, the script said the "the desperation facing the Palestinians today is a direct extension of the tragic dilemma of the Jewish people after Hitler's holocaust." In the context in which that statement was made, the Council believes that it referred to the creation of the state of Israel as a solution to the Jewish refugee problem *following* the holocaust. It did not say that Palestinians were meeting the same fate as Jews did *during* the holocaust.

Differing interpretations can also be ascribed to the complainant's contention concerning the origins of the Palestinian problem and the film showing Arab refugee camps.

There are two significant contentions of factual error in the complaint. The first concerns the use of Movietone News film which purportedly showed refugees fleeing from a section of Jerusalem during the 1948 war.

The complaint contended that the film clip actually depicted Arabs looting and sacking a "centuries-old Jewish quarter of Jerusalem" and that the narrative described the scene as "Jews driving the Arabs out of Jerusalem." According to the complaint, the film came from Movietone stock footage which "is correctly labeled in Movietone's catalogue as 'Arabs driving Jews out of Jerusalem on May 28, 1948'."

An examination of the transcript shows no wording about "Jews driving the Arabs out of Jerusalem." This was the narrative that accompanied that piece of film footage:

> Statehood and war arrived at the same time, but the Israelis fought to victory. Through fear and panic, a massive refugee problem was created. These frightened and suddenly homeless people became the Palestinian problem of today.

Council efforts to determine the correct identification for the film footage produced conflicting responses. The Council believes, however, that the film shown and the manner in which it was narrated were not misleading.

In the portion of the program in which Raanan Weitz was interviewed, and misidentified, the complaint contended that "the facts as to land acquisition by the Jewish National Fund were also erroneously portrayed."

Mr. Weitz is a member of the World Zionist Organization's executive board and head of its settlement and absorption department. He has no connection with the Jewish National Fund. In his job, however, he does place Jewish settlers on what was once Arab land and he was interviewed by ABC in this regard. The interview made no mention of the Jewish National Fund other than incorrectly identifying Mr. Weitz as its director.

The Council believes that ABC News should have acknowledged promptly the error concerning Mr. Weitz but does not believe that this misidentification contributed to any misconception of the main thrust of the program.

As a general matter, the Council is aware of the problems faced by television in handling corrections applying to documentaries, since these programs are usually shown only once. The Council believes that the broadcasting of corrections is of major value in the maintaining of journalistic credibility. It is moved to suggest that the networks consider the widely viewed nightly news broadcasts or some comparable place for corrections and that they be considered for use when the news flow is such that no important story has to be excluded in order to make room for the correcting of the record.

The Council believes that ABC News exercised proper news and editing judgments in the selection and preparation of material. It finds the complaint to be unwarranted.

**Concurring:** Ghiglione, Hauser, Huston, Isaacs, McKay, Otwell, Pulitzer and Roberts.
March 9, 1979


**COMPLAINT NO. 156**             (Filed Jan. 3. 1979)
GLASSER (American Civil Liberties Union)
against
WCBS NEWSRADIO

**Complaint:** Ira Glasser, executive director of the American Civil Liberties Union, complained that a WCBS Newsradio editorial urging the ouster of Manhattan Civil Court Judge Margaret Taylor was unfair. Broadcast on September 5, 1978, the editorial contended that Judge

Taylor, while on rotating night duty in Bronx Criminal Court, had exercised "dreadful judgment" in releasing a murder case defendant without bail, "despite the fact that the prosecution had a videotaped confession from him."

WCBS Newsradio called for Judge Taylor's removal or resignation and cited three constitutional methods for removing a judge from the bench.

Mr. Glasser was invited by WCBS Newsradio to respond to the editorial. He complained, however, that when he asked WCBS Newsradio for a copy of the transcript of the murder case bail hearing he was told that no one connected with the preparation of the editorial had seen one.

In his editorial rebuttal, broadcast over WCBS Newsradio several weeks later, Mr. Glasser charged that had the station consulted pertinent court records before formulating its conclusions about Judge Taylor "a very different story" would have emerged. He argued further that "a public apology" by WCBS Newsradio was in order:

> The law requires judges to release an accused person unless there is reason to believe he will flee and fail to show up for trial. In this case, there was no reason to think the accused would run away. He was in court, he had a lawyer, he was not a transient, he had family living nearby. Judge Taylor's decision to release him pending trial was the only fair decision she could make. If WCBS had taken the trouble to read the court transcript it could not possibly have come to the conclusion it did. . . . To have criticized Judge Taylor for this decision was bad enough. To have called for her removal was completely irresponsible. We think WCBS owes Judge Taylor and its listeners a public apology.

**Response:** The Council forwarded copies of Mr. Glasser's complaint and editorial reply to Robert Hyland, vice president and general manager of WCBS Newsradio. On February 23, 1979, the Council received a response from Mr. Hyland consisting of a copy of an editorial that was broadcast over the station six times that day:

> Last Fall, WCBS broadcast an editorial which criticized a decision by Civil Court Judge Margaret Taylor. In a case in the Bronx, she released without bail a man charged with murder. We stated that she made this decision despite the 'fact that the prosecution had a video-taped confession from the defendant.'
>
> We were incorrect. What was widely reported as a 'confession' was, instead, a statement from the accused. In it, the defendant gives his version of what happened. That account was repeated in court later on. Our characterization of the statement as a confession was misleading, and our criticism of Judge Taylor, based on this incident, was inappropriate.
>
> It is our objective in all of our editorials to illuminate issues and contribute to a better understanding of them. Most of the time, we think we succeed. When we do make mistakes, it is our policy to correct them.

**Council finding:** It is apparent from the record that Mr. Glasser of the American Civil Liberties Union was entirely correct in charging WCBS Newsradio of having acted unfairly where Judge Margaret Taylor was concerned. However belatedly, WCBS Newsradio has corrected the record and the Council considers this action to have closed the matter and the case is recorded as dismissed.

**Concurring:** Ghiglione, Huston, Isaacs, McKay, Otwell, Pulitzer and Roberts.

March 9, 1979

### COMPLAINT NO. 157    (Filed Dec. 14, 1978)
### FALA
against
### THE PHILADELPHIA BULLETIN

**Complaint:** Mrs. Eleanor M. Fala of Havertown, Pa., a registered dietician, complained that three articles on the subject of nutrition which appeared in *The Philadelphia Bulletin* "contained misleading and erroneous information." Mrs. Fala also charged that the articles promoted "a variety of false (or unproven) ideas which are rejected by the scientific community."

The specific complaints about each of the articles follow:

1. "They Say Proper Diet Can Help Prevent Illness" (October 8, 1978). In addition to containing what she said were inaccuracies concerning nutritional information, Mrs. Fala said this article presented an unrepresentative view of the "medical community's" attitude toward the preventive approach to medicine.

2. "Will a Vitamin Pill a Day Keep the Illnesses Away?" (October 11, 1978).

The complainant contended that there were factual errors in the article concerning the effects of particular vitamins and minerals on people who take them. She further questioned the qualifications of Dr. Bonnie Maniaci, whose work was the subject of the article in question.

3. "Benjamin Feingold: "The Kids Love Him" (October 25. 1978). The complainant took issue with Dr. Feingold's theories concerning treatment of hyperactivity in children. She charged that Dr. Feingold's theories were unscientific and that the article did not sufficiently note that they are dismissed by many scientists.

**Response:** Addressing the overall complaint, B. Dale Davis, executive editor of *The Philadelphia Bulletin*, wrote in a letter to the Council:

> The three articles Mrs. Fala refers to simply present nontraditional views on health and nutrition . . . In none of these cases is the *Bulletin* advocating a particular diet, medical practice or anything. We simply quote those who are involved and hold a particular view. Whether they are 'qualified' in the traditional sense is not our judgment to make. Finding unanimous agreement among medical people on almost any matter dealing with diet, health, medicine or what have you is extremely difficult, if not impossible. Who is to say that they are wrong and Mrs. Fala is right? Our role is to present all kinds of views, not just those we happen to agree with.

Regarding the question of Dr. Bonnie Maniaci's credentials as presented in the second article, Mr. Davis commented:

> Bonnie Maniaci calls herself 'Doctor.' So do chiropractors, which is annoying to many M.D.s. It wasn't many years ago that osteopaths were regarded as unworthy of the 'Doctor' title and this view is still held by some in the medical profession. . . . We report the extent of Bonnie Maniaci's education background. One can assume that if she is violating any law by doing what she does then the *Bulletin* is providing officials a service by calling attention to her operation.

Addressing Mrs. Fala's objection to Dr. Benjamin Feingold's theories in the third article, Mr. Davis stated:

> As Mrs. Fala points out, there are differences of opinion on what he proclaims. That's what our story emphasizes.

**Council finding:** There was no attempt to mislead the reader concerning attitudes towards the use of preventive medicine. All material in the first article is directly attributed to Drs. Kenneth Fordham, Melvin Page, and Arthur Hochberg, whose work was the subject of the piece. When the writer asks the question: "How has the rest of the medical community responded to this preventive approach to medicine?" it is clear in the context of the story that the questions are being asked of the doctors being interviewed, and not of the medical community as a whole.

The theories concerning vitamin therapy in the second piece were clearly attributed to Dr. Maniaci, who was to begin a series of seminars the following week in the area, a newsworthy event. Dr. Maniaci was clearly identified as a doctor of naturopathic medicine and a definition of naturopathology was offered to the readers. It is clear from the article that her views are not those necessarily prevailing in the majority of the medical profession.

The third article points out that Dr. Feingold's theories have "triggered hot debate among physicians, researchers and segments of the food industry . . ." Clearly, this was a profile of Dr. Feingold and his work, and was an appropriate subject for a newspaper article.

**General conclusion of The Council:** Mrs. Fala's complaint raises a troublesome point about the manner in which many news stories are perceived by readers and viewers. The complainant believes that because the newspaper published the stories in question it is responsible for all of the material in them — even that which is clearly attributed to the persons who are subjects of the stories.

Each of the instances cited by Mrs. Fala, the Council believes, is an example of something newsworthy about which the newspaper elected to do a story which did not require inclusion of extensive rebuttal material. Proper news and editing judgment was exercised throughout and the Council finds the complaint unwarranted.

**Concurring:** Ghiglione, Hauser, Huston, Isaacs, McKay, Otwell, Pulitzer and Roberts.

March 9, 1979


### COMPLAINT NO.158         (Filed Dec. 19, 1978)
### KHEEL
### against
### NEW YORK MAGAZINE


**Complaint:** On December 19, 1978, Theodore Kheel, New York attorney and labor mediator, filed a complaint that he was about to be the subject of an unflattering article in *New York* magazine and that a request by him for advertising space in the same issue to counter the article had been ignored. Mr Kheel said he had intended to say in the advertisement that the article had been "killed" earlier and had been reinstated because of his role in mediating the New York newspaper strike. The article appeared in the January 8, 1979 issue and on January 19, Mr. Kheel filed an amended complaint, charging that *New York*'s owner, Rupert Murdoch, who also owns *The New York Post*, had used the magazine as reprisal for Mr. Kheel's role in settling the strike.

The outlines of the controversy can be summarized as follows:

Free-lance reporter Richard Karp called on Mr. Kheel in August to interview him for the *New York* article. At an earlier time, Mr. Kheel had been counsel to *New York*. He asked that he be released from the attorney/client relationship so that he could discuss Mr. Murdoch's acquisition of the magazine. Mr. Kheel wrote to *New York* to this point. Editor John

38

Berendt declined to waive the attorney/client relationship, but Mr. Kheel said that in a telephone talk, Mr. Berendt told him the article had been "killed." Mr. Kheel asserted that he was also told this by the publisher, Joe Armstrong, whom he quoted as attributing the "kill" order to Mr. Murdoch. Mr. Kheel said further, that Mr. Murdoch had made the same statement to *Daily News* general manager Joseph Barletta and *Times* senior vice-president Walter Mattson. Both were quoted publicly as confirming this and expressing "surprise" that the article had been revived. Mr. Barletta has described these accounts as accurate.

Shortly after Mr. Kheel's entry into the newspaper strike negotiations, Mr. Murdoch withdrew from the publishers group, resumed publication of *The Post*, introduced a Sunday paper, and announced plans for a morning paper. Mr. Kheel said that following these developments, he received a call from reporter Karp saying the story had been revived. Mr. Kheel says that the settlement of the strike deprived Mr. Murdoch of what he described as a "free ride," forced abandonment of the Sunday paper and blocked plans for a morning paper.

Publisher Armstrong normally refused to accept the proferred Kheel advertisement as against policy and suggested a letter. Mr. Kheel submitted a 2,100-word letter. *New York* deleted two introductory paragraphs, ran the rest verbatim, including a clear mention of the reply on its page one cover. Mr. Kheel concedes that the "right of reply" has been accorded but maintains that an article once ordered "killed" was revived because of the publisher's resentment over the strike settlement.

The issue before the Council, therefore, comes down to this single consideration: Did the owner of *The Post* and *New York* make malicious use of the magazine's columns for the purpose of retribution?

**Response:** *New York*, through the law firm of Squadron, Ellenoff, Plesent and Lehrer, responded to the original and amended complaints by Mr. Kheel. A January 12, 1979, letter from Neal M. Goldman of the law firm, asked the Council to reject the original complaint concerning an advertisement on the ground that "the circumstances of the case have no bearing on freedom of speech or freedom of the press." The letter cited what it said was *New York*'s existing policy of not accepting advertisements which comment on editorial matter in the magazine. Mr. Kheel had previously been informed of that policy in a letter from *New York* publisher Joe Armstrong.

On February 26, Mr. Goldman made a seven-point response to Mr. Kheel's amended complaint which charged that the magazine had been used as an instrument of reprisal against him for his role as a mediator in the recent New York newspaper strike.

Mr. Goldman reiterated an earlier statement by Mr. Armstrong and John Berendt, *New York*'s editor, that the piece about Mr. Kheel had been assigned well before the newspaper strike and that it was withheld from publication "at Mr. Murdoch's request when Mr. Kheel complained in order not to jeopardize the negotiations, in which Mr. Kheel was obviously determined to play a role." Mr. Goldman further said:

> It is interesting that Mr Kheel finds nothing wrong with his ability to prevent publication of a critical article but cannot accept the decision to publish that article as anything but revengeful.

The letter also took issue with Mr. Kheel's motivation in seeking to place an advertisement in the same issue of *New York* in which Mr. Karp's article ran. Mr. Goldman said that this confirmed that his (Kheel's) intention "was not to bring information to the attention of the magazine's readership, but to engage in an attack on Mr. Murdoch and the magazine to detract attention from the content of the article."

The letter also termed Mr. Kheel's request to be released from his attorney/client privilege as *New York*'s former counsel as "typical holier-than-thou Kheel, lecturing the press on its obligations while ignoring the substance of an article that *New York* had every right to publish."

The letter also cited publication by *New York* of Mr. Kheel's lengthy letter of reply and said:

> He does not suffer from any disadvantage of not being able to respond to the substance of public criticism or unfavorable comment. We call your attention to the advertisement on the front page of *The New York Times* and the full-page coverage in *Cue* Magazine as the most recent example of Mr. Kheel's ability to respond. He is certainly not entitled to any special treatment or protection.

Mr. Goldman concluded by saying, "there is no basis whatsoever for considering Mr. Kheel's complaint."

**Council finding:** Through public statements made on several occasions, *New York* magazine has said that editorial decisions at the magazine are made by the publisher and editor-in-chief, Joe Armstrong, and the editor, John Berendt. In a *New York* magazine press release statement by Mr. Armstrong and Mr. Berendt issued shortly after Mr. Kheel publicly charged, in a press statement, that the article was "filled with inaccuracies," this policy was reiterated. Both declared that Mr. Murdoch "has steadfastly pursued a hands-off policy" on editorial matters.

In the face of these statements, we have several confirmations that Mr.

Murdoch intervened in decisions regarding publication of the article about Mr. Kheel. The publisher and the editor, in their press release statement, said that Mr. Murdoch asked "that the editors consider postponing publication of this particular piece (the Kheel story) until the sensitive newspaper negotiations were completed." In their response to Council inquiries, *New York*'s lawyers acknowledged that the article was "withheld at Mr. Murdoch's request." Joseph F. Barletta, General Manager of the *Daily News*, and Walter E. Mattson, Executive Vice President of *The New York Times*, were reported, in a *New York Times*' story of January 3, as having confirmed a statement by Mr. Kheel that they had told him that Mr. Murdoch had informed them that he had "killed the article."

It is apparent that Mr. Murdoch did intervene with the publisher and the editor — in contradiction of his stated policy of not intervening — by "killing" or "postponing" the article. In this respect, Mr. Murdoch has misled the public by not pursuing the "hands-off" policy on editorial matters that he has espoused. Such a policy may or may not be the best practice; we do not pass on that question. But if such a policy is proclaimed it depends on consistency for its credibility.

Regarding the decision to revive the article, the situation becomes muddled. If the article was "killed," as Mr. Kheel claims he was led to believe, then it never would have appeared. "Killed" means dead. If the article was "postponed," as the publisher and editor of *New York* state, "until the sensitive newspaper negotiations were completed," then this flies in the face of the fact that Mr. Karp received the call to resume his assignment on the article shortly after Mr. Murdoch had broken with the other publishers involved in the newspaper strike, denounced Mr. Kheel and resumed publication of the *New York Post* under his own interim settlement with the pressmen's union. The *Times* and the *Daily News* remained down and the "sensitive newspaper negotiations" were still very much in progress.

The Council has no clear proof that Mr. Murdoch personally ordered the article about Mr. Kheel revived, and therefore cannot find that he used his magazine as an instrument of reprisal, as the complainant contends. The Council can, however, suggest that special dangers to credibility are involved when a magazine publishes an article concerning an individual with whom the magazine has had a close, and special relationship — in this case attorney/client.

In a recent complaint, the *Boston Globe* was accused of not printing a story that might have damaged a friend. Here *New York* magazine is accused of printing a story that might damage a foe. In cases where friendly or unfriendly ties exist between a publication or its officials and a story or its principals, the publication has a great burden to show that the ties do not influence news judgment.

With respect to the original complaint by Mr. Kheel concerning the refusal of the advertisement he wished to insert in the issue of the magazine that contained the article, the Council believes that the requirements of fairness were satisfied by the extensive space the editors of *New York* made available to Mr. Kheel to challenge what he regarded as errors of fact and interpretation.

The remaining issue is credibility. *New York* magazine lowered its credibility by misleading the public on the "hands-off" rule of its owner.

**Concurring:** Cooney, Ghiglione, Hauser, Huston, Isaacs, McKay, Pulitzer, Roberts and Rusher.

**Dissenting:** Otwell

March 9, 1979

## COMPLAINT NO. 159      (Filed July 21, 1978)
## COHEN
### against
### ABC NEWS

**Complaint:** Professor Bernard L. Cohen of the University of Pittsburgh, complained that two segments on ABC's "20/20" program, aired July 4 and July 18, 1978, provided "one-sided" and unfair coverage on the subject of low-level radiation. Specifically, Professor Cohen contended that:

> 1. Nearly every portion of the presentations contained conclusions and implications that were contrary to prevailing scientific thought on the subject. (To support this contention, Professor Cohen listed six scientific organizations involved in the study of radiation which he thought were representative of majority opinion.)
>
> 2. ABC had "deceived" the public by "spreading misleading information and impressions" and was not qualified to make decisions on scientific subjects.
>
> 3. In view of the limited number of network programs on low level radiation, ABC's "misleading" report neglected the needs of its audience.

**Response:** Mr. William Sheehan, who was Senior Vice President of ABC News, wrote:

> In our judgment, ABC has been fair on an overall basis in treating this subject on "20/20" and other programs . . . To a large extent, "20/20" concerned itself with

aspects of nuclear power which we do not believe are controversial. In our judgment, there is no serious controversy concerning the fact that nuclear radiation can be dangerous to health. Furthermore, we do not believe that there is any serious dispute concerning the fact that in the past there have not been adequate studies of the risks of low-level radiation.

Regarding Professor Cohen's charge that the program was "one-sided" and lacked the nuclear industry viewpoint, Mr. Sheehan said:

> While "20/20" did present views that there are serious potential risks to low-level radiation, the question was treated as one to which there is no conclusive answer . . . In the concluding segment, Mr. (Dave) Marash also reported that the nuclear power industry says that there are many possible reasons why cancer and leukemia have been increasing in so many places, and they say that no link between low levels of radiation and these diseases has ever been proved. . . . In conclusion, we believe ABC has fairly presented representative and contrasting views on the nuclear power issue in its overall programming.

**Council finding:** Investigative reporting in the United States has built, for the most part, a long and honorable record. It calls for probing into issues that are controversial, provides documentation, and often draws pointed conclusions. ABC News chose to do just this in its two-part report on the effects of low level radiation. Challenged, ABC News has taken the position that its over-all coverage of the general subject over an extended period has presented "representative and contrasting views."

The program reported that many experts believe there are substantial dangers from low level radiation to which the public has not been sufficiently alerted. The program, while not balanced on the subject, also included the views of those who do not believe the danger had been proven.

In his complaint, Professor Cohen challenges the right of broadcast journalism to take such an unbalanced position. He argues that had such a presentation been made in print, "there are many other publications to present the other side" and he holds further that people "are accustomed to having newspapers taking sides on issues." The Council rejects the idea that broadcast journalism is relegated to a separate and lesser standard of freedom.

Professor Cohen also takes the position that "There is a long and commendable tradition in journalism of investigative reporting on matters where the reporter can understand the issues as well as anyone else, as in crime or politics. However this surely does not apply to scientific questions. Your people are not qualified to make decisions on scientific questions. . . ."

The Council rejects Professor Cohen's stance that scientific questions are beyond the scope of journalists. The Council believes, as do most responsible professionals, that the growth of specialists is both healthy and desirable. But to eliminate the vast bodies of journalists from the continued examination of public issues, scientific or otherwise, would, in the Council's opinion, be detrimental to the public interest.

The major portion of Professor Cohen's charge centers on the expertise of the persons interviewed on the ABC programs. The Council finds that the subject matter was pertinent for examination and that it was within ABC's editorial discretion to take the views it did.

The complaint is found unwarranted.

**Concurring:** Cooney, Ghiglione, Huston, Isaacs, McKay, Otwell, Pulitzer, Roberts and Rusher.

March 9, 1979


### COMPLAINT NO. 160      (Filed Aug. 8, 1978)
### NEWTON
### against
### ABC NEWS


**Complaint:** Jane Newton, president of Oregon Women for Timber, complained of bias, distortions and inaccuracies in one portion of an ABC "20/20" two-part broadcast on herbicides, telecast July 25, 1978 and August 1, 1978. The complaint focused on the August 1 installment which explored the effects of human and animal exposure to the herbicide 2,4,5-T, used domestically on rice crops, cattle ranges, forests and rights of way, and containing traces of the poisonous substance dioxin. Ms. Newton protested that the practicality and benefits of using the herbicide, 2,4,5-T, as well as its relative safety, were not adequately reported because:

● Only one person who "had anything to do with" 2,4,5-T actually appeared on the program. He was a Dow Chemical Company toxicologist.

● Only those "with a long adversary history to herbicides, although they are in the extreme minority among researchers or users with herbicide or forestry experience," were interviewed. Ms. Newton also contended that there was no conclusive evidence to connect those presented as victims in the broadcast with the effects of exposure to 2,4,5-T.

She maintained:

• The broadcast failed to interview people with "real" exposure to herbicides.

• The animals shown were, in fact, suffering from "severe nutritional deficiencies" and not from exposure to 2,4,5-T.

• No effort was made to compare such exposures to lab tests producing observable effects.

• Documentation from health departments and professionals "about the anecdotal health problems that make up the bulk of the program" was not included.

Ms. Newton argued:

> After 30 years of use, their (herbicides) field-study record is *unblemished*. As human activities go this is an almost unique record. The insistence of virtually all media reporters that the contrary must be true threatens the whole forestry resource with continued sickening exploitation . . . Programs such as '20/20' destroy people's trust in technology without offering documentation either of their thesis, or of the effectiveness of 'alternatives' which I presume they also tout.

**Response:** ABC News supplied transcripts and video cassettes of the two broadcasts. While ABC News did not directly respond to Ms. Newton's complaint, Jeffrey Gralnick, director and executive producer of special events, answered a similar grievance from another viewer. ABC News provided the Council with a copy of this correspondence, in which Mr. Gralnick wrote:

> In the August "20/20" report, Mr. (Geraldo) Rivera stressed that there are opposing views on whether 2,4,5-T as currently used in commercial applications is harmful.

Addressing the charge that viewers were misled as to the connection between the symptoms suffered by those interviewed and the spraying of 2,4,5-T, Mr. Gralnick said:

> A Dow scientist pointed out that the level of dioxin in his company's 2,4,5-T products was well within current government guidelines and that such levels were absolutely safe. . . . The report cited the views of industry scientists that the dioxin content of the 2,4,5-T chemical now being used in our forests is so low that no miscarriages could possibly result from such exposure. . . . Geraldo Rivera closed his report by noting that in considering further restrictions on the use of 2,4,5-T, Congress and the EPA would have to weigh the risks against the substantial economic benefits of this chemical. . . . In conclusion, we believe that the report presented an accurate and factual account of the controversy surrounding the use of 2,4,5-T and included a fair representation of the view that this chemical is safe and of considerable economic value.

**Council finding:** The issue of the effects of exposure to herbicides as currently used in the United States is clearly a controversial one. As pointed out in ABC's two-part broadcast, the matter has been under review by the Federal Environmental Protection Agency, Congress and the Veterans Administration.

On March 1, the E.P.A. issued an emergency ban on the further use of 2,4,5-T citing what it said was an "alarming rate of miscarriages among women in one area of Oregon during the months immediately after the spraying of 2,4,5-T in forests surrounding their homes.

The ABC report included mention of the Oregon situation as it existed before the ban, but was also careful to report on the uncertainty surrounding the use of herbicides.

At the close of the August 1 report, Mr. Rivera noted:

> . . . assuming that the EPA isn't outdistanced by Congress in this case. . . . after they weigh the risks, they have to weigh the economic benefits of using the spray, because the spray is useful obviously. And, it's only after they do risk/benefit analysis that they (can) make their decision.

He added that there was no collective perspective on the matter: "It depends on who you ask."

In examining the effects of herbicide spraying, ABC News raised the kinds of questions that should be expected from an investigative report of this nature. The report questioned whether proper safety standards were being met in the use of herbicides and included many statements maintaining that such standards were in effect.

The Council finds the complaint to be unwarranted.

**Concurring:** Cooney, Ghiglione, Huston, Isaacs, McKay, Otwell, Pulitzer, Roberts and Rusher.

March 9, 1979


## COMPLAINT NO. 161     (Filed Feb. 5, 1979)
### LOERA
### against
### CBS NEWS

**Complaint:** Leo T. Loera of Riverside, Calif., complained that a "60 Minutes" segment entitled "Stop! Police!" which was broadcast on Jan. 14, 1979, was poorly researched and contained "insensitive reporting."

The segment, which dealt with police training for survival in the face of ambush and similar attacks, concentrated on conditions and training of police in Riverside and examined conditions police encountered in Casa Blanca, a Riverside neighborhood with a predominantly Chicano population. Mr. Loera, who specified what he said were inaccuracies in the presentation, said that the segment "left a residue of ill feelings and depicted the Hispanic community as lawless."

Points which Mr. Loera said were in error or distorted were:

• The use of the term "the ambush rate for the Riverside Police Department." The complaint said "the use of the word 'ambush rate' . . . is wholly inappropriate; for what was intended was the assault rate citywide."

• Statements that the survival training of officers was developed "when two officers died in an ambush in 1974." Mr. Loera said this comment was made immediately after a statement that "to deal with Casa Blanca, these officers are taking special courses in survival training." He said "the two tragic deaths had nothing to do with the Hispanic community."

• The use of what Mr. Loera said was the lurid presentation of the Hispanic community by insinuations, "dated film footage and a camera focusing on a police car which only confirms the worst that people can imagine."

Those portions of the broadcast to which Mr. Loera referred are included here from the transcript:

> This is one area of Riverside called Casa Blanca, a tough Chicano neighborhood. The streets look innocent enough on a bright afternoon, but we'd be a little nervous making this drive at night; and we'd be especially nervous driving through in a police car. At night this neighborhood, where a lot of people are armed, can be a death trap for police. It's hard even for our special night lens to capture the eeriness of a place where most street lights have been shot out, and police cars run with lights out to avoid attracting attention and drawing fire. Mostly it's random potshots out of the dark, but it adds up to an ambush rate for the Riverside police that is four times the national average.
>
> REASONER: To deal with Casa Blanca, these officers are taking special courses in officer survival: how to react effectively within the law in crisis situations? Riverside developed its course when two officers died in an ambush in 1974; and now troopers from all over the area get the special training at the San Bernardino Police Academy.

**Response:** In response to complaints concerning the accuracy of "Stop! Police!" CBS aired a correction on its Feb. 11 broadcast of "60 Minutes." It said:

> MORLEY SAFER: On January 14, 60 MINUTES reported on a training program in Riverside, California in which policemen were being taught when they should and should not use their weapons. In that story we made two errors. We said the ambush

rate against the Riverside Police was four times the national average. We now learn it was not the ambush rate but the assault rate. Assault includes everything from shooting a policeman to throwing rocks at him. We also said Riverside developed its program when two officers were killed in 1974. Those officers were in fact killed in 1971. It wasn't until five years later in 1976 that the training program began.

In a letter to Mr. Loera, dated Jan. 17, Robert Chandler, vice president and director of public affairs broadcasts for CBS News, said:

We did not depict the Hispanic community of Riverside as being lawless. What we did do, and I am enclosing a transcript of what actually was said, was to refer to the sniping in the Casa Blanca neighborhood of Riverside as follows: "This is one area of Riverside called Casa Blanca, a tough Chicano neighborhood." If this is inaccurate, please let us know.

We said nothing about the Hispanic community in Riverside and indeed, the officer we interviewed in his squad car in Casa Blanca, who told us he has been assaulted seven times in the last year has a Hispanic surname. You asked for an explanation and a clear rebuttal to our "distorted presentation of the Hispanic community in Riverside," but we simply described one particular neighborhood in that community.

Responding to the Council on Feb. 13, Kay Wight, vice president for administration and assistant to the president of CBS News, enclosed a copy of the Feb. 11 correction, and addressed herself additionally to the point made by Mr. Loera about "lurid presentation of the Hispanic community":
"What we said was:

. . . The streets look innocent enough on a bright afternoon, but we'd be a little nervous making this drive at night; and we'd be especially nervous driving through in a police car. At night this neighborhood, where a lot of people are armed, can be a death trap for police. It's hard even for our special night lens to capture the eeriness of a place where most street lights have been shot out, and police cars run with lights out to avoid attracting attention and drawing fire . . .

. . . We were told by members of the Riverside police force that 'police cars run with lights out to avoid attracting attention and drawing fire.' We did not say the police run with their light out *only* in Casa Blanca. We believe our statement to be accurate.

Commenting on Mr. Loera's complaint concerning filming police cars in Casa Blanca, Riverside Police Chief Vic Jones told the Council that patrol cars in the Casa Blanca section do not routinely ride with lights out to avoid detection. He said this is done only in "tactical situations" and in all sections of Riverside.

**Council finding:** In its portrayal of Casa Blanca as a "tough Chicano neighborhood," 60 Minutes committed factual errors that the Council

48

believes were never adequately corrected. The Council also finds that the broadcast did create an impression of lawlessness among Hispanics in general, which was underscored when it hopscotched across the country to Spanish Harlem to show New York police in a tense confrontation with apparently lawless elements.

In acknowledging on air that the 60 Minutes segment contained factual errors about the origins of a police survival training program and about the ambush rate for policemen in Riverside, the CBS corrections made no mention of the fact that the original errors were linked to portions of the broadcast that mentioned Casa Blanca prominently.

Additionally, the original program made reference to the fact that police cars run with their lights out in Casa Blanca to avoid attracting attention. Although the Riverside Police Chief said this was done only in tactical situations and in sections other than Casa Blanca as well, CBS did not correct this apparent error.

In sum, the Council believes the original program was flawed not only by errors of fact but by the manner in which it referred to the Hispanic community of Riverside. The subjects of crime and ethnic communities are sensitive ones and added care should be taken in the filming, reporting and editing of any such stories.

The Council also believes strongly in adequate correction of errors that occur in the reporting and editing process. CBS has pioneered in broadcasting prompt corrections, but in this instance, the Council finds the corrections to have been inadequate.

**Concurring:** Cooney, Ghiglione, Hauser, Huston, Isaacs, McKay, Otwell, Pulitzer, Roberts and Rusher.

March 9, 1979

**RECONSIDERATION**      (Reconsideration request filed
**COMPLAINT NO. 161**      March 14, 1979)
LOERA
against
CBS NEWS

**Background:** On March 9, 1979, the Council issued its decision in a complaint against CBS News "60 Minutes" report entitled "Stop! Police!," which was broadcast on January 14, 1979. The segment, which dealt with police training for survival in the face of ambush and similar attacks, concentrated on the training of police in Riverside, California, and examined conditions police encountered in Casa Blanca, an area of Riverside which the broadcast described as "a tough Chicano neighborhood."

In its decision, the Council made the following findings: That factual errors in the original broadcast were not adequately addressed in a correction which CBS aired on a subsequent "60 Minutes" broadcast, and that "Stop! Police!" did "create an impression of lawlessness among Hispanics in general."

On March 14, 1979, CBS requested that the Council reconsider these two conclusions.

**Reconsideration and conclusion of the Council:** The Council reaffirms its belief that CBS's corrections, which were addressed to specific errors of fact, were inadequate without acknowledgment that the errors had occurred in those portions of the broadcast which referred to Casa Blanca.

On reconsideration the Council concludes that it was in error in saying that the "60 Minutes" report created an impression of lawlessness among Hispanics. The original broadcast contained no such implication and the Council withdraws that portion of its findings.

**Concurring:** Brady, Cooney, Isaacs, Otwell, Pulitzer, Renick and Rusher.

**Dissenting:** Ghiglione, Huston, McKay, Roberts and Scott.
June 11, 1979


## COMPLAINT NO. 162 (Filed Sept. 26, 1978)
### STANS
### against
### NEWSPAPER ENTERPRISE ASSOCIATION

**Complaint:** Maurice Stans, former Secretary of Commerce, and Chairman of the Finance Committee to Reelect the President (Nixon, 1972) complained that a column written by Martha Angle and Robert Walters and distributed by Newspaper Enterprise Association was inaccurate and irresponsible. Mr. Stans submitted the column as it had appeared in the *Las Vegas Review-Journal* of February 28, 1978. It was based on documents obtained under the Freedom of Information Act from the file of the Watergate Special Prosecutor and described various aspects of Mr. Stans' fund-raising efforts.

The principal thrust of Mr. Stans' complaint centered on differences between allegations contained in the documents obtained from the Special Prosecutor's file and what transpired later in court. Mr. Stans contended that "the sources from which the authors obtained their information . . . related primarily to other persons, and only incidentally to me, and the authors knew, or should have known, that the incidental references to me had been overtaken and contradicted by subsequent public disclosures."

What Mr. Stans was focusing upon was that in the later court proceedings he pleaded guilty to five misdemeanor charges, which he described as technical, and not wilful. The Angle-Walters column mentioned this aspect, but laid all the emphasis on what was contained in the Prosecutor's opened files.

Mr. Stans' attorney on March 30, 1978, wrote NEA, denouncing the column, asking for an apology and asking, also, that the letter be published. NEA's counsel responded, offering Mr. Stans "an opportunity to tell his side of the story" in an "op-ed type of article." Mr. Stans rejected this, asserting that it was unacceptable because it was not going to allow him to mention the original "devastating column." He termed the offer "specious and meaningless because such a step would have provided no remedy for the damages done. . . ."

After Mr. Stans filed his complaint with the News Council, NEA made another offer for a rebuttal column. This was also refused. In a letter to the Council on February 8, 1979, Mr. Stans said: "The only thing that will satisfy me at this time is a direct apology in the same column, printed in the same papers."

**Response:** David Hendin, vice president and executive editor of NEA, responded to the Council in a letter on November 16, 1978. Mr. Hendin also subsequently forwarded copies of the Special Prosecutor's memoranda on which the disputed column was based.

Mr. Hendin wrote that he was prepared from the outset to grant Mr. Stans rebuttal space even though he held that the column contained no substantive factual errors. Mr. Hendin wrote:

> The inability to get together on a solution was quite simple: I was insisting upon receiving an article written specifically for newspaper readers. Since the article I suggested Mr. Stans write would have appeared in newspapers a minimum of two months after the original column, it would seem ludicrous to refer to the original column. This is especially true since the Stans article would be distributed and thus considered for use by all of our clients — some of whom had not used the original column in question.

Mr. Hendin said that although he believed no reference should be made to the original column he had no objection to a rebuttal containing material which dealt specifically with issues raised by that column. Additionally, Mr. Hendin said the drafts which had previously been submitted by Mr. Stans' attorneys were of "poor journalistic quality" and, therefore, would not be used by NEA clients.

**Council finding:** The Angle-Walters column about Mr. Stans' fund-raising activities was accurate in the narrow context in which it interpreted material obtained from the Watergate Special Prosecutor's file. The use of such material was clearly privileged, but the Council does not believe the column accurately reflected the subsequent public record on many of the points cited in the memoranda. The column employed material from the Special Prosecutor's file accusing Mr. Stans of activities for which he was never formally tried. He was tried only on the five misdemeanor charges relating to the handling of cash donations.

In light of the record, the Council believes Mr. Stans was entitled to some form of rebuttal. As a matter of practice, most syndicates will offer to forward to the customers of a column a reasonable rebuttal to derogatory material appearing in the column, and NEA offered to do that in this case. It rejected what Mr. Stans' attorneys submitted, however, because it was in substance a legal document rather than a personal letter or a column-style communication — and on the further ground that it referred to the original offending column, at a time when the reference was too dated to be newsworthy.

The Council rejects the latter objection; Mr. Stans and his attorneys were entitled to identify what they were refuting. The former has more substance; newspapers understandably would rather print a personal letter or a column than a legal document. Perhaps Mr. Stans ought thereupon to have demanded the right to have his legal document forwarded by the syndicate to the relevant newspapers anyway, so they might individually decide whether to publish it. Perhaps he even did so, though the record is unclear. What actually seems to have happened is that the controversy raveled itself out in an exchange of letters between attorneys, culminating in a demand by Mr. Stans for "a direct apology." In these circumstances, and especially in view of the fact that NEA did not refuse to distribute some more orthodox form of reply, we are unwilling to hold the complaint "warranted."

**Concurring:** Brady, Cooney, Isaacs, Otwell, Pulitzer, Renick, Roberts and Rusher.

**Dissenting:** Ghiglione, Huston, McKay, and Scott.

**Dissenting opinion by Ms. Huston:** (Ghiglione, McKay and Scott concurring).

The Angle-Walters column was based on material from the Watergate Special Prosecutor's file, obtained under the Freedom of Information Act. The column may have been accurate enough in reporting allegations made in the early 1970s, but the authors failed to disclose subsequent developments, including the fact that the allegations had never been tested in court. The column reported allegations of wrongdoing with which Mr. Stans was never charged.

Although the material was circulated in the form of a column, it was a reportorial column. So, as with any article making an accusation, the Angle-Walters piece should have included a response from the person charged with wrongdoing. At the very least, the reporters should have reported that they attempted to reach Mr. Stans for comment.

The column was distributed by the Newspaper Enterprise Association, which, because of its nature as a syndicator, complicates the process of response, particularly since NEA will not disclose to the subject of a column the newspapers to which the column was offered.

The NEA's own policy statement entitled, "A Statement on Ethics and Principles," has delineated what it calls the "Right of Response." Its commendable statement reads: "In our editorial material, we strive to be fair and accurate at all times. Our editors, writers and contributors attempt to recognize opposing points of view . . ." However, in this case we found no evidence that NEA's editors or writers attempted to recognize opposing points of view.

Further, the policy states that in certain cases the NEA would "invite the complaining organization or individual to present its or his position in an article which shall be of similar length to the article or column in question. This will be distributed to those newspapers which received the original article and column."

In this case, NEA acknowledged Stans' right of response, but over ensuing months the whole matter became mired in disagreements as to the form and timing of the response. NEA acknowledged that this was a matter that warranted a response. The news organization contended that Stans' response was not in the proper journalistic form. But NEA should have found a way to accommodate Mr. Stans in his right to be heard. Newspaper reporters, rewriters and editors know how to translate legalese into newspaperese. They should have done so in this case, putting Stans' response into journalistic form.

By not forwarding any communication from Stans or his attorney to the newspapers it serves, NEA, in effect, made it impossible for each newspaper to reach its own decision about publication of a possible rebuttal to the Angle-Walters column. NEA and other editorial services should volunteer, as a matter of principle, to forward all significant rebuttals to their customer newspapers.

**Concurring opinion by Ms. Roberts:** I concur with the majority opinion that the complaint is unwarranted. However, I understand one majority conclusion is premised on a *right* of a person to reply to what he perceives to be derogatory material in a syndicated column, despite the fact the column contains no factual inaccuracy. I believe this places an impossible burden on the press, and amounts to an obligation of the press to provide access rejected by the Supreme Court in *Miami Herald Publishing Co. v. Tornillo*, 418 U.S. 241 (1974), and never before supported by the Council to my knowledge.

In this case the column purported to reveal material regarding Maurice Stans from a "series of memos prepared in 1973 and 1974 by the Watergate Special Prosecution Force but only recently made public after the Fund for Constitutional Government filed a lawsuit to force their disclosure." Unfortunately the columnists termed this material "evidence," but they were careful to point out to the reader that Stans "pleaded guilty to five misdemeanor charges" relating to other matters, and even with respect to these charges "he claimed the violations were 'not willful,' and (were) of minor, technical nature." Thus the reader could judge whether or not the material from the memos was suspect as to the reported activities of Stans since he was not in fact tried or convicted growing out of these alleged activities. The columnists repeatedly described such activities not as actual happenings but as matters "recounted" in one of the special prosecutor's memos, and remarks attributed to Stans are labelled statements "he is quoted as saying in a special prosecutor's memo."

While I believe the public is better served if a columnist seeks a response from a public figure who is the subject of a column, I do not believe 1) the record is clear in this case what, if any, effort the columnists made to obtain such a response, or that 2) the request of response is mandatory in each and every instance, especially when the reader is explicitly advised what is being related is from prosecutor's files, which material did not result in prosecution of Mr. Stans.

Such a right would be mandatory in my view in the event there is a danger the reader could be misled by untrue, inaccurate material. Here the reader was advised at the outset the source of the information and of the fact Mr. Stans was never prosecuted on charges growing out of the activities reported in these memos. Mr. Stans does not contend the memos did not in fact state what the column says; he contests the fact underlying the memos.

I believe the Council's conclusion in this aspect of the case can only mean syndicated columns, which so often deal with public figures such as Mr. Stans, must allow space for a riposte every time a public figure is depicted in any manner other than laudatory, and no matter how factually accurate or careful a columnist is to place the derogatory material in perspective.
June 11, 1979

**COMPLAINT NO. 163**      (Filed Feb. 27, 1979)
JANEWAY
against
ESQUIRE

**Complaint:** Economist Eliot Janeway complained that an article about him in the November 21, 1978, issue of *Esquire* magazine (with Mr. Janeway featured on the front cover) contained "documentable cases of malicious falsehood, distortion and misrepresentation."

The article, written by Chris Welles, was headlined, "Eliot 'Calamity' Janeway: An Old Bear Who's Largely Bull."

Welles' article dealt with Janeway's personality, his political and professional associations, his financial standing and presumed to give inside information on several major investment involvements. Welles described Janeway as a "consummate poseur," asserted that "his performance as a private investor has been lackluster and sometimes disastrous;" that "on Wall Street, State Street and La Salle Street, (he) is generally regarded as a somewhat comic figure." Welles treated Janeway's associations with such political figures as Bert Lance and Lyndon Johnson, and such Janeway investments as Medserco, Inc., a St. Louis health insurance firm; Florida real estate; and particularly Realty Equities Corp., which went bankrupt and about which Welles asserted that Janeway "did escape being charged by the SEC for helping to engineer the fraud."

Janeway's 21-page complaint on February 27, 1979, cited aspects he termed falsehoods. On April 6, Mr. Janeway filed a supplementary charge that in the March 13 issue of *Esquire*, an article titled, "Faking

Your Way to the Top," by William Flanagan, "escalates Felker's campaign of malice against me." (Clay Felker was editor and publisher of *Esquire* at the time both articles appeared). The Flanagan article said, "Economics guru Eliot Janeway has long led reporters to believe he was a Cornell graduate; he did attend but never took his degree." This same basic data had appeared in Mr. Welles' November article.

**Response:** *Esquire* magazine did not respond. However, Mr. Welles provided the Council with point by point answers to Mr. Janeway's charges, and tendered documentation, including some of his reportorial notes, which the Council had not requested. (The new editor of *Esquire* has now indicated he intends to write to the Council saying that the magazine stands ready to correct any provable errors.)

### Bert Lance Relationship

> *Esquire* article: (After describing Janeway's early relationship, Welles wrote that) Janeway was among Lance's friends who received loans from his banks. "I did Lance a favor," Janeway claims. "At his request, I did business with him." According to federal investigators, Janeway's loans from Calhoun First National Bank at one point totaled $103,500. The loans were moved to the National Bank of Georgia (NBG) when Lance moved, where they grew to at least $400,000. Like Lance's other friends, Janeway, say federal investigators, did not bother to make regular payments on the loans. Janeway, meanwhile, bought NBG stock. The new management of NBG has since forced Janeway to repay the loans.

Much later in the article, Welles wrote about Janeway's losses in Realty Equities and referred to "Lance loans and mortgages."

**Janeway's charge:** The loans never totaled $400,000 and payments on the loans were not made because of bank confusion over billing involving personal and corporate loans. When the confusion was cleared up, payments were made. "We labeled any allegation of a Lance mortgage as the lie it is and he (Welles) professed to be satisfied," said the complaint.

**Welles' response:** Welles did not speak to the challenge to his accuracy about the published amount of the loans. He conceded the "mortgage" reference was wrong and said *Esquire* had failed to make the correction he marked. He said Janeway did not deny the basic thrust of the description of his dealings with Lance.

**Staff addenda:** National Bank of Georgia documents show that the loans reached a maximum of $213,869 in 1977. Correspondence from the bank indicates that confusion over billing practice may well have caused the delay in repayments.

56

# Realty Equities Corp.

*Esquire article:* When it was all over, Realty (Equities Corp.) which was (Janeway's) largest business investment, cost (him) his entire investment . . . about $2-$3 million before taxes . . . Realty Equities was founded in 1958 by Morris Karp, an ambitious young home builder. Starting with $2 million in apartment buildings and other properties, Karp built the company by the end of the 1960's into a . . . conglomerate with $500 million in assets . . . During the money crunches and laggard economy of the early 1970s, it fell deeply into the red . . . In 1974, the SEC charged Realty and Republic National Life Insurance Co. of Dallas and several of the concerns' executives, including Morris Karp, with having perpetrated one of the largest real estate frauds in recent history . . . For nearly all its existence, Eliot Janeway was a member of Realty Equities' board of directors.

The article quoted one former officer as calling Janeway "the second most important person in the company . . . He gave it credibility . . . He opened doors." The article went on to say that "although (Janeway) opposed many of Karp's acquisitions (he) loyally stayed with the company until November 1973." It said:

> Whatever the case, Janeway did escape being charged by the SEC for helping to engineer the fraud.

**Janeway's charge:** "He ignored or distorted the facts he was aware of in his representation of my involvement." Janeway says he gave Welles all of the Realty story, claims Welles omitted "any consideration whatever" of the "clean bill of health" given Janeway's role by former Attorney General Herbert Brownell, former Federal Judge Simon Rifkind and the SEC. "The disposition of the class action suit brought against the directors of both companies confirms the record," asserts Janeway. "The Republic directors were assessed $1.6 million and Republic itself was assessed $5 million. The Realty directors were assessed nothing. By having access to the SEC records, Welles knew exactly what I knew . . ."
**Welles' response:** "Janeway emphasized that he was never charged with impropriety. I never said or implied he had been. I specifically said he escaped being charged."
**Staff addenda:** In this general connection, Janeway disputed a statement attributed by Welles to Ian McGregor, a Lazard Freres partner, that "Eliot has lost some of his credibility as a result of . . . Realty Equities." Welles stood by his quote and produced his notes, which, under the heading "RE" contain the notation "lost certain credibility." In a letter to *Esquire*, Mr. McGregor denied he had made the statement. He maintained that Realty Equities was a subject with which he was not familiar. Sources

57

at the SEC told the staff that there was no indication in the files that Mr. Janeway was ever considered a possible subject for prosecution in connection with the Realty Equities case.

## Janeway's Investment Record

> *Esquire article:* His performance as a private investor . . . had been lackluster and sometimes disastrous . . .
>
> He is a major investor in Medserco (a small St. Louis health insurance concern), is a paid economic adviser to it . . . until recently served on its board of directors, and is a business partner of its president. . . . The gold stocks have done well for Janeway and Medserco may also. But the same cannot be said for some of his other investments. . . . Janeway during the mid-1950s organized a group of investors, mainly Wall Street and business friends, to buy a 3,000 acre parcel of land near Tampa. It became Janeway's largest direct investment in real estate. Janeway assured the others that the land was directly in the path of local development and would almost certainly yield a handsome profit. But as the years went by, development . . . moved in other directions. The land remained undeveloped. It rose so slowly in value that much if not all the increase was eaten up by taxes and mortgage payments. . . . By the early 1970s, a number of the investors were so irate that they demanded Janeway have them bought out. . . .

**Janeway's charge:** In an approximately 1,000-word statement, Janeway asserted that Welles chose to disregard a wealth of material offered to substantiate Janeway's "body of positive information he was given about my investment performance." (The complete detail on Janeway's trusts and other involvements can be examined in the complaint letter of February 16.)

**Welles' response:** "Janeway challenges my statement that his performance as a private investor has been 'lackluster, and sometimes disastrous.' Yet he does not deny my evaluation of the investment results of perhaps his two largest private investments: The Florida land venture, his largest real estate holding, and Realty Equities, his largest securities investment from which he admits he suffered a $2-$3-million pretax loss . . . He offers no persuasive evidence that his overall investment performance has been any better than lackluster."

**Staff addenda:** Janeway's record in Realty Equities is recorded earlier. He insists that the Florida land transaction was profitable, although original landholders have been bought out. Many are now mortgagees.

Don Bleakley, who has managed the Florida land for Janeway, told Council staff that the land rose slowly in value because environmental considerations had prevented construction on much of the 3,000-acre site.

## The Janeway Network

*Esquire article*: A typical rank-and-file network member is Paula Hughes, a stockbroker with Thomson McKinnon Securities Incorporated and one of the highest producers on Wall Street. Hughes arranges speaking engagements for Janeway, sends clients to hear him, introduces him to her Wall Street friends, and once gave a reception at her house in his honor. In return, Janeway sends brokerage business to her, suggest to clients that they do likewise, gives her publicity in his column, and most recently was trying to secure Senator Russell Long ("One of my best friends," says Janeway) to speak before a women's investment group to which she belongs.

**Janeway's charge:** "Ms. Hughes has written a letter to *Esquire* nailing Welles' canard about my being the guest of honor at a sales pitch reception. In her letter, she documented my donation of an afternoon to a worthy cause whose purpose it is to donate books to backward countries. Welles did not confront me with this 'revelation' in order to give me an opportunity to set the record straight."

**Welles' response:** Defends the accuracy of his description of Paula Hughes as part of the "Janeway network" and notes that he did not, as Janeway charges, say that he (Janeway) was a guest of honor at a "sales pitch" reception given by Ms. Hughes.

**Staff addenda:** In a letter to *Esquire* on December 1, Ms. Hughes declared that she "had rarely read material so thoroughly distorted as to fact. . . ." She specifically denied the article's assertion that she had arranged speaking engagements for Janeway or that she sends clients to hear him lecture at his seminars.

## Relationship with Lyndon Johnson

*Esquire article:* Janeway had met Johnson in the late 1930s, when Johnson was first elected to Congress. For many years, the two were close. "They genuinely liked each other," says Michael Janeway, (Janeway's son) whom once worked for Johnson. "But it was more than a friendship. Johnson thought my old man was well connected with the media, New York, the Wall Street crowd, the money world."

. . . .

Michael Janeway says the break between the two men derived mainly from his father's opposition to LBJ's acceptance of the vice-presidential nomination in 1960. But, he adds, "Maybe they rubbed each other the wrong way. It had become a bit of a Rashomon situation: Am I using you or are you using me?

. . . .

When Johnson became president in 1963, some of Janeway's friends thought that Janeway nevertheless expected that Johnson would reward him for his years of loyal friendship—specifically Secretary of the Treasury or head of the Council of Economic Advisers. Elizabeth Janeway (Janeway's wife) says he expected to become a ranking member of LBJ's brain trust.

**Janeway's charge:** "I respect the editorial right of selectivity—but not for the purposes of hatcheting, distorting and suppressing facts. . . . The crowning lie Welles has fashioned out of the whole cloth . . . is the statement attributed to my wife." Janeway is also vehement about the material attributed to his son and asserts "it may be read as one of many examples of Welles' selective use of quotes and segments of quotes, taken out of context, given to him by persons, who, to their regret, honestly tried to help Welles understand the subtleties of a complicated relationship."

**Welles' response:** "Very little of the elaborate detail Janeway provides about Johnson is new to me. Most of the pertinent points were checked and rechecked with other sources. I stand by my interpretations and conclusions. . . . Though Janeway's wife denies the statement I attributed to her, I stand by it. Attached as Exhibit/12 is the applicable page from my handwritten notes of my interview with her."

**Staff addenda:** Mrs. Elizabeth Janeway denied to staff ever saying what Welles attributed to her. Michael Janeway said he was "taken aback by the rather arbitrary cutting" of the quotes attributed to him. He added: "The quotes were out of context in terms of the relationship I was trying to describe to him."

### Janeway's Economic Forecasts

*Esquire article*: Janeway's principal stock-in-trade, grim warnings of coming calamities such as stock market crashes and economic collapses, has come to be widely seen, in the economically ravaged 1970s as chillingly pertinent and imperative. He is widely known as "Calamity" Janeway. . . . The doomsday Janeway is almost total artifice, the furthest of the Janeways from reality. Away from a microphone Janeway is generally cheerful and ebullient. Indeed, he is an inveterate optimist.

**Janeway's charge**: "Despite Welles' claim that my 'principal stock-in-trade'. . . . is 'grim warnings of coming calamities such as stock market collapses', I have never written or spoken a bearish forecast that was not packaged with a bullish remedy calculated to turn a real danger into a false alarm."

**Welles' response**: "Janeway claims that my article exaggerates his bearishness and is erroneous in suggesting that his bearish outlook is designed at least in part, for its commercial appeal. It is true that during his early years his forecasts were often bullish. Yet in recent years, as evidenced by his popular sobriquet, 'Calamity' Janeway, it is indisputable that doomsday predictions have become his chief stock in trade."

**Staff addenda**: In support of his description of Janeway's personality, Welles quoted Donald Cook, a partner at Lazard Freres, and a friend of Janeway's. Cook told Council staff that the quotation attributed to him, "You can't find the real Eliot Janeway. All you'll find is an artichoke. There are twenty-five Janeways," was inaccurate. Mr. Cook said he had been complimentary about Janeway in his interview with Welles. He said the story was told about another individual and that Welles had taken it out of context and applied it to Janeway.

### Disclosure

*Esquire article*: Though he does not publicly disclose the fact, he (Janeway) regularly uses his media outlets to promote situations that he and his company are invested in. Over the past year, for instance, he has frequently recommended South African gold stocks in his column, newsletters, speeches, and at seminars
. . . .

A more specific example is Medserco Incorporated, a small St. Louis health insurance concern. Though Medserco has operated in the red for eight years, Janeway has promoted the company at his seminars and in one of his newsletters. He has not disclosed, though, the details of his personal involvement with the company
. . . .

Earlier in the article, Welles wrote:

Despite the image of independence and credibility he projects, Janeway often uses his column to sustain business relationships. For a long time Janeway has had ties with the insurance industry. He has been a paid consultant to a number of insurance companies and is a frequent speaker at industry gatherings. . . . Janeway has not disclosed his ties to the insurance industry in his column.

**Janeway's charge:** "I have no ties to the insurance industry. Welles never asked me to verify that I have ever been paid any kind of retainer by any insurance company or association. Consequently, I was not given the opportunity to refute that statement. . . ."

Janeway also attacked a portion of Welles' article dealing with term v. whole life insurance, saying "Welles has turned a difference of opinion, which allows for different priorities for different types of policy holders in different financial circumstances, health conditions and age groups, into an attack on my integrity which originated with his ignorance of the facts. He never asked me to discuss the relative merits of term v. whole life . . . nor did he ever ask if I had ever bought term myself or recommmended it to readers and listeners. . . . I have done both for reasons I would have been happy to explain to Welles if he had asked."

As to Medserco, Janeway says the company's documents show him to be an advisor to its board of directors and that this constitutes sufficient disclosure. He said the company's president offered these documents to Welles, who (he said) refused them.

**Welles' response**: "Acting as a paid advisor to corporations is a worthy and honorable occupation. It is much less worthy and honorable for an ostensibly disinterested investment analyst to be an investor in a company and on its payroll at the same time that he is promoting the sale of the company's stock to the public. And it is distinctly unworthy and dishonorable to promote the stock without making a public disclosure to those who read his recommendation of his relationship with the company.

"Janeway takes issue with my characterization of his relationship with the insurance industry. Yet while he disclaims any 'ties' with the insurance industry, he does not specifically deny my statement that he has been a paid consultant to a number of insurance companies. Indeed, he concedes his dealings with Phoenix Mutual and even adds that he recently received a retainer from an insurance company."

**Staff addenda:** A check with SEC discloses that Janeway's type of consulting service is not required to register with the SEC as an "investment adviser." Registered firms often voluntarily carry statements on their reports and newsletters indicating that they may or may not have holdings in stocks being discussed. The Janeway firm denies that it ever recommends specific stocks. Technically, this appears to be correct, even though a non-expert might be led into semantic difficulties about what constitutes a recommendation.

On insurance company ties, T. Lawrence Jones, president of the American Insurance Association, said he did not believe Janeway had served as paid consultant to any insurance company. Janeway himself reported to the Council in his complaint that "in recent months I have had one retainer from a specialty insurance company to advise it on its international financial, foreign exchange and non-insurance operations. But this company, far from being part of the organized insurance industry, is a maverick, as is evidenced from the boycott the life insurance companies organized of its recent private placement offering."

### Professional Standing

*Esquire article:* Very few economists and investment professionals take Janeway seriously. 'He's off in his own world,' says Albert T. Sommers, the widely respected chief economist of The Conference Board. 'None of the practicing or teaching economists I know communicate with him or listen to what he says.'. . . . On Wall

Street, State Street and La Salle Street, Janeway is generally regarded as a somewhat comic figure . . . He has few friends or followers in the upper echelons of the major money-center banks or Fortune 500 corporations . . .

**Janeway's charge:** "Welles never asked me how many Fortune 500 corporations, Wall Street firms, major economists or American and European banks subscribe to our services, pay us monthly consultation fees, retain me to lecture and attend my seminars; although he did have the list of September 1978 seminar participants, which clearly consists of more than 'small fry' . . . and lists as one of the speakers . . . Hans Baer, of Julius Baer and Co., the largest private bank in Switzerland. . . . Within a month after the publication of (the article) I appeared on the program of the New York Economic Club, which is the establishment forum; and its President, Edwin Locke, has previously told Welles . . . that I am indeed taken seriously nationally and internationally. He ignored this testimony by Locke."

(Locke wrote to Janeway after publication of Welles' article and termed it "a monstrous case of malice.")

**Welles' response:** Cited his own list of experts who support his argument that Janeway is not taken seriously by investment professionals. Concerning Locke, Welles said he was a member of the "Janeway network" and the fact that he interviewed him in preparing the article was evidence "of my attempt to get a wide range of views on Janeway."

## Academic Credentials

*Esquire article:* Janeway's own academic credentials . . . are negligible. He possesses no degrees. Though he has led interviewers to believe he is a Cornell graduate, in fact he left shortly before graduation for reasons he declines to discuss. His subsequent education was confined to three months at the London School of Economics. His career before he started Janeway Publishing and Research consisted mainly of writing for *Time*, *Fortune* and *Newsweek*. Though he has published two relatively serious books of political and economic history, his writings and especially his speeches tend to be rambling, disjointed, elliptic and lacking an overall coherence or framework. . . .

**Janeway's charge:** "Welles never asked me how I got my start . . . I have publicly spoken all over this country for a generation, explaining that in my day we remained graduate students only *until* we could get jobs . . . I was considered a prodigy as a graduate student because I got a job as early as 1935 . . . I am an associate fellow of Berkley College, Yale. I have just been reelected. Welles was aware of this. . . . The faculties of many colleges and universities have invited me to lecture over the years (beginning with Harvard . . . and Princeton). Welles did not ask me how many academic engagements I have taken."

**Welles' response**: "Intellectual abilities and ties to academia do not in themselves constitute 'academic credentials'."

**Council finding**: Eliot Janeway is clearly a public figure with complex business and personal relationships and he and his business organization are fit subjects for an investigative journalistic report. It was the prerogative of writer Chris Welles and *Esquire* magazine to seek to describe and assess Mr. Janeway's personality traits and his methods of wielding influence. As Mr. Janeway conceded in his complaint, there is an "editorial right of selectivity."

Selectivity, however, becomes open to challenge where factual material becomes an issue. The article appears to have been seriously in error in regard to the amount of loans Mr. Janeway had from banks controlled by Bert Lance and in referring to a "mortgage." Mr. Welles concedes that the mortgage reference was an error and showed copies of galley proofs from which he had excised the mortgage reference. The correction, however, seems to have been overlooked in the checking process at *Esquire*. The Council believes that a correction on both points is in order.

There also appears to have been an overreaching in the language dealing with Mr. Janeway in his role at Realty Equities, both regarding his association with the company and the extent to which it was detrimental to his financial position.

To assert, as Mr. Welles did, that "Janeway did escape being charged by the SEC for helping to engineer the fraud" would indicate a deliberate effort to discredit Mr. Janeway.

Other instances where overreaching seems to be indicated were in the description of Mr. Janeway as a paid consultant to a number of insurance companies, and in the protest of five individuals who assert that they were either misquoted, or that the statements attributed to them were taken out of context.

Confining its findings to what it perceives to be the journalistic flaws in the article, the Council believes that the errors of fact, combined with instances of overreaching including the cover treatment and the headline for the article, were sufficient to justify a finding that the complaint was warranted.

**Concurring:** Isaacs, McKay, Otwell, Pulitzer, Roberts, Rusher and Scott.

**Dissenting:** Brady and Renick.

**Abstaining:** Ghiglione and Huston.
June 11, 1979


### COMPLAINT NO. 164 (Filed Dec. 29, 1978)
### PHARMACEUTICAL MANUFACTURERS
### ASSOCIATION
### against
### ABC NEWS

**Complaint:** C. Joseph Stetler, president of the Pharmaceutical Manufacturers Association, complained that an ABC News *20/20* segment on prescription drugs, broadcast November 30, 1978, was "unbalanced, misleading and, in parts, inaccurate."

Mr. Stetler contended that the industry viewpoint was inadequately represented in the broadcast.

In addition, he maintained that the program made misleading comparisons among drug products, inaccurately reported on how they are manufactured, quoted incorrect drug prices and improperly characterized certain drugs as "interchangeable."

Mr. Stetler said that the "most specific inaccuracy" occurred in the program's presentation of how Mylan Pharmaceuticals, Inc., produced the antibiotic erythromycin for SmithKline & French, Bristol, and a third unidentified drug firm. ABC reported that although these drugs varied in price when dispensed, "We know for a fact that . . . the only thing that's different is the color coding and logo." Mr. Stetler asserted that according to Mylan, the drugs were made "at different times, using different raw materials, and according to different standards and specifications."

**Response:** Al Ittleson, ABC News vice-president and executive producer of *20/20*, included a research memo prepared by the *20/20* staff in response to the complaint. He wrote:

> In our judgment, the segment was factually accurate. Futhermore, we believe that ABC has fairly covered the controversy concerning prescription drugs.

To the charge that ABC erroneously reported on the manner in which Mylan Labs manufactured erythromycin for three drug firms, Mr. Ittleson replied:

> According to highly reliable FDA (Food and Drug Administration) sources, the erythromycin Mylan manufacturers for SmithKline and for Bristol is therapeutically

identical with Mylan's own erythromycin. Mylan's vice-president for marketing, Warren Hartman, confirmed this during our tour of Mylan's plant. Therefore, we believe that our statement, although presented in simpler terms, is accurate.

As to pricing, he said:

> The SmithKline prices we broadcast were accurately quoted from the *Drug Topic Redbook, 1978: the Pharmacist's Guide to Products and Prices*, the foremost authority for drug prices. In fact, the prices were taken from SmithKline's own advertisement in *Redbook*. The prices were properly attributed to *Redbook* on the air.
>
> With respect to the statement in the program that Abbott erythromycin and the Mylan generic versions are 'interchangeable,' 'interchangeable' was used in the sense that was expressed in the very next line of the script, that 'One is just as safe and effective as the other.' According to our FDA sources, the statement is entirely accurate in this context. In addition, with reference to bioavailability, two studies we have examined conclude that Mylan erythromycin performs equal to or better than the Abbott brand.
>
> . . . ABC has fairly presented the point of view of your (Mr. Stetler's) organization. The November 30 program included statements in which you justify the price differential between brand-name and generics.

**Council finding:** It is clear from the contrasting views presented in the program that ABC was attempting to present a fair report on the much-debated issue of brand versus generic drugs.

The Council finds no support for Mr. Stetler's complaint that the prices quoted in the broadcast were outdated or inaccurate. ABC made it clear in the program that it was relying on the 1978 *Drug Topic Redbook*, current at the time of its report.

There were two elements in the program, however, where the Council feels that the *20/20* program slipped from total accuracy.

One had to do with the use of language: The broadcast attributed to the FDA the statement that two versions of the antibiotic erythromycin are "interchangeable." This has been disputed by Gene Knapp, associate director for drug monographs at the FDA. He noted that the drugs cited by ABC perform differently when taken with food and so according to FDA terminology, they cannot accurately be described as "interchangeable" under all conditions.

The Council's second reservation involves Mr. Stetler's argument that the manufacturing of erythromycin at the Mylan facility was inaccurately portrayed in the program. Council research has determined that according to the Antibiotic Form Six papers filed with the FDA, two of the drugs in question, SmithKline's and Bristol's, have different formulations. ABC contended that the only difference between the drugs was their "color coding and the logo."

Although ABC News claims to have substantiation of this point, it declined to provide it to the Council. An FDA official familiar with the program told Council staff that while the drugs were "essentially the same," he believed that ABC's explanation in this instance was "over-simplified." The Council agrees.

Similar comparisons concerning other manufacturing plants later in the program included comments of officials at those places and they confirmed for ABC that a specific product was identical. At the Mylan plant, ABC's accompanying narration read: "We know for a fact that these three drugs were manufactured at the same plant and the only difference is the color coding and the logo."

In summary, the Council believes that ABC News presented an investigative report on an important subject. Most of the major points were essentially accurate. However, there appears to have been an overreaching in language involving the Mylan manufacturing operations; and the characterization of certain drugs as interchangeable was technically flawed. The Council does not find that these flaws invalidated the main thrust of the program and the complaint is, therefore, found unwarranted.

**Concurring:** Cooney, Huston, Isaacs, Otwell, Pulitzer, Renick and Scott.

**Dissenting:** Brady, Ghiglione, McKay and Rusher.

**Abstaining:** Roberts.

**Concurring opinion by Ms. Huston:** In finding the Pharmaceutical Manufacturers Association's complaint against ABC unwarranted, I do not want to quibble. If I were to quibble, it only would be with the word "batch" — used in the billboard or headline to this excellent investigative show that depicted in a pratical way how people can get more for their money at the drugstore.

Council inquiries were necessarily inconclusive because Mylan Pharmaceuticals, Inc., refused to have followup conversations with our researcher. If the program's headline, or billboard, as spoken by Hugh Downs, had said that the differently priced pills came from the same machine, instead of the same batch, I believe the headline might has been improved.

One point made in the *20/20* segment was that some erythromycin, wearing either the SmithKline/French or the Bristol label, is actually made, not at the drug companies' own plants, but at the Mylan Pharmaceutical Co., in Morgantown. W. Va.

"What we found at Mylan was one machine turning out white erythromycin tablets. . . ." said Geraldo Rivera. Mylan has not informed the Council that different machines were used to make the various companies' versions of erythromycin.

In another part of the show, some detractors point to Rivera's statement: "According to the FDA, these two products are interchangeable; they're chemically equivalent. One is just as safe and effective as the other. The only difference is the price you pay." Some will quibble with the phrase "they're chemically equivalent," preferring ABC to have said, "their active ingredients are equivalent," citing the difference in the dyes and possibly in the inactive ingredients.

To quibble over such phrases that will, most likely, mean the same to the viewer, is to pick away at the kind of television journalism the News Council ought to applaud.

**Dissenting opinion by Mr. Rusher:** As is too often true in journalism, there was an overreaching in language, and two portions of the program on the Mylan manufacturing operations were technically flawed: In the opener Hugh Downs spoke of "a single batch" of erythromycin as being sold at three different prices. Later on, Geraldo Rivera said that at Mylan "we found one machine turning out white erythromycin tablets" — duly shown on screen — and then added that they were separately colored, stamped and labeled for sale to separate brand manufacturers for resale at different prices. Both statements were important, and both, according to Mylan, were false: Batches of erythromycin manufactured by Mylan for different companies are manufactured separately — and in some cases are manufactured according to different specifications that produce different results in various respects, including bioavailability (which is not necessarily an unimportant consideration).

Accordingly, while reaffirming the Council's approval of ABC's decision to undertake a documentary on such an important subject, we (would) hold the complaint, to that limited extent, warranted.
June 11, 1979

**COMPLAINT NO. 165** (Notification filed Nov. 3, 1978)
ILIVICKY (Bryant High School) (Complaint filed Feb. 12, 1979)
against
WNET (Channel 13)

**Complaint:** Martin Ilivicky, the principal of Bryant High School in New York City, complained that *Bad Boys*, a documentary broadcast on

WNET (Channel 13) on October 29, 1978, had "misrepresented the school in an obvious disregard of the truth."

The program, produced for WNET by independent filmmakers Alan and Susan Raymond, focused on the problems of troubled youth. It began by examining a high school truant population and then moved to two correctional institutions, Spofford Detention Center in the Bronx, and Brookwood Center, an upstate New York maximum security facility for boys under 16. The report on high school truants took place in and around the Bryant High School area, and covered approximately the first thirty minutes of the two hour documentary. The complaint to the Council was concerned with only this portion of the broadcast.

Mr. Ilivicky charged that the broadcast had unfairly created the impression of "a school in total chaos" by presenting scenes that were factually inaccurate and by focusing on what he described as the "aberrant student."

He further charged that the producers had gained admittance to the school under false pretenses by claiming that they intended to make a documentary on "values and attitudes of high school students" and by stating that Bryant was one of the schools selected for this purpose. (No other school was depicted in the documentary.)

Mr. Ilivicky said that the documentary's assertion that Bryant had been chosen for inclusion in the program because it had been selected by a Presidential committee as "one of America's ten most typical high schools" was unverifiable.

Mr. Ilivicky also concluded that the Bryant segment was unbalanced because the many scenes of normal classroom and school activity which had been filmed were "left in the out-takes."

**Response:** In a 10-page response to the complaint, Robert N. Gold, general counsel for WNET/Thirteen, said:

> We believe that our actions in connection with *Bad Boys* were in all ways consistent with the special relationship that exists between WNET/Thirteen and independent producers. This relationship is one that must strike a reasonable balance between our commitment to truly diverse and independent producers and our responsibility to our audience for the programs we broadcast.
>
> Alan and Susan Raymond are independent producers. They conceived of the documentary *Bad Boys*, and produced it in association with The Television Laboratory (the 'TV Lab') at WNET/Thirteen. As independent producers, the Raymonds are the appropriate parties to respond to complaints of this nature.

The Raymonds have not responded to the complaint.

Mr. Gold said that "no one from WNET/Thirteen was present on the

Bryant High School premises during the shooting, nor at any other locale featured in the documentary." He went on to say:

> It was and continues to be our view that the thrust of the Bryant High School segment of *Bad Boys* was generally perceived as the Raymonds intended: namely a closer look at the small but significant portion of urban high school adolescents who 'hang out,' are truant and otherwise display the type of deviant behavior that may ultimately lead to more sophisticated forms of anti-social acts.

The letter took note of the complaints from the Bryant High School community and detailed WNET/Thirteen responses to the complaints. These included:

● Three script changes, made with the approval of the Raymonds, and inserted before rebroadcast of the program locally in January 1979. Those script changes, the response said, were "geared to reemphasizing the point that the Bryant segment was only about a small portion of the student body." The letter also described those changes as "minor."

● Broadcast of a Board of Education-produced rebuttal to the program, entitled *We're Not Bad Boys*, and assistance in attempting to arrange broadcast of the rebuttal on PBS stations which had aired *Bad Boys*.

Much of the remainder of the response went on to detail the nature of the special relationship between independent producers and a PBS station such as Channel 13, and a description of the TV Lab, which the letter said was created "to explore and experiment with the video medium."

**Council finding:** The Council is faced at the outset with a problem of responsibility. WNET has stated that it allowed the producers complete freedom in making the program. The program was produced as part of the station's experimental TV laboratory, designed to encourage the works of independent producers. Clearly, such independent production has a place in public television and WNET should be applauded for encouraging it. Nevertheless, the licensee cannot escape the responsibility for that which it airs.

The subject of truancy and its potential as a spawning ground for more serious forms of anti-social behavior was clearly in focus in *Bad Boys*. The selection of Bryant High School as a place to examine the subject was also appropriate. Bryant, like most city high schools, has a truancy problem.

However, the producers did not, as WNET suggested in its reply, concentrate wholly on the truant population in the Bryant portion of the program. They went into classrooms, and the class they chose to concentrate on to show the students' dislike for school was a typing class for problem students with serious learning difficulties. It was not typical of the school as a whole, wherein most students apply themselves to their classwork. The producers spent several weeks at the school and videotaped much of the normal classroom activity. Virtually none of this was used.

The program's script said that the problem truants "hanging out" at a nearby candy store were clearly visible from the school principal's office. They are not. The program depicted large groups of students outside the school as truant, making no effort to distinguish between those who were actual truants and those who were waiting to go to class or had finished their classes, on the school's staggered classroom schedule. The school operates at 125 percent of capacity.

The script said the Bryant High School had been chosen for examination because it had been "selected by a Presidential committee as one of America's ten most typical high schools." Neither school officials, the Board of Education, nor the Department of Health, Education and Welfare knew of any such designation having been made about Bryant High School.

As the complainant also notes, the producers gained admission to the school by telling officials that they intended to make a documentary on "values and attitudes of high school students." In a newspaper interview the Raymonds freely admitted this, adding: "If we said we were making a film about truants they never would have let us in." The use of such a ruse places a special responsibility on the producers to place their story in proper perspective, and the Council believes the Raymonds failed to do that insofar as the Bryant segment is concerned.

All of the above factors, the Council believes, add up to the fact that the producers overreached in the Bryant segment in their desire to highlight the problems of truancy. Because WNET failed to exercise proper oversight, the Council finds the complaint against it warranted.

**Concurring:** Brady, Isaacs, McKay, Otwell, Rusher and Scott.

**Dissenting:** Ghiglione, Huston and Renick.

**Abstaining:** Roberts.

**Note:** Council member Cooney absented herself during the discussion and vote on the complaint because she is a member of WNET's Board.

**Dissenting opinion by Mr. Ghiglione:** The question is not, as it was phrased by Martin Ilivicky, principal of Bryant High School, whether the program "misrepresented the school." The segment of the program in question was about truancy, not about Bryant, and the producers and WNET had no responsibility to even-handedly describe the entire student

71

population, "normal classroom and school activity," as well as the shenanigans of those who only hang out. Nevertheless, the majority opinion calls for such a balancing act: "The producers spent several weeks at the school and videotaped much of the normal classroom activity. Virtually none of this was used."

I disagree with more than the application of that standard to the program. The unwillingness of the Raymonds to talk to The National News Council about their program is unfortunate. But I am uncomfortable with the majority's reliance in part on a New York *Post* article for the conclusion that the Raymonds used a ruse to gain admittance to Bryant. That kind of evidence is insufficient.

The majority opinion notes a number of minor errors. I do not defend those mistakes, but I also do not believe they should cause the Council to find the complaint warranted.

**Dissenting opinion by Ms. Huston:** Council researchers commented that Bryant High School officials "whitewashed the Council's investigation," that few truants were in evidence during the researchers' visit, and that some students even asked Council researchers what important people were visiting the school that day. A police officer was reported to be stationed at the candy store, otherwise the turf of students. In other words, it was not business-as-usual when the Council stopped by to check the validity of Principal Martin Ilivicky's complaint that *Bad Boys* had "misrepresented the school in an obvious disregard of the truth."

What kind of truth can be obtained during a whitewashed investigation? My hunch is that more truth can be culled from 80 hours of videotape, which is what the Raymonds did.

Nor — remembering my own high school days — can I submit to the majority's view that "most students apply themselves to their classwork."

Everyone seems to agree that the Raymonds represented themselves as journalists intending to make a program on "values and attitudes of high school students."

The majority held that the Raymonds resorted to a ruse to gain entry. The record does not substantiate that.

In my opinion, *Bad Boys* was indeed a show describing "values and attitudes of high school students."

Here, difficulty arose, as one would expect, after the Raymonds did not discover a goody-two-shoes environment.

My dissent is intended to applaud journalists who, whether in print, on radio or on television, take the public beyond the superficial of society's institutions into the reality of life within.

**Dissenting opinion by Mr. Renick:** While WNET must assume the ultimate reponsibility for what it broadcasts, the NNC goes a step too far in interpreting this as meaning that WNET failed to "exercise proper oversight" by not being more closely involved with the outside producers of *Bad Boys* in the actual production of the segment—the videotaping, editing, writing and all other aspects.

Such interference would be a deterrent to the creative output of independent documentary producers.

There is a great need for more diversity of ideas, approaches and techniques in documentary programming. What the NNC suggests would discourage such contributions.

Stations have the right to air or not-to-air, but they should aim for a hands-off policy in the production process.

I further found the *Bad Boys* segment a most illuminating look at school truancy. It was not meant to be a balanced look inside Bryant High School. It was not.

June 12, 1979

### COMPLAINT NO. 166  (Filed Feb. 20, 1979)
### LITMAN
### against
### KDKA-TV

**Complaint:** Roslyn M. Litman, a Pittsburgh attorney who had been proposed as a candidate for a federal judgeship, complained that a critical news report about her on KDKA-TV was "grossly unfair, inaccurate and devoid of journalistic standards." Broadcast three times—on December 5 and 6, 1978—the report stated that Mrs. Litman had business associations that raised questions about her fitness for appointment to the federal bench.

Mrs. Litman, who was the first woman president of the Allegheny County Bar Association, charged that the broadcast "utilized television's unique visual appeal to implicate and distort by juxtaposing my photograph along with various mug shots of convicted felons, most of whom they (KDKA-TV) are aware are totally unknown to me."

> I fully understand the concept that when a person leaves relative obscurity and enters into the public arena, the media takes (sic) on an interest in that individual

and, by definition, rightfully assumes a watchdog function in the interest of keeping the community informed.

At the same time, however, the media has a responsibility to exercise prudent judgment and objectivity in presenting its report, particularly so-called investigative reports, because of, if for no other reason, television's wide reach in influencing public opinion.

On December 20 and 21, 1978, Mrs. Litman was granted time on KDKA-TV to reply to the news report. Concerning this she said:

In the opinion of some people my rebuttal set the record straight. That may or may not be. I do not believe, frankly, that anybody ever recovers and that there is always a lingering suspicion in the minds of many people.

In the rebuttal, Mrs. Litman charged that the broadcast attempted to "assassinate" her character and "undermine" her chances of obtaining the judgeship through innuendo, hearsay, inference, and guilt-by-association. She said that the government, which requires full disclosure by its judicial candidates, found her worthy of consideration for the judgeship and that the FBI had also investigated her fitness for the post.

The rebuttal also addressed what Mrs. Litman felt were specific inaccuracies in the KDKA report:

• She denied any improprieties in her connection with Tavern Lending Corporation, a company specializing in loans to people interested in opening bars. KDKA-TV said that the company had charged exorbitant interest rates and fees which sometimes amounted to more than 40 percent a year, and that it had financed bars controlled by various crime figures. Mrs. Litman, who, with her husband David, owns 30 percent of the company's stock, said that its interest rates are lower than "any company of its kind in the state of Pennsylvania" and that crime figures were never granted loans or had received them long before they had any conflict with the law. Mrs. Litman said further that she has no involvement in Tavern Lending's operation and that KDKA-TV was incorrect in identifying her and her husband as "major stockholders" in the company.

• She disputed KDKA-TV's contention that her law firm may have engaged in an unethical practice when it hired the official in charge of a county redevelopment authority project three months after he had concluded a deal with the authority for Mrs. Litman and members of her family.

• She challenged KDKA-TV's assertion that her business relationships with her brother-in-law, Eugene Litman, have led to associations with persons of notoriety. Mr. Litman is a business man in the Pittsburgh area whose investments include apartment complexes, and real estate and insurance interests.

In presenting her on-air rebuttal, Mrs. Litman said that she did not have sufficient time to deal with other specific examples of what she considered to be inaccuracies in the KDKA report. In all, in three separate appearances on KDKA, Mrs. Litman was granted a total of 21 minutes of rebuttal time. The original news report about her had totalled nine minutes. Two subsequent, condensed versions of the original report totalled 12 minutes.

In conversations with Council staff in New York, Mrs. Litman reiterated her contention that she had no personal or professional association with any of the underworld figures or other persons accused of crimes who were mentioned on the newscasts.

**Response:** In response to the charges made by Mrs. Litman, Richard K. Glover, news director of KDKA-TV, wrote:

> To whom were we unfair? Certainly not Mrs. Litman . . .
>
> Although Mrs. Litman accuses us of not being accurate, she has presented no evidence to support that allegation. During the months of preparation of our story, we asked Mrs. Litman repeatedly to answer our questions on camera . . . We conducted lengthy off-camera interviews with her and her husband in order to insure that her assertions were part of our story . . . After she repeatedly refused to be interviewed (on-camera), we gave Mrs. Litman time to present her views . . . Her response took considerably more air time than our original report. Even so, she still failed to address many of our allegations. We aired her response nonetheless without editing and without comment. . . .
>
> Mrs. Litman says we used distortion and innuendo. This isn't so. . . . In every instance in our report, Mrs. Litman, through her law firm or through a business in which she has a significant financial interest, had either a personal relationship or had done business herself, with every individual mentioned. Although she professes ignorance of some of these relationships, she is responsible under the Code of Professional Responsibility which requires an attorney to be fully aware of her financial interests. Additionally, the kind of pattern formed by her associations and insensitivities was relevant and important information in assessing her fitness as a candidate for the federal judiciary.

In a later letter, Mr. Glover asserted that KDKA-TV had confidential documentation for its statement that Tavern Lending had charged interest and fees exceeding 40 percent per year on some loans.

Mr. Glover and station manager Jonathan Hayes met with Council staff in Pittsburgh to discuss the specifics of the complaint. They reviewed the basis for much of the report, and noted where material about Mrs. Litman had been obtained from confidential sources. They also stressed that Mrs. Litman's 21-minute rebuttal had been presented unedited on the day that it was received from her.

**Examination and analysis:** Specific objections by the complainant, the response of KDKA-TV, and comments on those points follow:

I. Roslyn and David Litman own a 30% share of Tavern Lending Corp. and completely own the firm which actually manages Tavern Lending (Service Organization Inc.).

> A. Complaint—Mrs. Litman denies that she has any "involvement in the operation of Tavern Lending." She concedes that she and her husband jointly own 30% of the company which has a total of 38 shareholders. She denies that she is a "major" stockholder in Tavern Lending. She does not deny her and her husband's ownership of Service Organization Inc.
>
> B. Response of KDKA—Station officials said that the inclusion of the fact that the Litmans owned a 30% share of the business was germane to their report.
>
> C. Comment—The complainant objects to the implication that she is a "major" shareholder in Tavern Lending, but the record appears to contradict this. Moreover, it appears that at least David Litman's control over Tavern Lending (regardless of the amount of stock he holds) is very real since Service Organization Inc., which he claims is "merely" a management and consulting firm, apparently has only one client, Tavern Lending.

II. "Interest and fees on (Tavern Lending's) loans can amount to more than forty percent a year."

> A. Complaint—"No borrower has ever repaid a loan at the rate of anywhere close to 40%."
>
> B. Response of KDKA—The news director said he had confidential documentation of the fact that interest and fees charged by Tavern Lending can amount to 40% or more, particularly in cases where the Litman law firm represented the borrower in an application for a liquor license.
>
> C. Comment—Mrs. Litman makes her claim on the basis of "more than 700 outstanding and paid loans" checked by two of Tavern Lending's attorneys (Gil Helwig and Jack McLean). She showed us memos prepared by these lawyers outlining Tavern Lending's intricate loan arrangements and provided the names of six other loan companies in the state that specialized in financing liquor establishments—all of which charge higher set interest rates than Tavern Lending does. Mrs. Litman (and the Tavern Lending lawyers) maintain that no borrowing rate—even when the "add on" rate and service charge is taken into account—has ever exceeded 40%. She also cites a state law that limits interest rates for these types of loans. None of this, however, deals with the possibility of "under the table" arrangements negotiated by Tavern Lending and the Litman law firm with loan applicants. An article in the Pittsburgh *Post-Gazette* on David Litman's operations outlines one case in which a loan applicant at Tavern Lending was formally charged 10% per annum rate but actually wound up paying more in extraneous "fees." The KDKA report said that interest and fees on Tavern Lending loans "can amount to more than forty per cent."

III. "In one case Tavern Lending wanted a 20 percent return in one month."

A. Complaint—Mrs. Litman objects to the "false impression that Tavern Lending "had obtained a 20% return," and claims that "it never happened." However, Mrs. Litman showed us a memo from Tavern Lending attorney Jack McLean (dated December 27, 1978) which concedes that on one occasion, Tavern Lending did seek a 20% "payoff figure" because the borrower wanted a loan of very "short duration."

B. Response of KDKA—The news director pointed out that the script specifically said that Tavern Lending had *asked* for a 20% return, not that they had received it. They said they had documentation on the case in point.

C. Comment—In her conversation with the Council staff, Mrs. Litman conceded that Tavern Lending might have sought a 20% monthly rate on one loan, which is what the broadcast said.

IV. Two individuals (Robert Ficklin and John "Jocko" Heatherington) are among the undesirable persons who "control or allegedly control bars financed through Tavern Lending."

A. Complaint—Mrs. Litman does not deny that these individuals obtained loans from Tavern Lending but claims that neither of them had been convicted of a crime at the time the loans were made and that his fact should have been mentioned in the broadcast. She says that Ficklin "was involved in illegal activity three years after he . . . received the loan," and that Heatherington was charged with voluntary man-slaughter nine years after he received a loan and was not, as the broadcast stated, "convicted" of the charge.

B. Response of KDKA—The station aired a correction relating to Jocko Heath-erington. It stated that Heatherington's conviction had been overturned on appeal and that he was acquitted on a retrial. It also placed the earlier mention of him in the context of the report it had aired about Mrs. Litman. The station official also said that in the case of these two men, as well as others with criminal backgrounds, that their arrest record was not the only test the station had used to determine those back-grounds. Law enforcement officials had been consulted and had provided that background information, station officials said.

C. Comment—According to the Pennsylvania Liquor Control Board (LCB), Robert Ficklin has been an officer in a number of liquor establishments including the Rendezvous Lounge, Inc., which received loans from Tavern Lending in 1962 and in 1968. Ficklin's "rap sheet" shows that he was charged with bookmaking (lottery) in September, 1956—six years *before* his company's first Tavern Lending loan. He was subsequently indicted for receiving stolen goods (found not guilty in January, 1964), four years before his company's second contract with Tavern Lending. Heath-erington was sentenced for involuntary manslaughter in September, 1975 but was found not guilty at a retrial in August, 1978. This is the account which KDKA aired in its correction.

The broadcast's failure to mention conviction dates becomes significant *only* if these persons had never brushed with the law prior to the time they received their loans. The fact that any of these persons received approval for a Pennsylvania liquor license is no indication of a clean bill of health. There are currently two federal grand jury investigations into payoffs to Liquor Control Board members and a state investigation is under way as well. The point of this allegation is that Tavern Lending has been associated with unsavory characters and that some who are in the liquor business in the Pittsburgh area got financing through Tavern Lending. Therefore, it is fair to question the business practices of Tavern Lending and its 30% shareholders, the Litmans.

## V. "Convicted gambling racketeer" Joseph "Sykes" Talarico has been "connected to (a) Tavern Lending loan."

A. Complaint—Mrs. Litman says that it was Talarico's wife, not Talarico himself who received a loan from Tavern Lending and that his run-in with the law (a misdemeanor charge that was eventually dismissed) occurred 12 years before the loan was made.

B. Response of KDKA—Documentation was provided to show that both Talarico and his wife had obtained loans.

C. Comment—According to the Tavern Lending records which Mrs. Litman showed us, both Joseph Talarico and his wife, Rose, received loans from Tavern Lending in 1964 and in 1969. Mrs. Litman also showed us court records indicating a 1952 bookmaking indictment against Joseph that was eventually dismissed. The business of conviction dates is a tricky one and Mrs. Litman seems to use it both ways. In the case of Ficklin and Heatherington, the fact that the individuals had no record *prior* to the time they dealt with Tavern Lending (not true of Ficklin's case) is supposed to absolve Tavern Lending, while in the case of Talarico, the fact that he *did have* a record is also supposed to absolve the company. As with all the persons alleged in the broadcast to have had ties to Tavern Lending, the issue is not whether they had been convicted at the time the loans were made, but whether they were underworld figures with whom Tavern Lending should have been associated.

## VI. Two "convicted heroin dealers" (Cuyler Reynolds and Leonard Schumpert) and one "reputed Mafia member" (Joseph "Joey" De-Marco) "control or allegedly control" "bars financed through Tavern Lending." "Hijacker" Louis "Lolly" Volpe is "connected" to a Tavern Lending loan.

A. Complaint—According to Mrs. Litman, Tavern Lending "never provided loans to" these individuals "or to any corporation in which any of them had an interest."

B. Response of KDKA—As noted above, (KDKA response to IV) the criminal background of the persons mentioned as well as their associations with bars financed by Tavern Lending was obtained on a confidential basis from law enforcement officials. In addition, the station provided background from what they describe as law enforcement documents which they said showed that Tavern Lending was on a list of Pennsylvania businesses with connection to organized crime.

C. Comment—Mrs. Litman makes a direct denial of any association between Tavern Lending and any of the individuals mentioned by KDKA. She has also provided a copy of a letter Cuyler Reynolds had sent to KDKA from Danbury federal prison stating that he had "never had any dealings with Tavern Lending whatsoever." Faced with the Council rule to respect confidentiality of news sources, the staff offers the information on this portion of the report without recommendation.

VII. There is "an apparent conflict of interest" in the Litman law firm's hiring of David R. Brown, a county official involved in a real estate redevelopment project in which David, Roslyn and Eugene Litman had an interest. "Just three months after the (real estate) deal was finalized, Brown . . . went to work . . . in the Litman law firm. He then represented the Litmans in their dealings with his former employer until the project was completed."

A. Complaint—In the rebuttal, Mrs. Litman denied the allegation of unethical conduct but did not deny the facts as reported. Now she does deny KDKA's account. A letter to KDKA from "distinguished professor of ethics" Robert Potter and a memo prepared by one of the lawyers in the Litman firm, presents a slightly different version of the circumstances surrounding David Brown's change of jobs. According to this version, Brown did *not* represent the Litmans in the Frick Park development deal at all after he left the county government in June, 1969. But all acknowledge that David Litman did offer him the job while the two were negotiating the project in April, 1969, and that Brown did show up at the closings of the property sale in August, 1969 (at the request, Mrs. Litman claims, of his former employers, the Urban Redevelopment Authority).

B. Response of KDKA—Station officials noted that although they may have been technically incorrect in saying that Brown had "represented" the Litmans in their dealings with his former employers, the Urban Redevelopment Authority, he did appear at meetings concerned with the Frick Park transaction and was in receipt of correspondence from the Authority to him at the Litman law firm concerning the deal.

C. Comments—The ABA's Code of Professional Responsibility contains the following disciplinary rule: "A lawyer shall not accept private employment in a *matter* in which he had substantial responsibility while he was a public employee." The ABA's Canons of Ethics contain a similar provision as does a recent law enacted in Pennsylvania. According to the ABA's Code, the reason for such a rule is that accepting employment in these circumstances, "would give the appearance of impropriety even if none exists." Mrs. Litman's response to this charge was stated by KDKA reporter Charles Bosworth as follows: "Although this appears to be a conflict of interest, Roslyn Litman told me it was not, because Brown didn't grant favors while he worked for the (redevelopment) authority. . . ."

Although Brown did not formally represent the Litmans in the Frick Park negotiations, he did not scrupulously avoid involvement in the "matter." Even though Bosworth was not completely accurate in using the term "represent," he could have fairly characterized the situation as an "apparent conflict of interest."

VIII. Roslyn Litman's "business relationships with Eugene (Litman) and his associates are another cause for concern." The report continues that a tenant in a building owned by Roslyn and Eugene Litman was Tex Gill "the notorious madam . . . . (who) is considered an heir to the sex empire of prostitution kingpin George Lee." The report then mentions that Lee was killed in a gangland-style murder and ties another man, John Sabbatini, involved in prostitution, to the employ of Eugene Litman.

A. Complaint—Mrs. Litman states that she has "no dealings with any associates or tenants of my husband's brother, who is an ethical and moral man."

B. Response of KDKA—Station officials said the the mention of Gill and Sabbatini was relevant to its presentation of what it termed the "web of relationships" surrounding Mrs. Litman.

C. Comments—Mrs. Litman's views on these allegations were presented on the broadcast in part, when reporter Bosworth stated that "Roslyn Litman told me she had nothing to do with renting the space to Tex Gill." Mrs. Litman told the staff that she and her brother-in-law do own the building in which Tex Gill's company (Take-Me-Paint-Me) operates and that they are the sole owners. However, Mrs. Litman's connections with the other individuals appear to be even less direct. This could be an instance of extreme overreaching on KDKA's part (tying her to her brother-in-law's associates).

**Council finding:** A journalistic investigation into the background of a person who is a candidate for a sensitive post such as the federal judiciary is entirely in order. In the Council's view, it is the kind of investigation undertaken too infrequently by American news organizations. The Council believes that KDKA-TV's news objectives in studying Roslyn Litman's record were valid and that the news reports provided pertinent information.

However, the Council also believes that the news reports had shortcomings in two areas. The first occurs in the report's effort to bolster what the station chose to call "the web" of Mrs. Litman's relationships and associations. The Council believes this was the case in the emphasis placed on Mrs. Litman's connections with Eugene Litman and his business associations with persons such as Tex Gill. Eugene Litman is her brother-in-law, with whom she owns two Pittsburgh properties. In this particular respect, the station's accounts left an impression that Mrs. Litman was in some manner associated with criminal elements who were linked to Eugene Litman-owned properties or businesses. In arranging a photo montage of criminal figures and placing Mrs. Litman's photo in the center, the station was engaging in the technique of guilt by association.

The second shortcoming, the Council believes, was in the manner in which some of the confidential material obtained in the reports was presented. The Council is pledged to respect the confidentiality of sources but believes in the present instance that some better identification than "my investigation has turned up" or "we're told" could have been employed to indicate the type of source. It is possible to protect a source and still indicate the kind of authority or agency one is relying on.

The fact remains that Mrs. Litman is a substantial owner of the Tavern Lending Co. and a partner in the law firm which regularly has dealings with Tavern Lending. This was clearly set forth in the news reports the station aired and was information the public had a right to know about a candidate for the federal judiciary. In the 21 minutes the station afforded her for rebuttal, Mrs. Litman left unchallenged many of the original allegations, choosing instead to assert that some areas had not been covered because "KDKA will not permit me any more time." The 21 minutes represented as much time as KDKA-TV had taken to broadcast its reports about Mrs. Litman.

The Council' believes that except in the instances already indicated which do not vitiate the essential validity of the report, the complaint is found unwarranted.

**Concurring:** Brady, Dilliard, Ghiglione, Huston, Isaacs, McKay, Roberts, Rusher and Salant.

**Abstaining:** Lawson and Otwell.

September 20, 1979


## COMPLAINT NO. 167      (Filed March 1, 1979)
## GAVRIN
### against
## NEW YORK MAGAZINE

**Complaint:** Joseph Gavrin, executive director of the New York State Council of Voluntary Child Care Agencies, complained that an investigative article by Nicholas Pileggi in the December 18, 1978, issue of *New York* magazine constituted a "scurrilous attack on the New York . . . voluntary child care agencies."

The article, entitled WHO'LL SAVE THE CHILDREN? asserted that a "scandal is about to explode" in New York City's child-care services because of mismanagement of public funds and a lack of official scrutiny over the government-reimbursement system under which numerous charitable agencies operate.

Mr. Gavrin charged that the article inadequately represented the views of his organization and that it contained eleven unfair or false passages ("accusations"), each of which was specifically referred to in the complaint. Mr. Gavrin sent a letter to the editor of *New York* rebutting certain portions of the article. This letter appeared in abbreviated form in the February 12, 1979, issue of *New York*.

**Response:** Nicholas Pileggi responded to each of Mr. Gavrin's eleven objections. In most instances, he provided the specific documentation on which he based his conclusions.

**Examination and analysis:** Specific objections by the complainant are listed below, followed by a staff analysis.

1. A "scandal is about to explode" in New York's child-care services—The child-care reimbursement system in New York State and New York City has been under increasing criticism in the last three years. There have been at least six governmental investigations into fiscal irregularities at charitable child-care agencies, all of which have criticized the current reimbursement system and have urged more official oversight of child care. Mayor Edward Koch recently appointed a task force to investigate these charges. There have been, moreover, numerous news stories since 1975 detailing both the findings of various government panels and the complaints of parents and foster-reform groups. Editorials in New York newspapers and on television stations have also assailed child welfare and foster care in the state. This public criticism surely evidences the likelihood of a scandal ("indignation, chagrin or bewilderment brough about by a violation of morality or propriety") occurring.

2. Undue reliance on the 1978 report of Joint Action for Children (J.A.C.)—Mr. Gavrin alleged unfairness in Mr. Pileggi's reliance on a report that was critical of child-care agencies and which excluded eighteen agencies from its survey. Mr. Pileggi maintained that most of his information on agency reimbursements came from state financial records. The News Council staff was shown the income and expenditure forms submitted by over twenty-five agencies and on which Mr. Pileggi relied. He made reference to the J.A.C. report only once in the article and then clearly delineated its conclusions from his own. Certainly J.A.C.— an organization of child-welfare reform groups—is a legitimate source for comment on the state of foster care.

3. One child-care agency—Maimonides Institute—was investigated by the I.R.S. and state auditors for "phony child care costs"—Mr. Gavrin acknowledged that the investigation of Maimonides took place, but claimed that it was cleared of any wrongdoing and that this fact should have been mentioned in the article. "The point of the Maimonides story," however, said Mr. Pileggi in response, "was clearly that government auditing of child care was so weak that even agencies involved in . . .

questionable practices . . . were still paid by the city and state." Moreover, officials in the State Department of Social Services deny that Maimonides has been "cleared"; state and federal investigators are still examining payroll practices at the agency.

4. Four named foster agencies placed only ten of their 2,000 children after receiving $6 million from the city and state—This charge is misleading. Although $6 million may have been appropriated to the agencies in question for services including placement of children in their care, it was not, as the article suggested, earmarked specifically for that purpose.

5. First Deputy Comptroller Martin Ives has said that most agencies have refused to reveal their leasing and rental arrangements and that he had found exorbitant rents and illegal leasing arrangements—Mr. Gavrin did not directly deny that most agencies had not disclosed their leasing arrangements, but asserted that the "Comptroller's Office has access to whatever information they may wish." Officials in the comptroller's office said this was not so, and maintained that in the past four years only about half of the agencies had submitted rental records as required by law. Steve Newman of the comptroller's staff claimed that only 20 percent of the forms required by June 1, 1979, had been turned in by the due date. The comptroller's office now says that it has begun to get hold of the records at issue, partly because of new city regulations on disclosure. As to the charges of improper rental deals, a 1978 study by the State Welfare Inspector General documented rents paid by child-care agencies that "grossly exceeded the fair rental value of the properties." Even the City Department of Special Services for Children (S.S.C.), in a memo which Mr. Gavrin attached in support of his complaint, said that it had "been aware of this problem for some time."

6. Foster families are supposed to receive a $10,000 "allotment" from agencies for each child they care for, but many families have "begun to complain" that agencies are providing only "about half" this amount— Mr. Gavrin asserted that the $10,000 figure was wrong and quoted from an S.S.C. memo which claimed that the correct figure was $5,548. He also argued that it was "not possible for any agency to retain for overhead more than the state rate system has designated. . . ." Mr. Pileggi conceded that the $10,000 figure "mistakenly wended its way into the article," but defended what he termed the main point of this passage, namely that foster parents insist that they have not received adequate funds. He said that the sentence in question would have been completely accurate had it read, "the $3,500 to $5,500 a year allotment the city pays."

Like many aspects of New York's child-welfare system, the foster-family program (under which agencies temporarily place children with private families) is a maze of confusing and conflicting regulations. There has been no set fee provided for foster families, as both the article and Mr. Gavrin implied. Agencies have been reimbursed on a per diem basis depending on the needs of each child and foster family and where they live. The reimbursements for an individual foster case have ranged from $3,000 to $5,500 per year and, of that amount, the state has required that at least $2,100 go directly to the foster family. Thus, an agency has not had to be in violation of the state's requirements to pay a family—as the article stated—only "half" of the total appropriated for the child's care. The figures, which Mr. Gavrin provided, showed that only 40 percent of the total foster-care funds were directly provided to the families. According to state reimbursement records from 1977, in most instances the remaining 60 percent went toward the "administrative costs" of the family-boarding program and for the children's clothing. Thus, state financial reports (as well as News Council staff conversations with four foster parents) confirmed that foster families have routinely received only half of what the city and state paid for the foster program in which they have participated. The article did misstate the actual "allotment" families are entitled to and suggested that all families were entitled to the same amount, but the numerical error here (a figure that was about $6,000 off the mark) did not detract from the overall accuracy of the passage.

7. Many child-care agencies, including three named agencies, have "managed to accumulate multi-million dollar stock portfolios from child-care operations"—Mr. Gavrin argued that it was theoretically impossible for an agency to "build up a 'stock portfolio' from its 'profits' from the care of children." He acknowledged that many agencies had built up considerable investment holdings, but claimed that such "reserves" were "accumulated over time from legacies, bequests, theatre benefits and other appeals for contributions" and not from taxpayers' money. State records confirmed that significant investment earnings were reported by several agencies in 1977, but at the time there was no requirement that an agency show the source of these earnings or how they were used. The key to measuring the accuracy of this allegation is the use of the word "operations." (The word "profits" did not, as Mr. Gavrin suggested, appear in the article). Have child-care agencies invested funds out of their child-care "operations" (which could, of course, include public funds) or have they earned interest and dividends strictly from their bequested "reserves"?

No one, including several state and city auditors, was able to adequately answer this question. Indeed, one of the criticisms leveled against the reimbursement system has been its poor accounting of private-agency income. Nevertheless, the article's assertion that stock portfolios had been accumulated from "child-care operations" failed to give a complete picture of the problem. The public funds which agencies receive are more closely monitored than their private income and none of the state records suggest that operational funding has been used for investment purposes. The question of agency stock holdings is undeniably an area of legitimate concern, but the article's conclusion could not have been substantiated by the available documentation or from other sources on which Mr. Pileggi said he relied.

8. There have been such "meager fiscal controls" over the reimbursement system that Sister Cecilia Schneider, the executive director of a child-care agency, received a $44,592 salary in 1977, a figure 50 percent higher than the city's allowable reimbursement rate—Mr. Gavrin denied that the city contributed to a salary "beyond the maximum amounts it has set," as complained, and also asserted that Sister Schneider's correct salary for that year was $38,000. It is true, as Mr. Gavrin noted, that the city's maximum-salary reimbursement for someone in Sister Schneider's position has been $28,160 and that an agency could contribute whatever additional amount it wished. In this case, however, the 1977 "Report on Details of Operating Agency Salaries" submitted by Sister Schneider's agency (and signed by her) shows her total salary as $44,592, the figure stated in the article.

The sentence in question did not state that the city improperly contributed more than the allowable amount to Sister Schneider's salary. It did not dispute the propriety or legality of Sister Schneider's agency contributing $16,432 (or more than 50 percent above the city's own contribution limit) to her salary, but rather criticized a reimbursement system which allowed city funds to contribute to a total salary far above the city's own ceiling.

9. According to Clara Barksdale, executive director of the Council on Adoptable Children, "The agencies can get $24,000 a year in government money for the kids they have in their institutions. . . ."—Although Mr. Gavrin argued that this quote "implies that every agency is receiving $24,000 a year," a fair reading of this passage suggested that *some* agencies have received $24,000 while some of them received less.

10. Contacts between child-care directors (including Mr. Gavrin) and city officials have had a "chilling effect" on governmental scrutiny of the

reimbursement system and have meant that "some of the worst child-care agencies have gone unaudited for seven or eight years"—Almost every public and private child-care expert with whom the News Council staff talked acknowledged the considerable political influence of some of the charitable child-care agencies. Prominent city officials have served on the board of directors of some agencies. Most of those interviewed agreed that such influence has been one factor (among others) in producing the "time lag" in government auditing which Mr. Gavrin himself acknowledged.

11. "Some child-care agencies have purposely kept youngsters ware-housed in foster-care institutions . . . years longer than necessary in order to receive millions in government reimbursements"—One of the main findings in the city council president's May 1979 report on private-sector foster care was that the current reimbursement system "provides no incentive to an agency to reduce expenditures." To the contrary, it stated, "increased expenditures will ultimately lead to higher reimbursement rates." The temporary State Commission on Child Welfare in its 1978 report agreed that "Children stay in foster care too long (the statewide average length-of-stay currently approaches five years), all too often with no indication that meaningful plans are developed to move them toward permanent homes. . . ." In its 1977 audit of child-care services, the city comptroller's office charged that almost 11,000 New York City foster children had been kept longer than was necessary in foster care (in some instances as much as 5½ years). Relying on these official findings, it is fair to conclude that "some" agencies have, on occasion, "purposely" kept children institutionalized longer than was necessary. This may not be the result of malice or greed, but clearly has been the result of an inefficient and cumbersome system in which the child-care agencies have been operating.

**Council findings:** Mr. Pileggi's article contains a strong indictment of a government-initiated system which even Mr. Gavrin's organization would acknowledge rarely operated "in the best interest of" the child. The article does not constitute a "scurrilous attack" on the private child-care agencies, since the bulk of its criticism concerning "meager fiscal controls" and insufficient oversight is directed at government officials, auditors, and administrators. However, a piece of advocacy journalism such as this one, places a special burden on both reporters and editors to be thorough and accurate. There was a failure in some instances here to be either thorough enough or accurate. These include the passages about agency stockholdings, the amount of money earmarked for foster home placement and the numerical error concerning foster family allotments. Moreover, some of these inaccuracies were highlighted in subheads which appeared throughout the article.

The Council believes, however, that these errors do not undermine the article's essential characterization of abuses in New York's child care system. With the exception's noted, the Council finds the complaint unwarranted.

**Concurring:** Cooney, Dilliard, Ghiglione, Isaacs, Pulitzer and Rusher.
**Dissenting:** Huston.

**Dissenting opinion by Ms. Huston:** Reporters must exercise great care when using figures in a story to make a point. Throughout "Who'll Save the Children?" unlike figures were compared, thus leading to faulty conclusions—both implied and stated.

Granted, in many cities, child welfare systems are inadequate. However, irresponsible reporting such as this does not further public understanding, nor does it serve to pursuade policymakers to undertake improvements.

Initially, it was the reporter's obligation to use the figures correctly. That failing, it was the editor's job to spot the errors. In this case, both failed—to the detriment of the press and of the children.
September 21, 1979


**COMPLAINT NO. 168**        (Filed Aug. 17, 1978)
HAYES (BOISE CASCADE CORPORATION)
against
UNITED PRESS INTERNATIONAL

**Complaint:** Robert B. Hayes, director of corporate communications at the Boise Cascade Corporation, Boise, Idaho, complained that a United Press International story about the company was "grossly distorted, inaccurate and misleading."

Mr. Hayes submitted a copy of the article as it had appeared in the *Dallas Morning News* of April 29, 1979. Headlined "Boise ignored '72 skeleton," the article focused on the company's severe financial difficulties in 1972. Today, Boise Cascade, one of the nation's largest wood and paper products firms, is prospering, having had near record earnings for 1978.

Mr. Hayes maintained that the story created the false impression that the company was attempting to "cover up a negative period in its past."

It was "highly misleading," he said, for the article to have stated that Boise Cascade's library "conspicuously lacks" a 1972 annual report. He argued that copies of the company's financial statements are used to fill information requests and that the supply for 1972 "was only temporarily depleted." A company employee provided his personal copy to the U.P.I. reporter, he added.

Mr. Hayes said the "in an apparent effort to build intrigue" the U.P.I. report described the company's communications department as a "modest office tucked away on Boise Cascade's fifth floor. . . ." In fact, said Mrs. Hayes, the department occupies approximately 20 percent of the top floor of a building that covers an entire city block.

Mr. Hayes disputed the article's assertion that Boise Cascade was "reluctant to talk about 1972." He said that the company provided the U.P.I. reporter with annual reports for all the years dating back to 1970, and offered to arrange interviews with senior management, an invitation, said Mr. Hayes, which was declined.

In addition, Mr. Hayes contended that the story used quotes attributed to unnamed communications employees of the company, which were "erroneous and taken out of context." According to Mr. Hayes, the first statement was made "offhandedly" by an employee who discovered that there were no 1972 reports on file: "I can't believe it. This is the only one in the whole building." Mr. Hayes said that a second staff member spoke "facetiously" when he commented: "Why do you want to know about 1972? That's a skeleton in our closet that we'd just as soon forget." At the same time, said Mr. Hayes, the man provided the U.P.I. reporter with the materials he required.

Mr. Hayes said further that he was told by the company's founder and former board chairman that quotes in the story attributed to him were "inaccurate and or fabricated."

By way of contrast, Mr. Hayes provided a copy of an article, "There's No Looking Back at Boise Cascade," that appeared in *The Idaho Statesman* on May 13, 1979, and which he felt differed sharply from the U.P.I. account of the company's operations. He said that "Boise Cascade's investor-related communications are considered both open and credible," adding that the company received the Financial Analysts Federation Award for excellence in financial reporting four of the past seven years, including 1972. In two of the seven years, the award committee did not meet and no selections were made, he said.

**Response:** H.L. Stevenson, editor-in-chief and vice-president of United Press International, wrote:

United Press International stands by its April 25, 1979 story on the Boise Cascade Corporation. . . . We have reviewed the reporting of Steven K. Wagner, the correspondent who did the story, and are satisfied that it is accurate.

Robert B. Hayes, who wrote the letter of complaint, feels the story is grossly distorted, inaccurate and misleading. . . . I do not agree, especially on the matter of inaccuracy. . . . He is certainly entitled to his own judgment about the general thrust of the story. . . . We feel the story conveys that Boise Cascade, after suffering severe financial losses in the early 1970's, has rebounded and again is in the black.

Mr. Hayes contends, among his several allegations, that Mr. Robert Hansberger, the former board chairman, has denied his remarks to our reporter. . . . Mr. Hansberger has not challenged any of his statements in any communication with UPI. . . .

**Council finding:** The U.P.I. story placed heavy emphasis on Boise Cascade's missing 1972 annual report—a year of financial troubles for the company. But although this report was found in short supply, the reporter was readily given a copy during his visit to the company. It was no secret that Boise Cascade had financial difficulties in the early 1970's. It made headlines then and is a matter of well-publicized record.

The complaint is found warranted because the story was sloppily prepared and inadequately edited, exaggerated and misleading.

**Concurring:** Brady, Cooney, Dilliard, Ghiglione, Huston, Isaacs, Lawson, Pulitzer, Roberts, Rusher, Salant and Scott.
September 21, 1979


### COMPLAINT NO. 169        (Filed Oct. 24, 1979)
### SHELL OIL COMPANY
### against
### NBC NEWS

**Complaint:** The Shell Oil Company complained that an NBC Nightly News report on the activities of the big oil companies "grossly distorted the facts" and was "misleading, inaccurate and out-of-date." In a letter to the Council dated October 22, J. H. DeNike, Shell's vice president for oil products, said that the broadcast of October 15, titled "Fly Now, Freeze Later," the first of a five-part series, "left viewers with the distinct impression that we (Shell) suddenly made a business decision to emphasize the production of jet fuel and thus leave New Englanders without heating oil this winter, and that we took this action without considering our customers or the public."

Mr. DeNike provided the Council with a copy of a letter he had sent to

William J. Small, president of NBC News, dated October 16. On November 8, Shell forwarded to the Council its "views and comments" covering the "Fly Now, Freeze Later" segment. This material, as well as the letter to the Council of October 22, was forwarded by the Council to NBC News on November 9.

In his letter to Mr. Small, Mr. DeNike said that "despite an extensive interview taped with the NBC News Correspondent Mr. Brian Ross, and R. E. Hall, Shell's General Manager Oil Products Business Centers, in Houston August 8, which we felt fully explained the situation, "viewers were left with the impression that Shell had "abritrarily and callously" made its decision to withdraw.

"This kind of reporting, in our view, does a great disservice to your network and to your viewers' understanding of the current home heating oil situation."

After an introduction to the segment, John Chancellor said that Mr. Ross "has discovered" that some of the big oil companies "would rather sell fuel for jet planes than heating oil for home furnaces. . . .," Mr. Ross said:

> For the oil companies this year, there's been no better business than making and selling fuel for jet airplanes, jet fuel. It's delivered to the big airports in huge quantity, cheaply by pipeline. And the airlines, which are adding more and more flights, are willing to pay premium prices. . . .

Mr. Ross said that Texaco and Shell "have made plans to completely cut off some of their home heating oil dealers and customers who now have no guarantee that they can get heating oil anywhere else."

To illustrate its point about the "Freeze Later" consequences of the Shell decision, the NBC News report cited a Portsmouth, New Hampshire, dealer which "Shell tried to cut off." Mr. Ross went on to say that only after government pressure was applied Shell "backed down and agreed to sell this dealer some home heating oil."

In its complaint, Shell declared: "Our withdrawal began in 1975 when supplies were available. Further, we had stated publicly and to our dealers that we would not abandon them. Nor did we." And, "because we wanted to be open," said Shell, "various levels of government," including the Department of Energy, were informed of its decision to withdraw.

Shell said that its customers were informed that the withdrawal would take place "in an orderly way over a long period of time."

In his letter to NBC News, Mr. DeNike declared:

> Shell only sells to wholesalers and not to individual home heating accounts. The

> withdrawal was gradually done, and no wholesale customer of Shell was abandoned.
> No contracts were terminated. Beginning in 1975, each customer was advised of the
> withdrawal decision and was asked to find another supplier. Once that supplier was
> found, Shell allowed the contract to expire. Because of the recent Iranian crude oil
> shut-off and resulting product shortage, a few former Shell customers could not find
> alternate suppliers this year; and after determining that this was the case, Shell
> purchased home heating oil on the open market and sold it to those few remaining
> customers.

One dealer unable to find an alternate supplier, said Shell, was C. H. Sprague and Son, the Portsmouth, New Hampshire, oil company cited in the NBC News broadcast. Shell said that it had scheduled meetings with Sprague before the government became involved, that it never told the company it would "cut off" its supplies, and that it continues to supply Sprague today.

Mr. DeNike said that Shell was withdrawing from the home heating oil business in the Northeast because "the company has traditionally emphasized the production of gasoline, aviation turbine fuel and petrochemicals with the result that home heating oil has always been a very small part of the business. . . ."

In its follow-up analysis of the broadcast, Shell declared, in response to Mr. Ross' charge concerning the profitability of selling jet fuel, that "We have reduced our sales in the Northeast of turbine (jet) fuel and we have continued to try to reduce our sales of turbine fuel in the Northeast." This point was made by Mr. Hall in the NBC interview, the company said, adding that it's "an oversimplification" to say that jet fuel is delivered to the big airports "'in huge quantities, cheaply by pipeline.'"

"It's true, if you have the pipelines between your refinery and the 'large airports.' But that is not the case for Shell in the Northeast. . . ."

In answer to NBC's assertion that Shell planned to emphasize production of jet fuel at the expense of home heating oil, Shell said that this year it is making less jet fuel as well as less home heating oil as compared to last year.

**Response:** NBC News provided the Council on November 15 with a copy of Mr. Small's response to Mr. DeNike, dated November 1, as well as a transcript of the program. In his letter to the Council accompanying his response to Shell, Mr. Small wrote:

> I believe that the text of what we actually said in this letter should answer the
> questions that they raised.

At the time the response to Shell was prepared, NBC News did not have in its possession a copy of Shell's "views and comments" on the broadcast. Nor did it have the Council's follow-up letter of November 14 asking for its views on certain specific aspects of the complaint growing out of Shell's analysis. It has become apparent that the pressures of coverage of the explosive situation in Iran have made it difficult for NBC News' executives to respond immediately to these requests.

In his letter to Mr. DeNike, Mr. Small wrote:

> Your objections to the story appear to be directed to the "impression" it left on viewers, rather than any factual inaccuracies. We believe that the report was a fair presentation of the relevant facts and opinions, and did not, as you claim, "distort" Shell's role in the Northeast heating oil market.
>
> In preparing the particular story in question, NBC journalists were careful to solicit the views of both the oil industry, including Shell, and others who may disagree with you. We believe all significant points of view were aired, including Shell's. and we believe we exercised reasonable editorial judgments in determining what aspects our discussions with you and other interested parties were most relevant to the story.
>
> You do not dispute the main factual point of the report: That Shell and other oil companies have decided to withdraw from the home heating oil business in the Northeast. And I do not believe that the story suggests Shell made its decision in an "arbitrary" or "callous" manner. In fact, the Shell spokesman appearing in the story noted that the Company was convinced that its home heating oil customers would be able to find alternate suppliers.
>
> In reporting a complex issue in a limited period of time, NBC made various editorial judgments as to what information to include or omit. . . . Such judgments are a core of the news gathering process, and we believe NBC News made them in a professional and responsible manner.

On November 27, two days before the meeting of the National News Council and four weeks after a copy of the original Shell complaint had been hand-delivered to NBC News, Jay E. Gerber of NBC's Law Department asked that the Council delay action on this matter while it considered whether the network wished to provide any further information to the Council.

The chronology of communications between this Council and NBC makes it clear that NBC had ample notice and opportunity to respond to Shell's complaint before this meeting and, in fact, NBC News President Small appeared to do so in his letter of November 12, to Mr. Isaacs. If, however, Mr. Gerber's letter of November 27 intended to suggest that NBC nevertheless has further relevant evidence to put before the Council, NBC's attention is called to the provisions of the Council's rules concerning reconsideration.

**Staff analysis:** The central points at issue in this complaint are the charges by NBC News that (1) the Shell Oil Company, with total disregard of the consequences ("Freeze Later") had suddenly decided to cease supplying home heating oil to the Northeast area of the nation because (2) it was more profitable to sell jet fuel for airplanes ("Fly Now").

## The Decision to Withdraw

Regarding the suddenness of the decision, it is necessary to bear in mind only what the viewer and listener saw and heard when the segment was broadcast. During the broadcast, NBC Reporter Brian Ross declared:

> And NBC News *has learned* that two major oil companies, very active in the jet fuel business, Texaco and Shell, *have made plans to completely cut off* some of their home heating oil dealers and customers who now have no guarantee that they can get heating oil anywhere else.

Mr. Ross later added:

> At Shell headquarters in Houston, the company *is planning to pull out* of the home heating oil business in the Northeast.

The complaint concerns only the Shell Oil Company. There was clearly an implication in the two statements above (note the Council's emphasis) that the pull-out action by Shell was a new decision and that action in carrying it out now is in progress. The listener and viewer was not made aware that the Shell decision was made in 1975, long before the current world-wide oil situation was exacerbated by the situation in the Middle East.

Ivan Maple, Director of Marketing and Industry Liaison of the Department of Energy, told the Council staff that a letter from the Shell Oil Company, as well as from other major oil companies, was received by the Federal Energy Administration (predecessor to the Department of Energy) sometime in late 1975 or early 1976 which, paraphrased in part, read as follows:

> You have our assurances that we will continue to supply our customers for one year after the decontrol of products. We will continue to honor our contractual commitments to those customers who have extended contracts for the length of those contracts and for one year beyond. We will continue to supply them, even in areas where we are pulling out.

Home heating oil was decontrolled on July 1, 1976, but Shell lived up to its commitment, according to Charles H. Burkhardt, executive vice president of the New England Fuel Institute, an organization based in

93

Watertown, Massachusetts, representing 1,134 independent home heating oil distributors in the New England states.

"They gave us ample notice, in all fairness to them," Mr. Burkhardt told the Council's staff. He said that be became aware of Shell's decision to pull out of the New England home heating oil market "a year and a half to two years ago. I can't remember exactly." He said that Shell told dealers that it planned to withdraw completely on June 30, 1979. At the time of this notice there was no shortage of home heating oil, he declared. "I went to major and independent wholesalers who told me 'We can supply. It's no problem.'"

When Shell made its original announcement to withdraw, supplies were not that tight, Mr. Burkhardt said. But by the time Shell was to complete the cutback (June 30, 1979), "it was a different situation; oil supplies had become scarcer."

"It was a time," Mr. Burkhardt said, "when the President had mandated that 240,000,000 barrels of home heating oil be held in primary storage by the oil companies to provide adequate supplies to meet normal needs. This goal was reached. . . . During this period, and in the early stages of their announcement (to withdraw), Shell lived up to their commitments, and they did it intelligently."

The Council's staff notes that the President's announced goal of 240,000,000 barrels, according to Department of Energy sources, had reached 251,000,000 barrels by the end of October, and that Shell's commitment to this goal—5,000,000 barrels—had been surpassed on October 1 by 200,000 barrels.

Mr. Maple of the Department of Energy confirmed to the Council's staff that Shell, beginning in late 1975, when supplies were not tight, gradually began to phase out of its Northeastern home heating oil commitment, and that by the summer of 1979 had narrowed its customer list from approximately 340 (as of 1975) to about a dozen that had not found alternative sources of supply.

"Shell is countinuing to supply these companies," Mr. Maple said, "until alternative sources are found."

In a spotcheck of the 340 dealers, the Council's staff was informed, without exception, that Shell had not terminated a single contract. All said that they had found alternative sources of supply. All dealers checked said that they were notified of the Shell withdrawal at least a year ago. Several said that they were aware of the decision by Shell to pull out of the home heating market in the Northeast as far back as four or five years ago.

During the NBC News broadcast, reporter Ross declared:

94

> This summer, Shell tried to cut off this home heating oil dealer in Portsmouth, New Hampshire, who serves 45,000 homes here. Shell said the dealer would have to get his heating oil somewhere else. But nine other oil companies turned this dealer down.
>
> Finally, after a lot of pressure from senators and congressmen from this area, Shell backed down; agreed to sell this dealer some home heating oil. But Shell says it still plans to get out of the home heating oil business in this part of the country as quickly as possible.

The dealer, unidentified by NBC, was C. H. Sprague and Son. Sprague was one of the approximately twelve dealers Shell said had difficulty in finding replacement supplies. Henry Powers, president of Sprague, told the Council staff that he heard about the Shell pullout "at least a couple of years ago." Mr. Powers said that Shell representatives visited the company's corporate headquarters in Boston to discuss its plans to withdraw. (Sprague relocated its head offices to Portsmouth this past summer).

"In general terms," Mr. Powers said, "it (the announcement to withdraw) was put in public print. It was well aired and they did a good job of making it known. It was in every New Hampshire paper, on radio, television, all over. I wouldn't put all this on Shell. When they originally told us, they did a good job, and we tried to replace their volume."

Mr. Powers explained that one-third of Sprague's home heating oil comes from its own refinery and that two-thirds is supplied by Shell. When that portion of the broadcast pertaining to Sprague was read to him, Mr. Powers responded:

> Basically, that's right. But Shell didn't tell us this summer. They told us two years ago. It wasn't something that happened at a moment's notice. Still, we were unable to find someone to supply the home heating oil we needed. They implied that Shell did this overnight. The only inaccuracy was that they implied that we had momentarily been cut off. That was a wrong implication. They (Shell) gave us plenty of notice . . . Shell never said "No, we're going to cut you off."

Mr. Powers went on to say that Sprague's two-year contract with Shell expired on May 31, 1979. He said he was told by Shell in June 1979, that it had "completed all contractual arrangements" and that "it was standing by its previous announcement to withdraw. In effect, we were on our own after 22 years with Shell. We knew in advance two years ago that Shell wanted to get out and we tried every possible, conceivable angle of getting another supplier, but none could be found."

After informing government officials of the situation, Mr. Powers said he was notified, early in July, that Shell would supply Sprague on a month-to-month basis. Mr. Powers refused this offer, he said, stating "you can't live on a month-to-month basis. We would be failing the public. . . . I couldn't go to the governor in October and say 'Hey, no oil.'"

At his instigation, Mr. Powers said a meeting was held in Washington on July 12 in the office of Senator John Durkin of New Hampshire. Most of the New England congressional delegation was there, as were representatives from Sprague, the Department of Energy, and Shell.

"Shell has been a very, very good supplier," Mr. Powers said. "I wasn't there to castigate them. I had to merely focus the problem in the government's eye."

Shell and Sprague agreed at the meeting to continue talking, and on July 25, officials from both companies met at the Sprague office. According to Mr. Powers, they "drew up a concept" and then ironed out the details at a meeting on August 15. Shell agreed, said Mr. Powers, to supply Sprague on a "signed contractual basis" with one million barrels of heating oil for the 1979-80 winter heating season in return for all the naphtha produced in Sprague's northeast refinery. Mr. Powers added that the contract covers the current heating season only and that next year "We'll be on our own again."

Shell contends that governmental intervention was unnecessary; that it arranged, prior to the July 12 meeting, to meet with Sprague on July 25 to iron out the matter. Mr. Powers said they made that arrangement on July 11.

The results of all of this, according to a high-ranking official of the Department of Energy who asked that his name not be published, is that Shell simply reiterated its previous commitment. "They had never said they would cut off Sprague, and they didn't," he said. "They had tried for several years to get Sprague to find alternative sources. Sprague had not found such sources. There was a time when it could have found such sources, when anybody seriously looking for supplies could do so. The big refiners were looking for customers, there being somewhat of a glut. It was the season of 1977-78, following the disastrous season of 1976-77 in the Northeast, when waterways froze over and the weather was in the extremes.

"At the end of November 1977, a total of 270.6 million barrels was in reserve, as against 223.6 million on the corresponding date in 1976. Shell, itself," he said, "didn't particularly mind then that Sprague was a customer.

"Last summer, Shell prodded Sprague. It had been a long time since it announced its plans to withdraw. It put on the pressure. But it also had its commitment. It still has, and it's living up to it. I think it always intended to do so. The prodding from Washington didn't hurt, although it may have been unnecessary.''

The Department of Energy source then added:

> No oil company today can be dumb enough to shoot its own foot. Responsible oil companies today cannot afford to create a bad public image. And Shell is one of the better oil companies, with a reputation for fair dealing. It is a responsible company.

### The Profitability Factor

Shell, according to oil industry statistics, has never been among the top oil companies in providing the Northeast with home heating oil. The Department of Energy said that at most, Shell's share of that market, on a composite basis, didn't top 4 percent. The reason, as given by Shell, and confirmed by the Department of Energy, is that Shell had to supply the area from its nearest refining facilities, on the Gulf Coast, 1,500 miles away. It was a logistical problem not faced by Exxon, Texaco and Mobil, three of the area's top heating oil suppliers. Together, they supply from 30 to 35 percent of the area's requirements. All three have refineries in New Jersey.

Shell had tried, on two occasions, in the early 1970's to overcome this logistical handicap. Its efforts to build a refinery in Delaware were thwarted by that state's legislature when it passed a law prohibiting heavy industry and transshipment terminals in Delaware's coastal area. The company's efforts to build a refinery in New Jersey were abandoned as a result of the Arab oil embargo in 1973-74 and problems arising from environmental protests.

According to Department of Energy sources, Shell was placed at a competitive disadvantage in supplying its Northeast dealers with home heating oil. Logistics that required Shell to ship home heating oil by boat from the Gulf area also made it necessary that Shell charge more for the product. This amounted to anywhere from 1 to 3 cents more per gallon in 1975, when Shell made its decision to withdraw.

The company has announced that it also is gradually reducing its supply of jet fuel to the Northeast, to the many small airports far removed from the larger cities, for the same competitive reasons that apply to home heating oil. It continues to supply Logan Airport in Boston via pipeline or tanker from the Gulf to its Sewaren, New Jersey, terminal; from there by barge to its Fall River, Mass., terminal; from there by pipeline to its Waltham, Mass., terminal, and from there to Logan. At Logan, Shell supplies about eight percent of the total jet fuel.

Shell's jet fuel sales nationwide thus far for 1979 are running at a rate of eight percent less than such sales in 1978, according to the company.

Shell has been strong, traditionally, in the production of gasoline, aviation turbine fuel (jet fuel) and in petrochemicals which find their way in the production process into a myriad of consumer, agricultural, industrial products and processes.

"The company," according to the Department of Energy, "in reaching its decision in 1975 to pull out of the Northeast in home heating oil was simply making a business decision to place its emphasis on those production areas in which it was strongest. At the same time, it continued its marketing of home heating oil in areas where the logistical problem of distance from refinery to market created a favorable competitive position. In the Midwest, Shell has a refinery on the Mississippi River near St. Louis. It's competitive in that area."

Mr. Hall of Shell, in the interview with Mr. Ross of NBC News, said that "the company's long-range plan has been to continue to grow with the transportation sector, such as the gasoline business, and jet fuel business for the growing airline use. Also, to grow in the chemical end of our business. Shell is probably the largest petroleum based chemical company in the country. About 10 percent of our requirements." He continued:

> A certain amount of that heating oil diesel was feedstock for the petrochemical end of our business, which makes things like plastics that go into automobiles to reduce the weight to meet mileage requirements, medicines, fertilizers for agricultural needs.

Regarding the profitability of jet fuel sales versus home heating oil sales, a Department of Energy spokesman said that they have no way to validate such figures. "Currently, I would agree that jet fuel sales are slightly more profitable than home heating oil sales," he said, "but other factors are involved, such as the quantity sold and the logistics. When you talk about huge amounts of jet fuel going into an airport from nearby refineries there is a difference in profits from smaller amounts coming in from afar, by boat or by truck. Then, you have to add in the factor involved in how much of that jet fuel comes from oil imported from other lands, the Middle East for instance."

**Council finding:** Contrary to the impression that the NBC report was clearly intended to convey, the record provides strong support for the contention by Shell Oil Company that, from 1975 until the summer of 1979, the company acted in a responsible and careful manner in carrying out its 1975 policy decision to withdraw from supplying home heating oil to the Northeast area. This is documented by Department of Energy records and by the many dealers in the area, including even the C. H. Sprague and Son Company, which was featured in the NBC News segment.

The title, "Fly Now, Freeze Later," while catchy, was misleading insofar as Shell's performance record was concerned. The record is incontrovertible: There is nothing sudden about Shell's decision or subsequent actions. Moreover, in the light of the timing of the original decision—1975—there was a clear overstress in the report of Shell's desire for higher profits from jet fuel. The policy decision was made at a time when the oil situation in the Middle East and the price explosion had not fully materialized. Most certainly, profit played a role in Shell's 1975 decision, as it properly does in all such business actions, but the NBC News report's emphasis on sudden action to take advantage of high profits is unsupported. With respect to the supply of home heating oil it is clear that it was unfair to make it appear that Shell had a total disregard of any "Freeze Later" consequences.

The Council finds the complaint against the NBC Nightly News segment warranted.

**Concurring:** Brady, Isaacs, McKay, Roberts, Rusher and Scott.

**Abstaining:** Huston, Otwell, Pulitzer, Renick and Williams.

**Note:** Council member Salant absented himself from the discussion and vote because he is vice-chairman of the National Broadcasting Company.

**Concurring opinion by Mr. Brady and Mr. Rusher:** We join the Council majority in finding the complaint against the NBC Nightly News segment warranted.

We hold the NBC News report to be strident and accusatory. The distortions regarding Shell's actions in particular, and oil companies in general, reflect a mindset that translates into a biased and at times deceitful presentation. Such a report can only be termed irresponsible.

The broadcast contains several statements for which no supporting evidence is offered. Mr. Ross begins with the assertion that "for the oil companies this year there has been no better business than making and selling fuel for jet airplanes." This is an opinion which is not supported by the information given to Mr. Ross by Shell in the taped interview or by verification from outside sources.

In the same paragraph Mr. Ross says, "The fuel that goes into these airplanes is almost the same product as home heating oil. There is little difference." To people having no knowledge of oil refining this means the two products are virtually interchangeable when, in fact, they are not. Mr. Ross apparently made no effort to learn the difference, much less to convey it on the air.

The taped interview with Mr. Hall seems to have been edited to reinforce the thrust of the program title: "Fly Now, Freeze Later." Mr. Hall was quoted on the broadcast as saying Shell's decision to withdraw from the Northeast was a business decision. Immediately following this statement during the interview, Mr. Hall said the following:

> And time has proved that correct, to the extent that almost all of the 340 customers have found new suppliers except this handful. And this handful we continue to work with so that they do not go without product during the heating season until they can find an alternate supplier.

There was no reference in the broadcast to this follow-up statement.

We also find destructive of public confidence in the reliability of television news the projection on camera (as was done in this case) of unidentified silhouettes speaking with dubbed-in or muffled voices, which are then identified to the audience as those of authoritative industry or government officials, to convey opinions that square precisely with the theme of the broadcast but express views directly opposite to those set forth officially by the company or government agency.

Such representations inevitably inject a cloak-and-dagger element into the viewer's consideration of whatever issue is being presented in a way that distorts fair judgment. They also are subject to manipulation, both as to the authenticity of the statement being made and the competence of the person being quoted to speak from first-hand knowledge.
November 30, 1979

### COMPLAINT NO. 170     (Filed Nov. 2, 1979)
### BEAUDIN
### against
### THE BAY CITY TIMES

**Complaint:** Chris Beaudin, a city commissioner in Bay City, Michigan, complained that *The Bay City Times*, in handling letters to the editor, failed "to see that their public forum is not used as a weapon to coerce political actions." Mr. Beaudin added: "They have an obligation not to publish allegations in their letter column that they know to be untrue. They have an obligation to issue corrections when they have allowed untrue statements to be published."

Mr. Beaudin's complaint centered on (1) a letter written by Michael D. Martindale that appeared in *The Bay City Times* on September 16, 1979, and (2) a responding letter submitted by Mr. Beaudin published on October 10.

The Martindale letter denounced Mr. Beaudin's performance as city commissioner. Mr. Beaudin's letter of reply contained what he said were the "real reasons" behind Mr. Martindale's "attacks" on him.

Mr. Beaudin said Mr. Martindale had written to him earlier concerning property—"about $80" worth— that had allegedly been stolen from his impounded car.

"You could do me a great favor," said the Martindale letter offered by Mr. Beaudin to support his argument, "and make political hay by using your power as city commissioner to see I'm paid $100 for the items stolen. . . . Then I plug you with a letter to the editor . . . and others follow accordingly."

Mr. Beaudin attached to his letter to the *Times* a copy of the Martindale letter to him. His letter made mention of the copy, but this was edited out for publication.

On October 18 the *Times* published another letter by Mr. Martindale in which he denied writing the letter and accused Mr. Beaudin of attempting to "smear" him.

Mr. Beaudin said that in a meeting with the chief editorial writer for the *Times* on October 22, he was told that the Martindale letter "had somehow been lost," and he provided the paper with a second copy. Mr. Beaudin also said he was told that the *Times* would print a note stating that the paper had seen the Martindale letter. This, said Mr. Beaudin, was to appear under a letter to the editor written by his mother.

The *Times* printed Mrs. Beaudin's letter on October 24, but no editor's note about the Martindale letter accompanied it, nor was one forthcoming.

**Response:** Thomas E. Fallon, editor of the *Times*, said:

> Toss a couple of rather dubious, fringe-type characters into a friendship, have that friendship sour and spill out into a newspaper Forum because both are community activists . . . and what do you have?
>
> Name-calling, charges, counter charges!
>
> As I told you, Chris Beaudin has come under editorial fire for his conduct and his

performance as a city commissioner. We firmly rejected his candidacy for reelection in the primary and again, very recently, in the run-off. Sure, he's smarting.

Martindale is a wild-eyed Vietnam veteran who has opinions on everything. In recent years, we've reduced his Forum commentary to about one a month.

Now that their friendship has dissolved into a hate relationship, they're trying to make the Times Forum their battleground. We've sought to keep the issue between them in some kind of perspective.

Dave Rogers, our chief editorial writer, had indicated we would add an editor's note to the Beaudin letter acknowledging we had seen the Martindale letter to Beaudin.

In the meantime, however, we received the letter from Beaudin's mother and also one from another activist, Mable Cowgill, both acknowledging the Beaudin letter. We assumed that was sufficient. Now Martindale says the letter Beaudin raves about is a "forgery." And so it goes . . .

We've given space to both parties in this controversy. They've stated their charges and counter-charges. That's the end of it as far as we're concerned.

**Council finding:** Because this particular incident raises no issues of national significance and is, therefore, outside of the Council's purview, the complaint is dismissed.

**Concurring:** Brady, Huston, Otwell, Pulitzer, Renick, Roberts, Rusher, Salant and Scott.

**Abstaining:** Isaacs, McKay and Williams.
November 30, 1979

<br>

**COMPLAINT NO. 171**     (Filed: October 19, 1979)
RYBA
against
NEW YORK POST

**Complaint:** Debra Ryba of New York complained about a series of *New York Post* headlines, which she said were "of an extremely provocative and biased nature which lead to problem situations." Ms. Ryba said:

> The following are a few examples of sensationalism that the publisher, Mr. Murdoch, uses to sell his newspaper.
>
> 1. *Inflammatory atmosphere*: August 15, 1979, 'FIRE HIM.' This is the front-page headline published during the Andrew Young affair. The story quoted only one far-right Jewish organization, the American Zionist Organization, as demanding that Mr. Young be replaced.
> 2. *Political bias*: September 11, 1979, 'THEY'RE ALL CRAZY FOR KENNEDY . . .' This blatantly editorial headline capped an all-Kennedy issue filled with sensational stories that were all pro-Kennedy.

3. *Aura of fear*: Here the *Post* uses misleading headlines to create an atmosphere of crime. Reading some of the *Post*'s 'glorified' crime headlines almost parallels the 'yellow journalism' days of William Randolph Hearst.
   a. August 23, 1979, 'FURY AS POLICE KILL PSYCHO.' What is so urgent about this story and why does it take precedence over other major stories?
   b. September 11, 1979, (inside) 'TERROR IN THE TUNNELS.' Nobody was seriously injured.
   c. September 15, 1979, 'MAYHEM IN OUR STREETS.' The *Post* took two isolated criminal incidents and attempted to blow them up to panic proportions.
4. *Non-News Trivia*: July 11, 1979, 'WE'RE SAFE.' Here is another example of sensationalism used by the *Post* to inform the public about Skylab which was considered by NASA scientists to never have endangered the city in the first place.

Mr. Murdoch insults the intelligence of his readers daily. I am surprised that responsible persons or organizations have not had the courage or the desire to step forward and register their indignation at his high-handed publishing tactics.

**Response:** The *Post* declined to comment on the complaint.

**Council finding:** All of the instances cited by the complainant are examples of what she says were sensational headlines. But sensational headlines in themselves do not necessarily merit consideration by the Council. The Council is concerned when they go beyond sensationalism and are inaccurate or misleading.

The Council believes a report of the chairman of the British Press Council, Lord Shawcross, is applicable. He said:

> The (British) Council can condemn tendentious headlines. . . . It is, however, not an arbiter of taste nor can it attempt to control the manners of contemporary society.

The News Council believes that while the headlines complained about may have offended the taste of the complainant, there is no allegation that they were inaccurate. The Council, therefore, dismisses the complaint.

**Concurring:** Brady, Huston, Isaacs, McKay, Otwell, Pulitzer, Renick, Roberts, Rusher, Salant, Scott and Williams.
November 30, 1979

**COMPLAINT NO. 172**          (Filed Nov. 16, 1979)
EXXON CORPORATION
against
NBC NEWS

**Complaint:** J. G. Clarke, director and senior vice president of Exxon

Corporation, filed a complaint for Exxon against a segment of the NBC Nightly News of October 16, 1979, entitled, "Dirty Oil and Dirty Air." It was a second part of a five-part series on energy-related topics.

The segment focused on an Exxon marketing decision which cut low-sulphur fuel shipments to Exxon U.S.A.'s largest customer, Florida Power & Light Company, and how that decision affected the quality of the air in Florida.

The complaint contended specifically that the segment was permeated by "factual error, the selective use of information, lack of perspective, and the building of effect through innuendo."

The Exxon complaint continued:

> The way facts are strung together, the decision to mention some but not others, the tone in which they are presented and the hints scattered along the way can create indelible impressions. A decision merely to present information in a limited perspective can distort its significance. In varying degrees we believe that Dirty Oil and Dirty Air suffered from all these deficiencies.

The complaint cited five specific points in the broadcast with which Exxon took issue. They were:

1. *NBC*—One of the big multinational oil companies is Exxon, which has customers in many countries. Some of these customers get what we might call clean oil and some get shipments of dirty oil. Exxon decides and those decisions have direct effect on the air its customers breathe.

   *Exxon Complaint*—The implication, as becomes clear later in the program, is that Exxon diverted clean oil from Florida to Europe and substituted dirty oil here at home. The fact is that even the somewhat more sulphurous fuel oil now being burnt by Florida Power and Light is substantially higher in quality than the average fuel consumed in Europe. European customers are not being favored. To say that Exxon 'decides' who gets what is in a narrow sense true: The product *is* sold to *someone*. But then Exxon, and other companies, make such decisions every day, around the world. There is nothing sinister about this, and no one worries about it *except* when supplies are exceptionally short. At such times, companies such as Exxon have an obligation to explain the constraints and principles determining their decisions. Neither the constraints nor Exxon's efforts to distribute oil supplies on a fair and equitable basis among all its customers were given much of an airing in NBC's report although they were discussed at length with the reporter. One would gather from NBC's account that only whim and commercial self-interest may have been involved.

2. *NBC*—This is southern Florida. Tourists and people who live there have always breathed some of the cleanest air in the country. But now all that is changing. For five months the air in southern Florida has been getting dirtier and dirtier.

*Exxon complaint*—Implied in this statement is a progressive deterioration in the air because of Exxon's actions. But that is not true. The cutback in supplies of low-sulphur fuel oil to Florida Power and Light began March 1 of this year. There has been some easing of the reduction for portions of the period since March 1. Both Mr. Hess and Mr. Wolgast (both of Exxon) made this point to the reporter. Moreover, the average sulphur content of the fuel oil delivered by Exxon to the utility so far this year has been only minimally above that in the same period last year, about 1.5 percent for the first three quarters compared to 1.4 percent. Historically the sulphur content of the fuel oil burnt in Florida was much higher. Prior to the early 1970s it was 2.5 percent or more. and since then it has fluctuated between 1 percent and 1.6 percent. To imply a major retreat from long established standards, therefore, is misleading.

3. *NBC*-The emergency in Florida was the direct result of a change in operations in this huge refinery in Aruba in the Carribean, owned and run by Exxon.

   *Exxon complaint*-It is true that had the Aruba Refinery continued to produce as much low-sulphur fuel oil as in the past, the problem of Florida Power and Light would have been eased. But it could have been completely avoided only if Exxon's *total* supplies of low-sulphur fuel oil from *all* sources had been unimpaired, or if Exxon had favored FP&L over other customers. At issue was not just who would get scarce supplies of low-sulphur fuel oil but how much of this product would be produced at the expense of other products, such as heating oil and gasoline, which were also in short supply. All these products were under allocation. The point is that there was an overall shortage of the crude oil from which all these things are made. This was the underlying cause of the problem in Florida as well as in a great many other places. And it was the cause of the change in operations at Aruba. All this was discussed with the reporter prior to his broadcast. NBC presented the viewer with a fact that was trivially true, but false in its implication.

4. *NBC*—Exxon says the production changes at the refinery were made to meet pressing demands in the United States. But NBC News found that a number of tankers carrying petroleum products from this refinery ended up not in the U.S., but in Europe. When we asked Vice President Hess at Exxon about shipments to Europe, he said that they were rare.

   . . . a study done by Lloyd's of London for NBC News . . . shows at least fifteen tankers left for Europe in the first part of this year containing more than three million barrels of various petroleum products.

   *Exxon complaint*—It is hard for the viewer not to infer from this that significant volumes of product, relevant to the needs of Florida Power and Light, were sent to Europe and that Mr. Hess was wrong in suggesting that such movements were rare. The information made available to NBC by Exxon supports neither of these conclusions. The facts are these: (a) Of the total output of the Aruba refinery in the first half of this year, less than seven percent was shipped to Europe; (b) Only *three* of the fifteen tankers identified by Lloyd's of London carried product relevant to the clean air issue. The product in question was heating oil which can be combined with regular-sulphur fuel oil to produce the quality of fuel desired by Florida Power and Light. The other tankers carried jet fuel under contract to U.S. military forces, high-sulphur fuel oil and several small parcels of acidic chemical products. In several instances the ships identified in fact picked up no product at all from Aruba.

In Point 4, Exxon also claimed that the cargoes of heating oil shipped from Aruba to Europe during the time in question represented a net amount of 400,000 barrels. The company contended that if this fuel was "blended or otherwise converted to low-sulphur fuel it could have produced 800,000 barrels of fuel supply for Florida Power & Light at the outside."

This point of the complaint further contended that the NBC News report failed to mention that the shipments to Europe had "a well established historical base" and that "it was misleading to suggest, as the program did, an improper diversion of supplies." As was emphasized to the reporter, the cause of the continuing shortfall of this product (low-sulphur fuel oil) has been twofold: first, a shortage of the crude oil from which this and all other oil products are made, and, second, a decision to make somewhat less low-sulphur fuel oil, for which there are substitutes, so that more heating oil, for which there are no ready substitutes, could be made.

"One may quarrel with the latter decision, but in the circumstances we believe that it was a reasonable one."

> 5. *NBC*—But so far the power company, the State of Florida and even President Carter have all gone along with the dirtier air, because Exxon says that's the way it has to be.
>
> *Exxon complaint*—This implies remarkably little independent judgment by the State of Florida and our federal agencies. Exxon has never said this is the way it has to be. Exxon made certain supply decisions based on the facts available to it and consistent with its wish to allocate short supplies equitably among its customers. That the authorities have acquiesced in these decisions . . . or at least accepted their consequences . . . would suggest that they have concluded that they were not unreasonable.

**Response:** William J. Small, president of NBC News, responded to the complaint in a 13-page letter. He wrote, in part:

> . . . At no time did the NBC News report suggest that Exxon's decisions were made in an irresponsible manner. NBC News merely reported on an existing controversy and the viewpoints of those involved in the controversy.
>
> Exxon's complaint alleges 'factual error, selective use of information, lack of

106

perspective and the building of effect through innuendo.' However, an examination of Exxon's specific contentions reveals no factual inaccuracies or distortions. Rather, Exxon's principal and repeated complaint is directed to alleged implications or inferences in the story. . . . While NBC disagrees that its report was characterized by the shortcomings catalogued by Exxon, it is significant to note that the thrust of this complaint goes not to accuracy, but to editorial decisons. . . . NBC urges the Council not to become involved in judging the wisdom of these decisions. Complaints which focus on impressions, innuendoes or peripheral aspects of a news report divert attention from the essential elements of the story and their accuracy, fairness and completeness. Full-fledged investigations of such complaints are bound to chill investigative journalism.

Exxon's general and specific criticisms of the October 16 report, to which we will now turn, must be viewed against these concerns.

First . . . nowhere did the NBC report state, as Exxon charges, that Exxon's European customers were receiving clean oil, nor was that the point of the discussion of foreign shipments. Such shipments were relevant only insofar as *any* shipments might have resulted in reduced sulphur content in the oil delivered to FP&L.

Significantly, Exxon admits that the central point of the story was true: that Exxon decided who got what.

Contrary to Exxon's assertion that its efforts to allocate oil fairly and equitably were not given much of an airing, two Exxon representatives discussed these efforts, particularly in relation to the foreign shipments, in the body of the report. . . .

> *Ed Hess, Exxon Vice President*: 'We had to accept some modest degree of trade-off on the environmental constraints in order to provide oil products that customers need.'
>
> *A. K. Wolgast, Manager of Planning for Exxon International*: 'I can't really say we give priority to any part of the world, because we feel that we have a very interdependent system and we try to be fair to American customers. But at the same time we recognize that we have interests in Europe as well, and we try to balance these out and treat all our customers on a fair and equitable basis.'

Clearly, Exxon's point of view was fully aired—a point of view that emphasized its decisions were not based on 'whim and commercial self-interest.'. . . . Second, as Exxon is well aware, the fact that the level of sulphur in the oil shipped to FP&L may have changed by an average of only .1%, and has not been reduced further, does not mean that the air quality in Florida is not undergoing 'progressive deterioration.' . . . NBC News based its statement 'the air in Florida has been getting dirtier and dirtier' on information it received from Jacob Varn, Executive Director of Florida Department of Environmental Regulation, and EPA officials in Washington. The accuracy of this description was also confirmed to us by Steven Smallwood (chief of the Bureau of Air Quality Management, Florida Department of Environmental Regulation). Nevertheless, the October 16 report was careful to point out: 'There are disagreements about how serious a health problem this dirtier air is.'

Finally, Exxon does not refute the central and undeniable fact that Federal Clean Air Act opacity standards had to be suspended in order to permit FP&L to utilize the fuel now supplied by Exxon. Nor did Exxon representatives Hess and Wolgast contradict Brian Ross when, during the course of their interviews, Ross referred to the 'dirtier air' caused by the high-sulphur fuel shipped to FP&L.

Exxon's third point is basically a repetition of its first: that the report, while 'trivially true,' failed to fully discuss all the reasons for Exxon's cutback to FP&L, such as the worldwide crude oil shortage. As we have pointed out, the report did not fail to discuss the factors Exxon claims influenced its allocations decisions. . . . In its fourth point, Exxon recited a host of detailed facts relating to the amount and nature of oil products shipped from Aruba to Europe. But, basically, its complaint is that the report 'inferred' that 'significant volumes of product, relevant to the needs of FP&L, were sent to Europe,' when, in fact, the shipments would have accounted for only three days' additional low sulphur supply.

Once again, however, even Exxon's complaints as to inference and perspective are groundless. The report stated clearly that 'of the oil products that Exxon sent to Europe it is *unclear how much could have been used by Florida Power and Light.*'

The Lloyd's of London study commissioned by NBC News lists only the name, flag, dead weight, ports of departure and destination, and sailing and arrival dates of 15 tankers which sailed between Aruba and Europe in early 1979. The contents of those vessels is known only to Exxon. The study was useful in preparing the report only insofar as it indicated that there were fairly frequent shipments from Aruba to Europe by Exxon. The News Council has asked NBC to furnish it with a copy of the Lloyd's study to help clarify how much of the petroleum product shipped to Europe may have been 'relevant to the clean air issue.' However, the information contained in the Lloyd's study is not helpful in terms of indicating the nature of contents of the shipments to Europe. NBC got that information from Exxon and we trust the Council can do the same. . . . While Brian Ross did not physically show Mr. Wolgast the Lloyd's of London list, Ross carefully went over each vessel on the list with Wolgast during their interview to determine both the accuracy of the information contained in the Lloyd's study and the contents of each tanker—information known only to Exxon. . . . And while Exxon keeps arguing over the number of tankers, it has never contested the more significant statement that, whatever the number of vessels, its shipments to Europe contained 'more than three million barrels of various petroleum products.'

. . . Exxon contends that only three of the 15 tankers identified by Lloyd's carried product 'relevant to the clean air issue,' specifically, the heating oil cargoes. . . . Exxon wrote to the News Council noting that at the appropriate blending ratio this heating oil would yield at most 840,000 barrels of low-sulphur oil for FP&L. However, petroleum refining experts contacted by NBC News stated that the jet fuel transported to Europe by Exxon might also have been refined differently so as to supply FP&L with low-sulphur fuel. Moreover, while Exxon focuses on the tankers listed by Lloyd's, Mr. Wolgast's records listed several shipments of petroleum products that did not appear in the Lloyd's study.

Because of these differing pieces of information, the NBC story reported both Exxon's original statement that the petroleum sent to Europe could have constituted more than six weeks' supply for FP&L and its subsequent 'few days' supply' statement. More importantly, Brian Ross noted specifically that it was unclear how much of the oil shipped to Europe could have been used by FP&L.

Exxon then reiterates that it decided to make less low-sulphur fuel oil because of demands for other oil products, and notes that both its customers and federal officials were aware of these conflicting needs. It argues that shipments to Europe are customary and that the report was 'misleading' in its suggestion that supplies were improperly diverted.

108

Again, Exxon's characterization of the 'suggestion' or implication of the report is unfounded. The story did not imply that federal officials were unaware of the world energy crisis or conflicting demands for petroleum products. It did not suggest that shipments to Europe were a departure from prior practices. Nor . . . did the story contradict Exxon's contention that low-sulphur fuel was in short supply.

Exxon's fifth and final point adds little. It argues that the acquiescence of state and federal officials suggests they believed Exxon's decisions were reasonable. The fact is that they had no choice but to acquiesce. A proper question is whether officials acquiesced knowing all the pertinent facts about availability of low-sulphur fuel. Incidentally, the Florida Department of Environmental Regulation, after the Exxon experience, is not satisfied that it is equipped to handle fuel-related environmental questions, so it has hired a fuel consultant. Exxon's point has little relevance.

This point-by-point examination of Exxon's complaint reveals that despite the rhetoric about 'factual error,' 'distortion' and 'unbalanced reporting,' its complaint reflects little more than its dissatisfaction with the 'impression' it believes the report left with viewers and its disagreement with NBC's editorial judgments as to the inclusion and omission of material. Appearances by Exxon representatives constituted about 20 percent of the five-minute report. More importantly, *these representatives expressed precisely the points of view that Exxon now claims were omitted from the broadcast.*

NBC believes 'Dirty Oil and Dirty Air' was a responsible and fair account of the Florida air pollution controversy. We do not believe, therefore, that Exxon's complaint has merit.

**Shortage of low-sulphur fuel oil:** According to officials of the federal Department of Energy and the Florida Department of Environmental Regulation, there was a worldwide shortage of low-sulphur fuel oil in the early part of 1979.

"Trade-off decisions had to be made by Exxon," said Phil Keif, the Department of Energy's public information officer. "If more low-sulphur fuel oil was produced, cutbacks would be necessary in the production of gasoline and heating oil."

Jacob Varn, secretary of the Florida Department of Environmental Regulation and court officer at the series of state hearings held on the availability of low-sulphur fuel, said: "The fact that there was a shortage of low-sulphur fuel oil in Florida went virtually uncontradicted. Experts on the energy situation testified under oath at the hearings and their statements on the shortage went unchallenged. If someone had reason to believe that the people testifying were not telling the truth, they had their shot at it."

Mr. Varn said that the decision to ask for emergency suspension of clean air regulations was necessary because "we were faced with a possibility where 4.5 million people were going to have to do without electricity for four to six hours a day if we did not make contingency plans."

Jack Francis, Florida Power & Light's vice president, told the Council staff that following the NBC News broadcast the power company conducted its own study to determine the extent of the energy shortage. "We wanted to find out if we were being lied to by Exxon and the DOE," he said. Although the actual findings of the study are proprietary, Mr. Francis said that "we were covinced there was a worldwide shortage of low-sulphur fuel or we would never have asked the President of the United States to sign an exemption of air quality standards order."

Moreover, Marty Gitten, a Con Edison spokesman, told the Council staff that Con Edison's supply of low-sulphur fuel had also been cut by Exxon during the time deliveries to Florida Power and Light were being curtailed. He added that Con Edison's other suppliers also cut back low-sulphur fuel shipments during that period.

**Acquiescence of federal and state officials:** A related question raised by NBC News in its response is whether federal and state officials knew all the pertinent facts about the availability of low-sulphur fuel oil.

Mary Clark, assistant general counsel at the Florida Department of Environmental Regulation and court reporter at the state hearings, discussed the difficulties of making an informed independent judgment on the Exxon cutbacks: "We felt that there was nobody with any expertise present to make an independent judgment in the matter," she said. "So we started talking with people at the Environmental Protection Agency and the Department of Energy. We found, unfortunately, that they had no one with any expertise either. . . . I don't feel we were being lied to by Exxon or Florida Power & Light, but I don't know if we even asked the right questions."

Mr. Varn said he was confident of the fact-finding process used at the state hearings. Nevertheless, he did acknowledge that the Florida Department of Environmental Regulation has since hired two independent fuel consultants to, in part, better equip the agency for future hearings on energy-related issues.

Mr. Keif of the Department of Energy stated that the DOE has no control over Exxon's production decisions outside the United States—including the cutbacks of low-sulphur fuel oil production at Exxon/Aruba, which directly affected supplies to Florida Power & Light. Another DOE officer, Kathy Litwak, stated that although work is underway to improve its independent data gathering systems, the DOE's "major source" of information has been the oil industry.

**Quality of air in Florida:** The NBC News report said:

110

> For five months now, the air in Southern Florida has been getting dirtier and
> dirtier.

Jacob Varn and Steve Smallwood of the Florida Department of Environmental Regulation, both confirmed the accuracy of NBC News's
statement.

"Obviously, if you burn dirtier oil, oil that is higher in sulphur dioxide
and particulate emissions," said Mr. Smallwood, "the air is going to get
dirtier."

With the relaxation of clean air standards in Florida, Florida Power &
Light has been burning fuel from Exxon that is higher in sulphur content
than oil burned before the standards were changed, said Mr. Smallwood.

**Lloyd's of London study:** The NBC News report said:

> In a study done by Lloyd's of London for NBC News, a tanker movement out of
> the Exxon refinery shows at least fifteen tankers left for Europe in the first part of this
> year containing more than three million barrels of various petroleum products. All at
> the very time Exxon was telling Florida Power & Light that there wasn't enough
> crude oil to make low-sulphur fuel.

Pertaining to the Lloyd's study, NBC News said that "(it) is not helpful
in terms of indicating the nature or contents of the shipments to Europe.
NBC got that information from Exxon and we trust the Council can do the
same."

It was A. K. Wolgast, manager of planning for Exxon International,
who told NBC that the tankers in question carried a total of more than
three million barrels of various petroleum products. The Lloyd's study
contained no such data.

**Tanker contents:** In a breakdown of tanker movements from Exxon's
Aruba refinery to Europe during the first half of 1979, Exxon contended
that only three of the fifteen tankers identified in the Lloyd's study carried
product "relevant to the clean air issue."

Mr. Wolgast said in the NBC interview transcript that the remaining
twelve tankers in question contained four cargoes of jet fuel to the U.S.
military; four cargoes of residual fuel to third-party customers; and four
cargoes of chemical components to various Exxon customers. None of
which, said Exxon, could have been used by Florida Power and Light.

The Council Staff was able to independently verify with the Department of Defense that a number of jet fuel shipments were picked up from
Exxon/Aruba bound for Europe during the first half of 1979. The Department of Defense said that Exxon was fulfilling its contractual obligations

at the time these shipments were made and that the fuel was used to supply U. S. military bases in Europe and to refuel naval ships at sea.

**Council finding:** NBC insists that "the central point of the story" was simply "that Exxon decided who got what," and that "at no time did the NBC News report suggest that Exxon's decisions were made in an irresponsible manner." This Council, however, received a different impression. The opening announcement was that "For five months now the air in Southern Florida has been getting dirtier and dirtier;" the subsequent account of Exxon's decision to alter its mix of production and deliveries, to the detriment of Florida's air (to some unstated but implicitly harmful degree); the reported investigations whereby NBC News discovered that substantial shipments of Exxon oil had found their way to Europe, and even into the lucrative "spot market;" the reference to Exxon Vice President Hess's unavailability for a second interview (referring NBC to another officer instead). All of these gave the impression that Exxon was guilty of duplicity.

Perhaps that suggestion was unintentional. But news broadcasters (or for that matter news writers) who seek to compress complex stories are not relieved of the obligation to be reasonably fair just because time and space limitations make their task harder. Exxon's complaint is found warranted.

**Concurring:** Brady, Cooney, McKay, Otwell, Pulitzer, Roberts and Rusher.

**Dissenting:** Ghiglione, Huston, Lawson and Miller.

**Abstaining:** Isaacs.

**Concurring opinion by Mr. Brady:** This unfortunate TV program and its accusatory title are the product of unknowledgeable journalists who lack the qualifications to deal with the extraordinary subject of energy.

NBC News might have performed less ineptly had it checked its premises and facts with a few of the 20 or so energy economists at various American universities. NBC News might then have, as in my opinion it should have done, even based on the information obtained from Exxon executives in extensive interviews, complimented Exxon for its alertness in recognizing a serious imbalance in the supply of grades of crude oil; commended Exxon for its astute planning and timely action in adjusting its refinery operations so the American people would continue to have uninterrupted supplies of the necessary grades of refined products for heat, cooling (Florida) and transportation; and congratulated Exxon for its accomplishments under extremely difficult conditions.

**Dissenting opinion by Mr. Lawson:** (Huston concurring) I do not find the complaint warranted. The air in Southern Florida is getting dirtier with sulphur from Florida Power & Light plants which are burning oil with higher sulphur content. Exxon made the decision based on Exxon information and business considerations.

NBC has erred in that other causes for the air becoming dirtier are not mentioned. But then, was the air quality standard in Florida suspended for any other pollutant?

The press steadily prints many oil company ads and reports that attempt to show that our present energy crisis is caused by "fate" and not as a result of decisons by human beings and institutions.

Whatever the specific inadequacies of this report, NBC should be commended for at least reporting that Exxon made this decision that affects the human need for clean air.

I do not see that The National News Council's criteria of accuracy and fairness have been violated by NBC.
March 6, 1980.

## COMPLAINT NO. 173    (Filed: Nov. 26, 1979)
### HOGGE
### against
### THE COURIER-JOURNAL

**Complaint:** Dr. Gary A. Hogge of Louisville, Kentucky, complained that an article appearing in *The Courier-Journal* on October 14, 1979, was, "at least as it regards me, totally erroneous."

The article, headlined "Doctors' fees in Kentucky and Indiana vary greatly," was a comparative study of doctors' fees for a number of common medical procedures. The article contained a series of tables, each listing a particular medical procedure, a doctor's name, and what he or she charged for that service. The tables were arranged in descending order with those who charged the most listed first.

Dr. Hogge's name was the first to appear in a table captioned "Initial Office Visit/General Practice," where he was listed as charging $35 in both 1978 and 1976.

"The price puts me at the very top (as far as charges are concerned) of the Louisville area general practitioners," wrote Dr. Hogge. "This is, to say in the least, inaccurate." He said that he actually charged $15 in 1978 and $12 in 1976 for such visits, "even though it is usually more time consuming to examine a patient for the first time."

Dr. Hogge also said:

> When I called the reporter, Robert Peirce, to suggest that if he wanted accuracy all he would have to do was call me, he informed me that: (a) he did not have time to check to see if his figures were accurate and that (b) even if he had called me he would still not have changed the article to make it more accurate. This seems to be a classic example of 'Don't confuse me with facts, my mind's made up.' It concerns me to be misrepresented in this fashion particularly when it is done with so little concern for accuracy.

In an explanation accompanying the tables, *The Courier-Journal* said that it obtained its information on Kentucky's doctors' fees from the Medicare records of the Metropolitan Life Insurance Company and that the figures cited in the tables represented a doctor's median charge.

To this point, Dr. Hogge wrote that "I have never accepted assignment from Medicare. I have asked the patient to file for whatever reimbursement from Medicare they could obtain. Therefore, I have never dealt directly with Medicare. . . . I am in solo medical practice and, therefore, these charges could not be those of an associate."

**Response:** In response to the complaint, Frank Hartley, news ombudsman for *The Courier-Journal*, wrote:

> I believe that reporter Bob Peirce and his editors touched all of the right bases. In fact, they double-checked many of the records, and talked to about 60 of the 400 physicians listed in Medicare records in taking precautions against errors. . . . Furthermore, I believe, after discussing Dr. Hogge's charges with Peirce and City Editor Bill Cox, that Peirce's comments about checking the accuracy of his work were misunderstood by the doctor.
>
> Here are the facts I have learned:
>
> After Peirce was assigned to do a story on doctors' fees in the Greater Louisville area, he determined, after thorough investigation, that Medicare records were the only source of doctors' charges open to him. . . . Peirce and his editors next determined that billings to Medicare accurately reflect the amounts doctors charge. Medicare officials in Kentucky and Washington said that physicians should not charge Medicare patients more than non-Medicare patients, adding that it is illegal to do so. . . . Continuing his research, Peirce learned that Medicare information is an average charge based on at least three billings.
>
> After obtaining from Medicare a list of the types of medical procedures for which records are kept, Peirce and his editors settled on about 20 procedures common enough, they believed, to be of general interest. . . . Further research caused the list to be pared to 18 procedures because two procedures were not as common as had been believed and there did not appear to be a sufficient number of claims to get an accurate picture. . . . Peirce talked to some practicing physicians about whether any of the remaining 18 procedures should be dropped because they might not provide a fair test of fees. None of the physicians thought any of the 18 should be eliminated.
>
> After the reporter obtained a printout of 400 area doctors' charges paid by

Medicare for three years, 1976 through 1978, the newspaper hired an outside computer firm to prepare the information on a tape to be run and analyzed by our in-house computers. The newspaper, in fact, paid to have the information punched twice as a check against human error. . . . Peirce was provided with a printout showing the doctor's average charges for each procedure and he interviewed at random more than 60 physicians who were in the high or low range. . . . His purpose was to provide the doctors with an opportunity to challenge or explain the figures. Peirce also asked Medicare to recheck its records on procedures with the widest variations in charges.

It was at this stage in the preparation of the story that Peirce came upon what seems to be the heart of Dr. Hogge's complaint. It is this: Whether it was fair to use Medicare's "initial office visit" category. We learned from some doctors and Medicare that services in an initial visit vary, which accounts for part of the range in charges.

Therefore, in an attempt to make it clear to readers that such differences do exist, Peirce and his editors phrased an introductory paragraph to the category of initial office visits and it was in type as large as the doctors' names and charges. . . . The paragraph read:

'The initial office visit and follow-up office visit are categories used by Medicare. But one doctor may provide more services on initial or followup visits than other doctors. Thus, a doctor's charge might appear to be more expensive than another's when it really isn't. In some cases, these charges might not be what the doctor himself considers to be his initial and followup visit charges. It is important to ask a doctor what he includes in office-visit charges.'

That disclaimer, it seems to me, is evidence of the newspaper's interest in fair and accurate reporting. . . . Dr. Hogge benefited from the disclaimer more than some other physicians because he was at the top of the list, immediately under the explanatory paragraph.

Dr. Hogge called us to object to the story on the day of publication, October 14, 1979, and Peirce and Cox have talked to him several times since then. He said he believes that the explanatory paragraph was overlooked by readers although he has conceded that those who did read it should not have a problem understanding the difference in charges. . . . Also, he said he thinks he should have been called before the story was published.

Cox explained that more than 60 doctors were called and that it would have been impractical to have attempted to call all 400 listed by Medicare. Cox also shared with Dr. Hogge many of the other details involved in researching the story.

Dr. Hogge complains in his letter to his patients that when he called Peirce to ask for a correction, Peirce told him that '(a) he did not have time to check to see if his figures were accurate and that (b) even in he had called me (Dr. Hogge) he would still not have changed the article to make it more accurate.'

Peirce disputes Dr. Hogge's account of the conversation. And I, as an editor who has known Peirce since he joined The Courier-Journal some two years ago, believe that Dr. Hogge misunderstood Peirce. . . . Peirce says that he did tell Dr. Hogge that he did not attempt to call all 400 doctors and he says that he did explain the many checks for accuracy he made during the research of the story. . . . He also told Dr. Hogge, he says, that he talked with another doctor who was listed by Medicare as charging $35 for an initial visit. That doctor, he says he told Dr. Hogge, said that

115

some physicians perform more services in an initial office visit than others. . . . It was that same doctor, incidentally, who helped alert Peirce and Cox to the need for the introductory paragraph.

To reiterate, I believe the reporter and his editors took adequate precautions in researching and writing the story and I do not find any reason to believe that Dr. Hogge correctly understood Peirce during the conversation about which the doctor complains. . . . I am sorry that Dr. Hogge continues to believe he was mistreated by The Courier-Journal, but I think the accuracy and fairness of the story can be judged by the fact that only Dr. Hogge has found reason to be so critical. . . . As best I can determine, there were only two other complaints, one because a doctor's name was misspelled and another from a patient who said her doctor's fees were listed as being lower than she was charged.

## Staff Analysis:

1. Many doctors—perhaps as many as 40 percent of the total—do not accept the assignment of Medicare responsibilities. They wish patients to pay for services and for them then to seek reimbursement on their own. A doctor need not know that a patient is seeking reimbursement from Medicare. And, some doctors seem to think that because their patients do the filing, their charges do not become part of a Medicare "profile" or record. They are mistaken.

2. Where doctors do not provide itemization of tests and other procedures, patients may lose benefits covered by insurance. Blanket fee billing is treated as a "visit" in Medicare listings.

3. A Medicare profile of a doctor may become distorted because of: the doctor's method of itemization or lump sum billing; the very nature of the initial office visit category (It can be coded one of three ways—as a routine initial office visit, as a complete initial office visit involving an "established patient or minor chronic illness" or a complete initial office visit involving a "new patient or major illness." These last two categories may include the costs of a complete diagnostic history and physical examination and the initiation of diagnostic and treatment programs); the subjective element that enters into the coding process.

4. Dr. Hogge's billing form is less than ideal. Some of his patients may well have kept the itemized part of his bills, submitting only the blanket fee indicated at the top of the form. Also, in doing his itemization, the doctor simply lists "office visit," making no distinctions for the various Medicare classifications.

**Council finding:** Dr. Hogge's complaint was accepted for review on the ground that many news organizations consider it a public service to periodically check on medical costs and that a Council study might produce information useful to the media generally. The assumption was justified.

*The Courier-Journal* listing was accurate insofar as the Medicare computer records listed Dr. Hogge's charges. What seemed essential was a direct check with Dr. Hogge and all others listed in the top rank of fees recorded, the most sensitive area in the lists. It is clear such a recheck with Dr. Hogge would have brought instant protest and a deeper check. However, the newspaper opted for random checking. Moreover, the newspaper's statement seeking to clarify differentials was not fully informative. *The Courier-Journal*'s motivation was sound and the paper did publish a patient's letter supporting Dr. Hogge's view. Nevertheless, Dr. Hogge was done an inadvertent injustice and the complaint is found warranted.

**Concurring:** Brady, Cooney, Ghiglione, Lawson, McKay, Miller, Otwell, Pulitzer, Roberts and Rusher.

**Note:** Norman E. Isaacs, Chairman, did not take part in the vote because he is the former executive editor of *The Courier Journal & Louisville Times*.

March 6, 1980


## COMPLAINT NO. 174     (Filed: April 22, 1980)
AMERICAN-ARAB RELATIONS COMMITTEE
against
CBS NEWS RADIO

**Complaint:** Dr. H. T. Mehdi, president of the American Arab Relations Committee of New York, complained that CBS News, on April 7, failed "at least three times" to attribute to Israeli sources a report that a baby was killed in a raid by Palestinians on an Israeli kibbutz. Dr. Mehdi wrote that he called CBS News Radio's foreign news desk "and complained that they should attribute the news to its Israeli source. The editors refused and continued repeating the story without attributing it to its source."

In a mailgram to Brian Ellis, CBS News Radio's foreign news editor, Dr. Mehdi asked if the failure to attribute the report to an Israeli source was "the result of bad editing or was there some wicked influence somewhere to affect American public opinion against the Palestinians?"

In his letter to the Council Dr. Mehdi declared that "This 'information' must have been given either by the Palestinians directly to CBS or a CBS

117

reporter must have been on the spot at the moment of the raid and observed the fact that the Palestinians killed the child." Dr. Mehdi discounted these two possibilities.

"The other alternative," Dr. Mehdi wrote, "is that Israelis gave this information to CBS and CBS failed to do the professional work and refused to attribute the story to its source."

**Response:** In response to the complaint, Emerson L. Stone, Vice President CBS News, Radio, wrote:

> In the best of all worlds, most every statement in every newscast would be attributed; meantime, we report what seems reasonable to us, fairly and without the biases of those who would have things shaped one way or the other as a special pleading, nor have we any cause to do otherwise.
>
> CBS News tries to use reasonable judgment within a framework of what listeners can be expected to know or to judge about any given story.
>
> It seems then to come down to the three broadcasts at 7 a.m. and 11 a.m. and 4 p.m. Only in those broadcasts was it stated that the "terrorists" had "killed" one child. (Elsewhere, the fact of the death of that child—and of other persons—was reported, but additional specifics were not stated.) Three different writers produced those three newscasts; three different editors edited them. The consensus of those involved is that to their recollection the wire services on that day made the statement without qualification of reponsibility by the guerrillas for the death of the child. This is often done. In fact the vast majority of statements made in most news reports are made without attribution. Even in this same story, statements of the slayings committed by the Israelis were made without attribution to the obvious source of all information for that story that day, namely the Israeli military.
>
> Incidentally, it should be noted also that in some stories such as this one the facts are developed in an evolutionary manner and seeming contradictions or conflicts—even errors of fact—develop between periodic reports as additional information becomes available.

Mr. Stone stated in conclusion that "(a) because of the general aura of military security in which this story was cloaked, its location, its course, and the single nationality (Israeli) of its participants who lived, it can be reasonably expected that the listener would adduce the source of the information accordingly; (b) the timing and the sequence of events of the story logically support the contention, also put forward without attribution by others, that the child died in the hands of terrorists, and (c) finally, that indeed the evidence points to the fact that the guerrillas did kill the child, intentionally or not."

**Staff analysis:** Regarding the matter of attribution, all reports examined by the Council—AP, UPI, the New York *Daily News*, the *Washington Post* and the *New York Times*—said that there were five Palestinian raiders, and that all were killed. All of these reports originated in Israel.

Such being the case, it would seem obvious that the source of the reports had to be Israeli.

The two wire services and three newspaper reports examined attributed their information variously to "Israeli military sources," "Israeli military command," "Israeli authorities," and "Israelis." The *Washington Post*'s report was published under an italicized notice stating that "The following file was subject to Israeli Army censorship."

There were variations among the reports as to responsibility for killing the baby, 2½-year-old Ayel Gluska. For example, one UPI report said that "One adult and a child from the kibbutz died in the counterattack." An AP report said the "Palestinian terrorists attacked a nursery in this kibbutz on the Israeli-Lebanese frontier today, killing an Israeli baby and two adults before troops stormed the children's dormitory. . . ." The *New York Times*, after reporting on the Israeli counterattack, said that "A two-and-a-half-year-old boy in the dormitory was killed, possibly by the terrorists. . . ." The *Daily News* reported that "In a sneak attack under cover of darkness, five Palestinian terrorists early yesterday invaded a nursery . . . and in nine hours of terror killed a baby and two adults. . . ." The *Washington Post* reported that "All five guerrillas and two Israelis, including a 2-year-old child, died during the siege and attack."

It is essential to bear in mind what Mr. Stone said in his letter of response to the complaint, i.e., ". . . .that in some stories such as this one the facts are developed in an evolutionary manner and seeming contradictions or conflicts—even errors of fact—develop between periodic reports as additional information becomes available."

It is apparent that additional facts did develop as this story broke and unfolded during the night. As it developed, it became less clear as to when the baby died. Was it during the initial action by the terrorists or during the Israeli counterattack? *The New York Times* dealt with this by attributing to Mr. Weizman, after his arrival on the scene, a statement that it was not clear whether he (the baby) had been killed in the assault or earlier. *The Times* also reported Lieut. Gen. Rafael Eytan, Israeli Chief of Staff, as saying that preliminary evidence pointed to the baby having been shot by the terrorists during the night.

**Council finding:** The Council believes that attribution is important in many news accounts, and this should be kept particularly in mind where terroristic acts are involved. All wire services and newspaper reports examined by the Council make it evident that the information on the death of the baby came through Israeli sources. This is not similarly evident, however, in several of the transcripts submitted to the Council by CBS News Radio. Dr. Mehdi's protest should serve to remind all broadcasters that even in compact form there are instances, in new reports of this nature, where attribution is necessary. However, nothing in the record provides any support for imputations of bias on the part of CBS New Radio in the handling of these reports. The complaint is found unwarranted.

**Concurring:** Abel, Bell, Benson, Ghiglione, Isaacs, Miller, Pulitzer, Roberts, Rusher, Scott, and Salant.

**Dissenting:** Huston.

**Dissenting opinion by Ms. Huston:** This complaint is warranted, in my opinion, because CBS led its audience to believe that there was *no* doubt that the Palestinians killed the baby. In any war, there must always be doubt of *any* information released by either side. Therefore, I agree with the complainant's assertion that the coverage was "unprofessional" and further, that "such misrepresentation creates hostility in this country against the Palestinians and the Arabs at large."

June 12, 1980

## COMPLAINT NO. 175 (Filed May 1, 1980)
### CATHOLIC LEAGUE FOR RELIGIOUS AND CIVIL RIGHTS
against
### THE CAMDEN COURIER-POST
(Gannett News Service)

**Complaint:** The Catholic League for Religious and Civil Rights, a national organization with headquarters in Milwaukee, charged "inaccurate and unfair reporting" in a Gannett News Service story published in the *Camden Courier-Post* on February 29, 1980.

The article was headlined, "Paulines face foreclosure by bondholders." It stated that trustees for bondholders had taken legal action toward foreclosure on the holdings of the Order of St. Paul, First Hermit, The Pauline Fathers, in order to meet overdue loans. The story challenged by the Catholic League was the most current of a series of well more than 100 articles dealing with financial difficulties of the Pauline Fathers, which led from the sale of bonds to build a shrine at Doylestown, Pa. The shrine is still incomplete. The Pauline order was accused of mishandling the bond money.

The complaint asserted that some of the statements in the February 29 story "attributed to anonymous sources within the (First National Bank of Minneapolis) are in direct contradiction to the official position of the bank as stated in a letter to the *Courier-Post*, dated November 21, 1979, from Frank B. Krause, senior vice-president and official spokesman for the bank on this matter." The bank was trustee for some 1,500 individuals who bought the bonds.

In support of its position, the League cited what it termed "three significant points":

1. "With reference to the bank's decision to move toward foreclosure, the *Courier-Post* reports that, 'The bank officials say the action was triggered by overwhelming frustration with what they decribed as a series of stalling tactics, unfulfilled promises and contradictory statements by Camden Bishop George H. Guilfoyle.' Yet in his letter, Krause had said that 'the bank's relations with Bishop Guilfoyle . . . over the long period of default on the notes have been courteous, businesslike, open and aboveboard.' It is possible that some unnamed person with the bank expressed the opinion recorded by the *Courier-Post*, but Mr. Krause's position of November 21 still stands as the official position of the bank. . . . Even if there is a division of opinion within the bank . . . it would seem that the *Courier-Post* had an obligation to note that the official public position of the bank was one of satisfaction. On the contrary, they have left the public with the impression that Bishop Guilfoyle's dealings with the bank are not now and have not for a long time been 'courteous, business-like, open and aboveboard.'"

2. Concerns the use of funds collected through a special appeal which had, as one of its goals, the satisfaction of the defaulted notes. The *Courier-Post* writes, "(Philadelphia Cardinal John) Krol and Guilfoyle persuaded bankers to delay foreclosure with assurances that the proceeds from a national fundraising campaign would be used to satisfy the debt. . . . But instead of paying off the elderly Catholic lenders, Guilfoyle and Krol used about half of the cash to quietly liquidate what the Vatican described as 'legally questionable' loans, businesses and tax-dodge schemes in which the Paulines had involved themselves.' The clear implication . . . is that Bishop Guilfoyle and Cardinal Krol had conspired to deceive that bank by failing to use the funds gained from the Trust Appeal as the bank expected. Leaving aside the invidious choice of words . . . the *Courier-Post* report clearly leaves readers with the impression that the prelates had violated a trust, when in fact it had been planned well in advance and agreed to by the bank that the funds from the Trust Appeal

would be disbursed in the manner in which they actually were disbursed."

3. "Finally, the *Courier-Post* once again reports its self-congratulatory claims that the repayment of $1.5 million to bondholders in November, 1979, was due not to the sincere efforts of Cardinal Krol, Bishop Guilfoyle and the First Bank to see to it that the investors did not suffer financial loss, but rather to the pressure placed on these parties by the Gannett News Service. . . . What is particularly inappropriate about the *Courier-Post*'s version is that it refers . . . to the state of mind of the bank's representatives . . . long after the bank had made an effort to correct the previous erroneous statements, the *Courier-Post* persisted in putting forth to the public these same misrepresentations. . . . To repeat those same inaccuracies again, even after a correction has been made public must be viewed as irresponsible."

**Response:** John J. Curley, Vice President and General Manager of the Gannett News Service in Washington, wrote in response for the service and the Camden editors.

Mr. Curley wrote: "The basic question raised by the complaint . . . is this: In its reports . . . what responsibility did Gannett News Service have to (the letter written by Mr. Krause)?" He went on: "The bank's effort, as trustee, to recoup some $4.5 million owed to Pauline bondholders have been underway for 7½ years. They are still going on, despite repeated promises by the church to pay up. Mr. Krause has never had a direct role in these negotiations. Court records show that they were conducted until late 1979 by Charles Tilden, a bank vice president, and since then by James Anderson, corporate trust officer. . . . Mr. Krause's letter appeared out of the blue. It represents his only involvement. . . . It was, as we reported in a news story, a concession to church pressure. . . ."

He then turned to the three parts of the League's complaint:

1. "(This) objects to our characterization of the relationship between the bank and the church. Our contention . . . is that the relationship has not been smooth, that at times it has been fractious. . . . We have numerous documents to support the fact that the bank was increasingly frustrated and angered. . . . We have included just two of these documents as examples. The bank's actions . . . speak most clearly of this relationship. Bank officials took the church to court when the initial payments were defaulted; they subpoenaed church officials and records to see for themselves what the truth of the matter was; they forced an audit of the Pauline holdings (and found $800,000 the church had kept secret from them); and, most recently, the bank filed with church officials a 30-day

legal notice of foreclosure for nonpayment. Separately and together, these actions make mockery of the assertion that 'Bishop Guilfoyle's dealing with the bank are now and have for a long time been 'courteous, businesslike, open and aboveboard.'"

2. "(This) deals with how the money raised by Cardinal John Krol's appeal was to be used. The appeal was billed as one to 'save the shrine' by paying off those who contributed to build it: the Pauline bond-holders. . . . Until the Krause letter, no bank or church official had ever mentioned the existence of any other debts—and for good reason. Many of the Pauline debts which Bishop Guilfoyle was concealing and hoping to resolve by secret payoffs involved—in his own words—immoral and perhaps illegal actions. Krause's statement that these other debts were always recognized and accepted by the bank was itself an astounding admission . . . since the bank and church had always said the bond-holders were their sole concern. . . ."

3. "The last part of the complaint suggests that bank and church officials had long agreed on a release date for the $1.5 million in escrow money and that the Gannett reports played no part in the release of these funds. . . . No bank or church official has ever disputed that the bank's . . . 'get-tough' attitude was triggered by (our reporting). . . . We have many, many more documents to support all of the above. You are welcome to inspect them. . . ."

**Staff examination:** The News Council explored the three points at issue with an officer of the First National Bank in Minneapolis. He preferred to discuss the matter on an "off-the-record" basis, but said the bank would go on record if it became necessary.

Concerning the news report language, "Bank officials say the action was triggered by overwhelming frustration with what they described as a series of stalling tactics, unfulfilled promises and contradictory public statements," the bank official termed this an accurate reflection of the bank's position.

Part two of the complaint dealt with that portion of the story that read: "The drive, headed by (Cardinal) Krol, raised more than $5 million. But instead of paying off the elderly Catholic lenders, Guilfoyle and Krol used about half the cash to quietly liquidate what the Vatican described as 'legally questionable' loans, businesses and tax-dodge schemes in which the Paulines had involved themselves." The bank official was asked if the bank knew, as both the complaint and Mr. Krause's letter suggest, that funds from the fund drive would be used to pay off other obligations beside the bonds. The answer was yes. However, the banker said the bank had no idea of the extent of the other obligations. Because of the extent of these other obligations, he said, money to pay off the bonds did not come in as rapidly as the bank had expected. He added that meanwhile the bank received no formal, regular reports on the fund drive, it did not know how much was raised, and, he said, "We could not impose an audit on them."

The banker's attention was drawn to the paragraph saying, "Acting on the detailed information (supplied in the Gannett coverage), the Minneapolis bankers suspended negotiations with Guilfoyle and seized the $1.5 million escrow fund." The bank officer's reply was, "Had it not been for the Gannett (coverage), the distribution would have been later."

As to the emphasis placed on Mr. Krause's letter in the complaint, the Minneapolis banker said the letter had been "very carefully drafted" in response to what he termed a plea from the diocese "to give it some respectability after the appearance of the Gannett articles, if only so that they could continue to raise funds."

\*   \*   \*

(Informative note to the Council: On May 22, the *Courier-Post* carried a new Gannett News Service report that the church—Cardinal Krol, the Knights of Columbus and the Pauline order—had paid to the Minneapolis bank $2.9 million in checks, bank drafts and securities as payment in full for all known debts of the Pauline Fathers. The bank said it would send checks promptly to those holding the Pauline bonds. A bank spokesman credited Gannett coverage for the resolution of the conflict. There remain an unresolved number of continuing state and federal examinations).

\*   \*   \*

**Council finding:** The Catholic League for Religious and Civil Rights complaint placed full reliance on the letter written in November, 1979, by a senior vice-president of the First National Bank of Minneapolis. It is evident that the League believed the letter was an independent action by the bank and constituted a direct challenge to the accuracy and fairness of the published reports in the Camden *Courier-Post*. The Council, however, finds that the bank's letter was written in response to direct requests from church executives of the Philadelphia and Camden diocese and thus the weight of the assertions in it was diminished. Based on the record, the Council finds the Gannett News Service report of February 29, including its references to earlier developments, was accurate and fair. The complaint is found unwarranted.
**Concurring:** Abel, Bell, Benson, Brady, Ghiglione, Huston, Isaacs, Pulitzer, Roberts, Rusher and Salant.

**Abstaining:** Miller.

June 12, 1980

**COMPLAINT NO. 176**       (Filed: Feb. 27, 1980)

DURAND

against

COLUMBIA JOURNALISM REVIEW

**Complaint:** Enrique Durand, who was editor-in-charge of United Press International's Latin American Department in New York for seven years, complained that an article in the November/December 1979, issue of *Columbia Journalism Review* was a "biased, bigoted 'hatchet job' " and that it demonstrated a "lack of documentation, doctoring of news reports and unfounded attacks on both (the) moral and professional capabilities" of UPI.

The article, headlined "Inside the wires' banana republics" and written by the *Review*'s executive editor, Michael Massing, was a critical report on the operations of the Latin American desks of UPI and The Associated Press in New York. The desks provide Spanish-language news services for subscribers in Latin American and the United States. UPI's Latin American desk, for example, receives stories—some in English, others already in Spanish—filed by various UPI bureaus. From these, stories are selected, edited and translated into Spanish by the desk for transmission to UPI clients. Occasionally, the desk assigns reporters to cover New York stories with Hispanic angles, including, for instance, the visit of a Latin American dignitary or a conference at the United Nations.

The *Review* article contained charges that the Latin American desks essentially perform a translating function, that they are short on original reporting and low on editorial standards, and that they often fail to transmit stories that represent a broad and well-balanced cross section of world and Latin American events.

Mr. Durand's complaint pertained only to the *Review*'s account of UPI operations. It was divided into fifteen, as he described them, "false-hoods" and "distortions" purportedly contained in the article and included eighteen enclosures as substantiation. The specifics of Mr. Durand's complaint and the *Review*'s response to each charge appear in the "Points in Dispute" section of the Council report.

**Response:** The *Review*'s response was prepared by Michael Massing and was accompanied by a note from the *Review*'s publisher, Edward W.

125

Barrett, who wrote: "We should point out that the *Review*, by its very nature, is predominantly a magazine of opinion. This article of necessity involves a substantial amount of interpretation as well as factual reporting."

In prefacing his reply, Mr. Massing said:

> Mr. Durand's petition consistently misinterprets and misrepresents the article . . . and thus deserves to be dismissed. In some cases, he simply misses altogether the points the article tries to make; in others, he seems to try to discredit the article by misquoting it and ignoring evidence cited in it. He also skirts some of the article's most serious charges by making petty grievances against its language or registering protests against points it does not try to make.

Mr. Massing added:

> The *Review* published a letter from Mr. Durand in its January/February, 1980, issue, in which many of his allegations were aired; I responded to those charges there. I would also like to call The Council's attention to the editors' note following that exchange, which observes that, shortly after the article appeared, Mr. Durand was transferred to UPI's Washington bureau—a move resulting from the *Review*'s article, according to desk members.

## POINTS IN DISPUTE

1. The headline:

*Durand*:

> "Banana republics" generally have been read to refer to Central American countries in a bad light. The headline . . . is a bigoted insult to these Central American republics. . . . (T)he factual issue is that the article does not mention one Central American country that either produces or exports bananas . . . so (it) is very misleading.

*Review*:

> The headline . . . conveys a sense of the inept and unprofessional performance of the Spanish-language services as documented in the article; it is simply a play on words, and clearly no offense was intended. The fact that no Central American republic is mentioned . . . demonstrates that the phrase is used in other than its traditional context.

**Staff comment:** In *Webster's International Dictionary* (Unabridged), the term "banana republic" is defined as ". . . some small tropical countries . . . economically dependent on their fruit exporting trade; a small country usually in the tropics that is economically dependent on foreign capital and dominated by it."

While the term's usage in certain instances can be considered objectionable (one college professor of Spanish called it "derogatory without

126

question," "only appropriate when used in a political sense or in quotation marks," and likened its application to characterizing the entire South as a "cotton plantation"), the *Review*'s use of the term was clearly figurative. Ideally, the use of quotation marks might have been advisable and preferable.

2. Aldo Moro kidnapping story:

The *Review* article compared a March 17, 1978, English-language cable filed by the Rome bureau of UPI (". . . The ruling party said the secret service of an unnamed power may have staged the abduction to destroy freedom in Italy") with the same story after it left the Latin American desk ("The secret service of a foreign power was behind the abduction in order to procure the destruction of democracy in Italy in the same way that Argentina was enveloped in a wave of terroristic violence.") The article then stated: "A story about Western Europe, at the hands of the New York desk, had become a Latin American political parable."

*Durand*:

> It is Massing who doctored the original report, omitting the Argentine parallel, supressing the sources mentioned in the UPI Spanish version and changing a vital verb tense (from "may" to "was") in order to convey a false picture of manipulation of news. . . . We made a legitimate editorial decison incorporating into the lead the analogy made by the Christian Democratic magazine, which is clearly identified in the story as the source for it. . . . We did not add conceptually anything, but just moved . . . the body of the story to the lead—the Argentine parallel—as it was fit for (our) subscribers.

(Copies of the Rome and Latin American desk stories were provided by Mr. Durand.)

*Review*:

> The article is guilty of an honest, minor error of translation. . . . But what is important is that . . . the lead of the edited Spanish version fails to identify the Argentina reference as speculation by the organ of the Christian Democratic party, as the original cable did; the new version thus endows the reference with an authority it lacked in the English version. Secondly . . . the wording has been changed from the rather tame and exceedingly vague reference in the Christian Democrat magazine—"an Argentine-type situation"—to the highly charged Spanish version, "a wave of terroristic violence". . . . This represents a clear, if subtle, case of "editorializing," as the piece charges. . . . What the article describes here is not a sensational form of distorting a cable; in fact, the article nowhere charges either UPI or the AP with knowingly introducing falsehoods. What it does describe is a case of subtle bias that violates the canons of objective journalism—how "a story about Western Europe, at the hands of the New York desk, had become a Latin American political parable."

**Staff comments:** In the Rome bureau's story, the Argentine analogy appears in the fifth paragraph as a direct quote from the Christian Democratic Party's weekly magazine *La Discussione*. In contrast, the Latin American desk version places the Argentine analogy in the lead. It expands on and dramatizes the comment by *La Discussione* and identifies the paper as the source for the analogy seven paragraphs later.

These alterations by the Latin American desk can conceivably be considered a case of subtle editorializing. The story did deviate in thrust and tone from the Rome cable and it did fail to identify its source until much later.

However, the *Review*'s translation error was a significant one. It served to effectively change from speculation to fact what was conveyed in the Spanish-language story and created a much stronger argument for the *Review*'s thesis—that stories leaving the desk sometimes reflected political bias—than was truly the case. Moreover, it is important to underscore the fact that the Latin American desk caters to clients with a special interest in Latin American affairs. Given this reality, placement of the Argentine angle in the lead was, therefore, not unreasonable.

"It was a way to explain a situation to our subscribers and wasn't politically motivated," said Herman Beals, editor-in-charge of the Latin American desk, the position formerly held by Mr. Durand. "It is normal that we try to make a Latin American parallel."

Norberto Svarzman, a member of the desk for the past ten years, said "Whenever there is a Latin American mention in any story, we put it in the top."

3. "Anti-Pinochet" story

The *Review* article said:

> Last November 9, (1978), UPI's Madrid bureau wired a report in English on a meeting of the World Committee in Solidarity with Chile, an organization . . . opposed to the Pinochet government. . . . The Latin American desk editor (Durand) in New York decided to distribute the story, but only after he had changed the lead— and the story's political tone. . . . Durand responded (to a staff member's objection to the altered piece) by simply killing the story. . . .

*Durand:*

> I did edit (the story). . . . I cut out several paragraphs. . . . (T)he lead was rewritten to indicate the political nature of the meeting, substantiated in subsequent paragraphs. That is my job—to *edit*. . . . *I not only did not kill the story—but UPI subscribers did hear about the* anti-Pinochet sentiments for several days following.
>
> (A copy of the story in question and follow-up stories, dated November 10 and 12, were provided by Mr. Durand.)

*Review:*

> The article states that Mr. Durand decided to distribute the story "only after he had changed the lead—and the story's political tone"—all of which I maintain is accurate and which Mr. Durand himself seems to confirm in his complaint, where he writes, "the lead was rewritten to indicate the political nature of the meeting". . . . He also confirms that he cut several paragraphs from the story. . . .
>
> Unfortunately, while researching the story, I was *not* provided the opportunity to view the agency's file on the story, as Mr. Durand claims. I specifically asked Claude Hippeau for permission to do so, but after consulting with other executives, he declined, explaining, "We prefer not to resurrect this matter." Again, I was unable to confront Mr. Durand with the matter directly because of conditions imposed on me by my sources. I did, however, check the account with another staff member and was sufficiently convinced of its accuracy to include it in the story. I do concede that my source erred in informing me that the Madrid story had been killed and that no follow-up had ensued. Had I been provided the opportunity to see the cables, as requested, I would have been able to eliminate this error.

**Staff comments:** Neither Mr. Durand, UPI in New York, nor the Madrid bureau could provide a copy of the original story filed from Madrid. Claude Hippeau, vice president of UPI International and chief of its Latin American coverage, did say that a "letter of reprimand" was sent to Mr. Durand for his handling of that particular story because, in ways that Mr. Hippeau could not now recall, it did not meet certain UPI standards. Follow-up stories sent from the Latin American desk, said Mr. Hippeau, were faithful to their English counterparts.

The *Review*'s error in stating that the story had been killed by Mr. Durand was a serious one considering that it inaccurately depicted an act of suppression.

4. Staff profile:

The *Review* article said:

> The composition of the Latin American desk is largely responsible for the distorted mirror the . . . wire holds up to events. Of the desk's seventeen staff members, eight are Argentines, mostly middle-aged and politically conservative who together constitute what one person on the desk likes to call a mafia.

*Durand:*

> I explained to (Mr. Massing) that UPI used to have a large national service in Argentina, a situation not equaled in any other Latin American country, and that made Argentina a natural source of Spanish-speaking journalists for the desk. . . . I took over in 1972 with more or less the same number of people as we have now on the Latin American desk. We have always had a problem of staffing and do not have too many qualified applicants because applicants must know English and Spanish perfectly, they must be journalists and they have to have some knowledge of the Latin American media market. . . . *What is middle-aged?* We do not ask political

affiliation in our applications. It's against the law. How did Mr. Massing know their political affiliations or inclinations?

(Mr. Durand included among his enclosures to the Council a list of Latin American desk members, their ages, national origin, and visa status.)

*Review*:

> Mr. Durand takes great pains to point out that the desk's heavy Argentine presence—a presence he doesn't contest—predated him. Such may be the case, but the article makes no claim to the contrary; it merely states that "the stories sent out over the wire reflect the heavy Argentine presence on the desk."
>
> Mr. Durand also contests the article's description of the desk as "mostly middle-aged" but the data he provides serve only to confirm that characterization. And the article's description of the desk as mostly "politically conservative" (which Mr. Durand misquotes, omitting the word "politically") was based on long discussions with members of the desk.

**Staff comments:** Mr. Durand's list confirms that eight out of seventeen desk members are Argentine. Mr. Durand himself is Argentine. (The further implications of the Argentine "presence," as presented in the article, are discussed in subsequent sections of this report.) The list also confirms that desk members are "mostly middle-aged"; "middle age" is defined in the dictionary as "the period in life from about 40 to 60." Five desk members are in their thirties, five are in their forties, four are in their fifties and three are in their sixties. The average age of desk members is forty-six.

Politically, the desk staff breakdown is not quite as simple. Latin American journalists are "far more politicized" than their American counterparts, said John Virtue, UPI bureau chief in Mexico City. In Latin America, there is a great deal of crossing over from politics to journalism and vice versa, he said. "Sometimes people straddle both fields." However, Mr. Virtue said, this does not, for the most part interfere with the news judgment of desk members. One desk member, Rogelio Caparros, who was critical of operations when Mr. Durand supervised the desk and outspoken on the desk's shortcomings, said that there is neither a right-wing nor left-wing sentiment at the desk. "We print what we get," said Mr. Caparros. "I have never received any complaint of bias." Daniel Drosdoff, news deputy at the desk, said "You have every single stripe of political color at this desk. There are extreme hatreds and extreme differences politically."

5. Favoritism:

The *Review* article said:

Durand . . . is said to provide his compatriots with choice assignments, desirable work hours, and other favors. Those who question his decisions are likely to find themselves working the graveyard shift. "There is almost no reporting on the desk, but of the stories assigned, all the plums go to Argentines," says a staff member. . . . His protests, he says, have only earned him weekend assignments.

## Durand:

I am again not going to try and refute that except by fact. As you may know, this is a 7 days a week desk, 24 hours a day organization. We have a system where people who do not want to work on some shifts have the opportunity to ask for a change of shift, according to the union contract. Some people wish to work at night—for a while—some do not. There is constant change. People working on the night or overnight shifts got 5% to 10% extra pay. . . . Did Mr. Massing ask any of our editors? Did he check our files to see if Argentines got all the "plums?" Of course, he didn't. He never asked me or any of the desk editors, who are in position to know about (that). He never checked a representative period, except for a few hours of filing, to see the number of stories we sent out and who wrote them. On this flimsy basis, can you imagine a capable reporter saying that "all the plums go to Argentines?"

## Review:

As to Mr. Durand's . . . use of shift scheduling, the author's interviews revealed widespread, and strongly felt, dissatisfaction. Again, I was not free to ask Mr. Durand about these charges directly. The same is true with regard to Mr. Durand's criticism of the remark by one staff member that "there is almost no reporting on the desk, but of the stories assigned, all the plums go to Argentines." It should be noted that this is a direct quote and not the author's own statement. In any case, I did present this and other charges regarding favoritism to Mr. Hippeau, who replied that he had "been aware of this uneasiness for some time." He also noted, as reported in the article that he had appointed Herman Beals, a Chilean, as second-in-command on the desk, in an effort to "ease that (situation) up," but even Mr. Hippeau conceded, as reported in the article, that "I don't know whether my instructions and directives have been followed." As the article notes, they hadn't been at the time of publication.

**Staff comments:** Desk Member Rogelio Caparros said that for the six and one-half years he worked under Mr. Durand he was given "a bad shift. I worked Sundays and holidays—New Year's eve, Christmas Day, like that." Mr. Caparros attributed his work schedule to the fact that he sometimes opposed Mr. Durand's policies and openly voiced his dissatisfaction. "It was retaliatory," he said. "It had nothing to do with seniority." Caparros added that his wife, distressed by her husband's hours, wrote to the president of UPI, Roderick Beaton, requesting a shift change. Soon after, said Mr. Caparros, his situation improved.

Questioned about story assignment at the desk, Mr. Caparros, who is

Cuban-born and an American citizen, said "very few reporting assignments were given" to desk members. But when such assignments were doled out, they went "mostly to Argentines," excluding, he said, those Argentines who disagreed vocally with the way in which Mr. Durand ran the desk.

Noberto Svarzman, a desk member who is Argentine, said that "seniority and competence" largely determine shift scheduling and story assignment. Mr. Svarzman added, however, that with the recent changes at the desk, including the transfer of Mr. Durand to UPI's Washington bureau, "there is a little more rotation" of hours and days worked by desk members.

Herman Beals, a seven-year veteran of the desk and who has worked for UPI off and on since 1960, said "It is a natural reaction to put the best workers on the best shifts. . . . There are people here twenty years and they don't know anything about how stories go to a client. They pick up the story to translate it, put it in the hold file and say goodbye to it. They don't know what happened to the story. They don't care. They don't want to get involved." Such workers, said Mr. Beals, might get schedules that include weekends and holidays because the work flow is generally lighter and less demanding at those times.

6. Visa status:

The *Review* article said:

> . . . Many other desk employees live in this country on special visas that enable them to remain here only while they work for UPI, and they are not inclined to complain.

*Durand*:

> The list (of desk members) shows of 16 on our desk, 12 are either American citizens or residents of the U.S., so they can't be sent back. If 12 are either American or residents, how come "many" are afraid? Or that "many" are on special visas?

*Review*:

> It is significant that Mr. Durand does not challenge the article's assertion that in some cases desk employees are loath to criticize the (Spanish-language) service because they hold special visas that enable them to remain in this country only while they work for UPI; Mr. Durand merely objects to the use of the word "many" to apply to four desk members, a trivial matter of interpretation given the seriousness of the charges under discussion.

**Staff comments:** Mr. Durand's list shows that four desk members are American citizens, six have permanent resident visas, one has applied for a permanent resident visa and five are in the U.S. on special visas.

The special visa-types—I-visa and L-visa—named in Mr. Durand's list were defined respectively by the district counsel for the Immigration and Naturalization Service in New York, Nina Cameron, as a "representative of foreign information media" visa and an "intra-company transferee" visa. As she explained, holders of either of these visa-types can remain in the United States as long as they continue to be employed by the company that obtained the visa for them.

At most, the stay in the U.S. of six Latin American desk members is contingent on their maintaining employment at UPI and it can be argued that, mindful of the consequences, they would be cautious about falling into disfavor with their employer.

However, Mr. Svarzman said that in the ten years he has been on the desk "Nobody has ever been fired." In fact, he said, one desk member, prone to physically violent outbursts, received only a three-day suspension after hitting a colleague on the head with a chair.

Mr. Drosdoff remarked that "UPI makes a concerted effort to get green (permanent resident visa) cards for its foreign employees." In addition, desk members, American citizens and aliens alike, belong to the union, receiving the attendant privileges and protections this provides.

7. Executive scrutiny:

The *Review* article said:

> In spite of their central role as news suppliers, both Latin American desks are regarded as journalistic Albanias at their respective agencies. Working in a foreign language and staffed exclusively by people of Latin American origin, the desks have been virtually ignored by news executives and largely left to their own devices.

*Durand*:

> . . . . What is a "journalistic Albania"?
> Also, what is the basis of (Mr. Massing's) assertion that the desks "have been virtually ignored by news executives and largely left to their own devices."
> Did he talk to the Foreign Editor, Gerry Loughran, or the Vice-President and Editor-in-Chief, H. L. Stevenson? I report to them. We have at least one weekly meeting at which all editors come—the financial, foreign, Latin American, enterprise features, national and New York City editors. Did he talk to these people?

*Review*:

> Mr. Durand cites as evidence his attendance at weekly meetings held with all editors. These meetings, however, did not deal with such nut-and-bolts matters as what is transmitted over the Spanish-language wires, which is what the article is referring to, as the context makes clear. Although the quote following this passage in the article refers specifically to the AP desk, my research indicated the same was true at UPI. At the agency, coverage in each region of the world is supervised by a vice-

president working under Claude Hippeau, vice-president for UPI international. But Latin America has not had its own vice-president for several years; in the meantime, Mr. Hippeau told me that while he served officially as the desk's supervisor, "I haven't looked at the (Spanish-language) wire for a long time."

**Staff comments:** H. L. Stevenson, editor-in-chief, and vice-president of UPI International, said the Latin American desk is "an adjunct to the foreign desk" and is "physically integrated" with the rest of UPI. Mr. Stevenson said that editorial meetings are held weekly and that the editor of the Latin American desk participates in these sessions "I guess, as an equal."

Nevertheless, meaningful oversight of the Latin American desk by UPI executives has proven problematic. "Historically," said Mr. Stevenson, "it has been difficult for senior news executives to read the daily Spanish-language wire." Neither Mr. Stevenson nor UPI's foreign editor, Gerry Loughran, who have jurisdiction over the desk, speak Spanish.

This communication barrier was eradicated to some extent by the addition, three years ago, of Mr. Hippeau. Fluent in Spanish, Mr. Hippeau has the Spanish-language wire plugged into his office and he said he checks daily on desk operations. Mr. Hippeau's position requires that he travel "about two to three months scattered over the year" which keeps him out of direct touch with the desk in New York. He said that when he told Mr. Massing that he had not looked at the wire for "some time," he had just returned from one of those trips. "But when I'm not here," he told the Council staff, "There is someone else minding the store."

In January, Mr. Stevenson said, Daniel Drosdoff, formerly of UPI in Argentina and also fluent in Spanish, assumed the newly-created position of news deputy in charge of Spanish translations at the desk in New York. Other steps designed to centralize control at the desk have been "in the works for over a year," Mr. Stevenson said, reflecting the "growth and complexity of Latin American news over the years" and the resultant expansion of the Spanish-language wire from a ten-hours-a-day service to its present round-the-clock operation.

In April, UPI announced the formation of a UPI Latin American Advisory Board composed of Western Hemisphere editors and publishers from outside the United States who are to meet once a year with UPI executives. Mr. Stevenson said that the Latin American board, patterned after the UPI Newspaper Advisory Board of the United States, is intended to increase input from Latin American subscribers and to make UPI more

134

adaptable and suited to their special needs through organized meetings and consultations.

At the time of the *Review* article's publication, these administrative changes, although contemplated for some time according to Mr. Stevenson, had not been put into effect. Mr. Hippeau said that Mr. Massing was not alerted to these plans because, with the pending transfer of Mr. Durand and other personnel adjustments, "We didn't want it published. Mr. Massing was doing the story during an embarrasing period for us."

Mr. Hippeau said that he "was too candid" with the *Review* editor and that he was "dismayed" that the article did not contain "anything positive that I said. I expected some negative comments but the article focused on the negative aspects only and was a personal attack on Enrique (Durand)." Mr. Hippeau added that the article concentrated on "personalities and personality conflicts, something which happens in all organizations" and that "I'm sure if he (Mr. Massing) talked to people who were satisfied with the way the desk was run he would have had a more balanced story." Furthermore, Mr. Hippeau said, "If we really had such a bad Latin American service, do you think we would sell our service to so many Latin American papers? If we were so bad, they wouldn't buy it. They have a choice. It is one of the most competitive markets in the world."

8. Unnamed sources:

*Durand*:

> What staff members said that we have "political bias" and (are) in favor of the "status quo?" If, in fact, one person said it, is it not necessary to point out that we have another 15 people on our desk. What do they think? Is one person enough to interview to come to these conclusions? . . . . Mr. Massing talks about "journalists familiar with" and such words as "those familiar with." Who . . . . did Mr. Massing interview to reach such conclusions of our alleged low standards? Who at the desk called Argentine staffers a "mafia" and who called me a "godfather?" . . . Who said I run the desk "like Stroessner runs Paraguay"? Are the words *iron fist* (referring to Mr. Durand's management of the desk) which are not in quotes, Mr. Massing's editorializing or were the quotation marks in the wrong place? . . . .
>
> When Mr. Massing interviewed me during the preparation of his article, he did not ask me one single question about the allegations but concentrated his questions on the mechanics of (the Latin American desk) operation, number of bureaus and staffers in Latin America and so on.

*Review*:

> The article was based on interviews with more than twenty persons, eight of whom (including Mr. Durand) were UPI staff members. I am at liberty to name four of them: Mr. Durand, Claude Hippeau, John Virtue and Noberto Svarzman. The

remaining four UPI employees set anonymity as a condition for granting interviews; in some cases they said they feared retribution from Mr. Durand should he discover their identity. Their fears also help explain why I did not confront Mr. Durand directly with some of the evidence; my sources prohibited me from doing so before publication of the article. They felt that only the appearance of the piece in print would provide them adequate protection. To ensure the accuracy of my sources' information, I cross-checked my evidence thoroughly; in many cases, Mr. Hippeau frankly confirmed claims made by my sources on the desk. Mr. Durand also questions quotes from outside observers, which he apparently feels were fabricated; in fact, I interviewed numerous people familiar with the performance of news organizations working in New York and Washington (one of whom, Raymundo Riva-Palacio of Mexico's Uno Mas Uno, is quoted by name in the article); reporters with other news services; officials at the Organization of American States and at the United Nations; and news personnel at Hispanic newspapers and broadcast outlets in this country. . . . I am not at liberty to name the desk member who called the desk a "mafia," nor who likened Mr. Durand's regime to Stroessner's; such sentiments, however, were commonly expressed by desk members.

**Staff comment:** The question raised here is a nettlesome one. In protecting the confidentiality of sources, did the writer fail to make a conscientous effort to afford Mr. Durand opportunity to reply to the charges against him?

There is some credence to Mr. Massing's position that by confronting Mr. Durand with off-the-record testimony the identity of the sources might be revealed, thus leaving them open to retaliatory action. Only through publication of the article, maintained Mr. Massing, would the threat of retribution be lessened.

In the course of conversations with Mr. Hippeau, Mr. Durand, Mr. Svarzman and Mr. Beals, there were allusions and statements that they "knew" who some, or all, the anonymous sources in the article were, based on the published quotes.

This, however, does not negate the fact that damaging testimony attributed to unnamed sources was left to stand, without benefit, in many instances, of response by Mr. Durand, the individual most affected. The *Review* has conceded to two instances where, by not crosschecking thoroughly, factual errors appeared in the article.

9. Argentine datelines:

The *Review* article said:

> The stories sent out over the wire reflect the heavy Argentine presence on the desk, as did the Aldo Moro cable cited earlier. "Durand has an obsession with Argentine news," observes one (Latin American wire) worker. "He doesn't care about the rest of the world." An in-house study of the wire conducted in November 1978 revealed that a full 17 percent of all Latin American stories were datelined

Argentina, though that country was but one of twenty-two reported on in the survey period.

*Durand*:

> What Mr. Massing does not know, didn't ask or deliberately forgot, is that in November 1978, Argentina and Chile were close to war. Troops were called up, the Vatican sent an emissary, and it was only hours before the confrontation that it was stopped in December. And the factor was also mentioned in the same survey.
>
> We don't allocate news quotas regarding the countries in Latin America. Our report reflects what happens in the different countries, disregarding their size based only in the intrinsical news value of the events.

*Review*:

> Mr. Durand does not challenge the accuracy of the figures cited in the article regarding the percentage of material that was datelined Argentina as reported in an in-house survey. . . . What he complains about is that the article does not mention that at the time of the survey, Argentina and Chile were close to war. But that circumstance is irrelevant to the fact that the survey provided firm evidence in support of what all my interviews indicated—that Argentina received inordinate attention. Mr. Hippeau himself confirmed this to me in no uncertain terms, and he is in fact quoted in my response to Mr. Durand in the January/February 1980 issue of the *Review*: "Argentina has gotten undue coverage." Mr. Hippeau stated further in my interview with him, "We're giving too much importance to the southern cone (Argentina, Chile, Uruguay). One of the changes we want to make is to make coverage more balanced. We are aware of this. This is something that obviously is of great concern for us."

**Staff comment:** The study cited, conducted by Mr. Hippeau and distributed to UPI Latin American executives in the U. S. and abroad, states: "In Latin America, Argentina (16 items, 17.5% of the Latin American total) is still the most important news center. Admittedly, the border disputes between Argentina and Chile had its effect on the number of stories moved from Buenos Aires. However, it must be pointed out that although Chile was also a center of news about the border dispute, Santiago moved only an average of 6 times per day, or 6.39% of the Latin American total."

Mr. Hippeau said that the tensions between Argentina and Chile and the possibility that the two countries would go to war were responsible for the relatively high number of Argentine stories being moved during the survey week, as the study clearly points out. "We follow the news and change our emphasis accordingly," said Mr. Hippeau. The question is raised though as to why a lesser number of stories from Chile were disseminated during the period examined.

Mr. Beals said, in general, "I wouldn't say that we had too many

Argentine stories. Everything we sent out should have gone out. But too many of them had priority. Keep in mind that for the last ten years, Argentina has been a big news center for Latin America. Revolution, terrorism, thousands of killings, Mr. Peron returning from Spain, Mrs. Peron, the conflict with Chile, almost going to war, all produced a big amount of news for Latin America.''

John Virtue of the Mexico City bureau said that "historically," the Spanish-language services of UPI and AP have been geared toward Argentina. UPI's major Latin American subscriber was *La Prensa*; AP's was Argentina's other main newspaper, *La Nacion*. Also, Mr. Virtue said, both services have traditionally placed Argentines in charge of their Latin American desks. As a result, "the volume of Argentine news is probably out of proportion. Sometimes Argentine news would be moved at the expense of something else." This emphasis has persisted, Mr. Virtue said, despite the fact that Argentina no longer has the "importance it once had in Latin America. Latin America has changed, but we haven't."

10. Original reporting deficiencies:

The *Review* article said:

> . . . . In fact, New York's active exile community, and the visitors it receives, go virtually unreported at UPI. The same bias extends to Washington where UPI correspondent Adolfo Merino, a Cuban exile, is not known for keeping his political views out of his reporting. Says Larry Birns, director of the Council on Hemispheric Affairs, a Washington-based human rights group, "Merino will consistently go to hear some obscure retired general talking about the Red Menace in Latin America, but he'll never cover stories that involve dissident politicians or groups critical of dictatorship."

*Durand*:

> Mr. Massing is quoting an alleged human rights organization and Larry Birns for evidence that our crime is that we don't report on the "active exile community" and that is "bias". . . . Our job is to report news, not rhetorical press releases without question unless we deem them newsworthy. We do print on "exiles" but not because Mr. Birns tells us to. Mr. Massing, again, never looked at our files.

*Review*:

> Mr. Durand attacks my use of Larry Birns of the Council on Hemispheric Affairs as a source of information without giving any indication why. My facts about UPI's failure to cover Latin American exiles and visitors adequately were provided not only by Mr. Birns but also by desk staff members. . . .

**Staff comments:** The majority of executives and desk members who spoke with the Council staff agreed that enterprise reporting by the desk has been limited. Several reasons were given for the shortcoming.

Desk members are occupied translating and editing approximately 100 stories a day into Spanish and editing another 100, already in Spanish. "Everyone would like to cover more but we don't have the money or the manpower," said Mr. Beals. In recent months, he added, there has been an increase in original reporting "because people have been working overtime."

Close to half of the sixteen desk members function as translators and are either unwilling or incapable of assuming reporting responsibilities. "A caste system has developed," said Mr. Drosdoff. "Some editors consider themselves translators and do nothing more."

Many Spanish-language subscribers are simply not interested in certain stories. "We have one Latin American wire for about 23 countries," said Mr. Beals. "We have to satisfy all clients and not everyone is interested in, say, the Puerto Rican community in New York."

"That's not our job," said Mr. Virtue, who in December, 1978, issued an in-house study on wire-service usage in Latin American newspapers. The study noted, however, that UPI was weak, in terms of "play" in Latin American newspapers, on the goings-on of visiting Latin Americans.

Miguel Frankenfeld of the Organization of American States, told the Council that UPI's coverage is sometimes "superficial, in many cases affirming things that are not so and, in many cases even containing contradictions" with the other news service stories that the OAS receives—AP, Spain's EFE, Reuters-LATIN, Agence France-Presse and the Caribbean News Agency. In terms of "fast," said Frankenfeld, UPI does "quite well," but in terms of "how the news is presented," UPI does not compare favorably with the rest and there have been instances of "editorializing."

Roger Tatarian, UPI vice president and editor-in-chief until 1972, now professor of journalism at California State University, characterized the *Review* article as "overblown, overdone and exaggerated. It was a terribly unfair indictment." Mr. Tatarian said, ". . . . if news was coming up from Latin America and was being changed in thrust and emphasis (by the desk in New York) the correspondents who wrote the stories are bound to scream. The clientele, people receiving the news, clearly would speak up also. There are those kinds of checks."

Professor Tatarian, who has been engaged in special studies on the international flow of news, said that "UPI is not a perfect operation. But the wire services are generally the most misunderstood and underappreciated institutions and are the subject of more shallow journalistic generalities than any other institution. . . . Anyone who is going to go through one or two days of wire service files is going to come away with some erroneous conclusions." You cannot sample an operation of that magnitude without devoting at least a number of months to scientific, in-depth study, he said.

**Council finding:** Several serious departures from sound journalistic standards were committed in *The Columbia Journalism Review* article. These included:

• Factual errors: Of these, two were particularly damaging in the article alleging news manipulation by the UPI Latin-American desk. One was the mistranslation of a critical word from "may" to "was," thus creating the false impression that the Latin-American desk had, for political reasons, injected into a report from Rome the statement that "The secret service of a foreign power *was* behind the abduction" of Aldo Moro. (Italics ours.) Another was the incorrect assertion that Mr. Durand had suppressed a report on a Madrid meeting of opponents of the Pinochet regime in Chile.

• Unnamed sources. Reliance on unnamed sources as a foundation for broad generalizations and for aspersions on a person's character is always a peril-fraught process. It is totally unacceptable when the source gives his information with the explicit understanding that the substance of the charges cannot be conveyed to the person being criticized for response, even with the confidentiality of the source protected. The erroneous charge that Mr. Durand had "killed" the story on the anti-Pinochet meeting came from such a source and was never put up to the desk for verification.

• Sensationalist descriptives. The tone of the article, as reflected in the use of such pejorative terms as "mafia," "Stroessner", and "godfather" to describe Mr. Durand and his methods of operation, is of particular concern to the Council because all such terms originated with unnamed sources who, for whatever reasons of fear or animus, declined to take responsibility for these strong statements and opinions. Criticism can also be made of the use in the article's headline of the derogatory term "banana republic," a term made no more palatable by the *Columbia Journalism Review*'s disingenuous response that "clearly no offense was intended."

The comment in the headline was typical of the deplorable tone of the entire response by the *Review* to the Durand complaint. The *Review*, for example, called the translation error cited above "minor", though it drastically changed the thrust of the statement. Similarly, it glossed over the incorrectness of its charge that an article was suppressed for political reasons—a charge of utmost gravity in news practice—by asserting that other aspects of the anecdote about the handling of the anti-Pinochet meeting illustrate a valid point.

The Council agrees with former UPI executive Roger Tatarian's characterization of the article as "overblown, overdone and exaggerated." This make doubly distressing the defensiveness, lack of care and lack of analysis that flawed the *Review*'s response.

Because of the above shortcomings in the article, the Council finds the complaint warranted.

**Concurring:** Bell, Benson, Brady, Huston, Miller, Pulitzer, Roberts, Salant, and Scott.

**Concurring opinion by Ms. Huston:** The *Review* committed the cardinal sin of investigative reporting by relying on verbal assertions instead of putting in the necessary time and effort to (a) carefully examine the documents in question—in this case, wire service stories—and, (b) base any conclusions on the results of that examination.

**Additional opinion by Mr. Salant:** While I fully agree with the Council's opinion and conclusions, I want, additionally, to note my distress concerning, and distaste for, the *Columbia Journalism Review*'s practice in its letters to the editor segment, of reserving to itself the first word, in the article about which an initial letter is written, *and* the last word, in the rebuttal to the critical letter. Such a rebuttal may on rare occasions be warranted, but *Columbia Journalism Review* includes rebuttals as a general practice. This, I believe, is unfair.

**Note:** The following Council members disqualified themselves from any participation on this complaint:

Norman E. Isaacs, due to prior service on Columbia's Graduate School of Journalism faculty.

Elie Abel, former Dean of the School, for the same reason.

Loren F. Ghiglione, because he serves on UPI's New England Advisory Board.

William A. Rusher, Publisher of the *National Review*, which is in the "Leadership Network" of seven magazines, including the *Columbia Journalism Review*, which sells advertising at a group discount.

June 13, 1980

## COMPLAINT NO. 177      (Filed July 10, 1980)
## SAN FRANCISCO BOARD OF SUPER-
## VISORS, SAN FRANCISCO HUMAN
## RIGHTS COMMISSION, NATIONAL GAY
## TASK FORCE, RANDY ALFRED, ET AL.
### against
### CBS NEWS

**Complaint:** Relying principally on an original complaint by Randy Alfred, of San Francisco, California, a reporter; the San Francisco Board of Supervisors, by formal vote; that city's Human Rights Commission and the National Gay Task Force joined to complain that a one-hour CBS-TV network report, "Gay Power, Gay Politics," broadcast on April 26, 1980, "tends to demean, disgrace, and dishonor the entire journalistic profession . . . through the systematic use of hearsay, oversights, exaggerations, distortion, inflammatory buzzwords, leading questions and misleading and deceitful editing."

The documentary, described by Anchorman Harry Reasoner as a report on "how the gays of San Francisco are using the political process to further their own special interest, just like every other minority group before them," was produced by Grace Diekhaus and George Crile, with Mr. Crile serving as narrator.

Mr. Alfred asserted that the documentary "ignores major issues on the one hand while exaggerating and fabricating issues on the other."

The broadcast presented a succession of events, scenes and interviews leading into, and surrounding the city's mayoralty campaign of 1979. There were two elections, the first a primary on November 6 in which Acting Mayor Dianne Feinstein was opposed to Quentin Kopp, a member of the Board of Supervisors; David Scott, a gay businessman; and seven other candidates. Mayor Feinstein, as a Supervisor, had taken over as Mayor following the assassination on November 27, 1978, of Mayor George Moscone, along with Supervisor Harvey Milk, a gay.

A runoff election was forced when Mayor Feinstein received 42 percent of the votes to 40 percent for Mr. Kopp, and 10 percent for Mr. Scott.

Campaigning for the runoff between Mayor Feinstein and Mr. Kopp was lively and heavy during the 34 days following the primary, with both candidates publicly seeking Mr. Scott's support—and the support of the gay community. Mayor Feinstein was elected on December 11.

Mr. Alfred wrote that "Numerous 'minor' errors during the course of the broadcast tended uniformly towards the outrageous editorial stance of the producers: exaggerating preoccupation with sex, minimizing the gay concern for physical safety on the streets and in the bars, making all the phenomena under study appear more sudden, recent, and threatening, and making the mayor and the city's establishment seem craven and intimidated."

"The producers' view is revealed clearly in the opening of the show and in its conclusion," Mr. Alfred charged. "From the first, talk of politics is used to voice-over scenes depicting or suggesting sexuality. Sex and politics are repeatedly confused right through to the conclusion."

Referring to Mr. Reasoner's use of the words "special interest" in his opening comments, the complaint said that "The implication is that there is only one interest. Thus, the program is barely underway when the deceptive mixing of politics and sex begins . . . . For the last words on the show, after an hour of setting up its audience, CBS trots out Harry Reasoner with the unsupported declaration that gays in San Francisco demanded 'absolute sexual freedom.'

"In between, we have seen a major issue made of a question that is never asked of any gay leader: 'Should public parks be used for sex?' Private membership clubs, under attack throughout 1979, are made out to be free of government interference. An actual public controversy, the redesign of Buena Vista Park, is glossed over in typically inflammatory and one-sided fashion."

Mr. Alfred, in his 19½ page, single-spaced complaint, detailed 44 charges, many of which, he said "contribute to the cumulative effect of patterned distortion."

In its resolution approved on June 2 by 10 of the Board of Supervisors' 11 members and forwarded to the Council, "Gay Power, Gay Politics" was charged with "total disregard for principles of good journalism" by providing "a series of images of the 'darker practices of the gay community' intended to startle viewers and to show how gays are attacking traditional values and frightening heterosexuals."

The Supervisors charged further that "The program grossly distorted the many positive contributions that the gay community has made to the culture and politics of the City" and that "The CBS documentary has done great harm to San Francisco by slandering the City before a nationwide audience."

143

The resolution by the Board of Supervisors was signed on June 9 by Mayor Feinstein.

In a resolution adopted on May 22, and forwarded to the Council, the Human Rights Commission declared that "this alleged documentary claimed to represent the actuality of gay influence and practices relating to San Francisco's political structure," but instead "conveyed distorted information pertaining to the behavior and attitudes of the gay community, which contributed to the perpetuation of stereotypes."

The National Gay Task Force, in its letter to the Council dated July 18 and co-signed by Charles F. Brydon and Lucia L. Valeska, Co-Executive Directors, charged that the program "unjustly maligned and stigmatized gay people by presenting an inaccurate and unbalanced view of the political work of San Francisco's gay community."

The National Gay Task Force complaint further charged that "The program ignored those gay political and business leaders in the city who are outspoken in their concern for gay problems such as employment and housing discrimination, health care, child custody, the need for social outlets other than bars, public safety, and immigration issues. And it further ignored those gay people who are active in the political process, such as Supervisor Harry Britt and (Police) Commissioner Jo Daly among others, and the pioneering gay Democratic and Republican political clubs that provided the organizational base for mainstream political action."

The National Gay Task Force concurred with the analysis submitted to the Council by Mr. Alfred, referring to it as "detailed substantiation of our contention that this program was inaccurate, misleading, and distorted."

The National Gay Task Force refers to itself as "the largest gay civil rights organization in the U.S., with over 10,000 individual and organizational members." It declared that it had received nearly 1,000 letters and phone calls protesting the CBS program.

**Response:** CBS News responded to the complaint in a letter dated September 4 and received by the Council on that date. Writing on behalf of the network, Robert Chandler, Vice President and Director of Public Affairs Broadcasts, said that "The complaint presents a significant number of difficulties. By our count, it includes some 44 separate allegations, some of which are important, others of which are trivial, irrelevant or clearly represent matters of opinion or judgment.

"In our view," Mr. Chandler continued, "the complaint boils down to three essential grievances, which we would characterize as follows:

144

"1. *The Campaign Issues*—The complaint, in its essence, is that we distorted the nature of the mayoral campaign in the gay community, that we focused exclusively on the matter of 'community standards' and the demands for an apology to the exclusion of other issues of far more importance to the gay community. That in focusing on the issue of apology, we made it appear that the only concern of the gay community involved matters of sexual behavior when in fact that was a lesser or minor issue. In a larger sense, the complaint suggests that at a time when gays nationwide have not achieved what they believe to be equal rights and protection of the law, our broadcast portrayed them as obsessed not with the attainment of these objectives but with a desire only to maintain their sexual freedoms.

"2. *The Sexual Issues*—The essentials of these charges are that to support the above thesis, we brought into our broadcast sensationalized issues and materials, sexual in nature, that had no connection with the campaign, that were in part activities reflected in heterosexual behavior, and that were designed to portray gays unfairly by suggesting that the acts of an irresponsible minority were being generalized to the majority of gays. Specifically in this category were those parts of the broadcast devoted to public sex in Buena Vista Park and sado-masochism. To a lesser extent, the scenes of the Beaux Arts Ball and of Castro Street fall into this category. And finally, the Harry Reasoner observation that gay leaders had been insisting on absolute sexual freedom is a subject of complaint.

"3. *The Applause*—Although the allegation that there was no applause directly following the Mayor's apology is an issue that falls into the broader question addressed in #1 above, the specificity of the charge requires that it be addressed separately.

"The Applause Issue" refers to remarks made by Mayor Feinstein at a meeting of the Harvey Milk Democratic Club, a gay and lesbian organization, shortly before the runoff election. At that time, the Mayor, according to the narration by Mr. Crile, "apologized" for a statement attributed to her in an article published in the March, 1979, issue of *Ladies' Home Journal*. The published statement, as Mr. Crile paraphrased it, was "all she said was that gays should observe community standards . . . . That they shouldn't force their life styles on others. But this seemingly moderate criticism outraged the homosexual community." In the on-air presentation of "Gay Power, Gay Politics," applause followed the Mayor's "apology." Mr. Alfred charged that there was no applause at this point.

"It seems appropriate to deal with the allegations about applause first," CBS said in its response. "Mr. Alfred is correct. The audience did not applaud at that moment, but shortly thereafter, following her reference to the appointment of a new police chief.

"Our producers did not use the applause shot out of any desire to distort, but because they believed that the audience was in fact applauding the apology, that they were so surprised that it took them several moments to realize what had occurred and that they applauded at the next appropriate pause, two sentences later, some 25 seconds after the conclusion of the apology. And our producers also used the applause as a means of separating the Mayor's prepared speech from the question and answer period depicted immediately following her apology. They note that in interviews following the meeting, it was the apology that was for the gays the highlight of the meeting and was regarded as their victory. That view was shared in the *San Francisco Chronicle* the next day, which reported on the Mayor's apology (and drew the same conclusion as we did, reporting that the apology drew applause).

"Whatever the motivation, however, it is clear that our producers indicated the applause out of its actual time sequence and therefore misled our viewers. This, then constitutes an acknowledgement of error and an apology for a breach of our own journalistic standards."

The network, in addition to providing the Council with a response to each of the three issues, also presented a longer, detailed and numbered response to each of Mr. Alfred's 44 allegations.

**The Issues:** The Council's staff finds it helpful, in attempting to assess the detailed charges, to deal with them under the three main headings suggested by CBS News in its response. Such a grouping, we believe, keeps the central questions in focus and thus contributes to clarity in evaluation and presentation.

Mr. Alfred acknowledged in his letter to the Council that CBS has the right to make news judgments with which he might disagree. He said, for example, that he would have included some coverage of lesbians and some coverage of the election of gay Supervisor Harry Britt in a broadcast about gay politics.

The Council staff has excluded from detailed discussion here those allegations of Mr. Alfred's that seem to be matters of news judgment not seriously affecting the ultimate judgment of whether the broadcast taken as a whole was fair and accurate.

For example, it seems a matter of judgment, with little major impact, whether CBS ought to have used footage of protest marches or of "cruising" to introduce the audience to Castro Street in San Francisco's gay area.

Similarly, it is a matter of judgment, with minor impact, whether Mayor Feinstein "began to court the gay vote" in October or "well before that," as Mr. Alfred contended.

Allegations by Mr. Alfred that materially affect the judgment of the program as a whole are covered in the following examination of the "three essential grievances."

## The Campaign Issue

Mr. Alfred charged that CBS overstated the importance of Mayor Feinstein's apology for her comment on the gays and their relationship to community standards.

CBS responded that "There remains not the slightest doubt, so far as CBS News is concerned, that the issue of community standards, the demand that both the Mayor and Quentin Kopp apologize for past statements, became the transcendant issue of the campaign for the gay community. That is true of the specific meeting at which the apology was given, and of the campaign at large insofar as it concerned the efforts of the candidate to win the gay vote."

The *San Francisco Examiner & Chronicle,* on November 18, 1979, twelve days after the city's primary election, published an interview with David Scott, the defeated gay candidate for mayor. In that report, *Examiner* political writer W. E. Barnes wrote:

> David Scott, whose endorsement, many feel, could tip the balance in the mayor's race, has decided to withhold that endorsement until election eve because he believes both Dianne Feinstein and Quentin Kopp have been evasive and unresponsive to the concerns of the 18,500 people who voted for him in the primary election.
>
> Scott said he reached that conclusion after lengthy conversations in which 'both candidates either talked around the questions I raised or gave unsatisfactory responses.'

Questions raised by Mr. Scott, the *Examiner* report said, included concerns within "the homosexual and progressive communities" over the appointment of a new police chief, the appointment of police commissioners, affirmative action for women, the retention of district elections, rent control laws, the floating of low-interest mortage revenue bonds for moderate and low-income home buyers, and Mr. Kopp's "embrace of former Mayor Joseph Alioto, who refused to meet with organized groups of gay men and lesbians while in office."

Mr. Barnes wrote "But the major issue—even more important than the next chief, he (Mr. Scott) said—is specific 'highly offensive and degrading comments' made by both candidates in the recent past that continue to rankle the city's gay community."

What Mayor Feinstein said in the *Ladies' Home Journal* statement that

Mr. Scott, and others in the city's gay community, found to be "highly offensive and degrading" was the following:

> The right of an individual to live as he or she chooses can become offensive. The gay community is going to have to face this. It's fine for us to live here respecting each other's lifestyles, but that doesn't mean imposing them on others. I do not want San Franciscans to set up backlash.

Mr. Kopp, during a meeting of the Board of Supervisors in 1979. had said "tolerance yes, glorification no" when a Certificate of Merit was awarded to Del Martin and Phyllis Lyon, two lesbians, for their work on behalf of human rights causes in the city.

The *Examiner's* report continued, quoting Mr. Scott:

> I discussed these remarks with both candidates. These comments can set the tenor for their administrations, and I feel they should make some kind of modifying statement. They are completely offensive and unacceptable.
>
> I told each of them that, if elected, you are going to be mayor of the whole city, and that means representing everyone including lesbians and gay men. That's something our community wants addressed. As of now, neither candidate has chosen to do that, and that is certainly heavy in my mind.

Following Mr. Scott's primary defeat, in a note thanking members of the Harvey Milk Democratic Club for their support, he wrote that "These are some of the questions that I have been asking the mayoral candidates since the November 6th election." Included in a listing of ten questions was the following:

> Has either of you changed your mind about these anti-gay statements? If so, would you restate them to reflect your current attitudes about gay people?

Both Mayor Feinstein and Mr. Kopp appeared to plead their cases at a meeting of the Harvey Milk Democratic Club held on November 20, twenty days before the runoff election. The *San Francisco Chronicle,* on November 21, in a report headlined "Gays Hear Some Apologies," stated the following:

> San Francisco's two mayoral candidates, appearing contrite while courting votes that could sway the December 11 election, told a gay political club last night that they were both sorry for their allegedly anti-gay remarks in the past.
>
> 'If I said things that offended the community, I apologize,' Mayor Dianne Feinstein told the Harvey Milk Democratic Club, referring to her published remarks that gays should not flaunt their behavior publicly.
>
> 'Maybe my choice of words was wrong,' said Supervisor Quentin Kopp, of his slightly famous 'Tolerance yes, glorification no' comment about gays living together.

*****

148

When the votes were tallied, Feinstein had scraped together 73 votes to 14 for Kopp—exactly the 60 percent needed for the club's endorsement. Thirty-four members voted to endorse no one.

To Mr. Alfred's charge that CBS, in concentrating on the "community standards" issue, relegated other, more important issues to a minor role, CBS responded that "issues that surfaced other than the question of an apology were the issue of police protection against harassment from police and civilians alike, and to a lesser degree, the issue of proportional gay representation on non-elective bodies. These issues were covered in the broadcast. Early in the broadcast George Crile reports that as Mayor Feinstein began her campaign, 'the gays were mad at her for firing the pro-gay chief of police, a man counted on as their ally.'" CBS then showed the Mayor addressing a meeting of the gays on that subject:

> FEINSTEIN: It doesn't do any good to have a chief that may—may be the best thing since apple pie if the men won't follow his leadership.
> MAN: I suggest, Mayor, then, that without wanting to debate you, that maybe we need a new police department, not a new chief.

Later, in a further effort to substantiate the CBS claim that "Gay Power, Gay Politics" did cover other issues in the mayoralty campaign, Mr. Chandler cited Mr. Crile's depiction of Hallowe'en night on Castro Street:

> CRILE: For Captain Jeffries (George Jeffries of the San Francisco Police Department), Hallowe'en has become a nightmare. Each year on this night, more and more toughs have been coming into the gay areas to beat up homosexuals. The night of the City Hall riots (which followed the sentencing of Supervisor Dan White for the assassination of Mayor Moscone and Supervisor Milk), Jeffries' own men had burst into a bar on Castro Street, attacking with billy clubs. It had been called a police riot. But on this Hallowe'en night no matter what their feelings, Jeffries' men were supposed to protect the gays.

"The scenes which followed," CBS said, "include interviews Crile had with Captain Jeffries about police behaviour and with Cleve Jones (a gay activist who was serving as a "Monitor" within the gay community) about the gay hostility toward the police and their insistence that they rather than the police provide security in the area. Later we show the police moving in and the gays' anger at their actions."

CBS also referred to the sequence involving the Mayor's apology before the Harvey Milk Democratic Club, quoting Mr. Crile saying ". . . . it wasn't just an apology. She'd offered them a gay police commissioner and political appointments in proportion to their numbers in the city.

"In sum," Mr. Chandler said, "the *only* issues which surfaced above and beyond the community standards issue in the campaign in the gay community were these issues of police behaviour and protection and appointment to political posts, and these were covered."

Mr. Chandler cited other sections of the broadcast in support of the producers' belief that Mayor Feinstein's and Mr. Kopp's apologies were a condition of gay support in the election. These included a statement by the Mayor that it is the mayor's responsibility to establish and maintain community standards; a statement by a gay business man that "I, for one, have talked to her (the Mayor) specifically about these comments, and she wouldn't make them again . . . ," and another statement by the same person that "She would not have had it (the gay vote) if she had continued to make the same kind of comments she did in the *Ladies' Home Journal* throughout the campaign.

"In the opinion of our two journalists who had followed the campaign throughout," Mr. Chandler said, "it was their news judgment that the community standards-apology issue was transcendent in the gay community, that it was the single issue that separated the two candidates, that it was the issue that was most important to the gays in determining their support. This was, of course, an editorial judgment, but one based on months of reporting and close observation."

In response to Mr. Alfred's charge that Mr. Crile gave the audience "his own voice-over, truncated, watered-down and confused version of the *Ladies' Home Journal* comment," and characterized it as "'seemingly moderate,'" Mr. Chandler said "It is a matter of regret to us that we did not quote directly from the *Ladies' Home Journal* but chose to characterize the Mayor's words.

"In retrospect," Mr. Chandler said, ". . . it would have been more effective to have used the full quotation. Its inclusion would have made the escalating anger during the campaign about her statement more understandable.

"Finally, it should be noted that the fury and concern expressed over this issue from other parts of the country is understandable. We were careful to make it clear from the outset that San Francisco, by virtue of its traditions, its tolerance and the size of its gay community, had achieved a high level of progress in gay issues. Gays were part of the establishment, as we pointed out, in business, in law, in journalism, in medicine, in government. Housing and jobs were apparently not the problem in San Francisco they have been in other cities. Nor have other forms of discrimination.

"But in focusing on the community standards issue . . . . We incurred the anger of gays in other parts of the country, who felt *their* unmet objectives had been denigrated. One could hardly expect their anger to be directed at the gay leadership in San Francisco; instead it was directed at CBS News. As for San Francisco's gays, we can only speculate that they believed the broadcast had trivialized their problems and their objectives. But we reported what we found."

**Staff analysis:** In interview after interview, gay individuals told the Council's staff representative that the Mayor's remarks, either as reported in the *Ladies' Home Journal,* or as characterized by Mr. Crile, were "offensive to the gay community." And so was the remark by Mr. Kopp.

Apologies may not have been insisted upon, as stated by Mr. Crile. Mayor Feinstein told the Council's staff representative that no demand was made of her to apologize or, "as Mr. Crile put it, to 'atone' for my 'sins.'" But it was obvious to the Council's staff that apologies from both the Mayor and Mr. Kopp were high on the gay community's agenda for clarification pending a decision to support or not to support either one of the candidates in the runoff election.

The staff examination also revealed something which was not revealed on the broadcast itself: the reasons why the two statements (the Mayor's and Mr. Kopp's) were anathema to the city's gay community. Supervisor Britt, who stated that he was interviewed "at great length" by Mr. Crile, but who did not appear on "Gay Power, Gay Politics," put it this way:

> Basically, the Mayor was saying that she hasn't anything against gay people as long as they behave themselves. That's how it came across to us. She was giving support to that strategy for gay people which means think what other people want you to feel before you decide what you're going to feel. That's psychological death for gay people. And when we say we want to set our own standards, as Cleve Jones said on the broadcast, we mean simply that we want to be free to explore, in ways natural to us, who we are, and to have a moral sense that comes out of yourself and not out of conformity to the world.
>
> Mr. Crile's reference to hedonism on the broadcast comes through as an endorsement of what you see elsewhere on the program. It tells the viewer that what gay politics is about is hedonism; chain 'em to the bed and whip 'em. And that movement of thought is bizarre. People have been whipping other people long before the gay rights movement came along, and I think they're going to be whipping 'em less as we make sexuality less of an ugly, dirty word in the popular imagination.

David Weissman, legislative aide to Mr. Britt, who was present during the staff interview, said that "Also, historically, when gay people are told to conform to community standards that means don't hold hands in public, don't kiss in public, don't give any evidence to the outside world that you are anything other than a heterosexual. And that's how the

Mayor's statement was responded to. We have every right to hold hands on the street, as much as any couple does, and that was the response to the Mayor's statement. It's not let us have wild orgies in Buena Vista Park. We think our standards are perfectly fine. The implication is that gay standards are hedonistic and crazy and wild. They're not."

## The Sexual Issues

Mr. Alfred's complaint charges CBS with "exaggerating preoccupation with sex." In its response, CBS interprets this as meaning that the broadcast "unfairly portrayed the gays of San Francisco by focusing on sexual matters unconnected with the mayoral campaign. Specifically, they focused on the Buena Vista Park sequence and on the section of the broadcast devoted to sadomasochism."

Other questions concerning sexual matters were raised in the complaint, concerning in particular sequences involving San Francisco's annual Beaux Arts Ball, Castro Street on Hallowe'en night, and a program to "demystify" homosexuality in the schools. All of these will be examined in this section of the report.

## Buena Vista Park

Buena Vista Park is a 37-acre tract neighboring on San Francisco's Castro Street District. It was introduced on "Gay Power, Gay Politics" by Mr. Crile with a question: ". . . should public parks be used for sex?" He continued:

> Today it's one of the pieces of territory claimed by the men of the gay community. For the average person, it may not be dangerous to go into this park, but when we came here with our camera crew a group of gay men surrounded us and forced us to leave. A week later we came back without our crew, but with a home movie camera. This is what we found. From sunup to sundown, men everywhere—hundreds of them coming to this park each day for public sex.

There follows in this sequence an interview with a family living on the edge of the park. A young boy and a young girl tell what they have seen, and their mother and father express their anxieties.

In its response to Mr. Alfred's contention that CBS presented no evidence "that sex in Buena Vista Park was an issue in the campaign," Mr. Chandler said "it was germane. The Mayor never stated what she meant when she said that gays should not impose their lifestyles on others. In the absence of such specifics, it seemed to us mandatory to examine precisely those elements of gay lifestyles which involved impositions on the rest of the community, which were potential areas of the very sort of backlash the Mayor expressed concern about.

"It was also essential to differentiate the attitudes between private and public acts. As was pointed out, the 'glory holes' were, in the view of the city, legal because they involved private acts between consenting adults . . . . But the use of a public park for sexual intercourse clearly falls outside the category of private acts, and the fact that such activities were disruptive to residents of the neighborhood was relevant to any discussion of the 'imposition of lifestyles' on others."

In response to the charge that Mr. Crile at no point asked the question ("Should public parks be used for sex?") of any gay leader or spokesperson, Mr. Chandler responded that "we did, although such questions did not appear on the broadcast," and that "None of the gays we talked with . . . nor any gay leaders we know of, have publicly deplored public sex in Buena Vista Park . . . . One can only assume that their reasons, at least in part, relate to their concern about the imposition of standards, either by heterosexuals upon homosexuals, or by homosexuals upon their fellows."

Burleigh Sutton, a gay businessman, who was interviewed on several occasions on "Gay Power, Gay Politics," told the Council's staff representative that he was interviewed by Mr. Crile for from two and a half to three hours, and that not once did Mr. Crile ask him how he felt about Buena Vista Park. "I don't know of anyone who is responsible," he said, "who feels that the Buena Vista situation should be condoned or encouraged. It's a matter of embarrassment to most of the people I know. It's a small percentage of the gay population that's involved in that scene, and we don't even condone that."

In his complaint, Mr. Alfred took exception to Mr. Crile's use of the figure "hundreds" of them in reference to the number of gays who utilize the park, and also to the statement that "For the gay men of San Francisco, cruising in Buena Vista Park is done without shame."

"'Hundreds of them,'" Mr. Alfred said, "amount to no more than a fraction of a percent of Crile's own estimate ('from 75,000 to 175,000') of the number of gays in the city. Crile does not and cannot establish that all of the gay men there use the park for sex. And if it 'is done without shame,' why then do the men go deep in the bushes to do it, and why did a group of gay men allegedly chase the CBS camera crew out of the park?"

CBS responded that "Alfred . . . does not deny the essential facts that it is used for public sex."

Mr. Alfred contended that the real issue in the "community standards" controversy pertained to "glory holes," and not to Buena Vista Park. Responding to Mr. Crile's on-air statement that "The authorities take the position that government has no business interfering with them; that what goes on inside are essentially private acts carried out by consenting adults," Mr. Alfred said:

> The District Attorney moved against these clubs in March, 1979. Bitter and protracted negotiations took place during the spring. Then-Supervisor Dianne Feinstein's 1978 role in relaying the complaint that began "Red Light Abatement" proceedings against the clubs was a major issue in gay male circles during the campaign. It was also one of the substantive worries beneath concern about her remarks to the *Ladies' Home Journal*.

> This story was covered extensively by the *Bay Area Reporter,* the *Sentinel,* and other gay press in March and April of 1979. On June 26, the S.F. *Examiner* ran the story on its front page under the banner headline, "DA's gay sex club deal." The deal was an April out-of-court settlement which carefully defined the minimum standards for privacy.

### Sadomasochism

Aside from the fleeting earlier mention, the subject of sadomasochism comes into the documentary during the Hallowe'en party sequence on Castro Street when Mr. Crile encounters Mel Wald, a gay who identifies himself as a "bike commander," a part of the gay community's security force.

"During the day," Mr. Crile asks, "what's your ordinary work?" Mr. Wald responds: "My ordinary work is a sadomasochist and consultant, or best known as an S & M consultant," to which he adds that "Part of my profession is I teach police departments, coroners, doctors."

"Coroners?" Mr. Crile asks. "Coroners about S & M," Mr. Wald replies, "so that when they see a body with certain ties, certain implements around, how to distinguish whether it was a forcible, non-forcible, whether the bondage was something that they got into or didn't, whether it was willing or not."

Later during the broadcast, sadomasochism is reintroduced with a statement by Mr. Crile that "The problem for straight politicians courting the gay vote is that some things about the homosexual community here are undeniably troubling but politically dangerous to challenge. There are things which divide the straight and gay communities, and I suppose one of them are sexual mores." Burleigh Sutton replies "Very definitely," and the camera takes the viewer into an S & M "toy" shop, where Mr. Crile asks a clerk "What kind of people will use this sort of thing?

The—is it the lunatic fringe of the community?" The clerk replies: "It's—no, it's everybody. It's bankers, lawyers, doctors. We sell to all types of clientele."

A few moments later Mr. Crile poses a question to Charles K. (Rusty) Epps, another gay businessman who appears several times on the program:

> CRILE: There are a number of things that happen in the gay community, which go from the leather bars to the glory holes and to the S & M parlors. Do you all support all these things, or do you draw a line on some of them and say, "We ought to clean it up?"
>
> EPPS: I'm willing to take it. I support them, with the proviso that these are things that people are doing in private, that if—if you want to go to the glory holes or you want to go to an S & M bar, you go there knowing that's what it is. It's the choice of the individual to do what he or she wishes to do.

The sequence continues with a brief interview with San Francisco's Coroner Boyd Stephens and a visit with Mr. Wald in an S & M "torture chamber." Following the sound of crashing chains, Mr. Crile asks Mr. Wald: "What are these things, Mel, here?" And Mr. Wald replies, "They're different toys to be used in different manner through the different sessions."

> CRILE: We last met Mel Wald on Halloween. On this night he took us to one of San Francisco's commercial establishments where you can rent a torture chamber. This one is licensed, perfectly legal.
>
> WALD: Board of Education, very interesting. It has the holes, and when it's used it can leave a lot of interesting marks. Regulation night stick—wonderful to be used as a dildo.

Preceding and following the torture chamber scene, Mr. Crile interviews Dr. Stephens. His first question to the Coroner is "about a new kind of problem that you're facing. Could you tell us about it?"

> DR. STEPHENS: We've been seeing for a while now about 10 percent of our homicides related to homosexual behaviour, and this ranges from just homosexual-type behaviour—an individual who goes to a bar, picks up another person of their own sex—through and including sadomasochism with bondage and severe injury.

Mr. Crile's second question relates to "an institution in this city where people are involved in S & M activities . . . in which they're so dangerous that they have a gynecological table there with a doctor and nurse on hand to sew people up.

> DR. STEPHENS: Yes, I've heard of these places. We see right now—
> CRILE: Well, why are they allowed to flourish?
> DR. STEPHENS: Currently, there's no law against them.

155

Responding to the objections to the inclusion of sadomasochism in a broadcast titled "Gay Power, Gay Politics," Mr. Chandler said the "arguments . . . are somewhat different. Again, there is no denial that S & M is practiced by a portion of the gay community. The complaint is that it is also practiced by the heterosexual community, that the 'torture chamber' shown is owned by and caters to heterosexuals too, and that the S & M question bore no relationship to the issues in the campaign."

Mr. Alfred contended that S & M "is predominantly heterosexual," and gave as his reference a KQED-TV (Channel 9, San Francisco) documentary titled "S-M: One Foot Out of the Closet," broadcast on February 11 and May 26, 1980.

Phil Bronstein of KQED-TV, who reported and narrated the program, told the Council's staff that he determined in his research that S & M activity in the Bay Area was about 90 percent straight. " It is predominantly heterosexual," he said; to which he added that the "torture chamber" scene shown on the CBS program was filmed at "The Chateau," an S & M parlor that is "almost wholly heterosexual."

"The Chateau's" owner, James Hillier, told the Council's staff that his clientele "is about 99 to 99.8 percent heterosexual."

In its detailed response, CBS said ". . . we pointed out in the film (that) the Chateau was Mr. Wald's choice (presumably because its proprietor was agreeable to let us film there). There are many other S & M establishments in the city which cater exclusively to the gay community."

Mr. Hillier said "I was reluctant and uneasy when they came to my place to film."

Mr. Alfred said that Dr. Stephens acknowledged to him that the 10 percent figure included the killing of homosexuals by heterosexuals. He also said that "Crile earlier in the show estimated the gay portion of the population at 12 percent to 25 percent, but fails to remind his audience of that here. This omission fits CBS's editorial pattern.'

"No one really knows how many people are gay in San Francisco," Dr. Stephens told the Council's staff. "You'll have estimates ranging from a low of a few thousand up to an estimate that would make almost every person in the city a gay. If there are 100,000 gays in San Francisco and the rate of gay-related homicides is 10 percent, that makes a difference. Ten percent would be a low rate. It is going up. In approximately one half of the homicides involving homosexuals the killer either is not a gay, or the identity of the killer is unknown.

"I would say that S & M activities involve a relatively small portion of homosexuals in general, but it's somewhat higher here simply because we

156

happen to have a larger portion of people operating establishments in that field."

Dr. Stephens said that he was speaking from hearsay when he said during the broadcast that he had heard of the place referred by Mr. Crile as having "a gynecological table . . . with a doctor and nurse on hand to sew people up." The Coroner said that later on during his interview with Mr. Crile "I believe we explained that we were unaware of anywhere where there was a doctor in attendance . . . I personally know of no place where there is a doctor on duty, so to speak, to sew people up, but it's hard for me to say that CBS erred in not going back to what I said later in finishing the sentence that was cut off. They have to cut and fit into a time slot."

In its detailed response, CBS said that "We have spoken to the coroner since the documentary and his remarks stand as broadcast. Mr. Alfred suggests that our account of the S & M parlor . . . is based on hearsay and rumor. He does not, however, say that such an institution is non-existent . . . and for good reason. Dr. Stephens only confirmed that he knew about this establishment. Our attention was first directed to the S & M parlor in question by another city official who had formally investigated the S & M world and who related his findings to us."

Mr. Chandler said that "The complaint overlooks some significant differences between homosexual S & M and heterosexual S & M. For one thing, to the extent that heterosexual S & M exists, it is not institutionalized but in fact is an 'underground' activity. While it is true that its practioners buy or rent equipment from such establishments as depicted, there is no other public manifestation of their activity. Not so in the case of homosexual S & M, which is institutionalized to the extent that so-called S & M or 'leather' bars are an institution in the gay community. They are public establishments which serve as a gathering place for homosexual sado-masochists, and to one degree or another, some sado-masochism takes place in a number of them.

"A second significant difference is that while homosexual leaders are quick to defend homosexual S & M, we have observed no one among heterosexuals who would defend the heterosexual S & M, at least publicly.

### The Hallowe'en Party

A sequence involving a Hallowe'en party on Castro Street in the gay community is introduced on the broadcast as follows:

CRILE: The problem is that the gay life style was already creating a backlash in the city. Nowhere is this more apparent than Hallowe'en night on Castro Street. It's a custom in this old family neighborhood to begin Hallowe'en with a party for the children. The tradition remains, but since the gays took over here, they've introduced a new experience for the kiddies.

There follows a scene showing a frightened, or apprehensive girl, with film cuts back and forth from the girl to costumed men, one of whom was clad in a sexually explicit costume.

Mr. Alfred said that he talked with the girl's mother and that she said her daughter "was reacting to being shoved onto the stage. And she was generally freaked out, since she and I had just been separated from another mother and daughter. There was a real crush. It was terrible." According to Mr. Alfred, Mrs. Trina Robbins, the mother of the girl, blamed "the violence in the air" on "non-gay punks from outside the neighborhood" who were there to "hassle people."

William Paul, a lecturer on Interdisciplinary Studies at San Francisco State University, who attended the party as part of a research project sponsored by The Society for the Psychological Study of Social Issues, told the Council's staff representative that "I did not observe any sexually explicit costumes or inappropriate behaviour in the vicinity of the kids' party, which was actually quite early in the evening. I recall the girl and the filming and . . . felt she was suffering from stage fright . . . . It seems quite likely that serious distortions of actual events were made in editing . . . . The social atmosphere at the children's party, although quite crowded, was one of warmth and intergroup conciliation, hardly the lurid, threatening images portrayed. Parents and relatives participated."

In its detailed response, CBS declared that "as to the Alfred claim that one of the little girls seen on the stage at Hallowe'en was frightened by 'non-gay punks from outside the neighborhood' instead of by the stream of homosexuals dressed in bizarre costumes on the stage, we will allow the film to speak for itself."

Later in this sequence, following the children's party, Mr. Crile states:

As the night wore on, it looked as though there would be no major confrontation between straights and gays, but it had been an ordeal for Captain Jeffries' men. For hours now they had stood by silently as the gays provocatively taunted them.

Mr. Alfred said that the video "shows someone in a buglike costume acting like a bug, perhaps intending to amuse more than to taunt. In any case, the major taunting in this scene takes place as Crile repeatedly and unsuccessfully tries to elicit anti-gay responses from two policemen, one

158

a commanding officer. To their credit, and to the credit of the San Francisco Police Department, both officers remain absolutely calm, nonjudgmental, and professional . . . ."

CBS responded that ". . . surely he is aware that the gay leaders on Castro Street were deeply concerned about police attitudes. A number of policemen had recently attacked gays on Castro Street . . . . The questions Crile asked the police were the questions on the minds of the gay leaders that night. As seen at the end of the Hallowe'en sequence, those concerns were well founded. At about 2 a.m. the police moved onto Castro Street and began bullying the gays in a manner that only barely escaped breaking into a truly dangerous confrontation."

Captain George Jeffries, of the San Francisco Police Department, a District Commander, who was present at the party, told the Council's staff that "It is standard procedure for the department to meet with leaders prior to such events. We met with gay leaders before the Hallowe'en Party. We ran over the ground rules: How many police we'll have, diversion of traffic, the use of monitors. We agreed to take the side streets, to prevent trouble involving those coming and leaving the main street. The monitors from the gay community would take Castro Street, aside from a couple of squads and undercover personnel. There were from 30,000 to 35,000 people there that night, and after it was over we had made about 15 arrests, with one-half of them non-gays from outside the area. About three of the arrests were for assaults. The rest were for drunken behavior.

"I wrote in my report to the department that the night was totally orderly. There was a skirmish, but it occurred late, when only about 200 or 300 people were left—mostly drunks who didn't want to go home. We made eight of our arrests then, and withdrew. Things like that look bad on film, but it really was over in about ten or fifteen minutes. A relatively minor story. I don't think the presence of a television crew had any effect."

## The Demystification Program

One of Mr. Alfred's major charges is that Mr. Crile editorialized in the documentary when he commented on the Mayor's financial report of the Human Rights Foundation's program in the schools of "demystification" of homosexuality. The relevant segment of the broadcast went as follows:

> CRILE: For these men, political power is only one of many goals. Bob Sass is chairman of the Human Rights Foundation. He's doing something that frightens

many heterosexuals. He's working to introduce what the gays call a 'demystification program' into the schools.

SUTTON: Its basic goal is exactly what it says. It's the education of the general public. It's not an attempt to convert, but simply acquaint children of a formidable age that differences exist with respect to sexual orientation.

CRILE: And will it present homosexuality as a—alternative, normal lifestyle?

SUTTON: Yes.

CRILE: Because—

SUTTON: I consider it a normal lifestyle, certainly.

CRILE: Whether it's normal or not, scenes like this remain difficult for the straight world to accept. For Dianne Feinstein, the problem was more complex. She had an election to win, and her homosexual friends were now telling her that mere acceptance of this life style was not enough. She must become an advocate of their causes.

At this point, Jerry Berg, former president of the foundation, comments: "It was exciting for us when it came time to raise some substantial funds for the Human Rights Foundation. We invited a number of city officials, including the mayor. The price of the evening was $500."

CRILE: What you're saying is that the mayor of San Francisco personally contributed $500 to the Human Rights Foundation, which is working to introduce the teaching of homosexuality into the schools?

BERG: That's one of our programs.

CRILE: That's incredible, isn't it?

BERG: Well, it's—it's satisfying to us, because we feel so strongly about these programs that we love to have support from everywhere, and—in the mayor's office it's—it's most welcome.

Criticizing Mr. Crile's usage of the word "incredible," Mr. Alfred cited a comment made by Mr. Crile on a follow-up program titled "Has the Truth Been Told," broadcast by KPIX-TV, the San Francisco CBS affiliate, on the same evening as "Gay Power, Gay Politics." Mr. Crile said:

I think that . . . one thing that San Francisco can do, if Kinsey is right and one out of every ten Americans are gay, we all have to learn to live together. San Francisco should be the city which teaches the nation how to do that.

Mr. Alfred said that "The demystification program is a conscious attempt by straight and gay San Franciscans 'to learn to live together,' to replace queer-bashing hatred with understanding. If Crile found the progam so 'incredible,' maybe he should have covered it. He would have learned that it was motivated by the same problem of anti-gay violence which CBS ignored as an issue in the mayoral campaign."

In its detailed response, CBS said that "Mr. Alfred misrepresents the

Crile response ('incredible') by not citing the full exchange. That response was both a reaction and a question to the three interviewees. Crile was acknowledging the unprecedented action that Dianne Feinstein, a traditional heterosexual politician, had taken by publicly supporting such a highly controversial homosexual program. The interviewees acknowledged the novelty and uniqueness of the Mayor's position with a laugh," followed by Mr. Berg's remark that "It was exciting for us . . . ."

The Human Rights Foundation, incorporated in August 1977, is a tax-exempt organization whose purpose is to eliminate "those perceptions concerning human rights and human sexuality that limit the full self-expression of all members of society." In describing its "Demystifying Homosexuality Project," funded by the Playboy and Hazen Foundations, the Human Rights Foundation says it "provides carefully selected and trained gay male and lesbian speakers to Bay Area high schools and junior colleges (outside the city of San Francisco) who "are invited . . . to answer questions from students in such high school courses as 'Health Education' and "Family Life Education' and in such junior college courses as 'Counseling' and 'Marriage and the Family.'"

The project, which started in the fall of 1978 after a pilot program in 1977, has been invited by the San Francisco Unified School District's "Advisory Committee on Health and Family Life Education" to provide scheduling assistance for lesbian and gay male speakers in certain San Francisco high schools, to meet with administrators, counselors, teachers, or students in their classes.

Robert W. Sass, president of the Foundation (identified but not appearing on the CBS program as "chairman" of the Foundation) told the Council's staff that "The benefits of the program have been almost universally acknowledged and I have nothing in the foundation's record in the way of a complaint from anyone, teachers, students or parents."

Mr. Sass said that "What is very true is that what we hear consistently from teachers and students is that it is usually the first time that many of the students have had a chance to speak with someone who is gay. They carry around enormously strong stereotypes and myths about what gay people are like, and they find that gay people are really just like they are except that their sexual preferences are different.

"For me, the sadness was that there was no effort made by CBS to explore the program in depth and to look at it with real objectivity. Our program does not teach homosexuality. It introduces students to the fact that there are homosexuals living in their community, and that sometimes they are in their midst."

## The Beaux Arts Ball

Immediately preceding a sequence in the documentary photographed at the city's annual Beaux Arts Ball, a conversation takes place between Mr. Crile and Cleve Jones in which Mr. Crile asks the question: "Do you feel there'll be a gay mayor some day?"

> JONES: I don't feel certain about anything. There were a lot of gay people doing a lot of work in Germany before Hitler, and there was a huge movement—the German homosexual emancipation movement—and it was wiped out. The odds, I think, are still against us, but I'm optimistic.
> CRILE: It was a very decadent society, if you remember it.
> JONES: Yeah.
> CRILE: The Berlin cafe society. Isn't it a sign of decadence when you have so many gays emerging, breaking apart all of the values of a society?
> JONES: I don't see that as a sign of decadence. Perhaps the values of society are decadent. Perhaps they need to be broken up.

The scene shifts immediately to the Beaux Arts Ball at the Civic Auditorium, where Mr. Crile, in a voice-over, says "The Beaux Arts Ball. It's a tradition in San Francisco: a night when gay men dress up as women and anything else that suits their fancy; a night when men can compete in a beauty contest for the prettiest costume . . . . It's an old institution in the gay community but with a new wrinkle: this year, the Beaux Arts Ball became a major stop on the campaign trail."

Both Mayor Feinstein and Supervisor Kopp attended the ball, with the Mayor making a few on-stage remarks in the broadcast, and Mr. Kopp engaging in the following broadcast exchange with Mr. Crile:

> CRILE: The gay community of San Francisco.
> KOPP (laughing): Okay.
> CRILE: Tell me, why—why do you laugh when you think of the gay community of—of this city?
> KOPP: I didn't laugh.

"This sequence," according to Mr. Alfred, "is linked to Crile's own description of decadence in Weimar Germany. Cleve Jones was discussing not 'cafe society,' but work in a political movement that had been associated with Germany's Social Democrats since the late 19th century . . . . Crile is the one who changed the subject."

CBS, in its detailed response, said that "Again Mr. Alfred is seeking to tell us what he thinks Mr. Jones really meant to say. His assertion that Jones was talking about 'work in a political movement' associated with Germany's Social Democrats is not true. The question Mr. Jones was

responding to dealt with the possibility of a homosexual becoming Mayor
. . . ."

"CBS," Mr. Alfred said, "fails to inform its audience that the Beaux Arts Ball is a Hallowe'en charity event that benefits community organizations. Wayne Friday, president of the sponsoring San Francisco Tavern Guild Foundation, said that the foundation distributes proceeds from the ball to service organizations in the gay and straight communities. Reporting this would have made the ball seem less 'decadent' and more like a traditional costume ball appropriate to the season."

CBS responded that "He (Alfred) apparently would have us believe that this event, also known as the Drag Queens Ball, is not primarily a gay affair. But it would be a gross distortion to describe it in any other way."

In reference to Mr. Crile's description of the ball as "a night when gay men dress up as women . . . ." Mr. Alfred said that "Bob Ross, publisher of the *Bay Area Reporter* and a former 'Emperor' closely associated with the city's gay 'royal courts,' and Friday, both told me that about 40 percent of the costume competition entrants and 40 percent of the audience in 1979 were heterosexual."

Pam Brunger, Features Editor of the *San Francisco Examiner,* told the Council's staff that "No one can say with certainty how many of those in costume at the ball are heterosexual, and how many are gay. Do you ask them at the door? Most certainly, there are heterosexuals in the audience, and undoubtedly there are some in costume, but it is known as a 'gay event.'"

Mr. Alfred said that politicking at the ball has been going on for years, and that "State Senator Milton Marks, Mayor George Moscone, Sheriff Richard Hongisto and Supervisors Feinstein and Carol Ruth Silver, among others, had all attended the ball in years past."

"It is true," the CBS response said, "that certain San Francisco politicians have attended this event in the past. But so far as we know, 1979 was the first year that the principal candidates in the Mayor's race all came . . . . Last year marked the coming of age of gay political power in San Francisco and all the candidates acknowledged it with their appearances at the Beaux Arts Ball."

Mr. Alfred charged that "The entire interview with Quentin Kopp is fraught with manipulation. As edited it opens with Crile and Kopp both laughing and Kopp caught in midsentence . . . . Kopp reported to me that he and Crile were both reacting to humor that preceded the opening edit. Why didn't CBS show what th· two were laughing about instead of merely including Crile's unanswered question on this subject?

"It is not true . . . that Kopp was 'reacting to humor that preceded the opening edit,'" CBS said in its response. "Mr. Kopp initiated the laughter when Crile explained that he wished to talk about the gay community . . . . If there is any doubt here see Kopp interview."

Mr. Alfred charged that Mr. Kopp had left the ball but was chased by CBS and brought back for the filming of the interview. "This scene is not genuine but a recreation." To which CBS responded: "There is nothing unusual nor questionable about asking a politician to come back for an interview to a place that he had left just minutes before and where a film crew was set up."

A further charge by Mr. Alfred was that the appearance of a drag queen "in the midst of this 'interview' . . . was apparently shot either earlier or later and spliced into the scene. Kopp said it did not occur during the interview itself. Such editing is inflammatory, irresponsible, and disreputable."

CBS said that "The scene with the drag queen took place during the time Mr. Kopp was being interviewed."

## The Applause Issue

Mr. Alfred charged that CBS, by inserting applause after Mayor Feinstein's "apology" at the Harvey Milk Democratic Club meeting "willfully and wantonly misrepresented community response in this sequence. The reaction to the Mayor's apology, which CBS falsely set up as the major issue, was, speaking plainly, *staged*. CBS first watered down Feinstein's comment, and then created a false reaction to her apology for it."

Mr. Alfred submitted his own tape recording of the event, and referred to another taping made by David Lamble, a Scott aide during his campaign. The Council's staff has heard both tapes. Neither contains applause following the apology.

CBS has acknowledged that there was no applause at that moment. In his response to the Council, Mr. Chandler stated that the applause came "shortly thereafter," and presented an explanation as to why the applause was shifted. Mr. Chandler denied that this was done with "any desire to distort," but stated that "our producers . . . misled our viewers."

**Staff additions:** The Council's staff has come to believe that the central issue underlying all of the charges and countercharges contained in Mr. Alfred's complaint, and in the complaints by San Francisco's Board of Supervisors, the Human Rights Commission, and the National Gay Task

164

Force centers on the commentary by Mr. Reasoner that closed "Gay Power, Gay Politics." Those comments follow, in full:

> It may be that San Francisco is unique and it couldn't happen anywhere else. But if Kinsey is right, upwards of 20 million Americans are homosexual and as we saw at the march in Washington last October, gay political organizations are acting all across the country. The right of homosexuals to organize like any other minority seeking to further its own interests is no longer in question. The question is, what will those interests be? Will they include a demand for absolute sexual freedom, as they did in San Francisco? And if so, will this challenge to traditional values provoke far more hostility and controversy when it is put to the test elsewhere?
>
> It is no longer a matter of whether homosexuals will achieve political power, but what they will attempt to do with it.

The key words in this closing passage are "absolute sexual freedom."

Mr. Alfred said that "For the last words on the show, after an hour of setting up its audience, CBS trots out Harry Reasoner with the unsupported declaration that gays in San Francisco demanded 'absolute sexual freedom.'" The city's Board of Supervisors charged that the documentary provided "a series of images of the 'darker practices of the gay community' intended to startle viewers and to show how gays are attacking traditional values and frightening heterosexuals." The Human Rights Commission said it "conveyed distorted information pertaining to the behaviour and attitudes of the gay community, which contributed to the perpetuation of stereotypes." And the National Gay Task Force said it "unjustly maligned and stimatized gay people . . . ."

Mr. Chandler, in his response, stated that "We believe the characterization is valid, for all of the reasons cited in this response. The gay leadership has insisted on the right to set its own standards of sexual behaviour, it rejects any interference with glory holes or S & M bars and it avoids or refuses to condemn public sexual activity in Buena Vista Park. It is impossible to conclude otherwise."

Mr. Chandler called attention to another exchange in the documentary:

> CRILE: Burleigh, Jerry, Rusty, what if Mayor Feinstein had gone through the campaign making the same kind of comments she did to the *Ladies' Home Journal* and said there are too many sexual excesses and it's against the customs and traditions of this city. What would have happened to her in terms of the gay vote, Jerry?
>
> BERG: She would not have had it.
>
> SUTTON: Jerry can talk about the gay community and its standards, but the Mayor has difficulty. If you're not a member of our minority, I think you're on really shaky footing by pointing to it in general terms and saying clean up your act.

Mr. Sutton told the Council's staff that "I don't think that any responsible gay activist in San Francisco, or across the country, is advocating absolute sexual freedom as a criteria. What the gay community is concerned about is police harrassment, homophobic harrassment which transmits itself into physical violence, and an opportunity in the job market, basically, the same things that any minority is out to correct.

"In terms of sexual freedom, certainly there is an element of the gay movement—the minority exists because of its sexual orientation—which has to include the word sexuality in terms of its goals. But what the gay movement seeks to achieve is a fair, unbiased approach to an individual, irrespective of his or her sexual orientation. The gay and lesbian community doesn't ask for any favor with respect to sexual orientation. It asks simply to be treated fairly."

Mayor Feinstein, in an interview with the Council's representative, said that "The CBS people came into this thing with a personal bias. They did a show that permitted that bias to come through. They ignored a community, a community of gays who go to work every day, who are in the mainstream of the city's life, who are generally ideologically conservative. They concentrated on the fringe element. They did it to frighten."

The Mayor cited a letter she had written to Pat Polillo, general manager of KPIX-TV, the Bay Area CBS affiliate. In that letter she said "Certainly, to give the impression that 'glory holes,' S & M parlors, and bath houses, along with open-air sex in Buena Vista Park depicts the gay lifestyle accurately is unfair and false."

District Captain Jeffries of the Police Department said he felt that the documentary "dealt with extremes, overlooking the fact that the vast majority, I'd say 95 percent, of the gay population is going to work every day, just making a living, getting by, upgrading their property. Now, we, the police, deal with extremes. We don't deal with many normal people, so to speak. We deal with those who aren't. But extremes are news, I suppose."

Referring to Mr. Reasoner's comment on "absolute sexual freedom," the Mayor wrote: "That is a false assumption. The gay community did not demand, nor do they have, 'absolute sexual freedom' in San Francisco. Their sexual standards are different from those of the 'straight' community, but the laws that govern sexual conduct apply equally to gay and straight citizens."

"Missing from the program," according to William Paul of the University of San Francisco, "was any real effort to show the enormous number of straight people in our city who are supportive of the gay community, who are tolerant, and no real effort was made on the part of CBS to find—

166

and they can be found—those in the gay community who can, and do, speak out against public sex."

Rich Weatherly, Minister of Evangelism for the Metropolitan Community Church in San Francisco, a church ministering to gays and lesbians, told the Council's staff that he was "completely surprised" by the documentary. "What they said they were doing was not dealing with lifestyles, but instead dealing with the impact on political life of the gay community. Instead, their clear intention was to show that the reasons for gay political involvement were so that we could tear loose every civil and customary restriction on sexual behaviour so that we could dance naked in the streets, go to S & M parlors, have sexual license to do anything we wanted to do.

"True, for an outsider viewing our community the most alienating things about gay life are things like Buena Vista Park and S & M parlors. But these things are not typical of most gay people. They are regrettable. By concentrating on them, CBS trivialized all that the vast majority of gay people have been trying to do over these past ten years."

**Council finding:** The CBS documentary, "Gay Power, Gay Politics," touched many sensitivities and provoked passionate reaction and protest.

The central complaint is, as noted in the staff analysis, unusually complex. It has required grouping under three headings: the political campaign, the sexual issues and the applause issue.

On the political campaign issue, it is clear that the Mayor and her rival in the runoff election acted in standard political fashion in seeking to win the vote of the gay community. CBS News was not alone in its editorial judgment that Mayor Feinstein's apology for what she had said in *Ladies' Home Journal* about gays and community standards was a pivotal factor in her endorsement by the gay community. Both San Francisco daily newspapers accorded special importance to that apology. Its significance was further underscored by a respected gay leader's flat statement that Mayor Feinstein would not have received the gay vote if she had continued to make such comments. Elsewhere in the program, CBS did note other political issues and specifically the gays' calls for greater security against violence by heterosexuals and by what they consider police harassment.

For these reasons the complaint with respect to the election campaign is found unwarranted.

The Council finds unfairness in the presentation of the sexual issues. By concentrating on certain flamboyant examples of homosexual behavior, the program tended to reinforce stereotypes. The program also exaggerated political concessions to gays and made those concessions appear as threats to public morals and decency.

The Council exempts from this criticism the program's attention to Buena Vista Park. Inquiry by the Council's staff confirmed the existence of widespread opposition to the usurpation of the park for sexual purposes. The many hearings before public bodies show that its misuse was a subject laden with political significance, whether or not it arose specifically in the mayoralty campaign.

However, justification cannot be found for the degree of attention given to sado-masochism or the treatment of the Beaux Arts Ball and the Hallowe'en sequences.

Authoritative sources agree that sado-masochism is practiced extensively by heterosexuals, yet the broadcast treats it as distinctively homosexual. The Chateau, pictured as an example of sado-masochistic indulgence, is owned by and patronized almost exclusively by heterosexuals.

The Hallowe'en events were presented in a manner both confusing and misleading. The children's party early in the evening was made to appear frightening because of the gays' presence at the party, thus fortifying parental fears about the safety of their children.

The Council finds troublesome the abrupt transition from the discussion of decadence to the Beaux Arts Ball. The Beaux Arts Ball, held up as an example of decadence, is an accepted community event in San Francisco. While sponsored by gays, it is also attended by heterosexuals and the proceeds go to many community programs.

In dealing with the "demystification" program in the schools, CBS failed to make clear that supporters see as its purpose a reduction in the danger of harassment and violence by heterosexuals against homosexuals. CBS conveyed so little solid information that it left a frightening impression, fostered in part by pictures of men embracing and kissing. The Council's investigation showed, by contrast, that civic leaders generally view the program as a useful bridge for better understanding between the gay and the majority communities. While there is unquestionably room for argument on the appropriateness of such a project in the schools or on how it is executed, what came through on the CBS program was that the demystification project was simply a gay thrust to promote homosexuality in the schools, with the financial support of the mayor.

Mr. Reasoner asked at the end of the broadcast whether the gays' national political objectives will include a "demand for absolute sexual freedom, as they did in San Francisco." The undue emphasis on sadomasochism and the distortions of the Hallowe'en party and the de-mystification program contribute to a picture of what Mr. Reasoner means by a demand for absolute sexual freedom. The reality is that homosexuals are not monolithic in their behavior or their political objectives. Many abhor public sex; their principle objective is a climate of tolerance that permits them to operate in the mainstream of their communities. The unwillingness of gays in this category to break ranks with extremists by repudiating more flamboyant demands created reportorial problems for CBS, but did not relieve it of its obligation to present a fair picture.

The Council finds the complaint warranted as it applies to the treatment of sado-masochism, the demystification project, the Hallowe'en party and the transition from a discussion of decadence to the Beaux Arts Ball.

As for the applause issue, CBS News has acknowledged that through the insertion of applause where there was none after the mayor's apology it violated the network's own standards and has offered an apology for that violation. Also the network is candid in its response that it would have been wiser to have reported in full the mayor's comments in the *Ladies' Home Journal* instead of paraphrasing them. The Council welcomes CBS's candor in both these admissions.

**Concurring:** Abel, Brady, Ghiglione, Huston, Isaacs, Lawson, Maynard, Pulitzer and Williams.

**Concurring opinion by Mr. Lawson:** I concur with the majority but with an additional word. The CBS report did not do what Mr. Reasoner said it would do. The report did not assess the meaning of the political power of the gay community for the 1980's. Whatever "absolute sexual freedom" means, gay leadership did not make that the primary objective of political action. By omission of those objectives, and by omission of an analysis of those objectives this documentary is severely flawed. As news it fails to feed the public mind.

**Concurring opinion by Mr. Maynard and Mr. Williams:** We concur with the majority in its principal findings which essentially were that the network dealt with the visible and flamboyant aspects of gay life, but ignored other essential aspects of the life and concerns of that community.

The Council's findings gave too little attention to the overall thrust and effect of the CBS effort. That broadcast portrayed the gay political movement in threatening and sensational terms that ignored the facts of discrimination against members of the gay community. It failed to note the pervasive discrimination against gays in the job market. It failed to note the discrimination against gays in domestic relation disputes where the custody of offspring is at stake. It barely noted the problems of unequal justice with which gay people cope daily. Nor did it fully explain the phenomenon of anti-gay violence in the streets.

The interests of accuracy, fairness and balance were more poorly served than the majority opinion would suggest. To the degree that CBS News failed those interests in this case, it failed all those it sought to serve.

**Dissenting:** Bell.

**Dissenting (in part):** Rusher.

**Dissenting, in part, opinion by Mr. Rusher:** I concur in the Council's careful and discriminating assessment of various aspects of this documentary. But I disagree with the charge of "unfairness" in regard to sexual topics—not because the documentary was a balanced presentation of homosexual life, but because it never pretended to be one. In producing (as it chose to do) a documentary on the political impact of the gay community in San Francisco and elsewhere, including potential backlashes against it, CBS could hardly avoid depicting at considerable length certain sorts of homosexual behavior that are particularly visible and offensive to heterosexuals. In implying, as I believe the documentary does, that the producers share the sense of offense at such behavior, it is surely well within the protection of the First Amendment.

I also have some trouble agreeing that, as the Council seems to think, no sensible person could find anything "decadent" about the Beaux Arts Ball. We are in danger of hurting the feelings of its promoters.

**Dissenting opinion by Mr. Bell:** I cannot support the Council's findings in a number of specific features of the CBS documentary "Gay Power, Gay Politics," nor the overall finding of unfairness in the treatment of "sexual issues." Given what I take to be the thesis of the documentary— that the coming of age of homosexual politics in San Francisco has significantly altered the city's standard of acceptable public behavior—all of the scenes objected to are permissible and even desirable.

When looking for an alteration of community standards, one must search for the toleration of bizarre events in public. To dwell on the private or commonplace would be the height of irrelevance. CBS's decision to concentrate on "certain flamboyant examples of homosexual behavior" is therefore justified, even assuming the Council is correct in asserting that these examples will reinforce stereotypes.

I find no evidence, in the Council's opinion or elsewhere, that the program "exaggerated political concessions to gays" or unfairly made the concessions "appear as threats to public morals and decency."

I agree with the Council that CBS should have made it clear that sadomasochism has a heterosexual component, but can find no error in the overall depiction of sado-masochism as a widely accepted part of San Francisco's gay scene. Certainly its importance was underlined by Mayor Feinstein's decision to campaign in the so-called "leather bars" with gay political activist David Scott in the closing days of the runoff campaign.

The ambivalence of the scene at the children's party is not, in my view, sufficient to sustain an overall finding against the coverage of Hallowe'en. Nor is the sudden transition from the interview on decadence to the Beaux Arts Ball a reason to invalidate CBS's coverage of the ball and its social and political significance.

I find especially disturbing the Council's condemnation of the documentary for conveying "so little solid information" on the demystification campaign, particularly since nothing CBS did say was on its face either inaccurate or beyond the bounds of permissible opinion. The Council here is on the edge of second-guessing CBS on its selection of subject matter.

Despite some minor factual errors and the acknowledged major error of misplacing the applause, the documentary taken as a whole was, in my judgment, an effective examination of an unusually complex and troubling issue. The question of "community standards" is important and appropriate and the treatment by producers Crile and Diekhaus is well within the bounds of permissible journalistic practice. I hope the Council majority's finding will not discourage further examination of a growing issue in our society.

September 18, 1980

### COMPLAINT NO. 178 (Filed: May 23, 1980)
### VETERANS ADMINISTRATION
### against
### NATIONAL ENQUIRER

**Complaint:** The Veterans Administration, Department of Medicine and Surgery, complained that a *National Enquirer* article of April 8 "painted a ludicrously distorted image of the Veterans Administration's health care system."

"Briefly stated," wrote Robert R. Putnam, VA Public Information Officer, "the complaint is that the *Enquirer* published a story based on sensational allegations from irresponsible sources . . . . Further, *Enquirer* reporters and editorial staff ignored information and comments supplied by responsible sources that would have provided critically needed balance to the story."

The *Enquirer* article was headlined "Helpless Hospitalized Vets Preyed on by Violent Criminals." It claimed that an influx of "hardened criminals" had turned the nation's VA hospitals into "criminal cesspools where patients, staff and the VA's police fear for their lives."

The article stated that "an official estimates 40 percent of VA patients have been convicted of crimes." According to an unnamed VA police lieutenant quoted, conditions at VA hospitals are the product of a "mutually beneficial scheme" to fill empty VA beds and ease overcrowding in state prisons.

A VA medical center in Menlo Park, CA, was described by the *Enquirer* as a "tax-supported chamber of horrors where murder, extortion, dope dealing, theft, prostitution, drug overdose and suicide are commonplace."

"A one-year study of crimes at the Menlo Park and nearby Palo Alto VA facilities," the article went on, "shows narcotics thefts up 500 percent, assault with a deadly weapon up 400 percent and vandalism up 333 percent."

A former liaison officer between the Palo Alto and Menlo Park VA facilities was reported as saying that "murders at the two hospitals average about four or five a year and that drug overdoses occur weekly."

In addition, the article contained charges that "people are shooting up all over the place with heroin, cocaine, morphine"; that at the Menlo Park facility "there's a lot of stealing from patients—and they're terrified"; and that VA police officers across the country have been "attacked, beaten and wounded" on the job with some regularity.

In a letter to the *Enquirer*, the VA protested shortly after the article appeared. The letter said that an *Enquirer* reporter, in preparing for the article, was shown statistics refuting the published charges. The reporter was also told, according to the VA, that the VA's medical activities are monitored by some forty different agencies, including the General Accounting Office and the Joint Commission on Accreditation of Hospitals. None of these reviewing organizations, the VA said, have ever "found evidence to even come near supporting the sensational allegations accepted by the *Enquirer* as fact."

**Response:** Iain Calder, the *Enquirer*'s president, wrote:

> ". . . I have no hesitation in standing by our story . . . . It was handled by one of our most experienced editors . . . . We have a voluminous file, which I have read, and it leaves me little doubt that the charges in our article are, if anything,

understated. We did not have space to report all the anecdotes and shocking statements made by witness after witness . . . . We spoke to VA employees, VA policemen, former VA policemen, city police officers in areas where such hospitals are located, and many others with a knowledge of the situation . . . . After our story went through reporters, the story editor and an evaluator, it was passed on to our Research Department, whose function is to determine the accuracy and fairness of the file. I spoke to the researcher who says she okayed the final version with confidence after reading the extensive interviews . . . ."

With his letter, Mr. Calder enclosed a copy of an internal memo by the *Enquirer* editor who handled the story. The memo read:

Five reporters worked on this article . . . for a total of at least one month. They interviewed VA employees on the medical, nursing and police staffs of eight VA hospitals in seven states. They also confirmed the employees' statements with officials of local police departments and the Federal Bureau of Investigation—and with concerned citizens who were victims of crimes near these VA facilities.

If anything, we were restrained and mild in our story. There is a conscious and deliberate VA policy to keep security at a minimum. According to the VA police manual . . . "we know that crimes do and will occur on hospital property. Those not anticipated are embarrassing."

What's more, James Fasone, chief of VA security, readily admitted to (*Enquirer* reporter Ben) Bolton at their November 5, 1979 Washington meeting: "We took the fences down (around VA property) in the 1960's. We should have left them up a few more years. When the 1970's came, we were sorry we took the fences down. Little did we know what was going to happen."

At the same meeting Fasone cited statistics showing that no VA policeman, patient or visitor suffered any weapon-inflicted injury during the seven years the VA has had its own police force. Yet we interviewed VA policemen who have been shot, shot at, pistol-whipped and mugged, including some forced into disability retirement as a result. And PR officer Putnam told the California newspaper Peninsula Times Tribune: "Of course, we have had instances of weapon-inflicted injury in our hospital system."

Further, Fasone insisted in his meeting with Bolton that the chemical Mace is effective in stopping aggressive individuals despite being shown a letter in Bolton's possession in which Smith & Wesson, manufacturers of Mace, stated that Mace is ineffective against alcohol and drug-influenced individuals.

Finally, nowhere in our story did we characterize America's veterans as thieves, muggers and dope addicts.

**Background:** To illustrate what it presented as a nationwide epidemic of soaring crime rates and inadequate security at VA hospitals, the *Enquirer* article concentrated on VA medical centers in Palo Alto and Menlo Park, CA. The two facilities are seven miles apart, but are jointly run, sharing one police force, hospital director and chief of police. They gained some notoriety following an October 1979 five-part investigative series by the

173

*Peninsula Times Tribune* in which charges of crime and mismanagement were highlighted.

On November 27, 1979, following the *Times Tribune* series and congressional inquiries, an investigation of conditions at the Palo Alto/ Menlo Park facilities was launched by the VA's office of the Inspector General. Under investigation were current and former VA employee charges of drug illegalities, extortion, insufficient staffing, crime increases and enforcement problems. The investigation's findings were later detailed in an 18-page (May 23, 1980) report that concluded that "most of the specific complaints of criminal activity were unfounded or exaggerated" and were precipitated by VA police officers who were resentful and frustrated over what they considered low pay, needless restriction of their duties, and an unresponsive management.

The United States General Accounting Office, Human Resources Division, issued an analysis of the Inspector General's findings on August 13, 1980. In that analysis, the GAO reported that most of the major allegations were not fully pursued and that although specific incidents were addressed the Inspector General's office did not attempt to resolve the broader allegations, including the increasing crime rate at Palo Alto.

At a June 11, 1980 Senate committee hearing of the GAO and the Inspector General, agreement was reached on the GAO analysis and efforts to resolve remaining questions were initiated.

The Inspector General's staff returned to Palo Alto for further checking on September 2, 1980. No date has been set for release of the findings.

**Staff report:** The Council staff operated on two levels. On the national level, the staff dealt with officials in various government agencies in Washington. For a local view, the Council commissioned a west coast journalist to assist in its research.

Jay Thorwaldson, teacher of journalism at Stanford University and former *Peninsula Times Tribune* ombudsman with years of experience as reporter and editorial writer, conducted extensive interviews with present and past VA employees and local police chiefs in the area. He visited the VA facilities, and spent many hours speaking with nurses and patients on several wards and accompanying a VA police officer on patrol.

What follows first is a look at the Palo Alto/Menlo Park VA facilities based on information supplied in a report by Mr. Thorwaldson and his access to official documents:

About 60 percent of VA patients receive psychiatric treatment, presenting special challenges to the security staff at many facilities. At the Palo Alto/Menlo Park hospitals, which are largely psychiatric treatment

174

centers, there is the additional burden of limited police manpower.

While the total VA police force authorized to patrol both hospitals is 17, present staffing is 13 police officers, soon to decline to 12. The combined facilities have 1,339 beds. The hospitals receive approximately 200,000 out-patient visits per year.

The federal studies of Palo Alto agree that staffing of the medical center police section is insufficient and subject to high turnover.

The *Enquirer* article cited a "one-year study of crimes at the Menlo Park/Palo Alto facilities" which shows dramatic percentage increases in narcotics thefts, assaults with a deadly weapon and vandalism. The article did not indicate what was being compared; no base figures were provided and the time period examined was not identified.

It becomes clear that the percentages were taken from a crime statistics report by Jerome Hoban, the hospitals' police chief, dated January 24, 1979 and containing a statistical breakdown and comparison of criminal incidents in 1977 and 1978.

The 500 percent increase in narcotics thefts used by the *Enquirer* actually reflects an increase from two such thefts in 1977 to 12 in 1978. Chief Hoban explained that "this was due to employee thefts from ward stock." The 400 percent increase in assaults with a deadly weapon represented an increase from one such assault in 1977 to five in 1978, attributed possibly, said Chief Hogan, to a four percent increase in patient admissions and an increase in out-patient load, especially in the psychiatric areas.

Later crime statistics, presumably available to the *Enquirer* prior to its April 1980 edition, show three narcotics thefts for the first six months of 1979 and one assault with a deadly weapon case for the same period. Subsequent summaries of monthly crime reports prepared by Chief Hoban indicated drops in nearly all other crime-report categories except for the dollar value of losses from theft of personal property and especially government property.

Vandalism during the study period compared rose appreciably from 12 such occurrences in 1977 to 52 in 1978, a far greater jump in incidents than in the other categories mentioned, but a lower percentage rise—333—than the rest. However, a decline in vandalism incidents from 31 to 1978 to 27 in 1979 is reported by Chief Hoban.

The *Enquirer* article recited a list of "commonplace" offenses at the Menlo Park facility, including murder, extortion, dope dealing and overdose, theft, prostitution and suicide.

According to Chief Hoban, VA officials, police officers and staff members interviewed, suicides occur several times a year and perhaps could be considered common.

Concerning drug use, there are indicators that it is a problem, but to what degree is uncertain. There is the existence, not necessarily "dealing", of drugs—principally marijuana and pills—in and around the two facilities. VA officer Al Brown said that in his 28 months with the VA he has made "quite a few drug arrests, most just marijuana" and that "the hardest thing I ever had (to deal with) was cocaine and PCP."

One of the more vocal critics of the VA, VA Police Lieutenant Vernon A. Mize, said "I know a lot of marijuana smoking goes on" at the Menlo Park facility, adding that a spring 1978 memo from John J. Peters, then director of the hospitals, cited reports of drug activities involving patients and staff members.

Thomas Jackson, former court liaison officer for the two facilities, supported statements in the article, including one attributed to him, of drug abuse and frequent overdosing, both from illegal drugs and wrongly administered medications. Illicit drugs on the grounds "is big," said Mr. Jackson. "They were finding syringes, rubber bands, spoons."

"It's here, yes," Chief Hoban said of drug use. "A guy wants marijuana, he can get all he wants four blocks away (from the Menlo Park facility). Here (the Palo Alto hospital), he can go to Cogswell Plaza (a small park in downtown Palo Alto that is a hangout for VA patients and others). As far as being a tremendous problem on the wards, it's not reported as such by the nursing service."

Allegations of people "shooting up all over the place with heroin, cocaine, morphine . . ." were not supported based on Mr. Thorwaldson's observation of the facilities and interviews with hospital staff members.

Theft of personal and government property, although not identified by staff members interviewed as a serious problem, did occur with some frequency and could be classified, according to their testimony, as commonplace.

There have been instances of reported extortion attempts by staff against patients or patients against patients. These have been investigated by the Inspector General and GAO and dismissed. Extortion does not appear to be a prevalent feature of life in the VA wards visited by Mr. Thorwaldson.

The *Enquirer* article contained statements by an unnamed VA police lieutenant charging VA officials with soliciting incarcerated vets for hospitalization. Several VA employees interviewed, including VA Police

Lieutenant Vernon Mize, Police Chief Hoban and Albert Washko, recently-appointed assistant director of the hospitals, traced the statements to a misreading of a VA national employee newsletter article, "VA Reaches Past Steel Bars to Help." The September 1979 article reported that the VA made 75,300 face-to-face briefings on veterans benefits during the prior four years with veterans who were in prison, jail, on probation or paroled.

Lieutenant Mize said that he is aware of VA programs for prisoners and that the "criminal element (at the VA) is a real problem, but you've got me about whether they are direct from prison."

In a joint interview, Chief Hoban and Lawrence Stewart, Palo Alto VA's assistant director trainee, agreed that such out-of-prison-into-the-VA recruitment described in the *Enquirer* quotation not only does not take place, but that it is specifically against VA regulations.

"We can't take anyone who is on parole or pending court cases," Chief Hoban said, although seeking treatment might be a condition of parole if the judge involved deems it appropriate.

Mr. Stewart said that even in those cases where treatment is part of a veteran's parole "our main criteria (for admission) is medical eligibility."

Nor does there appear to be any immediate budgetary payoff for filling beds, as VA hospitals operate under a fixed annual budget. Each year's allocation is based on a projection of the workload for the past year, according to Assistant Director Washko.

On the estimate that 40 percent of VA patients have been convicted of crimes, Dan Walls, acting chief of mental hygiene at the Menlo Park Facility, said that actual statistics would be almost impossible to get, but "my best guess is about 5 percent. I don't know how by any stretch of the imagination you could make it 40 percent."

Chief Hoban called the 40 percent figure "an incredible exaggeration."

The *Enquirer* article did not explain what type of crimes (as serious as armed robbery or as minor as traffic violations) comprised the 40 percent "estimate." But based on the article's headline, "Helpless Hospitalized Vets Preyed on by Violent Criminals," and its lead sentence, "A nightmarish invasion of hardened convicts . . . ," it would appear that serious criminal offenses were involved.

Thomas Jackson was one of the two named sources used by the *Enquirer*. Attributed to Mr. Jackson was the claim that "murders at the two hospitals average four or five a year and that drug overdoses occur weekly."

Mr. Jackson said about that statement: "I can't truthfully say in my mind that I said it, but I can't truthfully say I didn't. It sounds a little heavy." He said he wondered about the statement when he first read the article, adding that he personally would not be surprised if there were unreported murders but that he cannot document this, does not know about and will not stand behind the four or five murders a year charge. He did support the statement on drug overdoses.

A search of newspaper clip files and interviews with VA staff, turned up one recorded murder at the facilities in the past several years. The Inspector General's report stated that corrobative evidence for Mr. Jackson's published charges could not be found and the GAO analysis that followed said that no further investigation of the matter was warranted.

Mr. Jackson also raised the issue in the article of VA "coverups" of crimes.

*Peninsula Times Tribune* editors consulted felt that they have carefully documented such "cover-up" cases, and said they have additional information not yet put into print.

Lending force to the allegation of "cover-ups" is a report by Chief Hoban that discusses his views of deficiencies in the VA police setup locally and nationwide. Hoban's repeated references to the need for a police system that cannot be controlled at the local level "to ensure that no collusion to squash or coverup an incident is perpetuated" indicates a concern about the possibility of censorship within the present system. When interviewed, Hoban said he knows of no such instance at the facilities in his charge.

There are two allegations which the GAO analysis faults the Inspector General's office with not investigating adequately. One is the "VA's failure to pursue legal action against employees and patients suspected of being involved in criminal activities." The other is an allegation of a $7 million coverup in the supply section books.

Also quoted in the *Enquirer* article was the statement of John Strickland, a former VA police officer, that VA police are assaulted "all the time."

A survey by the psychology division, covering February through April, 1979, reported 43 assaults by patients on staff members resulting in injuries. Division officials then instituted a "crisis intervention training program" for staff members and a similar survey for the same months this year showed only 14 injury-producing assaults.

A composite study of engineering division incident reports, workers' compensation reports and police reports came up with these figures for assaults—presumably the more serious assaults, not the day-to-day ward scuffles—for the period since 1977: August, 1977-July, 1978—34 assaults; August, 1978-July, 1979—36 assaults; August, 1979-July, 1980—21 assaults.

The GAO analysis of police officer injuries states that based on the Inspector General's study, medical center police sustained slightly less injuries per employee than the nursing, dietic, engineering and house-keeping employees considered as a group."

There was some anxiety expressed by Officer Al Brown of policing buildings at night with only a can of Mace for protection.

Ward staff members expressed concern by Mr. Thorwaldson for their safety, tempered with observations that they know they are working in a mental hospital. One of the safety problems cited several times was the increase in women hired as nursing aides. Hospital administrators agreed that this is a problem but said equal opportunity hiring requirements constrain the VA from insisting on strictly male aides.

Now for the national perspective:

As of December 31, 1979, VA provided care in 172 medical centers, 220 outpatient clinics, 92 nursing homes and 16 domiciliaries. There are 1.1 million inpatients, 15.5 million outpatients and nearly 200,000 employees at VA hospitals nationwide, plus millions of visitors yearly.

Providing a broader, albeit preliminary, picture of conditions at VA hospitals, Bill DeSarno, supervisory auditor at the GAO's VA audit site in Washington informed the Council staff of an in-progress GAO review of eleven medical centers in various parts of the country.

The review, begun at Congressional request, will evaluate allegations of crime, cover-ups, underreporting of crime, intervention in criminal investigations and other security-related questions about the VA medical system.

With the bulk of the field reports in, said Mr. DeSarno, the GAO is working to pull together its findings which should be available in the fall. Commenting on the progress of the investigations based on the raw data and stressing the tentative nature of the material, Mr. DeSarno said: "Basically, the situation isn't nearly as bad as what has been reported in the press. We have found no evidence of cover-ups. While there is a certain amount of crime, which is not surprising in psychiatric settings, most incidents are minor, like disturbances between employees and patients, petty theft and some drugs. There were very few serious crimes."

Mr. DeSarno said it is his understanding that, in general, the crime rate at VA hospitals has a direct correlation with the crime rate of the communities in which the hospitals are located. (The Menlo Park facility is in a high crime area.)

Asked about the attitude of VA police officers and media charges of frequent work-related injuries, Mr. DeSarno said that of those surveyed there was general contentment with the job and no evidence of greater injuries to VA police officers than any other VA hospital employee and that overall such injuries were minor. He added, however, that on the issue of carrying firearms, a majority of police officers interviewed felt it would be useful to have guns available or with them on the grounds surrounding VA facilities but not within the hospitals. Mr. DeSarno added that some officers felt "lucky" that they have never had "any really serious confrontation to require firearms" although the possibility of encountering a highly dangerous situation is very much on their minds.

Regarding press and governmental attention to conditions at the Menlo Park/Palo Alto facilities, Mr. DeSarno said that the two hospitals present "a unique problem," primarily because of their physical makeup and because of tensions between officers, including the police chief, and the hospitals' administrative staff.

On other charges contained in the *Enquirer* article, Mr. DeSarno commented:

The GAO to his knowledge has never had any indication or information to support the charge of prisoner recruitment by the VA;

The GAO cannot validate the estimate that 40 percent of VA patients have been convicted of crimes. It would involve a massive study of patient records, said Mr. DeSarno, something which has never been attempted, for any conclusion to be reached.

On the 40 percent estimate, Robert Putnam, VA public information officer, said "there is no way anyone can know this. The *Enquirer* simply took a statement from an uninformed source and used it as a fact." He said it is not legal "to ask people if they have ever been convicted of a crime before admission to a VA facility." Mr. Putnam said that as a group veterans comprise about 30 percent of the country's prison population.

The GAO first reported on shortcomings in the VA's control over drugs in 1975. In a June 24, 1980 follow-up report, the GAO stated that "millions of potentially dangerous drugs are vulnerable to pilferage and abuse . . . . The VA does not have any effective program for controlling the use of, or accounting for, drugs dispensed by many of its pharmacy units."

Currently, the report said, VA estimates of annual drug dollar losses is $17.4 million. Contributing to the problem, according to the GAO, are weak controls over VA prescription filling procedures and unused VA prescription pads that are readily accessible to unauthorized persons.

The GAO report did not involve the question of outside drugs introduced into VA facilities.

A reading of a VA Department of Medicine and Surgery memo of April 1980 on security and law enforcement disclosed apprehension over property thefts at VA hospitals. The memo, which went to the directors of VA medical centers across the country, stated that reported losses in government equipment and supplies exceeded $2.8 million in the last fiscal year and recommended increased police presence at nightfall and in parking lots at certain times of the day and night.

**Council finding:** Using sweeping assertions and offering no verification to readers, the *National Enquirer* constructed a story that likened VA hospitals to "chambers of horrors" and "criminal cesspools." The Council has been unable to unearth evidence to support such a blanket characterization.

There is some crime in VA hospitals, some dissension and occasional abuse within the system. There are also questions, not yet answered, of the reliability of VA-collected crime statistics.

But it is the Council's belief that the *Enquirer* article sensationalized, generalized, exaggerated and, in some cases, misrepresented the facts of crime in VA hospitals.

The Council finds the complaint warranted.

**Concurring:** Abel, Bell, Brady, Ghiglione, Huston, Isaacs, Lawson, Maynard, Pulitzer, Rusher and Williams.
September 18, 1980


### COMPLAINT NO. 179      (Filed: July 23, 1980)
### MILLER
### against
### CBS NEWS

**Complaint:** Dr. Robert W. Miller protested that in a "60 Minutes" segment CBS news unfairly pictured New York State Health Commissioner David Axelrod and the health department as negligent and uncaring in their response to warnings that toxic material in Love Canal might endanger more residents of the area than had been originally thought. Dr.

181

Miller is a former chairman of the Committee on Environmental Hazards of the American Academy of Pediatrics. He was supported in his complaint by Dr. Laurence Finberg, present chairman of the committee.

The broadcast was part of the "60 Minutes" show of May 25, 1980. It was narrated by Harry Reasoner and entitled, "Warning: Living Here May Be Hazardous to Your Health." Mr. Reasoner makes two assertions in the introduction. One is that there is still no agreement on how dangerous the Love Canal wastes are even though two years have passed since the discovery of the health hazard. The other assertion is that the State of New York had begun to fear that a costly precedent might be set if additional Love Canal residents were moved away at public expense without a clear showing that their health was in peril.

The program focuses on Beverly Paigen, a researcher at the Roswell Park Memorial Institute in Buffalo, NY, as the person who warned of new levels of danger. It focuses on Dr. Axelrod for response. Dr. Axelrod was state health commissioner at the time of the program. He was the state's chief environmental investigator at Love Canal in 1978.

Dr. Miller complained that Mr. Reasoner "disparaged" a 1978 health department report on the Love Canal crisis as a "fancy brochure," and did not describe its contents.

Dr. Miller complained further that Dr. Paigen "was presented as a knowledgeable investigator of human disease." He said that her competence is in the field of molecular biology, not in clinical medicine or epidemiology or public health, which he called "the areas of principal importance in studying the residents of the Love Canal."

Dr. Miller noted that Dr. Paigen played a part in what he called "the fiasco" of a leaked study report that there was an unusual number of damaged chromosomes among some residents of the Love Canal area. Dr. Miller said that the study in which Dr. Paigen participated with Dr. Dante J. Picciano, should have included a contemporary control group against which to measure the chromosome damage found among Love Canal residents. Dr. Miller wrote, "Clearly they should not have agreed to the study design, and by doing so, they contributed monumentally to the psychological disturbance among residents at the Love Canal."

Finally, Dr. Miller complained that Dr. Axelrod was portrayed in the program as having been "negligent" in that he did not evacuate families quickly enough from the danger area. He said that Dr. Axelrod "came off badly" and that Dr. Paigen "appeared to be a heroine."

**Response:** CBS defended the description of the brochure as "fancy" by noting that it was "on glossy stock, was printed and contained pictures."

The network denied that the program ignored the contents of the brochure. CBS pointed out that Reasoner says in the broadcast:

> It was a horror story, and the State of New York treated it like one. They declared a health emergency. At a cost of $10 million, the state bought 239 homes and permanently moved the people out of the first two rings around the vicious ditch. Then they put up a chain link fence around the area which was to define the limits of the danger.

"Obviously the brochure described the same steps Mr. Reasoner described," CBS said in its response.

CBS defended Dr. Paigen as "a very reputable environmental carcinogenecist whose work for the last five years has involved sophisticated use of the tools of epidemiology. A panel of scientists convened by HEW and EPA to examine her Love Canal studies not only did not challenge her competence, but, in the main, recommended following the leads suggested by her work."

As for Dr. Paigen's part in the chromosome study, CBS said that the study report contained its own warnings about the lack of a control group. CBS said further, "She, as much as anyone else, was appalled by the premature and inappropriate leak of the findings, having taken the position that it was a pilot study."

**Staff analysis:** A partial chronology may be helpful in analyzing the complaint:

April 25, 1978. New York State Health Department declares that a health hazard exists at Love Canal and orders various studies and protective actions.

August 9, 1978. State says it will evacuate at state expense some 236 families in the two rings of homes closest to the canal.

September, 1978. Health department publishes report to governor and legislature on what's been done in the four months since the discovery of a hazard.

February, 1979. State health department recommends that pregnant women and children under 2 be evacuated temporarily from an additional area outside the area that was previously cleared.

May 17, 1980. Pilot study for U.S. Environmental Protection Agency (EPA) suit against Hooker Chemicals and Plastics Corp. is leaked. It shows a higher number of damaged chromosomes among some residents of the Love Canal area than might normally be expected.

May 18, 1980. A study by Dr. Beverly Paigen and Dr. Stephen Barron, researcher at the medical school of the State University of New York at

Buffalo, reports nerve damage in a majority of 35 residents of the Love Canal area.

May 20, 1980. President Carter declares a federal emergency at Love Canal and agrees to provide federal funds for evacuation and temporary housing of 710 more families. Dr. Stephen J. Gage, director of research and development for the EPA says, "The last two studies have pushed us over the edge."

Gov. Hugh Carey complains that federal action is not enough; asks federal government to buy homes of the threatened families. Mr. Carey asks for a "valid and scientifically reliable study to follow up the findings" in the chromosome study. Dr. Axelrod says the chromosome study is "uninterpretable." (*New York Times,* P1A, May 22.)

May 25, 1980. "60 Minutes" shows "Warning: Living Here May Be Hazardous to Your Health."

June 4, 1980. Gov. Carey names panel of six physicians to "evaluate all medical and scientific data related to Love Canal, including studies done for the state and the federal EPA" and to report in 30 days. (The panel had not reported Sept. 11, 1980.)

July 31, 1980. Federal government agrees to provide $15 million in grants and loans to buy homes of the new evacuees at Love Canal.

** ** **

The brochure was a report to the governor and the legislature on the first four months of the Love Canal crisis. It was a 32-page booklet with a two-color cover prepared by state health department employees and printed by the state contract printer for 20 cents a copy, according to Frances Tarlton, executive assistant to Dr. Axelrod. The department prepares some 200 reports a year at an average of 50 cents a copy, she said.

** ** **

CBS calls Dr. Paigen a 'cancer research scientist' in the broadcast, and it describes her as an 'unpaid expert working with the Love Canal homeowners . . . .'

The description seems to be accurate. Dr. Paigen works for the state's Roswell Park Memorial Institute at Buffalo, a facility for cancer research and treatment. The job category for Dr. Paigen and for most other degreed people at Roswell Park is "cancer research scientist." She is at the highest level in that category.

Taking a broader look at her qualifications in the light of Dr. Miller's complaint, Dr. Paigen received her Ph.D. from the State University of New York at Buffalo in 1967. It was in biology. Since 1974 she has been

184

researching the biochemical basis for the genetic factors that make one person more vulnerable than another to chemicals in the environment.

She says she went to Love Canal in the summer of 1978 because she had heard that there were some families in which all the members were sick following exposure to the chemical wastes. If that were true, it might have provided her with a study group of people whose genetic characteristics predisposed them to harm from chemicals.

Dr. Paigen told the Council staff that she found the illnesses were related to geographical factors instead of familial factors; specifically that the illnesses were related to distance from the sites of exposure to the toxic wastes. Among other phenomena, Dr. Paigen said, she found a "whopping" increase above normal expectations for the number of miscarriages outside the previously circumscribed danger area. That finding contradicted the state's finding. Dr. Paigen told the staff that she went to Dr. Axelrod privately with her discovery. The following Friday, as indicated on the chronology and in the CBS broadcast, Dr. Axelrod did recommend that pregnant women and children under 2 move out of the next area outside the initial danger zone.

Dr. Axelrod acknowledged to Council staff that Dr. Paigen's work has been helpful, but, he said it had not "served as a substantive basis for any action taken by the health department."

As for an objective appraisal of Dr. Paigen's work, Dr. David Rall, director of the National Institute of Environmental Health Sciences, confirmed what Dr. Paigen said in the program about the reaction of a panel of epidemiologists to her studies.

> The top-notch panel of epidemiologists spent a day listening to me and my information and they spent a day listening to the Department of Health studies, and they came out and said that my data in—was substantial enough to warrant further studies.

Dr. Rall was chairman of the panel of epidemiologists to which Dr. Paigen refers. The panel was called together at the request of Rep. John LaFalce of New York to evaluate research on Love Canal. The panel heard Dr. Paigen April 12, 1979.

Does the program make Dr. Axelrod appear negligent?

Dr. Miller and Dr. Finberg say yes. Dr. Miller backed up his view in his letter to CBS with this contention: "In fact, with each new increment of medical information, outside scientists were consulted, and their advice was acted upon."

That process is demonstrated in the CBS program. Dr. Axelrod is shown in February, 1979, recommending that pregnant women and children under two move away from homes outside the area covered by his earlier recommendation. The program dwells at length on the fact that a blue ribbon panel did assess the state's research.

If Dr. Axelrod appears unsympathetic in the broadcast, it is not because of anything CBS did to him. It is the result of his having willingly accepted professional and legal restraints that prevent him from answering questions about the state research.

The key question is whether Dr. Axelrod is responding to political pressure in refusing to recommend further evacuations with the consequent public cost.

Reasoner asks Dr. Axelrod that question directly and Dr. Axelrod has ample opportunity to say no and to expand on his answer.

Dr. Axelrod was asked by Council staff if he thought the "60 Minutes" segment was unfair to him and his department. He replied through his executive assistant, Frances Tarlton, that he thought the program exhibited an "inappropriate bias in that it seemed a selective effort was made to put forward a political perspective rather than a presentation of factual evidence relating to the state's activities at Love Canal."

Dr. Axelrod told Ms. Tarlton that he would not have initiated a complaint against the broadcast despite his disappointment in its focus. Ms. Tarlton said she believed that Dr. Axelrod acknowledged the right of CBS to choose its own focus.

**Council finding:** The Council finds that Dr. Beverly Paigen was accurately described in the CBS "60 Minutes" segment, "Warning: Living Here May be Hazardous to Your Health" and that Dr. David Axelrod and the New York State Health Department were not characterized as negligent and uncaring. The complaint is found unwarranted.

**Concurring:** Abel, Bell, Brady, Ghiglione, Huston, Isaacs, Lawson, Maynard, McKay, Pulitzer, Rusher and Williams.
September 19, 1980.


**COMPLAINT NO. 180**    (Filed: July 18, 1980)
DRS. BARRETT and HERBERT
against
US MAGAZINE

**Complaint:** Stephen Barrett, M.D., and Victor Herbert, M.D., complained that an article in *US* magazine misled the public by giving the appearance of reliability of Dr. Kurt Donsbach and his Donsbach University School of Nutrition in Huntington Beach, Calif. Dr. Barrett is chairman of the Lehigh Valley Committee Against Health Fraud, Inc. in Allentown, Pa. Dr. Herbert is vice-chairman of the committee on public information of the American Institute of Nutrition.

The article appeared in *US* May 27, 1980, under the headline, "Maverick nutritionist Kurt Donsbach shatters diet myths." It says that Dr. Donsbach is dedicated to "promoting the truth and sifting out the chaff in nutritional information." It says that Dr. Donsbach holds Ph.D. degrees in nutrition and naturopathic medicine and that he has opened "the first—and so far only—university in the country dealing with the various aspects of nutrition."

The article says Dr. Donsbach's school "is licensed by the California department of post-secondary education and is authorized to grant degrees (B.S., M.S., and Ph.D.) in nutrition. In other words, it's the real thing, boasting a faculty of seven and a staff membership of 25 who function much like any other university professors, correcting lessons and evaluation papers."

Dr. Barrett in his complaint said that Dr. Donsbach's Ph.D. was not from an accredited school; that there is no such thing as a Ph.D. in naturopathy; that the description of Donsbach University as "the real thing" and the only university teaching nutrition is misleading, and that the faculty includes at least two members whose competence Dr. Barrett questions.

Dr. Barrett said the description of Dr. Donsbach's previous enterprise is inaccurate, and he says the article should have included the fact that Dr. Donsbach pleaded guilty to practicing medicine without a license. Dr. Barrett criticizes the article for what appears to him to be a suggestion that Dr. Donsbach's teaching was effective against multiple sclerosis in one of his students.

Dr. Barrett argued against the article's description of some of Dr. Donsbach's programs as "revolutionary" and against the article's statement that "MDs have neither the time nor background to determine whether a patient has nutritional deficiencies."

Dr. Barrett included with his complaint a pamphlet entitled "The Unhealthy Alliance," which is a chapter from a book entitled "The Health Robbers," edited by Dr. Barrett in 1980. The chapter discussed an organization called the National Health Federation (NHF) of which Dr. Donsbach is reported to be chairman. Dr. Barrett writes that the NHF lobbied against marketing rules proposed by the U.S. Food and Drug

Administration (FDA) to reduce public confusion about food supplements and health foods. Dr. Barrett writes in "The Unhealthy Alliance":

"The reason for NHF involvement in this issue is suggested by the backgrounds of its leaders. Many of them write or publish books and other materials which support unscientific health theories and practices. Many sell questionable 'health' products, and some have even been convicted of crimes while engaged in this kind of activity."

**Response:** Peter Callahan, president and publisher of *US*, turned the complaint over to an attorney, Michael Pantaleoni. Mr. Pantaleoni replied with a note saying that he had advised *US* not to respond to the Council because the matters raised in the complaint were in his views matters of "internal editorial discretion."

**Staff analysis:** The complaint boils down to a charge that *US* magazine gave unwarranted respectability to Dr. Donsbach and his school through factual errors, omissions and "use of words in ways that will clearly mislead the average reader."

Conventional wisdom cries out against the magazine's claims, but it is difficult to find objective criteria against which to test them. Discussing his own degrees, for example, Dr. Donsbach said the magazine article is factually wrong in saying that he has a Ph.D. in Naturopathy. The degree he does hold in that discipline is a Doctor of Naturopathy (D.N.), he said. The degree is from a now-defunct school and, therefore, impossible to check, but Dr. Donsbach noted (and the State of Oregon confirmed) that he is licensed as a naturopathic physician in that state. That would appear to give him the right to use D.N.

Western States College of Chiropractic in Portland, Ore., confirmed that Dr. Donsbach holds a doctor of chiropractic degree from that school. His Ph.D. in nutrition came from Union University in Los Angeles, Dr. Donsbach said. Robert Pfeiffer, the current president of Union, said he has seen the Ph.D. on Dr. Donsbach's wall, but that he has no record of Dr. Donsbach as a student. Dr. Donsbach replied that one of the reasons he left Union (where he was an administrator for a time) was that he had no confidence in the school's record-keeping.

M. T. Bogumill, fraud co-ordinator for the Food and Drug Section of the California Department of Health Services, confirmed that Dr. Donsbach pleaded guilty in 1971 to one count of practicing medicine without a license. He was charged with "prescribing vitamins, minerals and herbs as treatment for serious diseases." In 1973 Dr. Donsbach pleaded no contest to "selling, holding for sale, or offering for sale, new drugs without having the proper applications on file with either the State of

California or the U.S. Food and Drug Administration," Mr. Bogumill said. In 1974, Mr. Bogumill said, a municipal judge in West Orange County found Dr. Donsbach guilty of violating a condition of his probation on the 1973 charge, a condition requiring that he divest himself of all proprietary interest in a company called Westpro Labs.

Dr. Donsbach admitted his difficulties with the law. He said he had incorporated what he has learned from them into a course at Donsbach University called Jurisprudence of Nutrition Consultation. The questions that arise from those difficulties when assessing the *US* article are: Should they have been included: and, in view of the divestiture order, was it misleading to describe Dr. Donsbach's separation from the business as a "retirement"?

As for the magazine's claims about Donsbach University, the description of its status with the State of California is correct with the minor exception of the word, "licensed." The university is not licensed, but it is "authorized" to grant degrees. Section 94310C of the California Education Code provides that an institution may be authorized by the Office of Private Post-Secondary Education to grant degrees upon filing a statement that it meets certain financial requirements and has a curriculum and a faculty, according to John Peterson of the post-secondary education office. The state does not evaluate institutions in the authorized status, Mr. Peterson said. To be evaluated, an institution must apply for another status in which it is "approved" to grant degrees. (An approved institution must apply to regional or national bodies, not the state, for the "accredited" status to which most schools aspire.) Some 170 of California's approximately 400 degree-granting institutions are in the "authorized" status with Donsbach University, Mr. Peterson said. Donsbach does not have the option of applying for approved status yet, according to Frances Louie of the post-secondary office; the school was authorized January 2, 1979, and has not had time to establish the track record necessary for evaluation, he said.

Peterson spontaneously gave evidence of the intensity of feeling among critics and supporters of Dr. Donsbach. He said, "Dr. Donsbach is well respected in many circles. He is as well known as anybody in the United States in his field. The fact that he can put out so much so fast bothers a lot of people."

To provide standards against which to measure the education—as opposed to the credentialing—of Donsbach University, Dr. Myron Winick, director of the Institute for Human Nutrition at Columbia University Medical School, suggested that Council staff compare the requirements for the M.S. in nutrition with the requirements for the same degree at a conventional university. The M.S., said Dr. Winick, is the degree held by dietician-nutritionists. Dietician-nutritionists are the health professionals who, when they are teamed with medical doctors, do provide the background to evaluate and advise on nutritional deficiencies. The *US* article said that medical doctors do not have that background. (There is an element of truth in that statement, said Dr. Winick, but it is a distortion of that truth to suggest that practitioners without medical training might be better equipped.)

Dr. Donsbach lists 10 courses in a core curriculum that must be completed for the bachelor's degree at his school. He said the courses could be completed in 11 months under the school's new outreach program. Outreach involves meeting for two full days a month with faculty from Donsbach University. When the core curriculum is complete, it might take nine months to complete the combined master's and Ph.D. program, Dr. Donsbach said. The time would depend on how adaptive was the student to home study. (Tuition for the B.S. program, incidentally, is $1,495, which covers books and study guides. The M.S. cost $1,695 and the Ph.D. $2,195. All three may be combined for $3,795.)

The titles of the courses in the core curriculum at Donsbach University are Introduction to Chemistry, Physiology of Nutrition I and II; Food and Nutrition Principles I and II, Principles of Nutrition and Disease, Dietary Management, Jurisprudence of Nutrition Consultation and Nutrition and Health Care Management. A sample program for the master's degree consists of Pediatric Nutrition, Psycho-nutrition, Geriatric Nutrition, General Nutrition and a thesis. A sample program for the doctorate consists of four more courses in general nutrition and a doctoral dissertation.

By contrast, the B.S. program in Nutrition and Dietetics at the University of Minnesota requires general undergraduate courses in areas described as "Communication, Language, Symbolic Systems," "Man and Society" and "Artistic Expression." The physical and biological science prerequisites to the major are: two courses in General Chemistry; Elementary Organic Chemistry with a laboratory course; General Biology; Biochemistry with a laboratory course; General Microbiology and Human Physiology.

Courses required in the major are: Sociocultural Aspects of Nutrition; Principles of Nutrition; Food Chemistry with a lab; Experimental Foods; Principles of Food Purchasing; Food and Nutrition in the Life Cycle;

General Seminar; Human Nutrition; Clinical Nutrition with lab; Pathology and Clinical Medicine for Allied Health Students I and II and Management. Also required are 4-5 credits in sociology or anthropology; three credits in the psychology of learning, and 3-5 credits in statistics or computer usage.

In addition the student must complete requirements in one of the five following areas of emphasis: General Dietetics; Therapeutic and Clinical Dietetics; Community Nutrition; Nutrition Science, or a program including field experience. Finally the student must take electives sufficient to provide 185 credits.

The master's program at Minnesota requires 20 quarter credits in the major field and a minimum of eight in one or more related fields plus a thesis. (An alternative program without the thesis requirement demands 44 quarter credits and an investigative project.) The Ph.D. program requires nine quarters (three years) of course work plus preliminary oral examination, a thesis and a final oral examination.

A bachelor's degree at Minnesota normally requires four years of study; a master's two more and a Ph.D. three more, according to Kim Goodfellow in the Department of Food Science and Nutrition. Using the current $385 per-quarter estimate for tuition for Minnesota residents, that comes to $4,620 for a B.S., $2,310 additional for the M.S. and $3,465 additional for the Ph.D., a total of $10,395 in tuition for the Ph.D.

To discuss other elements raised tangentially in the complaints—the claim that Dr. Donsbach's teaching helped a victim of multiple sclerosis, for example, or the suggestion that megavitamins may be effective against heroin addiction—would require extensive research and would not help in making a judgment on the central issues.

The *US* article allows the reader to believe that the degrees held by Dr. Donsbach and offered by his university are comparable with degrees offered by more conventional schools. Even Dr. Donsbach does not make that claim. He says in his catalogue that his program is for people "who desire a degree but do not want to spend the great amount of money and time involved in going to college." He calls his method "alternative education." He says it is based on home study. He says in his application to the post-secondary education office that the program is designed for the person who "in all probability will never re-enter the education mainstream of on-campus classes." He says the program is designed to let such people "receive a credential in their chosen field with a minimum of inconvenience."

In short Dr. Donsbach makes no pretense that his university is what is conventionally considered "the real thing." If the magazine had quoted from Dr. Donsbach's own material it would have been on solid ground. The only criticism that could have been raised would have been from people who disagree with Dr. Donsbach. Instead the article leaves itself open to being judged misleading.

**Council finding:** The complaint is basically that *US* magazine made Dr. Donsbach and his university appear to meet conventional standards that even Dr. Donsbach does not claim for himself or his school. The Council finds the complaint warranted.

**Concurring:** Abel, Bell, Brady, Ghiglione, Huston, Isaacs, Lawson, Maynard, McKay, Pulitzer, Rusher and Williams.
September 19, 1980

## COMPLAINT NO. 181      (Filed May 9, 1980)
### DOCTORS OUGHT TO CARE (DOC)
### against
### NBC NEWS

**Complaint:** Alan Blum, M. D., president of "Doctors Ought to Care, Inc.," a non-profit organization headquartered in Chicago, complained that a segment on NBC News' "Prime Time Saturday" on February 9, dealing with fires and fire deaths attributed to inflammable polyurethane furniture, "ignored the central issue of the polyurethane fire controversy—smouldering cigarettes . . . ."

Dr. Blum contended that the NBC News report was inaccurate and unfair when it placed the blame for such fire deaths on the furniture makers rather than on "the real cause of home fire deaths—the chemical-laden cigarette . . . ." He called attention to two bills in Congress, known as the "Cigarette Safety Act," which he said state "quite clearly that 'the careless use of smoking materials is the leading cause of fire-related death and injury in residences in the United States.'" Both bills, Dr. Blum said, were ignored on the program.

**Staff analysis:** Noting that Dr. Blum's complaint dealt almost solely with charges that NBC News had omitted references to smouldering cigarettes as a cause of residential fire deaths, the Council's staff examined the NBC News segment. It noted that the report did not attempt to absolve cigarettes; that it reported with vigor on the role of cigarettes in many fires. The thrust of the report, as determined by NBC News' reporters and editors, was directed toward the dangers related to untreated polyurethane

192

furniture. Included were references to long delays on the part of the federal Consumer Product Safety Commission in promulgating standards calling for the addition of a fire retardant chemical to the other chemicals which make polyurethane. The cost factor was included, with one manufacturer of the retardant concluding that it would be 50 cents to make a chair safer than it is without the retardant.

**Council finding:** After careful examination of the program's transcript, the Council concluded that while the complaint was well motivated, the protest could only be considered one that sought to change the reporting thrust. NBC News was on sound journalistic ground in centering on the dangers arising from untreated polyurethane furniture.

The complaint is unwarranted.

**Concurring:** Abel, Bell, Benson, Brady, McKay, Miller, Pulitzer, Rusher, Scott and Williams.

**Abstaining:** Salant.

September 19, 1980

## COMPLAINT NO. 182     (Filed May 17, 1980)
### THE REV. LYNN BERGFALK
### against
### THE NEW YORKER

**Complaint:** The Rev. Lynn Bergfalk, pastor of First Baptist Church of Fairfield, Iowa, complained that an article in *The New Yorker* March 24, 1980, "projects false and disparaging impressions of our congregation as sponsors of the Yang family," and that the magazine did not give him an opportunity to reply to the article.

The *New Yorker* article by Calvin Trillin was headlined, "U.S. Journal, Fairfield, Iowa—Resettling the Yangs." The Yangs are from the Hmong tribe in the highlands of Laos. Theng Pao Yang arrived in Fairfield Dec. 1, 1979, with his wife, Yi Ly, daughter, Bay, and three other children. Seven weeks later, on the evening of Jan. 22, 1980, one of the Baptist sponsors stopped by with a bundle of clean laundry, and, as Mr. Trillin reported, "He found Yi Ly distraught. Her son, So, was lying on the living-room sofa. The boy's eyes were closed. He was cold to the touch. Theng Pao and Bay seemed to be moaning or grieving in the bedroom."

Theng Pao and six-year-old Bay were taken to the hospital by ambulance seriously injured. Eight-year-old So was pronounced dead at the scene. In the basement of the house, Mr. Trillin reported, "Some of the

Yangs' possessions were on the floor: five dollars in American bills that had been cut up with scissors, a Hmong flute that had been shattered, a knife whose blade had been broken. Over a pipe, there were six cords with nooses tied in them."

Yi Ly, who spoke no English, told several stories, first in sign language and then to a Hmong interpreter. The story that investigators came to believe, *The New Yorker* reported, "was that the entire Yang family, upon the decision of Theng Pao and with the acquiescence of Yi Ly, had tried to commit suicide—with the parents hanging the children who were too young to hang themselves. Apparently, Yi Ly had changed her mind at the last minute, and had finally managed to cut everyone down—too late for So."

Mr. Trillin went to Fairfield three weeks after the hanging. He wrote about the impact on the community of the incident and the grand jury investigation that followed it. The *New Yorker's* March 24 article was reprinted in the *Des Moines Sunday Register* April 13.

Mr. Bergfalk complained to the News Council that the article "contains statements and insinuations which are demonstrably false as well as more subtle distortions" that "called into question" the good name of the church. Specifically, he wrote in an article that appeared in part in the *Des Moines Sunday Register* May 4:

> The *New Yorker* article neglects to mention that First Baptist has assisted six refugee families in resettlement during the last decade, beginning with a Cuban family in 1970. Three families from Burma, which shares its eastern border with Thailand and Laos, have remained in the community and are active members of the church . . . .
>
> What puzzles us at First Baptist is not so much that *The New Yorker* article chooses to ignore the church's past record of refugee work in human need, but a series of factual blunders that generate a false impression of our sponsorship of the Yangs. Unnamed sources suggest that we may have "smothered the Yangs or treated them like pets." Mr. Trillin not only allows that degrading, paternalistic insinuation to stand unquestioned but reinforces it with a catalogue of factual errors.
>
> Under the question of "what the Baptists might have done wrong," Trillin raises "the possibility that Theng Pao's self-respect was threatened when he saw his wife carted off here and there without his permission." The fact is that Mrs. Yang went nowhere unaccompanied by her husband, let alone without his permission. Even trips to the doctor and dentist were scheduled as family appointments. The article states the wife, Yi Ly, "was taken to the beauty parlor for a haircut and the doctor for a checkup." But she never went to a beauty parlor, and only went to the doctor in the company of her family. The article suggests possibly the Yangs were insulted at "having other people decide when a haircut was advisable." In fact, Yi Ly did have her hair cut—at her own request, in the home of another Asian refugee . . . .
>
> Besides the factual errors and insinuations about our sponsorship of the Yangs,

*The New Yorker* contains other distortions. It reports how sponsorship of refugees by Fairfield churches "quickly turned ecumenical." Only the Baptists—apparently—failed to act in concert with other churches: "Even with an ecumenical minister in ecumenical times, First Baptist has stood a bit apart."

What Mr. Trillin has done is create a double falsehood which impugns the good will and long-standing ecumenical commitment of First Baptist, while at the same time supposing a conscious level of cooperation among other sponsors which never existed. Persons involved say they were not aware of any group consultation such as implied by *The New Yorker*. Lutheran pastor Keith Lingwall is grateful for a combination of circumstances and the friendship between Lao families in Fairfield which served to draw sponsors together on an informal level of personal contact. But he says this development happened "after the fact" rather than by design or as a result of any formal ecumenical cooperation.

The idea of a conscious ecumenical effort by refugee sponsors would be a harmless enough misreading of facts if it were not used to set up a false contrast with the Baptists. Assertions that "First Baptist has stood a bit apart"—or that "there remain limitations on the Baptists' ecumenical participation, and there remains in the minds of Fairfield Christians some residue of the old notion that Baptists tend to go their own way"—simply fly in the face of obvious fact. The church's record of community involvement and unwavering participation in ecumenical events speaks for itself. Keith Lingwall of the Lutheran church, who was among those interviewed when Trillin visited Fairfield in February, called the comments in *The New Yorker* a "bum rap" and said the author "drew an absolutely false deduction in suggesting limitations in First Baptist's ecumenical involvement . . . ."

Why *The New Yorker* utterly disregards our church's established reputation I don't know; it is an injustice to our congregation and only serves to create an artificial backdrop for the reports of "hard feelings" among churches sponsoring refugees which subsequently are introduced into the article.

Later Trillin uses an episode which never happened to further highlight this theme of "conflict." "When Lynn Bergfalk and Keith Lingwall (the Lutheran pastor) arrived at the grand-jury investigation of the death of So Yang," Trillin reports, "they exchanged perfunctory greetings and then sat silently outside the jury-deliberation room." On the day this incident occurred I happened only to run into Lingwall in a hallway of the courtroom, after I had been waiting nearly two hours to testify to the grand jury. We exchanged greetings before conversing with other persons who had been involved in the hearing. At no time did we sit together in silence.

Mr. Bergfalk also complained in his article in the *Register* that Mr. Trillin interviewed him three weeks after the tragedy but reached back to a newspaper report at the time of the crisis for a comment on the issue that caused community division. That issue was a report that the Yangs had attempted suicide because of a threat from one of the Lowland Laotians that they would kill Theng Pao, parcel out the children to the other Laotian families, and give Yi Ly to a Laotian widower for his wife. The *New Yorker* article said:

To Lynn Bergfalk, it was the first explanation that made sense. "The whole situation, from my perspective, is that the hanging is totally inexplicable unless there was an external factor like a death threat," he told the local paper. "They were a happy family, with no reason to do something like this."

Mr. Bergfalk complained that "in lifting my quotation from the original news story, Trillin unfortunately ignores the context of the article and also the context of the events, which had changed considerably by the time he visited Fairfield."

Mr. Bergfalk raised an additional complaint in a letter to the Council Oct. 18. He quotes the *New Yorker* article as saying, "When Lynn Bergfalk, the pastor of the First Baptist Church, walked into the daily English class with the Yangs, it was the first the other sponsors had heard about the Baptists' sponsoring a refugee family."

Mr. Bergfalk wrote:
This statement is totally false. Our sponsorship of the Yangs was discussed informally with pastors and members of other churches and two other Laotian families and some of their sponsors were contacted about the Yangs on the day of their arrival in Fairfield. (Also it should be pointed out that the Yangs arrived "unexpectedly" about a month earlier than we had planned, and if I remember correctly, only three to four weeks after it was confirmed that we would sponsor their family. Given that time frame, our interaction with other sponsors was certainly as much as could have been expected.)

Mr. Bergfalk said further that members of two, and possibly all three, of the other Laotian families were in the Yangs' home on the day of their arrival in Fairfield, days before the Yangs went to English class. Mr. Bergfalk wrote, "I think it should also be pointed out that this error is central to the whole context and the deliberate 'setting off' of the Baptists from the other churches who sponsored refugees."

Mr. Bergfalk wrote in a letter of complaint to *The New Yorker* that both he and Mr. Lingwall were asked by the magazine's checking department about points that he now disputes. "I was asked if Yi Ly was ever taken to a beauty parlor," Mr. Bergfalk wrote. "I said 'no' but yet found this error not only included in the article, but buttressing the insinuation of paternalistic attitudes toward the Yangs by our congregation." Furthermore, he wrote, "Keith Lingwall said he twice told your checker that he felt Mr. Trillin's statements about First Baptist 'standing apart' were inaccurate, and yet these statements remained in the article unchallenged."

Mr. Bergfalk complained about *The New Yorker*'s treatment of his challenges to the article. In his first letter to the News Council he wrote, "Since the magazine does not even have a letters-to-the-editor department, I am bringing my complaint to the National News Council, and asking for your assistance."

Mr. Bergfalk said he called *The New Yorker* as soon as the March 24 issue appeared and raised his objections with the checker who had talked with him before publication. He said he assumed that his complaints were to be taken under consideration and was, therefore, disappointed when the article appeared unchanged in the *Des Moines Sunday Register* April 13. Mr. Bergfalk said he phoned *The New Yorker* again and was assured that an editor would call him back early in the week of April 21. When he had not heard anything by May 6, he wrote to *The New Yorker* that he would appeal to the News Council unless he received a satisfactory response by May 13. Mr. Bergfalk's complaint to the Council is dated May 17. After mailing it, he received a letter from Robert Bingham, executive editor of *The New Yorker,* dated May 16 and saying that Mr. Bingham was satisfied that the article was accurate.

**Response:** *The New Yorker* responded to Mr. Bergfalk May 16 with the following letter:

> Dear Mr. Bergfalk,
>
> We are sorry that you did not like Calvin Trillin's article "Resettling the Yangs," but we cannot agree that it contains what you call "factual errors and false impressions." Mr. Trillin is an experienced reporter with an indefatigable insistence on accuracy, and his work was carefully verified by our Checking Department. In this checking process, we got in touch with a number of people aside from you, and I must tell you that we were satisfied—and are satisfied—that the report is accurate. Indeed, many of the points you raise seem to have to do with the subjective interpretation of facts, on which opinions will certainly differ in such a matter. You have written your article from your point of view, and I wish to thank you for letting us have a chance to read it. But Mr. Trillin set himself the task of reporting on an event and the reactions to it throughout the community, and we believe that he did it justice.
>
> Sincerely yours,
>
> Robert Bingham
> Executive Editor

Mr. Bingham has been courteous and helpful to the Council's staff since his telephoned response to Executive Director William Arthur's letter July 16. On the matter of alleged errors, his attitude is expressed in this paragraph from a letter to the Council Oct. 31:

> When all the talk about "errors" (plural) is sifted, we come down to the matter of whether or not Yi Ly "was taken to the beauty parlor for a haircut." We tried hard to check this, and Trillin was certainly told that that's what happened, but it may be

197

wrong. If it *is* wrong, how seriously does it undermine the validity of the article? We think very little.

Mr. Bingham said he didn't know whether Theng Pao "saw his wife carted off here and there without his permission" or whether "other people" did decide "when a haircut was advisable." Both allegations were among speculations that Mr. Trillin heard in Fairfield about what may have contributed to the Yang tragedy he said.

Mr. Bingham, said *The New Yorker* was satisfied that the incident involving Mr. Bergfalk and the Lutheran pastor outside the grand-jury room was correctly reported.

In answer to a staff question, Mr. Bingham reported that *The New Yorker* has published four corrections in 18 years as follows: July 14, 1980, the name of the French magazine, *La Vie;* March 12, 1979, acknowledgement that a slice of turbot eaten in a New York restaurant had not been frozen; April 8, 1967, a three-column reply from a translator to criticism from a Soviet author whose work she had translated; and May 5, 1962, a denial by the mayor of Bradentown, Fla., that seating was segregated racially at a spring-training ball park.

Mr. Bingham said in a followup letter:

> The list of corrections we've printed may seem risible when you look at it. But I would stress that if the list is a short one and the issues minor, it is not because we have refused to admit gross distortions. No one has accused us of any gross distortions. We work very hard to get our facts right and to be fair.

Mr. Bingham said in an interview that *The New Yorker* editors did not consider the alleged errors in the Trillin story serious enough to warrant correction. "It would be different if he (Mr. Bergfalk) were seriously wronged or if the material were importantly untrue," he said. "We have had no complaints from anyone except the one person who might be expected to be embarrassed." Mr. Bingham stressed his view that "we are dealing with subjective views of the situation." The article was not, in his view, a "judgmental piece;" it was a piece "pointing out the irony of people wanting to correct an evil but not knowing how to help."

The discussion of fact with Mr. Bingham led naturally to a discussion of the interpretation of facts, and whether *The New Yorker* ought to publish letters from people like Mr. Bergfalk who might dispute *The New Yorker*'s interpretation. Mr. Bingham said the magazine did not feel the obligation of a newspaper to print all sides of an issue or to publish the opposition viewpoint. "But," he said, "that may be a mistake."

He said he could see how Council members might be critical of the magazine's reluctance to publish letters taking issue with *The New Yorker*'s reporting, particularly since the magazine does publish barbed comments about errors in other publications. Mr. Bingham made the same point that Dick Cavett made last spring in an interview with Mr. Trillin: Given the readership of *The New Yorker*, the magazine would probably get some excellent letters. However, he said, the magazine's editors were not about to start publishing such letters with Mr. Bergfalk's, because to do so would make "too big a deal" out of a complaint that the editors did not consider warranted. To publish a letter from Mr. Bergfalk might have made it appear that the magazine and the reporter were backing off from the reporting, Mr. Bingham said.

**Staff analysis:** Mr. Bergfalk's complaint divides into three parts: First, he makes eight specific criticisms of the article. Second, he charges that Mr. Trillin exploited negative aspects of the tragedy and reported hard feelings that did not exist. Third, he complains that *The New Yorker* should have provided him an opportunity to answer in print the implied criticism of him and his congregation.

Dealing first with the specific criticisms:

1. That the article ignored First Baptist's past work with refugees.

This is not entirely true. The article does note that First Baptist sponsored a Burmese technician and his wife who immigrated in 1975.

2. That Mr. Trillin reported incorrectly that Theng Pao "saw his wife carted off here and there without his permission."

The sentence in which the clause appears reads as follows:

> There are expressions of compassion in Fairfield for the anguish the Baptists must have suffered over the death of So Yang, but there is also talk about what the Baptists might have done wrong—the possibility that they "smothered" the Yangs or treated them like pets, the possibility that Theng Pao's self-respect was threatened when he saw his wife carted off here and there without his permission, the possibility that the Yangs were insulted rather than pleased at having their laundry done for them or having other people decide when a haircut was advisable.

The sentence has four elements in it: smothered, carted off, laundry and haircut. Smothered is introduced with the words, "possibility that they were." It is, therefore, clear that it is not an accepted fact that the Yangs were smothered. The three other elements seem to be listed as facts. The fact that other people did do the Yangs' laundry is reported elsewhere in the article. When the questions of carting off and deciding about haircuts are listed in the same construction, it gives them the aura of facts. Two families who were close to the Yangs in Fairfield (the John Heckenbergs and the John BaTins) make it seem unlikely that Yi Ly was carted off without Theng Pao's permission. Mrs. BaTin says that Yi Ly asked for her first haircut and Mrs. Heckenberg says Yi Ly asked to have her hair set by the Heckenbergs' daughter on the day of So's funeral. *New Yorker* editor Robert Bingham said the magazine simply does not know whether Yi Ly was carted off or whether others decided when a haircut was necessary. The magazine's intention was to list those elements as part of the community speculation. The failing, then, is one of construction, not reporting.

3. That Mr. Trillin reported incorrectly that Yi Ly "was taken to the beauty parlor for a haircut."

The complainant is right. Rosabelle BaTin, a Burmese woman resettled in Fairfield under the sponsorship of First Baptist, told a Council staff member that she cut Yi Ly's hair in the BaTin's house. "She came here and asked," Ms. BaTin said.

4. That *The New Yorker* incorrectly supposed a "conscious ecumenical effort" among refugee sponsors.

This does not seem to be a valid criticism of the article. The writer uses the word "ecumenical" in a broad sense, and he describes specifically the informal nature of the relationship among individuals of various denominations dealing with refugee sponsorship.

5. That the article was incorrect to say, "Even with an ecumenical pastor in ecumenical times, First Baptist has stood a bit apart."

It was on this statement that the Rev. Keith Lingwall, pastor of the Lutheran church, said First Baptist got "a bum rap." Mr. Lingwall told a Council staff member that he insisted to a *New Yorker* checker that the statement was wrong; that the checker called him back after consulting with Mr. Trillin and said that Mr. Trillin considered the statement correct despite Mr. Lingwall's protests. This point is an important one for members and friends of First Baptist, because they believe that their church has been more open to ecumenical participation than many other American Baptist congregations. The Fairfield Area Ministerial Alliance, of which Mr. Bergfalk is a former president, passed unanimously a resolution recording its "conviction—in light of an article in *The New Yorker* magazine, reprinted in the *Des Moines Register,* concerning the refugee tragedy in our community—that the First Baptist Chruch has consistently demonstrated its ecumenical concern and readiness to participate in community cooperation." Larry W. Johnson, managing editor of the *Fairfield Ledger*, said the suggestion that there was a division before the hanging was wrong. "He (Trillin) may have seen the division after the fact as existing before," Mr. Johnson said.

For all the protestations that First Baptist was ecumenically open, however, Mr. Lingwall, who twice told a *New Yorker* checker that its statement was wrong, told a Council staff member, "But I think that in the refugee question, there could be a case made (for First Baptist being less ecumenical than other sponsoring churches), and I, for one, would have desired it, because they had more experience than anyone else. On the other hand, I didn't ask." Mr. Lingwall added there was little interaction among the Baptist and the other sponsors after the Yangs came to Fairfield, until the crisis.

Clearly it is a matter of opinion how ecumenical First Baptist of Fairfield was before the Yang tragedy. The weight of opinion after the *New Yorker* article seems to be that the congregation was strongly ecumenical. Mr. Trillin had every right to reach and report a different conclusion. It is significant that he stuck to that conclusion despite a challenge before publication. The real question is, should people who were deeply affected by Mr. Trillin's conclusion have an opportunity to reply with an opposite conclusion.

6. That Mr. Trillin reported incorrectly that Mr. Bergfalk and Mr. Lingwall "exchanged perfunctory greetings and then sat silently outside the jury-deliberation room of the Jefferson County courthouse."

To the extent that the report implies that the two clergymen sat silently together, it is wrong. Mr. Bergfalk said, and Mrs. Lucille Taylor, one of the Methodist sponsors, confirmed that Mr. Lingwall and Mr. Bergfalk did not wait in the same room. However, Mrs. Taylor confirmed the suggestion that tension between Mr. Bergfalk and the non-Baptist sponsors was manifest in the waiting period. "I felt strange because we were not conversing," said Mrs. Taylor, who waited in the room with Mr. Bergfalk. "My heart just ached for (Bergfalk) because of what they had gone through, I wanted to comfort him, but that was not the place to do it." Mr. Lingwall made a similar point. He said *The New Yorker*'s description may have been wrong in specifics, but, "From my perspective it was a true picture. I felt very uncomfortable in Lynn's presence."

7. That Mr. Trillin used a quote from an old newspaper story to demonstrate Mr. Bergfalk's acceptance of the theory that a lowland Laotian may have threatened Theng Pao.

This does not seem to be a valid complaint. Mr. Trillin makes clear in his article that Mr. Bergfalk's quote came at the time the theory became public and that Mr. Bergfalk's acceptance of the possibility of a threat antagonized sponsors of the Laotian families.

8. That the other sponsors did not know of the Baptists' plans to

201

sponsor a family until Mr. Bergfalk walked into English class with the Yangs. Sponsors of two of the families knew. Sponsors of the third did not. The statement is not absolutely correct. But Barbara Hill, the English teacher, was surprised that the family came to class so soon after their arrival. And there may have been less advance notice of their arrival, partly because, as Mr. Bergfalk points out, they arrived sooner than they were expected, and partly because the local newspaper was no longer writing stories in advance of the arrival of each new refugee family.

The second part of Mr. Bergfalk's complaint is best expressed in this sentence from the response he submitted to the *Des Moines Sunday Register:*

> Trillin chooses to exploit some negative dimensions of a complex situation; that is his prerogative, but not at the expense of accuracy. Reporting "hard feelings" is one thing, creating them is another.

In a letter to Council staff Oct. 18, Mr. Bergfalk said, "Personally, I feel that the alleged feelings of ill will particularly among sponsors reported by *The New Yorker* are basically the creation of Mr. Trillin."

Dan Shepherd, moderator of First Baptist, told a Council staff member that he was not conscious of criticism of the Baptists' handling of the Yangs or of a division in the community. Yet he recalled that Mr. Lingwall was "hyper" when he talked to Mr. Bergfalk about Mr. Bergfalk's acceptance of the theory that a lowland Laotian had threatened Theng Pao.

Edwin Kelley, Jefferson County prosecuting attorney, told a Council staff member that people "chose up sides" after the tragedy. It was as if "they were running for a lifeboat," he said. Mr. Kelly said he felt pressure from Mr. Bergfalk to "do something" about the lowland Laotians, who he believed had threatened Theng Pao. Mr. Kelley said he felt pressure from Mr. Lingwall to "do something" about Hmong visitors from other parts of Iowa, who he feared might have come for retribution against the other Laotians.

Fairfield residents told Council staff that English classes were suspended; police patrols were alerted, and, as Mr. Trillin reported, sponsors sat with the wives and children of lowland Laotian families while husbands worked night shifts.

Colleen Shearer, director of the Iowa Department of Job Services and of the Iowa Refugee Service Center, knew that there was tension between groups over the threat theory and speculation in Fairfield about what the Baptists might have done wrong. She and Marvin Weidner, director of the refugee service center, heard it from staff members they sent to Fairfield to provide translation and background on Hmong culture.

Mrs. Taylor, the Methodist woman whose heart ached for Mr. Bergfalk was nonetheless "really upset that they (the Baptists) believe the story" that Laotians under her church's sponsorship might have threatened Theng Pao. Her voice tightened as late as November when she recalled saying to the Methodist congregation the Sunday after the threat theory became public, "I hope I live to see justice."

Su Thao, Hmong interpreter from the Iowa Refugee Service Center, recalls that Mr. Lingwall interrupted a spontaneous conversation between Su Thao and one of the lowland Laotians outside the grand jury hearing and hurried the Laotian away. Mr. Lingwall does not recall the specific incident, but says it is typical of the kind of thing that happened during the tense period immediately after the hangings. Those tensions diminished as the community "healed," said Mr. Lingwall. Mr. Trillin was in Fairfield three weeks after the incident. "If he had come two weeks later, he would have written a different story," Mr. Lingwall said.

The third part of Mr. Bergfalk's complaint involves *The New Yorker*'s refusal to either correct those elements in the report that were incorrect or to publish a response in which he could take issue with Mr. Trillin's interpretations.

Mr. Lingwall spoke of the healing process that had taken place in the community. He said neither Mr. Bergfalk nor First Baptist had been "hurt" in their community standing by the events themselves. But some saw in the Trillin article what Richard Whitaker referred to as the "smell" of criticism of First Baptist. Whitaker, coordinator of communications and publications for the Refugee Service Center, urged Mr. Bergfalk not to respond. He and Mr. Weidner, manager of the refugee center, thought a response would give more publicity to the matter than was warranted. Nonetheless, Mr. Weidner helped Mr. Bergfalk obtain a statement from the Iowa Joint Volunteer Agencies that First Baptist had been a good sponsor to the Yangs. The statement was for use in Mr. Bergfalk's response to the Trillin article.

Mr. Shepherd, moderator of First Baptist, provided insight into why Mr. Bergfalk has persisted in his quest for some reply to *The New Yorker* article. "I said the errors reflect on the Lord, and therefore, I encouraged him," said Mr. Shepherd. "If this thing isn't pursued, how do we know it won't happen again?"

The *Des Moines Sunday Register* published Mr. Bergfalk's response in keeping with its policy of granting space to "the other side." Mr.

Bingham, the *New Yorker* editor, said he does not feel the same obligation as a newspaper might to print the other side. Fairfield Managing Editor Johnson thinks that the major defect in the magazine's handling of the story lies in its reluctance to print a response. He said, "If they are going to take the responsibility for doing that kind of story, then there has to be some give and take."

**Council finding:** Calvin Trillin and *The New Yorker* ventured much in the Yang article. They delved into an emotional crisis in an intimate community. The gain was great. The article forced an insight into refugee problems upon a national audience which has a stake in resettlement.

The article dug more deeply into the emotions of individuals than articles in regional newspapers had done. It was a delicate task, and despite the considerable reporting and editing skills brought to the task, the magazine made some mistakes: It reported that Mrs. Yang was taken to a beauty parlor; apparently she was not. A sentence was structured in such a way that Mr. Trillin appeared to report that the refugee family was carted about without the husband's permission and that others decided when a haircut was advisable. These statements are probably not true, and the magazine intended only to list them as what people in the community were saying. Another sentence suggested that two clergymen sat together in hostile silence outside a grand jury room. The sentence is wrong to the extent that the men did not sit together. The article reported incorrectly that none of the other sponsoring families knew of the Baptists' refugee family until the Yangs walked into English class.

None of the defects taken singly or together twists *The New Yorker*'s correct report that the Yang tragedy caused agonies of soul-searching, fear and anger in Fairfield and that it left an agony of frustration because the cause of the tragedy may never be known.

Mr. Trillin reported that First Baptist Church stood a bit apart from the ecumenicity of other churches in Fairfield. The reporter held to that opinion despite a challenge before publication, but the opinion appears to be subject to dispute. One view of the combined effect of the opinion on First Baptist's ecumenicity and of the minor errors about the congregation's handling of the Yangs is provided in the following passage by the Rev. Wayne Bartruff in *The Herald* of his First United Methodist church in Fairfield: "It seems to present Lynn and his congregation either as dummies or non-cooperative with other churches or paternalistic."

*The New Yorker* was slow to respond to the protest of the Rev. Lynn Bergfalk about the article. The response did not deal with the specifics of Mr. Bergfalk's complaint. The magazine did not publish a correction.

The Council found two reporting errors in this otherwise perceptive and useful article.

The Council finds the complaint warranted as it refers to those errors, the question of a haircut and the question of whether others knew of the Baptists' plan to bring in a refugee family. Those errors caused concern to residents of the community. The magazine's handling of those concerns displayed insensitivity. Therefore, the Council also finds the complaint warranted as it applies to the magazine's handling of the complaint. The reluctance of *The New Yorker* to provide rebuttal space for those people it writes about was an important part of the problem in this case. The opportunity for such a response would have been particularly appropriate in this highly emotional situation.

**Concurring:** Abel, Bell, Benson, Brady, Ghiglione, Huston, Isaacs, Lawson, Maynard, Pulitzer, Roberts, Rusher, Scott and Williams.

**Dissenting:** Miller.

**Dissenting opinion by Mr. Miller:** Mr. Trillin's report on the tragedy in Fairfield was an outstanding job of reporting. The errors do not seem to me to be serious enough to warrant a complaint against the report. I do not believe that Mr. Bergfalk or this Council, either, can measure the impressions other people received from this or any other piece of reporting. But I agree that Mr. Bergfalk's complaint about the magazine's response to his letter is warranted.

December 5, 1980

### COMPLAINT NO. 183         (Filed June, 1980)
### HOWARD RUFF
### against
### CHICAGO TRIBUNE-NEW YORK NEWS SYNDICATE

**Complaint:** Economic advisor Howard Ruff complained that Dan Dorfman distorted facts and misrepresented Mr. Ruff's views in a column published April 10 and distributed to 85 newspapers by The Chicago Tribune-New York News Syndicate, Inc.

Mr. Dorfman reported that a subscriber to Mr. Ruff's newsletter had "shoddy experiences" with four vendors approved by Mr. Ruff in his book, *How to Prosper in the Coming Bad Years*. Mr. Dorfman wrote in the column, "His sad experiences indicate that they are hardly the kind of companies that will help you prosper during bad years."

205

Specifically, Mr. Ruff complained that Mr. Dorfman "Never even called three of the four vendors . . . . to get their side of the story or to verify the allegations of 'shoddy' handling." He said three of the four allegations were "wholly unfounded."

Mr. Ruff also charged that Mr. Dorfman "materially misrepresented the activities of one highly reputable vendor firm" leaving the damaging and undeserved impression that the firm was made up of "schlock artists and crooks."

In a third element of his complaint, Mr. Ruff said that "Mr. Dorfman created the false impression of a covert requirement that vendors recommended by Ruff are somehow influenced or persuaded to advertise on Ruff's syndicated TV show."

Finally, Mr. Ruff complained that Mr. Dorfman failed to report that the incidence of complaints against recommended firms is "tiny" and that Mr. Ruff has a "thorough procedure for monitoring and immediately resolving any such complaints equitably."

**Response:** Don Michel, vice president and editor of the news syndicate, replied that he had reviewed the Ruff complaint when it was brought to his attention by a client newspaper some months ago. He wrote:

> My conclusion from talking with Mr. Dorfman and from reading the text of the complaints (was) that while there was an impression left that some caution should be exercised in dealing with Mr. Ruff and his associates, it was fully justified.
>
> Dorfman says that he made more contacts than the Ruff people claim. Additionally, the publication of the column brought forth more complaints.

Referring to the suggestion that one must advertise on Mr. Ruff's show to win a favorable recommendation, Mr. Michel wrote, "It appears that many sponsors feel that it does help."

As an aside, Mr. Michel noted that the letter of complaint was sent to the Council more than three months after the publication of the column April 10. Norman Isaacs, Council chairman, said that he received the complaint by telephone from Mr. Ruff's public relations counsel, Michael Bayback, sometime earlier and that the July 11 letter furnished the details in writing.

**Staff analysis:** The part of the Dorfman column that refers to the four firms reads as follows:

> The most flagrant complaint centers on *North American Coin & Currency, Ltd.*, of Phoenix, Ariz., one of the country's largest dealers in the sale of physical precious metals. The Ruff client says he bought, but refused to accept, five double eagle $20 gold pieces for $3,450.50. The reason: two of them, according to an appraiser, were counterfeit.

Another of Ruff's acceptable vendors, *Gemstone Trading Corp.* of New York, sent him a bum check for $1,000 in returning a deposit he had made toward the purchase of a $6,000 diamond; after complaining, he got a new check from Gemstone that did not bounce.

A third vendor in Ruff's book, New York based *Joel D. Coen & Co.*, quoted a bid of $13.31 an ounce for decorative silver art when spot silver was above $10; that's a steep discount of more than 25 per cent and a bid that was made before the sharp run-up to $50.

And a fourth vendor, *Investment Rarities* of Minneapolis, turned out to be one of the highest-priced firms from which to buy coins.

Dealing with the firms one at a time:

*Investment Rarities.* Mack Greenberg, general sales manager, told a Council staff member that none of his staff recalled Mr. Dorfman calling for comment on the firm's allegedly high prices. That is not to say, said Mr. Greenberg, that Mr. Dorfman may not have called to get prices for comparison. In any case, said Mr. Greenberg, his firm had no complaint against the Dorfman column, because the firm bases its reputation on reliability, not price. It should be noted that the Ruff subscriber on whose experiences the column was based, had no complaint about Investment Rarities either. He told Council staff that the firm quoted him a "decent price."

*Joel D. Coen & Co.* Mr. Coen was emphatic in saying that Mr. Dorfman did not contact his firm for a comment on its prices. The Ruff subscriber said he may have expressed indignation to Mr. Dorfman at the 26% spot silver offered by the Coen firm. However, he said he subsequently learned from a coin dealer that the discount was reasonable. That view is backed up by an article on page one of *The Wall Street Journal* Feb. 12, 1980, several weeks before the Dorfman column. *The Journal* reported that the most advantageous discount quoted to a reporter sampling the market was 48%.

In the cases of Investment Rarities and the Coen firm it appears that Mr. Ruff is correct in his complaint that the allegations of shoddy handling were unfounded.

*North American Coin & Currency Ltd.* Mr. Dorfman did call Sherman Unkefer, president of North American, to ask if he had checked to see if two of the returned coins were indeed counterfeit. Dorfman wrote in the column:

> Surprisingly, Unkefer said he hadn't done so yet, but would immediately get to it and let me know. Later, he called back to say the coins in question were inadvertently mixed up with a batch of other coins, and there was no way of telling which was which. At my prodding, he had them all checked, and, lo and behold, there were some counterfeits among them.

207

It wasn't until our third chat that Unkefer told me his company had knowingly bought some counterfeit coins, but he hastened to add that these were to be melted down to gold scrap.

'There have been a large number of these gold coins effectively counterfeited in Lebanon, and I suppose we may have inadvertently shipped some of them,' he says.

Neland Nobel, National Sales Manager for *North American Coin and Currency*, made the following points in a letter to Mr. Dorfman: That the coins were sent to the customer's bank on a "sight draft" basis, that is, with payment subject to the inspection and approval of the customer; that the customer refused the coins without paying and, therefore, suffered no injury; that judging the authenticity of coins is subjective and that the customer refused to supply the name of his appraiser, raising in Mr. Nobel's mind the question, "were the coins switched?" Nobel wrote that all dealers inadvertently buy bad coins sometimes and that North American cannot to this day determine whether any of the coins sent to the customer were bad, because the customer did not complain until after the coins had been returned to inventory. Mr. Nobel emphasized that the main business of North American is bullion, not numismatic coins.

The customer told Council staff that the sight draft did not constitute an "on approval" arrangement but only an agreement that the bank would remit the money on delivery of the coins to the bank. He said he only had an opportunity to assess the coins because the banker who received them did not understand the arrangement and called the customer for instructions. The customer did take the coins to a coin shop. The owner said two were counterfeit. The customer returned the coins to the bank next day, and asked that they be sent back and payment withheld.

The customer told Council that he expected a call from North American asking why he had returned the coins. When he didn't receive such a call after some days, he called the company. A salesman subsequently talked with the customer and the customer made his charge that two of the coins were counterfeit.

Mr. Nobel told a Council staff member that North American called the customer on its own initiative; that he did not know how many counterfeit coins were found in the search referred to in Mr. Dorfman's column; that he guessed there were three to seven in an inventory of 50 to 75 of the $20 gold pieces, because, he said, that would be a normal expectation, given the subtleties of authenticating coins. (Mr. Nobel had the inventory checked Dec. 2 and found two questionable coins among 53 double eagles.) He again stressed that North American's main business is bullion, not numismatic coins, and that he considered it unprofessional for

Mr. Dorfman to have blackened the reputation of the firm on the anonymous report of a single alleged misadventure.

Council staff interviewed representatives from the following agencies about the norms for numismatic dealings: The American Numismatic Association; *Coin World*; *Numismatic News*; Bowers & Ruddy of Los Angeles, and Manfra, Tordella & Brookes of New York (both firms associated with the Professional Numismatic Guild).

All said that the appearance of two counterfeits in a shipment of five coins would be a major departure from the norm. All said that while it could happen inadvertently, it would have to be considered a serious accident. While some of those authorities acknowledged that the on-approval basis of shipment gave the appearance of forthrightness, others were not impressed.

Louis Vigdor, vice president of Manfra, Tordella & Brookes, said, "I don't expect my customer to know a good from a bad coin." David Bowers, partner in Bowers and Ruddy, said that both law and custom dictate that the customer can recover for the purchase of a counterfeit coin any time the counterfeit is discovered, even years after the transaction. Both men said it was not normal, and Bowers said it was illegal, to have counterfeit coins in inventory or to sell them.

It does not appear that Mr. Dorfman did, as Mr. Ruff charges, materially misrepresent the activities of North American. Mr. Dorfman did give Sherman Unkefer an opportunity to answer the allegation against his firm. The significant element that Mr. Dorfman left out of his report was the firm's contention that the coins were shipped on approval. But the customer denies that, and Council staff research suggests that such an arrangement is not the protection on which coin buyers normally depend. The firm acknowledged that it had two questionable coins in its inventory Dec. 2 and Mr. Nobel said he considered a 10 to 15 percent counterfeit count to be "fairly normal."

*Gemstone Trading Corporation.* Gemstone officers insist that Mr. Dorfman did not call the company for comment on the allegation that the company sent a customer a "bum" check that "bounced," as Mr. Dorfman reported. The company says it stopped payment on the check.

Michael Freedman, president of Gemstone, wrote to Howard Ruff after the Dorfman column as follows:

> These are the facts on the James Kramer incident.
> Mr. Kramer ordered a diamond from us on August 4, 1977, for $4,437. He sent us a check for $1,000 made payable to Bank Leumi Trust Co., Escrow Account. (All client payment normally goes into our escrow account).

Mr. Kramer decided to cancel his order, and in early October, requested a refund of his deposit. Inadvertently we sent him a check drawn on our corporate account. When the error was realized, we requested Mr. Kramer to return the check to us, and also to write to Bank Leumi requesting the bank to return his escrowed $1,000. Naturally, Gemstone stopped payment on its corporate check. Bank Leumi, having received Mr. Kramer's request, returned his $1,000 deposit.

To say that Gemstone sent a "bum" check, is certainly erroneous and a serious distortion of the facts.

I have enclosed copies of the relevant documentation for this transaction, sequentially numbered. I have also enclosed a letter from our bank that I thought you might be interested in seeing.

Unfortunately, the documentation of which Mr. Freedman speaks never reached Mr. Ruff. Mr. Freedman told Council staff that it was sent via Emery Air Freight to Mr. Ruff's post office box by someone who did not realize that air freight cannot be delivered to a box. Since then Gemstone has not been able to find either the copies sent to Mr. Ruff or the file documents from which the copies were made, Mr. Freedman said. Mr. Freedman did send the Council a copy of the following letter to him dated April 16, 1980, from Bank Leumi Trust Co. of New York:

Gemstone Trading Corporation
30 Rockefeller Plaza
New York, N.Y.

Attn: Michael Freedman
President
_____

Dear Mr. Freedman:

As per your request I would say our experience in the past four years has been superb, without any discrepancies in the handling of approximately 3,000 items to date. Furthermore no checks on Gemstone Trading Corporation have been returned to us due to insufficient funds.

Always at your service, we remain,

Very truly yours,

Rosemarie Watkins
Assistant Secretary

Contrary to the letter's assertion, the customer insisted to Council staff that the first check he received from Gemstone was returned for insufficient funds and that the second check bore the same account number as the first. The customer did not save the original check after he received the second. The stamp on the original check would settle the issue.

Bank Leumi was asked to look into the matter. It had not reported back to the Council's staff by Wednesday night (immediately preceding the Council meeting).

Since neither side has produced documentation that would remove all doubt, it is difficult to decide whether the original check was returned for insufficient funds or because Gemstone stopped payment. It does appear, however, that Mr. Dorfman did not give Gemstone an opportunity before publication to answer the "bum check" allegation.

There are two other elements in Mr. Ruff's complaint: that Mr. Dorfman implied that firms must advertise with Mr. Ruff to win his approval, and that Mr. Dorfman should have reported that Mr. Ruff receives few complaints about his recommended firms and has a mechanism for settling what complaints he does receive.

The first element seems unwarranted. Mr. Dorfman quoted Mr. Ruff in the column denying that any advertising tie-in is required. The column also said that "some" approved firms do advertise. The implication seems clear that some others do not.

As for Mr. Ruff's contention that Mr. Dorfman should have said more about his handling of complaints against the firms he personally recommends, it too appears unwarranted. The column specified that Mr. Ruff personally monitors the firms on his personally approved list. (Quite incidentally, the column reported incorrectly that none of the four firms mentioned in the column was on the personally approved list. Investment Rarities is.)

**Council finding:** Careful substantiation of information is a hallmark of good reporting. The Council's investigation of this case indicates that Mr. Dorfman did not seek substantiation of some charges as assiduously as might reasonably be expected.

The Council finds the complaint warranted as it applies to two of the four firms listed in Mr. Dorfman's column and unwarranted as it applies to another.

Neither Investment Rarities nor Joel D. Coen & Co. appears to have subjected Mr. Dorfman's informant to "shoddy" or "sad" experiences or "rough times," as Mr. Dorfman reported. In the case of Investment Rarities, even the informant did not have a complaint. In the case of the Coen firm, its bid for silver appeared reasonable to the informant after he consulted with another dealer.

The complaint is found unwarranted as it applies to North American Coin & Currency, Ltd. Mr. Dorfman did give the firm a chance to reply to the allegation against it. The Council's staff found no evidence of distortion in Mr. Dorfman's report of the firm's practices.

The Council finds unwarranted the complaint that Mr. Dorfman did not report adequately Mr. Ruff's denial that a firm must advertise with him to win approval. The Council also finds unwarranted the complaint that Mr. Dorfman did not report adequately Mr. Ruff's provisions for dealing with complaint against firms that he approves.

Without documentation, it is impossible to determine whether Mr. Dorfman's allegation against Gemstone, Inc., was "wholly unfounded," as Mr. Ruff complained. It is reasonable, however, to criticize Mr. Dorfman for not giving Gemstone and two of the other firms an opportunity before publication to answer the allegations against them. There is no indication in the column or in the answer to the complaint that Mr. Dorfman did provide such an opportunity.

**Concurring:**   Abel, Bell, Benson, Brady, Ghiglione, Huston, Isaacs, Lawson, Maynard, Miller, Pulitzer, Roberts, Scott and Williams.
December 5, 1980

**COMPLAINT NO. 184**    (Initiated: July 7, 1980)
THE ASSOCIATION OF    (Formally Filed: Nov. 18,
AMERICAN RAILROADS    1980)
against
ABC NEWS

**Complaint:**   The Association of American Railroads complained that a segment on ABC News' "20/20" "Working On The Railroad" was "a blend of half-truths, distortions and outright misrepresentations," and that the ABC production team "misused factual information and film footage to buttress a predetermined scenario that could not have been supported by an objective airing of the factual materials."

The ABC report featured Geraldo Rivera as the oncamera reporter and was produced by Peter Lance. Much of the investigative work was done by employees of the Better Government Association, a nonprofit, privately-financed organization with offices in Chicago and Washington. The BGA describes itself as a "watchdog" organization "dedicated to promoting efficient use of tax dollars and high standards of public service." In recent years the BGA has been associated in a number of investigatory pieces with both the print and electronic media, including the "sting" operation conducted by the *Chicago Sun-Times* in 1977 when

212

that newspaper purchased and operated a tavern in order to expose civic corruption. In 1970 investigative work by the BGA helped win a Pulitzer Prize for *The Chicago Tribune*.

It was a similar cooperative effort between the BGA and *The Washington Star* that led to the "20/20" report on railroad safety. In March 1980 the *Star* published three articles entitled "Our Unsafe Railroads," written by its reporter Michael Kiernan, and based upon an investigation into railroad safety by the BGA. The *Star* articles contained some of the same allegations used in the television report, most particularly the charge that despite millions of dollars spent by the railroads during the past decade to upgrade track conditions, "railroad lines in many parts of the country appear to be getting worse, not better," and despite a new Federal Railroad Administration's "get-tough policy with the industry to reduce accidents . . . . the monetary losses from track-caused accidents remain at near-record levels."

As a result of the articles in the *Star* ABC's "20/20" production team asked the BGA to collaborate on a television report about the dangers posed by the shipment on rail lines of hazardous materials. The resulting segment was the major story on the "20/20" program aired on the evening of June 5, 1980.

Two weeks after the telecast, Lawrence H. Kaufman, the AAR vice-president for information and public affairs, wrote to Roone Arledge, president of ABC News, protesting what he called the misuse of facts "in such a way as present a totally unfair report." A month later, on July 21, having received no response, Mr. Kaufman again wrote Mr. Arledge, this time notifying him of the AAR's intention to run an advertisement in several professional publications customarily read by journalists, including the July 28 issue of *Broadcasting* magazine, in which an edited version of his first letter would be printed. Mr. Arledge said he did not receive this second letter until after the publication of the ad in *Broadcasting*. On July 31, three days after the publication, "20/20" broadcast a rebuttal to the ad and its charges as part of its weekly program.

**Staff analysis:** The complaint is divided into three major parts: the so-called "misrepresentations" made by the "20/20" team in initial approaches to the AAR; the charge of "distortion of facts" in the broadcast report; and a charge that ABC made "false and misleading statements" in its follow-up rebuttal broadcast.

Concerning the pre-production phase, the AAR said it had met with producer Lance and that in the course of this meeting he stated as his "working premise" that the railroad plant was bad and continuing to deteriorate; that shipments of hazardous materials by rail were increasing; and that the confluence of these two circumstances posed a dangerous situation. The AAR complained that Mr. Lance held to this premise even after documented evidence was supplied which AAR maintained destroyed the premise Mr. Lance had advanced.

The AAR contended that Mr. Lance's "integrity and devotion to fair reporting" were contradicted by his actions, specifically in filming examples of "bad track" in the Memphis yards of the Illinois Central Gulf Railroad after denying he had any desire to gain access to railroad property for that purpose; in allowing the camera crew to board a Conrail freight train in Indiana in violation of railroad safety rules; and in refusing to use portions of a taped interview with Thomas Phemister, director of the AAR's Bureau of Explosives, which AAR held contradicted statements made in other parts of the broadcast.

The complaint conceded that "actual errors of fact . . . . are relatively few" but insisted that a deliberate effort was made to misrepresent these facts to uphold a predetermined "line." The following statements in the broadcast were singled out as misrepresentations or errors of fact:

1. "20/20" reported that in 1978, the last year for which statistics were available, more than 11,000 rail accidents occurred, thus ". . . once an hour on the average, a train derailment or collision" takes place, the resultant damages amounting to more than $800,000 a day. The AAR did not challenge the statistic but challenged the manner in which it was stated, claiming it obscured the fact "that the overwhelming majority of these accidents are extremely minor in nature and are reported only because the Federal Railroad Administration required a report in 1978 on any mishap that resulted in damage greater than $2,300." A comparable statistic was used in the *Washington Star* series—that "derailments and collisions took place at a rate of about one every hour"—although the *Star*'s report of $850,000 a day in damages was slightly higher than "20/20"'s $800,000 a day.

The AAR also took exception to the manner in which another statistic was reported. Following a film sequence in which five "major accidents" were depicted, Mr. Rivera summed up with: "Those are just some of the more than 1,000 rail accidents reported in the past seven weeks." Other than pointing out that two of the depicted accidents were leakages and therefore "incidents" and not "accidents," the complaint did not challenge the statistic but did object to what it held was the implication that the five "major accidents" were representative of the 1,000.

2. Mr. Rivera reported that "the amount of hazardous materials

shipped by rail has increased, up to 25% in the past three years to almost 100 million tons . . ." The AAR said that "technically, this is true." At the same time the AAR complained that while the *amount* of hazardous materials shipped has increased, the *number* of shipments has remained at the same levels for the past five years, and that "it is the number of carloads which is relevant in a safety sense." The difference is accounted for by the introduction in recent years of larger tank cars.

The News Council staff queried the National Transportation Safety Board on whether the larger tank cars posed additional danger and was told that like the jumbo aircraft in the airline business, size was no greater risk until or unless an accident did occur, in which case the potential for catastrophic accident was greater.

3. To illustrate "how a single hazardous materials train accident can have catastrophic effects," "20/20" showed newsfilm of a freight train derailment in Mississauga, Ontario—a Toronto suburb—in November, 1979. Mr. Rivera reported that "dozens were injured, more than 217,000 people were evacuated . . . the explosions which followed caused more than $5 million in damages." The AAR complained that "these words were spoken before film footage of people in some sort of distress being helped aboard emergency vehicles," and that "this film was of a nursing home being evacuated—not of persons injured as a result of the accident." Council investigation revealed that while the derailment was "catastrophic" in terms of property damage and the disruption to the lives of those evacuated, some for as many as six days, there were, miraculously, no casualties. The evacuation of more than 200,000 persons occurred the day following the accident and was caused not by the explosion (which occurred immediately after the derailment the previous evening) but by the dangers posed by a leaking tank car containing chlorine. Among those evacuated were the elderly residents of a nursing home. The film used by "20/20" showed emergency personnel evacuating the nursing home.

4. In a sequence in which "20/20" showed three major types of accidents that can occur with tank cars carrying hazardous materials (explosions, leaks, and toxic spills), the first—termed by railroad men as a "bleve," an acronym for Boiling Liquid Vapor Explosion—was illustrated with newsfilm of three tank car explosions, all of which, complained the AAR, occurred more than six years ago. Mr. Rivera described the third type of accident—a toxic spill—as a situation in which "a ruptured tank car doesn't explode or leak toxic gases into the atmosphere (but) can still cause severe environmental damage." This was illustrated

with film of a November, 1979 derailment in Indiana which spilled six different kinds of chemicals on adjoining farm land. Six months after the accident, Mr. Rivera interviewed the farmer on whose land the chemicals spilled. He asked the farmer when his land might be usable for crops again. Mr. Rivera reported that neither the farmer nor the dozen men "working around the clock to get the poison out of the ground" had any idea. The AAR complained that "a balanced report would have mentioned the fact that the owner had been made whole for all damages."

5. Another sequence showed Mr. Rivera and the film crew riding a Conrail freight train in Indiana. A brakeman was interviewed about the hazards posed by the poor trackage. The AAR complained of "several reprehensible elements in this passage," the first being the boarding of the train by the film crew in violation of the railroad's safety rules, and the second the failure of the film to reflect Mr. Rivera's description as "like taking one of those scary rides at the local amusement park." The sequence was used to make the point that Conrail, created by the government in 1976 to combine most of the facilities of six bankrupt railroads in the Northeast, had itself fallen on hard times and was spending $200 million less than it planned on track maintenance—with the consequences ostensibly depicted in the film segment. Any observer could recognize that the film team had not forced its way onto the train. The collaboration of the railroad crew made it self-evident that whatever the line's regulations may be, the railroad employees had shrugged them off.

6. The AAR complained that a 45-minute filmed interview with Mr. Phemister went largely unused when portions of it would have "clearly contradicted assertions in the broadcast." Although the AAR complained that the small portion which was used on the broadcast dealt with a subject on which Mr. Phemister is not an expert, his response to a question posed to him did provide the AAR the opportunity to correct two points which the complaint cited were misrepresented, namely, that the number of shipments of hazardous material has not increased significantly in the past five years, and that during the same period the railroads "have turned the corner on deferred (track) maintenance."

7. The AAR complaint said that the ABC crew, with the announced intention of testing the quality of the Federal Railroad Administration's track inspection system, made a "random visit" to the Memphis freight yards of the Illinois Central Gulf Railroad. The AAR complaint challenged the "random" nature of the visit, arguing that to contend a New York television crew would choose to visit Memphis randomly "strains all credulity." In the context of the broadcast it was not clear what was

intended by the word "random." In view of the description of Memphis as "the fourth busiest center in the nation for hazardous material" Council staff concluded that the usage was intended to convey "unscheduled and unannounced." At the Memphis yards, ABC shot pictures of badly maintained track. In one shot, the tracks were so bowed as to resemble nothing so much as a bobby-pin. The AAR accused ABC of using a long lens to exaggerate the condition of the track. Council investigation was unable to confirm or deny the allegation, although the BGA representative present with the film crew held that the track pictured was just as bad as it appeared on the screen. The Council staff was advised by experts that while a lens could exaggerate the poor condition of the track, no lens could disguise the fact that it was clearly below minimal standards. In one sequence, two tank cars labelled "hydrocyanic acid" were shown sitting on track that was partially submerged in water and in a state of disrepair. The AAR complained the two cars were empty and so labeled. Council staff found no way to determine if it was so, or that it was known to the film crew. It is a matter of record that after the condition of the track was called to the attention of the FRA inspector he told the ABC crew he would recommend the track be "taken out of service."

8. "Particularly reprehensible as a journalistic practice," said the AAR, was an interview with a railroad employee who "was not trained to deal with network 'stars' nor was he authorized to speak for his company." Study of the sequence shows that he was not questioned about company policy, but asked why the tracks he supervised had not been repaired seven weeks after an FRA inspector had reported finding 45 defects in them. The employee's reply was that he did not have the manpower to make the repairs. To Council staff, this appeared neither to exceed his range of authority nor his area of specialized knowledge.

9. Citing Mr. Rivera's statement that ". . . in at least a half dozen major train derailments in the past six years, the FRA either failed to notice track defects prior to the crashes or failed to see that the reported defects had been repaired," the AAR complained that throughout the broadcast Mr. Rivera maintained "an apparent belief that virtually all serious rail accidents are caused by track problems." The AAR asserted that while track has been the leading cause of minor accidents, it has been identified as the cause of very few serious accidents. In support of its charge, the broadcast cited two derailments within the past two-and-a-half years where FRA inspectors had completed inspections just prior to the accidents. In one, a 1977 derailment near Pensacola, Florida, in which two people were killed by leaking anhydrous ammonia gas, the

FRA reported "no defects" in the stretch of track on the day before the derailment, but found 38 serious defects in the same track six days after the accident. The AAR did not challenge the facts of the two accidents cited, though in subsequent response to the BGA investigation on which the "20/20" broadcast was based, the FRA argued that the defect which caused the Pensacola derailment ("tight track gauge") was rare and impossible to spot without specialized equipment. In that response, the FRA added that, "only the railroads themselves are capable of assuring the safety of their operations on a day-to-day basis." The FRA took exception, however, to any implication that the Federal program was not effective in monitoring railroad compliance and promoting remedial action because of poor performance by inspection personnel.

10. In a passage describing the safety improvements on tank cars, the broadcast noted that while virtually all the larger tank cars (described as "105" cars and constituting 85% of the tank car fleet) have not been fitted with top and bottom shelf couplers (a device that prevents the puncturing of tank cars by the couplers in derailment or collision) despite repeated recommendations of the National Transportation Safety Board over the past three years. The AAR complained that the broadcast described the situation "as though there is strong resistance" to the fitting of these cars with safety devices, and said the interview with the president of the Railway Progress Institute seemed to support this thesis. The broadcast made no reference to resistance on the part of the railroads. After an interview with Elwood T. Driver, vice-president of the NTSB, in which Mr. Driver spoke of the board's recommendations since 1977, Mr. Rivera said the board "only makes recommendations so the '105' tank cars have not been retrofitted." No reason was given why the board's recommendations had not been followed. Later, in an interview with Robert Smith, president of the Railway Progress Institute, Mr. Rivera asked, "Why has the *industry* resisted the National Transportation Safety Board's recommendation?" Since tank cars are largely owned by the chemical industries that use them, the "industry" referred to could have been the chemical industry. Mr. Smith, spokesman for the tank car industry, responded, "I don't think the industry has flatly resisted." Council staff believes that an explanation in the unused portion of the Phemister interview that delay in retrofitting "105" tank cars was due to a shortage of materials would have given additional clarity to this aspect. The broadcast made the point that whatever the reason for the slow progress in retrofitting "105" cars, these cars pose a continuing threat to public

safety until such time as they too are retrofitted with the safety devices used on the larger tank cars.

11. In what the AAR described as "a melodramatic little playlet," the "20/20" crew discovered a leaking tank car in a Chicago rail yard and summoned the fire department. On arriving, the battalion chief was unable to determine the contents of the tank car and, in fact, took two days to learn it was diesel fuel. The AAR complaint suggested there may have been some complicity when it stated the battalion chief "obligingly" agreed he could not discern the contents. According to the AAR complaint, a call to the yard office would have given an immediate answer. The fact that a fire official would be unaware of the most expeditious way to learn the contents of a leaking tank car sitting in a rail yard would seem to bolster ABC's point "that most fire departments in this country are totally unequipped to deal with hazardous material rail accidents."

The episode was designed to demonstrate the need for more specific labelling (placarding) of tank cars carrying hazardous materials. The program noted that a proposal for more specific placarding had been proposed by the Department of Transportation but that "five years later that proposal has been stalled, under pressure from the rail and chemical industries." The AAR complained that the broadcast "leaves the clear impression" that "the railroads oppose a 'more specific' placarding system" when in fact they do not. The broadcast made no mention of railroad opposition to a more specific placarding system, but only to the railroad's opposition to the DOT plan—which has now been mandated for all railroads. The AAR complaint acknowledged the railroad's opposition to the DOT placarding system on the grounds that it would be more confusing to emergency personnel than the former system. The complaint again made reference to the failure of the "20/20" team to use those portions of the Phemister interview which would have made the AAR's point that the railroads favor more specific placarding but not the system now mandated. The DOT system, Council staff was informed, was adopted largely because of its universality; it was proposed by the United Nations for use in all countries and on all modes of transport for hazardous materials.

The AAR said it made the July 31 follow-up broadcast a part of its complaint because it was "shocked by the malice conveyed by the rebuttal." Four instances were cited to demonstrate ABC's "lack of regard for fact," including an account of a Kansas City Southern freight derailment near Dallas. ABC termed the June 6 derailment as the kind of "catastrophic train accident . . . just waiting to happen" that was predicted on the June 5 telecast. The ABC report added that the "National Transportation Safety Board has blamed bad track." Council investigation disclosed that at the time of the rebuttal broadcast the NTSB had not yet issued its report on the cause of the derailment.

In its "Open Letter to Roone Arledge" advertisement, the AAR charged that ABC used "ten-year-old film clips in an effort to prove that the predetermined story line was accurate." In its rebuttal, ABC responded that "20/20" used film clips from more than 26 freight train accidents, only one of which was 10 years old; that 19 of the accidents had happened "in the past two years," and that the report was begun "with film and tape of seven different derailments all in the seven weeks just prior to Geraldo Rivera's report." The AAR complained that ABC News was inaccurate in its count and of its dating. AAR's statement that the program began with *five*, not *seven*, film clips was easily verifiable. It was not, however, possible by Council staff to identify or date the full volume used in the "20/20" segment. The staff was able to confirm that in those instances where the date was relevant, the program properly identified the accident by date and place. In those instances where film was used either to illustrate types of accidents, or as visual background for narration, there was no dating or placing. In a medium where visuals are in constant demand, Council staff found it impossible to assess or target what AAR called deliberate misrepresentation.

The AAR's complaint that "20/20" used "blame" to mean "determining the cause," the use of "accident" to describe a leaking tank car, and saying "catastrophic" to describe the Dallas derailment in which no fatalities occurred, found Council staff involved in what appears endemic in the current national cycle, that of imprecise language. It is often as evident in print journalism as in broadcasting—and, unfortunately, in complaints alleging malice when the issue is clearly whether information relayed was factual, or not.

Council staff could conclude only that accident statistics are open to easy misinterpretation—particularly in light of the changing standards of reportable railroad accidents over the past decade, and the inflationary rates which affect property damage. After immersion in such debates about differing interpretation, there remained a question about whether all of these statistics offered any way to determine the degree of danger posed by the transport of hazardous materials. The National Transportation Safety Board told Council staff that, in general, the trend in the number of accidents and injuries resulting from the shipment of these materials was downward, but the number of fatalities remained steady. Although there were no fatalities in 1979, there were two in 1980, both after the broadcast of the "20/20" program.

**Response:**  Av Westin, vice-president and executive producer of ABC News, responded to the complaint by letter on December 8, 1980. He denied the charge that ABC had failed to acknowledge or respond to the AAR's letter of July 21, citing Peter Lance's telephone call to Mr. Kaufman on July 30. He said that in his call Mr. Lance raised several questions, among them the AAR's justification for naming 1979 as the railroads' safest year. Mr. Westin said the AAR's reply—that there were fewer fatalities in 1979 than ever before—was insufficient to justify as "safest" a year in which the AAR admitted, according to Mr. Westin, that injuries had continued to increase. Mr. Westin added that "our interpretation of safety on the railroads is a function of the increase in shipments of hazardous material; the increase in the accident rate; the continual deterioration of the railbed and, finally, the practice of the Federal Railroad Administration to allow railroads to police themselves."

Following its own study and analysis, Council staff posed, in a meeting on February 19, a series of questions to Mr. Westin, seeking clarification of certain points.

In this meeting, Mr. Westin conceded that the selection of the Memphis railyard was "random" only in the sense that the visit had not been scheduled for a particular time when the shipment of hazardous materials might be at their peak. He said the "20/20" team was aware of the high volume of shipments through Memphis and chose it for that reason. Mr. Westin acknowledged the impreciseness of the term.

He said ABC was also aware that the film clip of emergency personnel loading an ambulance following the Ontario derailment was indeed the evacuation of a nursing home—the clip was from ABC News' own coverage of the 1979 accident and that the juxtaposition of the film clip with the erroneous statement about "dozens of injuries" was "an inadvertent and wrong edit." He could not recall the source of the erroneous information on the nonexistent injuries, nor could he recall the source of[1] the information that the "NTSB had blamed bad track" in the derailment near Dallas in the hours following the original broadcast. He speculated that the judgment on the cause of the derailment was unquestionably checked out with ABC's Dallas office and may have come from erroneous news reports immediately following the accident.

**Council finding:**  It is clear from the Council staff's examination and assessment that ABC News sought to educate the public about an issue of importance, that of the ever-present danger of major accidents in the shipment of hazardous materials by rail. The indignation of railroad executives over factual errors can be understood. The errors reveal something less than careful checking and a weakness in editing (as was the case in the incorrect reporting of "dozens of injuries" in the Canadian accident and the failure to identify the scene where emergency personnel evacuated a nursing home). These and several other errors of fact noted by the staff were regarded by the Council as sufficiently minor that, while they may have tended to weaken the credibility of the "20/20" segment, they do not, in the Council's view, demonstrate a willful effort to "misrepresent the facts," as the complaint asserted.

The refusal of the railroad companies to allow the ABC production team to enter their properties dilutes the credibility of the AAR's complaint. Their refusal suggests defensiveness and a reluctance to be candid and open. The companies chose to forego an opportunity to tell their side of the story and thereby educate both journalists and the public in the economic, logistical and technological complexities of track and roadbed maintenance.

As is often true in journalistic enterprises, internal communications are surprisingly convoluted, and there is no excusing ABC News' slowness in processing more adequately than by a telephone call a protest by a major organization about a program broadcast nationally.

The most difficult of all of the areas of disagreement between the parties rests in the differing interpretations of statistics. One example can be cited as illustrative. The Federal Railroad Administration informed the News Council staff that 90% of the accidents caused by bad track (which constitute almost half of all derailments) happen at speeds under 20 miles an hour. This is an interesting figure, but not necessarily useful. It is obvious that accidents, or incidents, involving the shipment of hazardous materials can happen at any speed, or even in situations where a tank car is motionless in a rail yard. It is not alone the frequency of accidents, nor even their severity, that poses the danger to public safety. It is the danger posed by the singular nature of the materials shipped and a single incident moving, or stationary, could result in major loss and injury.

ABC News was at fault in the "20/20" segment of overdramatizing some aspects of the problem in its search for strong visualization. But we do not find that the program "demonstrated a cavalier disregard for generally accepted journalistic standards of accuracy, objectivity and fairness." Other than in the specifics noted above, we find the complaint unwarranted.

**Concurring:**    D. Bell, J. Bell, Benson, Brady, Cooney, Decter, Ghiglione, Hornby, Huston, Isaacs, Maynard, Miller, Pulitzer, Scott, Stanton, and van den Haag.

March 6, 1981

## COMPLAINT NO. 185    (Filed: Jan. 9, 1981)
## DR. VICTOR HERBERT
### against
## PEOPLE MAGAZINE

**Complaint:**   Victor Herbert, M.D., complained that an article in *People* magazine "misled the public by giving the appearance of reliability to 'Dr.' Richard Passwater and 'his Ph.D. from Bernadean University in Las Vegas' and for promoting in that article that readers should take large quantities of vitamins, selenium, and zinc (as sold by Passwater's employer, the Solgar Vitamin Company, and other nutrition vendors)." Dr. Herbert is vice-chairman of the Committee on Information of the American Institute of Nutrition.

The article, published in the December 15, 1980, issue of *People* under the title "It was love at first bite when George Hamilton discovered mega-vitamins," was done, according to Dr. Herbert, despite a telephone call he received prior to publication from Judy Gould, one of the two persons who wrote it. In that call, according to Dr. Herbert, he raised a question about the legitimacy of Passwater's credentials. He also sent Ms. Gould a copy of a book he (Dr. Herbert) had written titled "Nutrition Cultism," which contained "a long listing of harms from vitamin mega-doses, collected from peer-reviewed scientific literature."

Dr. Herbert said that he had received a letter dated December 31, 1980, from Merlin D. Anderson, administrator of the Nevada Commission on Postsecondary Education, indicating that Bernadean University "was a diploma mill, which was never authorized, approved, or accredited by Nevada, and which is forbidden by the Nevada courts to offer any courses or degrees in Nevada."

Dr. Herbert charged that *People* should have referred to Passwater as "Mr." instead of "Dr." and that "to indicate his Ph.D. was from Bernadean University in Las Vegas without pointing out that Bernadean was a diploma mill forbidden by Nevada to offer courses or degrees was deceptive and misleading, and falsely conveyed Passwater's promotion of his company's products was based on sound courses leading to a sound doctorate.''

Dr. Herbert said that he had sent three letters on December 11 and 23, and January 6, to Richard Stolley, managing editor of *People,* and that he had received no replies. In these letters, Dr. Herbert, in addition to questioning the credentials of Passwater, charged that the large doses of vitamins (megavitamins) he recommends "can result in harm to a substantial number of people." He said that he had given such a warning to the writers of the article and that they had left it out.

**Response:** Richard A. Burgheim, Executive Editor of *People,* wrote that the article was ''an examination of the widespread popularity of taking heavy doses of vitamins and minerals daily in pursuit of better health and vitality.'' He further stated that ''the story also pointed out that the extreme use of vitamins and minerals as an aid to health is disputed by many authorities in the medical and nutritional fields.''

Regarding Passwater, Mr. Burgheim said that he: ''. . . . was cited as an author of several books on nutrition who is one of the leading advocates of multi-vitamin use. Dr. Passwater was interviewed by a *People* correspondent from our Washington bureau. In the course of the interview, Dr. Passwater gave our correspondent a copy of his personal vitae which included his educational background. In addition to an undergraduate degree from the University of Delaware, he listed a Ph.D. from Bernadean University. This information was also reported in his biography in *Who's Who in the East.*''

Mr. Burgheim said that Passwater's views, ''as well as warnings from his critics,'' were presented in the article. ''As the author of numerous successful books on multiple-vitamin nutrition, Dr. Passwater was quoted in the article without emphasis on his educational credits. If our story had been based entirely or even largely on Dr. Passwater, we certainly would have looked into his background and presumably would have checked out Bernadean University. But our story dealt with the mega-vitamin boom in this country, not on Dr. Passwater, and mentioned him only as a zealous proponent and popularizer.

''In summary, we feel we treated a controversial subject fairly and that any critical assessment of Dr. Passwater's academic history was beyond the scope of our story.''

**Staff analysis:** The use of mega-vitamins is, as *People* stated, ''controversial." The article took note of such controversy through statements such as the following:

> Passwater's enthusiasm is not shared by many.
> Even Passwater sounds a cautionary note: "Not everyone can tolerate a sudden concentration of vitamins . . . ."
> Passwater remains undaunted by the controversy over his theories.
> Passwater is not without supporters in the scientific community, most notably two-time Nobel Prize winner and vitamin C proponent Dr. Linus Pauling, 79. He says Passwater is 'reliable, with a good background and knowledge.'

The magazine quoted Dr. Herbert, the complainant, as saying "Passwater is talking nutrition nonsense."

To discuss the theories—both pro and con—that surround the use of mega-vitamins demonstrably would require extensive research, and even with such research in hand, the argument, it seems, would continue.

Theories aside, the central issue in this complaint is the charge by Dr. Herbert that *People* magazine "misled the public by giving the appearance of reliability for 'Dr.' Richard Passwater and 'his Ph.D.' from Bernadean University in Las Vegas."

Merlin D. Anderson, Administrator of the Nevada Commission on Postsecondary Education, told the Council's staff that Bernadean University is forbidden from operating in the State of Nevada. "Bernadean University operated without any State authorization until January of 1976," Mr. Anderson said. "At that time this Commission denied Bernadean University's application to continue operation. The decision was appealed to the courts and the agency decision was upheld at every level. Bernadean University has never been an approved or accredited school in this State, and the courts have decreed that no degrees or courses may be offered by the institution in Nevada."

Mr. Anderson said further that "a Bernadean University degree represents nothing more than a piece of paper."

Bernadean University also has a facility in Van Nuys, California. A catalog mailed from its address there, at 13615 Victory Boulevard, Suite 114, states that it has seven colleges—Liberal Arts, Law, Health Sciences, Agriculture, Police Sciences, Theology and Fine Arts. According to an information sheet titled "BU in a Capsule," the university is a part of the Church of Universology. "As such," the sheet states, "it is a church school and its educational function is a primary function of the church activities."

The university claims it is not subject to state regulatory agencies "because it is a church operation and because of the separation of church and state concept."

The university's College of Health Sciences' prospectus states that a course in basic nutrition, resulting in a "Certificate as a Nutritionist," costs $120. A "Cancer Researcher" certificate can be obtained after a two-credit-hour course costing $80.00.

Although the university has a certificate of incorporation in the State of California that certificate, according to Dr. Robert D. Welty, consultant to the Office of Private Postsecondary Education, "gives them no authorization, whatsoever, to operate a school or to issue degrees."

"Bernadean University is operating outside the law in California," Dr. Welty said. "We don't know if it is intentional or unintentional. They have not applied for authorization to operate as a university under the State's Educational Code. We are attempting to investigate their operations." Dr. Welty said "we have no evidence that the courses offered adhere to the principles of the Church of Universology. Judging by what I have seen and heard, they do not."

The University's catalog states that "If you hold a baccalaureate but not the master's degree, let us know and we can arrange for you to write a thesis or take some short course with the school for the master's degree. For example, we have a course in Applied Nutrition that will result in the award of the Master of Science (M.Sc.) degree."

The catalog states further:

> After you have both the baccalaureate and master's degree, you may either take a series of subjects to study on the graduate level until you attain 36 graduate hours or you may write a dissertation equivalent to 36 graduate hours. The title of the dissertation must first be submitted for approval.

Tuition, according to the catalog, is $40.00 per credit hour, which would total $1,400 for a Ph.D. if the 36 hours of graduate study procedure is followed.

Because the University is not authorized, according to state authorities, to grant degrees, either in Nevada or in California, state authorities have been unable to examine the school's records to determine who has obtained degrees, or how they were obtained.

In response to a Council letter seeking his answer to Dr. Herbert's charge that Bernadean University is a "diploma mill," Passwater wrote that "Bernadean University did have full legal authority to grant me a Doctor of Philosophy degree at the time that I earned it." He enclosed a description of the university as published in 1976 in *Lovejoy's College Guide*, 13th edition.

226

Passwater further said, "It is my understanding that Bernadean University did not grow to meet accepted standards of accreditation and was forced to discontinue. However, their alternative educational programs were a positive contribution to our free society and to myself."

As noted earlier in this analysis, Bernadean University, according to Nevada authorities, operated without authorization in that state until January, 1976, and since then has been denied its application to continue to operate. However, the 1981 Las Vegas telephone directory still lists the school in its "Yellow Pages" under "Schools—Universities & Colleges/Academic."

The school also still is listed in the Lovejoy Guide, but in the state of California rather than Nevada. According to Mrs. Barbara McCoun, research editor for the guide, Lovejoy's requirements for a nonaccredited institution to be listed are (1) that it be a degree-granting institution, and (2) that the institution have a state charter or license.

Mrs. McCoun said that apparently when Bernadean was first placed as an entry in the guide someone failed to check with the state (Nevada). Then when the school moved to California it was merely an editorial decision to move the Bernadean entry from under Nevada to under California in the 14th edition of the guide, published in 1979, and no effort was made to check with the California Office of Education as to Bernadean's status.

There is no questioning the legitimacy of Passwater's degree from the University of Delaware. His B.S. degree in Chemistry has been confirmed by the Council's staff. It was obtained in 1959. This degree, plus his record of experience, may well make him a researcher of competence and skill.

**Council finding:** The issue for the Council appears to be whether *People* exercised checking care to ascertain whether the doctorate Passwater obtained from Bernadean University in Las Vegas was a legitimate one.

Mr. Burgheim in his letter of response to the Council said that "the *People* story was about the mega-vitamin boom and not on Dr. Passwater, and mentioned him only as a zealous proponent and popularizer."

An examination of the story itself reveals that out of its total of 151 lines, at least 100 lines relate to Passwater, his theories and his family. Fifteen lines are devoted to dosages of mega-vitamins, selenium and zinc recommended by him.

"If you're interested in optimum health, think about supervitamins," Passwater is quoted as saying.

The reliability of the credentials of a person espousing a theory that "large quantities of vitamins up to 100 times the recommended dietary allowances will bestow exceptional health and vitality" becomes important in light of the Council's staff investigation of the university itself. When such a theory is supported by the use of photographs of personalities such as George Hamilton ("toasts his own health with herbs and vitamins"), Lynda Carter ("she neded an energy boost and quickly noticed the difference"), Rod McKuen ("I feel sluggish without my vitamins"), Pam Dawber ("depends on more than an apple a day"), Senator Strom Thurmond ("perhaps the best advertisement for mega-vitamins"), there is danger that others will adopt heavy doses of mega-vitamins on their own. Any audience deserves to know the credentials of the proponent in order to judge the efficacy of a treatment or theory.

This is where *People* failed. The authority credited to Passwater as a proponent of better health through mega-vitamins required the magazine to check the status of the university and its authority to grant degrees in Nevada and California, the states in which it operated and operates. Such checking would have established the accuracy of what Dr. Herbert had charged in his prepublication conversation with one of the writers of the article—and what the Council staff verified beyond serious contest—that Bernadean University was not authorized to grant degrees by the states in which it operated and operates.

The incorrect impression was reinforced in the article by a sentence that readers might easily have interpreted as indicating that Passwater had "medical" credentials. This was the sentence saying that "Passwater's enthusiasm is not shared by many of his medical colleagues." There also was a later sentence referring to him as "the doctor." These references represented a seeming identification of Passwater as a physician in an argument with his professional peers.

Reporters, as a matter of course, should check the academic credentials of persons expounding controversial subject matter of a scientific nature and should make the results known to their readers or viewers.

The inclusion of such additional information in the *People* article would not necessarily have destroyed Passwater's mega-vitamin argument, but putting that information before the reader represented an elementary and necessary exercise of journalistic responsibility that would have put the public on notice.

228

Dr. Herbert's complaint regarding this lapse by *People* is warranted.
**Concurring:**    D. Bell, J. Bell, Brady, Cooney, Decter, Ghiglione, Hornby, Huston, Isaacs, Maynard, Pulitzer, Scott, Stanton, and van den Haag.
**Dissenting:**    Miller.
March 5, 1981


**COMPLAINT NO. 186**    (Filed:  Jan. 26, 1981)
RUPERT ALLAN
against
LOS ANGELES HERALD EXAMINER

**Complaint:**    Rupert Allan, a long-time friend of President and Mrs. Ronald Reagan, complained that he had been erroneously quoted about the Reagans in a feature article published just before the election in the *Los Angeles Herald Examiner* and syndicated nationally as part of a series. Mr. Allan said he was interviewed by reporters Caroline Cushing and Wanda McDaniel because of his knowledge of the Reagans' lifestyle. He charged that the article violated his request not to be quoted personally about anything he said and that, more importantly, it was totally in error in attributing to him two statements:  (1) "The Reagans are drowning in rich friends" and (2) "She will make the White House comfortable with good food, cocktails and lunches. All their non-Jewish friends will be there."

Mr. Allan complained:  "I never made a statement on either subject, and I did not say those two quotes." Mr. Allan asked for a retraction, but did not pursue it when told by editor James Bellows, that the paper was willing to publish a letter, but would add an editor's note saying both writers confirmed he made the quotes and more. "(Mr. Bellows') proposed statement," Mr. Allan said in his complaint, "would only have added fuel to the fire and do more harm." He provided copies of his denials of the statements as carried in other newspapers.

> (*Council note*: Because the examination of this complaint resulted in later exchanges with the *Herald Examiner* and would complicate ready understanding of the competing issues if contained in the Council's normal "response" form, what follows is the newspaper's *first* reply. Subsequent comments by the editors are covered as they were made during the assessment).

**Response:**    In a letter February 9, 1981, Editor Bellows wrote:

> "The Rupert Allan complaint boggles the mind.

1) "Rupert Allan acknowledges (not once, but twice) that the *Herald Examiner* was willing to run his letter. What lack of adequate access?

2) "Rupert Allan complains about what was said by him for the record. We beg to disagree on this issue, which is as old as caveman communications.

"Please let me know what else I should do about this for the Council."

**Staff examination:** Titled "The Reagan Reign," the writers produced five articles. The one in which Mr. Allan was quoted appeared in the *Herald Examiner* on October 30, and was headlined: "Queen Nancy and Her Loyal Court," and sub-titled, "The Woman Who Would Be Queen." It was written in a gossipy style, containing phrases like, "Her majesty's bandwagon" and "will ascend to the throne" and described "a change in administrations from down-home Southern to worldly Western as dramatic as the restoration of the Hapsburgs." The article concentrated on what was called "a startlingly tight-knit social group" and named a number of Mrs. Reagan's closest friends. The quote about "non-Jewish friends" was ascribed to "pal Rupert Allan."

This aspect drew criticism in *The Sacramento Bee*, one of the newspapers that published the article. *The Bee*'s ombudsman, Art Nauman, protested in a column that "nothing that came before in the series laid any groundwork for that kind of grave implication. In fact . . . earlier in the same installment there were names of several people said to be part of the Reagan inner circle who are themselves Jews. Among them:  Mrs. Jack Benny and Betsy Bloomingdale." Mr. Nauman quoted Mary Anne Dolan, *Herald Examiner* managing editor, as saying "We stand by the story and by the quote." Nauman's published response was that it was "questionable journalism." He said that if the writers and editors "believed there was an element of truth behind the quote, they owed it to readers to explore it fully and openly." Mr. Nauman wrote that *The Bee* should have asked the authors or the editors for substantiation of what amounted to an accusation, and for more precise identification of the man making it . . . Failing that, I think the quote should have been dropped."

(For the record, Mr. Allan has been an executive in a Los Angeles public relations firm for some years. A St. Louisan, he was with *The Post-Dispatch* for a time and a writer for that newspaper's radio station, KSD. He went into the Navy in 1942 and left in '45 as a lieutenant commander; then became a State Department public affairs officer before joining West Coast film companies; and later being in the old *Look* magazine's West Coast bureau for five years. In his protest to Mr. Bellows, he referred to himself as part-Jewish. He recorded himself as Episcopalian in Who's Who).

There is unanimity in the Council staff that there can be no quarreling

230

with Mr. Bellows' point that disagreements about who-said-what-when trace back to the first humans' abilities to communicate verbally.

However, in this electronic age, there is no paucity of good quality pocket-sized tape recorders. Because of its policy of not intruding into reporters' notes or out-takes, the first staff appraisal was not to pursue the "impression" conveyed in Mr. Allan's complaint that one of the reporters had made mention of a recording. Instead, the emphasis moved to an appraisal of the various sides of access and subsequently focus anew on the possibility of a tape.

Where access was concerned, Mr. Bellows was firm in refusing to discuss the matter, even with *The Chicago Tribune*, one of the newspapers that purchased the *Herald Examiner* series. Acknowledging reader comment and inquiry about the "non-Jewish friends" quote, *The Tribune* published a long news account carrying Mr. Allan's strong denial he had said such a thing. That story carried this passage:

> Jim Bellows, editor of the *Herald Examiner*, refused to discuss the story with *The Tribune*, answering only, "We stand behind the story."

There can, of course, be no legal challenge to this position. In its *Tornillo v. Miami Herald* decision, the United States Supreme Court held that a Florida statute requiring such access to a complaining individual was unconstitutional and that an editor had an unchallengeable right to refuse to publish any letter.

The overwhelming majority of journalists praised the Tornillo decision, but there were also reservations held by some about the long-range philosophy. This latter view was outlined in the February, 1981, issue of *The Bulletin* of the American Society of Newspaper Editors, by Professor Ben Bagdikian, widely known media critic, in this manner:

> Papers continue to depend more on legal protection in fairness than in simple professional ethics. There was relief, including my own, when *The Miami Herald* won the Tornillo case. Few of us want judges making news decisions. But the fact is that *The Miami Herald* was wrong to have published a slashing attack on a candidate for office just before election and then to have refused to give him space for a response. The paper had the law on its side but not basic fairness.

Professor Bagdikian's comment is included not to register a point against the *Herald Examiner*, but to provide the Council with a broader framework about access.

Clearly, Mr. Allan's first mailgram to Mr. Bellows contained a different element. He asked for retraction of the quotations attributed to him. It is, therefore, understandable that Mr. Bellows would consider it mandatory

231

that this type of demand be followed by a response, either by the writers or by the newspaper. Equally understandable was Mr. Allan's decision that any further reinforcement of the newspaper's stand would harm, rather than aid, his effort to rebut the statements.

This is a type of problem facing news organizations all the time and Council staff found itself exploring the subject to see if anything new or useful might be on the scene. The most concrete appraisal came from the Council's Associate Director Richard P. Cunningham, who has had years of success as *The Minneapolis Tribune* ombudsman. He wrote:

> When a complaint is a matter of interpretation or opinion, it is clearly unfair for a newspaper to tack such a note on a complainant's letter. In a dispute over facts, the reader and the newspaper have interests that may go beyond the complainant's interest in fairness. The reader has an interest in getting enough information to decide who is right. The newspaper has an interest in explaining its position or in defending itself against an outright lie. None of these interests is properly served by the newspaper-stands-by-its-story rebuttal. This manifests a newspaper's refusal to engage in responsible rebuttal. On the other hand, I don't think the complainant should oppose an editor's note that limits itself to the facts upon which the newspaper based its belief that the disputed matter was correct."

It was at this stage that the staff felt emboldened to inquire about tape. If it existed and confirmed the *Herald Examiner*'s quotations, then any issue about access would evaporate instantly and the complaint would clearly be without merit.

Hence, Mr. Allan's statement in his letter of complaint, that Harvey B. Schecter, regional director of the Anti-Defamation League of B'nai Brith, had checks made with the newspaper about the "non-Jewish friends" statement and had relayed word that reporter Wanda McDaniel had given the impression that a tape recording existed, brought staff inquiry to Mr. Schecter. He confirmed Mr. Allan's assertion. Mr. Schecter said an ADL staff member had asked to borrow the tape or hear it and that the conversation was changed.

The matter was then posed to Mr. Bellows on a purely voluntary basis, with the offer to send a senior staff representative of the Council to Los Angeles immediately if this was agreeable. Mr. Bellows declined promptly. "We don't want to get into that," he said. "You ought to stick with the matter of access." He suggested a conversation with Ms. Dolan, the managing editor. She said that yes, there had been a taping, but added that she agreed with Mr. Bellows that the tape should not be made available. "I don't know where the tape is now," she said. "I have the transcript."

Totally unresolved is the matter of truth or falsity to Mr. Allan's assertion that he had stipulated that any conversation with the reporters was to be off the record and that if direct quotes were to be considered, he was to be checked. Neither Miss Cushing nor Miss McDaniel were available for comment. Both were reported out of the city on holiday.

In a later response to Council inquiries, Mr. Allan expressed bewilderment over what was described as a first interview on the telephone with Miss Cushing. "It was not an interview," he insisted, "but a social call. I've forgotten whether I called her or she called me. We chatted about her husband and her baby and she later mentioned Nancy Reagan and suggested lunch." He said that there had been a clear violation of his agreement with both reporters at the luncheon table that if they felt the need of a direct quote they would call him.

One of Ms. Dolan's remarks might possibly be interpreted to offer support for another of Mr. Allan's statements, that he had been told the original copy did not contain the controversial quote. Ms. Dolan said the quote was not in what she called "the raw copy." "I picked it up directly from the transcript," she said.

Ms. Dolan went on to say that she had put "more effort into trying to (soothe) Rupert Allan's feelings than anything I can recall." Asked about access and tape both, Ms. Dolan said: "I think the problem of access is serious. I really worry that a person's complaint might be right and whether we are doing right. But finally I had to throw up my hands over Rupert Allan. There is no question in my mind that Rupert Allan said what he did. Even if we were to produce tape, he would say it had been manufactured. There is no winning him over."

Mr. Allan's position to the Council was "I wish there had been a tape. If there is one, I hope the Council can hear it and judge accordingly. I have been damaged by the false quote. If there is tape evidence let it come out. I am confident it will vindicate me totally."

In summary, the staff can do no more than report the competing views. Mr. Allan's denials have been published in the two Chicago papers and in the *New York Daily News*. His position has not been reported in Los Angeles and he may have erred in not making his views clear, even with a strongly rebutting editor's note. At least, the conflict would have been public. It should be noted that in several aspects, his versions have not been shaken by subsequent analysis.

Granted that out-takes are generally considered protected work papers, this does not appear to the staff to be a matter of momentous proportions (except to Mr. Allan). If tape exists, it is difficult for the staff to fully grasp why it should not be produced in a challenge of this type. If, as the paper's executives hold, it verifies the published report, the newspaper's record for accurate reporting would be enhanced. It would set no legal precedent since the individual involved is willing and submitted his complaint with the required waiver of any subsequent legal recourse.

**Council finding:**  The appearance of the quote without examination is on its face bad journalism, and not only on the part of the *Herald Examiner*, but on the part of other newspapers that published it. The editors on these newspapers should have raised the questions that would have provided a framework for the quote or exposed it as not a reliable comment on the Reagans.

The Council finds the complaint warranted to the extent that it exposes poor journalistic practice in the editing of the quote. This poor practice is doubly indefensible when it involves a damaging imputation against a candidate on the eve of an election without the opportunity to reply.

**Concurring:**  Brady, D. Bell, J. Bell, Decter, Ghiglione, Hornby, Huston, Isaacs, Maynard, Stanton and van den Haag.

**Abstaining:**  Miller and Pulitzer.

March 6, 1981

(Filed: Feb. 6, 1981)
CHARLES MOHR, NAN ROBERTSON AND
JAMES WOOTEN
against
LIFE MAGAZINE

**Complaint:** In its February, 1981, issue, *LIFE* Magazine published an illustrated story on the career of the slain Dr. Michael Halberstam and Bernard Welch, the burglar accused of the killing. Charles Mohr, Nan Robertson and James Wooten, all journalists, complained of (1) *LIFE*'s conduct in the preparation of the story; (2) *LIFE*'s payment of $8,000 to Mr. Welch for the photographs provided through his literary agent; and of what they referred to as (3) "*LIFE*'s grotesquely choos(ing) to depict the biographies as parallel tragedies involving two high achievers with differing career specialities." The whole was submitted as "a particularly deplorable and professionally unwholesome case of bad editorial judgment and journalistic practice."

**Response:** On February 24, Philip B. Kunhardt, Jr., managing editor of *LIFE*, delivered the following reply:

"In answer to the charges that have been made to the National News Council about *LIFE*'s story *The Ghost Burglar and the Good Doctor*:

"*LIFE* agreed to pay Bernard Welch, through his attorney, for album pictures of him in the possession of Welch's parents and common-law wife. The price agreed upon was $1,000 for each picture used, a sum higher than we usually pay for pictures but certainly not as high as we have sometimes paid. No other arrangement between *LIFE* and Welch was ever discussed or implied. We never sought an interview. It was before we had even seen the Welch pictures that Welch decided he wanted to talk to our reporter. What was in Welch's mind is anyone's guess. It was our feeling then, and still is now, that the purchase of the pictures was justified since they made a real contribution to understanding the tragic dimensions of the terrible encounter between Dr. Halberstam and Welch.

"Parallel textual and photographic biographies of Michael Halberstam and his alleged killer were certainly *LIFE*'s aim. In retrospect I think the Welch quote in large type at the beginning of the story was unfortunate. To many of those close to Dr. Halberstam it sounded sympathetic to his killer and may have given the effect of "top billing" for Welch in their eyes. In a less heated atmosphere the self-serving insanity of the quote would be clear. But to suggest that the entire story gives equal credit and honor to both men is a charge without basis. The story speaks for itself.

"The most serious charge against *LIFE* in my opinion is that our reporter deliberately misled Michael Halberstam's widow. That is totally inaccurate. Elliott Jones was informed that the story would involve her husband and his murderer, and that was all our reporter knew at the time she interviewed her. It has been suggested that *LIFE* should have got back in touch with Elliott Jones after we had acquired the Welch pictures two weeks after she had lent us the pictures of her husband. We did not do so because Elliott Jones had put no restrictions on their use and because we saw no reason to assume that she would find our story offensive. 'I want to know everything about his killer . . . .' she was quoted in the *New York Times* of December 12. 'I would like to see his baby pictures. I would like to know who his mother was and what she thought of him as a kid . . . .' No one assured Elliott Jones or anyone else interviewed for the *LIFE* story that we were working on a journalistic memorial to Dr. Halberstam. After the story had closed and had gone to press and the nature of its content had been discussed, I said in a phone conversation to David Halberstam that I felt the story did honor to his brother and was, in part at least, a memorial to him. To my knowledge, that was the only instance in which the word "memorial" was used.

"One final thought. *LIFE* certainly underestimated the extremely emotional climate in the Washington area created by the killing of Michael Halberstam and the years of wanton robberies by his alleged killer. At least for those many people touched personally by Dr. Halberstam, there could be no satisfactory story. In fact, many of these shocked and saddened friends could only vent their frustration at whatever appeared in print."

**Analysis of complaint:** The three central elements of the complaint are clear: how *LIFE* conducted itself in the preparation of the story, whether payment to the individual accused of the murder was journalistically proper, and the challenge to editorial judgement and practice.

### The Magazine's Conduct

In his response, Mr. Kunhardt said that "The most serious charge against *LIFE* in my opinion is that our reporter deliberately misled Michael Halberstam's widow. That is totally inaccurate. Elliott Jones was informed that the story would involve her husband and his murderer, and that was all our reporter knew at the time she interviewed her."

Elliott Jones denounced this as "a deliberate lie—absolutely a lie."

She went on to assert that the reporter "never once mentioned doing a story on Welch."

However, several of the closest friends of the Halberstams said they were told from the start by the reporter, Hillary Johnson, that her central focus was on the man charged with the murder. Stephen Lesher, who with Michael Halberstam, wrote the best-selling book, "A Coronary Event," said that from the very first conversation he had with the reporter, she made it "very clear that her editors were greatly interested in Welch. I told her that Michael was the one who ought to be assessed because he was such a remarkable man. She said that she would talk to her editors, but she made clear that it was essentially a Welch story she was interested in." At the funeral service, the reporter approached others (Nancy Ball Lesher, a former magazine reporter; Fred Graham of television; Stephen Banker, another journalist). Most of these said they knew from the outset the reporter's intentions.

Mr. Lesher said that when the reporter was welcomed at the Halberstam home to go through the pictures there and check the details of Dr. Halberstam's career he gave thought to mentioning to Elliott Jones that the magazine's central focus was on Bernard Welch, but he decided not to report it for fear of upsetting her.

Mr. Lesher said that one added reason for his deciding not to mention it was that, from his journalistic experience, he had concluded that what was produced about Dr. Halberstam would be in the nature of a "sidebar" (an accompanying short feature) and that such an arrangement might also upset Elliott Jones.

Elliott Jones said that Ms. Johnson, in introducing herself, noted that she had written a story about Dr. Halberstam two years earlier in *Women's Wear Daily*. "Michael liked the story very much," said Elliott Jones, "and I felt that if anyone could do a good article about Michael, this young woman certainly could. But she lied to me. All she told me was that it was to be a story about Michael. I can't remember the exact word she used, but I think it was 'tribute.'"

Elliott Jones said she understood the necessity of adequate coverage about Welch in the final article. She said she recognized that this aspect would have to be included, but that the reporter's approach and as-surances were convincing enough that she fully believed the reporter was working principally on a story focused on her husband.

In a letter to David Halberstam February 5, Mr. Kunhardt wrote that "It is understandable that Mrs. Halberstam, in her great distress and in her unwillingness (under her lawyer's instructions) to discuss the case, did not absorb our reporter's statement that *LIFE* intended to do a story on both your brother and Bernard Welch."

## The Payment to Welch

If there was indignation in the Halberstam family and among the family's friends about the gathering of the information, there was fury about the payment of $8,000 to Welch, through his attorney and literary agent, for the snapshots published in *LIFE*.

Payments to outsiders for pictures have long been standard practice in journalism. Some of the most striking pictures over the years have come from free-lancers, and high bidding for exclusive rights is not uncommon. The issue posed here is not simply payment, but payment to an individual charged with murder.

David Halberstam called it "contemptible checkbook journalism." "It devastated me," said Elliott Jones.

In his February 5 letter to Mr. Halberstam, Mr. Kunhardt said: "Many criminals, alleged and convicted, have been paid for their cooperation on stories by magazines, newspapers, book publishers and television. The list includes Gary Gilmore, Sirhan Sirhan, James Earl Ray, and Sam Shepard, among others."

That is correct. It appears that the practice was imported from London's Fleet Street. As long ago as 1966, the British Press Council, in a declaration of principle, stated:

> No payment should be made for feature articles to persons engaged in crime or other notorious misbehaviour where the public interest does not warrant it.

Quite apart from the ambiguity of the phrase, "where the public interest does not warrant it," the declaration is evidence that many in journalism deplore the practice of paying fees to criminals for cooperation in news coverage.

Mr. Kunhardt's letter to the Council contains a long second paragraph about *LIFE*'s payment to Welch. One portion reads, "The price agreed upon was $1,000 for each picture used, a sum higher than we usually pay for pictures but certainly not as high as we have sometimes paid." This does not say that higher sums have been paid by *LIFE* to individuals involved in criminal episodes.

Journalist Stephen Banker had a number of conversations with the *LIFE* reporter during her several trips to Washington. He appears to have been the only one to keep notes on what was said, and his phone billings, he said, show a 32-minute conversation with her on January 14. She had

238

told Mr. Banker earlier that money would not figure anywhere in the undertaking. In the January 14 conversation, Mr. Banker's notes show that the reporter repeated this as having been in order when she first looked through the Halberstam photo files. However, she said, at what she called "the eleventh hour," Mr. Kunhardt decided he couldn't do the story without pictures of Welch. The reporter told Mr. Banker that "our page rate is somewhere around $500. That's what's paid first-time contributors." She said that she had talked with Martin Firestone, Welch's agent, and he (a) had said there would be "nothing for nothing," and (b) had suggested a *LIFE* book and motion picture contract. She said this was rejected immediately. She reported that Mr. Kunhardt had authorized $1,000 a picture. The staff notes that one of *LIFE*'s pages had six pictures, making this a $6,000 page, an escalation by twelve times the going rate the reporter mentioned.

At this point in the conversation, Mr. Banker says he entered some words of protest about the episode and called it "highly debatable."

Mr. Banker's notes show that the reporter told him she did get the interview with Welch before she had ever seen any of his pictures, but David Halberstam would have none of this. He said, "Kunhardt, to use his own word, worked out a formula to get Welch to collaborate. He will pay the magazine's top rate for pictures and then double it. Kunhardt says it is not 'checkbook journalism' because *LIFE* did not pay for the interview. In public relations terms, it is slick. We accuse Kunhardt of paying Welch for his *participation*, which is the crucial word."

Mr. Halberstam proposed a general principle that would cover any journalistic payments to anyone involved in criminal activity. "The reader is entitled to know on what basis either stories or photographs are obtained," he said. "If news organizations had to say publicly that they had paid for certain stories or pictures, there would be no payments."

A further reference to Mr. Kunhardt's February 5 letter to David Halberstam seems justified. It said, "If I had to do it over again, I probably would have told Mrs. Halberstam about the agreement with Welch for his pictures which was made two weeks after Mrs. Halberstam loaned us her pictures . . . . Maybe that was insensitive of us, and thoughtless, but it was certainly not the act of duplicity that you made it out to be."

In *LIFE*'s February issue, the so-called "title page" which lists the contents of the edition, also carries at the bottom "*Picture sources*." For the pages applying to the Halberstam/Welch story, the credits are extended to Blanche Halberstam, Harvard University Archives and Elliott

Jones, all for pictures dealing with Dr. Halberstam. There is no credit listed for the Welch photographs. Indeed, there is credit listed or placed next to or near every photograph in the issue except the Welch pictures.

Jonathan Larsen, news editor of *LIFE*, explained—in the absence of the picture editor—the omission of credits for the Welch snapshots: "We knew where the photos of Dr. Halberstam came from," he said, adding that they were collected personally by *LIFE*'s staff. The Welch snapshots, he said, came from his common-law wife and from his family in upstate New York. They were not collected personally by *LIFE*'s staff, and in the absence of certainty as to who, specifically, supplied each one, *LIFE* decided to skip crediting them.

A good deal of the Halberstam family indignation arose from the fact that its members learned about *LIFE*'s $1,000-a-picture arrangement not from the magazine, but from *The Washington Post*. That newspaper, said its executive editor, Benjamin Bradlee, got its information from Sol Rosen, Welch's lawyer.

## Judgment and Practice

No assessment could convey the antagonism expressed by those who entered the complaint and those who have added their protests in conversations.

In his response, Mr. Kunhardt used the word "unfortunate" about the large-type quote at the beginning of the article. It appears above the heading which read, "The Ghost Burglar and the Good Doctor." The quoted portion is in type only slightly smaller and says: "I had everything going for me and he had everything going for him. But now he's dead and I'm in prison. They say I destroyed his life, but he destroyed mine."

Mr. Kunhardt said that "in a less heated atmosphere the self-serving insanity of the quote would be clear."

Later in the letter, he recognized that *LIFE* underestimated the "extremely emotional climate in the Washington area created by the killing of Michael Halberstam and the years of wanton robberies by his alleged killer."

\* \* \*

NOTE: In a letter received by the Council twenty-seven days after its decision, Hillary Johnson criticized the analysis in this report as "illogical, muddle-headed and often vicious." She faulted the Council for not having given her a direct opportunity to reply to criticism of her journalistic conduct, instead of relying solely on the unequivocal defense of her actions given by her managing editor and included in full in this report.

The Council's established policy is never to go to reporters or sub-editors for comment on complaints unless that course is suggested by the publication. Ms. Johnson contended that in her case the Council's failure to do so made it "deliberately or unwittingly" a participant in a vendetta organized by friends of the Halberstams, which unfairly reflected on her professional integrity.

The Council Chairman wrote Ms. Johnson on April 9 inviting further discussion. Copies went to *LIFE* executives. No reply was received.

\* \* \*

**Council finding:** The Council has three questions before it: Did *LIFE* use deception in gathering its information? Was *LIFE* justified in depicting the lives of the two men as "parallel" tragedies? Should *LIFE* have paid a convicted criminal awaiting trial on charges of murder for news material?

First, on the matter of deception, the Council is being asked to make a judgment between complainants who say "evidence will show that representatives of *LIFE* secured the cooperation of Dr. Halberstam's widow and other persons by assuring her that they were preparing a journalistic 'memorial' to Dr. Halberstam," and an editor who says, "That is totally inaccurate." Both sides have presented evidence to back their assertions. Some of the evidence is compelling, but none of it conclusive. The Council cannot decide which side is right.

Second, as for *LIFE*'s depiction of the two men, the Council has always sought to restrict its purview to "the accuracy and fairness" of the reporting in question. The Council has tried to avoid substituting its judgment for that of editors in matters of news treatment. For that reason, the Council resists the temptation to censure *LIFE* for the headline given to Welch's remark—"They say I destroyed his life, but he destroyed mine"—and for the treatment of the lives of Dr. Halberstam and his alleged killer as parallel tragedies.

But the Council does question whether a national news magazine of great repute has kept faith with the highest professional standards. *LIFE*'s editor has acknowledged as "unfortunate" the large type headline portion of the article. Perhaps more than the headline—including the attempt to compare the lives of the two men—was unfortunate.

The Council also feels a responsibility to question *LIFE*'s $8,000 payment to Welch for snapshots. Dr. Halberstam's widow, Elliott Jones, says she would not have provided *LIFE* with photos of her husband if the magazine had told her of its $1,000-a-picture arrangement with Welch.

Furthermore, the magazine's payment causes the Council to ask

241

whether any news organization ought to pay a convicted criminal awaiting trial on charges of murder for interviews, photos, or other news
material. Such a payment throws into question the integrity of the
organization involved. Was *LIFE*, by agreeing to purchase and publish
photos that portrayed Welch as just another person (riding a bicycle,
playing a guitar, holding fish he had caught), appearing to sacrifice its
professionalism for the sake of a good story?

Was *LIFE* leaving itself open to the charge that it was giving Welch a
favorable pretrial interview as a reward for letting the magazine buy his
photos? Was it perverting the newsgathering process, encouraging what
could have developed into a bidding war among news organizations?

As *LIFE* indicates in its defense, other criminals, alleged and convicted, have been paid for their cooperation on stories by magazines,
newspapers, and broadcasters. A better practice—one designed to eliminate any possible questions by readers or viewers about the motives of the
news organization—would be adoption of a policy not to pay criminals
for news materials.

Short of that, a news organization should report to its readers or
viewers the payment to criminals it has made, thereby allowing the
readers or viewers to take that payment into account in evaluating the
published or broadcast report.

The Council's call for disclosure is consistent with its 1975 statement
on "Checkbook Journalism." That statement came in response to a
$50,000 payment by CBS News to H.R. Haldeman, former White House
aide, for his contributions to two hour-long programs: on-camera interviews, discussions with CBS staff, and 25 hours of 8mm. movies that he
had taken during his years at the White House.

The Council opted for disclosure of the circumstances of the payment
to Haldeman for two reasons: first, to better inform the public, and
second, to encourage more careful review by news organizations of
situations in which payment is deemed appropriate . . . or inappropriate.
The Council suggested the following guidelines:

> If compensation beyond actual expense is made to any person for news in the form
> of an interview (published or broadcast), for information to be used in a news story
> or broadcast, or for an article by a person in the news, that fact should be disclosed.
> A prefatory note or on-the-air statement immediately preceding the article or
> program should be published or broadcast.
>
> Such notification to the reader or viewer is not intended for the publication of
> articles or photographs or radio and television productions actually written or
> produced by an individual or supplier and marketed to the news organization
> through commonly accredited practices that do not deceive the public.

242

Reviewing *LIFE*'s article in light of that 1975 guideline, the Council believes the public would have been better served had the magazine disclosed to its readers the $8,000 payment to Welch for the photos. Such disclosure would have at least permitted the article's readers to evaluate in perhaps a slightly different light the magazine's treatment of an alleged murderer it billed as an accomplished thief "in pursuit of his rainbow."

Insofar as the Council proposes a higher standard for *LIFE* and other media with regard to payments for news material, the complaint is warranted.

**Concurring:** D. Bell, J. Bell, Benson, Brady, Ghiglione, Hornby, Isaacs, Pulitzer and Stanton.

**Dissenting:** Decter, Huston, Miller and van den Haag.

**Dissenting opinion by Ms. Huston (van den Haag concurring):** On the Halberstam case, the Council in its majority opinion crossed what I consider a potentially hazardous boundary line. Instead of properly confining its decision to fairness and accuracy, it marched blindly into the quicksand of values, news judgment and good taste, by suggesting that it was "unfortunate" for *LIFE* to compare the life of a prominent doctor to that of an alleged murderer. The Council is going dangerously too far when it questions a publication's "professionalism" for portraying someone "as just another person."

It is a grave mistake, in my opinion, for the News Council to assume the role of super-editor and start second-guessing editorial judgments as to what constitutes appropriate material—be it subject matter or approach—to of all things, a human interest story!

Unfortunately, it could easily appear to the outside observer, that the Council measures a case involving aggrieved fellow journalists with a different yardstick than it uses for other aggrieved readers.

**Dissenting opinion by Mr. Miller (van den Haag concurring):** I do not applaud the *LIFE* article on Dr. Halberstam and Mr. Welch. But this complaint does not convince me this Council should impose its concept of taste or judgment on the editors of this magazine.

**Abstaining:** Maynard. (Mr. Maynard explained that while he was employed in Washington, D.C., Dr. Halberstam was his physician.)

March 6, 1981

COMPLAINT NO. 188    (Filed April 24, 1981)
HOWARD UNIVERSITY
JOURNALISM FACULTY
against
THE WASHINGTON POST

**Complaint:** Ten members of the journalism faculty at the School of Communications of Howard University in Washington, D.C. filed with the National News Council a charge that the chain of events touched off by publication of a fabricated news story in *The Washington Post* on Sept. 28, 1980, had "posed a new and unnecessary danger to the First Amendment freedom of the press in our nation."

The complaint was drafted by Professor Samuel F. Yette and subscribed to by nine of his departmental colleagues, including the school's dean, Lionel C. Barrow, Jr. It asserted that the story, entitled "Jimmy's World," which purported to be an eye-witness account of the injection of heroin into the arm of an 8-year-old black child in the presence of his mother by her lover, a drug pusher, "defamed the journalism profession, disserved this community by imposing needless financial and emotional burdens upon this city and the nation and . . . maligned a group of people racially identified" with the non-existent victim.

The Howard group asked for an impartial investigation by the Council into what it termed "the inaccuracies and unfairness perpetrated by *The Washington Post*" in publishing the article, its subsequent winning, then relinquishing, a Pulitzer Prize for the story, and the actions attendant on "the resignation and virtual disappearance of Janet Cooke, whose name was the by-line used for the story."

The specific points raised included:

1. The faculty members rejected as unworthy of belief the notion that Miss Cooke, a young black reporter, had "hoodwinked and conned seasoned Watergate editors into publishing a fabricated story—replete with blind attributions—without their ever being suspicious enough to question the validity of her story."

2. They characterized as "willful and malicious ignorance" the failure of the editors and top managers at *The Post* to question either the story's validity or Miss Cooke's veracity after both had been challenged by Washington's mayor and police chief following an extensive and fruitless search for the child.

3. They charged that Publisher Donald Graham and Executive Editor Ben Bradlee were guilty of "what in other circumstances would be called

244

criminal negligence, given that they either knew or should have known what was being printed in their own newspaper."

4. They termed inconceivable any idea that Miss Cooke did not have "the sure-handed assistance of top management" in the submission of her story for a Pulitzer Prize or in its subsequent switch by the Pulitzer board from the local news writing category, where it did not win, to the feature category, where the board adjudged it the winner even though the nominating jury in that field had never had the Cooke story before it and had, in fact, recommended three other entries in order of preference for the award.

In urging an independent Council inquiry, the Howard faculty members contended that the public had been obliged to rely on a unilateral explanation by *The Post* while Miss Cooke, they alleged, had been "pressured to resign, forced into hiding, shielded from press and other inquiry, blamed for one of journalism's major hoaxes and labeled emotionally unstable."

The complainants argued that neither *The Post* nor any other recognized American newspaper would allow a county sheriff, a mayor, a governor or even the President of the United States, if involved in a hoax of such magnitude, to give a one-sided view of what took place. Impartial examination was important, the signers held, to arrive "not only at the truth but also a public perception of truth in this matter vital to the welfare of the profession, this community and the entire nation."

**Response:** *The Washington Post* cooperated fully with the Council. The paper's executives, from Donald Graham and Ben Bradlee down, answered questions at length. No restrictions were imposed on access to staff, and all the reporters or subeditors contacted set forth their views freely. *The Post* did not, however, submit any formal reply to the Howard group's complaint. There were two principal reasons for the absence of such a reply.

The first was the belief, expressed repeatedly by its top officials, that all the relevant information anyone in authority at the paper could supply on what had gone wrong and why was contained in the analysis of the case by *The Post*'s ombudsman, Bill Green, published in *The Post* Sunday, April 19, 1981, four days after Miss Cooke acknowledged for the first time that the story was a fake and five days before the filing of the complaint. The Green analysis, which started with a Page One display summarizing its highlights and including seven specific bold-face criticisms of *Post* performance in connection with the journalistic fraud, covered three and a half pages inside the paper's first section.

The second deterrent to a formal response was *The Post*'s reluctance to lend dignity to a complaint which, in the words of Mr. Graham, it regarded as "silly and frivolous on its face," particularly in its intimations that *The Post* was holding Miss Cooke hostage and that its executives had conspired to concoct the hoax. The leading role taken in preparation of the charges by Professor Yette was cited by both Mr. Graham and Mr. Bradlee as evidence that the accusations were designed largely to grind a political axe which Mr. Yette held against The Washington Post Company.

Their strongly expressed sentiment on this score stemmed from prolonged litigation that arose out of the professor's filing of charges of racial discrimination and abridgement of his First Amendment rights after his discharge in 1972 from the staff of the Washington bureau of *Newsweek*, a sister publication of *The Post*, where he had worked for four years. Incompetence was the basis cited by the magazine for the dismissal. A victory by Mr. Yette before the District of Columbia Commission on Human Rights was reversed in favor of *Newsweek* by a three-member bench of the District of Columbia Court of Appeals after more than two years of deliberation. An appeal by Mr. Yette for reconsideration by the full nine-judge court en banc resulted in a second judicial ruling upholding *Newsweek*. The Supreme Court denied a petition for certiorari, closing the case with the plaintiff defeated.

(Professor Yette says that there was absolutely no connection between the dispute over his firing and his submission of the complaint, except that his experience with *The Post* company in matters which he felt bore on its attitude toward ethics, race and questionable journalism "did possibly equip me better to understand some of the intracacies and dangers involved in this present matter." He adds that "those who contend that I carried a vendetta should also note that nine of my colleagues concurred in this complaint, none of whom to my knowledge was ever fired by *The Post*.")

In lieu of a direct comment on the complaint, *The Post* stood on the ombudsman's report by Bill Green. It had been prepared from memoranda, interviews and other information gathered by Mr. Green after a "full disclosure" mandate had been issued to the staff by Messrs. Graham and Bradlee. Members of the Council have received copies as part of their background material, but it is summarized here both for the light it sheds on issues raised in the complaint and as a jumping-off point for the Council's exploration of the larger questions for journalism that flow from the Cooke story and its aftermath. The supplemental data gathered by Council staff in its investigation will be covered in the staff analysis.

## Capsulization of the Green Report

Janet Cooke, then 24, attracted the attention of executive editor Bradlee with a letter she wrote July 12, 1979, asking for a job. She wrote that she had two years' experience on *The Toledo* (OH.) *Blade* and had graduated Phi Beta Kappa from Vassar in 1976. She enclosed clippings of six stories she had written for *The Blade*. Her academic credentials were not checked. Tom Wilkinson, *Post* assistant managing editor for personnel, vaguely recalls talking with somebody at *The Blade* about her experience there. No other checks were made.

Miss Cooke was interviewed by at least four *Post* editors and was hired Jan. 3, 1980, as a reporter on the District Weekly staff. (The Weekly is a suburban supplement to *The Post*). In the next several months 52 stories by Miss Cooke appeared in *The Post*. In August Vivian Aplin-Brownlee, editor of the District Weekly, assigned her to find out about a new kind of heroin on the streets of Washington, which was said to ulcerate the skin of its users. Mrs. Aplin-Brownlee decided that the material Miss Cooke accumulated in the pursuit of the heroin story was suitable for use in the Metro section of the newspaper. In describing her material to City Editor Milton Coleman, Miss Cooke said she had heard of an 8-year-old child who was addicted to heroin. Mr. Coleman directed her to go after that story, assuring her it would make Page One.

Mr. Coleman is quoted in the Green report as follows:

> It appeared that the kid was at RAP, Inc., a service organization for drug addicts. I went to Managing Editor (Howard) Simons' office . . . and we talked it through. If RAP gave us permission to talk with the boy, could we reveal the name? We agreed that we would not under any circumstances. Would RAP let us talk with the parents? We didn't know. Janet went back out.

Two weeks passed and Miss Cooke reported that she could not find the child, but a week later she asserted that she had found another 8-year-old addict, Jimmy. She said the child's mother had called her after Miss Cooke left cards in a number of places where she had inquired about an 8-year-old addict. In answer to a question, Mr. Coleman told Miss Cooke that she could promise the mother anonymity. He did not ask her for the family's name or street address. Mr. Simons, who had concurred in the pledge of confidentiality for Miss Cooke's sources, sought no details on identity from either her or Mr. Coleman. Nor did Bob Woodward, assistant managing editor in charge of the Metro staff, when he saw the story at a later stage. The reporter told Mr. Coleman that the drug pusher/lover had said to her, "If I see any police, Miss Lady, or if any police come to see me, we (he glanced at a knife in his hand) will be around to see you."

Miss Cooke produced a 13½-page double-spaced memo describing a visit to the child's house during which she assertedly interviewed the child, the mother, and the mother's lover, and watched the injection. Mr. Woodward said later that if he had seen that memo he might have asked questions about the long and seemingly perfect quotes.

Mr. Coleman made some suggestions on a lead and on reorganization of the material, preliminary to preparation of a second draft by Miss Cooke. When it was turned in, he checked one element of the story—whether its description of the exchange of blood and fluid in the syringe during the process of "shooting up" was credible. Boisfeuillet Jones, Vice-president and Counsel for *The Post*, suggested a couple of changes to make the guarantee of anonymity to the pusher more perfect.

Mr. Woodward saw the story for the first time at this point and called in Miss Cooke to tell him about her experiences. Nothing in the account or in the story made him suspicious.

On this theme, the Green report notes:

> None of *The Post*'s senior editors subjected Cooke's story to close questioning. Simons was on vacation in Florida the week before it appeared . . . . Ben Bradlee read the story that week and thought it was "a helluva job."
>
> Are they satisfied with the preliminary screening on "Jimmy's World"? Simons answered: "Yes, there was no reason to disbelieve the story." Bradlee said: "I am not satisfied now—but I was then."
>
> Coleman, who was editing Cooke's copy, reflects on this: "Much of my attention was concentrated on the story and formulating it. Subconsciously, I think I firmly believed that the extra eyes of the backup system would catch anything that I missed."

Now Mr. Coleman believes other editors were relying on him. "We never really debated whether or not it was true," he said. "I think—if I can gore my own ox—they kind of took it for granted that Coleman should know."

Mr. Bradlee, who was on duty the weekend the story was to appear, designated it for Page One. On Friday night Mr. Coleman told Miss Cooke that Mr. Simons had asked him to warn her that she had seen a crime and might be subpoenaed; that *The Post* would stand behind her if she were, but that if she refused to reveal her sources, she might be found in contempt of court and have to spend time in jail. If she did not want to face that, Mr. Simons had said, *The Post* would not run the story. Miss Cooke considered the warning overnight. Saturday she told Mr. Coleman to let the story run.

Readers began calling *The Post* as soon as the story reached them. According to the Green report: "Readers were outraged. The story was described as racist and criminal. The concern was for Jimmy. 'What about the boy?' was the central question. It was repeated for the next four days in as many versions as the human mind can invent."

Mayor Marion Barry ordered a search for the child. Police Chief Burtell Jefferson threatened to have the reporter and her editors subpoenaed if they did not reveal the name. *The Post*'s attorneys replied that the newspaper had a right under the First Amendment to protect its sources.

"*The Post*'s telephones never stopped ringing. Between 50 and 60 letters to the editor arrived," Mr. Green reported. At one point the mayor announced that authorities knew who Jimmy was and that he was under treatment; later that statement proved erroneous, the ombudsman wrote.

On Oct. 15 Mr. Barry said, "We're kind of giving up on that . . . . I've been told the story is part myth, part reality. We all have agreed that we don't believe that the mother or the pusher would allow a reporter to see them shoot up."

Mr. Coleman had assigned 11 reporters to follow up on the Jimmy story—five to cover news developments and six to find a second Jimmy. The first doubts recorded inside *The Post* about the original story came to Mr. Coleman from Courtland Milloy, a black reporter assigned to accompany Miss Cooke on the search for a second young addict. He told Mr. Coleman that she did not know the area in which Jimmy allegedly lived.

Vivian Aplin-Brownlee, who had been Miss Cooke's supervisor on the Weekly staff, also voiced doubts about the story to Mr. Coleman because the language and ideas attributed to the child did not seem to fit an 8-year-old and because it seemed unlikely to her that Miss Cooke could gain access to a "shooting gallery."

Other staff members had doubts but didn't express them to the appropriate editors at this point, Mr. Green reported. Mr. Bradlee recalls going to Mr. Woodward or Mr. Coleman, asking if anything should be rechecked, and going away reassured. Publisher Graham recalled raising the same question with Mr. Coleman and being satisfied with the answer.

Three weeks after the story appeared, Mr. Simons said to Mr. Coleman, "That kid is still out there, and nobody's looking for him. Let's find him. Take Janet with you."

Mr. Coleman told Miss Cooke about the plan, but before he could arrange to go out with her, she came to him and said that there was no need for them to go; she herself had visited the house and found that the family had moved to Baltimore. Mr. Woodward found it logical that the mother would have taken the child away, but Mr. Coleman was angry at Miss Cooke's going out on her own. When he expressed his anger to Mr. Simons, it raised doubts in the managing editor's mind for the first time. "But all I had was a hunch and the fact that she had ducked the visit. How do you prove a negative?" Mr. Simon asked.

Mr. Coleman recalled talking with Mr. Simons at the time of Courtland Milloy's expression of doubt and of his own uneasiness that the police had not found Jimmy. He said:

> I voiced my concerns to Howard and he said in so many words that they were legitimate. But he urged me to find the most creative way to examine them, stressing that I, more than anyone else, had to stand by my reporter. At the point that I even began to hint to her that I thought she had not been truthful, her trust in me could be destroyed.

Mr. Simons told Mr. Green that he could not recall talking with Messrs. Coleman or Woodward about doubts at that point.

According to the report, Mr. Woodward and Mr. Coleman insisted that the latter meet personally with a 14-year-old prostitute about whom Miss Cooke was planning to write a story. The purpose of this insistence, as stated, was "mainly to protect Cooke from more staff jealousies and to establish once and for all the soundness of her reporting." Miss Cooke kept arranging times and places for the meeting, but each arrangement was canceled. Mr. Woodward found this only "mildly troubling," he told Mr. Green.

Among the reasons the report gives for *The Post*'s failure to reexamine the Jimmy story were the mayor's early statement that authorities knew who Jimmy was; a letter from a psychiatrist Nov. 10 that seemed to say he knew of many Jimmys; the attribution of some internal doubts to staff jealousy; the failure of staff members to press or, in some cases, even to express their individual doubts, and the adoption of a defensive stance. "We went into our Watergate mode: Protect the source and back the reporter," was Mr. Woodward's description for that posture.

Pride also contributed, according to Mr. Coleman. "We had published the story in the first place and stood by it. We probably put too much faith in the hope that maybe things were not the way so many indicators suggested they might be."

Whatever doubts there might have been appeared quiescent by Dec. 10 when Mr. Coleman recommended the Jimmy story for entry in various prize competitions with a memo calling it readable, accurate and complete and saying, "I can't think of another story that shows more enterprise and resourcefulness on the part of a reporter in overcoming obstacles."

The proposal to enter the Jimmy story for a Pulitzer produced a new expression of doubt, this time from Jonathan Neumann, himself a past Pulitzer winner. He voiced his reservations to David Maraniss, the Maryland editor, who was pushing for entry a series by a member of his own staff. Mr. Maraniss, on rereading the Jimmy story, decided that it did not ring true and urged Mr. Woodward to reread it before it was nominated. In hindsight, Mr. Maraniss told the ombudsman he did not put his doubts as strongly as he might have lest he appear to be lobbying for his own entry.

Mr. Neumann is quoted in the Green report:

> A number of people felt strongly that it should not be nominated because it could disgrace us. A couple of dozen people talked about it, but we didn't go to top editors. I think we felt that it wouldn't be fair to put her on the carpet when we couldn't prove anything.

The upshot was a decision by Mr. Woodward to ignore the internal doubters and send the nomination forward. "I have used the phrase 'in for a dime, in for a dollar' to describe my overall conclusion about submitting the Cooke story for a Pulitzer or any other prize," he informed the ombudsman.

Mr. Bradlee, Mr. Simons and Richard Harwood, deputy managing editor, made the final decisions on which stories should be submitted for Pulitzer awards. Mr. Bradlee said he had heard of no skepticism about the Cooke story. "Nobody ever came in this room and said, 'I have doubts about the story' before or after publication, and nobody said someone else had misgivings about the story," he said.

Mr. Harwood knew of no doubts. Mr. Simons said, "I didn't know of any staff doubts, but I had some of my own. I had reason to doubt but no reason to disbelieve, and Woodward supported the nomination strongly."

The Pulitzer Prizes were announced April 13. *The Toledo Blade* told The Associated Press that the wire service description of Miss Cooke's academic attainments contained elements that *The Blade* knew to be untrue. The AP report was based on material received by the Pulitzer board from *The Post*. It said that Miss Cooke had studied at the Sorbonne, graduated magna cum laude from Vassar and received a master's degree from the University of Toledo. The Associated Press checked with Vassar and learned that Miss Cooke had not graduated. The wire service called her. She said that she had. Louis D. Boccardi, executive editor of AP, called Mr. Simons about the same time that a Vassar official called Mr. Bradlee. By this time, it was Tuesday afternoon, April 14. *The Post* editors found that nobody at the paper had checked the biographical form Miss Cooke had filled out to accompany her Pulitzer entry. They also found that it differed from the original resume she filed at *The Post*. Specifically, it mentioned the Sorbonne, whereas her resume did not. It said she had reading knowledge of four languages compared with two on her resume. It said she had won six prizes from the Ohio Newspaper Women's Association; her resume said one.

Mr. Bradlee told Mr. Coleman to take Miss Cooke aside and find out about the discrepancies. After much questioning and telephone conversation with Miss Cooke, she acknowledged that her biographical material was false but continued to insist that the Jimmy story was true. Mr. Bradlee and other editors joined the interrogation and discovered additional flaws in the Cooke self-description. Finally, Mr. Bradlee asked about Jimmy's identity. Miss Cooke—unveiling the boy's full name for the first time to a *Post* editor—said that Jimmy was Tyrone Davis; his mother was Candi Davis, and her lover was Robert Jackson Anderson. They lived on Xenia Street, she said. Mr. Bradlee gave her 24 hours to prove that the Jimmy story was true. Mr. Woodward said flatly that he didn't believe the reporter. They sent Mr. Coleman off with her to see if she did, indeed, know where the house was.

Meanwhile, Miss Cooke's 145 pages of notes and her tape-recorded interviews were returned to *The Post* from the attorneys' office. They had been sent there when a subpoena was threatened. Mr. Woodward began going through the material with Messrs. Maraniss and Wilkinson. It was the first time that any editor at *The Post* had inspected the source data. Mr. Woodward said later that he saw "echoes" of the Jimmy story all through the notes, but no evidence of an interview with a child using heroin. Elsa Walsh, Miss Cooke's roommate and also a *Post* reporter, was called in. She revealed that she had gone through Miss Cooke's notes once without finding Jimmy. She said she had not believed the story but had not told her editors. Miss Walsh also recalled that Miss Cooke had once told her she was valedictorian at Vassar.

Mr. Coleman, out with the reporter, found that she could not identify the house where the interview had taken place. He became convinced that the story was a fake. On their return, they joined Messrs. Maraniss, Woodward and Wilkinson in the newspaper's fifth-floor conference room, and the questioning became more insistent. Mr. Woodward pressed and Mr. Maraniss, who had befriended Miss Cooke earlier, took a more gentle approach, according to the Green report. Miss Cooke reiterated 15 or 20 times that Jimmy did exist, but under continued grilling, the report says, "a subtle change crept into her answers."

Her own version of the meeting could not be obtained by Mr. Green because she declined to be interviewed by him, but the reconstruction he pieced together from the accounts of her questions had her saying such things as: "I have to believe the story," and, "What am I going to do?" When the others left the room, the report quotes Miss Cooke as saying to Mr. Maraniss:

> I was afraid I was going to be left alone with you. The first time I saw you today, I thought, "Oh boy, he knows, and I'm going to have to tell him." I couldn't lie to you. I couldn't tell them. I never would tell Woodward. The more he yelled, the more stubborn I was. Wilkinson represents the corporation. It means so much to Milton. You guys are smart. Woodward for the mind, you for the heart . . . .

It was at this point, according to the report, that Miss Cooke confessed that Jimmy was a composite. Woodward, Coleman and Wilkinson were told, and each of them hugged and kissed Miss Cooke. Then, alone again with Mr. Maraniss, she talked freely about what she had done. She is quoted as saying that she thought she knew enough to bring off the fake when she wrote the original draft for Coleman. The basis for her confidence, as stated, was threefold: (1) the police would not be able to find the boy because he did not exist; (2) she would not be afraid of the city officials; and (3) before the story was published she had been assured by Mr. Simons that he was not going to ask her the name of the boy or his mother. (The Green report notes that, according to others' recollections, Mr. Simons did direct Miss Cooke to tell Mr. Coleman the names.) Mr. Maraniss drove Miss Cooke to her apartment, where she stayed up the rest of the night talking with friends. Mr. Bradlee, having conferred over breakfast with Publisher Graham, instructed Mr. Maraniss to get Miss Cooke's resignation and a written statement. She wrote in longhand:

> "Jimmy's World" was in essence a fabrication. I never encountered or interviewed an 8-year-old heroin addict. The September 28, 1980, article in The Washington Post was a serious misrepresentation which I deeply regret. I apologize

to my newspaper, my profession, the Pulitzer board and all seekers of the truth. Today, in facing up to the truth, I have submitted my resignation. Janet Cooke.

**Staff Analysis:** The Council staff canvassed the elements in the Green report and found it to be in truth as comprehensive as it appeared to be. We found no evidence that Mr. Green or *The Post* editors and staff members to whom he turned for information had tried to cover up about things that reflected badly on the newspaper or on themselves. Nothing discovered in dozens of personal and telephone interviews raised any serious question about the report's basic accuracy. Primarily, the differences that surfaced involved interpretation and detail, not suppression of essential facts.

This staff report is defective in the same element that Mr. Green's is: It does not contain Janet Cooke's own story of what happened at *The Post*. However, the Council staff found no evidence that Miss Cooke was either forced into hiding or shielded from inquiry, as the complaint suggests. The staff established that she was in her apartment in Washington and often appeared socially in the community. She was contacted by mail and through several intermediaries. A staff member spoke to her mother by phone at Miss Cooke's apartment. Miss Cooke may have answered some of the calls directly, though the answerer identified herself simply as a "friend." Council staff is satisfied that she had received the messages, knew our identities and what was wanted, and had decided of her own free will not to talk.

This belief was confirmed by Miss Cooke herself when on June 9, two days before the opening of the Council meeting, staff made a final effort to speak with her in the hope that the passage of time might have lessened her reluctance to tell her side of the story. This time Miss Cooke did identify herself as the answerer of a call to her Washington apartment by Richard P. Cunningham, associate director of the Council. She said she had nothing to say about the circumstances of her story or her departure from *The Post*, though she was well aware of the Council's interest in obtaining her version. When Mr. Cunningham asked whether the decision not to talk was her own or whether it was part of an agreement with *The Post* to remain silent, Miss Cooke's response was: "Oh, certainly no. It's, it is absolutely my own decision."

To a follow-up question on whether she was in general agreement with Bill Green's account of what had happened, she replied: "Oh, I have absolutely no comment beyond telling you that my decision not to speak with you is my own." Miss Cooke was informed by Mr. Cunningham that the Howard University complainants had urged the Council not to decide the case at this meeting, in hopes that she might at some future time change her mind about talking. He asked whether she thought there was any chance such a change in her attitude might come within the next month. Her answer was: "Well, there's nothing I can tell you except that if I were you I'd proceed as scheduled."

The staff believes that this report is useful even without Miss Cooke's story, because *The Post*'s experiences with the Jimmy story raised so many issues of interest and importance to journalists and to the readers who are dependent on them for trustworthy information. Even though the Green report was comprehensive, it left questions unanswered about some of the issues. For example, did *The Post*'s editors ever consider before publication whether the newspaper had a citizen's responsibility to report to police that one of its reporters had seen a pusher inject heroin into a child? Was one editor specifically delegated to find out who Jimmy was before the story appeared?

This report contains information gathered by the staff on those issues as well as on the impact of the Jimmy story on Washington and *The Post*. It contains separate sections on the role of the ombudsman and on hoaxes at *The Post* and at other newspapers.

### Whether To Tell Police

On the question whether *The Post* had an obligation to report to police what Miss Cooke had observed and more particularly who was involved in the criminal acts she professed to have witnessed, the newspaper's position after publication is clear: Its lawyers cited "First Amendment provisions of the U. S. Constitution" when they defied the threat of a subpoena to obtain Jimmy's identity. A *Post* editorial Oct. 1 sounded the note that was echoed by other *Post* columnists: "No article could have been written if reporter Janet Cooke had not agreed to protect the confidentiality of her news sources. And what if there had been no story at all? Would the public know or care at all about what is happening to this boy and others like him?"

When Mayor Marion Barry suggested that the reporter might have broken the law by not reporting the crime, *The Post* reported in its news columns that several legal sources had told reporters after the Barry statement that "merely observing criminal conduct is not a violation of the law."

The community was torn with concern about Jimmy. Carolyn Bowden, supervisor of the Child Protective Services division of the Department of Human Services, was reported as saying that the child was in danger of a fatal overdose because of his age and his small stature (as described in Miss Cooke's story). "This newspaper article could be this child's epitaph," she said. Audrey Rose, acting commissioner of social services, was quoted as saying that the danger was increased by the fact that the heroin then being sold in Washington was of unprecedented strength and purity.

The conflict between the human concern and *The Post*'s stand on principle involved community readers in a conflict that is an old one for journalists. Peter Arnett, a 1966 Pulitzer laureate for Vietnam war coverage, has told of his wrestle with that crosspull while watching a monk covering himself with gasoline preparatory to burning himself near Saigon. He was quoted in an article in the *St. Louis Journalism Review* in May as saying, "I could have prevented that immolation by rushing at him and kicking the gasoline away. As a human being I wanted to, as a reporter I couldn't." *New York Times* columnist and a 1976 Pulitzer prizewinner for his reporting on Cambodia, Sydney Schanberg, asked a New York Deadline Club audience May 14 what they would do if as reporters they stumbled into an execution—a situation which was not entirely hypothetical for him. If the reporter thinks an injustice is about to be committed he or she will try to talk the executioners out of it, he said. "You are a human being. You will decide each time and then decide whether to rewrite your code of ethics. You decide what is the right thing. You can't make a rule."

Did editors consider before publication the implications of not going to the police? The Green report makes clear that Mr. Coleman did consult with Managing Editor Simons about guaranteeing anonymity for the mother if an 8-year-old addict should be found. (Mr. Coleman said he consulted with Mr. Simons instead of Bob Woodward, his immediate superior, because he customarily goes to Mr. Simons with legal questions). Mr. Coleman told Council staff that Mr. Jones, *The Post*'s counsel, was involved in the early meeting about anonymity. Mr. Coleman said his own purpose in the meeting was to find out for Miss Cooke, who had been at the paper only nine months, and for himself, named as city editor just five months before, "what kind of promises a reporter could make." The question of criminality did not come up, Mr. Coleman said, because he thought that whatever child they might find would be in counseling or under treatment. The lawyer's answer was yes on backing by the paper for a promise to keep identities secret.

When Miss Cooke came in weeks later with her story, she brought two elements that had not been discussed: She had assertedly seen the child injected, and her life had been threatened if she called police.

The memories of *Post* editors differ on the extent to which the new elements provoked prepublication discussion of whether the newspaper should report to the police.

Mr. Simons said, "I did not hold any discussions on that." But Mr. Bradlee said, "I met with the lawyers and with the staff before this thing was published and on that issue. It may have been the week that Simons was gone, but it's inconceivable that I didn't, and I did." Mr. Bradlee said he came down in favor of publishing the story and not telling the police.

Neither Mr. Coleman nor Mr. Woodward recalled any significant advance discussion of whether to go to the police. Mr. Woodward said "maybe half a sentence" of question was raised. He thought one of the problems with the story was that the issue should have been discussed fully beforehand.

The Green report does say that on Friday night, 24 hours before the Jimmy story went to press, Mr. Coleman passed on to Miss Cooke a message from Mr. Simons. The message noted that she had witnessed a felony, that she might be subpoenaed, and might have to go to jail; if she didn't want to face that, the story would not be published. Mr. Simons told Council staff that the message is his standard speech to reporters facing subpoena, but he cannot recall sending that message to Miss Cooke in this case.

The matter is further confused by the assertion in the Green report that Mr. Jones, *The Post*'s counsel, recommended changes in the Jimmy story that would protect the anonymity of the pusher more completely. Mr. Jones said he was prevented by his own professional and ethical commitments from commenting on his conferences with people in the newsroom and, therefore, could not clarify the confusion.

Mr. Coleman said that if someone had suggested to him that the police be informed he would have opposed it. This was his reasoning: "We had not gained knowledge of the crime as citizens but as reporters . . . . Reporters are reporters and law enforcement (people) are law enforcement—the two do not necessarily mesh." In this particular case, an important element in Mr. Coleman's thinking, he says, was his belief that "the cops would get the guy in three or four days." *The Post* did cooperate in one limited respect with searchers for Jimmy. When Audrey Rowe, acting commissioner for social services for the District of Columbia, called to inquire whether the child might have been a girl, not a boy,

Mr. Coleman said, he consulted with Miss Cooke and assured Ms. Rowe that Jimmy was a boy. (Ms. Rowe called because her department had received a tip on its child-abuse hotline that a contract was out to kill a pre-teenage girl who, it was alleged, was *The Post*'s Jimmy). Mr. Coleman told Council staff that he had fully expected the police to make a similar call within days after the original story appeared asking if a child named Tyrone was Jimmy. Mr. Coleman said he thought a carefully shaded reply to such a query might give the police the guidance they needed without violating the reporter's commitment.

Mr. Coleman said the one person who did raise the question of whether to inform the police or not in the prepublication phase was Miss Cooke. He said she told him that she considered not telling him about witnessing the heroin injection so that she would not have to face the dilemma. *Post* staff members recall that Miss Cooke asked at a training session less than two weeks before the story appeared about the obligation of a reporter who witnesses a crime. According to reporter Pat Tyler, Mr. Simons responded that the question was one of the toughest in journalism and must be answered on a case-by-case basis. Mr. Tyler recalled being told by another reporter at the meeting that Miss Cooke was working on a story about a child she saw "shoot up."

While community officials were pleading and demanding that *The Post* identify Jimmy, its editors stood fast in their refusal. But later, some had second thoughts about the rightness of the original decision to publish instead of reporting to the police.

Mr. Woodward, assistant managing editor of the Metro desk, said *The Post* had been wrong. He said *The Post* was in a "morally untenable position" having witnessed a crime and saying "to hell with" the 8-year-old victim.

Mr. Simons was moved by compassion for the child three weeks after the story appeared when he told Mr. Coleman to take Miss Cooke with him and find Jimmy.

Mr. Bradlee told Council staff he had not decided whether *The Post* was right not to report the injection of Jimmy to police. There can be no rule, he said. Yet deciding on a case-by-case basis has its perils. He said journalists would undoubtedly report an assassination attempt, at one extreme, and would probably not report pot smoking, at the other. He was uncomfortable with the thought that in less extreme cases journalists might report violations only of laws they approved of.

Ombudsman Green, in retrospect, says it was the obligation of the newspaper to recognize that a life was at stake. However, he still says he cannot answer to his own satisfaction whether it is enough for the paper to call attention to the situation. He noted that the question arose with more poignancy in the case of an 8-year-old than it might have in the case of a 14-year-old.

It is pertinent to note that the recent Public Agenda Foundation report, "The Speaker and the Listener: A Public Perspective on Freedom of Expression," says citizens—by a 47 per cent to 36 per cent plurality— believe that a reporter has the right to refuse to reveal the source of a story about drug abuse, even if it means criminals might not get caught. Harris and Gallup suveys had similar findings.

Charles Seib, Mr. Green's predecessor as *Post* ombudsman, wrote in the June issue of *presstime*, a publication of the American Newspaper Publishers Association, that the lack of concern for Jimmy before publication "spotlighted a blind spot that the news business had better do something about."

Mr. Seib wrote that a *Post* editor suggested to him, after the fact, a course of action that might have allowed the newspaper to avoid the charge of heartlessness without going to the police. The editor, whom Mr. Seib did not identify, said the newspaper might have put pressure on Jimmy's mother to get the child into treatment. *The Post* could have footed the bill, the editor said. Mr. Seib wrote:

> The irony here, of course, is that if he had done that—if he had allowed a humanitarian instinct to rise briefly above the enthusiasm for a smashing story— there is a good possibility that he would have uncovered the deception and the story would have died aborning.

The policy that *The Post* did follow of not informing the police was in line with what the News Council found to be the dominant view of editors and broadcasters in a survey it made last year, long before the Janet Cooke episode and reported in a booklet entitled "Covering Crime: How Much Press-Police Cooperation? How Little?" One question in that survey sought editors' views on when to report a crime to police. There was a top-heavy consensus among editors that news organizations had no obligation to report their findings confidentially to presecutors or police before the material was released.

The report continued:

> However, more than half of those holding this view said their answer would be different if they had reason to believe that persons who should be arrested and tried for crimes the news agency had unearthed would escape punitive action if there was no advance notice enabling the authorities to collect usable evidence. Such notice was considered especially in order where potential violence was involved.

## Responsibility to Know

Of the statement that Mr. Simons specifically delegated to Mr. Coleman the responsibility for learning "Jimmy's" identity, Council staff was told that the source for the statement was Miss Cooke. Nobody else has an independent memory of the incident. It comes up in the Green report in the form of a quote attributed to Mr. Coleman: "Howard said she should deal with me and tell me the child's identity. 'I don't want to know,' he said, somewhat jokingly."

Mr. Coleman told staff that the report makes his memory appear more concrete than it was. He said David Maraniss, the deputy Metro sub-editor who received Miss Cooke's confession, told him that the reporter decided she could get away with the hoax when she realized that she was not going to have to reveal Jimmy's identity to Howard Simons. Mr. Maraniss said that Miss Cooke recalled a meeting at which Mr. Simons said, "I don't want to know." Trying to find a framework for Mr. Maraniss' report, Mr. Coleman came up with a vague recollection that some such exchange might have taken place at a meeting about the Jimmy story. He included that possibility in a memo he was preparing for Mr. Green even though it contradicted another statement earlier in the memo, Mr. Coleman said.

Mr. Simons told Council staff that he cannot remember making any such statement, although he acknowledges that he has a short-term memory "like a short order cook." He said further that Mr. Jones, the lawyer at the meeting, could not recall Mr. Simons making the I-don't-want-to-know statement. However, Mr. Simons said the statement does conform with what he believes—that the managing editor need not know but that the sub-editor directly in charge of a story should know the source.

Mr. Coleman emphasized to the staff that he thought he did know enough to identify the child. "I knew the child's name was Tyrone (from Miss Cooke's first memo). I knew he was supposed to be a student at Washington Highlands Elementary School," Mr. Coleman said. He said he also knew the area where the child lived, "I felt that that was enough to identify the lad if we had to," Mr. Coleman said.

In any event, he did not believe having the name would help much. The people were not likely to be in the phone book or the city directory, he noted. If an editor went to the house of if Miss Cooke went back to the house, would that risk identifying the news source? he asked. His concern about identification was exacerbated by his fear that the pusher might make good on his threat to harm the reporter. Mr. Simons agreed and said further that it would have shown distrust for the reporter to send someone else to visit the family.

Mr. Coleman said he never did ask Miss Cooke for the identity of the child, "not in a knock-down, drag-out fashion." He said he believed that if there were doubts about the authenticity of the child, the last person to raise them would be the immediate surpervising editor. "Somebody has got to stand with the reporter," says the city editor.

Mr. Green said it was his impression that whatever Mr. Simons did say about learning the name of the child, was of an as-long-as-Milt-is-satisfied nature.

It seems clear that the managing editor counted on the city editor to be convinced of the authenticity of the story and that the city editor was convinced—at least until much later. However, Mr. Coleman is undoubtedly correct that, while he relied on the "extra eyes of the backup system" to catch anything he missed, the editors in the backup system "kind of took it for granted" that Mr. Coleman did know who the child was.

## Unattributed Sources

Discussion of whether a *Post* editor ought to have known Jimmy's identity leads inevitably to a discussion of *The Post*'s policy on confidential sources and unattributed material—a topic currently under intense discussion throughout journalism.

The *Post*'s style book, originally issued in 1978, lays down a basic standard on attribution of sources in a chapter written by Mr. Bradlee. It says:

> This newspaper is pledged to disclose the full source of all information unless disclosure would endanger the source's security. When we agree to protect a source's identity, that source will not be made known to anyone outside *The Post*.
>
> Before any information is accepted without full attribution, reporters must make every reasonable effort to get it on the record. If that is not possible, reporters should consider seeking the information elsewhere. If that in turn is not possible, reporters should request an on-the-record reason for restricting the source's identity, and should include the reason in the story.
>
> In any case, some kind of identification is almost always possible—by department or by position, for example—and should be reported.

Although this rule does not state explicitly that an editor, in evaluating the believability of the information on which a sensitive story is based, is entitled to know the identity of a reporter's confidential source, all the editors interviewed by staff said that they and the news staff had always operated on the principle that this was what the rule meant. Managing Editor Simons told the Council representatitives that he believed the use of the unknown "Deep Throat" in *The Post*'s Watergate stories was the only departure from that interpretation of the rule.

(Mr. Bradlee told a Columbia School of Journalism audience May 5 that he did know who "Deep Throat" was. That assertion—if designed to indicate that he had the knowledge at the time the Watergate stories appeared—threw into question whether even the use of "Deep Throat" had indeed been a departure from the rule. It also seemed to conflict with Mr. Woodward's statement in "All the President's Men" to Katharine Graham, chairman of *The Post*'s board, that he had not revealed "Deep Throat's" identity to anyone. Neither Mr. Woodward nor Mr. Bradlee would clarify that question for Council staff.)

Long before either the Janet Cooke case or Watergate, *The Post* exhibited sensitivity to the danger that reliance on confidential sources and unattributed material could be a form of journalistic malpractice. Its concern developed out of what it felt was manipulation of the press and of public opinion through "deep backgrounders" of the type given by Cabinet officers, with Henry Kissinger a principal practitioner of this particular art form in his period as National Security Adviser and Secretary of State in the Nixon Administration.

In the wake of the Nixon-Pompidou monetary conference in mid-December, 1971, Mr. Bradlee informed his editors and reporters that *The Post* would no longer allow its columns to be used as launching pads for stories that government officials or others in positions of authority wanted to get into circulation without assuming personal responsibility for them. He knew that a solo fight against self-serving leaks by people in high places would mean that *The Post* would find itself scooped frequently by its competitors and that the only effective resistance to the "deep backgrounders" lay in a general refusal by media leaders to participate in them. On this basis, Mr. Bradlee says, he sought to persuade *The New York Times* and the two large wire services to join *The Post* in boycotting such anonymous briefings. These efforts failed, and *The Post* abandoned its policy after three or four months of missing out on stories that *The Times* put on its front page.

In the aftermath of the Jimmy story, *Post* Publisher Graham has backed Mr. Bradlee and Mr. Woodward in their announced determination to cut down substantially on *The Post*'s use of material from unattributed sources. In his talk at Columbia, Mr. Bradlee expressed the view that laziness accounted for much of the tendency among reporters to use blind quotes. It was much easier, he told a student-faculty audience, "to write 'one source said' if you can't remember which source it was going through your notes of if you don't know or, God forbid, you should have made it up."

Mr. Woodward told the Council staff that the new policy is already bearing fruit. He told of sending a reporter out to talk to the parents of juvenile offenders and of instructing her to get their stories on the record. The reporter's response was that the parents would refuse to be identified by name. He instructed her to try anyway. "She came back surprised," Mr. Woodward reported. All the parents had agreed to talk for attribution.

Where confidential sources are required in stories dealing with corruption or other topics on which informants feel a need for protection, Mr. Bradlee has directed that the ambiguity which surrounded the original rule be removed. In meetings with his editors and *The Post* reportorial staff, he has said that he wants an editor to know the source of all sensitive material and, if some extraordinary circumstance makes the reporter feel he cannot tell, Mr. Bradlee personally must approve printing the story.

All *The Post* editors are convinced, however, that even if the rule had been enforced in the Jimmy story, it would not have safeguarded the paper against being duped by Miss Cooke. Publisher Graham is equally certain that insisting an editor know the family's name would have been of little help. "I think that Janet, if pressed, would have given us the name and other checkable information concerning those people," he told the Council staff. The circumstances of the case and particularly the supposed threat of the drug pusher/lover to knife the reporter if anyone came looking for him almost certainly would have discouraged any independent check by the paper in the absence of any tangible evidence of the story's falsity.

Perhaps out of a recognition that even the most rigorous policy of guarding against abuse of unattributed material has its limitations—and without implying that *The Post* will ever be able to forego all use of such material—the paper began many months before the "Jimmy's World" earthquake to instruct reporters engaged in some of its long investigative projects to have everything in their stories on the record and for direct attribution. Mr. Woodward cited as two examples of this new approach a series that ran some months ago on the Job Corps and another on the reconstruction of Union Station as a national visitors' center.

"You become philosophical after something like this," says Mr. Woodward. "You recognize that there is a time when certain techniques are needed, and a time when they are not. It is a good thing to have more things on the record. That will be the trend, though there won't be a time when you don't need source reporting on some stories. I recognize that I am one of those who helped popularize the mode of using unattributed sources. It has become fashionable. But, like any ship or any business, you have to loosen things sometimes and tighten things other times."

As a further cautionary step against misuse of blind quotes, Mr. Woodward says he intends to team reporters together to conduct interviews on sensitive stories. In that way the paper will have two witnesses to attest to the accuracy of material it prints that cannot be directly attributed. "This is an inclination I had a long time ago," says Mr. Woodward. "I've done it a lot, and I'm doing it even more now."

Having a corroborative witness is a device for increased accountability that reminds the co-author of "All the President's Men" and "The Brethren" of something he learned while serving in the Navy on the Presidential flagship. The contol mechanism for launching a nuclear attack or counterattack was in a safe aboard ship, Mr. Woodward says. The safe had two locks, one of which was under his control and the other a shipmate's. "Two-person control is not a bad thing," he declares.

The one consolation he derives from the Cooke affair is his belief that, for all the pain it caused *The Post*, it was a victimless crime—one in which there was no personal injury to anyone in the community. For the future, he says: "We must maintain a tough, skeptical edge to our reporting. We must be concerned with doing incisive, imaginative reporting. We can take the rattle out of things without taking out the spark."

### The Mayor's Jimmy

Every *Post* staff member to whom Council staff spoke reminded us that Mayor Marion Barry had said two days after the Jimmy story appeared that he knew who Jimmy was. That assertion turned out to be incorrect, but it delayed the growth of a suspicion that there might be no Jimmy at all and caused *Post* editors to discount the mayor's subsequent assertions to that effect.

On Wednesday, Oct. 1, the day the mayor's first statement was reported, *The Post* editorialized that the question of whether the newspaper should divulge Jimmy's identity "has now been mooted by the city's discovery, through other channels, of the boy's identity."

But the doctor on whose information the mayor had based his claim had called *The Post* the day before to say she thought Jimmy was fictitious. That incident is not reported in Bill Green's review, and it cannot be reported completely here, because Dr. Alyce Gullatte, psychiatrist and drug counselor at Howard University, declined to speak to Council staff. It appears from what little is known, however, that in the confusion over Dr. Gullatte's statements to the mayor and to the newspaper, an opportunity was lost to discover the hoax. Pat Tyler, a *Post* reporter, received information from Dr. Gullatte—phoned from the Mayor's office—on Monday, the day after the Jimmy story appeared, that Dr. Gullatte had been trying to find an 8-year-old heroin addict for Miss Cooke, but had been unable to make contact. Therefore, she thought Miss Cooke's Jimmy must be a fabrication. Mr. Tyler told Council staff that he interpreted Dr. Gullatte's call as an effort to be protective of Mr. Barry and thus insure continued municipal funding for her addiction program. He said he told her that on the phone, then communicated the substance of their conversation to Mr. Coleman. Mr. Tyler also passed on to Miss Cooke Dr. Gullatte's assertion that the child addict she wrote about was not the one Dr. Gullatte had been trying to reach for her. Miss Cooke replied, "There must be two Jimmys, then," according to Mr. Tyler.

Mr. Coleman said that he did take note of Dr. Gullatte's call and "We were assessing that," when, next day, the mayor said he knew who the child was. At that point his staff stopped checking on Dr. Gullatte's assertion, Mr. Coleman told the Capitol Press Club. Next day a spokesman for the mayor said that city officials had been premature in their initial comment; that they did not, in fact, know the name and address of the child; that Dr. Gullatte was the only person who knew the child's family. The Howard drug counselor had said earlier that the family had fled to avoid arrest. Dr. Gullatte refused to cooperate further with investigating authorities, *The Post* reported Oct. 16 in a story saying that the city had given up the search on the assumption that Jimmy was, at least in part, fictitious. In an interview on a television talk show after the revelation in mid-April that the Jimmy story was a hoax, Dr. Gullatte denounced *The Post* for having impugned her motives when she sought unsuccessfully to warn it about the story.

### The Dr. Hamlin Letter

A letter published in *The Post* Nov. 10, 1980, was another element that helped blind *Post* editors to the possibility that Jimmy might not be real.

The Nov. 10 letter was from Dr. Willie T. Hamlin, a psychiatrist. The Green report quoted the letter as saying in part, "The Washington metropolitan area, as well as hundreds of other large metropolitan areas in the country, are full of Jimmys. I know, I work with them."

The letter, as it appeared in *The Post*, went on to say, "I'm speaking of

265

children currently housed in the residential treatment facility at Hillcrest Children's Center." Dr. Hamlin referred later in the letter to the difficulty of finding places for "a child who needs residential treatment for emotional problems." He noted that Hillcrest was to close in December, and he urged the community to find ways to keep it open "if we truly want to do something for the Jimmys of our city."

Dr. Hamlin told Council staff that when his letter was mentioned in the Green report he was annoyed to find that it had reassured *Post* editors about the reality of Jimmy. He told the Council he had not meant to suggest that the area was full of 8-year-old heroin addicts, but that it was full of abused children in general.

### Blaming the Authorities

One element that does not come clear in the Green report is the degree to which *The Post*'s opinion columns flayed the officials in charge of police, schools, social services and drug abuse programs for their "failure" in the case.

Thus, in a column published on Sept. 30 Richard Cohen defended the reporter's commitment of anonymity as necessary to get the story to the public and asked how it was possible that "the drug enforcement people with their trillions of dollars in federal aid and their computers and their police officers did not know of this kid—could not do what a reporter could do."

"Somewhere in all this," he wrote, "is a story of failure—of massive failure. Somewhere in all this is a story of agencies not caring or not doing their jobs, of money being spent on the wrong things, of schools not paying attention, of well-meaning but defeated teachers who cannot cope and, also, maybe just as important, neighbors who knew or suspected and didn't do a thing . . . . An 8-year-old boy is about to die. Somebody, for crying out loud, ought to care."

In another column Oct. 12 Mr. Cohen said: "Clearly, Jimmy could not exist if people cared. Clearly, he could not be an 8-year-old addict if the cops cared or the school really cared or the welfare people really cared . . . . You might notice there have been no more stories about Jimmy, and without the stories there will be little done about him. He has become an embarrassment—to us, to the police, to the welfare department, to the schools . . . . Goodbye, Jimmy."

In the same Oct. 1 editorial in which it said the argument over Miss Cooke's pledge of confidentiality had been mooted by the Mayor's assertion that the city knew who the child addict was, *The Post* argued that the public outcry stirred by her story had been necessary to arouse officials to the need for a crackdown on drug abuse. "Maybe now more of the people who have been around these children—those who didn't, couldn't or wouldn't tell this story—will be moved to do something about it," the editorial said.

In his Oct. 3 column William Raspberry reported that some readers had called Miss Cooke a killer and a murderer for her withholding of the child's identity and he speculated that, if she went to jail rather than break her promise, public sentiment would in all probability be against her. But he saluted her for her courage on the ground that without her commitment to conceal the name there would have been no community outrage and "as far as the public is concerned, no Jimmy." On the same day in the ombudsman's column Bill Green asserted that all the promises society had made to Jimmy for a world of opportunity and respect for law had been broken. The only promise to him that had not been broken, he asserted, was the one that could not be broken—Miss Cooke's—and that had galvanized the city and caused it "to see the horror that lies on the detritus of promises unkept."

### Impact on the Community

No official estimate of even the most approximate kind could be obtained of the extra financial burden put upon the Washington community by the search for the non-existent Jimmy, but the Council survey left no doubt that the emotional burden on the community was heavy and the disruption of key municipal services severe, especially in the poor, black neighborhood where the boy was alleged to live.

Lt. Hiram Brewton, public information officer for the District of Columbia Police Department, said up to 35 community relations, youth service and narcotics policemen were mobilized in the hunt for Jimmy, some of them for as long as ten days. Some put in overtime shifts; all were diverted from their normal duties.

But in Lt. Brewton's view, the search did not interfere with the police department as much as it did with the school system. Dr. Vincent Reed, superintendent of District schools at the time of the story, said, "I turned the school system upside down." He said he "berated" his regional superintendents for not finding the boy. Audrey Rowe, acting commissioner for social services, assigned two highly-experienced field workers in the child protection division to spend full time on the search.

Representatives of police, schools and social services said their people knew within three or four days that the story was faked. Lt. Brewton said,

"We were convinced that it was not true as reported." Dr. Reed said school people turned up four or five pupils who appeared less than lively in class—one with a scratch on his arm—but none proved an addict. Ms. Rowe said that she and the police realized that a reporter would not have been allowed to see what she saw without a "tremendous cash exchange. But we couldn't get a fix on a large sum of money changing hands," she said.

Jonetta M. Bumgardner of the child protection section said, "Once it hit the paper, it should have hit the grapevine. It wasn't on the grapevine." Her colleague, Edward T. Shepherd, said, "Nobody was dropping a dime." (The phrase denotes tipping police on the identity of someone they are looking for in hopes of a favor later.)

But none of the agencies felt it could risk giving up the search. Lt. Brewton said, "It was not our job to knock holes in the story." Dr. Reed said, "If you say it's not true, it cuts off your willingness to search." Ms. Rowe said, "You can't beat 'I saw' with 'I can't find him.'"

The most irritating factor to Ms. Bumgardner and Mr. Shepherd was that the original story and the subsequent stories about the search reflected badly on the predominantly black and poor section in which Jimmy supposedly lived. The stories suggested that residents in that community didn't care enough about the child to report. In truth, they said the child-abuse section gets many calls from precisely the neighborhood in which the search for Jimmy focused—calls from neighbors concerned about neglected and abused children. One of their most consistent and reliable sources for such information lives on Xenia St. (where Miss Cooke said Jimmy lived in her last effort to persuade *Post* editors that he was real). They considered it a libel on people of that kind for *The Post* to suggest they were indifferent or inured to child abuse.

Ms. Rowe expressed the view—shared by many in a city that is 70 percent black—that the story would never have been printed if the child had been reported as living in the more affluent neighborhoods of the Northwest or Southwest sections of Washington. The fact that it was printed, Ms. Rowe said, reflected a misunderstanding of the minority community on the part of *The Post* and its reporters—a misunderstanding she feels persists despite the fact that *The Post* has hired many black reporters and editors.

On that score, Mr. Bradlee told the American Society of Newspaper Editors in Washington April 22 that he invested an extra measure of trust in Miss Cooke and her city editor on the Jimmy story because they were black and he considered them to be experts in the poor, black section of the city where Jimmy allegedly lived. Mr. Woodward told Council staff that in his view *Post* editors have not done enough to develop for themselves the same degree of understanding of the black community that they try to acquire in understanding such subjects as medicine, business and politics in which they supervise reporters who are experts.

## Hiring Practices

What tore the fabric of falsity in which Janet Cooke had enveloped herself in her brief career at *The Post* was an inflated catalogue of educational attainments that she prepared for the Pulitzer board and that was not checked by anyone until she had won the feature writing prize. The speed with which the whole tissue of lies unraveled after these scholastic credentials were discovered to be fraudulent has caused *The Post* and many other newspapers to decide that more alertness in verifying academic and employment records is an essential safeguard for the integrity of their publications when new reporters or editors are hired.

The item that caught Ben Bradlee's eye when Miss Cooke first wrote seeking a job two years ago was a statement in her resume that she had been a Phi Beta Kappa graduate of Vassar in 1976. That and six *Toledo Blade* clippings were sufficient to get her a series of interviews in which her intelligence, attractiveness and poise so impressed the several *Post* editors who talked to her that she was hired and assigned to the staff of the paper's District Weekly on Jan. 3, 1980.

No one bothered to check with Vassar—a check that would have disclosed before her first day on the job that Miss Cooke had left there after a year. Tom Wilkinson, *The Post*'s assistant managing editor for personnel, told Council staff that the neglect of such a check was normal rather than unusual in the case of reporters *The Post* hired from the staffs of other papers.

Except in the rare cases in which people were added to the staff fresh out of college, Mr. Wilkinson said, *The Post* tended to put little stress on academic credentials. Rather, it based its judgment of job applicants' capacity on the clips they brought with them, the impression they made in interviews, and on follow-up calls to editors *Post* people knew at the publications from which they came.

As a result of the Cooke case, however, *The Post* intends to make verification of both scholastic and past job records part of its standard operating procedure on additions to its staff. Mr. Wilkinson says the only reporter hired in recent weeks has already been put through an extensive check. Similarly, future job applicants will be required to sign forms authorizing their colleges to send academic data to *The Post*. In addition, Mr. Wilkinson says, an effort will be made to check beyond the references volunteered by the job-seeker so that the paper receives maximum information on experience and character.

No one at *The Post* fancies that the multiplication of such checks, even when supplemented by the filters the paper's own system of examination of clips and personal interviews provides, can furnish absolute guarantee of the probity and dependability of everyone hired. Conversely, however, *Post* editors say they have no intention of letting the "Jimmy's World" debacle steep them in such cynicism that they pass over newcomers of zeal and promise on the ground that every job-seeker must be deemed guilty until proved trustworthy.

A Council survey of the practices of other newspapers and broadcasters indicates that even the most formalized requirements for checking academic and employment records of new professional employees are far from failsafe. That is partly because of the limitations that an increasing array of protections for employee privacy put on the freedom of past employers to pass on job information that might be deemed derogatory and actionable at law.

Most editors who responded to a Council survey of hiring practices indicated that, wherever there had been a past failure to check on credentials, such attention would now be standard. On the question of any possible adverse effect of the Janet Cooke hoax on minority hiring, some feared there might be, although all insisted there shouldn't. Thus, John G. Craig, Jr., editor of *The Pittsburgh Post-Gazette*, noted: "I think the Janet Cooke case will reconfirm the prejudices of people who are already prejudiced. I also think that racial prejudice is a problem in newspapers, as it is a problem in the United States." From Burl Osborne, executive editor of *The Dallas Morning News*, came the view that what happened at *The Post* had no racial overtones. "The pressures generated by cutthroat competition and intense, sometimes blind, ambition are color blind," he said.

At the National Broadcasting Company Laura Nurse, manager of employment, told the Council that its general practice in taking on new professional employees is to check both scholastic and employment credentials. A similar policy exists at ABC, according to Tony Sproule, its personnel director. On staff positions, he says, it is routine to verify degrees and past employment. Where the academic check is made after hiring, the new employee is obliged to sign a standard release form authorizing his university to supply the network with the required information. "We have had a couple of last-minute confessionals when we ask them to sign a waiver," says Mr. Sproule.

Robert Chandler, vice-president of CBS News, reports that it has no fixed policy in the hiring of new reporters, on-air personnel or producers because much of the CBS hring involves people from other news organizations whose work is well known to the network. On that basis, a good deal of routine credentials checking is dispensed with, Mr. Chandler says. However, he makes it clear that this does not mean CBS is casual about satisfying itself that the people it is taking in are worthy of trust. If CBS were caught in a news fabrication of the type perpetrated at *The Washington Post*, Mr. Chandler notes, it could find itself in hot water with the Federal Communications Commission and in danger of losing station licenses.

### Pressures in the Newsroom

The newsroom of *The Washington Post* is an intensely competitive place, one in which many reporters tend to compete with one another for Page One prominence. The extent of this internal pressure is set forth starkly in the Green report, and Council staff in its interviews with individual reporters found plentiful confirmation for the resulting picture of a newsroom in which temptations are strong to court editors' favor by stretching every story to the ultimate—and perhaps, as in Miss Cooke's case, beyond.

Mr. Bradlee himself provided the key in his comment to Ombudsman Green: "People want to succeed. They bust their ass to succeed here. There's only a couple of places you want to work in this business, and when you get here you don't blow it." It is, of course, a fact of journalistic life that most reporters—and certainly those with talent and drive—want to work on stories that have importance or that will intrigue the reader by their unusual character or the deftness with which they are written. Newspapers would be dull, indeed, if this were not the case and so would the people who write them. More important, there would be too little of the enterprise and initiative that enable newspapers to discharge their essential function in a democracy of informing the citizens of corruption or social neglect or other problems in need of public attention.

The problem for editors is to make sure that reporters in their eagerness to get ahead do not make stories better than the facts justify. The dangers on that count have been heightened in recent years by a variety of developments that have caused many newspapers to move more and more toward magazine-model brightness in writing style and further and fur-

271

ther from their traditional emphasis on hard news, rooted in factuality. One such factor is the competition of television, now capable of instant delivery to almost every home of the highlights of breaking stories, with full details of those of maximum consequence or interest. The emergence of TV as a mainstay of news dissemination has brought two handmaidens in its train. Video newscasters have become household favorites, known to millions of viewers; and the result in newspapers has been a hunger among reporters for increased personalization of the news. By-lines, once a reward for superior performance, are now almost universal, and many writers strive to put a personal trade-mark on their stories by the flashiness of their writing or the provocativeness of the news treatment they give their material.

Along with that has been a slopping over into journalism of many of the techniques of the novel—the so-called "new journalism," with Tom Wolfe, Norman Mailer and Truman Capote among its high priests. This school of news writing blends fact and fiction, without clear indication to the reader of where one ends and the other begins, in the belief that such a free-wheeling approach allows the writer to arrive at the larger truth of his story, the truth beyond the truth. The increasing permissiveness many newspapers have adopted in recent years toward use of unattributed sources has vastly expanded the opportunity for wandering away from facts into the limitless frontiers of imagination.

How much the fusion of all these general media trends into the superheated atmosphere of the post-Watergate *Post* affected Miss Cooke must remain a matter of speculation in the absence of any willingness on her part to tell her story to the News Council, or so far as we have been able to establish, to anyone else. One who does feel that this atmosphere helps explain the Cooke episode is Ken Ringle, a *Post* reporter and former assistant city editor, who has been away on leave for more than a year but who returned to attend a Metro staff meeting called by Mr. Bradlee to discuss the incident.

"The real villian," Mr. Ringle told Council staff after the meeting, "is glamor journalism, the cult of personality. As long as people are writing stories so that the reader remembers who wrote it rather than what the subject is, then we're going to have these kind of things happen." Mr. Ringle extends his theory to explain why reporters with doubts about the story hesitated to carry them to the top editors. He describes the newsroom as a place where rivalry is so keen that "people are constantly torpedoing other people in order to get a little higher up on the notch." One result, he says, is that many uneasy about a particular story or what they see as a trend toward lax editing standards, especially in the style and magazine sections, keep a low-profile lest they be shot down as actuated by jealousy or other selfish motives. Mr. Ringle stresses his own pride in the paper, despite these criticisms.

His assessment is viewed as exaggerated by almost all the other *Post* people interviewed, though several dissented only in degree on the complaints of backbiting, toadyism and loose editing. However, none found in any of such defects a cause for Miss Cooke's aberrant conduct. The consensus supported Mr. Bradlee's description of her as "a one-in-a-million liar" determined to scale the heights whatever the means she had to employ. It is pointless to fill this report with instances of her asserted mendacity or opportunism given to staff by her former intimates at *The Post*. Without exception, however, those who reproach her for these qualities attest to her intelligence and her writing skill. All feel that a large talent was misused and there seemed genuineness in the universality with which editors and reporters alike expressed the hope that her life would not be irreparably injured.

Since her departure, *The Post* has been checking back on the other stories written by Miss Cooke to determine whether others were fabricated. Thus far, according to Mr. Woodward, one woman who figured in a Cooke story claims to have been misquoted and her claim is being looked into. Other stories contain blind quotes and are proving difficult to verify in the absence of cooperation from the ex-reporter. *The Post* will wait a bit before asking her. "She's got to get her life in order; that's more crucial for her," says Mr. Woodward.

At *The Toledo Blade*, where Miss Cooke worked for two years before coming to *The Post*, Publisher Paul Block, Jr. reports that his editors sent her out on the toughest stories because she was so intelligent. He adds, however, that her ambition was "overriding."

## The Pulitzer Entry

The most baffling question to answer, the Council staff found, is how *The Post* could have nominated the Jimmy story for a Pulitzer Prize in view of the suspicions that story had engendered within the newsroom. Perhaps the best answer is found in the resentment Managing Editor Simons says he feels at even being asked the question—because it implies either one of two things: That the paper put the story forward knowing it was a fraud, or that the mistake it made was to attract to the story the extra attention that resulted in its being exposed as fiction.

On the first point, the staff study confirmed what Mr. Green had found—a great number of people with doubts they could not pin down, doubts which they either did not communicate or did so weakly that their suspicions were discounted as too vaporous or as the product of jealousy in an intensely competitive newsroom. So far as staff could establish, Mr. Bradlee knew next to nothing of any skepticism inside the paper on the validity of the story. Mr. Woodward, on whose recommendation Messrs. Bradlee and Simons sent the entry in for a prize, had had warnings from several aides but none had anything concrete to back up his doubts. On that basis, the Metropolitan editor hunkered down behind the shield he described as "in for a dime, in for a dollar." The story was brilliantly written; it illuminated a critical social problem; the paper had confidence in it; it deserved entry. These were the thoughts in his mind and in the minds of his superiors. After all, *The Post* had weathered the storm of community attack on the Cooke story by adopting its Watergate mode, "protect the source and back the reporter."

In its letter of submission, sent to the Pulitzer Board on Mr. Simon's stationery, *The Post* said the Cooke story had "ignited a new awareness of the drug epidemic in the District of Columbia and the nation." Of the furor stirred by the story, the entry had this to say: "There was a burst of protest and disbelief about Jimmy's existence until social workers and teachers stepped forward to say on the record that heroin was being used by others Jimmy's age in elementary schools."

The story was one of 27 entries submitted by *The Post* in the twelve journalistic categories. It was the only one put forward in the local news category. In feature writing, where the story eventually won the prize as a result of reclassification by the Pulitzer Board, five entries were put in by *The Post*, none of which received endorsement by the jury in that field.

In his talk at Columbia three weeks after the crumbling of "Jimmy's World," Mr. Bradlee said, "It never occurred to me not to submit it because I had no doubt." Not to have submitted it, he declared, would have been "saying things about race—that I would submit a white person's work but not a black's—and I didn't want to say that." Among the factors that contributed to Mr. Bradlee's belief in the story's validity, he told Council staff, was the poignant drawing prepared by Michael Gnatek, Jr., to illustrate the story. The executive editor found the sketch of the boy shooting up so upsetting that he insisted it run inside the paper but he also found it totally believable. "I felt like I know that kid," he says.

On the second point about the prize bid, it is incontestable that *The Post* would—for the present at least—have escaped the embarrassment that now besets it if it had never submitted "Jimmy's World" for a Pulitzer. But would that have been a good thing for it or for journalism? Had the hoax not been uncovered after the award, Miss Cooke, with her active imagination and her inordinate ambition to scale the heights in a hurry, would have stayed in the newsroom—a time bomb waiting to go off. And quite apart from the potential for damage in that situation, the function of journalism is to arrive at the truth and communicate the truth to readers. That obligation is as strong or stronger where the exposure of facts is painful to the newspaper as it is where outsiders are wounded. That helps explain why the interrogation of Miss Cooke by *Post* editors after they discovered the fabrications in her personal history took on many aspects of a third degree. Obliged to face the reality that they might have perpetrated a fraud on their readers, the editors recognized that their first duty was to establish the facts, however embarrassing, and make them public. That duty they fulfilled—spectacularly.

The Green report contains human insights into *Post* people involved in the Jimmy drama that are essential to understanding how the tragic chain could have developed. Council staff were impressed with Mr. Simon's admission that he is not blessed with the kind of memory that enables others to dredge up months-old recollections in rich detail and with Mr. Coleman's acknowledgment that his attempts to match his memories with those of others sometimes resulted in "weird sequences" and nuances in the Green report. A reporter who remains a close friend of Miss Cooke confesses that he didn't face his own suspicions about her story, "because I didn't want to know."

Mr. Bradlee was equally frank in acknowledging that he had suffered a personal blow aside from that involved in the revelation that the story was false: He was hurt that he had not caught the suspicions and that no one at any level had come to him with them. It was particularly painful for someone who "works on" being close with the staff, as he described it. He said he "hangs out;" that he's good at it; he's a good reporter. He wanted not to be separated from the staff when the newsroom was remodeled, and he accepted a glass wall only because it was forced on him for security reasons. He said he makes five or six "sweeps" through the newsroom daily and has a pick-up lunch at the Madison coffee shop with whomever is in the newsroom on the one Saturday in three when he is on duty. He said he sees staff members socially and is lucky to have a wife 20 years younger than he to keep him in touch with younger staff members.

"People tell me they're afraid of me. I don't get it. I don't know why. I have not done it effectively," he said.

With reference to the specifics of the complaint before the Council, staff found no evidence that *The Post*'s management manipulated the award of the Pulitzer Prize to Miss Cooke. Every member of the Pulitzer board with whom the question was discussed ridiculed the notion that any attempt had been made by the paper to influence the board's decision.

The staff's inquiry into the production of the original story leaves it convinced that Miss Cooke did write the article herself with some help from Mike Sager, a *Post* reporter with more training on *The Post* than she had. Mr. Sager said he helped Miss Cooke with her writing while he was on the night police beat and she was "working 24 hours a day on the Weekly." His help consisted of making suggestions, frequently about getting rid of excess words. He said he played that role on the Jimmy story as well as others.

Additional help came from Mr. Coleman, but it appears to have been minimal considering her junior status on the paper. He says he assisted her in deciding on a lead and on organizing her material. When she turned in the story, Mr. Coleman reports, it was in much the same shape and approximately the same length as when it was published. After its appearance, he recalls, it was referred to inside the shop as "the best 42-inch story ever in *The Post*."

## Changes at *The Post*

The humiliation of the Cooke episode inflicted a profound jolt on *The Post*'s editors and administrators. Their reaction has been equally profound—and in many respects as heartening as the experience itself was dismaying.

The demoralizing effect of the initial shock was reflected in an early statement to Council representatives by Reporter Pat Tyler that *The Post* staff was damaging itself with destructive questions. "The paper's got to get past this," he said. Publisher Graham put the damage into perspective with his appraisal of the task facing *The Post*: "We are trying to rebuild a newspaper organization here."

To that end Mr. Bradlee held meetings with five news staffs—national, metro, sports, business and style. His aim was to gather staff views before sitting down with Managing Editor Simons and Deputy Managing Editor Harwood on what should be done. A parallel aim was to make a start toward unclogging the lines of communication between staff and editors that had proved so faulty in the Cooke episode.

Two constructive reforms in general *Post* practice have already been decided on: The use of unattributed material will be reduced and editors will be under strict mandate to know the identity and accept responsibility for confidential sources. Also the claims of job applicants will be more strictly checked, although the credentials of present *Post* personnel will not be reviewed. (Mr. Bradlee told a Columbia School of Journalism audience facetiously that *Post* editors had considered establishing 34 to 36 hours of clemency so that staff members could go to the personnel files with erasers and amend their own.)

There is a recognition that the measurement of truth in reporting is an inexact science, no matter how vigilant the paper. In a talk with Council staff, Mr. Bradlee stressed that tightening up on blind sources was only a limited answer. "When the President is lying and you quote the President, you are lying," he observed. The most interesting revelation in the Pentagon Papers, so far as Mr. Bradlee was concerned, was its disclosure that Secretary of Defense Robert McNamara had told President Johnson in a private White House conference that the American military position in Vietnam was deteriorating rapidly—a statement he made only 20 minutes after painting a rosy picture of the situation for reporters who met him at Andrews Air Force Base.

"The truth is not something that can be grasped," Mr. Bradlee said. "It is revealed in increments. There may be more truth to the Jimmy story than we are acknowledging."

Perhaps the most eloquent statement of the altered approach at *The Post* comes from Assistant Managing Editor Woodward. He and City Editor Coleman took full responsibility at a staff meeting in Mr. Woodward's home just before the Green report for allowing the fraud to be published and to be entered for the Pulitzer Prize. He told the Council staff later that the whole debacle had "driven a spike in my head" about the double standard the paper often applied. He said he personally had gone along for 10 years taking it for granted that reporters always tell the truth and government officials always lie. "That's not a good mode to be in," he says.

He believes that the remedy lies in applying the same skepticism inside the paper that it applies outside. "I mean it's not a reduction of skepticism, it's probably an increase of skepticism," he says. With that, according to Mr. Woodward, goes an obligation to exercise more care, more caution, more debate and more sense of fairness in all the paper's day-to-day operations. He feels that is already happening. He says he often finds himself going out into the newsroom when a story is turned in and saying: "Get a better statement of the other side. This is not balanced. This is a cheap shot. Let's think about what we're doing a little bit more." The result is much more reflectiveness, Mr. Woodward says.

He wants to see the accent on fairness and accuracy carried to a level that makes it obligatory on an assistant managing editor or his representative, before going home, to read all stories going into the paper from his desk. To counteract the notion that the only way to get ahead at *The Post* is by concentrating on blockbuster stories—and at the same time to improve *Post* service to its readers—Mr. Woodward also wants to see more attention paid on a regular basis to coverage of the daily grind—zoning boards, county councils, local court decisions, planning commissions and the like.

Publisher Graham is in full accord with the idea that there ought to be no imbalance in either attention or rewards for beat reporters covering the suburbs or black community organizations or federal regulatory agencies, as against those on high-visibility assignments. Indeed, he is convinced that is pretty much the way things are now, a belief not widely shared by others with whom Council staff spoke.

At every level of command an exploration seems under way to determine how most effectively to fuse needed changes into a structure that the administrators and editors regard as sound. Mr. Bradlee emphasized at his meetings with his reporters that no revolution is in prospect at *The Post* and certainly no ease-up in its pressure for hard-nosed investigative reporting. The trick, says Mr. Woodward, is "to tighten down but not so much as to break the bolt, just to get rid of some rattles."

Increased training for both reporters and editors will be part of the effort to heighten performance and responsibility. Up to now, training for newcomers to the staff has consisted almost entirely of two one-hour sessions over two days. The program is held twice a year for the benefit of summer interns as well as new employees. Miss Cooke was exposed to that program shortly before writing "Jimmy's World." What is now envisioned is a much more comprehensive orientation and training regimen with heavier emphasis on rules and ethics.

In one of his interviews with Council staff Mr. Bradlee indicated that he was also contemplating similar attention to the training of editors. "How do you make an editor?" he asked. "Do we bring them along too fast?" He expressed great admiration for Mr. Woodward and Mr. Coleman, the editors with pivotal roles in the Cooke story, but noted that both had moved up rapidly. Mr. Woodward, now 38, was promoted to Assistant Managing Editor with direction over more than a hundred members of the metro staff some two years before the Jimmy story. He started at *The Post* in 1971, nine months before the Watergate articles that brought fame to him and Carl Bernstein. Mr. Coleman, 34, joined the paper in 1976 and covered Montgomery County and City Hall before becoming assistant city editor four years later. He moved up to city editor in May of last year, after only two months in the No. 2 spot.

On the hiring of minority journalists, an area in which *The Post* has been a trailblazer, Katharine Graham, chairman of *The Post*'s board, had this to say in her keynote address May 4 as president of the American Newspaper Publishers Association:

> I am also troubled by the suggestion that the Janet Cooke episode is somehow the result of the pressures on papers to recruit and promote minorities. That suggestion is an insult to hundreds of promising young reporters and editors. The problem we should be focusing on in connection with minority journalists is there are not enough of them working for newspapers.

As *The Post* shakes off the traumatic effects of Jimmy's ignominious end, the predominant endeavor seems to be to create an atmosphere of two-way trust in the newsroom. Everyone recognizes that success in that effort is an indispensable foundation for any plugging of the holes in the safety shield that was supposed to protect the paper's credibility. Editors cannot check everything in the paper, Mr. Bradlee notes, adding: "If you're not on enough of a team to trust each other, it's not worth playing."

Mr. Woodward believes that within five years people at *The Post* will be looking back on the Cooke incident as "a good thing" because of the self-criticism and change it engendered. A similar hope is expressed by Donald Graham. He says he does not see the Jimmy story as something that was caused by, or symptomatic of, the institution. On the contrary, he sees it as a spur to all-around improvement. He told Council staff:

> This episode gives this newsroom a chance to react, an opportunity to stop relating everything back to Janet Cooke but to recognize that there is an unending, 365-day-a-year job of making this paper better, and draw some lessons from this episode, some lessons from what people in this newsroom are saying, some lessons from what critics on the outside are saying, but let us channel all the energy that is generated by this story in ways that will make this paper much better, perceptibly better in every way, without backing off any of our commitments to do aggressive and tough reporting. If we've failed in providing any kind of coverage that our readers deserve from us, then let's apply ourselves now and immediately to filling those holes.

**Council finding:** In approaching its assessment of this complaint, the

National News Council is evaluating the conduct of a newspaper which has already acknowledged fault and apologized editorially.

A lie perpetrated by Janet Cooke produced a monstrous miscarriage of journalism. *The Washington Post* was negligent in the editing process that preceded publication of her false story. Following the publication, it failed to react in any constructive manner to questions from the community and from a few members of its staff regarding the existence of Jimmy.

Once *The Post* discovered that the story was a fraud, however, the manner in which it reacted was rare in journalism. *The Post* gave its ombudsman carte blanche to determine what had gone wrong and why. It instructed its editors and reporters to cooperate unreservedly in making these facts available, no matter how great the embarrassment to *The Post*. The massive 18,000-word self-indictment that resulted was an impressive demonstration of a newspaper's acceptance of public accountability.

The independent investigation the Council has conducted in response to the complaint by the Howard University Journalism Department has confirmed the essential accuracy of the report by *Post* Ombudsman Bill Green. Nothing discovered in interviews by Council representatives with 24 staff members at all levels of *The Post* organization raises any suggestion that information derogatory to the newspaper or to its editors and administrators was soft-pedaled or covered up in that report.

However, the Council, as representative of both public and press, would be derelict if it did not recognize that the issues raised in this case go to the credibility of all news organizations. The Council feels obligated to pass on the individual charges contained in this complaint as well as to note some lessons the "Jimmy's World" case underscores for journalism generally.

The story did indeed, as the complaint suggests, impair the credibility of journalists not only because it was a fake but also because a reporter invoked the First Amendment as a shield against disclosure that her supposed confidential source did not, in fact, exist. It imposed an emotional burden on the Washington community, interfered with police, social service and school functions, and unfairly implied that a poor and black community does not care about its children. Without embracing the specific language of the complaint, the Council finds these aspects of it warranted.

No evidence was found to sustain the charge that Miss Cooke had been forced into hiding and muzzled by *The Post*. The one statement she has made to the Council is that her refusal to discuss the case represents a personal decision made of her own free will.

The complaint also asks the Council to make judgments on other specific questions. The material in the Green report and the investigative findings of its own staff lead the Council to assess these issues, as follows:

- No evidence was found to sustain the charge that Miss Cooke had "the sure-handed assistance of top management" in perpetrating her fraud and rigging the Pulitzer award process to win her prize. Unwarranted.

- The Council found no evidence that Miss Cooke did not write the story substantially herself. Unwarranted.

- The Council finds warranted the charge that *Post* editors were negligent in failing to challenge and investigate the validity of the story, especially when doubts were expressed, first by the outside community and then increasingly from within its own staff.

- The evidence does not support the charge that this failure was willful and malicious. Unwarranted.

- The Council finds unwarranted the charge that *Post* editors knowingly recommended a false story for the Pulitzer Prize, but this is not to say they were blameless in proceeding with the submission despite the doubts at least two of them say they were beginning to feel on the basis of questions raised by staff members.

- The imputation that *The Post* manipulated the Pulitzer award process to insure a prize for Miss Cooke and "Jimmy's World" is found unwarranted. No evidence gathered by the Council supports this suggestion and it is explicitly denied by members of the Pulitzer Board.

*The Post* damaged journalism and the Washington community by the failures which it has acknowledged in such internal matters as making clear the responsibilities of editors, checking credentials and cautioning beginners against the potential danger of competition for journalistic prizes and the big-hit story.

Neither the complaint nor the ombudsman's report addressed what the Council believes to be a pivotal issue in this case: the human concern that a journalist as citizen ought to have for an 8-year-old child whose life is being criminally endangered. The Council's investigation shows that there was no adequate discussion among *Post* editors of a question that admittedly presents an uncomfortable dilemma for news organizations— whether to fulfill their obligation as citizens and report the crime to the police or to stand on the principle that it is the journalist's obligation to publish the story to call attention to a social problem. The Council regrets that even after the story was published, *The Post*'s editors failed to try to help the mortally endangered child they believed to exist.

The Council also finds that the ombudsman's report ignored a critical failure by the ombudsman himself. As a bridge between the *Post* editors on one side and the community and staff on the other, it was his responsibility to insist that an inquiry be made early on when suspicion that Jimmy was not real was expressed by many District of Columbia officials and other readers. He did not. Nor did he heed concerns of some *Post* staff members about the truth of the story until after Miss Cooke's confession.

\* \* \*

In the wake of the Jimmy hoax, editors at *The Post* and at newspapers throughout the country are making changes and tightening procedures to lessen the danger of more such journalistic debacles. A survey by the Council brought swift responses from more than 30 editors, all attesting to the depth of the soul-searching now under way. One theme recurs: the central obligation for keeping papers truthful belongs to editors. Among the editorial practices suggested by those editors as needing revitalization for better journalistic performance are these:

● Checking the credentials and the credibility of new staff members and applicants.

● Systematic training of new reporters. Ethics and accuracy should be emphasized as much as a concern for writing style.

● Prompt, conspicuous public admission of error.

● Avoidance of the fortress mentality that obstructs acceptance and action on valid complaints.

● Less automatic responses as to where to draw the line between citizen responsibility and journalistic function in each case when a reporter witnesses a crime, especially one where lives are in jeopardy.

● Greater care in the selection of editors and, beyond that, training for those chosen in the specific attitudes and skills that make an editor's job different from a reporter's.

● Insisting on minimal use of unattributed information.

● Making invariable the right and duty of editors to know the identity of confidential sources.

● Guarding against a blurring of the line between fact and fancy. Guarding against such techniques of the New Journalism and docudrama as tampering with or inventing quotes, rearranging events and guessing what goes on in the recesses of people's minds.

● Encouraging two-way trust and two-way communication between editors and reporters by fostering an atmosphere of candor and cooperation, not competition carried to the lengths of backbiting.

282

- Keeping the pursuit of prizes from becoming an obsession in the newsroom.
- Applying inside the newsroom the same skepticism that journalists apply in reporting on the world outside.

**Concurring:** Abel, J. Bell, Benson, Brady, Cooney, Decter, Ghiglione, Hornby, Isaacs, Maynard, Pulitzer, Scott, Stanton, van den Haag and Williams.

**Dissenting:** Huston and Miller.

**Concurring opinion by Mr. Hornby (Mr. Isaacs concurring):** The overall tone of the Council's finding suggests that the *major* responsibility for the Cooke affair lies with negligent editing practices at *The Washington Post*. That is not true. Janet Cooke was the principal villain of this piece. A practiced liar can shove falsehoods past even the best of editors. No one can quarrel with or ignore the lessons for improvement of editing which the Council abstracts from the Cooke affair, but *The Washington Post*, its news system, and its reaction to the fraud once discovered deserve more respect than the Council's summary indicates. The Janet Cooke "hoax" was an aberration in American journalistic practice, and the Council's findings should not be taken as implying indirectly that normal editing at *The Post* or most other American newspapers encourages widespread publication of fabricated stories.

**Dissenting opinion by Ms. Huston:** In my opinion, the News Council wrongly exceeded its scope by taking on this complaint because, as the majority rightly states, *The Washington Post* had already "acknowledged fault and apologized editorially."

It has long been my understanding that the News Council's grievance procedure exists primarily as a recourse for persons who (1) feel as if they've been wronged by a news organization and (2) fail to get an adequate response from that news organization.

Instead of devoting its resources to rehashing a journalistic failure that has been properly addressed by the offending news organization, the News Council should attempt to resolve more of the complaints it receives against those news organizations which improperly refuse to re-examine their own actions. Then the News Council would more adequately be performing its vital function as a watchdog of the watchdogs, the nation's news media.

**Dissenting opinion by Mr. Miller:** The Janet Cooke case was unfortunate. *The Washington Post* took the appropriate action.

I am not sure what the complainants' motives are, but I am satisfied that

the complaint is totally and completely unwarranted in all its aspects.
June 12, 1981


**COMPLAINT NO. 189**                    (Filed May 4 and
LARRY LOWENSTEIN AND                       May 6, 1981)
JAMES A. WECHSLER
against
THE VILLAGE VOICE AND
TERESA CARPENTER

**Complaint:** Immediately after the awarding of a Pulitzer Prize for feature writing to Teresa Carpenter for three articles in *The Village Voice*, two complaints were filed with the Council about one of the articles, "From Heroism to Madness: The Odyssey of the Man Who Shot Al Lowenstein." One complainant was Larry Lowenstein, brother of Allard Lowenstein, the former Congressman from New York's Fifth District, who was shot fatally in his Rockefeller Center law office by Dennis Sweeney, a former student and, at one time, a political protege of Allard Lowenstein. The other complaint was filed by James A. Wechsler, Associate Editor of *The New York Post*, a long-time friend of the former Congressman.

*The Village Voice* is a New York weekly tabloid (circulation 144,000), founded in 1955 as an anti-establishment, counter-culture publication. The article under challenge was published in *The Voice* on May 12, 1980, two months after the March 14 murder. The article was reprinted, somewhat edited, by *The Washington Post* a week later, on May 18.

Mr. Sweeney was first charged with second-degree murder, but later changed his plea to "not responsible by reason of mental disease and defect" and was adjudged legally insane and committed earlier this year to the Mid-Hudson Psychiatric Center, New Hampton, N.Y.

Miss Carpenter's three articles dealt with murders committed under bizarre conditions. "From Heroism to Madness" dealt with the early years of Mr. Sweeney; his enrollment in 1961 at Stanford University, where he studied under Mr. Lowenstein, who was then a professor and associate dean of men; their involvement in the Mississippi civil rights movement in the '60s; their break, brought about through differences in political approaches, and the events which led to the murder.

Both Mr. (Larry) Lowenstein and Mr. Wechsler complained that *The Voice* article was a distorted portrayal of Allard Lowenstein. Mr.

284

Wechsler wrote two columns in *The Post* attacking Miss Carpenter's account. In his column on April 21, he wrote:

> Miss Carpenter was guilty of irresponsible defamation of a dead man. It very seriously raises the question of what I view as journalistic malpractice in repeatedly invoking anonymous 'sources' against a dead man who cannot answer back and whose family has no recourse to the laws of libel. In such a situation, The Council becomes in effect a court of last resort for the survivors.
>
> Miss Carpenter's pseudo-psychological study of the relationship between Lowenstein and his assassin was a melange of unattributed gossip-mongering and political malice that could shadow the lives of Lowenstein's family—and especially his three children, now 13, 11 and 10 . . . Surely these paragraphs warrant dishonorable mention in any textbook in elementary newspaper standards . . .

In his second column on May 8, Mr. Wechsler wrote that he had personally confirmed in a telephone call to Miss Carpenter that she had never spoken to Mr. Sweeney. It was both Mr. Lowenstein's and Mr. Wechsler's contention that her article conveyed a direct reflection of such a conversation. "She told me she did not feel her article had claimed any direct conversation," wrote Mr. Wechsler. "Can that passage ('Now from his cell at Riker's Island . . . .') conceivably be read as anything other than an account of a reporter's purported interview with Sweeney?"

The awarding of the Pulitzer Prize and the attendant national publicity clearly made moot the Council's normal rule of a 90-day limit on the filing of a protest after publication and the complaints were accepted.

**Response:** In a telephone conversation with Council staff on May 19, 1981, David Schneiderman, editor-in-chief of *The Village Voice*, said that his organization "respectfully declines to cooperate with the Council in its investigation." He appeared to be reading from a prepared statement. The Council offered to pick up the statement by messenger, but Mr. Schneiderman said he would have it typed and sent the next day. It has never been received.

Even though Miss Carpenter had already made a number of comments publicly, Mr. Schneiderman said *The Voice*'s refusal to cooperate covered her as well.

In the May 27-June 2 issue of *The Voice*, using his initials, Mr. Schneiderman carried a three-paragraph comment, saying that "none of the allegations undermines the accuracy or newsworthiness of the . . . 6,000-word story." He wrote that it "was reviewed by the editors of this paper at every stage; her sources were known to her editors and to our counsel, who reviewed the article line by line. *The Village Voice* stands behind every word in the story."

The comment ended: "We have been critical of the National News Council in the pages of *The Voice* for the last six years because it is troublesome that a quasi-official body attempts to police the press. *The New York Times* takes essentially the same position. *The Voice* believes that the way to deal with this issue and with similar issues is to present our readers with the facts, not to encourage censure from a self-appointed group."

**Analysis:** Study of both the complaints and the article led Council staff to decide that there were four issues in contention:

1. Whether the general characterization of Allard Lowenstein was reasonably accurate?
2. Whether there was validity in incorporating homosexuality as a potential motive in the slaying?
3. Whether there was over-use of anonymous sources?
4. Whether the story in its totality, met standards of basic accuracy, fairness and balance?

One attempt was made to treat each of these in individual sections. It failed because the arguments overlap at every point.

Miss Carpenter's article brought both the characterization and the homosexual aspect into single focus with one passage that clearly deeply offended both Mr. Lowenstein and Mr. Wechsler. It read:

. . . . There was suspicion, even back at Stanford, that Lowenstein never dealt quite honestly in personal matters. There was an undeniable tension between Lowenstein and the young men in his following. "I know that many of us, most of us had passes made at us from Al," says a friend of both Sweeney and Lowenstein from the Stanford period. Often they weren't overt proposals "but clearly testing . . . to be offered an overnight room and to discover that there was one bed."

After the shooting, in fact, there were rumors that Lowenstein and Sweeney had fallen out as the result of a lover's quarrel. Everyone simply assumed that Lowenstein approached Sweeney. (Now, from his cell at Rikers Island, Sweeney denies they ever had a relationship. Once while he and Lowenstein were traveling through Mississippi together, they checked into a motel. According to Sweeney, Lowenstein made a pass and Sweeney rebuffed it. Sweeney is not angry with Lowenstein, he claims. Nor does he feel any shame. It's just that Lowenstein wasn't always above board.)

In itself, this excerpt leads to the matter of anonymous sources. Mr. Schneiderman, in public comment, has said that Miss Carpenter conducted 48 interviews during her research. Staff examination confirms that assessment. But not verifiable to any reader are the identities of at least 36 of the 48 (75 percent) of Miss Carpenter's sources. This technique is studied later in this report. Of the 12 who were named in the article, almost all appear to have been associates of Sweeney. They were identified as:

> Patty Hagan, a friend at Stanford
> *The Stanford Daily*
> Mary King, to whom Sweeney was married for a brief time.
> Rodney Gage, a black musician who at one time "became Sweeney's closest friend."
> Ed Pincus, a filmmaker whom Sweeney met in Mississippi.
> Mendy Samstein, "who lived with Sweeney in McComb (Miss.)."
> Leni Wildflower and Paul Potter, of Students for a Democratic Society (SDS).
> David Harris, who became a leader in the war resistance movement.
> Mr. and Mrs. Herman Hamilton, Sweeney's landlords in New London, Conn.
> "Martin." This source, who recalled how Sweeney "was so flustered (when he met Mary King) that he could hardly speak, had not been identified previously, nor were there further references to him in the article.

A strikingly different assessment of Lowenstein was offered in a letter in *The Washington Post* June 22, 1980. It was signed by 18 persons, 15 of them members of Congress. Signers were:

> Congressmen: George E. Brown, Jr. (D-Calif.), John Buchanan (R-Ala.), Don Edwards (D-Calif.), Dave Evans (D-Ind.), Tom Harkin (D-Iowa), Andy Jacobs, Jr. (D-Ind.), Pete McCloskey (R-Calif.), Andy McGuire (D-N.J.), G.V. Montgomery (D-Miss.), Richard Ottinger (D-N.Y.), Richardson Preyer (D-N.C.), Pat Schroeder (D-Col.), Morris Udall (D-Ariz.), Doug Walgren (D-Pa.), and Ted Weiss (D-N.Y.).
> Others: Jed Johnson, Jr., former U.S. Representative from Oklahoma, a Democrat; Richard Celeste, Director of the Peace Corps, and Edith Wilkie, Executive Director of "Members of Congress for Peace Through Law."

The writers said that the article ". . . . measured against even the loosest of journalistic standards . . . . is grossly deficient . . . . It is devoid of any attributable quotes. For that matter, it has hardly any supporting quotes at all. It is rife with unsubstantiated assertions and gratuitous innuendo."
The letter continued:

> The tone of the article suggests that somehow Dennis Sweeney was the victim, not Al Lowenstein. It paints Al as an insensitive, selfish gadfly preying on the innocence of young people.
> Such a portrait is deeply offensive and completely at odds with reality. As William F. Buckley, Jr. said at Al's funeral, "Of all the partisans I have known . . . his was the most undistracted concern, not for humanity . . . but for human beings."
> Indeed, it was his very concern for people, and Dennis Sweeney in particular, that led Al to set up an appointment to help this troubled young man.
> Dennis Sweeney's life is certainly worth examining. But the examination should be responsible and not include farfetched and ridiculous gossip.

> The damage and pain caused by Ms. Carpenter's piece has been done. But we could not stand silent and let it pass without registering our assertion that many of her assertions are not only unsubstantiated but patently false.

Mr. Lowenstein told the Council's staff that he wonders if this letter ever came to the attention of the Pulitzer Prize jury and board. The Council staff checked and found that it had not been mentioned.

Miss Carpenter's language raised questions about Mr. Lowenstein's personal honesty, about "undeniable tension between Lowenstein and the young men in his following" and of "passes" made by him on his following.

Council checking brought strongly contrary views. Kenneth Cuthbertson, Administrative Vice-President of the Irvine Foundation in San Francisco, who was Vice-President for Financial Affairs at Stanford during Mr. Lowenstein's year on campus, said:

> Al was an absolutely straightforward and open guy. You knew where he stood on everything. I am totally surprised that anyone would suggest that he made passes at the young men who became his proteges. The first time I heard such rumors was when *The Voice*'s story came out. I had never heard anything like that from anyone who knew him. We were close friends, and my life clearly was affected by him.

Dr. William Craig, who was dean of students at the time and Mr. Lowenstein's superior officer, challenged one comment in Miss Carpenter's story that someone in the administration in 1961 had expressed "chagrin" when Mr. Lowenstein "set about politicizing students." "There was no concern on my part," said Dr. Craig. "What administrators was she talking about? There was nothing in her story quoting anyone by name in the administration. Al raised a lot of concerns, and if you will recall that period you'll know there was a lot in the country to be concerned about."

Others who were at Stanford at the time spoke to Council staff readily.

John Steinbruner, a former student of Mr. Lowenstein who now is with the Brookings Institution in Washington, said he was aware of the charges made about Mr. Lowenstein in *The Voice* article. "The references to his personal honesty, to his making passes, to his political motives, are inaccurate," Mr. Steinbruner said. "They are based more on assumptions than on facts. They are extremely uncharitable in their construction, revealing an element of hostility on the part of those who reportedly said such things. Al was a charismatic person with passionate supporters and passionate attackers. I do not know of any evidence that would support the charges that were made."

288

Armand Rosencrantz, of Inverness, Calif., who was elected head of the Stanford student body during the Lowenstein period, and who is now Executive Director of the Pioneer Fund in California, said he got to know Mr. Lowenstein quite well. Mr. Rosencrantz took issue with Miss Carpenter's statement regarding tension between Mr. Lowenstein and the young men in his following. "That simply is not true," Mr. Rosencrantz said. "There was no tension. Al was the kind of person who would get to the nitty-gritty quickly. He took a strong interest in those with whom he came in contact. If they had a problem, he would listen sympathetically, and then would do something to help.

"There were many times when a student would visit in Al's room and rap late into the night. Typically, Al would say that if the student wanted to stay to crash he was welcome to do so. While in bed he may have put his arm around the shoulder of the person, and the ambiguous circumstances of that perhaps is what gave rise to the report written by Miss Carpenter. She didn't probe further and find that that was just Al's way of showing affection. It is my strong belief that this show of affection never got more specific than that. I know of no one who ever had an improper overture from Al, and I personally never saw any untoward behavior by Al toward the young men around him. Unfortunately, a show of affection by one man toward another often is misunderstood."

James Woolsey, a Washington attorney and former Under Secretary of the Navy, who, as a Stanford student was associated with Mr. Lowenstein in efforts which led the university back into the National Student Association, said he was "quite surprised at the allegations concerning homosexuality when they were published in *The Voice*. My attitude was one of anger. This was the sort of thing you would hear from people who were hostile to him. It was an almost gratuitous reference, and anyone saying such a thing should be able to substantiate it. I never knew Al to be anything except above board. He was very straightforward. He did not create the tensions ascribed to him in the article. He was charismatic. He changed people's lives. In the entire time I was at Stanford, and in all the years that followed, until the article came out I never heard anyone say, or imply, that he made homosexual passes."

Rick Saslaw, a Los Angeles realtor, called the Council's offices on June 8 and said that he wanted to speak in reference to the allusions in *The Voice*'s story to gay relationships on the part of Allard Lowenstein.

Mr. Saslaw, who identified himself as an open gay and a gay political activist, said that he had known Mr. Lowenstein from the time he (Mr. Saslaw) was 15 years old; that he had baby-sat with the Lowenstein children when he was a teenager and later had escorted Mrs. Lowenstein to various political events; that he had worked with Mr. Lowenstein as a volunteer during his Fifth District Congressional campaign, and that he also served as a volunteer in Congressman Lowenstein's Long Island office.

"Al, in those later years, often confided in me regarding many confidential aspects of his life," Mr. Saslaw said. "We would discuss his economic situation, problems he was having with his wife, his relationships with his children—he was away from home so much of his time—and the issue of gayness never came up, except as a civil rights issue. If there was a personal gayness issue it seems strange to me that it never came up.

"I question the motives of those who infer that Al was gay. There are people—who for the sake of self-aggrandizement—pretend to have knowledge that they never really had. In the 13 years I knew him I never witnessed anything that could be construed as gayness. He never questioned me regarding my own gayness, and he was aware of that."

Franklin D. Roosevelt III, a New York attorney and grandson of President Roosevelt, offered another perspective "on the basis of a fairly intimate relationship with Al from 1960 until his death in 1980. I was one person who never knew that Al was gay, as *The Voice* so intimated. I traveled with Al in Mississippi in the summer of 1964 for ten days in a car and nothing in that experience ever occurred that would lead me to such a conclusion. I was very much affected and influenced by Al. He taught me to be politically responsible."

Mr. Roosevelt said that he first met Mr. Lowenstein after a lecture by him at the Yale Law School on the subject of South Africa. "It was in the Fall of 1960, and I had recently been to South Africa. I introduced myself and we went to his room, got on the same wave-length and rapped all night."

An associate of Mr. Lowenstein during his later years, Gregory Stone of Alexandria, Va., wrote in a letter to the editor of *The Voice* dated May 19, 1981, that "for much of the last ten years" he had traveled with Mr. Lowenstein, "was a guest in his home, etc. There was nothing in my observation or experience resembling the kind of gossip or keyhole rumor of which Miss Carpenter seems so fond." A copy of the letter, not yet published by *The Voice*, was obtained by the Council's staff from Mr. Stone.

*Voice* Editor Schneiderman justified the handling of the homosexual issue in a letter published in *The New York Post* on April 25, responding to

Mr. Wechsler's April 21 column. Mr. Schneiderman said, "In order to understand why Mr. Lowenstein was murdered, it was necessary to confront delicate issues. Miss Carpenter handled these matters with great sensitivity."

In a statement in the May 13-19 issue of *The Voice* Mr. Schneiderman wrote that "while Miss Carpenter, during her research recorded accounts attesting to homosexual advances by Mr. Lowenstein, her feature article comes to no conclusions on the matter. Mr. Lowenstein's alleged sexual preferences during the early '60s was *not* (his emphasis) the pivotal point of this piece. It was mentioned only because Sweeney told our sources that Mr. Lowenstein had once made a homosexual advance toward him— a fact which merited scrutiny as a possible motive for murder. The article also reported Sweeney's denial that this encounter had provoked any rancor or that there had ever been a homosexual relationship between the two men."

Mr. Schneiderman continued:

> Second, the article did not suggest that the author interviewed Sweeney; in fact, the absence of quotation marks indicates that the information came not from Sweeney directly but from interviews with sources close to him. None of the recent allegations challenges the fact that those views were expressed by Sweeney while at Riker's Island and that they accurately reflected the state of mind at the time. . . .

The Council's staff obtained a 31-page document written by Mr. Sweeney for his court-appointed counsel, Jesse Zaslav. Autobiographical in nature, it described his relationship with Mr. Lowenstein from the time they first met in 1962 to the time of the murder. It was written by Mr. Sweeney while he was imprisoned at Riker's Island. In addition, the Council staff has in hand five other pieces of legal documentation—three psychiatric reports, the transcript of the District Attorney's staff aide's interview with Mr. Sweeney immediately after the shooting, and the transcript of Mr. Zaslav's interview with Mr. Sweeney at Riker's Island. There is not one mention at any point by any individual, including Mr. Sweeney, of any homosexual aspect.

What emerged from these reports was a portrait of a paranoid schizophrenic, who believed that Mr. Lowenstein was trying to control his life through mental telepathy and had power to cause major accidents. Both this aspect and Miss Carpenter's article came under scrutiny in a *Wall Street Journal* article on May 14, under the headline, "Some Journalists Fear Flashy Reporters Let Color Overwhelm Fact." *The Journal* reproduced the following paragraph from *The Voice* story on the murder:

Sweeney was utterly alone. . . . Lowenstein, he was sure, had willed the murder of San Francisco Mayor George Moscone in 1978, as well as the 1979 DC-10 crash in Chicago. . . . The plan he devised contained a simple and chilling logic. He would confront Lowenstein and demand that in the future he would leave Sweeney, his family, and others alone. If he got those assurances, Sweeney intended to drive home to Oregon. . . . If not, he would have to destroy his tormentor.

"Sounds as if Miss Carpenter had a searching interview with Mr. Sweeney, right?" *The Journal* asked rhetorically.

"Wrong. . . ." *The Journal* responded, adding that Miss Carpenter had never met Mr. Sweeney.

*The Journal* used the *Village Voice* reference as an example of "liberties taken in the name of the so-called New Journalism," a literary style often described as the adaptation of fiction techniques to the realities of reporting.

Miss Carpenter told *The Journal* that she didn't mean to imply that she had talked to Mr. Sweeney. "It's very cumbersome to say, 'According to sources close to Sweeney,'" she said.

The passage about Mr. Sweeney's thoughts just before Mr. Lowenstein was killed was derived, Miss Carpenter told *The Journal*, from interviews with the accused man's attorney and with another person who talked to Mr. Sweeney after the killing and who requested anonymity. Since the attorney was planning on pleading innocent by reason of insanity, Miss Carpenter added, "If I had not been able to corroborate the material, I might not have used it.

"I knew in my gut that this is what Sweeney was thinking," she added. "It's incumbent upon me to make judgments. Otherwise I'm shunting off responsibility and being terribly cautious, and being a clumsy writer in the process. . . ."

Mr. Zaslav, referred to by Miss Carpenter as one of the two sources for information contained in the paragraph quoted by *The Journal*, told the Council's staff that he had two interviews with Miss Carpenter, one at "some length." He was asked by Council staff how the homosexual matter had come into the episode. "I don't know," he said. "Perhaps there were rumors within the prison. Things like that get around in prisons."

There is no question about Miss Carpenter's writing style being provocatively powerful. Her material evokes a feeling that she was present when certain events occurred. She employs imaginative words and phrases, such as "the laid-back life of the commune," "the all-consuming milieu of the civil rights movement," "Sweeney wavered at the fringe of radicalism," "The caravan was a political dud," and "The severing stroke came." Throughout the article, Mr. Lowenstein "descended," "surfaced," "floated," was in a "breathless frenzy," "dropped out," and "flew hither and yon."

In the disputed article, Miss Carpenter referred to her sources through a number of writing techniques, including the following:

". . . commentators cast about for reasons."

"Some tried to explain the murder . . ."

"Some said privately . . ."

"A more bizarre tale circulated that Sweeney was an assassin . . ."

"No one, however, expected to find in politics alone why Sweeney was driven to such intimate violence . . ."

"But people who had known the two men as friends have wracked their memories for some foreshadowing . . ."

"Nearly everyone who was close to Sweeney . . ."

" 'He (Sweeney) was an attractive guy,' says one woman who knew him as a freshman at Stanford . . ."

"To the chagrin of the Stanford administration, Lowenstein set out politicizing students . . ."

"Al, he (Sweeney) told a friend, showed you how to get out on a limb . . ."

" 'The relationship Al had with Dennis,' says one man, 'is the same he had with a thousand other people. Al had a need for adulation from a host of admirers . . .' "

"They (the blacks) sensed that Lowenstein saw the movement as a vehicle for his personal ambitions . . ."

"No one realized when Sweeney left (Stanford) in 1964 . . . that he would not return . . ."

". . . Lowenstein confided to mutual friends . . ."

"There was suspicion, even back at Stanford . . ."

". . . says a friend of both Sweeney and Lowenstein . . ."

"After the shooting, in fact, there were rumors . . ."

"Everyone simply assumed . . ."

"He (Sweeney) was exuberantly reporting back to friends . . ."

"Sweeney later told someone . . ."

"While friends in the movement could tell he (Sweeney) was wrestling with internal problems . . ."

" 'His upset seemed so political,' recalls one friend . . ."

"They (women) found him (Sweeney) 'angelic' and 'sweet' . . ."

"He was, as one friend put it 'rerunning old films in his head. . . .' "

"Lowenstein, it was rumoured, also had ties to the CIA . . ."

"Lowenstein later told a friend that he had met Sweeney at Penn Station in Philadelphia. . . ."

" 'Why,' he (Lowenstein) would ask friends later, 'does Dennis hate me so much?' . . ."

"Sweeney . . . carried on a correspondence with a Stanford psychologist. . . ."

" 'She was just out of his control,' says a friend . . ."

At one point, Miss Carpenter wrote:

Lowenstein, meanwhile, surfaced occasionally in the Bay Area. After the 1964 elections he too had floated. He married and for a while he dropped out altogether to attend to his family's restaurant business. On one visit to Palo Alto he met with Sweeney. The two men embraced, and Lowenstein, noting his former disciple's apparently successful shift from civil rights to resistance, remarked: "You are at the center of things now, Dennis. I am not." Sweeney was flattered, but could not help feeling that Lowenstein was being ironic. By 1967 Lowenstein was back in the fray. Attacking resistance for not working within the system, he flew hither and yon mustering support for a "Dump Johnson" initiative, then made his successful run for Congress in New York's fifth district.

In reference to the statement that his brother dropped out "to attend to his family's restaurant business," Larry Lowenstein, who operated the business at that time, declared that his brother's only connection with the restaurant business "was as an eater." Mr. Lowenstein also said that his brother "may have surfaced, and he may have floated, but he never dropped out. He was involved in something at all times. There are many sources who could tell you, and could have told Miss Carpenter, if she had asked, what Al was doing during those years, and why he was doing it."

Mr. Lowenstein also called attention to a dating error in Miss Carpenter's article. In reporting about Sweeney's purchase of a gun, she wrote that "On Tuesday, March 13, Sweeney picked up the Llama and a box of 50 bullets." The flow-line of the story continues in such form that her account would have had the murder committed on Thursday, March 15 instead of the proper date, Friday, March 14.

Mr. Lowenstein and Mr. Wechsler, referring to the letter *Voice* editor Schneiderman wrote to *The New York Post* in defense of the article (". . . a brilliantly reported and thoroughly documented portrayal . . .") said that "If this is so, how come they got the wrong dates for this major story on a crime?"

One other aspect of looseness applies to the longer passage about the "Palo Alto" meeting and "the two men embraced." In Mr. Sweeney's document given to his lawyer, he wrote:

> I remember a phone conversation in 1967 after a long period of absence (from Lowenstein). I was working with students and friends in the anti-draft movement in California, when a call came one evening to our lodging directed to someone else. I was asked to pick up the phone since Mr. Lowenstein heard I was there, and after a brief explanation of what we were doing I remember his saying: "Well, you're at the center of things now. The forms we were in together have disappeared, and it is up to you and those like you to provide leadership to the new wave of recruits coming along."

There is a similarity between what Miss Carpenter wrote about the Palo

Alto encounter and what Mr. Sweeney wrote. Both said "You are at the center of things now." But there the similarity ends. In Miss Carpenter's version the two men met and embraced. In Mr. Sweeney's version, he talked with Mr. Lowenstein by telephone, which ruled out any embrace. Mr. Sweeney doesn't have Mr. Lowenstein saying "I am not" ("at the center of things"). And Miss Carpenter has Mr. Sweeney "flattered" and "feeling that Lowenstein was being ironic."

In reference to Miss Carpenter's statement that Mr. Lowenstein returned to the fray—following the 1967 "meeting" with Sweeney "Attacking the Resistance for not working within the system," *The New York Times* reported on April 23, 1969, that on the previous day Mr. Lowenstein, then a Congressman, had arranged a news conference in Washington at which a dozen students, representing 253 student leaders from leading universities throughout the country, vowed "they would go to jail rather than serve in the military 'as long as the war in Vietnam continues.'"

Another phrase of the article has been challenged by a Boston filmmaker. Miss Carpenter reported that Mr. Sweeney, ". . . during 1965, while floating in Amite Country (sic) . . . had run across a filmmaker named Ed Pincus, who was shooting a documentary about civil violence in Natchez."

Mr. Pincus, who says he was interviewed by Miss Carpenter, told the Council's staff that "I have never been in Amite County. I met Sweeney, not in 1965, but in 1964 in Cambridge, Mass. He didn't meet me while I was filming a documentary in Natchez, and in fact the documentary was not about civil rights violence."

Mr. Pincus later became one of the "voices" communicating with Mr. Sweeney and became, in Mr. Sweeney's tortured mind, a person he had to stop. "Sometime in 1976," Miss Carpenter wrote, "when Dennis was working at a mattress factory in Lynn, Massachusetts, he contacted Pincus and told him to call off the voices. Once he even visited his former associate at his home and threw a punch. (The blow was blocked by a visiting friend.) Pincus came to think of gentle Sweeney as a potentially dangerous man. He feared for himself and his family."

Mr. Pincus told the Council's staff that the encounter didn't happen at his home. "He didn't know where my house was. I had to keep it secret so he wouldn't know where I lived. The encounter happened in front of a restaurant in Cambridge and in fact the blow was not blocked by a visiting friend. There were many blows and he had me on the ground pummeling me until friends who had accompanied me to protect me pulled him off."

Although Mr. Schneiderman's decision of non-cooperation with the Council also covered Miss Carpenter, there were a number of public comments made by her in defense of her article and of her reporting and writing technique.

In an interview with *The New York Times* May 11, she said, "In my research I was satisfied that what the story says was true. The reader has got to trust me when he or she is reading the piece. I do not feel compelled to attribute each and every piece of information to its source. I don't mean to sound arrogant, but I do mean to sound confident."

Miss Carpenter told *The New York Post* (May 8) that only "unsophisticated" readers would think she had obtained the information directly from Sweeney.

"My stories are excellent," she told *The Post*. "They stand on their own merit."

New York's *Soho News*, another weekly tabloid, quoted Miss Carpenter as saying that "Lowenstein's family was upset because my story didn't come out the way they wanted it to. It seems a little cheap to do it after I win the prize. There was no malice involved. . . . My story was an attempt to understand Sweeney. I was trying to unravel the motives of a sick man."

In an interview on the Caryl Ratner Show over New York's radio station WPLJ on May 17, Miss Carpenter described how she does a story. She said that it starts with an idea, with the choice not made on a rational basis, but rather like love: See an idea and everything feels right. She then does her research, utilizing public records, such as court documents and publications. She reviews the material and then sets up interviews. She said it took three weeks on each story (referring to the three Pulitzer Prize entries) to do the research and reporting, and ten days to do the writing.

At *The Voice*, Miss Carpenter said, there was "light-handed editing," followed by "backchecking". She said that because she was a free-lance writer at the time she did the three stories (she now is on the staff) she was subjected to heavier backchecking than normally occurs, and that this took two to three days of examination by lawyers and editors. Miss Carpenter called Mr. Wechsler's criticisms in his column "a sloppy and irresponsible attack."

She further said that she was at a natural juncture in her career and that she was thinking of pursuing work in screen plays or books. She called the Pulitzer Prizes the "Academy Awards of Journalism."

**Council finding:** Under the patterns followed on most newspapers, the inclusion of many critical comments about an individual's actions and motivations would bring requests from editors for further investigation and broader interviewing to make certain that the general characterization being drawn was well-founded. There is no evidence of any such attempt in this *Village Voice* story, even though the Council's research promptly brought forth a number of strongly differing viewpoints and flat contradictions from individuals who were closely associated with Allard Lowenstein during his career.

Teresa Carpenter has made it clear she was a free-lancer at the time she submitted her articles and has said that because of this *The Voice* applied stringent checking to her copy. Despite Editor David Schneiderman's reiteration of such checking and his confidence in the article, a number of valid challenges have arisen to cast doubt on the story's accuracy and its depiction of Mr. Lowenstein. The Council is further disturbed by a paragraph that reads as if Ms. Carpenter had interviewed Dennis Sweeney in his cell at Riker's Island when in fact she did not.

In sum, the Council finds the article to have been marred by the over-use of unattributed sources, by a writing style so colored and imaginative as to blur precise meanings, and by such reckless and speculative construction as to result in profound unfairness to the victim of a demented killer. The complaints are found warranted.

**Concurring:** Abel, J. Bell, Brady, Cooney, Decter, Ghiglione, Hornby, Huston, Maynard, Pulitzer, Scott, Stanton and van den Haag.

**Dissenting:** Miller.

**Abstaining:** Isaacs.

**Dissenting opinion by Mr. Miller:** I would have to be convinced that Teresa Carpenter made up what she wrote before I could agree with the majority that this complaint is warranted. I am not convinced that she did and I cannot assume that she did.

I agree that her use of unidentified sources was reckless, but this practice is unfortunately very widespread and spreading. Many editors today appear to believe they have done their duty when they publish or broadcast an item that says, "Sources say . . . ."

BARRETT (LEHIGH VALLEY COMMITTEE
AGAINST HEALTH FRAUD, INC.)
against
PARADE MAGAZINE and
JACK ANDERSON

**Complaint:** Dr. Stephen Barrett, M.D., chairman of the Lehigh Valley Committee Against Health Fraud, Inc., complained about an article by Jack Anderson in *Parade* magazine April 26, 1981. The article was headlined, "Dear Mr. President . . . an Open Letter from Jack Anderson." The article was a plea to President Reagan to cultivate and to protect the "whistle blowers" upon whom Mr. Anderson said the president must depend to make good his campaign pledge to root out fraud and waste in the federal government. Mr. Anderson listed nine such whistle blowers who he said had suffered for their efforts. Dr. Barrett's complaint was directed specifically against the following paragraph:

> DR. J. ANTHONY MORRIS. An eminent microbiologist, he challenged the government's 1976 swine flu immunization program. He was proved right in warning that the predicted epidemic would not occur and that mass inoculations would prove hazardous. Many who submitted to the shots suffered serious side effects. Some died. Damage suits against the government have totaled more than $3 billion. For trying to prevent this disaster, Morris was locked out of his laboratory and fired. He is now blackballed from further government employment.

Dr. Barrett called that paragraph a distorted account of the firing of Dr. Morris. He acknowledged that Dr. Morris spoke out against the swine flu program and that he was fired by the U.S. Food and Drug Administration. However, said Dr. Barrett, the firing process began well before Dr. Morris spoke out against the program. Furthermore, he said, "The official record indicates that (Dr. Morris) was fired for 'inefficiency' related to his scientific procedures, a charge ultimately upheld by the Civil Service Commission." Dr. Barrett also complained that it was not true that Dr. Morris was locked out of his laboratory for trying to prevent the swine flu disaster.

Dr. Barrett recalled that he complained in 1977 that a longer article in *Parade* on March 13 of that year was biased and that the News Council had found his complaint warranted. He concluded, "I charge again that *Parade* has published a one-sided, editorially irresponsible account of Morris' firing. I wish this complaint to be brought against both the magazine and Mr. Anderson."

**Response:** Murray M. Weiss, managing editor of *Parade*, said he sent Dr. Barrett's complaint to Jack Anderson and that Mr. Anderson ascribed the dispute to a difference in interpretation of the firing of Dr. Morris. Mr. Weiss replied along those lines to Dr. Barrett and sent a copy of his letter to the Council to serve as *Parade*'s answer to the complaint. He wrote in part:

> The case involves the government getting rid of a dissenting scientist and then covering up its tracks by implying that the man was inefficient. That the Civil Service Commission upheld Morris' dismissal is meaningless. The Commission almost always upheld the government against its employees in appeals cases. The facts simply happen to be that Morris, the *only* government scientist who opposed the swine flu program, was fired.

Dr. Barrett sent Mr. Weiss the face sheets of government documents showing that the process of firing Dr. Morris began in May of 1975, nearly a year before the swine flu program became a public issue. "I don't know how your theory of cause-and-effect is compatible with the enclosed documents," Dr. Barrett wrote.

"Moreover," he continued, "The issue before the National News Council is not whether Morris was or was not fired for speaking out or whether his firing was or was not justified. The issue is whether reduction of a highly complex set of circumstances to a brief, one-sided account is proper journalism or improperly biased reporting."

Mr. Weiss did not reply further.

**Staff report:** Dr. Barrett does not challenge—nor does he support—the view that Dr. Morris was fired because of his opposition to the swine flu program. Instead he attacks Mr. Anderson's report on the same ground from which he attacked the 1977 *Parade* article—that both were so one-sided and simplistic as to be editorially irresponsible.

To evaluate the present complaint, some review of the firing of Dr. Morris is necessary, but the Council's staff has not set out to reevaluate the original complaint. The following account is based on the original article; the material gathered in 1977 to evaluate that article, and, in addition, a portion of Dr. Morris's testimony before an appeals review board of the U.S. Civil Service Commission.

Dr. Morris began investigating viral diseases in the U.S. Army in World War II. In the 1950s he was assigned to the National Institutes of Health to assess the risks in vaccines. By the middle 1960s he was reporting that flu vaccines might be dangerous. Following his reports (The original *Parade* article implies a cause-and-effect relationship.), Dr. Morris was relieved of his duties as influenza control officer and moved out of his laboratory at NIH. This is apparently the incident to which Mr. Anderson refers when he says that Dr. Morris was locked out of his laboratory. It happened several years before the swine flu program became a public issue. Nonetheless, it appears reasonable to characterize Dr. Morris's efforts in this period as "trying to prevent" some of the effects that did show up later in the swine flu program.

John Gardner, former secretary of Health, Education and Welfare, enlisted the help of Ralph Nader's organization on Dr. Morris's behalf. James Turner, a Nader lawyer, took up his cause. There followed: a memorandum charging irregularities in the handling of flu vaccines by the NIH; hearings called by the late Sen. Abraham Ribicoff; an investigation by the General Accounting Office, and the transfer of Dr. Morris from the NIH to the U.S. Food and Drug Administration.

At FDA Dr. Morris reported that live vaccines, on which the government was beginnning to pin its hopes for an effective weapon against flu—and which had already been tested on some humans—accelerated the growth of tumors in test animals.

Feb. 19, 1975, Dr. Morris requested "a detailed investigation into the current state of my research program, the program of the Bureau (of Biologics) in general and an evaluation of the general state of national vaccine policy. . . ." The review was conducted by the FDA's Panel on Viral Vaccines and Rickettsial Vaccines. It found Dr. Morris's research "grossly unsatisfactory."

July 11, 1975, Dr. Harry M. Meyer, Jr., director of the Bureau of Biologics, notified Dr. Morris that he intended to remove him from his position for inefficiency and insubordination. Dr. Morris appealed.

Feb. 14, 1976, swine flu diagnosed at Ft. Dix, NJ.

March 16, 1976, hearing on Dr. Morris's appeal.

May 24, 1976, hearing examiner upheld a majority of the charges against Dr. Morris but recommended a five-day suspension instead of firing.

July 12, 1976, Dr. Alexander M. Schmidt, commissioner of food and drugs, rejected the examiner's recommendation and fired Dr. Morris.

March 13, 1977, *Parade* article.

June 3, 1977, Civil Service Commission upheld firing.

In his response to the 1977 complaint, Jess Gorkin, then editor of *Parade*, told the Council that Dr. Morris wrote a letter to Dr. Schmidt a few days before Dr. Schmidt fired him. The letter raised questions about the manufacture of swine flu vaccine. Furthermore, wrote Mr. Gorkin, Dr. Morris had been quoted in *The Washington Post* attacking the swine flu program; HEW took the attack seriously enough to deliver a reply from its chief health official. (Dr. Meyer is sending a transcript of testimony in an appeal hearing in which he says Dr. Morris himself acknowledged that he did speak out against vaccine risks in the period immediately before his firing.)

An argument can be made on either side of the question, "Was Dr. Morris fired because he spoke out against the swine flu program?" The data does not answer the question, for example, "Would the commissioner have agreed to a lesser punishment, as the appeal examiner had suggested, if Dr. Morris had not been speaking out against the swine flu program immediately before his firing?"

The answer is a matter of opinion.

In 1977 the Council concluded that there was no dispute over the facts that Dr. Morris did fight the flu program and was fired. But, the Council said, the *Parade* article was defective in that it did not provide any indication "that there might be some substantive arguments on any side other than Dr. Morris's arguments. . . ."

The Council said further, "The Council, thus, does not challenge the right of the authors to champion Dr. Morris's case. Rather the issue before the Council is whether in this instance the presentation was so one-sided as to have strayed beyond an acceptable range of editorial judgment."

In that instance the Council concluded that the article did stray beyond acceptable limits. The question before the Council today is whether the same limits should apply to an 82-word paragraph by Mr. Anderson that applied to a 1,300-word feature story in 1977.

The Anderson article comes in different trappings from the earlier article. The 1977 article appeared as an expository feature article entirely about Dr. Morris under the headline, "He Fought the Flu Shots and the U.S. Fired Him." The paragraph now under examination is, by contrast, a part of an article in which Mr. Anderson expresses his opinion that whistle blowers tend to be punished.

The question arises: Is the present article adequately labeled so that the reader can recognize it as opinion? The answer appears to be yes. The article bears the title, "Dear Mr. President," and a descriptive line in equally large type, "An open letter from Jack Anderson."

If then the article is opinion and so labeled, the Council's only concern can be whether the facts were significantly distorted to justify the opinion. (The Council's brochure says, "It does not concern itself with editorial expressions of opinion, except when there is evidence to indicate facts have been manipulated.")

The Council staff has not rereported the original article. It has reviewed the material gathered to evaluate that article. That review suggests that the facts do not prove conclusively whether or not Dr. Morris was fired because of his opposition to the swine flu program. They provide the basis for an argument either way.

It did not require any significant manipulation or distortion of those facts for Mr. Anderson to justify his opinion.

**Council finding:** In 1977 the Council found that an article about the firing of Dr. J. Anthony Morris was "so one-sided as to have strayed beyond an acceptable range of editorial judgment." Now, the same complainant asks the Council to make similar judgment of a capsulized report by columnist Jack Anderson of Dr. Morris's firing. The article at issue in 1977 was a 1,300-word expository article entirely about Dr. Morris. In it a reader might reasonably have expected some reference to all sides of his controversial firing. By contrast, the article now under scrutiny seems to the Council to be an expression of opinion labeled, "Dear Mr. President . . . an open letter from Jack Anderson."

Any attempt to compress a complex set of events occurring over several years into a single, one paragraph judgment on an issue of right or wrong may be open to challenge. However, the Council does not concern itself with expressions of opinion unless the facts have been significantly distorted. A review of the facts available to the Council in this case does not reveal any such gross distortion. Therefore, the complaint is found unwarranted.

**Concurring:** Abel, D. Bell, J. Bell, Benson, Brady, Decter, Huston, Isaacs, Scott, Stanton, van den Haag, Williams.
September 24, 1981

### COMPLAINT NO. 191 (Filed May 28, 1981)
### BARRETT (LEHIGH VALLEY COMMITTEE
### AGAINST HEALTH FRAUD, INC.)
### against
### LOS ANGELES TIMES SYNDICATE

**Complaint:** Dr. Stephen Barrett, M.D., chairman of the Lehigh Valley Committee Against Health Fraud, Inc., complained that the Los Angeles Times Syndicate had distributed a misleading article. The article appeared May 27, 1981, in *The Morning Call* in Allentown, PA, which is Dr. Barrett's local newspaper, under the headline, "The Bathing Suit

Diet." The article said that readers could lose from 15 to 30 pounds by adopting a balanced diet of 1,300 calories a day. Fourteen days of suggested menus were published along with the article.

Dr. Barrett complained that the article suggested that readers could lose 15 to 30 pounds in 14 days. As evidence he noted that the newspaper claimed specifically in a promotion announcement over radio station WFMZ that the weight loss could be achieved in two weeks.

"The diet is perfectly fine," Dr. Barrett wrote. "Someone who follows it will lose from 1 to 3 pounds a week, depending upon how many calories are burned off as energy. . . . We don't know whether the wording of the article is accidentally or deliberately misleading, but something should be done to counteract the impression it gives that people can lose 15 to 30 pounds in two weeks. Even starvation won't do that."

The article appeared in *The Call* under the following introductory editor's note:

> Can't squeeze into that bikini? Paunching out over your trunks? That's just about everyone's problem when the summer duds get hauled out this time of year. Here, from weight-loss specialist Dr. Neil Solomon, is a diet with specific menus that takes the guesswork out of calorie counting. Each day's menu adds up to about 1300 calories and meets standard vitamin recommendations.

The second and third paragraphs of the article read as follows:

> With his assistant, Registered Dietician Marion Hanna, Dr. Solomon has devised a special diet, including two weeks of menus (breakfast, lunch, dinner, snack).
>
> "Men and women can lose anywhere from 15 to 30 pounds on this diet," says Solomon, "if they pay careful attention to their eating habits."

The menus were printed under headlines reading, "Day 1, Day 2, Day 3 . . ." The article refers specifically to the menus once after the second paragraph; it says that the dieter must "brown-bag" lunch except on Day 11.

The script for the newspaper's radio promotion May 27 shows that the announcer did say, "With this diet you can expect to lose anywhere from 15 to 30 pounds in two weeks, just in time for the beach."

**Response:** Jane Amari, editor of the Los Angeles Time Syndicate, sent the Council the copy for the diet articles as it was distributed to syndicate customers. She noted that the copy did not say that all the weight would be lost in two weeks. "As a matter of fact, the wording suggests otherwise," Ms. Amari wrote. "The second paragraph says, '. . . Dr. Solomon has devised a special diet, including two weeks of menus. . . .' He does not say a special diet consisting exclusively of two weeks of menus. In fact,

Point 8 of our copy says dieters can stay on the program for several months, because it is a balanced diet. Allentown cut that graph.

"Because only two weeks of menus were included, it seems that *The Morning Call* and Dr. Barrett jumped to the conclusion that we were suggesting all 15 to 30 pounds would be lost in that period. I think reasonable people would agree that it is impossible to include menus for the entire time span of a diet to lose 30 pounds. That could conceivably take 15 weeks. Newsprint is dearer than that. This is why Dr. Solomon, and virtually every other diet in magazines and newspapers, offers menus for a limited time only.

"We are also syndicating a year's worth of columns by Nathan Pritikin. His diet plan lowers serum cholesterol. But we only include one recipe per week with his column. Following Dr. Barrett's reasoning to the extreme, it could be charged that Pritikin claims to lower cholesterol with one meal.

"However, having been made aware of the confusion resulting from Dr. Solomon's diet (although Allentown and Dr. Barrett were apparently the only cases of misinterpretation), on our next diet we will add a phrase clearly indicating that any sensible weight-loss plan is a long-term project."

**Staff report:** The introductory editor's note, which was supplied by the syndicate, can be understood to mean that the entire diet program consists of the 14 days' menus accompanying the article ("Here . . . is a diet with specific menus that takes the guesswork out of calorie counting.").

The 14-day idea is reinforced by the second paragraph (". . . Dr. Solomon has devised a special diet, including two weeks of menus . . ."). It is reinforced further by the headlines over each day's menu reading, "Day 1, Day 2" etc. Lawrence J. Burnagiel, promotion manager for Call-Chronicle Newspapers in Allentown, said the 14-day idea was still further reinforced for him by a specific reference in the article to the 11th day; then the dieter might break his or her brown-bag lunch routine with a fast-food hamburger.

Both Mr. Burnagiel and Mary Millan, the *Morning Call* copy writer who wrote the radio promotion for the diet article, noted that the diet was obviously designed for a quick weight loss, because its stated goal was to shed pounds before the swimming season. (The diet was published in Allentown May 27. Memorial Day is the traditional start of swimming there, said Mr. Burnagiel.)

Ms. Millan noted that the amount of weight that might be lost is suggested in the third paragraph ("'Men and women can lose anywhere from 15 to 30 pounds on this diet," says Solomon, 'if they pay careful attention to their eating habits.'"). Ms. Millan took that to mean that one could lose 15 to 30 pounds if one stuck to the diet for two weeks. She said she had some familiarity with dieting and she believes that such a goal is possible.

Ms. Millan ascribed her misinterpretation to the wording of the article. She said she had read and reread the article when she learned of the complaint, and "I still think I was not all that wrong. It is open to interpretation."

**Council finding:** To the extent that the word "misleading," which is used in this complaint, carries some suggestion of purposeful deceit, the complaint is found unwarranted. The Council has found no evidence that the Los Angeles Times Syndicate set out purposefully to deceive readers with its bathing suit diet. However, the wording of the article was somewhat ambiguous. That ambiguity was evidenced by the fact that the complainant and a copy writer for *The Morning Call* thought the diet promised a weight loss of 15 to 30 pounds in two weeks. There are millions of readers who want to lose weight. Many of them do not know that there are no safe shortcuts. Their prospects for losing weight might be damaged by disappointment in a diet that did not do what they thought it would. For that reason it is important that editors make it clear that safe dieting is a long-term project. The Council commends the Los Angeles Times Syndicate editor for her commitment to include cautionary language in future diet articles.

**Concurring:** Abel, D. Bell, J. Bell, Benson, Brady, Decter, Huston, Isaacs, Scott, Stanton, van den Haag.
September 24, 1981

## COMPLAINT NO. 192          (Filed July 21, 1981)
### SUNKIST GROWERS, INC.
### against
### THE NEW YORK TIMES and TIME

**Complaint:** Jack J. Heeger, vice president, public affairs, Sunkist Growers, Inc., Van Nuys, CA, complained about articles in *The New York Times* March 25, 1981, and in *Time* April 6, 1981. Both articles were about the diversion of part of the bumper 1980-81 crop of California navel oranges from the retail food market. The diversion was effected under a federal marketing order. Marketing orders are devices dating from the 1930s that allow the growers of some 47 crops to control to some degree the marketing of those crops. The *Times* article reported that the marketing order system is under attack by some consumer groups, economists and growers, and that its administrative costs are scheduled for scrutiny by the Reagan Administration.

Opponents of the marketing order charged that more than half of the 1980-81 California navel orange crop was being kept off the market by the order. "The inference is that the other half is destroyed, dumped or otherwise wasted," said Mr. Heeger.

Actually, Mr. Heeger said, about 56 percent of the crop went to the domestic fresh fruit market; 8 percent went to fresh export, and 26 percent went to juice products. "Thus, about 92 percent of the total crop reached the consumer as fresh fruit or juice in the U.S. and abroad," he wrote.

Normally, he said, all of the fruit that cannot be marketed fresh because it is too small or its quality is too poor would be turned into juice. However, this year it was not. He wrote:

> The fruit this year was late in maturing and the sugar-to-acid ratio was quite low in the early season. Thus, during those early months, it cost more to extract the juice from the oranges than the juice was worth. Hence, an economic decision was made—rather than incur a loss on processing the fruit into juice, some of this fruit would be used as cattle feed. About 5.4 percent of the total crop was utilized in this way.

The Sunkist complaint focuses on pictures and articles in both *The Times* and *Time* of fruit that Mr. Heeger said was being dried preparatory to processing as cattle feed. Both publications reported, incorrectly according to Mr. Heeger, that the fruit had been abandoned to rot.

The *New York Times* article said of the fruit, "Stretching in all directions are millions and millions of navel oranges, some stamped with the Sunkist label, all abandoned to rot in the California sun." Under a picture accompanying the article, *The Times* published this line: "Carl A. Pescosolido, an orange grower, examining oranges dumped by other growers in California's San Joaquin Valley."

Under a similar picture *Time* magazine published this line: "Grower Carl Pescosolido amid a sea of navel oranges left to rot in Kern County." The three-paragraph article accompanying the *Time* picture said in part:

> Even amid the lush groves of California's San Joaquin Valley, the sight is startling. Covering acre after acre, mammoth mounds of navel oranges lie rotting in the sun. This season's crop hit a record 1,421,250 tons, but nearly half of it will

never reach the fresh-produce markets. The result: a large navel orange costs as much as 70 cents in Chicago, up from 50 cents last year.

The oranges are being dumped because of U.S. Department of Agriculture "marketing orders." . . .

The fruit pictured in *The Times* and in *Time* was at the Famoso drag strip near Bakersfield, which was rented by Don Smith, president of Sun-Gro Commodities, Inc., for use as a cattle feed processing station, according to Mr. Heeger. He said Mr. Smith dries the fruit in the sun, then grinds it up and sells it to dairy farmers and feed lot operators. Mr. Heeger added that Mr. Smith dries and uses other commodities, including peaches, plums and potatoes, in the same way. Mr. Heeger wrote:

> A reporter for *The New York Times*, Ann Crittenden, while investigating a story on marketing orders, was taken to this Bakersfield location by one of the opponents of the marketing order. While there she talked with two other gentlemen who explained that the fruit was being used for cattle feed. Statements from these two gentlemen, John Wollenman and Solon Boydston are attached.
>
> Ms. Crittenden also was told about the use of the fruit as cattle feed by two others, Bill Peightal, manager of the Navel Orange Administrative Committee, and Marshall Anderson, then president of Citrus Mutual. Statements from these gentlemen also are attached.
>
> Although she referred to Sunkist several times in her story, Ms. Crittenden spoke only briefly to Russell L. Hanlin, president of Sunkist Growers, Inc., but he said the conversation was very general in nature. He said it lasted no more than 5 to 10 minutes, but he is certain that the subject of use of oranges as cattle feed arose. Ms. Crittenden refused to speak with me, although I am Sunkist's principal spokesman in matters of this type.

Miss Crittenden's story appeared on page one of *The Times* with no mention of the use of diverted fruit as cattle feed, Mr. Heeger noted. As for *Time*, Mr. Heeger wrote:

> Following the appearance of *The New York Times* article, *Time* magazine dispatched a reporter, Joe Pilcher, to cover the story. Mr. Pilcher never talked with anyone at Sunkist, and the only person I can be certain he talked with was Mr. Peightal (manager of the Navel Orange Administrative Committee), with whom he spoke for two and one-half hours. Mr. Peightal indicated that he went into great detail about the use of the fruit as cattle feed, and suggested that he contact Don Smith. Mr. Pilcher did not do so. . . .

Mr. Heeger wrote a letter to the editor for publication in *The New York Times* to correct what he called the erroneous impression left by the story. The newspaper published his letter April 21. Mr. Heeger and, he said, others also wrote to *Time*, but he said the magazine did not publish their letters. Instead it published two letters that, he said, were critical of growers for letting the oranges rot. Mr. Heeger continued:

> Then *Time* sent me a response which clearly ignores the content of my letter. I realized later that it was a form letter because a grower who had also sent them a complaint received the identical response, except that it was signed by a different person.

**Response:** In response to a letter from the Council's staff, Seymour Topping, managing editor of *The New York Times*, wrote that he would not depart from that newspaper's policy not to engage with the News Council. He said further:

> We have dealt with the Sunkist complaint and we do not feel that it is necessary to take any further action. We stand by the story of our reporter, Ann Crittenden, as being fair and accurate. We agreed to the publication of the letter from Sunkist simply to allow that company to have a say, and not as a substitution for any correction. We have done this frequently in the past to illuminate all aspects of complex circumstances.
>
> You may be interested to know that as a consequence of the Sunkist statements, a news program was planned by Hodding Carter on Channel 13 which would have dealt with the Sunkist allegations. Following a response to the Channel 13 people by Miss Crittenden, the program's segment was dropped and to the best of my knowledge, it was never broadcast.

Staff called Miss Crittenden and asked her if she would send a copy of her reply to the inquiries from "Inside Story," the Carter program. She declined to do that, but she replied to the Sunkist complaint as follows:

She said there was no material difference between dumping the fruit and processing it as cattle feed.

"When were orange groves planted to feed cattle?" she asked.

She denied that anyone had told her that the oranges were to be processed for cattle feed. "All I had been told was that they had been dumped and that a portion of them might be disposed of in some other way," she said.

Miss Crittenden said that the oranges she saw at Famoso had been "given away" and were definitely rotting. She said she also saw grove after grove where the oranges were not even hauled to disposal sites but had been left on the ground to rot.

In response to a question about whether her article gave the reader enough information to decide whether there was no material difference among methods of disposal, Miss Crittenden said that she had gone through that analysis. She said the story was not a nuts-and-bolts story about the orange crop; it was a national story about marketing orders with the orange crop used as a lead. She said she made the decision that she didn't need to get into details that would bog down the reader.

Miss Crittenden said she considered the complaint to the News Council an effort by a public relations executive to manipulate an agency of redress on behalf of Sunkist. She said she stood by her story, and, she said, "Nobody has a right to say what you should put in a story."

While *Time* declined to respond to the Council about the Sunkist complaint, Jason McManus, an executive editor, pointed out to Council staff that the magazine had not published the Sunkist letter. It is the magazine's practice to publish letters taking issue with its reporting only when *Time* believes it was wrong. Since *Time* did not publish the Sunkist letter in April or in August after the Council's inquiry, it is reasonable to infer that the editors decided their article was essentially correct.

**Staff examination:** At the heart of this dispute is the concept of waste. Those who oppose the marketing order considered any use of oranges except as human food to be wasteful. Carl A. Pescosolido, a grower who is also a leader in the attack on the marketing order, dramatized this interpretation of waste by giving away oranges to an Oakland, CA, food cooperative in defiance of the marketing order, and by giving fruit to charitable organizations. In articles in *The Tribune* in Oakland, in the *Los Angeles Times* and in the *Visalia Times-Delta* there are quotations from Mr. Pescosolido making it clear that he believes that processing for cattle feed amounts to the same thing as dumping or destroying.[1]

On the other hand, those who support the marketing order see a difference between methods of disposing of the diverted fruit and a difference in the words used to describe those methods. They considered it less wasteful to process fruit for cattle feed than to dump it in a landfill, for example. That differentiation is suggested in a United Press International article datelined Sacramento, Feb. 14. It predicted that four out of 10 navel oranges in the huge crop "will be provided to cattle for feed or given away to juicing plants." The article continued, "In case the glut of oranges becomes too great, space has been reserved at the Tulare County dump in southern San Joaquin Valley to dump oranges at a cost to farmers of $1 a ton."

Mr. Pescosolido's challenge to the marketing order generated extensive publicity in the spring and summer. It was the subject of television news broadcasts from KNBC-TV in Los Angeles, March 10; KNXT-TV in Los Angeles March 16, and the "Today Show" March 19. After *The New*

---

*Tribune* Feb 28; *Times* June 10; *Times-Delta* May 15.

*York Times* picture and article March 25, for three days a part of the "Ken and Bob Show" on KABC-Radio in Los Angeles was devoted to whether or not the oranges at Mr. Smith's operation were being wasted or utilized.

Similarly, after the "Today Show" March 19 and the *Times* picture March 25, national attention on the effects of the marketing order seemed to focus on the Famoso pile-up and its significance. An article April 8 in Gannett Westchester Newspapers by columnist Jack Murdich referred to "a picture that recently appeared on the front page of another major newspaper." Under the headline, "Story of an expensive rotting shame," Murdich wrote:

> The newsphoto showed huge mounds of California oranges left to rot in the fields. There were literally millions of oranges. The growers deliberately had destroyed fruit to prop up market prices.

The *Chicago Sun-Times* published a UPI picture of the Famoso oranges March 26 and described them in a headline as "dumped" in quotation marks without specifying what would be their ultimate disposal. The *Time* publication followed on April 6.

On April 9, the *New York Daily News* twitted *The Times*, *Time* and the "Today Show" for having been misled into thinking the Famoso oranges were abandoned to rot. Columnist Richard Stern said the three had been "bushwhacked" in "California's dirty little orange war."

On March 20, in response to the controversy Rep. George Miller of California called for a General Accounting Office (GAO) review of the marketing order.

The GAO report dated July 2 said in its introduction:

> Our objective was to provide information on the California-Arizona navel orange marketing order in response to Rep. George Miller's specific questions. His primary concern was whether the composition of the California-Arizona Navel Orange Administrative Committee assures adequate consideration of the overall public interest. Also, the use of navel oranges as cattle feed had led to allegations that oranges have been dumped and otherwise destroyed to enhance the navel orange price. In addition, some growers have expressed concern about not being able to sell all of their navel oranges in the fresh domestic market because of restrictions imposed by the marketing order.

The part of the GAO report that is pertinent to this review says:

> We found no evidence that good fruit was being dumped or otherwise destroyed. However, 82,800 tons of navel oranges have been processed as cattle feed through May, 1981 . . . . Whether oranges are shipped to the fresh market or processed as byproducts, including juice and cattle feed, is largely the result of economics. Growers generally pay handlers to pick, pack, haul, and sell their oranges. Packing-

310

houses charge growers for oranges picked plus an additional amount for oranges packed for the fresh market. The poorer quality fruit is processed as byproducts. Some of this fruit may be good tasting but of small size or inferior appearance and may not demand enough price on the fresh market to pay for the packing.

Whether byproduct fruit is processed for its juice or fed to cattle depends largely on its value in the juice market. Before the fruit is squeezed for juice, the price of juice concentrate must exceed the processing cost. If it does not, the fruit is sold as cattle feed to avoid a total loss.

In support of her view that cattle feed and dumping amounted to the same thing, Miss Crittenden said that fruit processed for cattle feed was given away. This season, the GAO report says, diverted fruit was sold as cattle feed at one time and at another time Sunkist had to pay shippers to haul it away. One shipper said that Sunkist paid him $1 a ton to haul away fruit that he later sold as cattle feed.

In July there was a hearing on the marketing order before a U.S. Department of Agriculture administrative law judge at Exeter, CA. It went on for six days and produced 1,359 pages of testimony.

Don Smith, president of the company that was processing the oranges pictured in *The New York Times* and in *Time*, testified that the use of diverted oranges in cattle feed was not a waste. He said his company had developed the drying technique to allow the orange material to be stored like other feeds. He said his firm spent more than $100,000 to buy and transport some 17,000 tons of oranges for feed this season. He said his firm would have received more oranges if what he called damaging, inaccurate publicity in *The New York Times* had not made some handlers reluctant to provide oranges to his company.

One opponent of the marketing order said he didn't think Mr. Smith's fruit was fit to be used in cattle feed at the time *The Times* pictured it. Richard Pescosolido, brother of Carl, said he took the pictures of the Famoso fruit "that got this whole thing going." As a result of his pictures, he said the fruit piles were featured on a Public Broadcasting System "Market to Market" program last spring. At that time, Mr. Pescosolido said, the fruit was piled as high as the head of a 6-foot PBS cameraman; it was not spread out to dry. Mr. Pescosolido said the fruit was starting to mold and ferment. Once that happens, he said, the fruit is "gone" as a source of nourishment. Miss Crittenden also emphasized to Council staff that the fruit was unquestionably rotting when she took her pictures of it. Mr. Pescosolido speculated that the fruit may have indeed been abandoned to rot early in the spring and that the effort to turn it into cattle feed came after the initial publicity.

Mr. Smith told Council staff that the speculation was "totally incorrect." Five or six days of consecutive sunshine are required to dry high-moisture fruit like oranges, and the required weather conditions are not likely to obtain in November, December and January. He said the firm was able to stockpile fruit for as much as four or five months and still obtain the guaranteed levels of protein, fat, fiber and ash required under the firm's license from the California Department of Agriculture. (He said he would send the Council copies of the results of spot checks indicating that the Famoso fruit had met the requirements.)

Mr. Smith said the oranges might well appear to be rotting. "We do let them ferment." He said the process brings out the citrus molasses; "It does not hurt the product at all."

Carl Pescosolido shared his brother's view of the suitability of the Famoso fruit for cattle feed. Nonetheless, he told Council staff, he was satisfied that the fruit was indeed processed for that purpose. He said he saw the Smith firm spread the fruit in April and bring in a machine that "flails and chops" the oranges.

Concluding this part of the staff examination, the GAO report differentiates between dumping and processing for cattle feed. Along the same line of differentiation, Council staff determined that the dump referred to in the Feb. 12 UPI article as being available in case the orange glut became too great—was not used.

The *Los Angeles Times* took cognizance of the specific controversy over the Famoso orange piles in a comprehensive article June 10 on the challenge to the marketing order. It said in part:

> Pescosolido seized upon the controversial issue of dumping as a way to arouse public opinion on behalf of his fight to end the marketing order. Soon, he was pictured in the national publications standing by great piles of oranges that were reported to have been dumped and left to rot in the California sun.
>
> When Pescosolido's photo appeared, committee (Navel Orange Administrative Committee) and Sunkist spokesmen howled in protest, pointing out, correctly, that the oranges had not been "dumped" but were being dried, like raisins, before being mixed as cattle feed.
>
> Pescosolido shrugged off the protest, saying the point was that food was being diverted from human consumption.

In sum, the information gathered by the Council's staff indicates that the specific oranges in the *Times* and *Time* pictures probably were not simply abandoned to rot. However, John Lawrence, administrative assistant to Rep. Miller, warned that one can get into what he called a syllogistic game about their disposal. Without challenging the GAO assertion that few oranges were actually dumped, Mr. Lawrence charged that the report did not reflect the oranges left on trees to rot.

Furthermore, Mr. Lawrence noted that the GAO reported 44 percent of the 1980-81 crop was kept off the market by the action of the Navel Orange Administrative Committee under the marketing order. "Once you've said that, it doesn't make much difference what happened to that fruit," said Lawrence. In his view the issue is that through "artificial restraint" of the marketing order, farmers were prevented from offering fruit for sale and the consumer from buying.

(The final figures from the Navel Orange Administration Committee on the disposition of the 1980-81 crop are: 56 percent to the domestic fresh market; 8 percent exported; 28 percent to juice; 6 percent to livestock feed, and 2 percent to charity, parcel post sales, roadside markets and rotting.)

Mr. Lawrence represents one view of the controversy over the marketing order, and of the dispute over whether the diverted fruit was wasted. The Sunkist complaint represents another view of the same issues.

The actual disposition of the fruit pictured in *The Times* and *Time* may not be the most significant test of the fairness and accuracy of their reports. A more significant test may be: Did the reports provide the reader with the information to decide whether the disposition of the fruit was a waste?

A secondary part of the complaint against *The Times* and, to a lesser degree, *Time*, is the claim that reporters were told certain things that they did not use and/or that reporters did not talk to the right people. The charges are uncomfortable to investigate. For one thing, they get into a question of whom do you believe. More important, though, they get into the area of a reporter's and an editor's discretion in choosing elements for an article. It is more comfortable to use the final articles to gauge whether that discretion was exercised fairly.

Finally, the complaint raised questions about how the two publication responded to Sunkist's protests. Mr. Topping wrote that *The Times* "agreed to" the publication of Mr. Heeger's letter. That wording suggests that the newspaper did consider Mr. Heeger's protest and decided that *The Times* report was accurate and a correction was not necessary. Nonetheless, *The Times* did publish the letter. That gave Mr. Heeger a chance to dispute the *Times* interpretation of the facts and to expand on the Sunkist view of the broader dispute.

By contrast, *Time*'s similar responses to three complaints did not disclose whether specific consideration was given to the charge of inaccuracy raised in those complaints. (The only one of the three letters before the Council is Mr. Heeger's. However, that letter does say, "The oranges that were depicted as rotting are, in fact, drying to be used in cattle feed. These were purchased by an entrepreneur who dries the fruit, grinds it, supplements it with other nutrients and resells it to dairy farmers and feedlot operators.")

*Time*'s response to the three letters seemed to recognize differences among the dispositions of diverted fruit. (". . . the phenomenon of half this year's crop being diverted to juice and cattle feed, or just plain dumped . . .") However, the responses do not deal with whether *Time* had correctly described the disposition of the fruit in its picture.

The thought that *Time* may not have seriously considered the Sunkist complaints is reinforced by the response of a *Time* researcher Sept. 10 that she was just then checking the report in response to the News Council's question.

Even though *Time* did not publish the grower's letters, it did publish April 27 two letters unfriendly to their cause. One commented on the waste represented by the "rotting oranges." The other charged that orange growers in the Depression soaked diverted oranges with kerosene to keep hungry people from eating them.

**Council finding:** The complaint is that *The New York Times* and *Time* described a particular quantity of California Navel oranges as having been left to rot; the complainant says those oranges were instead processed for cattle feed. The ground for the complaint is narrow. The broader issue is whether oranges that could be sold for human consumption should have been diverted from the consumer market under a federal marketing order. That issue was accurately raised by both *The Times* and *Time*. The Council, therefore, finds the complaint unwarranted on the grounds that the specific issue is not substantial.

The Council does note that *The Times* published a letter from the complainant allowing him to present his view. The Council finds it unfortunate that *Time* did not afford the complainant the same opportunity.

The Council directs its staff to make a study of the policies relating to publication of corrective letters in American publications.

**Concurring:** Abel, D. Bell, J. Bell, Benson, Brady, Cooney, Decter, Ghiglione, Huston, Isaacs, van den Haag, Williams.
September 24, 1981

## COMPLAINT NO. 193    (Filed July 30, 1981)
## AMERICAN-ARAB
## ANTI-DISCRIMINATION COMMITTEE
### against
### ABC NEWS

**Complaint:** James J. Zogby, director of the American-Arab Anti-Discrimination Committee, complained about ABC-TV's "Nightline" program of July 22, 1981. He charged ABC correspondent Bill Seamans with "biased, misleading and egregiously irresponsible reporting on the violence between Israelis and Arabs." He said that Mr. Seamans had presented a report on the then most recent cycle of violence that was "flagrantly erroneous" and "contradictory of established facts about the chronology of that violence."

In support of his charge, Mr. Zogby quoted the following portion of Mr. Seaman's account:

> After Begin was reelected on June 30, having made a campaign promise to stop the rockets from falling on northern Israel the PLO launched its new offensive and hit all along the border area, from Nahariya on the Mediterranean to the towns of Keryat Shemona and Litula on the east. It was a fearsome barrage. Salvos of 40 rockets at a time rained down without warning, and the heavy artillery shells crumping in and spraying razor-sharp shrapnel everywhere, killing five persons.
>
> Northern Israel was forced into the bomb shelters. Life came to a standstill. Most business shut down, tourism destroyed. Many left the area. This fact gave the PLO a victory it has never tasted.
>
> The Israelis answered back with heavier and heavier air strikes, which did not stop the PLO rockets. So, said Begin, they had to bomb PLO headquarters in downtown Beirut. Begin said the PLO would no longer be able to hide its deadly military headquarters behind civilian skirts. One Israeli official said wherever the snake's head, we will cut it off.

Mr. Zogby charged that "Mr. Seamans completely reversed the correct sequence of events leading up to the Beirut bombing." Mr. Zogby cited a *New York Times* report July 19, which said that the latest cycle of attacks and counterattacks "began with Israeli pre-emptive strikes on southern Lebanon 10 days ago. The raids ended a five-week lull during the Israeli election campaign and post-election negotiations."

Mr. Zogby also cited a *New York Times* chart entitled "Mideast Chronology Before the Raid on Beirut" published July 24. He quoted *The Christian Science Monitor* of July 20 as follows:

> It should not be overlooked that the recent Palestinian rocket attacks on Israeli

315

towns (resulting in only a few casualties) began after Israel launched these so-called preemptive strikes into Lebanon.

Finally Mr. Zogby quoted the following statement of Yitzhak Rabin, former Israeli defense minister. It was published in the Israeli newspaper, *Yediot Aharonot*, and reprinted in the Shalom Network Newsletter published in River Edge, NJ.

> It is important to remember that in the past few months, the terrorist organizations have not initiated any bombings of Israeli villages other than in response to activities that were initiated by the Israeli Defense forces.

Mr. Zogby also charged that film footage of Israeli casualties was incorrectly identified. He said the casualties were identified as victims of PLO attacks preceding the Israeli bombing of Beirut. In truth they were casualties of attacks that occurred after the Beirut bombing, Mr. Zogby said.

In a followup letter to the Council Aug. 18, Mr. Zogby said, "The Seamans account was presented with all the authority of an objective report (with accompanying file footage) and was left unchallenged." In an earlier protest to Ted Koppel, anchor of the "Nightline" show, Mr. Zogby had made the same point about the Seamans report. He wrote:

> His report, while it makes passing reference at the outset to the opinon of Israel's Chief of Military Intelligence, is clearly presented as an *objective* news account—why else did ABC-TV News see fit to use film footage to enhance the report? Is it a standard news reporting practice to use file films of real events to document mere opinions or fabricated historical accounts?

Mr. Zogby said also in his followup letter, "Our complaint about ABC is that, in general, its coverage failed to communicate the enormity of the Arab loss of life."

**Response:** George Watson, vice president, ABC News, replied to Mr. Zogby that he found Mr. Seamans' "Nightline" report both accurate and fair. He wrote:

> His broadcast is just what it purports to be, i.e., an explanation of Israeli actions as they were perceived by Israeli officials and others in the country from which he was reporting.
>
> Contrary to the allegation in your letter, Mr. Seamans did not describe the Israeli raid on Beirut as "retaliatory." In fact, he clearly reported that the Israelis "took the offensive" and launched pre-emptive strikes *before* the Palestinian rocket attacks and *before* the Beirut raid.
>
> The essential points of the report were attributed to the Israeli officials who made them. Israel's Chief of Military Intelligence, General Yehoshua Sagi, was quoted as saying that the immediate conflict with the Palestine Liberation Organization started

eight months before the Beirut raid. It was, he said, at that time that Prime Minister Begin changed Israel's strategy and "launched a pre-emptive campaign against the PLO."

Mr. Seaman's report went on to explain that in the Israeli view the pre-emptive strikes did not succeed in putting an end to border exchanges and that as a result Mr. Begin decided to bomb PLO headquarters in Beirut. . . .

Our analysis indicates that the chronology of the events surrounding the Israeli bombing of Beirut was essentially the same as that contained in the *New York Times* report which you enclosed. The only difference was that Mr. Seamans traced the sequence of events back eight months, not just ten days as the newspaper did.

Mr. Watson acknowledged that the Israelis pictured as casualties of an earlier PLO shelling were actually hurt in a shelling after the Israeli bombing of Beirut. He wrote:

You are correct in stating that one scene of civilian casualties in Israel which accompanied Mr. Seamans' narration incorrectly left the impression that it occurred before the Israeli attack on Beirut July 17-18. In fact, that picture was transmitted from Tel Aviv to New York via satellite on July 19. The picture was merely illustrative of PLO attacks on Israel which indisputably had taken place before and after the raid on Beirut. Nevertheless, within a chronological context the picture was out of sequence. Our error was unintentional and we regret it.

**Staff examination:** The newspaper material to which Mr. Zogby referred the Council supports the view that Israeli air strikes were the first hostile act between Israeli forces and the PLO after a pre-election lull. A chronology of PLO attacks submitted to the president of the United Nations Security Council by Yehuda Z. Blum, Israeli ambassador to the U.N., on July 20 shows no attacks between April 30 and July 10. In debate on a Security Council resolution July 21, Sir Anthony Parson, United Kingdom, said in part, "The Israeli air force broke a longish period of relative tranquility with air attacks on southern Lebanon on July 10. These attacks continued over the next few days. On 15 July, large-scale PLO retaliation began. . . ."

Elizabeth Jones, country officer for Lebanon at the U.S. State Department in Washington, told News Council staff, "As it happened, this particular time, the Israeli strikes did precede the PLO attack." She said the *Times* chronology was correct.

Mr. Zogby complained that the "Nightline" show made it appear that reporter Seamans was making an objective statement that the PLO struck first. In support of that view, Mr. Zogby quoted in his complaint three paragraphs of the Seamans account. However, the two preceding paragraphs contained the attribution to which ABC referred when saying that

Mr. Seamans was quoting Israeli sources. Those paragraphs read as follows:

> BILL SEAMANS: The events leading to the current PLO mini-war began about eight months (ago), according to Israel's chief of military intelligence, General Yehoshua Sagi. It was around that time, he said, the Israelis detected an alarming new PLO development in southern Lebanon. The Palestinians were receiving huge supplies of Soviet-made heavy weapons, rocket launchers, 130 millimeter cannon and T-55, T-54 and T-34 tanks. These were coming from Libya and Soviet-bloc countries and were turning the PLO into a small, but very dangerous army whose sole objective, according to Sagi, was to kill unarmed Israeli civilians, not attack Israeli military positions.
>
> Prime Minister Begin, who is also Defense Minister, changed Israel's tactics. From then on they would not wait until Israelis were killed before retaliating. They took the offensive, hitting PLO bases to prevent the use of the new heavy weapons. Israel launched a pre-emptive campaign against the PLO.

There are additional references back to Gen. Sagi and to Mr. Begin in the concluding paragraphs of the Seamans account. Another clue that the report may rely on Israeli sources came in Mr. Koppel's introduction. He said, "Bill Seamans reports on what seems to be behind current Israeli tactics." Two questions arise: First, did the attributive references make it clear that Mr. Seamans was relying on Israeli sources for his account of the chronology? Second, did the use of news film along with the Seamans account make it less clear that the account is attributed to Israeli sources?

The Council will have an opportunity to see the complete broadcast before deciding those questions.

ABC News makes the point that the Seamans account of recent hostilities covered an eight-month period, not just the few days after the elections in Israel.

The longer time frame raises the question: How can one ignore the lull in hostilities and the circumstances leading up to their resumption?

It is consistent with the Israeli analysis to ignore the lull. But perhaps the reporter should have interjected a note on his own that the lull had occurred. That suggestion raises a question of news judgment. Judging on its past performance, the Council would not second-guess such a judgment in this case unless the broadcast failed to make clear that Mr. Seamans was recounting a purely Israeli perspective of recent events.

Another point in connection with the clarity of the attribution is the language used by the reporter to describe the first shellings of what he called the PLO's new offensive. Mr. Seamans said:

> It was a fearsome barrage. Salvos of 40 rockets at a time rained down without

warning, and the heavy artillery shells crumping in and spraying razor-sharp
shrapnel everywhere, killing five persons.

The language contains some suggestion that it was an eyewitness account. Does that suggestion make it less clear that the account is a detached report of Israeli views?

ABC News does not answer Mr. Zogby's charge that the use of news film gives Mr. Seamans' account the force of objective reporting. The network does acknowledge that Israeli civilian casualties in one PLO attack were incorrectly identified as victims of another PLO attack.

There is nothing extraordinary in broadcast or print journalism about illustrating a story with film of something like the story. One danger is that the film of something like the story may produce emotional impact that is not appropriate to the story being illustrated. The way out of the danger is precise labeling of the pictures. While the pictures were not precisely labeled in this case, there is no showing that the substitute film was intended to or, in fact, did produce an emotional impact inappropriate to the story being illustrated.

Finally, Mr. Zogby complains that the broadcast does not adequately reflect the Arab loss of life, but Mr. Koppel reports at the outset that the casualty ratio is 80 Arabs to 1 Israeli.

The report of the chronology of recent fighting is only part of the treatment of the Arab-Israeli conflict in the July 22 "Nightline" broadcast. A significant portion of the rest of the program was devoted to criticism of Israel or of Prime Minister Begin for the Beirut bombing. Sen. Richard Lugar and Meyer Berger, a Philadelphia philanthropist devoted to the Zionist cause, are interviewed and are directly critical. Criticisms are recalled from earlier that day by Defense Secretary Caspar Weinberger and Sen. Charles Percy. As a result, the broadcast taken as a whole has balance.

**Council finding:** The complaint charges that ABC's "Nightline" broadcast of July 22 distorted the chronology of recent Israeli-PLO hostilities so that the PLO, rather than Israel, appeared to have broken a lull in the fighting after the Israeli election June 30. As a result, the Israeli bombing of Beirut July 17 appeared as a retaliatory attack rather than a preemptive strike, the complainant says.

To support this conclusion, the complainant depends upon a sentence in the "Nightline" account saying that the PLO launched a new offensive after the election. However, the broadcast is based on an Israeli interpretation that traces the current violence back eight months earlier. Without specifically mentioning the election lull, the account does emphasize that Israel adopted preemptive strikes as an ongoing tactic months before the elections.

A point where clearer attribution in the account would have been helpful is the point at which the post-election PLO attacks are described as a new offensive without any mention of the Israeli bombings that immediately preceded them. However, even without attribution at that particular point, the account as a whole does seem to be properly attributed.

A mistake—acknowledged by ABC News—in identification of pictures of Israeli casualties illustrates the importance of precise labeling, particularly when pictures are not directly related to the story being told. But again, the mistake does not seem likely to have produced an impact inappropriate to the story being illustrated.

The Council finds the complaint unwarranted.

**Concurring:** Abel, D. Bell, J. Bell, Benson, Brady, Decter, Ghiglione, Huston, Isaascs, Stanton, van den Haag, Williams.

September 24, 1981


### COMPLAINT NO. 194      (Filed Sept. 14, 1981)
### ROBERT GULACK
### against
### NEW YORK DAILY NEWS

**Complaint:** On Sept. 13, 1981, U.S. Secretary of State Alexander Haig implied that communist forces had used toxins derived from living organisms in Laos, Kampuchea and Afghanistan. The New York *Daily News* headlined the story, "Haig charges: Soviets Use Germ War."

Robert Gulack complained that "germ war" was (1) not what Mr. Haig was talking about, and (2) was far more frightening. Mr. Gulack suggested that "chem war" would have been correct to describe the poisons (which have been referred to as "yellow rain").

Mr. Gulack said, "This distortion comes at the worst possible time: a period of superpower confrontation, when the American people are themselves reconsidering the option of deploying such nightmarish weapons."

Mr. Gulack called *News* managing editor W. L. Umstead the day the story appeared and complained that "germ war" was not the proper term. "But," he said, "I was left with the impression that I had not made much of an impact."

He wrote a letter to the editor saying in part:

> "Germ war" is something quite different and far more scary than the use of poisons, because germs reproduce themselves in an uncontrollable manner. It is important for your readers to realize that Haig did *not* charge the Soviets with using plague as a weapon of war.

The letter was not published.

**Response:** John H. Metcalfe, assistant to *Daily News* editor Michael J. O'Neill, said he thought Mr. Gulack was "straining at a semantic gnat."

> "Germ" is not a scientific word, and "germ war" does not connote "plague" to the average newspaper reader. . . . The distinction between a living microorganism and a poison produced in nature by living organisms is not likely to be readily made by the reading public—or considered all that significant.
>
> On the otther hand, my dictionary defines "chemical warfare" as "warfare with asphyxiating, poisonous, corrosive or debilitating gases, oil flames, etc." This definition doesn't exactly fit "yellow rain."

Mr. Metcalfe quarreled with the complainant's assertion that germ warfare is inherently more frightening than chemical warfare, and he continued:

> Thus, if biological poisons allegedly employed by the Soviets are not made of living microorganisms but do not qualify as chemical warfare weapons, we contend that "germ war" is an acceptable vernacular phrase for use in a newspaper.
>
> This usage is all the more valid in page-one headlines because of space limitations, as Mr. Umstead tells me he attempted to explain on the phone to Mr. Gulack. Mr. Gulack's suggested alternative, "chem warfare," would be meaningless to most readers.
>
> You'll note that the text of the AP story published (a followup story) in *The News*—where space constraints of headline writing did not apply—made no use of the phrase "germ war."
>
> As managing editor, W. L. Umstead is directly responsible to the editor and ultimately to the publisher for the headlines and news content of *The News*. It is our policy to attempt to answer complaints from the public courteously and to correct errors when they occur. Neither Mr. Umstead nor *The News* can surrender editorial direction of the paper to telephone callers, as Mr. Gulack appears to have expected.
>
> Nor can *The News* publish all of the hundreds (sometimes thousands) of letters to the editor which arrive weekly.

Mr. Metcalfe closed with a vigorous defense against a suggestion in Mr. Gulack's complaint that *The News* had chosen the term, "germ war," to sell newspapers.

**Staff examination:** Definitions for reference:

> Germ. Any microorganism, especially any of the pathogenic bacteria; a microbe.
> —Webster's New Collegiate Dictionary, 1959.

Germ. A microorganism, especially one that causes disease.
—Taber's Cyclopedic Medical Dictionary, 1977.

Chemical and biological warfare. The tactics and technique of conducting warfare by use of toxic chemical agents and the introduction of disease-producing organisms into populations of people, animals or plants. The chemicals include nerve gases; agents which cause temporary blindness, paralysis, hallucinations, or deafness; eye and lung irritants; mustard gas; defoliants; and herbicides. Organisms which have been considered suitable for use in biological warfare include anthrax, brucellosis, plague, Q-fever, and tularemia.
—Taber's Cyclopedic Medical Dictionary, 1977.

Only two of 13 newspapers sampled by the staff used "germ" warfare, as *The News* did, in headlines over the Haig story. One was the *News-Sun* in Waukegan, IL, which changed to "chemical warfare" the next day. The other was the *Los Angeles Times*, which used "germ warfare" on the 14th and 15th, but changed to "biological weapons," "yellow rain" and "toxins" on the 17th and 18th. Five of the sampled newspapers were tabloids like *The News*. None of them used "germ war."

Robert Trounson, assistant foreign editor of the *Los Angeles Times*, said in response to a Council query:

As far as I know, no readers complained that we were being inaccurate in using the term, "germ warfare" in headlines. However, there was considerable discussion among our staff here as to whether Secretary Haig was talking about biological or chemical weapons in his Sept. 13 speech.

As well as I can determine, Haig spoke of "toxins," the ordinary dictionary definition of which could well lead most laymen to believe that Haig was speaking of biological, or "germ" warfare. It was on this belief that we based our use of "germ warfare" in headlines.

However . . . we avoided the use of the term after the first two days of the story and we went to considerable lengths to explain just what Haig was talking about.

"Germ warfare" would never have been used in *The Times* had it been immediately clear that the toxins Haig referred to were indeed chemical, rather than biological, weapons. Our use of the term was not thoughtless or intentionally sensational. The exigencies of headline writing being what they are, I presume that we will use the term in the future, but only to refer to biological warfare.

None of the wire service stories—including the United Press International story used originally by *The News*—used the term "germ warfare." UPI used in its lead, "illegal biological poisons;" the other relevant reference was to ". . . poisons described as chemicals produced by biological organisms such as fungus or mushrooms." Associated Press used "chemical weapons," "lethal weapons," "toxic chemicals," and "lethal chemical weapons."

The words used in Secretary Haig's speech were: "Toxins," "lethal chemical weapons," "three potent mycotoxins," which he described as "poisonous substances not indigenous to the region and which are highly toxic to man and animals." Mr. Haig said the use in war of such toxins was prohibited by the 1925 Geneva Protocol and the 1972 Biological Weapons Convention.

A fact sheet distributed by the State Department the day after Mr. Haig's speech traced the concern over the use of "chemical warfare agents" in Southeast Asia back to 1976 and said:

> Specifically we believe we have obtained good evidence that rather than a traditional lethal chemical agent, three potent mycotoxins of the trichothecene group have been used. A mycotoxin is a poison typically produced in nature by living organisms.

The fact sheet contained this note:

> I want to caution you that there are certainly other agents being used that we have not yet identified. Incapacitating and riot control agents as well as other possible lethal agents may be involved. We are attempting to obtain additional information from Laos and Kampuchea in an effort to obtain corroborative evidence.

Robert Mikulak, physical science officer in the Multilateral Affairs bureau of the U.S. Arms Control and Disarmament Agency, said it is not correct to refer to what Mr. Haig was talking about as "germ warfare." "Germ warfare," Mr. Mikulak said, is usually used as a synonym for bacteriological warfare, which means using bacteria (or viruses) that grow and reproduce and have the capacity for spreading through a population on their own.

Mr. Mikulak pointed out that the language in the 1972 convention prohibiting the "development, production or stockpiling of bacteriological (biological) and toxic weapons" differentiates between "microbial or other biological agents" on the one hand, and "toxins, whatever their origin or method of production" on the other hand. "Bacteriological agents" refers to germs and viruses, Mr. Mikulak said. "That is not what is at issue here. Toxins are at issue."

Even though it is not correct to refer to the use of toxins as germ warfare, Mr. Mikulak said it was common for people—"even people in this building"—not to differentiate between chemical and biological warfare because up until the 1972 convention the two have been linked in efforts to control them.

Indeed, Council staff found that distinctions among weapons have been critical in the efforts to control chemical and biological warfare. The 1925 Geneva Protocol was not ratified by the U.S. Senate until 1976 partly because the U.S. did not want the controls to apply to nontoxic riot-control gases and herbicides. The efforts to produce a more contemporary treaty in the United Nations got nowhere until 1969 when the British suggested a treaty governing biological weapons only. First the United States and then, in 1970, the Soviet Union agreed that the control of biological weapons should not be held up by the more difficult problems of reaching agreement on the control of chemical weapons.

The importance of differentiations in the efforts to control chemical and biological weapons points up the importance of the State Department warning that other poisonous agents are involved in Southeast Asia besides the mycotoxins reported by Mr. Haig in September. It will be important for newspaper editors to make distinctions as the story develops of new agents and the efforts to control them.

The staff's examination suggests that there has been a difference between chemical and biological warfare—a difference that is becoming blurred by just such developments as the ones Secretary Haig was reporting. Germ warfare, however, remains a distinct sub-category of biological warfare.

**Council finding:** The complaint against *The New York Daily News* is warranted. While a precise distinction was difficult to make in this case, and while headline space was a factor, nevertheless, there was an obligation to be as accurate as possible and not to mislead. The complainant made the distinction *The News* failed to make in the letter he sent for publication to *The News*. It is unfortunate that *The News* did not publish that letter or a correction.

**Concurring:** Abel, J. Bell, Benson, Decter, Ghiglione, Huston, Isaacs, Maynard, Miller, Pulitzer, Stanton and Williams.
December 3, 1981


**COMPLAINT NO. 195**          (Filed Sept. 22, 1981)
JAN REYNOLDS AND JUDY GIBSON
against
WINFIELD (KS) DAILY COURIER

**Complaint:** Two women who were victims of a rapist complain of sensationalism against a small Kansas daily for the explicit reporting of their testimony in a preliminary hearing of the case in the district court. Following their testimony, the rapist pleaded guilty and now awaits sentencing (Kansas laws permit up to 30 years imprisonment). The detailed and vivid report in the *Winfield Courier* brought a large volume of protesting letters and the temporary withdrawal of some advertising. Some other Kansas newspapers carried accounts of the reporting and the protests. The Winfield paper published many of the protesting letters and followed with an editorial. The Council pointed out to the complainants the probability of national publicity. Their response has been that they consider the issues involved to be of major importance for all journalists to weigh and are, therefore, willing to forego anonymity in the interest of making these issues clear through public examination.

**Staff examination:** Under the headline "Assault victims testify," the challenged story appeared on page 1 of the August 27, 1981, edition of the *Winfield Courier*. The account began, "Testimony from two women assaulted on the nights of July 31 and August 2 in Winfield was heard in district court here this morning. . . ." The women were not identified in the 28-paragraph, 21-inch long story.

Using direct quotes, the account reported in detail what the women told the court about the rapes and subsequent sodomy. In a telephone conversation with the Council on November 18, the newspaper publisher said that in a city of Winfield's size (11,067), it was a good assumption that many in the community knew the women's identities. He said he had learned later that about 30 people attended the hearing.

Two protesting letters appeared in the paper the next day, August 28. One called the article "sensational journalism that was an invasion of privacy" and went on to say "This type of reporting will discourage future rape victims from going to the police because of fear of exposure by the press." The other letter, from a doctor, called "the blow by blow description . . . unnecessary and inappropriate" and added, "Such reporting . . . may prolong the psychological trauma (of the victims)."

The next three days' editions carried 21 more letters, bearing in all 182 signatures. Of these, 84 were affixed to a letter representing the faculty, administration and staff of Southwestern College.

One letter approved the story, saying "If more blow by blow accounts were given it could make a few more stronger feelings about crime."

The other letters were in the same tone as the first two. "Sensationalism" was a word used frequently. Several referred to the possible deterrence of testimony by future victims. Almost all objected to the detail carried in the story and some raised the issue of its appearance in "a family newspaper."

On September 23, the newspaper published an editorial, titled "The newspaper and the victims of violent crime." It was a careful review of newspaper responsibility to report news of crime. It went on to say, "Without any intent to cause pain, mistakes can be made." A later comment was, "An editor's guide in these decisions is a sense of what is necessary to serve the community's best interests, keeping in mind that the victims, too, are members of the community. Community standards and expectations should be taken into account in reporting the crime and subsequent events."

In her letter of complaint, Mrs. Jan Reynolds of Winfield said the published letters "most articulately describe the pain, trauma and humiliation that the other victim and I have experienced since the original report of the hearing."

"Mr. Dave Seaton (publisher of the paper)," her letter continued, "has offered his verbal apologies for the item appearing in the manner in which it did. However, until I see a personal apology and a reassurance to the women of Winfield that news coverage of such a despicable crime of violence will not be approached in this manner, I will not rest. It is my desire that the National News Council find it appropriate to address the issues involved . . . particularly as it affects the future well-being of other potential rape victims."

In a telephone conversation November 18, Mrs. Reynolds told Council staff that she was not satisfied with the editorial. She said there were two aspects to the affair that concerned her most: The detail in the account and the fact that she and the other victim were known. "There's no doubt about that," she said. "Just walking downtown people would stop talking on the street. You knew what they were talking about."

She added that it was difficult enough to call the police and go through the embarrassment of making the initial report. To go through a second trauma as a result of the publicity must discourage some victims from coming forward, she said.

Judy Gibson, the other victim, was hospitalized under the care of a psychiatrist after the incident. She did not blame her hospitalization directly on the newspaper's reporting, but she said she might have weathered the rape and the experience of testifying had it not been for the report. She said the report had a direct effect on her four children, aged 11 through 17. They were out of town when she was raped. She told them about it in general terms, but when the newspaper report appeared, she had to explain in more detail. She said she was asked, "What did he do to you, Mother?" and "What does that sentence mean?" The *Courier* story identified the rapist as black, and that presented problems for her 11-year-old adopted son, who is black, said Mrs. Gibson.

Mrs. Gibson said the publicity may have presented particular difficulties for her because she is well known in the community. She is sales manager and conducts a morning talk show for radio station KWKS-FM. She also is active in public affairs and music. Her station manager editorialized against the *Courier* for several days, and it pained her to hear some people say the outcry over the reporting would have been dismissed if it had been anybody but Judy Gibson. She said young members of a 60-voice choir that she directs stopped her on the street and asked, "Mrs. Gibson, did you get raped?"

"They didn't know what it meant, but they had heard their parents talking about it," she said.

Mrs. Gibson has participated in rape seminars since the report, and she feels that they may have done some good. She said that she and Mrs. Reynolds thought they had "helped" by standing up and reporting the rapes, but, "We thought the newspaper article was 10 steps backward. If this is what women can expect, no one's going to tell anyone."

**Response:** On October 22, Publisher Seaton sent to the Council a copy of the editorial with the series of letters published earlier. In his letter he said:

> There was a period of about a month between the original story and the editorial. The reason I waited before writing the editorial was to allow emotions to subside in this matter. Also, we as a newspaper had been subject to some pressure from advertisers to apologize and/or state our policy on such reporting in the future. I was not willing to write an editorial in response to such pressure.

In a telephone conversation on November 18, Mr. Seaton went into much more detail about the entire episode. He described the events of August 27 in terms familiar to all journalists. Although he had been on the newspaper for three years, he had held the publisher role for three weeks. The managing editor was on vacation so he had stepped in to provide supervision. The reporter of the rape hearing was three months out of college. He had no conversation with the acting editor before writing his account. He turned it in at deadline time. The story struck Mr. Seaton as "rough," but he said that since there was no identification of the two women he "leaned in the direction of using it." He said that in the hurried moments that he was considering it, two thoughts were strongly in mind. One was his feeling that the paper had often been criticized for being too cautious and protective of the community. The other was a concern that the citizens of Winfield needed "to know how severe rape cases are. I felt the town was very reluctant to face the danger. It seemed to me there was a sound case to be made for having people face the harsh realities. Both these rapes occurred because of the long habit of keeping doors unlocked. I had not expected so vivid and detailed a story, but since the names were not used it seemed to me then to be justified. I cannot accept the charge of sensationalism. That implies deliberate motivation. Our purpose was totally different. We were trying to alert the community."

After reflection, Mr. Seaton said, he felt conscious that he was also "pressing" in his desire to try to improve the paper and inspire creativity. He said that if confronted with the same circumstances now, he would not hesitate to have other senior staff members look over the story and give their opinions, nor would he hesitate to hold the story a full day in order to have an account that conveyed the seriousness of the situation and yet used more delicacy of touch. "We learn by experience," he said.

What this experience taught the *Winfield Courier* is that explicit reporting of rape can have a huge impact on the community. But that is only one of the problems that face journalists in covering cases involving rape. In Virginia and in North Carolina controversy has arisen over the identification of complainants in rape trials.

When he was editor of *The Washington Post*, James Russell Wiggins was the accepted spokesman for editor's groups on freedom of information matters. He wrote the book, "Freedom or Secrecy." In it he took up the issue of the reporting of sex offenses. He wrote:

> Many legislatures have sought to protect the identity of victims of rape attacks. Much can be said for the motives behind such protection. It can be argued that the humiliation of publicity may deter the bringing of complaints. . . . Sound as the motive of the lawmakers may be, however, even this sort of secrecy has its price, in terms of the public good and the processes of justice.
>
> Some prosecutors fear that such laws may protect complaining witnesses too much. Under such secrecy, irresponsible persons, or accusing witnesses with an ax to grind, may expose innocent persons to all the disadvantages of defending themselves without putting the complainant to much trouble or inconvenience. The crime of rape is a capital crime in some jurisdictions. Perhaps those who allege it has been committed ought to be under all the normal restraints that operate on citizens who bring serious charges. There is a risk that victims will be deterred by publicity from making a charge that ought to be made; but there is also a risk that the utter absence of any publicity will encourage an alleged victim to bring charges that ought not to be brought.

It was within this general context that Herman J. Obermayer, editor-publisher of the *Northern Virginia Sun* in Arlington, challenged the accepted journalistic pattern of never naming prosecuting witnesses in rape cases. Mr. Obermayer said he was led into the confrontation by a case involving a number of men and young women, who had spent several days and nights in a motel. The women were under 18. Under Virginia law, the charge of statutory rape applies when minors are involved. Mr. Obermayer said by using the charge of statutory (forced) rape, the prosecutor was able to legally seal the record on the identities of the women.

"It creates an enormous prosecutorial advantage," said Mr. Obermayer. "It can create contrived situations where every witness can be promised anonymity. It mocks the intent of the Sixth Amendment for public trial."

Responding to a Council question on November 19, Mr. Obermayer said that "only yesterday we published the name of a woman who testified in a rape case. It fit under our guidelines."

These guidelines at the *Northern Virginia Sun* instruct the staff not to report preliminary hearings in rape cases, or hearings before lesser judges. "We do not report original arrests," he said. "We do not name the victim. We do name the accused. A case has to go all the way to trial before we cover it. If there is a plea of guilty we do not publish the victim's name." In the November 18 case Mr. Obermayer said the woman's name was published because the accused man was found not guilty in a one-day trial in the Arlington Circuit Court. He said that if the verdict had been guilty the victim's name would not have appeared in the paper.

Where controversy arose, Mr. Obermayer said, was in the reporting of trials that ran longer than one day. In these instances, he said, "What we have here is a legal contest of credibility. I am among those who believe that public disclosure is the greatest deterrent to perjured testimony. It is the one most critical period in a trial. A man is facing what in Virginia is a life term. The names of witnesses would be published in a murder trial. The accused in a rape trial faces almost the identical penalty. To accept a principle of total anonymity for prosecuting witnesses is, I think, journalistically irresponsible."

The *Durham* (NC) *Herald* has followed a similar course and, after a challenge to its policies, published and later distributed in booklet form an 18-part series detailing all the issues involved in the coverage and reporting of rape cases.

In the *Northern Virginia Sun*, there have been a dozen such episodes of identifying adult prosecuting witnesses. Mr. Obermayer has maintained a policy of having reporters refer all questions to him. "Our policy is now better understood," he said. "At the outset we faced constant complaint, stirred in large part by inflammatory TV coverage and by the open editorial criticism of the policy by *The Washington Post* and *The Washington Star*. Now, it is rare to hear a protest or criticism. Juveniles, or those who have been adjudged by the law to be mental incompetents, are not affected by our reporting. All others are. When there have been remonstrances I have held to the position that the credibility of the courts is only as good as public scrutiny is available. I do not see how you can have a type of crime in which the accused is denied the protection of the law and I cannot sit by and accept the premise that there is a crime where an individual can go to prison for life without the witnesses being publicly identified."

As was the case with the *Northern Virginia Sun*, the *Durham* (NC) *Morning Herald* openly challenged the prevailing pattern of not publishing the names of complainants in rape cases. Michael Rouse, managing editor of the *Herald*, said the paper was deluged with letters spurred by a campaign of the city's Rape Crisis Center. Out of this confrontation came the 18-part series of editorials.

"We use the name of a rape complainant only when a formal charge has been made against a specific person who must then defend himself in court," said Mr. Rouse. Names of girls 16 and under are not published.

In the editorials, the *Herald* said, "No one seems concerned that the newspaper, along with the police and courts, could be exploited as a weapon against a man by a woman seeking to ruin him."

It also raised the matter of a "double standard on due process." "In any other criminal case," one editorial said, "the concern for the rights of the defendant seems paramount; great suspicion is directed at the motives and integrity of the prosecution witnesses, the police, the entire judicial system . . . until it comes to a rape charge. Then it is unbelievable . . . how suddenly they have faith in the judicial system. Suddenly they don't seem to have ever heard of the idea that a defendant might possibly be innocent—the victim either of honest mistake or malice."

The Raleigh *News & Observer* follows the Durham pattern for the most part. When a formal charge of rape is made against a man, the name of the complainant is also used. Executive Editor Claude Sitton says that in the case of married women, the Raleigh papers use the woman's first name and married surname. When victims testify in trials, their names are again used. Names of complainants are not used a second time in Raleigh when guilty pleas are entered before open trial.

A comprehensive study of news practice nationally apparently has never been made on this issue, but leading editors believe that the overwhelming majority of newspapers withhold the names of rape victims automatically, although most reserve the right to publish the name if the victim is prominent or the circumstances of the rape were such that the victim is publicly identified. Such an example was the case of singer Connie Francis, who sued a hotel chain for failing to provide adequate security.

Illustrative of the complexities and delicacies surrounding the reporting of rape is the most recent example—that involving Susan Byrne, daughter of New Jersey's governor. The three New York City newspapers did not hesitate to identify her, even though police would not confirm any details because of departmental regulations, including identity. The *Daily News* began its account by saying Miss Byrne had been "attacked." *The Times* used the word "assaulted." Only the *Post* said flatly: "Miss Byrne . . . said the assailants ripped a gold necklace from her neck, then raped her." The following day the family attorney said there had been no rape and up to November 23, only *The Times* had carried this report.

Both the *Arizona Daily Star* and *The Cincinnati Enquirer* have recently run into stories that tested their commitments to protect rape victims. Leo Della Betta, ombudsman for the *Star*, reported that the newspaper followed its policy and did not name the victim when a recent rape was first reported. However, when the assailant went on trial, the charge was dropped from rape to attempted assault. Then the victim was named. Mr. Della Betta argued in his ombudsman's column that the spirit of the newspaper's policy dictated that the victim should have remained protected despite the lesser charge.

*The Enquirer* published the name of a woman who was held hostage by her brother-in-law while he killed her sister. When the man came to trial, he was charged not only with murder and kidnapping, but with rape of his sister-in-law. The newspaper published her name—despite its policy—in the first stories of the trial. It dropped her name only when the judge suggested it. *Enquirer* ombudsman John Caldwell wrote, "Why do news columns regularly withhold the name of a woman caught and raped in a parking garage, but publish the name of a woman who undergoes the triple horrors of rape, kidnap and watching a murder? If there is logic there, I can't find it."

**Council finding:** The complaint does not question the accuracy of the report in the *Winfield Daily Courier*. Instead it raises issues of needlessly explicit reporting and its impact on the victims, their families and the community. While these impacts may have been traumatic, the Council cannot be in the position of advocating that accurate reports of open court proceedings should not be published. Therefore, the Council finds unwarranted the charge that the reporting was sensationalized. The editor has already published many letters indicating that the community was offended by the reporting. Furthermore, he has indicated in an editorial that future coverage will be handled more cautiously.

The Council staff has discovered in connection with this complaint that some newspapers—the *Durham* (NC) *Morning Herald* and the *Northern Virginia Sun* at Arlington, for two—have raised thoughtful questions about the complicated business of reporting rape and other sex crimes. The News Council recommends that the leading organizations of newspaper editors and broadcast journalists institute a major study of community attitudes towards sex crimes and of the attendant problems of reporting on them.

**Concurring:** Abel, J. Bell, Benson, Cooney, Decter, Ghiglione, Huston, Isaacs, Maynard, Miller, Pulitzer, Stanton and Williams.

**Concurring minority viewpoint:** We do not understand what the majority of the Council means by the word "sensationalized." That is not the gravamen of the complaint.

The complainants would have the Council condemn the *Winfield Daily Courier* for reporting in detail their testimony describing the crime as committed.

The Council properly refused to do this.

The publication of such details in a small community in itself may be considered sensational—indeed, letters to the editor refer to the story as such. A similar report in a large metropolitan area may not be so considered.

Therefore, we find it irrelevant and unnecessary to refer to "sensationalism" and to make a finding that such a charge was not warranted.

**Concurring:** Decter, Ghiglione, Huston, Maynard, Stanton and Williams.

December 3, 1981

**Note:** As a result of the *Winfield Daily Courier* case, Carol E. Oukrop, Associate Professor of Journalism at Kansas State University, made a study of rape reporting. The American Society of Newspaper Editors felt that her study accomplished the goal set out by the News Council. It publicized her study and decided not to make one of its own. The study, "Views of Newspaper Gatekeepers on Rape and Rape Coverage," is available from Dr. Carol Oukrop, Department of Journalism, Kansas State University, Kedzie 104, Manhattan, KS 66506, at a cost of $3.50.

**COMPLAINT NO. 196** (Filed Oct. 5, 1981)
LARRY L. CONSTANTINE
against
TIME

**Complaint:** Larry L. Constantine, a family therapist in Acton, MA, charged *Time* with "systematic distortion and misrepresentation" in an article entitled "Cradle-to-Grave Intimacy" September 7, 1981. He said that he and a number of other professionals with concern for sexual health were made to appear to advocate sexual relationships between adults and children. He said, ". . . none of those professionals cited is in any sense an advocate of adult-child sex."

Furthermore, he said, ". . . a position was attributed to me in an indirect quotation which I had specifically denied and corrected when asked by *Time* for a confirmation."

Mr. Constantine said he contacted seven of the professionals cited in the article and reported to the News Council that "only one was not misquoted or quoted out of context." He said four of the seven sent corrective letters to the editor, but none of the letters was published.

**Response:** Jason McManus, executive editor of *Time*, declined to respond to the News Council's inquiry about Mr. Constantine's complaint. Mr. McManus wrote, ". . . we take most seriously any complaints directly to *Time* about inaccuracies and make every effort to double-check that the facts that we have printed are correct." However, he wrote, ". . . we have concluded that the admission of the National News Council into this process does not serve a significantly useful purpose. In view of our consensus on that principle, I must respectfully decline to respond to your questions about this particular story."

**Staff report:** The full-page article appeared under a headline, "Sexes," at the top of the page. Under the main headline, "Cradle-to-Grave Intimacy," was a sub-head saying, "Some researchers openly argue that 'anything goes' for children." The page included a picture of the cover of what *Time* called "the controversial children's book, Show Me!" by Will McBride and Dr. Helga Fleischhauer-Hardt. The book cover included a picture of two naked children, five or six years old.

Since Mr. Constantine has alleged that several researchers were misrepresented in the *Time* article, this analysis will take up the researchers' comments in the order that they appear in the article. The second sentence of the article sets the stage:

Now, however, a disturbing idea is gaining currency within the sex establishment: very young children should be allowed, and perhaps encouraged, to conduct a full sex life without interference from parents and the law.

## Mary S. Calderone

The second paragraph leads up to a quote from Mary S. Calderone, M.D., president of the Sex Information and Education Council of the U.S.:

The idea is rarely presented directly—most of the researchers, doctors and counselors have the wit to keep a low profile and tuck the idea away neatly in a longer, more conventional speech or article. The suggestion comes wrapped in the pieties of feminism (children, like women, have the right to control their own bodies) and the children's rights movement (children have rights versus their parents). According to the argument, children are sexual beings who need to develop skills early in life. The child has a fundamental right, says Mary S. Calderone, head of the influential Sex Information and Education Council of the U.S., "to know about sexuality and to *be* sexual."

Dr. Calderone was one of the researchers who wrote corrective letters to *Time*. She wrote in part:

You quoted me as saying that the child has a fundamental right "to know about sexuality and to *be* sexual." I could never apply this statement to your article, because it was said in my address to the American Psychiatric Association with specific reference to the obligation of parents to protect their child's fundamental sexual rights. You see, not enough parents have the information yet, that they no longer have to try to extirpate or punish the naturally occurring sexual interests and activities of young children. Instead, as leading child psychiatrists today teach (and I am only their echo)—parents can learn how to socialize their child's sexuality without harming it. They can guide it gently toward maturity by providing adequate and appropriate sexual information at various developmental stages. They can—and should—teach family personal values about *all* behavior, including sexual, but without fear-inducing guilt about "sin." In this way, I believe that they can keep the talk so ongoing that by adolescence children will still be in communication with their parents, as they are not today. In other words, sexuality which we all have from birth is not something nasty, nor does (being sexual) call for instant intercourse or any form of inappropriate genital behavior.

. . . I have an uncompromising Quaker—and professional—conscience. I will stubbornly continue, in my conservative, 77-year-old way, to insist until proven wrong by adequate studies that sexual contacts between adults and children are inappropriate and indefensible. And I am on record as holding that same opinion about most teenage sexual intercourse. With all this, please accept that I am a firm believer in freedom of the press—but not in unfair reporting that is at the expense of my personal integrity and professional credibility. Where does *Time* stand on the question of fairness to the reportee?

*Time* did not publish Dr. Calderone's letter. Instead the magazine sent her the following reply:

> Dear Dr. Calderone:
>
> Editor-in-chief Henry Grunwald has asked me to reply to your letter about *Time*'s September 7 sexes story.
>
> In using a statement you made before the American Psychiatric Association and reiterated to *Time* Researcher Nancy Williamson, it certainly was not our intention to suggest that you condoned adult/child sexual relationships. The record clearly indicates that you do not. But the statement did serve to illustrate a basic point in our story: that many noted sex researchers and educators are pressing for fundamental sexual rights of children.
>
> Thank you for letting us hear from you.
>
> Sincerely,
> Joan D. Walsh

Dr. Calderone wrote back to Henry Grunwald, editor-in-chief of *Time*, calling the Walsh letter "naive and laughable." If, as the Walsh letter said, it was not *Time*'s intention to "suggest" that she condoned adult-child sex, it was certainly the magazine's intention "to imply" it, wrote Dr. Calderone. Otherwise, the magazine would have quoted from the record, which Ms. Walsh acknowledged "clearly indicates that you do not." Dr. Calderone continued:

> It is astonishing to see a story woven out of three or four-word quotes from respected researchers that in all probability belie what they actually said. I could as well accuse Jerry Falwell of having said that "I don't believe in" Jesus Christ. Somewhere in his writings I know that he has said those four words in quotes, and all I have to do is impute by juxtaposition. I doubt if the copies of this very lame and inept reply that I shall send to those of my colleagues who have written to *Time* will strike them as anything but evasive. To tell you the truth, I am embarrassed for the kind of journalism that this represents.

Dr. Calderone had not received a reply to that letter by December 1. On that date she wrote again to Mr. Grunwald saying, "I am afraid that the damage done by your September 7th article will continue to haunt me and many fellow colleagues for a long, long time." She enclosed copies of an exchange of letters between her and Dr. Panos D. Bardis, a physician she had met some years ago.

Dr. Bardis expressed alarm that such "radical pronouncements" as the one attributed to her in *Time* might set back the cause of sex education and family life education. He asked, "Is it possible that you have been misquoted?"

Dr. Calderone replied:

> It is definitely and clearly not only possible but true that I was misquoted—not

really misquoted, but taken completely out of context. The quote given was correct, made when I presented one of the Special Medical Lectures before the American Psychiatric Association last May in Louisiana. I was speaking very specifically of *childhood sexuality* as it is beginning to be understood by such people as Albert Solnit at the Child Development Institute at Yale University; another child psychiatrist, James Anthony at Washington University; and many others. I was saying that in the light of these facts, parents do not have a *right* to teach their children about sexuality, they have an *obligation* to do it. It is the children who have the right to this kind of teaching from parents, but the parents will not be able to do the kind of fostering that children need unless they accept the child's fundamental right to "know about sexuality and to *be* sexual." It is the manner in which the child will be sexual, in terms of interests, questions, development of body image and self-esteem, that is important.

On December 3, Mr. Grunwald replied to Dr. Calderone with an apology for not answering her Oct. 14 letter. (He had been on an extensive trip.) He wrote:

I do not believe that your characterization of the story as a whole—as woven from quotes taken out of context—is accurate or fair.

As for the use of your own quotation, I am sorry to learn that some readers found it ambiguous and that you believe it to be unfair. A story presenting your views more fully may be possible at a later date. We will watch for an opportunity to run such a story.

In answer to a Council staff inquiry Dr. Calderone replied that she had been interviewed by *Time* on the telephone. She wrote:

I most certainly said that "children are sexual and should be allowed to be sexual," but this referred not in any way to sexual activities with adults or even older children. I am on record on this, of course, as being totally inappropriate.

A number of psychiatrists who had heard me wrote to *Time* magazine, knowing, of course, that I was being misrepresented not only in the context of the quotes but in the context of the "anything goes" attitude of a couple of people mentioned in the article . . . . All of us received exactly the same (first) letter, but signed by different people.

Dr. Calderone outlined the following background for the dispute with *Time*:

A long chain of misquotes began with a serious article by James W. Ramey, Ed.D in the May 1979 issue of the *SIECUS Report*, called "Dealing With the Last Taboo." Ramey suggested that harm could be done to "victims" of incest by labeling them as such, and by subjecting them to processes of investigation that made them feel culpable, guilty and ruined forever. In the March 1980 issue of *Psychology Today*, appeared a diatribe by one Benjamin DeMott (a professor of *English* at Amherst College) titled "The Pro-Incest Lobby". . . .

In the same month the columnist, George F. Will, picked it up under the headline "A Researcher Puts in a Good Word for Incest." (I defy anybody to find a "good

336

word for incest" in Ramey's article). The inference of all this is, that if you don't thunder against it, then you must be for it. I myself in a *Sexual Medicine Today* long interview with me (June 1980) stated my position clearly on this question.

A health writer, Susan G. Sawyer, interviewed me at length and had the good conscience to try to correct some of the mess in an article in *Family Health* for June 1980. . . .

Also in June 1980, Ramey prefaced a paper he was giving on "Positive Socialization of Incestuous Desires" at a plenary session of The Family Sexual International Symposium, University of Minnesota Medical School, as follows: "In the light of recent media comments, I wish to preface my remarks by stating flatly that I am not an advocate of incest. I will read this paper verbatim in hopes that by doing so I can ensure that I will be quoted accurately."

In any case, the *Time* smear was utterly without provocation, and totally unfounded as far as I was concerned. Wardell Pomeroy was also misquoted, as Larry Constantine stated that he was. All of this illustrates the hysteria with which most people approach almost any sexual topic you can name—and it is just this kind of hysteria that SIECUS has been trying to overcome ever since our formation in 1964.

In the June, 1980, interview with *Sexual Medicine Today*, Dr. Calderone said of incest:

Our article said that since it is apparently more widespread than previously thought, we need to know much more about it. We should not automatically deduce that everybody is severely damaged by incestuous experiences simply because the people we hear from are the ones who have gone to clinics or the police. We say: "Let's get the data."

Everyone is scared of incest and they rear back at its very mention. Every time I mention it, I have to point out that description does not mean advocacy. Nobody in their right mind would advocate incest, but when you have a study reporting on people who have been damaged by incest, it is scientific to ask whether there are people—who knows in what proportion—who have not been damaged. There is a study now going on that might cover this ground but it is two years from being completed. My point is that we should not jump to conclusions but try to seek more properly gathered and analyzed data.

In the May, 1979, issue of *SIECUS Report*, the one in which the Ramey article appeared, Dr. Calderone recalled in an editorial the furor following publication of the Kinsey reports on the sexual behavior of men and later of women. The editorial said, ". . . because the researchers did not condemn, they were accused of advocating the sexual behaviors they had described, A to Z, in their two studies." The editorial continued:

The scientific method puts on all of us the obligation to react objectively to evidence and data. In this process of reacting, we should remind ourselves that analysis plus reportage does *not* equal advocacy . . . . It is evident that what Ramey is *reporting* is the present situation in which a number of conclusions about the effects of incest have been drawn on the basis of insufficient or nonexistent data. What he is *advocating* is adequate and properly conducted research to find out the

337

true facts about incest and its effects. In the absence of such research, to take for granted that the results will show up either as positive or negative is unwarranted and, either way, can, in the absence of hard data, be of genuine harm.

## Larry Constantine

*Time* called the complainant "the most intellectually disheveled of the new apostles of child sex" and said that his views "sound like a satire on how to raise children." Mr. Constantine does not dispute the accuracy of the quotation attributed to him, "Children really are a disenfranchised minority. They should have the right to express themselves sexually, which means that they may or may not have contact with people older than themselves."

However, Mr. Constantine does object to the construction of the following two sentences and to their characterization of his views. The sentences read:

> What about older men preying on four- and five-year-olds? Constantine would argue that if children were properly educated about sex, a child who did not want sex could always say no.

Mr. Constantine complained in a letter to the editor of *Time*:

> I have said many times that children need to learn about sexual situations they are likely to encounter, that they need to be taught assertiveness and independence, to learn that they do not have to comply with the misguided desires of adults who would exploit them.
> The idea that children need to know they have a choice and a right to say "no" to sexual approaches is advocated by many professionals and forms the core of model prevention programs. *Time* attributes to me a perverse distortion, a ridiculous position which I have never argued.

*Time* did not publish Mr. Constantine's letter. Instead Ms. Walsh replied to him as follows:

> We are, quite frankly, puzzled by your comments about the statements attributed to you in *Time*'s September 7 Sexes report. We see no difference between our quoted material and the way in which you expressed the point in your letter. The quoted statements, as you know, came directly from the paper you delivered in Wales as well as from previous interviews with you. *Time* would never knowingly misquote anyone, we assure you, and no exception was made in this case.
> Thank you for your letter.

The dispute is not over the direct quotations, but over the hypothetical question, "What about older men preying on four- and five-year-olds?" Mr. Constantine commented to Council staff that the passage sounds as if

338

he had been asked that question. He wasn't, he said. And if he had been, he would not have answered the way *Time* says he would have. He would have insisted that he didn't think anyone ought to be preying on four- and five-year-olds. He said:

> My statement says that children need more knowledge to recognize attempts to exploit them and they need the assertiveness to know they don't have to comply. I can see how their statement derives from mine, but it's so condensed that it no longer means what I said. It's like a headline in the *National Enquirer* or *Midnight Sun*.

Mr. Constantine echoed a position of Dr. Calderone in defending his view that more research is needed into the effects of adult-child sex.

> But to report honestly on research that shows there to be a wide range of effects is not to say that children *should* have such experiences. I am not and never have been an advocate of either incest or child-adult sex.

### Dr. John Money

The *Time* article quotes Dr. John Money, Ph.D., professor of Medical psychology and associate professor of pediatrics at Johns Hopkins University School of Medicine, in two places, There is no dispute over the first quote—"As sexologist John Money of Johns Hopkins wrote in *The Sciences* magazine, 'It is almost certain that human beings, like the other primates, require a period of early rehearsal play.'" Dr. Money did dispute the second quote—"Money claims that a youngster's 'rehearsal play' with adults 'affects them beneficially.'" Dr. Money protested to *Time* in a letter September 2, 1981, in which he said:

> This is a misrepresentation. The words, *with adults*, were editorially inserted, and are not my own. I do not, nor ever have, advocated sex between adults and juveniles. Quite to the contrary, I am codirector of a clinic at Johns Hopkins that specializes in the treatment of sex offenders, among whom are included pedophile offenders.

*Time* replied over the signature of Ms. Walsh that the sentence to which Dr. Money objected had been originally reported by *Time* correspondent Ruth Galvin (in an April 14, 1980, article headlined "The Last Taboo—Researchers are lobbying against the ban on incest") and checked with Dr. Money before the September, 1981, publication by Nancy Williamson. Dr. Money replied to *Time* that the assertion was "absolutely not true." He wrote on October 30:

> Ms. Williamson did not discuss with me the topic of "childhood sexual rehearsal play with adults . . . . If you look at the offending quotation, you will see that the words, "with adults," was inserted outside of the quotation marks. I consider this a

knowing misquote, and I demand that you publish my letter to the editor in which I declare I was misquoted.

To that *Time* replied on November 9:

On receiving your reply to our letter, we again checked all of our records on this story and found that we erred, not in the story, but in one respect in our initial reply to you: attributing the quote that troubles you to Ruth Galvin's reporting. That is not the case. It turns out that we paraphrased your views from your 1976 article "Childhood: the Last Frontier in Sex Research" in which you wrote: "A childhood sexual experience, such as being the partner of a relative, or of an older person, need not necessarily affect the child adversely."

Nancy Williamson, the reporter-researcher on the story, phoned you as we were closing it to be certain you still held this view. To her surprise, you were willing to change the double negative to a positive and say that a youngster's "rehearsal play" with adults "affects them beneficially". When you said this, Mrs. Williamson responded, intoning with a question, "Affects them beneficially?" You said, "Yes." She then read the entire sentence, as amended by you, back to you, including the words "With adults", and you approved it.

Under the circumstances, we believe we acted with full responsibility in this matter, checking and rechecking the article before publication, and must stand by the story, on which we greatly valued your cooperation.

Dr. Money commented to the News Council on that *Time* response with one word: "False."

Without the benefit of a response from *Time*, it is hard to be sure what happened between the reporter and Dr. Money. However, judging from Dr. Money's statements in the 1976 article in *The Sciences*, it seems possible that the reporter and Dr. Money were talking about two different things. It seems possible that the reporter was talking about Dr. Money's views on adult-child sex, which were expressed as follows in the 1976 article:

By contrast, a childhood sexual experience, such as being a partner of a relative, or of an older person, need not necessarily affect the child adversely.

It seems possible that Dr. Money was talking about his views on rehearsal play, which are expressed in the 1976 article as follows:

Although there is no firm knowledge of what constitutes a natural program of sexual rehearsal, nor what effect various experiences may have on sexual development, it is almost certain that human beings, like the other primates, require a period of early sexual manifestation of funtional mating behavior during puberty and later.

Note that there is no suggestion that Dr. Money thinks adult-child sex may be beneficial. The word, beneficial, comes in only when he talks about rehearsal play, which in the primates he describes in the 1976

340

article, does not involve either intercourse or interplay between adults and children.

In any case, given some demonstration that Dr. Money, a respected professional, did not believe what *Time* said he believed, it is surprising that the magazine did not publish his letter stating what his belief truly is.

## Dr. Wardell B. Pomeroy

Dr. Pomeroy, who is academic dean of The Institute for Advanced Study of Human Sexuality in San Francisco, was quoted just after Dr. Money in a paragraph that started:

> Almost all sexologists publicly state that they oppose adult-child sex, but a number of researchers maintain that such sex is basically harmless to the child.

*Time* then says, "Wardell Pomeroy, co-author of the original Kinsey reports, says incest 'can sometimes be beneficial' to children."

In answer to a Council inquiry Dr. Pomeroy commented:

> The statement by me in the *Time* article implies that I approve of incest. This, of course, is not true. It is a fact that incest can be beneficial to children (research data show that the older the child, the more likely it is to be beneficial, or to put it another way, the less likely it is to be traumatic). As a research scientist I am not concerned with making judgments about incest, or any other kind of sexual behavior, but I am concerned with learning as much about what people do sexually as possible. Hence I will stand on my statement that I have known cases where incest appears to be beneficial.

## Dr. Floyd Martinson

*Time* said:

> Sociologist Floyd Martinson of Minnesota's Gustavus Adolphus College thinks adults involved in affectionate sexual relationships with tots should not go to jail. "Intimate human relationships are important and precious," he feels. "I'd like to see as few restrictions placed on them as possible."

In answer to a Council staff inquiry Dr. Martinson recalled that a *Time* staff member read him the quotation, which was from an old article. He wrote:

> I remember my response to that 1977 quotation quite accurately. I said something as follows, "That's beautiful! Did I say that? I am proud of myself. By all means use it."
>
> The paraphrase that appears in the sentence that precedes the quotation was not read to me . . . . I refer to the sentence that ends with ". . . adults involved in affectionate sexual relationships with tots should not go to jail." I would have

objected to that statement if I knew it were to appear along with the quotation, for without qualifiers that statement is patently false.

The two items attributed to me and used in the context in which they were used do not represent my views and have been something of an embarrassment to myself and to Gustavus Adolphus College. For instance, up to five of the respondents have in one way or another called for my dismissal from the faculty. This will not occur, however.

Dr. Martinson enclosed a copy of a news story that appeared September 19, 1981, in *The Free Press* in Mankato, MN, under the headline, "Professor: Magazine mishandled quotes." The story said in part:

ST. PETER—Gustavus Adophus professor Floyd Martinson said he was flattered when a *Time* magazine reporter called to ask his views on child sexuality.

But when the article appeared, lumping accredited sex scholars together with pedophiles, the white-haired sociology professor knew he had been taken.

Martinson said the article in the Sept. 7 issue of *Time* used a five-year-old quote and a half-statement to make him sound like an advocate for incest. He suspects that the views of others quoted in the article may have been similarly mishandled.

Martinson, who has been answering calls and letters complaining about his purported views in the article, said the magazine piece on childhood sex was irresponsible and mischievous.

"They were out to inflame rather than inform," the professor said of the article, which he described as a "collage of quotes" that mixed serious scholars with crackpot advocates of unrestricted sex for children.

Martinson's views are introduced in the article in the midst of a discussion of adult-child sex. The article states that Martinson thinks that adults involved in affectionate relationships with children should not go to jail. That opinion is followed by a direct quote from Martinson, a quote taken from a conference on infant and child sexuality that he attended in Wales five years ago.

"Intimate human relationships are important and precious. I'd like to see as few restrictions placed on them as possible," Martinson was quoted in the article.

Taken alone, the quote isn't likely to raise any eyebrows. But placed in the context of adult-child sex, it takes on an entirely new meaning, the professor said.

As for his thoughts on jail terms for incest offenders, Martinson said the magazine was remiss in not fully explaining his opinion.

Martinson's full view: "Very often, the inclination in an incest case is to lock up the father. But in many instances, counseling benefits the family more than locking up the father."

Martinson said that jailing the father may result in guilt feelings for the abused child, who may feel that he or she is responsible for his or her father's predicament. Family counseling instead of jail terms may not only be more beneficial to the family, but would also help relieve overcrowded conditions in our prisons, Martinson said . . . .

As for the *Time* article, Martinson said he has no plans to press the issue. However, he sent back his recent subscription renewal with a letter chiding the magazine for the way his views were presented.

342

## Douglas H. Powell

Douglas Powell, Ed.D., is psychologist to the University Health Services at Harvard University. He was quoted in *Time* on the subject of "adult-child sex" just after the quote from Dr. Martinson as follows:

> I have not seen anyone harmed by this so long as it occurs in a relationship with somebody who really cares about the child.

Dr. Powell told the Council staff that the quotation is wrong: that he told *Time* it was wrong before publication; that a magazine staff member called him back with a changed quote. He approved the changed quote, but, he said, the magazine published the first and erroneous one anyway.

Dr. Powell protested to *Time* as follows:

> In your September 7, 1981, article on cradle-to-grave intimacy I was quoted as saying that sex between parents and their children is all right as long as affection exists between them. I believe my words were the recipient of creative editing. What I said was, "I have not seen anyone seriously harmed by this as long as there are compensating relationship with others who really care about the child.
>
> I do not believe that sex between parents and their offspring enhances psychological growth any more than an auto acccident.

To which *Time* replied, again over the signature of Ms. Walsh:

> Thank you for your letter commenting on the statement attributed to you in *Time*'s September 7 Sexes report. In the context in which that statement appeared, the subject in question was adult/child relationships, not parent/child relations or incest. We are fully aware of your position with regard to incest and nothing in our report should have led any reader to conclude that you advocated incestuous relationships. As for the statement itself, it was checked very carefully, I am advised, by *Time* correspondent Ruth Galvin.
>
> Our thanks, again, for letting us hear from you.

The *Time* response is true to the extent that the first sentence of the paragraph in which Dr. Powell's statement appears mentions "adult-child" sex. However, so does the first sentence of the previous paragraph, and yet it is in that paragraph that Dr. Pomeroy's comment on incest appears. It is clear that if there was not a purposeful effort to blur the distinction, there was not purposeful effort to make the distinction clear. As a practical matter, Dr. Pomeroy does not make a significant distinction between the effect of adult-child sex and the effect of incestuous adult-child sex. He recommends neither. However, if such a relationship does occur, he holds that it may not be seriously damaging if there are other compensating relationships with others who care about the child. *Time* simply got it wrong when the magazine quoted Dr. Pomeroy as saying the

343

nature of the relationship between the adult and the child involved in the sexual relationship was the critical factor.

He and the *Time* reporter were talking about incest, Dr. Powell said. When asked by Council staff if he had a different view about non-incestuous adult-child sex, Dr. Powell replied, "That's an interesting question. I've never been asked that before."

Furthermore, he said there was no question in the minds of his friends and, more important, the friends of his daughter, who is a Harvard senior, that Dr. Powell was talking about incestuous relationships.

Dr. Powell said that the *National Enquirer* called him to arrange an in-depth interview on the basis of the *Time* article. When he told the *Enquirer* that he had been misquoted, the magazine dropped its proposal for an in-depth article. However, it did publish a shorter one on his views about compensating relationship. "I thought it was ironic," said Dr. Powell, "that the *Enquirer* got it right when *Time* did not."

**Staff summary:** Except in the cases of Dr. Money and Dr. Powell, where *Time* is accused of incorrectly reporting their positions, the magazine can defend the wording of the actual sentences in which researchers are quoted or paraphrased. But the staff feels that it does not matter that the actual wording of a sentence can be defended. The sentence in which Dr. Calderone is quoted, for example, might be defended on the basis that it did not say specifically that she favored "a full sex life" for children which might include sexual contact with older people. However, such a defense would be narrow and legalistic. The context provided by the headlines, and second sentence of the article and the three sentences in the second paragraph leading up to the Calderone quote make it likely that a reader who does not know her position will come away believing that Dr. Calderone, in the words of the paragraph, is one of those who "has the wit to keep a low profile" about it, but who, nonetheless, believes that children "should be allowed to conduct a full sex life"—with all that that might imply to a lay person including, as is suggested by the next paragraph—to "have contact" (sexual contact is the inescapable implication) "with other people older than themselves." Indeed, the paragraph that follows Dr. Calderone's statement quotes Constantine as saying specifically that "to express themselves" sexually does mean that children may or may not have such contacts.

In this case the fairness of the reporting seems properly tested by the fact that several professionals who knew Dr. Calderone's position felt strongly enough to write letters to *Time* saying that the article distorted her position.

A similar distortion of the context makes Dr. Money appear to endorse what *Time* calls "early sex"—with its implication of sexual intercourse—when he actually is talking about rehearsal play, which, in the primates he describes, does not include intercourse. Dr. Money is quoted correctly, "It is almost certain that human beings, like the other primates, require a period of early sexual rehearsal play." But the sentence preceding that quote sets up the reader to believe that Dr. Money is advocating something he is not. It reads, "Even stranger is the theory that children will grow up askew if they do not have early sex."

Equally offensive is *Time*'s treatment of those scientists and their peers who protested that their positions were reported with a twist, or, in the case of Dr. Powell at Harvard, reported erroneously. Not only did *Time* not publish their letters, but the magazine's responses to their complaints manifested an obtuseness to the issues that seems studied. This is particularly true in the case of the complainant, Larry Constantine. In his case the difference between what he believes and what *Time* said he believes is more subtle than in some of the other cases. Nonetheless, the difference is possible to discern if one listens without defensiveness.

In *Time*'s defense, it does separate the views of the sexual health researchers from what the magazine calls "the pedophiles." However, even there, the article twists. It says, "Unfortunately, few responsible child experts have reacted . . . bluntly so far to the radical writing on child sex." Then it quotes two psychiatrists and a psychotherapist who warn that they have found people damaged by childhood sexual experiences.

The suggestion is that the sexologists like Mr. Constantine and Drs. Calderone, Martinson, and Powell are not aware of the possibility of such damage. In each case the sexologists say they are aware. And in each case they say that it is unfortunate that so many of the insights about child sex should come from those cases that do end up in the courts or in the offices of psychiatrists. In each case they ask only to widen the research to include those people whose early sex experiences were not so damaging. Such research would provide insight into why some experiences are damaging and others are not, they say.

**Council finding:** *Time* reported quotes from some professionals in the field of sexual health in such a way as to suggest that those professionals (1) shared the view that children should be allowed to conduct a "full sex life" and (2) shared a permissive view of adult-child sex. Further, in two cases the professionals say they were misquoted. In other cases the quotes, while accurate, are preceded by sentences in such a way that the quoted speaker appears to be taking a position more extreme than the quote itself suggests.

This article does not meet accepted journalistic standards for fairness and accuracy in reporting. The complaint that it distorts and misrepresents some of the views of the professionals who protested is found warranted.

It is unfortunate that *Time* did not publish any of the letters protesting that the professionals had been misrepresented. *Time* has explained to the Council in the past that its policy is not to publish such letters unless *Time* believes it was wrong. That policy works an injustice.

**Concurring:** Abel, Ayers, Benson, Brady, Hornby, Huston, Isaacs, Pulitzer, Scott and Williams.

**Note:** van den Haag dissented on Paragraphs 1 and 2 of Council action; concurred on paragraph 3.

April 22, 1982

## COMPLAINT NO. 197     (Filed Oct. 24, 1981)
### BRUCE CAMERON and LEONEL GOMEZ
#### against
### THE WALL STREET JOURNAL

**Complaint:** Bruce Cameron, director of the Human Rights project for Americans for Democratic Action, and Leonel Gomez, who identified himself as a former advisor to Rudolfo Viera, assassinated head of the Salvadoran Peasants Union, complained that an editorial in the October 19, 1981, edition of *The Wall Street Journal* under the headline "Forgotten Trabajadores," contained "three indisputable misrepresentations about the situation in El Salvador." They demanded, in a letter to *The Journal*, "that the record be set straight by a formal correction."

The editorial that prompted the complaint began as follows:

> Thanks to a disturbingly effective left-wing propaganda campaign, the Reagan administration has been largely stalled in its efforts to gather public support for a U.S. counter-attack against the Soviet-Cuban conquest of Central America. But it is far too early to give up the fight. The propaganda lies are by now so transparent that even the most liberal Congressmen, newspaper editors and churchmen surely cannot avoid recognizing them.

After offering evidence regarding Communist operations in Nicaragua, Costa Rica, Honduras and Panama, the editorial turned to El Salvador where, it stated, ". . . the Salvadoran government is proving

346

harder to vanquish on the ground than in the North American press." It continued:

> We received a clue to why last week when four Salvadoran union leaders, including the secretary general of the equivalent to the AFL-CIO, and the head of the campesino or peasants union, visited New York. All are under daily threat of death and in fact have all succeeded men who were murdered . . . .
>
> Their message: The war in El Salvador did not result from an indigenous worker and peasant uprising, as Communist propaganda insists. "The war involves 10% of the people, with 90% in the middle," declared Jose Luis Grande Preza, the labor federation leader. It is true that the Salvadoran army has committed brutalities and the group would like U.S. military aid to be accompanied by greater U.S. efforts to train Salvadoran troops in combatting guerrillas so as to avoid civilian casualties. But the five had no doubt that the origin of the killing was the campaign of destruction and terror conducted by the FMLN. The FMLN and FDR, so romantic sounding to the cocktail liberals of Washington, are not loved by the trabajadores (workers) and campesinos in El Salvador who must brave their bombs and bullets each day. "They have the guns but they don't have the people," says the country director in El Salvador for the AFL-CIO's American Institute for Free Labor Development, which attempts to encourage formation of free labor unions.
>
> There is bitter irony in all this. The American government is not taking a more forceful role in Central American in part because so many Americans have been convinced that this would be making war on the common man. But representatives of the common man are pleading for help in driving out what they know full well is a foreign-backed army that will enslave them if it wins . . . .

The editorial had earlier described the FMLN as the "Cuban- and Soviet-supported Farabundo Marti Liberation Front," and the FDR as "something called the Democratic Revolutionary Front . . . ."

Mr. Cameron and Mr. Lopez claimed that the editorial suggested that the courage of the five Salvadoran leaders (the four union officials and a former mayor of San Salvador), "confirms the *Journal*'s claim that the Salvadoran government has widespread popular support. The men, the editorial says, 'have all succeeded men who were murdered.' This is incorrect and intentionally misrepresents facts crucial to the understanding of the subject being discussed."

The complaint continued:

> First, the predecessors of two, not all five, of the men were murdered; a third's brother was killed. Second, and most importantly, it is reasonably certain to the Salvadorans themselves that all three killings were carried out by government forces or their right-wing allies . . . .

The third complaint challenged the editorial's statement that "representatives of the comman man are pleading for help in driving out what they know full well is a foreign-backed army." Mr. Cameron and Mr.

Lopez charged that "The utterly unmistakable meaning that this sentence intends to give is that these five Salvadoran men support the policies that the editorial supports, the policies of the Duarte government and the Reagan administration. This is a deliberate lie."

The complaint continued:

> The men belong to the Popular Democratic Union (UPD), an organization explicitly opposed to the Duarte and Reagan policies. In a press conference two weeks ago in Washington, the men emphasized that the UPD represented "neither the government of El Salvador nor its opposition . . . much less the two extremes," the military and the guerrillas. The spokesman for the group went on to say that the UPD favors a "dialogue among the various parties to the conflict . . . a non-military solution." The men, in fact, had come to the United States on their way back from Europe where they had explored diplomatic openings for such a dialogue. The *Journal* editorial led readers to believe that the men essentially agreed with the Reagan administration's policy on El Salvador when in fact, the men were actively pursuing an alternative to it. It is inconceivable that the author of "Forgotten Trabajadores" did not know the true position of the UPD and its delegation. We can only conclude that the editorial was intended to mislead readers.

**Response:** Robert J. Bartley, editor of *The Wall Street Journal*, said in a letter to the Council that "While there was a misunderstanding over precisely who was killed and some differences in nuance, our editorial was an accurate capsule description of the position of the Salvadoran labor leaders."

Mr. Bartley said that "it is Mr. Cameron's complaint that willfully distorts—both Mr. Grande's position and our editorial . . . ."

Mr. Bartley included with his letter a copy from the paper's March 5 issue of a lengthy interview Suzanne Garment, associate editor in *The Journal*'s Washington bureau, had with Mr. Grande and two other Salvadoran labor leaders, in Washington during the last week of February. "The original purpose of the interview," *The Journal* stated, "was to follow up on a controversy regarding what we had printed (in the October 19 editorial) about a previous meeting with a group of Salvadoran labor leaders led by Mr. Grande." *The Journal*'s reference to criticism was to the complaint by Mr. Cameron and Mr. Lopez subsequently filed with The National News Council, and "a more modest letter" (of complaint).

**Analysis:** It was important to recognize that two *Wall Street Journal* interviews with the Salvadoran labor leaders are involved. The first, which was held in New York City under informal circumstances, formed the basis for the editorial about which Mr. Cameron and Mr. Lopez complained. They were not present at the interview and no transcript was kept of what was said by the five Salvadorans to George Melloan, the *Wall*

*Street Journal* editor who did attend. Their remarks were all in Spanish and were then translated. The complaint by Mr. Cameron and Mr. Lopez stemmed from what they considered basic inconsistencies between the views attributed to the unionists in the editorial and those the Salvadorans had expressed in subsequent general press conferences in Washington.

The second *Journal* interview was held in Washington four months after the first and the charges in the Cameron-Lopez letter were specifically directed to the attention of the three Salvador labor representatives then in the capital, two of whom had been present at the New York meeting. This time a transcript was kept and substantial excerpts were published in textual form on the editorial page in the March 5 *Journal*. Included in these excerpts were specific comments on questions raised by complainants. The publication at first hand of the unionists' views did not alter the belief of the complainants that *The Journal* remained at fault.

A fundamental precept of The National News Council has always been that its processes ought not be susceptible to use in ways that would inhibit the free and vigorous expression by the media of editorial opinion on any side of controversial issues. The Council's original Rules of Procedure set forth that precept in these words: "The Council concerns itself with editorial comment only insofar as allegations of fact are in dispute." In 1980 the rule on this subject was revised to limit even more explicitly the circumstances under which it might be appropriate for the Council to entertain complaints about editorials or other expressions of journalistic viewpoint. The new formulation said. "The Council concerns itself with editorial comment only insofar as allegations of willful distorton of fact are made."

The change reflected the Council's recognition that, in almost any matter on which feelings run high, those arguing for opposite positions are likely to differ sharply on the interpretation of facts and on the fidelity or fairness with which facts are presented. To make the Council arbiter in such disagreements would thrust it into a realm of judgment in which, by definition, standards of objectivity are not expected to control. This would represent a role very different from the one the Council endeavors to discharge in assessing complaints that relate to the accuracy and fairness of news reports. For that reason, the Council confines itself to considering cases affecting editorials only where allegations have been made that the factual basis on which the editor's conclusions rest has been deliberately misrepresented.

The staff's inquiry into this complaint indicates the wisdom of circumscribing so rigidly the basis on which editorials will be reviewed. Any more intrusive rule would be difficult to reconcile with a commitment to keeping untrammeled the robustness of debate in the opinion sections of the nation's press. That is especially true in a situation such as this where material is subject to translation and people's interpretations of what has been said may not jibe. Different questions are asked on different occasions and different weighting may be given to responses in one setting as against another. The nuances of any answer are often subject to a variety of readings. and never more so than when the appraisal is being made by a person who starts with well-defined preconceptions of where truth and justice lie in a tangled situation.

The interview with the four Salvadoran unionists and the former mayor of San Salvador, on which the October 19 editorial was based, took place in the Manhattan apartment of Mary Temple, executive director of the Land Council, an independent agency concerned with land reform in developing countries, which has served as a consultant to the AFL-CIO and the American Institute for Free Labor Development in their activities in El Salvador. The purpose of the gathering was to acquaint American journalists and molders of public opinion with the views of the Latin American labor leaders.

The discussion was free-wheeling, but Ms. Temple says she found nothing in the editorial that she considered inconsistent with remarks made by one or all of the unionists that evening. She adds, however, that she might have phrased differently some of the views ascribed to the Salvadorans in the editorial, particularly the statement that "the five had no doubt that the origin of the killing was the campaign of destruction and terror conducted by the FMLN."

While she does not contest that comments along this line may have been made in the course of the evening, she says many others were made that underscored the apprehension and revulsion the unionists felt toward terror by right-wing extremists associated with the military, not just toward the killings by left-wing guerrillas. The central message the unionists sought to convey was that they represented a third force concerned with promoting a dialogue among all the political elements in El Salvador with a view to setting the stage for truly free and democratic elections.

With respect to United States military aid to El Salvador, the unionists did say, according to Ms. Temple and her husband, Robert Kleiman, a member of the editorial board of *The New York Times*, that its purpose ought to be exclusively to train Salvadoran security forces in the maintenance of order so that peasants and workers would not be killed but only those practicing terror and violence. Both also confirmed the statement in the editorial that, in the view of the union leaders, 90 percent of the Salvadoran people stand apart from both sides, right and left, in the war and that it does not represent an indigenous uprising from below.

Ms. Temple was also present at the second *Journal* interview conducted by Suzanne Garment in the Washington offices of the American Institute for Free Labor Development. She reports that what was said there by the two original participants, Jose Luis Grande Preza and Francesco Zaldana, was essentially the same as had been said at the meeting in her apartment prior to the editorial. On the question of terror directed against Salvadoran labor, she said the unionists felt some of the killing had been by the right and some by the left. The general political attitudes of the Salvadoran laborites, both on internal affairs and on American aid, are set forth in some detail in the published transcript.

By coincidence, A. H. Raskin, associate director of the Council, had been invited to attend the original session with the group in the Temple apartment, but had been obliged to decline because of absence from the city. Instead, he met with the five unionists and their AFL-CIO escorts, including Ms. Temple, a few days before the more general interview. The discussion covered much the same range of subject matter, and there was no question in Mr. Raskin's mind that the point the unionists were most eager to have him grasp was the desirability of United States support for dialogue among all the elements in the Salvadoran political spectrum, looking to a genuine expression of the popular will through elections. They had many harsh things to say against the guerrillas and the reinforcement they were receiving from left-wing revolutionary sources outside El Salvador, but they were no less condemnatory of those elements in the military which they accuse of seeking to wreck land reform in the service of the propertied classes.

On that basis, if what appeared in *The Journal* had been presented as a news story aimed at telling readers what position the Salvador labor delegation took, a complaint might have been in order that it was too one-sided and failed to give the paper's readers all the information they required for a balanced appraisal. But that obligation need not weigh on a writer of opinion, who is free to select those facts that support a viewpoint he considers valid and ignore those that get in the way. Thus, an editorial writer with a different perspective might have come away from the same session with material he felt justified an attack on the right wing or, more in line with the group's own goal, a plea for attempts to arrive at a meeting of minds among all factions on terms for a free and uncontrolled election.

Any one of the three versions would have been defensible as an editorial outside the Council's province of appropriate review on charges of "willful distortion" of the facts on which the opinion was predicated. However, in *The Journal's* case, the whole question of the factuality of its editorial was rendered academic by its decision after the letter of complaint was received to publish on its editorial page for March 5 an extended interview with two of the five Salvadorans who had participated in the original meeting, plus a third unionist not originally present.

The transcript of that second interview went into considerable detail on many of the positions bypassed in the October 19 editorial. It also gave Jose Luis Grande Preza, Lane Kirkland's counterpart in the Salvadoran labor movement, a chance to address himself to the specific complaints made against the editorial. The unionists' emphasis on the need for dialogue among the various parties was explicitly mentioned in the transcript, along with dozens of other details and clarifications of their position.

**Council finding:** Complaints against expressions of editorial opinion are outside the province of The National News Council, except to the extent that they may involve charges of "willful distortion of fact." The staff study supports no finding of "willful distortion of fact" in connection with this editorial in *The Wall Street Journal.* On that basis, the Council rejects the complaint.

The Council notes with approval, however, the action taken by *The Journal* on its own initiative after the complaint was filed to bring the matter to the attention of its readers and to give the Salvadoran unionists an opportunity, through follow-up interview on the editorial page, to set forth in detail their views on the issues raised in the complaint.

**Concurring:** Abel, Ayers, Benson, Brady, Hornby, Huston, Isaacs, Pulitzer, Scott, van den Haag and Williams.
April 22, 1982


## COMPLAINT NO. 198      (Filed Nov. 3, 1981)
### HERBERT D. KERMAN
against
### THE WASHINGTON POST, ABC NEWS
"20/20," and MOTHER JONES


**Complaint:** Dr. Herbert D. Kerman, M.D., president of the Association of Community Cancer Centers, complained that three recent news reports on cancer research exhibited unfairness and irresponsibility. He specified a four-part series in *The Washington Post* October 18-21, 1981; an hour-long ABC News "20/20" program October 22, and an article in the September-October issue of *Mother Jones*.

The *Washington Post* articles focused on defects in the testing of experimental cancer drugs by the National Cancer Institute. Dr. Kerman called the articles lurid recitals of complications and deaths which "may be partially factual," but "are written in a manner as to substantially impugn the entire effort of drug development of the NCI." He said, "The positive results which have occurred in the fight against cancer, while mentioned, are de-emphasized. The articles show no evenhandedness or fairness in presentation, and are so distorted as to deny the very great advances made in the experimental drug research effort."

Dr. Kerman said, "The ABC '20/20' show also de-emphasized the benefits of cancer research and the National Cancer Program and empha-sized some scientifically unproved drugs and methods. In essence, a pro and con report was lacking." He said a more recent "MacNeil-Lehrer Report" from WNET/Thirteen on cancer research "was more even-handed and afforded an opportunity for open debate between scientists with differences of opinion and an opportunity for a reasonable discus-sion on controversial issues ensued."

Dr. Kerman said, "A more flagrant and thoroughly distorted article appeared in *Mother Jones* about a research effort in Oak Ridge about which I have intimate firsthand knowledge, and I can state unequivocally that the article's implications were false. This latter report resulted in a congressional investigation by Rep. Albert Gore of Tennessee and, in essence, refuted the statements of the journalist."

Dr. Kerman said his concern about the three reports grew out of 30 years of treating cancer patients during which he has seen "slow but progressive positive results of ever increasing small improvements and sophistication in care, techniques, equipment and drug management of cancer which translates into improved survival and lessened morbidity for patients. He feared that:

> The present interest of the media in cancer and the way it is being presented results in erosion of confidence and questions the credibility and integrity of, not only the medical research scientists, but also the practicing community oncologists who apply the methodology evolved from the research efforts in the treatment of over 85 percent of all patients with cancer. While the public eagerly awaits a monumental "breakthrough" in cancer management, this is more than likely never to occur and

353

the benefits and progress of treatment methods must rely on small increments of increasing knowledge which can be applied to cancer management only through the present methods of investigation.

It would be my hope that the media itself, perhaps through the influence of The National News Council, could be urged to develop a more evenhanded approach to their reports and give as much emphasis to the compassion, quality of patient care and support, and concern of the investigators who overwhelmingly are concerned with the humanistic factors as well as the scientific factors of research which involves patients and their families. The medical and bioscientific community has little opportunity to be heard in the same forum and under the same circumstances as the media, and we can only rely on the journalistic profession to impose the characteristics of professionalism and ethical behavior in journalism.

**A note on this report:** The News Council employed two people with specialized knowledge to analyze this complaint. They are David Zimmerman, a free-lance science writer, and Gerald Delaney, director of Public Affairs for Memorial Sloan-Kettering Cancer Center in New York. Mr. Zimmerman was recommended by Barbara Culliton, news editor of *Science* magazine and president of the National Association of Science Writers, after Ms. Culliton discovered that she did not have time to do the analysis herself. She recommended Mr. Zimmerman as an experienced science writer who enjoyed the respect of his colleagues for his integrity and his concern with the ethics of science writing. Mr. Delaney was recommended by Lewis Cope, science editor of the *Minneaplis Tribune*, as a person within the cancer establishment who had enough detachment to make a reliable evaluation of attacks on that establishment.

Their analyses were sent to Council members as background material. So were an article from the January/February, 1982, issue of the *Washington Journalism Review* and an "explainer" article from the October 23, 1981, issue of *The Boston Globe*. Richard A. Knox, *The Globe*'s medical writer, felt compelled to write the explanatory article because he and *The Globe*'s ombudsman received a number of phone calls and questions after *The Globe* published parts of the *Washington Post* series.

The three complaints are dealt with separately here.

### The Washington Post

**The series:** The *Post* series consisted of four articles and a number of sidebars about the National Cancer Institute's Phase One testing program for experimental cancer drugs. The Phase One program is the first phase of human testing after laboratory tests have shown some results against cancer in animals. *The Post* described its series as follows in the first article:

A one-year study by *The Washington Post* had documented 620 cases in which experimental drugs have been implicated in the deaths of cancer patients . . . . And they amounted to merely a fraction of the thousands of people who in recent years have died or suffered terribly from cancer experiments conducted in the nation's hospitals.

*The Post* devoted its first two articles to case studies of 21 of the experimental drugs tested under the NCI's Phase One program. The third article focused on one of the clinics in which experimental drugs are used. The fourth article described the slow path of an experimental drug from hunch to the point where it can be used in human experiments.

**The Post's response to the complaint:** Ben Bradlee, editor of *The Post*, said it was unsophisticated to take Dr. Kerman's complaint seriously. He implied that the complaint was part of a "full court press" mounted against the articles by "the cancer establishment." He noted that the complaint did not allege inaccuracy and said, "I see no reason why, in the absence of anything like a specific charge, *The Washington Post* or any of its staff should share its thinking and insights or anything else with you."

Staff replied that the complaint did allege that the articles were unfair and that unfairness, as much as inaccuracy, was a concern of the News Council. Mr. Bradlee replied that the complaint, to the extent that it implied that the cancer series was not fair or not in the proper context, differed little from hundreds of other complaints he received in the course of a year. He said, "If you want to investigate us, be my guest," but he did not offer his thinking or that of his staff on the allegations in the complaint. That being the case, Council staff did not consider that his second response differed significantly from his first.

The Council received on April 6 from Vincent T. DeVita, director of The National Cancer Institute, a 52-page list of what he called "inaccuracies, omissions, or distortions of fact" in the *Post* series. Council staff was concerned that the list might consist of new criticism that *The Post* had not had an opportunity to answer. However, it appeared from references within the DeVita list that the gravamen of the criticisms had been communicated to *The Post* in one or more of three letters from Dr. DeVita—one that was published in *The Post* October 19, and two others dated October 19 and 21, which were not published. Nonetheless, the appearance of the DeVita criticisms at the last minute led Council staff to try again to elicit a response from *The Post* to the DeVita complaints and to the original Kerman complaint. Richard Cunningham called Mr. Bradlee April 9; told him about the DeVita material; said he was uncomfortable about not having a response from *The Post*, and offered to make himself and the material available to receive a response from Mr. Bradlee and/or his staff. Mr. Bradlee declined. He said it ought to be clear that Dr. DeVita had an axe to grind.

Mr. Cunningham sent a copy of Dr. DeVita's criticism to Mr. Bradlee. Mr. Bradlee replied with a letter noting that in his view the DeVita material did not constitute a challenge to the accuracy of the series and that the complaints had been largely dealt with in a statement from Dr. DeVita published by *The Post*.

### The complaint against ABC News

**The program:** The "20/20" segment against which the complaint is directed was an hour-long program entitled, "The War on Cancer: Cure, Profit or Politics?" The program opened with the question:

> The national war on cancer—ten years and $10 billion of your tax money, sophisticated research, free-flowing federal grants, power politics, relentless publicity, and public pressure for a breakthrough—has it done any good? Critics charge scandal, cover-up, manipulated statistics, monopoly of research funds, and they say worthy researchers with innovative treatments are harassed, stifled, discouraged.

Hugh Downs said:

> . . . 10 years and $10 billion later, we are in the midst of a cancer epidemic. Both the incidence and the death rate from cancer have climbed higher than ever before. Why so little progress after so long a battle? Well, here with our report is Geraldo Rivera.

Rivera reported:

> . . . So despite sophisticated new technology, and despite the expenditure of billions of tax dollars, the odds today are the same one-in-three odds that faced the cancer patient back in May of 1958 . . . . But cancer is not just a disease, it's a political and economic phenomenon, a $30 billion-a-year business—one that reaches deep into the halls of Congress, deep into the national pocketbook, and deep into the soul of the nation.

Mr. Rivera reported that an interlocking leadership existed between the National Cancer Institute and the American Cancer Society. That interlock, critics said, created a monopoly on cancer research funds and information. Mr. Rivera outline the stories of Dr. Stanislaw Bruzinski and Dr. Joseph Gold, who were allegedly frozen out of funds and credit for their innovative efforts to find new cancer therapies. Mr. Rivera outlined what he called "press misbehavior" in hyping the promising cancer therapy, Interferon. He concluded the program:

> Declaring our so-called war on cancer 10 years ago was a grand public relations

gesture, but as every year passes without victory, frustration and fear continue to mount. And as the multi-billion dollar campaign enters its second decade, all of us—the scientists, the politicians, the press, and the people—have to be more careful, because, it's been said, in all wars—and that includes this figurative one—the first casualty is often the truth.

**The response of ABC News:** George Watson, vice-president of ABC News, supplied the News Council with a complaint about the "20/20" program from Dr. Robert P. Hutter, president of the American Cancer Society, and his answer to that letter. Since the Hutter letter is more specific in its complaints than the Kerman complaint to the News Council, both it and Mr. Watson's response are incorporated into this report as a fair insight into the network's defense of the program.

Dear Mr. Goldenson (Chairman of the Board and Chief Executive Officer, ABC-TV):

Cancer is the disease most feared by people all over the world. Thus the television news media must be especially careful not to create undue fear or hopelessness in current patients or those recently treated. This is why the American Cancer Society is deeply concerned with a recent "20/20" special program on cancer.

The program's opening assumptions began with: "We are in the midst of a cancer epidemic."

This is a totally inaccurate thesis. The United States is most definitely not in the midst of a cancer epidemic. Except for lung cancer, 85 percent of which is caused by the smoking of cigarettes, the age-adjusted death rate of almost all cancer is flat or declining. Actually, five-year survival of all cancer patients with serious cancer in the United States has now risen to 45 percent.

It is important to separate lung cancer deaths from those of other forms of the disease, because these tumors are highly fatal. Yet the cause of the great majority of lung cancers is completely controllable through personal lifestyles. This basic truth was obscured by "20/20." When Dr. Vincent DeVita, Director of the National Cancer Institute, tried to explain this to Mr. Rivera, the latter asked: "Aren't we playing games?"

Mr. Rivera described cancer as a "thirty billion dollar a year business." This sounds sinister. What does it mean? This was never explained. Since the program dealt in the main with cancer research, it might have pointed out that the total research budget of the Society is currently $55 million annually; and the total research portion of the budget of the Institute is $600 million a year. This money is divided among hundreds of scientists and physicians. The Society's average grant to researchers is about $63,000 a year.

Dr. Samuel Epstein was introduced on the program as a "world renowned expert of the politics behind cancer research." Dr. Epstein went on to say that "our ability to treat and cure the major cancer killers has not materially advanced for decades." This is completely false and a disservice to the thousands of patients undergoing treatment at this time. In the past decade alone, the longterm survival rate for 17 out of 35 sites of cancer has increased significantly among U.S. men and women.

Dr. Epstein's accusation of "overlap in virtually every single area of boards,

357

committees, grants, even publications" between the Society and the Institute is also completely inaccurate. The Society receives no funds from the Institute as a matter of policy. And there is no representation on its board or committees by members of the Institute. This practice ceased four years ago. With this misinformation Dr. Epstein posited a "cancer establishment" on "20/20."

Building further on this wrong evidence, "20/20" devoted undue emphasis to the work of Dr. Stanislaw Bruzinski and Dr. Joseph Gold, identified as researchers with so-called cures slighted by the "cancer establishment." Dr. Bruzinski practices entirely within the state of Texas and has not submitted his drug to the Federal Food and Drug Administration. Dr. Gold's substance is currently under clinical investigation by the Institute, again a fact unreported by "20/20."

A viewer of the program could easily misconstrue that the purported therapies offered by these two physicians provide the panacea to cancer. What a shocking piece of information to offer cancer patients. Each year hundreds of applications for grants are turned down for lack of funds or proper protocols. Why single out these two cases as the possible answer to cancer?

In the past, ABC has shown sensitivity in this area. We hope that there may be an opportunity to present a balanced portrayal of cancer control to your vast viewing audience. We would be more than pleased to work with your staff toward that end.

Sincerely yours,
Robert V. P. Hutter, M.D.
President (American Cancer Society)

Dear Doctor Hutter:

Leonard Goldenson asked me to respond to your letter about the program "The War on Cancer: Cure, Profit or Politics?" which was broadcast by ABC News as a special report on "20/20". Since the broadcast last October, we have recently received a number of similar letters from various affiliates of the American Cancer Society. I want to address this correspondence at some length because of the seriousness of some of the charges made and our concern that the purpose and procedures we employed in making the program are better understood.

Let me begin by saying that the program was the result of many months research and careful documentation. Several hundred physicians and researchers were consulted. Our purpose was to examine issues involving policies, politics and attitudes toward cancer research and funding. The program did not endorse any form of treatment, established or experimental, and that point was emphasized in written replies to viewers who wrote or telephoned ABC News about it. We are acutely aware that desperate or distraught persons may seize on any information that seems to offer hope, or at the other emotional extreme, hopelessness. At the same time, we do feel an obligation to inform the general public about significant issues affecting its health and welfare. Therefore, we believed that the broader public interest was in fact served by forthrightly dealing with the topic. Indeed, we felt that this area of investigation is of great concern and has been largely neglected.

Let me now turn to the specific points of your letter and take them in the order that you raised them:

1) When speaking of a cancer "epidemic," we primarily had in mind the incidence of the disease. While there is, as we reported, a "confusing array of

statistics from a variety of sources," we concluded that "epidemic" was an accurate word to describe the increasing incidence of cancer.

We also observed that not only had the incidence increased, but that also the death rate of cancer was rising. We consulted many statistical sources. To take one conclusion from the ACS publication, "Cancer Facts and Figures, 1981," "There has been a steady rise in the age-adjusted death rate."

We decided we could not ignore the death rate from lung cancer because it happens to be the greatest killer of all. Additionally, we did not feel the death rate could be excluded just because some preventative measures are known.

While the statistics we reported are bleak, we also noted at the beginning of the program significant progress in treating some forms of cancer. Both Dr. Vincent DeVita, Jr., director of the National Cancer Institute, and Dr. Frank Rauscher, Jr., of the American Cancer Society, pointed out the accomplishments of cancer research. The correspondent, Geraldo Rivera, also recognized the progress made in treating several forms of cancer.

2) You questioned Mr. Rivera's statement that cancer is a "thirty billion dollar a year business." That described the total cost our society pays in detection, diagnosis, treatment, research and economic loss to individuals and the economy. I would agree that "business" is a rather loose word in this context and should have been explained more fully. The statistic itself, however, is substantiated by our research.

3) Dr. Samuel Epstein's assertion that "our ability to treat and cure the major cancer killers has not materially advanced for decades" refers back to the statistical question. Dr. Epstein is discussing the *major* killers such as lung cancer where there has been little or no progress according to the statistics.

4) On the matter of whether a cancer "establishment" exists, we were convinced that it does. In a general sense, establishments can be found in virtually all government, institutional, corporate or organizational endeavors. Specifically, there does appear to be substantial overlap on the boards and committees of the National Institute and the American Society. For example, when we cross-referenced the ACS advisory board members with the NCI Research Index we found that of 169 advisory board members, six were employed by the NCI, and that 84 persons were recipients of a total of 184 grants.

5) On the work of Dr. Stanislaw Bruzinski and Dr. Joseph Gold, ABC News did not endorse or debunk the work of either. We focused on these two doctors and their experiments because they were illustrative of what we believed were important issues concerning the funding and encouragement of cancer research. We discussed both the apparent positive results of their work and the criticism expressed by other cancer specialists. We did not portray their work as the "possible answer to cancer." We did ask the question whether potentially significant research is being effectively supported. In responding to inquiries from the public, we emphasized that the program "does not endorse any specific therapy or treatment for cancer, as this is a medical decision between patient and physician."

Since the program was broadcast, we have learned that important members of the international community of onocologists will be joining certain U.S. colleagues in a clinical evaluation of both treatments. It is my understanding that Dr. Bruzinski will soon submit various peptide compounds to the Food and Drug Administration. As for Dr. Gold, we are aware of three clinical trials approved by the F.D.A. It is our further understanding that these results are to be presented at a forthcoming ASCO meeting. We stated that hydrazine sulfate was recently used in clinical trials.

Finally, I would like to make several observations in response to your more general concerns and similar ones expressed in other letters from affiliated groups. There seems to be an implication that we should report only the good news about cancer research and treatment. We have reported positive aspects many times and shall continue to do so in the future. At the same time, we cannot ignore more critical or even negative aspects of the subject. Our responsibility is neither to encourage nor discourage the public. It is simply to provide information on which informed citizens can reach their own conclusions. Another implication in some letters to us suggests that we have a special obligation to amplify the voices of the medical and bioscientific community. They are in fact often heard on ABC News broadcasts, and indeed in the program to which you object, virtually all of the voices are those of physicians and scientists, even if they are ones with which you disagree. It is a debatable subject of enormous consequence to all citizens.

We are committed to accuracy and fairness in all of our reporting, and to stimulating debate on important issues. We believe those commitments were met by the program. You can be assured that in future reports we shall be attentive, as we have in the past, to the activities and views of the American Cancer Society.

Yours Sincerely,
George Watson

**Council finding:** Hard-hitting reporting on the battle against cancer has been overdue. The news reports complained of represent attempts to provide that kind of reporting.

The News Council finds that it is neither necessary nor desirable to establish special standards for the reporting of medical research in general or cancer research in particular. However, it is most important to be accurate and fair in reporting these fields.

The Council rejects the suggestion of the complainant that the medical and bioscientific communities are somehow cheated in the arena of public discussion of their programs. The press has developed some specialized reporters and editors competent to handle the complexities and subtleties of bioscientific subjects. The bioscientific community has developed public relation skills. Unfortunately those skills have often been used to limit rather than increase public discussion of the ethical issues in medical science. The cancer research program appears to both of the experts employed by the News Council to be one of the areas in which there has been too little public discussion.

## The complaint against *The Washington Post*

The News Council commends *The Washington Post* for spending months of reporting time on a series of articles focused specifically and in

360

depth at the complex and little known experimental drug testing program of the National Cancer Institute.

Unfortunately *The Post* adopted a sensational, accusatory tone and failed in some cases to supply information that would help the reader make up his or her mind independently about the issues involved in the experimental drug program.

As one example of the inappropriate tone of the articles: "Cancer did not kill Sheri Beck. Her treatment for cancer did. She died of congestive heart failure brought on by Mitoxantrone, an experimental drug derived from a dye used in ballpoint pen ink." The article does not report what the Beck child's doctor said: That the child was not responding to any other chemical therapy; had received maximum radiation treatment, and had survived under treatment with Mitoxantrone with a diminution of tumor size for five months before her death. The mention of ballpoint dye is egregious. Many drugs are related to harmful substances—nitroglycerin to explosives, coumadin to rat poison, and the cancer drug, MOOP, to mustard nerve gas—yet the reporters mention the relationship of Mitoxantrone to ballpoint ink three times. Furthermore, they report at one point that the drug changes the colors of bodily secretions; so do a number of other conventional drugs.

The *Post* series left no doubt that the writers found it unacceptable that some experimental drugs were continued in testing long after the *Post* writers thought they should be discontinued. But the *Post* writers, perhaps because they are not science reporters, did not present the NCI's explanation of how a drug might legitimately be under test against one type of cancer long after it had proved ineffective against other types: the NCI selects 6 to 8 of the more than 100 types of cancer for testing. Tests are conducted in 30 patients with each type of cancer, and they are tested at different dose levels and different schedules of administration. With only two dose levels and two schedules of administration almost 1,000 patients are required and the full test may take years.

Similarly the *Post* writers in many cases use numbers to draw a negative picture of a drug when numbers might be used to draw a positive picture. As an example Dr. Vincent DeVita, head of the NCI, cites the *Post* report that Mitoxantrone had been tested on 586 people with only one complete and five partial responses—and many cases of heart toxicity. *The Post* failed to note that the reporting was complete on only 314 patients—not 586— and *The Post* did not report that one complete response and three of the partial responses were among a group of only 84 terminal breast cancer patients, a quite different picture of the drug, which is still considered promising as an anti-cancer therapy. In general *The Post* does not put the number of drug-related deaths it discovered into a context that might suggest what is an appropriate number of deaths.

The reporters also point out that some of the drugs they judge to be unacceptable were on a "high priority" list created by Dr. DeVita. They do not describe the process by which those drugs were selected for testing from hundreds of other experimental drugs, nor do they make clear that "high priority" indicated only that the drugs had had some effect against animal cancers, not that they had aroused unusual hope that they might be effective in humans.

Furthermore, the *Post* writers do not emphasize adequately that therapies now accepted in cancer treatment once produced the same kind of side effects the writers deplore; or that any response at all in a terminally ill patient may warrant using a drug in combination with others. Nor do the writers provide adequate information on animal testing of experimental drugs or on the system that does exist to supervise testing.

It is a significant demonstration of accountability that *The Post* did publish well displayed along with the third article in the series a protest by the head of the NCI and that it did publish letters to the editor critical of the reporting.

While the News Council cannot accept the broad charges of the complainant against the useful and important *Post* series, it does find the series flawed to some extent by sensationalism and failure to supply important information that would allow the reader to put the defects of the testing program into reasonable context. The series, therefore, falls below *The Post*'s own standards for journalistic fairness.

**Concurring:** Abel, Ayers, Benson, Brady, Hornby, Huston, Isaacs, Pulitzer, Scott, van den Haag and Williams.

## Complaint against *Mother Jones*

**Note:** The complaint against *Mother Jones* was dismissed, because the mother of a child whose treatment was described in the article sued the Oak Ridge hospital using the allegations in the article as the grounds for her suit.

## Complaint against ABC News "20/20"

Dr. Kerman complained that "20/20" unfairly and irresponsibly de-emphasized the benefits of cancer research and overemphasized a couple of "scientifically unproven drugs and methods." Dr. Robert P. Hutter, president of the American Cancer Society, charged more specifically that the program was wrong in saying that cancer is epidemic in the United States; in implying that our ability to treat and cure cancer has not advanced, and in suggesting that the American Cancer Society and the National Cancer Institute have formed a monopoly on cancer research funds that has denied a chance to at least two researchers with promising therapies.

The News Council commends ABC News for investing months of reporting time in what "20/20" calls a "hard, cold look" at the "well-intended efforts" of the national war on cancer.

The impression comes through clearly that "20/20" believes that although billions of dollars have been spent, little progress has been made, and that the fault lies with a cancer "establishment" consisting of the American Cancer Society and the National Cancer Institute. However, the program's use of innuendo and its failure to supply adequate samples of contrary views raises suspicion about the validity of that message.

The program makes statements that cancer is "no longer the other guy's disease;" that we are in a cancer epidemic, and that cure rates have not improved. Yet there are no figures from biostatisticians who would dispute those conclusions; "epidemic" has a specific meaning not justified by the present incidence of cancer, and viewers are not given an opportunity to hear and judge for themselves the NCI's argument for leaving 85 percent of lung cancer out of the death rate statistics.

An example of tilting the information is provided by the "20/20" treatment of Dr. Frank Rauscher's assertion, "We're winning this war . . . ." The reporter translates that statement into a "claim that victory is at hand."

"20/20" clearly believes that the NCI-ACS "monopoly" has shouldered researchers with promising therapies out of the path of research grants and had denied them recognition. The report appears to place the blame on the peer review system, which, whatever its shortcomings, is essential to the prudent expenditure of research funds and to the reliable evaluation and supervision of research.

The report did not answer any number of "why" questions as it detailed the difficulties of two cancer researchers in obtaining funds or peer acceptance of their work. Such failure, which frequently occurs in adversarial reporting, tends to detract from the believability of the reporting.

The ABC News response to Dr. Hutter indicates that the program's treatment of two outsiders with promising therapies did prompt queries from the public about those therapies. Those calls illustrate the sensitivity that news media must take to the task of reporting on medical research.

A news program that takes a point of view has a right, the Council has held, to marshal fact in support of that point of view. However, the producers must be accurate and fair.

The Council rejects the charge that ABC was deliberately unfair. However, it finds that this program fell short in accuracy and responsibility.

**Concurring:** Abel, Ayers, Benson, Brady, Hornby, Isaacs, Pulitzer, van den Haag and Williams.

**Dissenting:** Huston

**Dissenting opinion by Huston:** The majority of the Council has rejected what it said was the "charge that ABC was deliberately unfair." I cannot concur. The complainant never charged that "ABC was deliberately unfair." In fact, the precise nature of the complaint was never defined to my satisfaction. Even David R. Zimmerman, the science writer who was employed by the Council to examine the complaint, noted: "The original complaint and its restatements are imprecise."

In my opinion, the Council must make a great effort to define the precise nature of each complaint. I have long suggested that forms be used as a starting point and that complainants be required to pinpoint their particular problems. Only then, can the News Council responsibly address the concerns. Anything less is shooting in the dark.

April 23, 1982


**COMPLAINT NO. 199**     (Filed Nov. 25, 1981)
ALBERT G. DANIELS
against
READER'S DIGEST


**Complaint:** Albert G. Daniels, a retired electrical engineer from Winnsboro, South Carolina, complained that he had not received a satisfactory answer from the *Reader's Digest* when he challenged facts in an article entitled "Nuclear Power in Perspective." He accused the *Digest* of "stonewalling."

The article appeared in the June, 1981, issue of the *Digest*. That was well over 90 days before Mr. Daniels' complaint to the News Council. However, Council staff waived the 90-day rule, because Mr. Daniels demonstrated that he had searched continuously for an appropriate forum to air his complaint. He learned of the News Council from Richard R. Cole, dean of the school of journalism at the University of North Carolina, on Nov. 22, 1981.

Mr. Daniels wrote to the *Digest* on May 20, 1981 challenging four assertions in the article by Ralph Kinney Bennett.

Receiving no answer, he followed up with another letter June 20, to which the *Digest* replied in part:

> We respect the opinions of those opposed to nuclear power and realize they can cite statistics to back up their claims. In our opinion, though, nuclear power is a vital U. S. energy source. That view is based on careful and extensive research. And, it seemed to us that with all the publicity those opposed to nuclear power have been receiving, the time had come to balance things: to bring to our readers' attention some of the positive aspects.

Mr. Daniels, who participated in the design of a nuclear power plant for South Carolina Electric and Gas Co., replied, "I am not an opponent of nuclear power. I am a proponent of the truth." He applauded the publication of such an article as Mr. Bennett's, but he charged that Mr. Bennett had made the four disputed assertions with no reference to supporting technical data.

"This would be all right if what he said agreed with known facts," Mr. Daniels wrote. "It does not. The public will believe it because it was published in *Reader's Digest*, a magazine held in high regard."

**The article and the challenge:** The *Digest* article set out to dispel what it called a fog of doubt and fear about nuclear generating plants. The writer promised facts "about some of the most misunderstood topics in the nuclear debate: plant safety, meltdowns, radiation and disposal of radioactive wastes."

The article concluded:

> Studies . . . have shown that those who understand nuclear power believe in it. They do not underestimate its risks. But they are able to see them in proportion to the greater risks to life and health—and to the economy—posed by other energy sources. In the end, the decision the American public makes on nuclear power will reflect whether we still have the technological faith in ourselves that has been the key to unparalleled progress.

The four assertions that Mr. Daniels challenged were:

1. "There are elaborate systems to control or completely stop the nuclear chain reaction."

Mr. Daniels wrote, "One of the most basic facts about nuclear power

. . . is that once nuclear action is started and the reactor has been in use generating power the nuclear reaction cannot be completely stopped."

2. "The top of the core at Three Mile Island was exposed intermittently for a total of about eight hours, but the heat reached only about 2,000 degrees Fahrenheit, far below meltdown temperature."

Mr. Daniels quoted from a Nuclear Regulatory Commission report (NUREG 0683) to the effect that the uncovering of the top of the core resulted in temperatures in the core in excess of 2,500 degrees, and in "possible melting and fusing together of various stainless steel parts on adjacent fuel assemblies."

Mr. Daniels also quoted from Mitchell Rogovin's "Three Mile Island—a Report to the Commissioners and to the Public" as follows: ". . . a portion of the core probably crumbled or slumped down badly."

3. "The accident at Three Mile Island came nowhere near such a catastrophe" (which Mr. Daniels interpreted to mean a core meltdown).

Mr. Daniels quoted from the Rogovin report, ". . . Three Mile Island came close to being the accident we had been told by many in the industry could not happen: a core meltdown." Also: ". . . our projections show that within 30 to 60 minutes a substantial amount of the reactor fuel would have begun to melt down."

4. "It had been assumed that meltdown would occur within a few minutes of such an exposure."

Mr. Daniels asked who made such an assumption. He said he had not found any reference to contradict his understanding that with the control rods fully inserted, as they were at Three Mile Island, it would have taken much longer than "a few minutes" for meltdown to occur.

**Response:** The News Council staff sent Mr. Daniels' complaint to the *Digest* on January 27. The *Digest* provided the Council—and Mr. Daniels—with an answer from Mr. Bennett on April 5. Edward T. Thompson, editor-in-chief of the *Digest*, apologized for the delay in responding; apparently there had been a mixup at the magazine.

Mr. Bennett answered Mr. Daniels' four challenges in essence as follows:

1. It is possible to stop a nuclear reaction. He cited three references to demonstrate that truth and to demonstrate that the insertion of the control rods did, in fact, stop the nuclear reaction at Three Mile Island.

2. Mr. Bennett insisted that his article specified only that the temperatures did not rise above 2,000 degrees in the exposed top of the core. He enclosed references to show that heat varies from one part of the fuel assembly to another. He also insisted that none of Mr. Daniels' references

indicated melting of the fuel itself.

3. Mr. Bennett said that Mr. Daniels made an incorrect assumption that the writer meant a core meltdown when he referred to "such a catastrophe." He didn't, he said. He referred to "a previously posited *combination* of circumstances involving the 'worst case' accident—complete core melt, breach of containment and meteorological conditions which would move the 'cloud' of radioactive material over populated areas without dispersing it."

4. Mr. Bennett conceded that the *Digest* could be faulted for saying it had been assumed that a meltdown would "occur" within a few minutes of exposure to the fuel core. The article should have said a meltdown would "start," Mr. Bennett said.

**Staff discussion:** Mr. Daniels challenged the *Digest*'s April 5 response with a new letter to Mr. Thompson, the editor. Mr. Daniels acknowleged that Mr. Bennett was technically correct that the chain reaction could be stopped, but he introduced another issue: He said the article should have noted that even after the reaction is stopped there is a danger from the heat generated by radioactive decay. Mr. Daniels also provided a new reference to bolster his contention that the heat had risen to close to or above meltdown temperatures in some parts of the fuel core at Three Mile Island.

Council staff came to the view that Mr. Daniels or any other serious, credentialed challenger ought to receive a response to factual questions. The *Digest* was remiss in not providing such a response to Mr. Daniels' first challenge. His pique is understandable at receiving a letter ignoring his questions and lumping him with opponents of nuclear power.

However, once the *Digest* did gear up to provide an answer, it provided a serious and detailed one, an answer that furnished Mr. Daniels with what he had asked for—the writer's sources.

It is clear from Mr. Daniels' new challenge on the question of the heat within the fuel core at Three Mile Island that all the information is not in yet on the Three Mile Island accident and that the "facts"—even though they involve concrete physical data—may not yet be subject to objective proof. That being the case, the *Digest* does not appear to have an obligation to continue the dispute with Mr. Daniels. The Council certainly has no obligation to continue as a mediator in such a dispute.

**Council finding:** It is understandable why Mr. Daniels suspected the *Reader's Digest* of "stonewalling"—refusing concrete answers to his concrete challenges of four factual assertions. First he recieved no answer at all to his challenge. Then, after the followup letter, he received a letter lumping him with the opponents of nuclear power and failing to answer his questions.

It would be impossible for news organizations to engage in personal dialogue with all the readers and viewers who want to argue. However, it is also true that publications and broadcasters ought to reply seriously to qualified challengers of factual assertions. Admittedly, it is sometimes difficult to distinguish the qualified challenger. That distinction may have been particularly difficult in this case, because Mr. Daniels printed his challenge by hand on plain paper and did not indicate that he was an engineer with experience assisting in the design of a nuclear power plant.

When a news organization fails to properly assess a letter writer as a serious challenger of the facts, the organization frequently replies with a bland, formula letter. Mr. Daniels, understandably annoyed at receiving such a letter, is to be commended for following through and finding a way to have his challenge treated seriously.

The *Digest*, too, performed commendably when, as a result of the Council complaint, it did take Mr. Daniels seriously. The magazine gave him precisely what he had asked for: the bases for the article's factual conclusions. Mr. Daniels' new challenge to one of those conclusions makes it clear that the "facts" remaining in dispute are not yet susceptible to objective proof. That being the case, the magazine does not seem to have an obligation to continue the dialogue

The *Digest*'s ultimate response was candid and full. Therefore, the complaint that the magazine was "stonewalling" is unfounded.

**Concurring:** Abel, Ayers, Benson, Brady, Hornby, Huston, Isaacs, Pulitzer, Scott, van den Haag and Williams.

April 22, 1982

**COMPLAINT NO. 200**    (Filed March 15, 1982)

LYLE M. NELSON

against

ABC NEWS "20/20"

**Complaint:** Lyle M. Nelson, professor of communications at Stanford University, complained that ABC News' "20/20" inaccurately portrayed a visiting Polish scholar "in a way that can have serious consequences for him and his career."

Professor Nelson complained on behalf of Marek Samotyj, a Fulbright scholar participating in Stanford's Professional Journalism Fellowship program. Mr. Samotyj was interviewed on a "20/20" segment March 4 entitled "A Target for Spies." The segment described the theft by the

368

Soviet Union of high technology equipment and knowledge, particularly from those microchip manufacturers clustered near Stanford in what has come to be called Silicon Valley.

Professor Nelson, who is director of the journalism fellowship program, complained that "20/20" did not warn Mr. Samotyj that the program was about espionage, and that the program left the impression that Mr. Samotyj himself might be a spy.

Specifically Professor Nelson complained that:

1. An interview was obtained with a visiting journalist, Mr. Samotyj, unsophisticated in the ways of U.S. television journalism, on an entirely false and unprofessional basis.

2. A short unrepresentative segment of approximately 10 seconds was taken out of a 20-minute interview and used on a totally different subject to give an impression directly contrary to that of the full interview itself.

In support of the complaint Mr. Samotyj himself wrote to Richard Wald, executive vice-president of ABC News:

> Your producers, and therefore your network, in effect used my face and my name to suggest that every educated man coming to the USA from Eastern Europe should be looked upon as a spy. The selection of 10 seconds of unrepresentative tape from a 20-minute interview, done here at Stanford, left the clear impression that I really could be a spy. Not only is this untrue, but it also is an impression clearly contrary to the material that was edited from the interview.
>
> From the outset I had many objections to the interview because it is not prudent for me to be interviewed by American TV when martial law exists in Poland. Even American journalists, and especially executives such as yourself, must be aware of the political conditions of martial law and its consequences. I realized that anything I said might be used against me upon my return to Poland. I am editor-in-chief of "Przeglad Techniczny", one of the most respected weekly magazines in Poland and my interview therefore could not be a private matter. I explicitly said this to Mr. John Stossel and Mr. Eric Tait, but they informed me that they wanted to interview me about scholarly exchanges. I agreed on that precise condition. *In essence, they used false pretenses to get my interview.*
>
> In the 20-minute interview, we discussed my professional skills, scholarly issues and interests, experiences that I have had during my stay in the USA. However, the person responsible for the final editing took only the last question from the interview which was such a stupid one that I couldn't answer it adequately. In Poland we have a saying: "It's not your fault somebody asks you a stupid question."

**The program:** The program was heralded in newspaper advertisements as "A Spy Story." The ads displayed a hammer and sickle on a field of stars and stripes and read:

> Soviet intelligence agents are now concentrating on America's last bastion of

superiority—high technology. Their methods: Theft. Blackmail. Bribery. And they're even being helped by some naive Americans. John Stossel reports.

The first word in the introduction to the segment was "espionage." The message of the introduction was that this was a story about a new kind of Soviet spy who was "stealing science," "and plenty of it."

The bulk of the segment dealt with the theft of both high-technology equipment and information from the microchip manufacturers of Silicon Valley. The seriousness of the threat was underlined by John Shea, a Defense Department spokesman, who said:

> The only way we're going to, candidly, whip the Soviet Union is by technology. They out-man us, out-plan us, out-gun us, out-ship us, out-submarine us.

The part of the program in which Mr. Samotyj appeared was introduced by a defected Soviet agent named Sakharov who said the Soviets lacked the know-how to put the blueprints and the devices they were stealing to productive use. It was to gain that know-how that Soviet students, engineers and scientists were studying in this country, according to Shea. John Stossel, the ABC correspondent, then says in a voice-over as Mr. Samotyj appears on the screen:

> To do that, their scientists need to learn the latest technology, and some people say we're teaching it to them, by letting them attend American universities. And it's true—visit engineering seminars here at Stanford on the edge of Silicon Valley, and you find many students from communist countries. Some people say they shouldn't be allowed to study here.

Mr. Samotyj says, "But why, I—"

Mr. Stossel answers, "Maybe you're a spy." And the following exchange occurs:

> SAMOTYJ: Of course, I decided to take engineering courses, not on the political science, or education, or Asian-African studies, no. Only engineering, and—
> STOSSEL: Makes one think, maybe you're a spy.
> SAMOTYJ: And—yeah, and after our talking I ought to be expelled from the USA, yeah? Because I cannot answer your question. I repeat this once again, I can't prove that I am not a spy.
> STOSSEL: But are you a spy?
> SAMOTYJ: No, I am not. I am a Fulbright scholar.

The frame is frozen on Mr. Samotyj's last words and immediately, with no separation, Mr. Shea appears on the screen saying:

> They are absorbing the very technology that we've talked about, and they will return to their countries, and they will be put to work on government military projects.

370

The program concludes with an interview with Professor Bernard Roth of Stanford who scoffs at the idea that significant advantage can accrue to the Soviets through academic interchange. Then in his last words to announcer Hugh Downs, Mr. Stossel says, "Our society is open and we like it that way. It's one of our freedoms."

**Response:** George Watson, vice-president of ABC News, sent two letters to Professor Nelson in response to his complaint. In the first, March 11, Mr. Watson noted as background to the "20/20" report that students of high technology from communist nations are in fact being accused of spying "and it may be reasonable to assume that some in fact are either active or passive conduits of sensitive information to their home countries." He noted that there is a growing body of opinion, expressed in this case by John Shea, that these students should be barred from U.S. colleges and universities or at least severely restricted in their studies. He continued:

> The representative man in the middle of this issue was Marek Samotyj. I thought he quite effectively and engagingly made the point that he could not prove a negative, i.e., that he was not a spy, at the same time he strongly denied being one. The interview was conducted in a sympathetic, not accusatory, manner. It even had elements of humor. The interview no more implied that he was in fact a spy than did the earlier sequence of patrons of a Silicon Valley bar imply they were engaged in treason.
>
> If the point needed further clarity, it was provided by the interview which ended the report in which Professor Bernard Roth criticized efforts to restrict the free flow of ideas. This was further emphasized by John Stossel talking with Hugh Downs in the studio after the report had concluded, "Our society is open and we like it that way. It's one of our freedoms."

In a second letter April 7 Mr. Watson replied specifically to Prof. Nelson's charge that the interview was obtained by deception. He wrote:

> That is simply not so. The producer of the report, Eric Tait, set up the taping at Stanford. He explained to three officials of the university and to Mr. Samotyj that the thrust of the report was the transfer of high technology information to communist nations, efforts of the Reagan Administration to crack down on this transfer and how those efforts were affecting the academic and scientific communities. This was explained to Lee Ziegler of the International Center, Bob Beyers, director of the university News Service, and Harry Press, the manager of the Stanford Professional Journalism Fellowships.
>
> In fact, Mr. Press suggested that we might interview Mr. Samotyj and made the first contact with him on our behalf. Before taping the interview, Mr. Tait also explained to Mr. Samotyj what the interview was to be about. Mr. Samotyj did say that he needed to be careful of commenting on the present political situation in Poland. Mr. Tait and John Stossel, the correspondent, assured him that there would

be no questions about the political situation in Poland. There were none. The interview was conducted in a friendly fashion. Mr. Samotyj raised no objections to it before, during or after the taping. Afterward, he signed a release giving us rights to the material.

As for the charge that the interview was unfairly edited, Mr. Watson wrote:

> You claim that "a short unrepresentative segment of approximately ten seconds was taken out of a twenty-minute interview and used on a totally different subject to give an impression directly contrary to the interview itself." This is quite untrue. The entire fifteen-minute interview consists of questions and answers relating to the subject of spying and espionage. Mr. Stossel's first substantive question was, "You know some people say that you should not be allowed to study in this country. You're from a communist country. You should not be allowed to be here." Mr. Samotyj's response was, "But why?" Mr. Stossel replied, "Maybe you're a spy." No other subject was discussed. The edited excerpt of about fifty seconds used in the report was an accurate reflection of the views expressed by Mr. Samotyj.

Mr. Watson enclosed a transcript of the interview to demonstrate that the entire interview that was actually taped did deal with questions about Mr. Samotyj as a possible spy.

**Staff discussion:** This complaint separates into three issues: (1) Whether Mr. Samotyj was fairly warned that the "20/20" segment was going to be about the theft of high technology; (2) whether the interview was conducted and edited unfairly, and (3) whether the segment left the impression that Mr. Samotyj might well be a spy.

### Fair Warning?

The ABC producer, Eric V. Tait, Jr., himself a former fellow in the professional journalism program, contacted Harry Press, managing director of the program and associate editor of the Stanford News Service on Januray 21 or 22. Mr. Tait said later in a memo to George Watson that he informed Mr. Press that the "20/20" segment "was about high technology transfer and the government's attempted crackdown on the flow of hardware and ideas to Soviet bloc countries." Mr. Tait said that Mr. Press responded with the suggestion that he speak to Robert Beyers, director of the Stanford News Service, "about the controversies on visiting Soviet scientists that Stanford and other universities had been and then were embroiled in with the Reagan administration."

Mr. Press' memory of the conversation, as contained in his Memo for the Record dated April 6, is "that Eric told me just two things:"

> "20/20" wanted to look at the theft of material from Silicon Valley and its

transmittal overseas; and (2) visiting scholars, a topic brought up because of the current proposed visit of a Russian robotics expert, and what such scholarly exchange means and its value.

Did I suggest Eric Tait contact Marek? Yes, I did, because of No. 2 above, and because during Eric's PJF year there was a Polish journalist here, I thought here was a logical contact. I also am quite sure I suggested he talk with Lee Ziegler at the international center, to find other visiting scholars. (He was interested in Eastern European scholars.) Eric never mentioned the word "spy" or "spying" to me.

Next (before January 26) Mr. Tait contacted Mr. Beyers, who did—as Mr. Tait reports that Mr. Press said he would—background him on the academic freedom issue as it applied to visiting scholars from communist and Soviet bloc countries—"from troubles a visiting Republic of China scholar had at Cornell University in November of 1980 right up to the controversy over a Soviet disarmament specialist not being allowed entry to lecture at Stanford in January of this year, as well as the restrictions on freedom of access and movement the Administration was trying to impose on the visit of a Soviet expert in walking machines who was expected in March of this year."

Mr. Tait also gave Mr. Beyers the working title of the "20/20" segment, which was "Spies in Silicon Valley." Mr. Beyers suggested that Mr. Tait contact a number of people to discuss the academic freedom issue, two of whom Mr. Tait did interview. One of those was Prof. Roth.

There is no question that Mr. Beyers understood the nature of the proposed segment. That raises the question: Is it possible then that Mr. Samotyj was not warned? Some suggestion of the answer comes in comments from Mr. Beyers to Norman Isaacs, chairman of the News Council:

> Unlike many public information offices, we encourage direct contact between news media and sources in the interest of speed, clarity and openness. We do not go through a lot of layered communication and heavy controls, such as sitting in on interviews. We assume the best, and only occasionally are discouraged as a result.

Mr. Tait called Lee Ziegler, director of the Bechtel International Center, at the suggestion of Mr. Beyers. Again, Mr. Tait said, he explained the thrust of the proposed report: "High technology transfer and the government's attempt to stop the flow of high-tech hardware and ideas to the Soviet bloc, and the academic freedom—free flow of ideas issue. I told him I'd like to interview students from Soviet bloc countries on that subject."

Mr. Ziegler's understanding of the nature of the report is indicated in his later comments to Mr. Isaacs. Of the subject of the piece he said,

"This, of course, was readily understandable to me in the light of all the difficulties arising out of the new thrust to restrict visiting scholars."

Mr. Ziegler recommended Mr. Tait to Professor Roth.

On January 28 or 29 Mr. Tait called Professor Roth, who had been suggested by Mr. Beyers and Mr. Ziegler because he was involved in the controversy over the visit of the Soviet expert (Professor Umzov) on walking machines. Mr. Tait learned from Professor Roth that he had a mechanical engineering seminar with students from Soviet bloc and other communist countries. He said, "It seemed a natural microcosmic setting that could well illustrate how the exchange of ideas could be seen by the Administration as flowing from the U.S. academic community to the benefit of the Soviet bloc."

Professor Roth clearly understood the nature of the program as indicated in comments to Mr. Isaacs. He wrote:

> When I was called, Mr. Tait or Mr. Peterson (Ray Peterson, associate producer)—I'm not sure which—said they understood I had a class with a lot of foreign students. They wanted to come over and film the class on the idea of technology transfer. In light of all the discussions about Umzov and the business of visiting scholars, my filter translated this to the idea of technology leakage . . . .
>
> On their arrival, Mr. Stossel told me there was great concern in Silicon Valley about letting Russians into the United States and I told him my position. He wanted to interview students from Eastern Europe. I said I would have to get the class's permission. They were willing. Stossel picked out only those from Eastern European countries and the questioning ran along the lines of, "Where do you come from?" . . . That's a communist country, isn't it?" . . ."You know that a lot of people say you should (not) be permitted to come here?" . . . "Are you aware of the worry over scholars stealing secrets?"
>
> My students looked at him in surprise. A couple of them said, "What is there to steal here?"

On January 29 Mr. Tait said he called Mr. Press to thank him for his help and to tell him when he could arrive at Stanford. It was then that Mr. Press suggested Mr. Samotyj as an interview subject. Mr. Tait recalled, "I thanked him and said that if I could not get any others, I'd be very interested in his checking with Samotyj on whether or not he would be willing to sit for an interview with us on the high-tech transfer/academic freedom issue."

When the crew arrived in Palo Alto, Mr. Peterson called Mr. Press to say that they would like to talk with Mr. Samotyj. When Mr. Peterson subsequently made phone contact with Mr. Samotyj, he was expecting the call.

It seems clear from this reconstruction of the contacts leading up to the

374

interview with Mr. Samotyj that the only faculty member to contact Mr. Samotyj was Mr. Press. It also seems clear from Mr. Press's memo, that he did not have the sense that the segment was going to be about spying. Therefore, he would not have alerted Mr. Samotyj to that possibility.

Mr. Samotyj himself recalls only that Mr. Press told him that Mr. Tait was a former program fellow; was in the area to do a "20/20" segment; was interested in putting Mr. Samotyj into the segment but that it was up to Mr. Samotyj. The other three faculty members who might have had an understanding of the nature of the program and of the possible danger to Mr. Samotyj—or to any other Soviet bloc scholar who might be interviewed—did not put out a warning to Soviet bloc students in general or to Mr. Samotyj in particular.

The last opportunity for Mr. Samotyj to have learned that the interview and the report itself was to concentrate on espionage was in the pre-interview discussion with the "20/20" crew. The reports of that crew and of Mr. Samotyj on that discussion are in conflict.

Much of the indignation from Mr. Samotyj's colleagues and professors focuses on their view that the ABC team did not tell people at Stanford that the program was going to be about spying. In his recounting of those contacts Mr. Tait says again and again that he told people the program was about "high-technology transfer and the government's attempt to stop the flow of high-tech hardware and ideas to the Soviet bloc, and the academic freedom—free flow of ideas issue." Whether that phraseology translated or should have translated into espionage and spying for American speakers of English, it apparently did not for Mr. Samotyj. The clarity of the promotion ads for the broadcast and of the opening language is in stark contrast to the language used by the producer in the preliminary arranging. The question arises whether the ABC crew ought to have used language equally clear in setting up the interviews with people in the precarious position of Mr. Samotyj and the other Soviet bloc and communist subjects they interviewed.

Mr. Watson noted to Council staff that the producer did not intend to be deceitful on the subject; if he had, he would not have given the working title of the program to the university official who might normally be expected to be in touch with people on the campus who were interview subjects.

### The Interview

Mr. Samotyj told Mr. Isaacs that he received a call from Mr. Tait (undoubtedly Mr. Peterson) the day of the interview. The caller said he was interested in Mr. Samotyj because he was a Fulbright scholar and he wanted to interview him on scholarly exchanges.

Mr. Samotyj said that when he arrived for the interview, Mr. Stossel (This may have been Mr. Tait) first asked if Mr. Samotyj was aware that there was discussion that perhaps the best way to protect American high technology was to bar all foreigners from such scholarly programs. Mr. Samotyj said he was aware. He said the questioner then asked if he was willing to discuss high-tech. Mr. Samotyj reports that he said no, that because of martial law in Poland, he would have to get an advance clearance for any such interview on American television. He said, "I told him I didn't want to make any comment on this subject."

Mr. Samotyj said he and Mr. Stossel then agreed on a limited interview to include his name, his background, what he was doing at Stanford, what courses he was studying and why he had chosen Stanford instead of another university. In answer to a question about his background, Mr. Samotyj said he explained that he was editor-in-chief of *Technical Review*, the weekly magazine of the Polish Federation of Engineering Associations. He said he told Mr. Stossel that he was taking courses in operational research (the analysis of energy news); energy and economic systems; economy and the environment; and all the courses in energy that he could take. In addition, he said, he had attended some seminars on politics and Eastern European cultures.

He said he was asked if any professor had monitored his class attendance (No); if Stanford was open enough for foreign students (yes). Mr. Samotyj recalls saying, "very open without any restrictions."

Mr. Samotyj told Mr. Isaacs that he recalls Mr. Stossel asking why, as a journalist, he had not taken courses in humanities. He recalled his answer as "Because this is not my field. I am an engineering specialist. I took some journalism courses to improve my writing skills. I wrote a book on Three Mile Island. My goal here is to improve my technical knowledge and my professional skills."

He said that Mr. Stossel then asked if it was not required that he take some humanities courses. He said he answered, "I don't know. If I am supposed to, then I am not doing what I am supposed to be doing and should be expelled from the university."

Then, said Mr. Samotyj, came the question, "Are you a spy?" He told Mr. Isaacs the question was like a thunderbolt to him. "I never expected such a question. Everybody knows who I am and what my record is. This was the first time I had ever heard that they had espionage on their mind. If

376

there had been any word about espionage, I would have said, 'No, I can't talk with you.'"

The memory of the ABC crew differs significantly, as evidenced by this portion of the transcript of an interview by Mr. Watson of the crew members:

JOHN STOSSEL: Yes, we were preparing for a sit down interview, but he was standing up talking to Eric and seemed nervous and a little bit. . . . I didn't know for sure whether he was going to do anything. He was asking Eric questions about it and Eric talked to him for a while. I don't know exactly what Eric said because after the introduction I wandered off. And I came in later and just said, "Look, there are people in this country who feel that people like you, exchange students, from communist bloc countries shouldn't be allowed to be here and we just interviewed a guy who said that, because you might take things you learn here and use them against us back in your own country. And there're people who say people like you shouldn't be allowed to stay here. Now, this is your chance to present another point of view. I mean, I personally happen to agree that there should be an open exchange and, and this is what we want to ask you about, this conflict."

GEORGE WATSON: I see. When you say that during the set up you wandered off and Eric was talking to him and you said something, that you weren't absolutely certain that he would do the interview. Why was that?

JOHN STOSSEL: He came in and he was shy and nervous, like what's this about. Sometimes people walk in and they sit right down in front of the lights and he wanted to hear what it was about first. And, so, while Eric talked to him I was going around trying to find other East bloc people who would also be interviewed. He was just one of several we did.

GEORGE WATSON: What did he say to you, Eric, that expressed his concern or his nervousness?

ERIC TAIT: Well, basically it was just before, if I remember correctly, just before we actually got into the actual interview, he did say he was a little nervous about doing the interview. He was already seated, you know, in the position where we would be doing the interview. Because of the political situation in Poland, he said, you know, "I have to be very careful," and, and I reassured him. I said, "I understand, I know the martial law situation makes it difficult but, the particular purpose of this interview does not even discuss the current political crisis in Poland and as such we won't even raise any such question in the course of this interview." And he seemed reassured by that answer. I know John in effect also reassured him we would not be dealing on that subject.

GEORGE WATSON: And was that the, did he raise any other concerns?

ERIC TAIT: Not to my recollection. That was the only concern that I heard him say.

GEORGE WATSON: Did he indicate any unwillingness to talk about the transfer of technology from this country to the communist bloc or Poland or to any other country?

ERIC TAIT: Not to me. He knew that was the specific purpose of the interview. He was willing to discuss that particular subject with us.

GEORGE WATSON: Did he raise any concern or reservation about that with you, John?

JOHN STOSSEL: No, I don't recall him making any specific concerns at all.

GEORGE WATSON: Did he do that with you, Ray?

RAY PETERSON: Not to my recollection. Except during the course of the interview he did seem a little concerned about what he was being asked.

GEORGE WATSON: But that is reflected in the transcript?

RAY PETERSON: That is reflected in the transcript.

The ABC crew members said the preliminary talk with Mr. Samotyj took about 10 minutes. After the interview they said they spent another 15 minutes with Mr. Samotyj. During that time Mr. Samotyj signed the release permitting ABC to use the interview, and Mr. Tait asked him if he knew anyone else who might want to be interviewed. Mr. Tait told Mr. Watson:

> And he said he had a friend who was either Polish or Russian who he thought might, and he went to the phone book and we spent a good 10 minutes trying to locate this person and then establishing that we would call him back or we would leave our number with him and he would, for tomorrow, try to find this guy to talk to us. And he was cheerful and happy to cooperate and offering to provide another person. Later on, apparently that persons elected not to do it, but we did again talk to Marek, the next day, and he was still, raised no objections about the interview, he just apologized that this other guy was unavailable.

Given his insistence that he would not have consented to an interview on high technology transfer, one wonders why Mr. Samotyj did not walk out of the interview or at least refuse to sign the waiver when the question of spying was introduced. Some insight into the answer may come from these comments by Mr. Samotyj to Mr. Isaacs.

> At the time they asked the question it seemed to me so far from anything that I was sure they would not use this on the air. It has no point. Energy is not a high-technology transfer. It is a basic economic course.

Mr. Samotyj also said,

> Transfer of technical information is going on all the time. The word doesn't mean espionage. I am not involved in high technology. I can't comment on any U.S. government decisions. I know nothing about Silicon Valley. I have never been there.

Mr. Samotyj's comment that he cannot comment on U.S Government decisions is the closest thing to common ground between his memory and the ABC crew's memory of what was ruled off limits for the interview. By their lights the ABC crew was probably not violating that agreement by asking Mr. Samotyj if he were a spy.

The complainant and Mr. Samotyj insist that the spy portion of the interview was a hooker thrown in at the last minute. ABC demonstrates that that is not so, at least as far as the recorded interview is concerned. The transcript of the recorded interview starts with Mr. Stossel saying, "You know some people say that you should not be allowed to study in this country. You're from a communist country. You should not be allowed to be here." That prompts the response from Mr. Samotyj, "But why? I—"

ABC furnished the transcript of the interview from a cassette labeled "Side B," and, at the request of the Council, then furnished a transcript of Side A of the same cassette to show that the previous material was from other interviews.

It is not inconceivable that Mr. Samotyj thought he was on camera before he actually was, but there is no question but that from the point when the camera started, the interview was about whether or not he was a spy.

Council staff asked Mr. Watson if Mr. Stossel had asked the spy question of other communist students. Mr. Watson read from transcripts of unused interview tapes with a Jugoslavian and a Chinese student. The questions were essentially the same.

### The Impression

While so much of the concern about the "20/20" segment is directed at whether Mr. Samotyj was given fair warning that the segment was about spies; and while much of the concern centers on the editing of the interview; a third element may have done more to label Mr. Samotyj as a possible spy. That element was the freezing on Mr. Samotyj's last statement ("No, I am a Fulbright scholar.") and the immediate juxtaposition without any intervening material of Mr. Shea's statement, "They are absorbing the very technology we've talked about.. . . ." There can be no doubt that Mr. Shea's "they" includes Mr. Samotyj.

It is ironic that Mr. Tait chose to freeze on Mr. Samotyj's Fulbright statement in order to enhance his credibility. He said in a letter responding to a protest from Mr. Press:

> As I indicated over the phone, Marek was my counterweight to John Shea's "Don't let any of them in" philosophy. I personally elected to identify him as a Polish "exchange student" for two reasons: First, I felt it would not have reflected well on him to be identified as a Polish journalism student and then have him say on camera that he was taking a great many engineering courses. That would just tend to reinforce the idea that he was here simply to get as much of our technology as possible (to the possible advantage of a Soviet bloc country). Secondly, I wanted the

strong emphatic declaration of Samotyj that No, he was NOT a spy, but a Fulbright scholar, to be as forcefully telling, as surprising to the viewer, as it was to us when we recorded the interview. I believe it was. I also emphasized the point that by freezing the video at that precise instant. (Although I knew Marek was in the professional journalism program, I was unaware it had been arranged via the Fulbright route.) But I was more than happy to hear him say that, knowing the instant recognizability and high degree of acceptability accorded Fulbright scholars by the general public.

I agree with you that the fact of Marek being immediately followed by John Shea's charges that he and other foreign students were all spies stealing our technology, may have lessened Marek's credibility in the eyes of some viewers, but it is my firm belief that the majority of viewers believed Marek to be just what he said he was, a Fulbright scholar, hard to prove himself not a spy, but nonetheless, not a spy. We who did that interview believed him, and I'm convinced that the bulk of the viewers believed him also.

In his Memo for the Record, Mr. Press quotes George Watson of ABC as saying to him in a phone call that it was not ABC's intention to imply that Samotyj was a spy, but that he could understand how that impression might have been left.

It is dangerous for producers or editors or viewers to speculate on how "most people" are going to interpret a device either in print or broadcast journalism. However, in this case one small indication of how an objective viewer interpreted the program in which Samotyj was interviewed came from a viewer in Pennsylvania. As part of its efforts to be accountable, ABC News has started showing segments of "20/20" to selected groups throughout the United States and asking for comment from the group. This "20/20" segment was screened for a PTA group in Pottstown, PA.

Robert Hoffman, of the Pottstown PTA said, "The thing that concerned me about the . . . piece was when the interviews were done with the students, it made it seem—and while that information is in the universities and is given out rather freely—I was concerned that it made it seem as if each foreign student was then a spy."

Finally, it was basic to the concern of his colleagues and professors that Samotyj has been endangered by his appearance on the ABC program. He told Mr. Isaacs:

I face a lot of problems when I return. The consulate called me right after the program and said that I had violated the martial law rules—that I had been told I could not be interviewed by American journalists. I will not have a job in journalism on my return. I will not be able to teach. I may go into work as an electrical engineer some place if there is anything open. It is also bad for the Fulbright program. It will be badly damaged in Eastern Europe. I am in trouble.

Since his violation of the martial law rules seems to have been that he was interviewed at all, one wonders why Mr. Samotyj consented to appear on the program whether or not he knew its nature. His answer, according to Mr. Isaacs, is that he believes in free academic exchange. He though that an interview on simply the exchange of scholars might help the cause of free exchange and might not be offensive to Polish officials.

**Council finding:** The News Council dealt with the complaint in four parts.

One—Professor Nelson charged that "20/20" obtained an interview with a foreign journalist who was unsophisticated in the ways of American television journalism "on an entirely false and unprofessional basis."

The Council decided not to address itself to this part of the complaint because, in its view, it was Mr. Samotyj's word against ABC's on what he was told would be the subject of the interview before the interview, and there was no objective data on which to base a judgment.

**Concurring:** Brady, Huston, Pulitzer, van den Haag and Williams.

**Dissenting:** Ayers, Benson and Hornby.

**Dissenting opinion by Hornby (Ayers and Benson concurring):** The Council chose not to address the method by which ABC arranged the interview with Samotyj. We believe that ABC did not properly and widely enough emphasize that its program content was to center on espionage, and that Samotyj and Stanford officials were led to the interview by false pretense.

Two—The complainant charged that a short unrepresentative segment was taken out of an interview and used to give an impression contrary to the full interview.

That does not seem to be true. Because he is unfamiliar with television, Mr. Samotyj thought that his preliminary discussion was part of the interview. But ABC News has presented convincing evidence that the full recorded interview was about spying, and the portion used—while it suffered from too tight editing—was not a distortion of what Mr. Samotyj said. The Council notes that portions of quotes are spliced together from different parts of the interview so as to appear to be one continuous quote. While the resultant quote is not a distortion in this case, the example shows how easy it would be to distort a quote, and the Council deplores the use of this splicing technique. Nonetheless, this portion of the complaint is found unwarranted.

**Concurring:** Ayers, Benson, Brady, Hornby, Huston, Pulitzer, van den Haag and Williams.

Three—the complaint charges that the "20/20" report left the impression that Mr. Samotyj might be a spy. No matter how vigorously the producer and the network argue that it did not intend to leave that impression, the juxtaposition of Mr. Samotyj's denial that he is a spy with John Shea's charge that all Soviet bloc students are spies clearly encompassed Mr. Samotyj in an accusation by a consultant to the Defense Department. The Council finds that this juxtaposition unfairly raised suspicion about Mr. Samotyj. This portion of the complaint is found warranted.

**Concurring:** Ayers, Benson, Hornby, Huston and Pulitzer.

**Dissenting:** Brady, van den Haag and Williams.

**Dissenting opinion by van den Haag (Brady concurring):** We do not find warranted the Council's acceptance of the charge of unfairness against the "20/20" program of ABC based on the interviewer asking the Polish Fulbright scholar "Are you a spy?" and the subsequent suggestion "Maybe you are a spy."

This section of the program was preceded by a section dealing with convicted Societ bloc spies. Samotyj, a journalist, freely admitted taking many engineering courses, but denied being a spy. Samotyj never was charged with any unlawful act and there is not reason to believe that he committed any.

However, in addition to its now legalistic meaning "spy" has a wider connotation referring to someone who means to acquire information which others would prefer to deny him (a fashion house may send a "spy" to a competitor's show. I may send a "spy" to someone's kitchen to learn a recipe).

Now, there is no law against Eastern European, or for that matter Soviet students, taking courses in advanced engineering at American universities, thereby acquiring American technological knowledge. Yet, it may be in the American interest to prevent that acquisition by appropriate laws and practices. Those who favor such preventative practices may well refer to Soviet bloc students who utilize the absence of legal prohibitions and legally acquire American technology as "spies."

I find nothing unfair in the charge and in the opportunity given the student to deny it. The context made it clear that he was not being charged with unlawful behavior. He has a right to enroll in any course of study he wishes. But the interviewer on the TV program for which he volunteered has a right to suggest that his purpose is to spy—to acquire and transfer technological knowledge that may not be in the American interest to have transferred to the Soviet bloc.

**Dissenting opinion by Williams:** Mr. Samotyj is a big boy. He is a journalist, and after having responded to all of the questions asked him he freely signed a release. He must be responsible for his own actions.

Four—Reporters do from time to time inject an unexpected and offensive question into an interview, a technique called sandbagging. The impact of sandbagging is not so great on the subject of a report in the print press; the interviewee can refuse to answer, and the most the print reporter can do is to report that refusal. The television camera changes the dynamics and presents a different danger to the interviewee. He or she is in full view of the audience as the sandbagging question is asked. His or her refusal or difficulty in answering can have more impact on the broadcast audience than the print report. That fact calls for greater sensitivity on the part of television. The requisite sensitivity was not exhibited by "20/20" in this instance. The Council asks the staff to make a deeper examination of television's use of this confrontational technique for consideration by the Council

**Concurring:** Ayers, Benson, Brady, Hornby, Huston, Pulitzer, van den Haag and Williams.

**Abstaining:** Abel and Isaacs abstained from all discussion and votes on the complaint by Professor Nelson because of their connections with Stanford University's Department of Communication. Scott abstained from the discussion and votes because of his connection with Satellite NewsChannels, a joint venture of ABC and the Westinghouse Broadcasting Company.

**Note:** Ayers asked that the record state clearly that he participated in the complaint although he is a member of the Board of Foreign Scholarships which supervises the Fulbright Scholarships.

April 23, 1982

**COMPLAINT NO. 201**      (Filed March 22, 1982)
PUBLIC AFFAIRS COUNCIL
against
CBS NEWS

**Complaint:** Richard A. Armstrong, president of the Public Affairs Council, complained that a series on political action committees by Bill Moyers, on the CBS Evening News "smacked of intellectual dishonesty," and was "a disservice to the truth." The series was broadcast on five consecutive evenings, February 22 through 26.

The Public Affairs Council describes itself as "a non-profit nonpartisan, professional organization of corporate public affairs executives." It is headquartered in Washington, DC.

Mr. Armstrong wrote to CBS News as follows:

1) It would appear that Mr. Moyers has bought the Common Cause line on PACs. Fred Wertheimer (president of Common Cause) appeared four or five times during the series, and the Common Cause philosophy was woven in and out of the reports.

This is not to suggest that the Common Cause arguments should not be heard. It is a responsible organization and represents a particular point of view.

What was *not* said, at any time, was that Common Cause has it own agenda—hidden only by CBS—for Common Cause itself is quite outspoken in citing its goal: public finance for all congressional elections. How can it get members of the public (and their representatives) to accept it? By attacking the current system, as CBS has done. If PACs were abolished tomorrow, Common Cause would zero in on individual contributors.

I feel that it was dishonest *not* to report *why* Common Cause feels the way it does—and not to report that it spends hundreds of thousands annually to expound its position.

2) All PACs were referred to and discussed in pejorative terms in the CBS reports. A PAC is a political committee—no more, no less. It is a group whose members voluntarily decide to pool their giving to support a cause—an institution like labor or business—an issue—or even a hobby. But why must all be referred to as evil and sinister?

3) The second segment on February 23 was particularly odious. We see the Eckhardt/Fields race discussed in terms of dollars—$173,000 to $297,000—Eckhardt's from labor, Field's from business and oil. (Why business *and* oil? Sounds more sinister, right?) No one mentioned that as an incumbent, Bob Eckhardt had a staff of 20 (paid by the taxpayer), the franking privilege, free WATS lines, generous travel allowances, an office and probably an office van in his district. (The value of all these perks is at least $300,000, or 5-1 in Nick the Greek terms). This is why so many thoughtful people oppose public finance. Public finance virtually guarantees an incumbent re-election, unless he or she is opposed by a wealthy person.

Why then wasn't Eckhardt re-elected? The real question is how he held on so long. Any 14-year-old in Houston can tell you he was out of sync with his district. (Look up his voting record).

Ironically, when it comes to Field's election in 1982, you tell us a little, not much, about the powers of incumbency.

4) Why couldn't some of the positive aspects of PACs have been mentioned? More individuals are giving to the political process (through PACs) than ever before. Is this all bad? I think not.

Most people feel helpless because the small amount they can or care to give to the political process represents only a drop in the bucket. By pooling their money with others of similar interests, however, they *can* make their dollars more effective.

The average individual contribution to a business PAC in 1980 was less than $80. Half of the donations were under $50 each. Why was there no mention of these statistics?

Only a little over 20% of the total costs of the congressional election came from

PACs. Where did the rest come from? It came from *individuals* (including a small chunk from parties—which had come from individuals earlier).

Can you honestly say—or believe—that a contribution from a group of people has a more deleterious effect on the system than a fat sum from Mr. Gotrocks? *Few members of Congress would!*

We know that people who give to a corporate PAC are more apt to take an interest in the election—and more apt to vote. This is a highly positive fact. Why couldn't it have been mentioned?

5) There are some genuine authorities on the subject of political finance: Herb Alexander of the University of Southern California; Alexander Heard, former Chancellor of Vanderbilt University; FEC Commissioners, etc. Where were they? Where were Congressmen Bill Frenzel and others who worked so hard on the legislation enabling PACs? Were they too impartial for Mr. Moyers' purposes?

6) Business PACs got kicked around all last week on CBS Evening News. Fairness cries out for objectivity—and rebuttal.

Mr. Armstrong closed by saying that "Everything CBS said was true. But by telling only part of the story, CBS did grave damage to the truth. . . ."

**Response:** CBS News provided the Council with a copy of its response to the complaint and transcripts of the five CBS Evening News segments. The response, by Van Gordon Sauter, president of CBS News, read as follows:

1) You say that Moyers "bought the Common Cause line on PACs" and that we were dishonest because we did not report that Common Cause favors public financing for all Congressional elections.

Quite frankly, you are asking to have it both ways. On the one hand, you are accusing us of somehow espousing the Common Cause objective by virtue of the very fact that we did not—intentionally—refer to that objective at all in the series. On the other hand, had we done so you no doubt would have been just as quick to accuse us of advancing their cause by referring to it.

The fact of the matter is that when it came to alternatives to PACs, the only voices heard were those of Congressmen who believe the alternative is not public financing for Congressional elections but a limit on the money politicians accept from PACs. So far from advancing the Common Cause position, we gave time for an entirely different one and one which is antithetical to the Common Cause stand.

2) We disagree most forcefully with your statement that "PAC is a political committee—no more, no less." That, in our view, is a disingenuous position. If that's all a PAC is, how do you explain the effect of contributions on specific pieces of legislation? We made many such connnections between the relationship of PACs to the action of Congressional committees, and no one—yourself included—has come forward to refute the connection. It is clear to anyone who looks at PACs in a disinterested fashion that they have clout far beyond what such a simplistic assertion as yours would have us believe. No one called PACs "evil and sinister," as you mistakenly allege, but we did say they are changing the political system, and behind that conclusion is the support of one significant study after another by some of this country's most respected political scientists.

3) You simply failed to hear what was said in the second segment on February 23. We called the Eckhardt/Fields race "a showdown of PAC," and made no suggestion whatsoever that one group of PACs was better or worse than the other. And you raise another red herring: the piece was not about the advantages of incumbency but about the role of PACs. Had we chosen to do a segment on incumbency, we could easily have explored why so many PACs back one candidate in a race, then immediately switch to the opponent if he or she wins. If they were indeed merely "a political committee—no more, no less," one would think that having discharged their civic obligation to participate in an election, that would be that. But you know as well as we do that they switch allegiance so casually because it is access they are trying to buy with the incumbent.

4) We did not go into the argument that PACs are "a group whose members voluntarily decide to pool their giving to support a cause" because, as you also know, it is more complicated than you make it. In some cases there is a lot of pressure on employees to contribute, and in most cases a small committee of executives decide to whom the contributions are made. But that's a story for another day, to which we no doubt will return.

5) As for saying "that a contribution from a small group of people has a more deleterious effect on the system than a fat sum from Mr. Gotrocks," we didn't make such a statement. You're putting words in our mouths. We made no comparison with individual contributions. We just talked about the impact of PACs on the system, not the impact of anyone else. I note your assertion, however, that "few Members of Congress" think that PACs are not (sic) having a deleterious effect on the system, and I beg to disagree. The House of Representatives even passed legislation limiting contributions Members can accept from PACs, which suggests anything but indifference; the Senate, as we said, refused to go along, under the heavy influence of pressure from PACs.

Quite frankly, I have to state that what you have accused us of doing is not what we did. If you have forgotten what we did, I enclose the transcript of the final report which quotes Members of Congress talking about the effects PACs are having on politics and quotes Mr. Moyers' commentary about the need to protect private giving but the need, as the Congressmen pleaded, to balance the scales. It would be one thing if PACs were roughly balanced in our pluralistic society. There is no balance, and that's the reason more attention was given to business PACs than to others. They're the most powerful and persuasive.

I can understand your strong feelings. That often happens when journalists shed light on activities of powerful groups which would prefer to work out of sight. But that's precisely our job and that of Mr. Moyers, and we're entirely satisfied that far from performing a disservice to the public, it accomplished exactly the opposite.

**Analysis:** It is obvious from the outset of the CBS Evening News series that the network was attempting to make the point that PACs have put the power of money into politics. In introducing the series, Anchorman Dan Rather said the following:

This, of course, is a congressional election year, and because it is it may be worth reminding ourselves that every year it takes fewer and fewer votes to win but more and more money. What was supposed to be election reforms put a limit on money individuals can contribute to candidates for federal office. But that law has a loophole. It allows huge group contributions through a device called political action committees, known for short as PACs. . . .

Mr. Moyers then said:

Power is what PACs are about—the power to raise and give money to political candidates who, in turn, will at least give them a hearing and, at best, do their bidding.

Mr. Moyers explained that the first PAC was started by a labor union—the AFL-CIO; that in 1974 they numbered 608 and today almost 3,000, and that they now are sponsored by single-issue groups, ideological allies, trade associations and corporations. "Acting together, they can pass legislation or kill it," he said. "They can make politicians and break them. You will hear it said by politicians themselves that PACs are becoming more important than the parties and their dollars more powerful than your vote. . . .

"Their contributions to congressional candidates have more than quadrupled to over $55 million in 1980 alone. . . . Contributions from political action committees alone will exceed $100 million" in the 1982 elections, "the most expensive in history."

**Council finding:** In his letter of complaint, Mr. Armstrong does not dispute the truth of what CBS said. He does, however, take issue with the fairness of the presentation. ". . . By telling only part of the story, CBS did grave damage to the truth. . . ." he wrote.

CBS made no pretension in the five-part series that it was endeavoring to arrive at a balanced presentation, that it would present the views of those who support PACs. CBS News, obviously concerned over the growing influence of PACs on the political process, expressed those concerns. It selected individuals to appear on camera who were generally supportive of Mr. Moyers' opinions. Some of them espoused changes that would place limitations on the money politicians accept from PACs. Curbs were called for on campaign spending, including curbs on costs of political campaign spending on television itself.

The Council, whether or not it agrees with the opinions expressed, is on record in support of robust opinion journalism. It believes that the interests of free expression are best served through a wide variety of views, including those which express strong points of view.

The complaint is found unwarranted. However, in news programming, point-of-view journalism should be more explicitly labeled as such.

Furthermore, appropriate as was the airing by CBS News of a strong editorial viewpoint on the dangers it envisaged in the spread of corporate PACs, the complaint by Mr. Armstrong does point up the failure of the network news programs to develop any adequate device through which people who disagree with opinions expressed under network auspices can present an opposing view. The news programs carried by the three principal networks represent a primary, if not a principal, source of information for millions of Americans. Opinion conveyed along with the news has unquestioned impact in shaping the view of these listeners.

Despite the time constraints under which they must operate, network investigative news programs have found it possible in a limited way to air dissenting views or use dissenting letters. They are now a staple on both "60 Minutes" and ABC's "20/20." Some such device on the regular news broadcasts would go a long way toward easing the sense of unfairness that understandably stems from those who now complain that access for contrary viewpoints is shut out entirely.

**Concurring:** Abel, Ayers, Benson, Brady, Hornby, Huston, Isaacs, Pulitzer, Scott and van den Haag.

**Abstaining:** Williams.

April 23, 1982

### COMPLAINT NO. 202
(Filed January 5, 1981)
### WILLIAM KALIS
### against
### WTVJ-TV MIAMI

**Complaint:** William Kalis, editor-in-chief of the Bahamas News Bureau, complained that WTVJ of Miami employed a priest who was an activist in the Haitian exile community to create a news story.

Specifically, Mr. Kalis complained that the television station sent the Rev. Gerard Jean-Juste via helicopter to Cay Lobos in the Bahamas, where 118 Haitians were about to be evacuated after being stranded for more than a month. In a letter to Ralph Renick, news director and vice-president of WTVJ and a former member of the News Council, Mr. Kalis charged that Father Jean-Juste incited the Haitians to resist evacuation from the cay. As a result, said Mr. Kalis, the Haitians refused to board a government tender, making it necessary for the authorities to send a patrol vessel with a police detachment to carry out the evacuation the next day. Mr. Kalis wrote:

> This example of participatory journalism was a deliberate and provocative act to create and manipulate the news. It was an astounding demonstration of irresponsible judgment.

Mr. Kalis wrote that Mr. Renick's published claim that Father Jean-Juste was serving as an interpreter, was a "feeble excuse." (Mr. Kalis' use of the term, "published," apparently referred to a news story in *The Miami Herald*, which quoted unnamed CBS spokesman as saying that Father Jean-Juste had been sent as an interpreter.) Mr. Kalis asked Mr. Renick for whom the clergyman was interpreting. The WTVJ crew, he said, was composed solely of cameramen.

Mr. Kalis said further that it was illegal for Father Jean-Juste and the helicopter to land at Cay Lobos without prior permission.

In his complaint to the Council, dated December 12, 1980, Mr. Kalis said that all three television networks "carried footage of the Haitians being incited to resist evacuation by the Rev. Jean-Juste." However, he said, he did not believe that any of the networks reported that the priest had been carried to the cay aboard a press helicopter.

Mr. Kalis also said that he had not received a response from Mr. Renick.

**Response of the news organization:** A copy of Mr. Kalis' complaint was sent to Mr. Renick January 8, 1981, with a suggestion that Mr. Renick respond to Mr. Kalis. Mr. Renick replied on January 21 with a copy of a letter dated December 23 he had already sent to Mr. Kalis. In that letter Mr. Renick said 1) the Reverend Jean-Juste served as an interpreter for the CBS correspondent on the story Charles Gomez, who was the third passenger aboard the WTVJ helicopter, and 2) their entry into the Bahamas was cleared with Bahamian immigration officials at Nassau. (While Mr. Renick's second point does not directly address Mr. Kalis' charge of illegal landing, the issue is not within the Council's purview.) Mr. Renick said:

> It was never our intention to "create and manipulate the news" as you accuse us of doing in your letter.
> The stranded Haitians at Cay Lobos constituted, in every measure, a bona fide news story. To cover that story in the best way possible was the sole motivation behind our selection of people to send to Cay Lobos.

(The copy of the Renick letter came to the Council at a time of changing staff. An assumption was made that the letter satisfied the complainant, and staff did not write to Mr. Kalis to make sure. A year later, in December 1981, Mr. Kalis asked the Council what had become of his complaint. At that time the staff began its present investigation.)

389

In a telephone conversation with the staff in April, 1981, Mr. Renick said that prior to the events on Cay Lobos, Father Jean-Juste was not identified as a "flamboyant, arousal type" individual. Mr. Renick said, "If we had known he was a rabble rouser type guy—as he has subsequently turned out to be in the public mind—it would have been the last thing in our minds to employ him."

Mr. Renick told the staff that Don Brown, head of the NBC news bureau in Miami, had called and lodged a formal complaint with WTVJ about Father Jean-Juste's involvement in the Cay Lobos coverage.

**Staff analysis:** In the WTVJ broadcast, Father Jean-Juste is shown being warmly greeted by the stranded Haitians and then leading them in prayer. Council staff was unable to tell from the tape what the clergyman said to the Haitians on camera.

In an attempt to get a first-hand account of exactly what happened on Cay-Lobos, the staff talked to three network reporters who were on the island at the same time as Father Jean-Juste.

CBS's Charles Gomez, who accompanied the priest to the island, told the staff that either there were not enough helicopters or that there was a shortage of crews. For one or the other reason CBS hitched a ride with WTVJ (a CBS affiliate) and used the WTVJ cameraman (the helicopter seated only three passengers). The decision to use Father Jean-Juste as an interpreter was made by WTVJ. Mr. Gomez said WTVJ thought the minister would be an effective interpreter. Mr. Gomez recalled that upon arrival at the island the minister received a warm greeting. Mr. Gomez left Father Jean-Juste with the Haitians and went off to interview at a nearby lighthouse, where there was an English-speaking person. After one and a half to two hours on the island the pilot wanted to leave because night was approaching and weather conditions were not good, said the correspondent. Mr. Gomez said that he left the island, accompanied by Father Jean-Juste, approximately 15 minutes before the arrival of the Bahamian government tender, Lady Moore. The ship was to have taken the Haitians back to Haiti, but the Haitians refused to get on board. Asked by the staff if the clergyman incited the Haitians' resistance to board the Lady Moore, Mr. Gomez replied that he did not hear Father Jean-Juste tell the Haitians to resist evacuation. The correspondent said he does not speak Creole. Mr. Gomez said that he "and everyone else" was "surprised" when they found out what happened.

"I did not think there was a deliberate attempt to incite the Haitians or create any brouhaha," Mr. Gomez said. He believed WTVJ was totally innocent.

ABC's David Garcia told the staff that he had interviewed Father Jean-Juste as a spokesman for the Haitians and that the clergyman spoke on camera about the plight of the Haitians. Mr. Garcia told the staff that he was surprised that Father Jean-Juste was brought in as an interpreter considering his connection with the Miami Haitian community. His presence added a new factor, he said.

Staff also spoke with Ike Seamans of NBC News, who was on the island when Father Jean-Juste arrived. Mr. Seamans said that those on the island "couldn't believe it" when he got off the helicopter. Seamans said he thought, "What is he doing here?" Asked if the minister incited the Haitians to resist evacuation, Seamans replied, "I can't tell you that he said resist. But by knowing what he's done in the past he could have. He's a well-known news maker. Every time there's a news event with the Haitians, you interview him. . . . The first thing he did was lead them in prayer. An interpreter wouldn't do that—that's hardly what an interpreter does. We were all upset that he was there."

Transcripts of CBS, NBC and WTVJ broadcasts of November 11, 1980, did not show Father Jean-Juste inciting the Haitians to resist evacuation. NBC news carried only a short report by John Chancellor that told of the Haitian's refusal to board the ship, but made no mention of Jean-Juste. CBS Evening News reported the Haitians' refusal to board the vessel and mentioned Father Jean-Juste's appearance on the island as follows:

> Cronkite: . . . Earlier, Charles Gomez arrived on the island with a Haitian leader, and here's his report.
>
> Charles Gomez: (For the) 118 stranded Haitian refugees, the unexpected arrival of Miami Haitian leader Father Gerard Jean-Juste was more than a welcome sight. For the weary and hungry Haitians, it was a chance to celebrate. Jean-Juste offered reassurances to the men and women who have survived an ordeal that has already left five dead, reportedly due to starvation. . . .
>
> These two pregnant women told Jean-Juste that they fear they will die soon.
>
> Miami Haitian leaders say that the plight of the refugees here raises serious questions about how far the U.S. is willing to go to extend humanitarian assistance. . . .

The partial WTVJ transcript below shows that the station did say that Father Jean-Juste had accompanied the WTVJ news crew and did indicate that he was a Haitian leader:

> WTVJ Voice-over: A Channel 4 news crew helicoptered to Cay Lobos today accompanied by Haitian priest Gerard Jean-Juste.
> The refugees recognized the man who has fought for Haitian rights in America . . . and greeted him with joy. . . .

> A Channel 4 news crew spent several hours on the island today before the boat arrived . . . and Chris Blatchford has prepared a report on the ordeal of the refugees. . . .
>
> Chris Blatchford: The Miami-based Haitian leader Father Jean-Juste . . . airlifted to the island today with a Channel 4 news crew . . . was greeted like a hero . . . but called the scene "inhumanity at its peak.". . .
>
> Father Jean-Juste led the group in prayer . . . asking God to send relief. And not to send them back to Haiti where Jean-Juste says . . . survivors face death. . . .
>
> Jean-Juste (from tape): It will be worse for these people who have internationally shamed the government of Haiti and anybody who insults that government will suffer . . . will be tortured. That's the law of the Duvaliers.

(Except at the end of Mr. Blatchford's first paragraph, all the ellipses are part of the transcript, indicating pauses in speech or words missed by the transcriber.)

All the material so far has to do with the first day of a two-day episode. It was on the second day, Wednesday, November 12, that the Bahamian government sent a vessel with a police detachment and forcibly removed the Haitians to be returned to Haiti. There is even less documentary material about what happened that day and what part Father Jean-Juste played than there is for the first day. Broadcast and written news reports were less extensive. The explanation lies partly in the fact that the police sent reporters away from the cay before the actual removal of the Haitians and partly in the fact that one news crew was lost in a helicopter crash on the way back to Miami from the cay. Finally there is the memory factor; after so long a time, many of the people involved cannot separate the events of the two days. An example of the confusion: Ruth Sperling, assistant news director of WTVJ, said the station sent reporter Chris Blatchford to the cay with a cameraman and a load of sandwiches for the Haitians on Wednesday. She said Father Jean-Juste did accompany the crew in the third-passenger seat. Mr. Blatchford, however, said he did not go.

*The Miami Herald* reported on Thursday, November 13:

> A CBS crew from Miami landed on the island *Wednesday* morning bringing 100 Cuban sandwiches, two cartons of yellow rice, and Miami Haitian minister Gerard Jean-Juste. . . . (Editor's note: It was actually a WTVJ crew.)
>
> It was Jean-Juste who accompanied CBS *Tuesday* to the island and urged the Haitians to refuse to be taken anywhere but the United States. CBS said it had brought Jean-Juste as an interpreter.
>
> But Ralph Renick, news director of the CBS affiliate WTVJ, said: "Our concern beyond the story was that there were 108 (sic) humans out there starving to death. If anyone could help them, why would anyone object? Jean-Juste is the man who knows the problems of his people. He gave them some needed hope."

392

Sara Rimer and Guillermo Martinez wrote the *Miami Herald* article. Ms. Rimer said she did not get to Cay Lobos, and she did not know why that information was not attributed to a source. Ms. Rimer said she did not recall where the information came from. She vaguely remembered having seen a film of Jean-Juste on the island. (A note: *The Miami Herald* employed a Creole-speaking woman as an interpreter for its news crew on one trip to Cay Lobos.)

NBC News reported on Thursday, November 13, that Father Jean-Juste went to the island again Wednesday, November 12:

> Seamans: . . . Yesterday a Haitian exile priest from Miami, the Reverend Gerard Jean-Juste prayed with the refugees, he told them no matter what happens they should avoid violence.
>
> Jean-Juste: If they act that way there will be no harm to them.
>
> Seamans: An hour after the priest left, Bahamian police in battle dress stormed ashore with automatic weapons, tear gas, and riot sticks. They immediately told the small group of reporters and photographers to get off the island.
>
> Man: —pack up and get out.
>
> Man: We have—
>
> Man: I said pack up and get out.
>
> Seamans: The frightened Haitians sat quietly, not knowing what to expect. They refused to leave, and the officers started to beat them. Tear gas was fired. A Bahamian government spokesman said the police had been instructed to use force only if absolutely necessary. They did use force, and the Haitians were taken off Cay Lobos to begin the trip to Haiti.

Father Jean-Juste told Council staff that WTVJ took him to Cay Lobos as an interpreter both days. He said, however, that he was not hired by WTVJ and did not receive any money for his services. He said he had "volunteered," but he could not recall how the arrangement was made. (Ralph Renick said Ruth Sperling telephoned Father Jean-Juste and asked him to go along with WTVJ as an interpreter. Mr. Renick said WTVJ did not offer to pay the clergyman.)

Father Jean-Juste said that he was not the only interpreter brought to the cay be the media. He said that AP, UPI, and *The Miami Herald* all had interpreters on the island. The priest said he could not recall what he said to the Haitians on the cay. He said he could not remember if he told them to resist boarding the ship that would take them back to Haiti.

In sum, there is no direct evidence of what Father Jean-Juste told the stranded Haitians to do. The *Miami Herald* assertion November 13 that the priest had told the exiles two days before "to refuse to be taken anywhere but the Unites States" is unattributed, and the reporter cannot recall the source. The recollections of the reporters at the cay add up at most to surprise that the activist priest should show up with a news crew.

393

Having those thoughts in mind and bearing in mind the statement of Charles Gomez, the CBS reporter who accompanied Father Jean-Juste, a statement to the effect that he did not believe the priest did make a deliberate attempt to create a "brouhaha," it is difficult to find the charge warranted that WTVJ sent the priest as a "deliberate and provocative act" to create and manipulate the news. Indeed, the transcript of the WTVJ news broadcast of the second days' events is skimpy, and it does not indicate that Father Jean-Juste was on the island.

The fact is inescapable, however, that whatever he said to the Haitians, the mere presence of the well-known priest did inject a new and dynamic element into the episode and did, perhaps, change the news situation.

**Council finding:** There is plenty of evidence that Father Jean-Juste believed that the stranded Haitians should resist being returned to Haiti. There is no direct evidence, however, that he specifically incited them to resist removal from Cay Lobos. There is some evidence in the CBS report that the priest may have done some interpreting; specifically there is Mr. Gomez' report that two pregnant women told the priest that they feared they would die soon. That being the case, the Council cannot find warranted the charge that WTVJ sent the priest as a "deliberate and provocative act to create and manipulate the news."

There is evidence, however, in the reactions of the Haitians and in the surprise expressed by other reporters in seeing the priest arriving with a news crew that Father Jean-Juste was widely known as a partisan activist in the Haitian community despite what Mr. Renick said to the contrary. And there is evidence that his mere presence on the cay added a dynamic element to the news situation that may have changed the outcome.

News organizations should take pains not to create news and particularly not to tip the balance towards violence in a tense situation. The Kerner Commission told the American press and the American public as much in its report on coverage of the urban riots of the late 1960s. Mr. Renick knows as much as evidenced by his statement that he would not have sent Father Jean-Juste if he had recognized his capacity for arousing the Haitians. WTVJ did not take adequate pains to avoid tipping the balance when it took Father Jean-Juste to Cay Lobos. There were other interpreters available. At least one other news organization hired one who was not an obviously partisan activist. Therefore, the Council finds warranted the charge that WTVJ exercised questionable judgment in sending Father Jean-Juste to Cay Lobos.

**Concurring:** Abel, Ayers, Benson, Brady, Decter, Hornby Huston, Isaacs, Kennedy, Miller, Pulitzer, Scott, Stanton, van den Haag and

Williams.
September 23, 1982

AMERICN IRISH UNITY COMMITTEE
against
THE NEW YORK TIMES


**Complaint:** The American Irish Unity Committee complained that *The New York Times* left out part of a sentence in a quotation from Garret FitzGerald, who was then prime minister of the Irish Republic. The effect of the omission was to give a "false picture of the Irish Republic," said the complaint.

Furthermore, said the Irish group, *The Times* published the incomplete quotation twice again, even though the omission was called to the attention of the newspaper, and even though a spokesman for *The Times* acknowledged that if the omitted portion was indeed part of the original statement, it ought not to have been left out.

The quotation appeared first in *The Times* on October 9, 1981, in a story from Dublin by William Borders, the *Times* deputy foreign editor, who was then in the *Times* London bureau. Mr. Borders reported that Mr. FitzGerald had launched an effort to make the Irish Republic more appealing to Northern Ireland's Protestants by reducing the official status of the Catholic Church in the Republic. Mr. Borders reported the following quote from a FitzGerald interview on Radio Telefis Eireann (RTE), the Irish national radio system:

> If I were a northern Protestant, I cannot see how I could be attracted to getting involved in a state which in itself is sectarian.

The Rev. Maurice Burke of Our Lady Help of Christians Church on Staten Island wrote a letter to the editor of *The Times* saying that the Borders story "misquotes" Mr. FitzGerald "and leaves out an important phrase." Father Burke said the complete quotation appeared in *The Irish Times* as follows:

> If I was a northern Protestant today, I can't see how I could be attracted to getting involved in a state which is itself sectarian *although not in the acutely sectarian way Northern Ireland was in which Catholics were repressed.*

Father Burke's letter said he feared that the omission of the qualifying phrase from the quote would provide material with which the enemies of Irish unity could attack the south. And Father Burke included a statement by David Rosen, described as the chief rabbi of Ireland, describing the Irish Republic as a "paradigm of how well different communities can live together."

William W. Humbach, assistant to the executive editor of *The Times*, replied to Father Burke October 20 thanking him for his letter and saying:

> I have had a copy of it forwarded to William Borders, and I have told our Foreign Newsdesk that if Prime Minister Garret FitzGerald's speech included the phrase, ". . . although not in the acutely sectarian way Northern Ireland was in which Catholics were repressed," it should not have been dropped.

When Father Burke received Mr. Humbach's letter, he called Mr. Humbach to protest that the incomplete quotation had appeared again October 18 in a Borders story in the Week in Review section of *The Times*. Father Burke's version of that phone conversation is as follows:

> They said they would not publish the letter calling attention to the misquotation; they would not publish the correct version of the FitzGerald quote: they were not in fact obliged to do so as it was Borders, not *The New York Times* who was responsible for the error; they would not publish the statement of the Episcopal Bishop in Ireland disagreeing with Prime Minister FitzGerald's use of the word sectarian; they refused also to publish the statement of David Rosen, Chief Rabbi of Ireland, who had spoken highly of conditions in the south and of the good relations there between people of different creeds. These statements, it was agreed, were newsworthy, particularly in the light of Mr. FitzGerald's statement, but no, *The New York Times* would not publish them.

On January 28, 1982, *The Times* published the incomplete quote once more in a Borders story reporting the defeat of the FitzGerald government. Without contacting *The Times* again, the Irish Unity Committee complained to the News Council. Said Raymond Quinn, publicity director for the Irish group:

> We feel that *The Times* engaged in inaccurate and unfair reporting by first, not publishing a correction of the Prime Minister's statement and secondly, by not publishing relevant statements from leading Irish religious figures challenging other parts of the Prime Minister's statement.
>
> The Unity Committee feels that this type of inaccurate and unfair reporting by *The New York Times* is one of the prime reasons why peace has not come to that part of the world.

**Response of the news organization:** William Borders said in a response to the Irish complaint June 16 that he was unable to document that his version of the quote was accurate because he had thinned out his file of

FitzGerald speeches and statements. "But," he said, "Here is what I think happened":

> In common with some other politicians, Mr. FitzGerald often picks up a phrase or an idea from one of his formal speeches and uses it again in another forum, sometimes changing the wording or the context. I can only conclude that that's what happened this time. I certainly would not have quoted the first half of the sentence in the RTE interview without quoting the second half as well. But I suggest that the version I was quoting, accurately, was from some other time or place—a television interview, a speech or a comment in parliament in which Mr. FitzGerald was, in effect, quoting himself. This theory is reinforced by the fact that there is also a slight variation in the wording of the sentence ("which is itself sectarian" vs. "which in itself is sectarian").
>
> It is certainly not correct to say that *The New York Times* "acknowledged the error and repeated it" (a reference to wording in the News Council letter forwarding the complaint). Indeed, your letter is the first I have heard of this complaint, and as you can see, I do not acknowledge an error, although I certainly will not use the partial quotation again, now that I see that on at least one occasion Mr. FitzGerald put it into a particular context. And although I understand the feelings of the American Irish Unity Committee, I honestly cannot agree that we have been guilty of unfair or inaccurate reporting in this instance, nor do I think that anything that *The New York Times* has ever done can be cited as "one of the prime reasons why peace has not come to that part of the world."

Responding to Father Burke's assertions that he had disclaimed *Times* responsibility for the incomplete quote and has refused to publish Father Burke's letter, Mr. Humbach said he did not recall the conversation in detail, but he speculated that he told Father Burke that if *The Times* is wrong, its editors prefer to publish a correction rather than use a letter to the editor as a kind of backdoor correction. Mr. Humbach said that what he had from Father Burke was a clipping from an Irish newspaper; not enough, he said, to justify a correction in itself. For that reason he directed the complaint to Mr. Borders via the foreign newsdesk. Apparently Mr. Borders never got it, he said.

Mr. Humbach said that in his description of *Times* policy and of his procedure, "I assume there was a communications breakdown. I never would tell him that *The Times* was not responsible for an error."

**Staff analysis:** It appears from Mr. Border's response and from Mr. Humbach's recollections and his description of *Times* policy that *The Times* was victim of a situation that is not uncommon on newspapers that will not use letters to the editor instead of corrections. *The Times* has not told the News Council staff specifically how Father Burke's letter to the editor was routed to Mr. Humbach. However, on other newspapers such a letter alleging an error is commonly received by the editor of the letters column, an editorial page feature. Because it alleges an error in a news story, the letters editor sends it to a person in the news department who deals with such allegations. (On *The Times* Mr. Humbach is one such person.) That person sends it to the appropriate sub-editor or reporter for analysis and response to the allegation. If there is no follow-up, the issue may wind up with neither a correction nor a published letter.

In this case the allegation that Mr. Borders had misquoted someone would have caused the letter to be routed to Mr. Borders. But from his assertion that he would not use the incomplete quote again, now that he knows of the complete statement, it is reasonable to assume that Mr. Borders truly did not receive Father Burke's protest and that the follow-up was defective. That assumption is strengthened by the fact that Mr. Borders used the incomplete quote a second time October 18 and a third time January 28. While Mr. Humbach was not specific on this point, the fact that his letter to Father Burke was dated October 20 suggests that Father Burke's letter may not have reached Mr. Humbach in time to cut off the second use of the incomplete quote in the October 18 Week in Review section. However, there was plenty of time to get the material to Mr. Borders before January 28 when he used the incomplete quote a third time.

**Council finding:** There is a significant difference between the complete and the incomplete Fitzgerald quote—a fact that is not disputed by either Mr. Humbach or Mr. Borders. For that reason *The Times* should have given readers an opportunity to see the complete quote either in a correction or in a letter to the editor, or, at the very least, the newspaper should have assured that the incomplete quote was not repeated. It seems clear that the failure to take any of those actions was a failure of administration, not of intent. Nonetheless, the News Council finds warranted the first part of this complaint, specifically, that it was inaccurate and unfair not to set the record straight.

The second part of the complaint—that *The Times* was unfair not to publish statements of Irish leaders who took issue with Mr. FitzGerald—is found unwarranted. The choice of whether or not to publish such statements is clearly a matter of news judgment, and neither choice would have significantly affected the fairness of the reporting of Mr. FitzGerald's crusade against sectarianism.

**Concurring:** Ayers, Benson, Brady, Decter, Hornby, Huston, Isaacs, Kennedy, Pulitzer, Stanton and van den Haag.
**Dissenting:** Miller, Scott and Williams
September 23, 1982

## COMPLAINT NO. 204   (Filed April 27, 1982)
## CHARLES MENDELSON
### against
## NEW YORK POST

**Complaint:** Charles Mendelson complained that the *New York Post* "savagely violated the right to privacy and society's protection" of a 14-year-old rape victim by publishing her name, picture and general location.

Mr. Mendelson called the publication "an immoral act carried out with the duped cooperation of the minor forsaken of intelligent adult protection." He asked that the *Post* be publicly censured for what he called its "gross indecency," and he asked:

> Where are the public and private authorities and moralists, to protect children's rights? The Civil Liberties Union advised (that) the *Post* is protected by the First Amendment. I refuse to believe we are so corrupt.

Mr. Mendelson's complaint referred to the publication October 26, 1981, in the *Post* of the picture and name of a 14-year-old girl, who the *Post* reported, was raped by three youths, thrown unconscious into the Hudson River and left for dead.

The *Post* reported that the child regained consciousness, trod water till her attackers left and then sought help from a 67-year-old widow, Helen Zackos, who lived nearby and who had befriended her sister. The *Post* published a picture of the child with Mrs. Zackos; it said the victim lived in Washington Heights and the rape took place in Washington Heights Park.

Mr. Mendelson, a Brooklyn resident who had no connection with the case, phoned the Civil Liberties Union, he said, and learned that there were no legal restraints on the publication of the victim's name. He wrote to Stanley Fink, speaker of the New York State Assembly, to express his concern that a newspaper could publish the name of a child rape victim with impunity. Rep. Fink responded sympathetically and pointed out that the State Legislature had in 1979 passed legislation prohibiting the disclosure by a public officer or employee of the identity of a sex-crime victim under 18. The purpose of the statute, said Mr. Fink, "is to prevent the embarrassment and added trauma imposed on those young victims by publicly linking their names with the details of a violent sex crime." Mr. Fink continued:

> Unfortunately, the scope of this legislation is limited by the First Amendment of

the U.S. Constitution from applying to the press when, through whatever means, they obtain a victim's name. Occasionally the most basic of our freedoms are abused in ways never envisioned by our forefathers; but the Supreme Court has continuously held that the freedom of the press is so basic to our democracy that it refuses to limit it. Nevertheless, while there is no journalistic code that applies to this type of case, many newspapers have adopted a policy of restraint and basic decency which adheres to the intent of the civil rights statute. Others, however, have found it convenient to exploit and sensationalize the violent, sick and tragic aspects of human behavior in order to sell newspapers.

The Legislature has clearly expressed its policy regarding the public disclosure of the identity of young sex-offense victims. Now, concerned citizens such as yourself must unite and let your feeling be known. This can be done by writing the offending newspaper, or by refusing to purchase it, so long as it continues journalistic policies the general public finds repugnant. If enough people do this, it may very well have an impact.

**Response of the news organization:** Council staff forwarded the complaint to Roger Wood, executive editor of the *Post*. At one point, Mr. Wood's secretary said he was preparing a response. However, a few days later the Council received a response not from Mr. Wood but from Howard M. Squadron, attorney for the newspaper. Mr. Squadron said the *Post* would not respond to Mr. Mendelson's complaint and said: "Indeed, since he has absolutely no personal connection with the story in question, it seems to us highly inappropriate that the National News Council should pursue the matter at all."

**Staff discussion:** The impact of the reporting in this case startled and ultimately disgusted Mrs. Zackos and her family. The raped child was not dismayed by the publication of her picture and her location. Instead she collected as many as 20 copies of the *Post* from neighbors in and around the apartment buildling and cut out the clippings to save "for the future," she said. She leaned out the window, waved the clippings, and asked passersby if they saw the story about her in the newspaper, according to Mrs. Zackos.

Mrs. Zackos' 21-year-old granddaughter, Dawn Allen, was the person who took the injured child to Columbia-Presbyterian Hospital's emergency room. The girl's face was three times normal size, she said, "and to forget that and wave those clippings around . . . it was the reverse to her than it would be for anyone else."

Ms. Allen said the child wanted to be on television. Indeed she was interviewed by a WABC-TV crew, and was disappointed that the interview was not aired.

Fourteen and fifteen-year-old granddaughters were living with Mrs. Zackos at the time, and she was discomfited for their sakes by the raped girl's behavior. "I've got a bunch of girls here; I can't let them see that it's glamorous to go out and get raped," she said.

The last straw for Mrs. Zackos was that the girl decided not to testify against her assailants. Again, said Mrs. Zackos, "I've got girls here, and she wants to let them run around loose!"

Carlos Pagan, child protective services case worker who dealt with the raped child, reinforced the recollections of the Zackos family about the girl's reaction to the publicity. "She thought it was something out of this world," said Mr. Pagan. She was "very proud of the attention."

But she was clearly unbalanced, he said. On the one hand she told an adult social worker not to say she had been raped; on the other hand, she told girls at a diagnostic center about the incident with apparent pride. The girl told Mr. Pagan after the rape that she wanted to be an actress; yet when he put her into a school where she might make a start toward that goal, she ran away.

Mr. Pagan does not believe that the publicity made the girl decide not to testify against her attackers; "She knew those boys," he said. However, he believes that if the child had been put into a therapeutic situation at once where neither the boys nor the *Post* could get to her, she might have reacted more appropriately. "The hospital mishandled the case," he said (A spokesman for Columbia-Presbyterian said there was no medical reason to hold the child and that the services of the hospital's rape intervention center were available to her.) Mr. Pagan placed the girl in an upstate shelter for girls. He did not believe she was still there in September, 1982.

Linda Fairstein, assistant New York County district attorney, acknowledged that the 14-year-old victim did testify on behalf of her assailants as the cases progressed through trial. Nonetheless, five males have been convicted in connection with the crime, she said. Ms. Fairstein said the victim was having a "good time" with the five boys before the rape.

The girl was so "disturbed" and her behavior so "inappropriate" that it was impossible to evaluate the impact of the *Post* story in this case, said Ms. Fairstein. However, she recalled that the effect of the identification by the *Post* of a 15-year-old rape victim four years ago was "devastating." In that case the newspaper did not use the victim's name, but it did publish the address where the 15-year-old girl was raped by a prison escapee in her own home. Since the address was a single-family home owned by the girl's family, her identity was revealed to an ailing grandmother and to her classmates, from whom she wanted to keep the incident secret, said Ms. Fairstein. As a result, the girl had to engage in extensive counseling, she said. She recalled that the father caller her in the middle of the night when the *Post* story appeared asking what he could possibly do; his daughter was overwhelmed by the story and was sobbing uncontrollably.

In the case before the Council, Mrs. Zackos said it was Channel 7, WABC-TV, that interviewed the raped child. Council staff called Cliff Abromats, local news director, to find out why the station did not use the interview. Abromats asked not to be put into a good-guy position over against the *Post* as the bad guy, because, he said, news judgments can differ legitimately without incurring a moral judgment.

That said, he outlined the policy elements that probably went into deciding not to air the interview with the raped girl. First, station policy is not to use the name of rape victims, he said. However, an exception can be made when the victim is killed and no further harm can come to the victim. An exception can also be made when the victim has no objection to being identified, Mr. Abromats said. "However, that becomes personally sticky for me when it comes to minors," he said.

The editor who has won considerable attention within newspaper circles for his forthright policy of naming rape victims also commented on the use of the name in this case. Like Mr. Abromats, Michael Rouse, managing editor of the Durham, NC, *Herald*, asked not to be played against the *Post*; "One person likes chocolate; another likes vanilla," he said. Nonetheless, said Mr. Rouse, even on his newspaper the victim in the present case would not have been named, because she was under 17.

The Council discovered last year in the investigation of a complaint by two Kansas rape victims that there are exceptions to what many people assume is a general rule—that rape victims' names are not reported. However, as Mr. Rouse's comment suggests, even in those newspapers that do go against the rule and do name victims, more caution is used when it comes to naming minors.

In this case the minor was, as the complainant suggests, deprived of the protection of a caring and concerned parent. Her mother, according to both the *Post* story in which she was named, and the assistant district attorney, had abused and turned the child out of her home. (The mother packed up and disappeared from the neighborhood some time after the *Post* story, Mrs. Zackos said.) The responsibility for the child was dropped on Mrs. Zackos unexpectedly. "Why are you bringing her back here, I have nothing to do with her," she told the police when they brought the child back from the hospital. She agreed to keep the girl overnight until authorities could find a more permanent place, but the stay actually extended for some weeks, she said. Mrs. Zackos is a widowed grandmother who makes no claims to worldliness. "I didn't see any harm in letting them take my picture with her," she said. The questions are inescapable: In a more conventional situation would her parents have exposed their 14-year-old daughter to the *Post*? Would the *Post* even have tried to get at the child in a different socio-economic and more conventional family setting?

A note: One of the principal reasons advanced by those who would keep rape victims' names out of the news is that exposure will discourage other victims from coming forward to testify against their attackers. In May the Council received a complaint on just those grounds against *Parade* magazine. The complainant was Susan Marie Coy of Honolulu, who was not the victim of the attack. Ms. Coy complained about *Parade*'s description May 9 of a program under which tourists who were victims of crimes were being flown back to Honolulu to testify against suspects. The article named a rape victim who had participated in the program.

Carlo Vittorini, president of *Parade*, responded sympathetically to Ms. Coy, and later in response to a Council follow-up, Mr. Vittorini called the Council's chairman and assured him that he had met with his editors to make them aware of the sensitivity of the issue. Because Mr. Vittorini had taken action internally with his staff, Council staff deemed the complaint to have been satisfied. Mr. Vittorini pointed out to Chairman Isaacs that a note in *Parade* stating his views on the reporting of rape victims' names might have conflicted with the policies of any one of the other editors who distribute *Parade* with their Sunday newspapers.

**Council finding:** The *New York Post* has suggested that it is inappropriate for the News Council to pursue this complaint because the complainant has no personal connection with the news report. The Council rejects that suggestion. It is fundamental to the Council's purposes that it be available to any person who raises a legitimate community concern about the performance of the news media with respect to fairness or accuracy.

This case indicates once again the broad range of questions involving the need for sensitivity on the part of news organizations in reporting on incidents of rape or other sex crimes.

In this case the News Council rejects the extreme charges of the complainant that the publication was an "immoral act" and a matter of "gross indecency." The essence of his complaint is that the *Post* violated the privacy of this child. That part of the complaint is found warranted.

**Concurring:** Abel, Ayers, Benson, Isaacs, Kennedy, Pulitzer, Scott, Stanton and van den Haag.

**Dissenting:** Hornby, Huston, Miller and Williams.

**Concurring opinion by Scott:** While I agree with the concluson of the Council that the complaint against the *New York Post* is warranted, I believe the *Post* was irresponsible in identifying this victim publicly, and this should have been so noted in the Council's decision.

**Dissenting opinion by Williams (Hornby, Huston, Miller concurring):** The complaint charges that the *New York Post* "savagely violated the right to privacy, and society's protection, of a 14-year-old . . ." and further requested that the *Post* ". . . be *publicly censured* . . . for its gross indecency . . . (and its) immoral act. . . ."

For response, the Council "rejects the extreme charges" of an "immoral act" and "gross indecency," and undertakes to state that the "essence of his complaint is a violation of "the privacy of this child;" and then finds such complaint "warranted." It is difficult to understand why the Council should find "warranted" a complaint not made to it.

Any one of us may feel the *Post*'s coverage of this story was in bad taste or, for that matter irresponsible. But, such stories, as we hope all members of the Council recognize, are protected by the First Amendment to the Constitution. In fact, that Amendment only comes into play where unpopular, distasteful or irresponsible stories are published.

What "privacy" right does this child or any other have when they are involved in a crime as a victim or perpetrator in the absence of legislation to that effect? In its absence, the decision to use, or for that matter, not to use, a distasteful story that invades or violates "privacy" lies squarely in the area of legitimate editorial judgment—and should not be condemned or censured by a Council concerned "about the performance of the news media with respect to fairness or accuracy."
September 24, 1982


**COMPLAINT NO. 205**          (Filed July 27, 1982)
AMERICAN ELECTRIC POWER SERVICE
CORPORATION, COLUMBUS, OH
against
CHICAGO TRIBUNE-NEW YORK NEWS
SYNDICATE


**Complaint:** American Electric Power Service Corporation complained that syndicated columnist Dan Dorfman published incorrect information about the company; quoted a faulty analysis of the company's health, and

404

violated the requirements of fairness by not calling the company for comment.

The column appeared July 25. In the Columbus, OH, *Dispatch*, the headline was, "Lights out for utilities, analyst says." Mr. Dorfman wrote that Martin Weiss, publisher of an investment newsletter, was warning holders of electric utility stocks to sell them. Other analysts disagreed, Mr. Dorfman wrote, but Mr. Weiss felt that electric utilities faced an unfriendly regulatory future, a decrease in demand for electricity, and, most important in his view, they were suffering from low liquidity ratios; that is, they had little cash on hand to cover short-term debt. A table from Mr. Weiss' publication accompanied the Dorfman column. It listed the liquidity ratios of 20 utility firms for 1965, 1976 and as of the firms' most recent report. In the table American Electric appeared to have 3.7 cents to cover each dollar of short-term debt as of the most recent company report, which was dated December 31, 1981. The 3.7-cent figure compared with 44.6 cents per dollar of short-term debt on December 31, 1976, and 40.5 cents on December 31, 1965, according to the table.

Gerald P. Maloney, vice-president of American Electric, denied in a letter to Mr. Dorfman that the 3.7-cent figure was correct. The correct figure for December 31 was 12.2 cents, he said.

Besides which, said Mr. Maloney, "Mr. Weiss' thesis that a low 'liquidity ratio' is the sole determinant of a utility company's financial propects would be ludicrous if it were not also harmful to investors who are disturbed and misled by your endorsement of his faulty reasoning and arithmetic." Mr. Maloney asserted that liquidity ratios are volatile and easily manipulated by a company wishing to present a better ratio. Therefore, it is a poor measure to demonstrate a trend, he said.

"Once, again," wrote Mr. Maloney, "I suggest that both you and your reading public would be better served if articles based on simplistic concepts such as this are tested first, seeking the views of uninvolved respected analysts, or even the companies affected, before this kind of material is permitted to find its way into print."

In his "once again" Mr. Maloney referred to a similar complaint filed with the News Council against Mr. Dorfman in May 1980. The circumstances were somewhat similar. Mr. Dorfman had quoted a brokerage firm, First Albany Corporation, as saying that electric utilities were in trouble.

In that 1980 column, however, unlike the column now at issue, Mr. Dorfman had focused on three firms specifically, American Electric and two others. He listed another handful of allegedly troubled utilities in a summary paragraph at the end of the report. Mr. Maloney complained then, as he did this time, that the data and the analysis were faulty and that Mr. Dorfman had not given the company a chance to comment. To that complaint Mr. Dorfman's editor, Don Michel, vice-president and editor of the Chicago Tribune-New York News Syndicate, responded by offering Mr. Dorfman an opportunity to write a letter in rebuttal, to be distributed to all the newspapers that had received the originial column. American Electric elected not to take advantage of that offer, because, in the company's view, too much time had elapsed since the appearance of the column. The column had appeared in May. The offer was made in September.

In the present case Mr. Maloney's letter was sent to Mr. Dorfman and Mr. Michel with a covering letter from William Loftus, senior vice president for public affairs of American Electric. Mr. Loftus spoke of the liquidity ratio figures as outdated, not inaccurate, and he said those figures could have been updated with one phone call to the company. Such an updating would have produced a different picture of the firm's financial condition, he said. In failing to make the call, said Mr. Loftus, Mr. Dorfman had again violated "a cardinal principle of journalism."

**Response of the news organization:** Mr. Dorfman and Mr. Michel referred questions on the accuracy of the figures to Mr. Weiss. Mr. Weiss said he relied on Standard and Poor's reporting service, which listed $1,487 million in short-term debt and $55.2 million in cash and cash equivalents for Mr. Dorfman as of December 31, 1981. Those figures produce a 3.7 ratio. Those figures compared with $740 million and $90.6 million in the American Electric annual report, which produce a 12.2 ratio. Mr. Maloney protested that the $55.2 million figure left out $35.5 million in "special deposits and working funds" which, he said were mostly in commercial paper and treasury notes and were, therefore, liquid. Howard Silverblatt at Standard & Poor's countered that the reporting service would have listed the $35.5 million as liquid if the company had reported it as treasury notes and commercial paper. However, the way the funds were listed in the company's report, there was no way Standard & Poor's could be certain that some or all of the $35.5 million was not tied up for example as "sinking funds" or deposits against credit, both of which appeared as categories later in the company's own report. Mr. Maloney acknowledged that some of the $35.5 million may have been in those categories but not a significant amount.

As for the difference in the short-term debt figure, Standard & Poor's included "other current liabilities such as trade payables, taxes payable, etc." which, Mr. Maloney asserted, were not "normally" accounted for as short-term debt.

Mr. Weiss told staff that the important thing was that he had used the Standard & Poor's schema consistently for his 1965, 1976 and most recent reports of the utilities' liquidity ratios; therefore, the basis for comparison was consistent.

On the question of the validity of liquidity ratios as measures of financial health, Mr. Dorfman and Mr. Michel pointed out that it was not the "sole" measure, as Mr. Maloney suggested. Mr. Dorfman said that Mr. Weiss had provided two other measures, interest compared with revenues and assets compared with liabilities, both of which reinforced his contention about the condition of the utility companies. Mr. Dorfman said he did not have the space to publish two additional tables. The two men also noted that the validity of the analysis seemed to be supported by a report from the investment firm, Morgan Stanley, to its clients the day after the Dorman column appeared. That report took a similar position on utilities, they said. (Neither Mr. Dorfman nor Mr. Michel claimed a connection between the Dorfman column and the Morgan Stanley report.)

The third element of the complaint provided the most discussion— whether Mr. Dorfman should have called American Electric and the other companies for a response to the negative analysis of their financial position.

It seemed to Mr. Michel that there may be a whole area of financial reporting in which it is not required to call the affected firms for a response.

He described that area as one in which columnists and reporters like Mr. Dorfman report the work of reputable newsletter writers and analysts. Mr. Weiss is one of a number of analysts Mr. Dorfman has come to rely upon as having a proven track record, he said. Mr. Weiss reported correctly that major banks were in trouble and that U.S. Steel was short of cash well before either story "broke," said Mr. Dorfman. He added that having accepted an analyst as reliable, he assumes that the figures supplied by that analyst are reliable. "You can't repeat their research," said Mr. Michel.

As for calling the affected companies, Mr. Dorfman said, "I don't have time to go to 20 companies."

Both men agreed, however, that there was a difference between the column at issue here and the 1980 column. In this column American Electric was not mentioned in the text of the column; it appeared only with

19 other companies in the accompanying table. In the 1980 column, in which American Electric and two other companies were singled out as examples of a negative trend, both men agreed that the reporter probably did owe the singled-out companies a chance to comment.

In this case, having found the liquidity ratio figures to be correct, Mr. Michel declined to make the same offer of a rebuttal to American Electric that he made two years ago. He said in a letter to the Council, "I am less inclined, in this case, to feel that a rebuttal is due. Weiss' comments were clearly labeled as such, and it was made clear that his was not the only point of view available."

**Staff analysis:** The accounting method underlying the liquidity-ratio figure in the table accompanying Mr. Dorfman's column is different from the accounting method underlying American Electric's calculation of its liquidity ratio. Standard and Poor's would have accepted the $35.5 million that the company included in its cash and cash equivalents if the company had reported it as treasury notes and commercial paper. Since that would have given the company a better ratio, one wonders why the company did not report the funds that way. The answer probably lies in Mr. Maloney's acknowledgment that some of those funds may not have been completely "available for the corporation to use"—the phrase used by the Standard & Poor's spokesman to categorize cash equivalents. Mr. Maloney counters that the proof of the availability of those funds is that a significant portion of them was actually spent by the company shortly after the annual report was issued.

Nonetheless, American Electric's challenge to the accuracy of the liquidity-ratio figures seems to fail. The accounting method is consistently used by the prestigious Standard & Poor's and was applied consistently to produce the three liquidity-ratio figures reported for American Electric.

As for the validity of liquidity ratio as a measure of a utility's health, it was not the "sole" basis on which the diagnosis was made. Mr. Dorfman reported that an unfriendly regulatory future and a falling demand for electricity were other factors. Furthermore, Mr. Weiss offered him two other measures that reinforced his analysis.

But the question of the validity of the liquidity ratio raises the third question in the complaint: should Mr. Dorfman have called American Electric and, by extension, the other 19 companies in the table for comment?

In this case such a call—judging from the after-publication complaints—would have produced a challenge to the validity of the liquidity-ratio measure and an offering of updated liquidity-ratio figures. Updating might have been important. The liquidity-ratio figures in the Weiss table were based on the most recent company report. In some cases that report was dated March 31, 1982, but in the case of American Electric and some others, the report from which the ratio came was dated December 31, 1981, nearly six months before the Weiss newsletter and the Dorfman column appeared. American Electric insists that newer figures would have produced a significantly different picture of their finances.

The practical problems of calling each company in a category (20 in this case) are imposing, as Mr. Dorfman said. It may be true that the column at issue here is of a kind that does not require a prepublication call for comment from each of the companies in the category. On the other hand, if two or three companies are singled out, as American Electric and two others were in a similar Dorfman report two years ago, the companies ought to have a chance to comment.

And in the first case, where a group of companies was the object of a negative report, the reporter did seem to open himself up to publish rebuttal from the affected companies, particularly in the area of factual accuracy. In this case Mr. Dorfman contented himself with Mr. Weiss' assurance that he could support the liquidity-ratio figures, and Mr. Michel did not ask for the specific numbers despite Mr. Maloney's challenge that they were wrong.

Why had Mr. Michel not asked for proof in the face of an accuracy challenge? "It's a good question," he said.

The answer, he said was not that the syndicate was ignoring the challenge, but that other concerns had priority and that the Council staff was pursuing the matter. Indeed, Mr. Michel's correspondence with Council staff and his and Mr. Dorfman's meeting with staff were characterized by an openness to correction if correction turned out to be necessary.

With the factual challenge out of the way, there does not appear to be a compelling reason to offer an opportunity for rebuttal in the case of this column. (There clearly was in 1980.) As Mr. Michel pointed out in his letter to the Council, the column made clear that Mr. Weiss' view of the condition of electric utilities was a minority view at the time the column was written.

**Council finding:** Discussion of the American Electric complaint with columnist Dorfman and his editor brought into focus the question: To what degree is the reporter or the news organization accountable when it reports another person's research and analysis? There can be no equivocation about the answer: The news organization takes on the responsibility to correct any factual error that may turn up in the original material. It may be virtually impossible to repeat the original research before publication, but the news organization must stand ready to check out challenges to the accuracy of the material after publication. Mr. Dorfman and the Chicago Tribune-New York News Syndicate were slow to pursue the data that would answer American Electric's factual challenge in this case, but since the figures turned out to be correct, the Council finds the complaint about their accuracy to be unwarranted.

Nor can the Council find warranted the complaint that Mr. Dorfman published an invalid measure of the financial health of the utilities. The validity of liquidity-ratio as a measure of health is clearly as matter of opinion, and Mr. Weiss' opinion was clearly labeled as such in the column.

The complaint also raises the question whether fairness dictates that a reporter give specific companies within a category that is subject to a negative report an opportunity to comment on the report. The view to which Mr. Dorfman and Don Michel, editor of the syndicate, seemed to subscribe is a reasonable one—that when a company is singled out it ought to have a chance to comment before publication, but when it is not singled out, the pre-publication opportunity to comment may not be required. Therefore, this element of the complaint is also found unwarranted.

However, if a company is not given a chance to comment before the publication, the obligation becomes very strong to offer an opportunity for rebuttal after the publication if the rebuttal raises substantive issues not covered in the original report and, particularly, if there are factual errors in the report.

In this case the original column said clearly that Mr. Weiss' opinion of the state of utilities was opposed by other analysts. That statement in the column seems to reduce the obligation to publish rebuttal that merely disagrees with Mr. Weiss or takes issue with the liquidity ratio as a measure. The liquidity figures were nearly six months old, though, and that fact argues for rebuttal. However, the table reporting the figures carried a legend telling readers that the figures were at best three and in some cases six months old. In view of that legend the Council agrees that it was not unfair of the syndicate to deny an opportunity for rebuttal in this case.

**Concurring:** Abel, Ayers, Benson, Brady, Decter, Hornby, Huston, Isaacs, Kennedy, Miller, Pulitzer, Scott, Stanton, van den Haag and

## COMPLAINT NO. 206    (Filed Aug. 9, 1982)
### JIM BOUMAN
### against
### THE MILWAUKEE JOURNAL AND
### THE MILWAUKEE SENTINEL

**Complaint:** Jim Bouman of Milwaukee complained on August 8, 1982, that *The Milwaukee Journal* and *The Milwaukee Sentinel* consistently failed to inform readers of their parent company's financial stake in a retail mall development. He said the situation came to a head recently when a construction industry work stoppage delayed the opening of the mall. The omission of consistent reminders of the company's investment had "a distorting effect on all the reporting of the economic conflict," said Mr. Bouman. He said further:

> What emerged was a consistent picture of irresponsible and selfish union workers holding the construction project hostage because the developers were in a precarious position of risk. Readers needed to know that The Journal Company was one of the developers in order to form accurate conclusions about whose claims were equitable.

Mr. Bouman wrote to the *Journal* op-ed section two years ago saying that the newspaper's integrity was threatened by its involvement in the financing of the project. In his view the reporting, analysis and editorial treatment of the downtown renewal in *The Journal* and *The Sentinel* over four years "reads just like something written by an investor in the project. And, indeed, it *was* written by an investor in the project."

Mr. Bouman charged that except for his own article in *The Journal* and his recent letter in *The Sentinel*, there were only two other mentions of the newspaper company's investment in the mall. He said one was a *Sentinel* article specifically about the investment June 7, 1978, and he said the other amounted to four paragraphs in a *Journal* article the same day. He said the newspapers should have made "timely and regular" mentions of the company's investment.

In the specific strike situation, editorials and news reports tended "to serve the financial interests of The Journal Company in shaping community opinion against the strikers . . .," Mr. Bouman said. He cited a news

411

article July 13 in which the Milwaukee Redevelopment Corporation, through which The Journal Company made its investment, was described as "a limited-profit organization formed nearly a decade ago to spur such renewal projects" as the mall.

He said that description was "patently false, a fiction, a willful distortion." He said that Ruth Wilson, Reader-Contact Editor at *The Journal*, acknowledged to him that the limited-profit description was not accurate. Yet 15 days later *The Sentinel* appended to a letter to the editor from Mr. Bouman an editor's note saying in part, "The funds are not intended as a speculative venture for The Journal Company, or any of the other contributors, but as an effort to strengthen the Downtown business community."

Mr. Bouman said that the alleged defects in reporting coupled with editorials in both newspapers and a cartoon in *The Sentinel* amounted to a willful distortion of the facts and did, therefore, qualify for judgment by the News Council as a comprehensive complaint involving both news reporting and the expression of editorial opinion. The editorials referred to were one in *The Journal* July 13 under the headline, "Electricians demand too much," and one in *The Sentinel* the same day under the headline, "Mall delay could hurt city, union." Accompanying the *Sentinel* editorial was a cartoon of a homeowner staring helplessly at a burned-out electrical circuit panel labeled "The Grand Avenue": an electrician wearing a sandwich sign saying "Electrician Strike" stood by apparently capable of repairing the damage.

Mr. Bouman agreed that his complaint could be accurately summarized as follows:

That it was unfair of the Milwaukee newspapers to omit in news reports "timely and regular mention" of their investment in the Grand Avenue mall.

That it was inaccurate for *The Journal* to report July 13, 1982, that the Milwaukee Redevelopment Company is a "limited-profit organization."

That is amounted to a willfull distortion of the facts for *The Sentinel* to say in an editor's note July 28 that the funds invested by The Journal Company "are not intended as a speculative venture . . . but as an effort to strengthen the Downtown business community."

That the omissions and the alleged inaccuracy taken together with the editorials against the strikers constitute a "willful distortion of the facts." That the distortion is sufficient to warrant the News Council making an exception to its policy of not judging editorial opinion; and that the Council ought to make a judgment on the fairness and accuracy of the news reports and the editorial comments taken as a whole."

Mr. Bouman added that the July 28 *Sentinel* editor's note said that not only The Journal Company but none of the other investors in the mall had any speculative interests. He wrote, "This heightens the malevolent intent in the midst of a "them-against-us" (strikers against developers) series of news, analysis and editorial pieces."

**Response of the news organizations:** *The Journal* and *The Sentinel* responded separately to the complaint.

### Reply of The Journal

Richard Leonard, editor of *The Journal* and senior vice-president of Newspapers, Inc., the Journal Company subsidary that publishes both newspapers, responded to the accusation that his newspaper had not adequately reported The Journal Company's investment as follows:

He said *The Journal* made its first report June 9, 1978, as Mr. Bouman notes, but then the newspaper mentioned the company investment in additional articles July 11, August 23, October 13, 1978, and January 11, 1979. He said the newspaper covered a Professional Journalism Society, SDX, ethics panel discussion at the Milwaukee Press Club February 21, 1979. The resulting article noted that *Journal* editors were asked by a *Journal* staff member if the investment didn't constitute a conflict of interest. Managing Editor Joseph Shoquist responded that the investment, which was made by top management, not the news department, did not influence the newspaper's reporting. Mr. Leonard noted that the newspaper had favored the downtown mall editorially before the investment was made: so the investment had not influenced the editorial position.

In his reply to the Council, Mr. Leonard also noted that *The Journal* did publish Mr. Bouman's piece examining the ethics of the investment on February 12, 1980. Mr. Leonard wrote:

> I think that all of the above refutes any notion that we were being secretive about our involvment in the financing of Grand Avenue. We didn't mention our investment in every story, because it was an established fact in the community. Further, we were having difficulty identifying the other investors, and it seemed immodest to give disproportionate attention to our role.

Mr. Leonard's response included the information from Reader-Contact Editor Ruth Wilson that she had asked reporters who had covered the mall if they had felt any constraint against reporting the company's involvement. He quoted Ms. Wilson:

One reporter, Linda Fibich, made the same point Mr. Leonard made, that since the financial investments of only three firms were known, "it seemed *The Journal* would be blowing its own horn by mentioning its involvement frequently."

Another reporter, formerly on the downtown beat, said that her editors were "always sensitive to The Journal Company's interest in Downtown projects . . ." She said it was never suggested that the firm's involvement be hidden. "To the contrary," she said, "I always felt my editors were interested in keeping this information up front."

Nevertheless, the newspaper apparently did not mention its parent company's investment in the mall after Mr. Bouman's op-ed piece in February 1980. "To my knowledge there wasn't any mention," Mr. Leonard said. He qualified his answer by saying that he didn't look at every story and that some of the stories were on microfilm, which he didn't get into at all.

"On August 25, 1982, we were able for the first time to get an almost complete list of the Grand Avenue investors," said Mr. Leonard. "We ran it that day."

"On August 31, 1982, we were able to identify the amount invested, and carried that in the paper."

Mr. Leonard said the investment did not influence *The Journal*'s reporting on the project. He cited "bad news" stories as follows:

September 22, 1980, a big department store was going to close because it had not been included in the mall; January 21, 1981, several small shopowners were bitter at being evicted to make room for the mall; July 26, 1981, 66 percent of shoppers said they would shop on the mall but they gave low ratings to the downtown area generally as a convenient place to shop and park; July 22, 1981, an op-ed column complained that revitalization of the poor areas of the city should take priority over such projects as the mall; October 8, 1981, Rep. Henry Reuss expressed fears about the future of downtown; November 18, 1981, a story on the plight of the elderly, poor and disabled being displaced by downtown development; April 6, 1982, a similar story on the plight of businesses being demolished to make room for the mall; and April 16, 1982, minority groups boycotted two major stores that are anchors of the mall and said they might broaden the boycott to all of the mall stores.

After the opening on August 27, 1982, *The Journal* reported that many

414

shoppers were going elsewhere to shop because of the crowds at the mall, Mr. Leonard noted.

"All of the above is convincing proof that we have remained objective about Downtown and Grand Avenue," he concluded.

Mr. Leonard acknowledged the validity of Mr. Bouman's second complaint, that the Milwaukee Redevelopment Company should not have been described as a limited-profit organization. The terms was used by an MRC official, and the reporter used it without checking, said Mr. Leonard. When the newspaper learned that there was no such thing as a limited-profit organization, it did not publish a correction. However, it did not use the term again and it did make subsequent references to Grand Avenue as a profit-making venture, Mr. Leonard said.

As for the contention that the editorials and reporting of the strikes provided a distorted picture of the union workers as irresponsibly holding the mall hostage, Mr. Leonard noted that a news story on July 13 reported differences of opinion as to whether labor disputes were solely responsible for the delay in the opening of the mall. The president of the AFL-CIO building trades council was quoted as saying other factors were involved.

Mr. Leonard commented on the two editorials on the subject as follows:

> The editorials concerning the electricians must be taken in context.
>
> The "Electricians demand too much" was tied to the mall because of the delay in a long-awaited opening. However, it was addressed to an area-wide labor dispute involving electricians who were working at the mall and electricians at work on other projects. We cited the facts that they were asking more than other unions had obtained and were exceeding the pace of the Consumer Price Index.
>
> The "New mall has suffered enough" editorial carried a tone of shared fate regarding Downtown development—that we all have a stake in the success of Downtown, including labor. We point out in the editorial that the Electrical Workers "commendably accepted a reasonable contract offer over the weekend."

Mr. Leonard introduces his response to Mr. Bouman's complaint with the statement:

> My reaction, after studying hundreds of clippings from 1977 to the present, is that our reporting was fair and well balanced. Further, we have no apologies to make for our editorials.
>
> The fact is that *The Milwaukee Journal* has been supportive of Downtown development since it was founded one hundred years ago.

His response concluded with:

> I would like to call attention to the August 26, 1982, editorial, "Milwaukee's new

chance to glow," in which we say, "If the (Grand Avenue) mall is a success, many enterprises, including *The Journal*, stand to profit."

That is how we feel.

### Reply of *The Sentinel*

Like Mr. Leonard, Robert Wills, editor of *The Sentinel*, denied that the company investment affected either the newspaper's editorial policy or its reporting. In response to Mr. Bouman's charges that the newspapers were guilty of boosterism, Mr. Wills quoted an earlier *Sentinel* editor as follows:

> The true measurement of a newspaper is how it serves its community. A good newspaper must devote a large part of its resources and manpower to the advancement of public interest.
>
> But reporting the news is not enough; the responsible press must work zealously for the welfare of its readers and people.

Mr. Wills commented, "*Sentinel* coverage of the Grand Avenue development has been consistent with that approach—on the editorial page as well as in the news columns."

Mr. Wills did not dispute Mr. Bouman's assertion that *The Sentinel* had not mentioned The Journal Company's investment in the mall after the original article June 7, 1978, until a special section published in conjunction with the opening of the mall August 26, 1982.

However, Mr. Wills noted that the 1978 article was prominently displayed on page one and that it said clearly that the company was putting up more than 10 percent of the equity cash from local investors. Mr. Wills continued:

> Since The Journal Company was one of many business firms investing in the mall project, no need was seen to list those investors on a regular basis. The Journal Company's financial investment was fully reported at the outset; there was no secrecy, no concealment. Also, as the Milwaukee Redevelopment Corp. was the actual developer, it made sense to premise stories on MRC, rather than its individual investors.
>
> More than 40 companies have invested in MRC. And this source of funds accounted for just $16 million of the $70 million invested in the Grand Avenue. Additional investments came from the Rouse Co. ($15 million to $20 million), the department stores (several million for renovation of their stores anchoring the mall), and public sources (city bonds and a federal grant—more than $30 million).
>
> The Journal Company's $900,000 equals less that 1.5% of the total investment and less than 3% of the private investment.

Mr. Wills also noted:

Mr. Wills said there was "abundant evidence" that the company investment did not bias news coverage in favor of the mall. He cited one story, July 2, 1981, that cost the mall-sponsoring Milwaukee Development Company $200,000, according to a company official. The story described a dispute between the MRC and the state over fireproofing of structural steel. Publication of the state's position in *The Sentinel* eliminated MRC's ability to bargain and apply pressure on the matter, the MRC president said.

Mr. Wills cited other stories that referred to a gloomy financial outlook for the project (February 6, 1982); documented unexpectedly high costs of property acquisition (August 2, 1980); raised the spectre of downtown vagrants on the mall (May 25 and August 26, 1981); discussed the problems of minority involvement in the mall (August 12, 1981, and June 10, 1982); covered the delay in opening the mall (October 3, 1981; July 9, August 3 and 5, 1982), and spoke of the traffic problems and future uncertainties of the mall at the time of its opening (August 26 and 27, 1982).

Mr. Wills noted that Mr. Bouman did not cite any *Sentinel* news articles in his charge that some reporting on the strikes affecting the mall was unfair. Mr. Wills said the news reporting of the strikes was consistent with routine *Sentinel* coverage of such disputes. He said, "Interestingly, neither the unions nor the contractors complained about *Sentinel* news coverage of the strikes."

As for the editorial in *The Sentinel* cited by Mr. Bouman, Mr. Wills said it was like many other *Sentinel* editorials in saying that strikers were pursuing their goals at public expense, "But," he said, "There was nothing inaccurate or distorted, willfully or otherwise, in the editorial."

Finally, in answer to Mr. Bouman's charge that the editor's note on his letter published July 28, 1982, was a repetition of *The Journal*'s inaccurate description of the MRC as a limited-profit corporation, Mr. Wills noted that the Bouman letter said The Journal Company was "a major investor in the consortium of high-rolling venture capitalists who are the developers of the Grand Avenue."

Said Mr. Wills:

> To describe the generally conservative Milwaukee business firms who have invested in the mall (which hasn't paid a penny in dividends in four years) as "high-rolling venture capitalists" is ludicrous.

417

> High-rolling venture capitalists seek quick and spectacular returns on their investments. They don't commit big chunks of money to redeveloping an aging downtown neighborhood where the return is not likely to be significant—or even soon.

Mr. Wills said *The Sentinel* was justified in adding an editor's comment noting that the company's investment had been reported and claiming that neither The Journal Company nor the other investors were primarily interested in profits, but were instead concerned with strengthening the downtown business community.

**Staff discussion:** There is no dispute in this case about the first element in Mr. Bouman's complaint, that the newspapers did not regularly remind readers of The Journal Company's financial interest in the Grand Avenue mall project. Mr. Bouman says there were no further mentions in either newspaper after the June, 1978, announcements except for his op-ed page piece in *The Journal* in February 1980 and his letter to *The Sentinel* July 28, 1982. That is not correct. Their investment was mentioned in at least five news stories in *The Journal* in the eight months after the announcement, and one of those stories, the story on the Society of Professional Journalists (SDX) ethics panel, revealed that at least one journalist wondered whether the investment might not present a conflict of interest.

It is true, however, that *The Sentinel* made no mention of the investment for four years, and Mr. Leonard appears to accept it as a fact that *The Journal* made no mention of the investment after Mr. Bouman's column in 1980.

It is also true, however, that the newspapers did not feel compelled ethically to mention the investment more often. Mr. Leonard said it was "an established fact in the community," and it might have seemed immodest to speak repeatedly of The Journal Company's investment when most of the other investors were not known. Mr. Wills also noted that The Journal Company was only one of more than 40 investors and that its investment was a relatively small part of the total of invested funds.

The Minnesota News Council dealt with complaints against *The Minneapolis Star* and the *Minneapolis Tribune* in 1979 growing out of the support of a downtown domed stadium by John Cowles, Jr., chairman of the company that owned the newspapers. In its finding on that case the state news council said in part:

> Thus, the fact that John Cowles, Jr. is chairman of the Chamber of Commerce Stadium Task Force and chief executive of the largest investor in the Industry Square

Indeed, during the years of contention over the downtown stadium in Minneapolis, it was routine for both newspapers to stick in a sentence, sometimes awkwardly, to be sure that readers did know of Mr. Cowles' involvement. However, there are at least two significant differences between the Minneapolis situation and the one the National News Council faces here: For one thing, the Minneapolis stadium was fought at every level of government—city, county, metropolitan and state. For another, Mr. Cowles carried most of the leadership of the pro-stadium fight. Milwaukee's Grand Avenue does not appear to have engendered the same kind of public dispute before governmental bodies. And The Journal Company's investment and its leadership role seem considerably less than Mr. Cowles'.

As for Mr. Bouman's second element, Mr. Leonard acknowledges candidly that the newspaper was wrong to call the Milwaukee Redevelopment Company a "limited-profit organization." There is no showing that the error was anything more invidious than what Mr. Leonard said it was, a reporter—and his or her editors—failing to check; it certainly does not appear to be what Mr. Bouman calls it, "a willful distortion." It is unfortunate, nevertheless, that *The Journal* did not publish a correction. A correction would have removed any suspicion of evil intent.

Regarding Mr. Bouman's third element, a correction might have caused *Sentinel* editors to modify the language of their editor's note on Mr. Bouman's letter two weeks later to make clear that while profit may not have been the main goal of the investing companies, profit was a prospect and there were no limits on the amount of those profits. It is important to add, however, that even as it stood, the editor's note did not constitute a willful distortion of the facts. It represents the opinion of *The Sentinel*'s editorial page editor that the firms' intentions in making investments in the mall were primarily to strengthen the downtown business community.

Mr. Bouman's fourth element is that the failure to remind readers of the investment, plus the "limited profit" error, plus the language of the editor's note, plus the criticism in editorials of the electrician strikers should be taken as willful distortion and the total performance of the newspapers in reporting and editorializing on the Grand Avenue mall should be judged unfair and innaccurate.

**Council finding:** That part of Mr. Bouman's complaint in which he asks the News Council to lump together the alleged sins of both *The Milwaukee Journal* and *The Sentinel* and to judge the reporting of both newspapers taken as a whole to be unfair and inaccurate is too broad. The Council finds it unwarranted.

The Council must deal with the specifics of the complaint and with each newspaper separately.

First, *The Journal*:

The complainant charges that the newspaper did not mention The Journal Company's investment in the downtown mall after the announcement in 1978. That is not true. *The Journal* mentioned the investment in at least five news stories in the eight months following the announcement. It also published the complainant's article in which he charges that the newspaper's reporting and editorializing had been affected by the investment of The Journal Company. Therefore, this part of the complaint is found unwarranted.

The complaint is warranted that *The Journal* reported incorrectly that the Milwaukee Redevelopment Corporation was a limited-profit organization. Furthermore, the Council finds it unfortunate that the newspaper did not publish a correction to defuse the suspicion of readers like the complainant.

As for the complaint that *The Journal*'s editorials on the strike willfully distorted the facts, the most that can be said is that in those editorials it would have been fairer to remind readers that The Journal Company had a financial stake in the mall whose opening was being delayed. The absence of such a reminder does not, however, amount to a willful distortion of the facts, and therefore, this part of the complaint is found unwarranted.

*The Sentinel:*

Even though *The Sentinel* after its initial announcement did nothing to remind readers of The Journal Company's investment in the mall, the Council cannot find warranted the charge that it was unfair not to repeat such reminders. Again, the key factor is that the newspaper did announce the investment.

The charge that the editor's note on Mr. Bouman's letter and *The Sentinel*'s strike editorial are willful distortions of the facts is found unwarranted.

**Concurring:** Abel, Ayers, Benson, Brady, Decter, Hornby, Isaacs, Kennedy, Miller, Pulitzer, Scott, Stanton, van den Haag and Williams.

420

Note: Council Member Huston absented herself from the discussion and vote.
September 23, 1982


**COMPLAINT NO. 207**          (Filed Aug. 24, 1982)
PETER ZEISLER
(THEATER COMMUNICATIONS GROUP)
against
*THE MORNING NEWS* (WILMINGTON, DE)

**Complaint:** The complaint is that a columnist, Otto Dekom, "seriously misrepresented the events and concerns" of a five-day theater conference, which he did not attend. Even though the writer was not at the conference, the column in *The Morning News* of Wilmington, DE, "unmistakably indicated that he had extensive and firsthand knowledge of the proceedings," the complainant said.

When the complainant wrote a letter to the editor charging that the report was inaccurate and the column deceptive, the newspaper published the letter with an editor's note acknowledging that the columnist was not at the conference but saying that he had "made clear" in his column that he had based his comments on press reports.

The complainant, Peter Zeisler, director of Theatre Communications Group, Inc., disagreed. He wrote:

> I believe that *The Morning News'* refusal to acknowledge Mr. Dekom's lack of factual information, and its patently false claim that he made his sources of information clear, constitute a breach—a minor one perhaps, but important in principle—of journalistic responsibility.

**Background:** The column starts with three paragraphs that do sound as if the writer was there:

> One expects some theatricality at a meeting of theater people. There was plenty of it during the recent New Brunswick, NJ, convention of people representing regional non-profit theaters.
> There was much ostentatious gnashing of teeth and agonized outcries of pain over Uncle Sam's tightening purse. Efforts by President Reagan's administration to cut government costs were decried in loud pejorative terms, most prominent among them being "New Philistinism." An administration that is not free with money must be Philistine.
> There was lament over the fact that the regional theater movement is now faced with a shortage of money because of reduced federal contributions and needs to find new sources of funding if it is to continue operating.

421

Mr. Dekom devoted the remaining nine paragraphs of the column to critcism of federal grants for local theaters.

The clue that the writer may not have been at the conference comes at the beginning of the fifth paragraph where Mr. Dekom wrote: "The press reports showed no evidence that the 250 theater delegates were troubled by the possibility that the country does not really need 175 regional theaters."

But two later references reinforce the thought that the writer was at the conference. In one he said, "Nor were any deeply concerned over the question of why the government in Washington should be concerned. . . ." In another he said, "Finally, there was no serious mention at the conference that one reason for the federal reduction. . . ."

**Response of the news organization:** As far as Mr. Zeisler is concerned, the editor's note represents the newspaper's response to his complaint.

The conference took place June 20–24. Mr. Dekom's column appeared June 30. Mr. Zeisler wrote to the newspaper July 8, and his letter appeared, after two follow-up phone calls, with the editor's note July 21. Mr. Zeisler complained to the News Council August 13.

When the News Council staff forwarded Mr. Zeisler's complaint to Sidney H. Hurlburt, executive editor of *The Morning News*, August 19, Mr. Hurlburt told staff he was going to urge Mr. Zeisler to make his complaint to *The News*' Public Editor (ombudsman) before pursuing it with the News Council. Mr. Hurlburt's letter so urging Mr. Zeisler is dated September 10. Mr. Zeisler told Council staff Sept. 13 that he wanted to pursue his complaint through the News Council without further dealings with the newspaper. He said he felt the newspaper's corrective machinery had its chance to operate when dealing with his letter to the editor.

**Staff discussion:** Mr. Zeisler insists that what Mr. Dekom wrote about had "nothing to do with the conference." He said the conference was a "think tank" to consider what regional, non-profit theaters are doing and what they should be doing. It was the fourth annual such conference, he said.

The fact of threatened Reagan administration cutbacks in the National Endowment for the Arts was regarded as one of the facts of today's world to be taken along with other facts into discussions of the role and direction of alternative theater, Mr. Zeisler said. There were no resolutions and no discussions in the scheduled seminars and sessions that were at all like what Mr. Dekom described in his column, Mr. Zeisler insisted.

A paragraph from the advance publicity release for the conference suggests the relationship of the conference to the facts of cutbacks:

> Theater Communications Group president Sara O'Connor, who is managing director of the Milwaukee Repertory Theater, said that the timing of this year's conference is particularly important in order to provide the profession with courage in the face of threatened federal budget cuts. However, she noted, "The conference is not expected to solve problems, but rather to raise questions, illuminate the issues of today and allow people engaged in all aspects of professional noncommercial theater to forge new connections *with those from other disciplines who observe and comment on society.* (Emphasis added.) In order to create a real theatrical community in a country this large, we need to come together periodically just to talk, to share and to find new creative energies so that we can go back home and do our work with renewed spirit.

Titles of the discussion panels tend to support Mr. Zeisler's description of the conference theme: "The American Theater, Where Are We Now?" "Reportage: The Drama of Life:" "How It All Began: Off—and Then Off-Off—Broadway;" "Creativity and Imagination: The Act of Communicating;" "Ways of Perceiving the World and the Process of Making Choices;" "Humor in Performance;" "The American Theater: Where Are We Going?" and "Collaboration: Investigating New Forms."

Finally, a report on the conference by William B. Collins, *Philadelphia Inquirer* theater critic who did attend, included statements from Mr. Collins on his own that the regional theater movement was "staggering under the pressures of the New Philistinism of the Reagan era as well as the withering blast of the economic recession." However, the report contained these paragraphs:

> So universal is the pinch on the theaters that the very subject of fund-raising was ruled out in advance of the TCG conference.
> "We're all in the same boat, and we know it stinks," said Sara O'Connor, outgoing TCG president. . . . She said that TCG officials decided to talk instead of the cultural mission of the theater movement. As (Donald) Schoenbaum (managing director of the Guthrie Theater in Minneapolis) expressed it, "Do the American people really want theater? And if they do, are we giving them the kind of theater they want?"
> Reporting on the discussion group he led one morning, Daniel Sullivan, artistic director of the Seattle Repertory Theater, said the emerging theme of the conference was fear, "fear of subscription bailout, of budget cuts, of conservatism."
> The conservative "bluenose" spirit that has led to a spate of book bannings was very much on the minds of the conferees.

It is difficult to judge whether Mr. Dekom—given the broad limits allowed a columnist—can be judged to have misrepresented the thrust of the conference and to have, thereby, been unfair and inaccurate. He said that wailing over federal cutbacks was an important part of the conference. What part such wailing actually played is a subjective matter, and he was giving his personal opinion.

What must be judged then is whether Mr. Dekom was fair in telling readers the basis for his opinion. Did he give readers the impression that his opinion was based on firsthand knowledge because he was at the conference?

*The Morning News* says Mr. Dekom did play fair. It says: "As he made clear in his column, he based his remarks on press reports about it."

The fact is that Mr. Dekom made clear to newspaper people that he was not at the conference. Newspaper people would pick up on the phrase, "The press reports showed . . ." in the fifth paragraph as an age-old device for saying, "I was not there."

**Council finding:** The Council dismisses this case on the grounds that the newspaper did publish the complainant's letter and did admit in an editor's note that the columnist was not at the conference.

**Concurring:** Abel, Benson, Brady, Decter, Hornby, Huston, Kennedy, Miller, Pulitzer, Stanton, van den Haag and Williams.

**Dissenting:** Scott.

**Abstaining:** Ayers and Isaacs.

September 23, 1982,

## COMPLAINT NO. 208     (Filed July 21, 1982)
## COALITION FOR
## ENVIRONMENTAL-ENERGY BALANCE
### against
### CBS NEWS

**Complaint:** A Midwestern organization called the Coalition for Environmental-Energy Balance (CEEB) complained that a CBS report on acid rain was unfair.

The complaint was made by C. Luther Heckman, a Columbus, OH, attorney who is executive director of the coalition. The coalition comprises 400 member organizations, including the electric utilities, in Ohio, West Virginia, Kentucky, Indiana and Michigan. The organization seeks to have acid rain "discussed in open dialogue using facts and science as the basis for a solution."

Mr. Heckman complained specifically about a report on the CBS

"Sunday Morning" program July 18. He said the program accepted as true the idea that Midwestern sources, particularly coal-burning power plants, are the cause of the acid rain that is causing a decline in aquatic life in the Adirondacks. "This," he said, "is a carefully-orchestrated thesis conveyed through the news outlets for the past two years, which is unproven by scientific studies or other proven facts."

The program consisted of introductory statements by Charles Kuralt and Jedd Duval followed by interviews with—

● Two Adirondacks residents who commented on the deterioration of their lakes,

● Allen Gottleib, Canadian Ambassador to the United States, who called for immediate action to halt sulfur emissions from United States industries that are upwind of southeastern Canada,

● Alan Hill, chairman of the U.S. Council on Environmental Quality, who defended the Reagan administration's determination to await more research before supporting such controls,

● Rep. Henry Waxman, D-CA, who attacked the administration position, calling it a repayment to big industry for its election support, and

● Rep. Clarence Brown, R-OH, who warned that the imposition of costly present-day control measures would have a devastating economic effect on the Midwest.

Mr. Heckman complained that the report was not a complete examination of the available facts. He cited studies which he said raised questions about the Midwestern source theory or about the rapidity of the deterioration in the Adirondacks. He charged that CBS reporters knew or should have known of the existence of those studies, and he said, "Fair, balanced reporting should have dictated at least mention of them. A desire to provide viewers with complete information would have motivated the 'reporters' to seek interviews with the presenters of these positions."

Mr. Heckman said balanced reporting was particularly important now because Congress is considering proposed revisions of the Clean Air Act, some of which would impose costly restrictions on emissions from Midwestern utilities with no assurance that those restrictions would lessen the damage to northeastern lakes.

Mr. Heckman also complained in a follow-up letter that the CBS response to his complaints about the program did not come until 64 days after the broadcast. One of the coalition's member organizations, the Edison Electric Institute, had complained to the producer of the program four days after the broadcast. Mr. Heckman complained to the News Council the day of the broadcast, but was urged to pursue the direct complaint to CBS before the Council considered the complaint. Mr. Heckman said the time lag between complaint and response was important, "because any effort to ensure fairness in such matters has to be measured by the timeliness of the response to the complaint."

Finally, Mr. Heckman asked the Council to request CBS to interview people connected with the reports he thought should have been noted in the July program and to present those interviews on a future "Sunday Morning" program.

**Response of the news organization:** Robert Chandler, senior vice-president/administration for CBS, denied that CBS had been unfair or had chosen up sides on the acid rain dispute as Mr. Heckman charged. He noted that the six persons interviewed on the program divided as follows on the issues:

> Two of the interviewees are neutral in the aired comments regarding just who is to blame for acid rain; two say there is inconclusive scientific evidence to justify imposing pollution controls on Midwest industries; two say there's enough scientific evidence to warrant immediate action.

Mr. Chandler said there were reports on both sides of the Midwestern-source issue that CBS did not cite. "The purpose of our story was not to examine conflicting scientific conclusions; the purpose was to talk with people knowledgeable about the issue and to explain what the issue was about. It did so flatly and dispassionately."

**The specifics:** The coalition produced a videotaped rebuttal containing 11 criticisms of the CBS program. The criticisms and the CBS answers to each follow:

1. The coalition asked why there was not attribution for this introductory statement by correspondent Jedd Duval: "Acid rain is on our cover this Sunday morning. Acid rain from the smokestacks of the Midwest and other regions of the country. Acid rain which can turn an incomparably beautiful pond into an incomparable greenish-blue lifelessness."

*CBS responded*, "It is true there was no attribution for the statement. It also is true that we know of no one, in the power industry, in the environmental field, in science, in government, who claims the Midwest and other parts of the country, through industrial pollution, are not a source of acid rain. The coalition's videotape does not refute the statement."

2. The coalition charged that CBS "ignored facts," one fact being research done by Dr. Kenneth A. Rahn of the Center for Atmospheric Chemistry Studies, at the graduate school of Oceanography of the Uni-

versity of Rhode Island. Mr. Heckman quoted from a memo of Dr. Rahn's on the movements of air masses:

> What does all this new evidence mean? We do not propose that it challenges the basic picture of long-range transport in the Northeast—such an allegation would be premature. But we think it is significant that the first attempt to confirm the accepted picture through direct evidence has given such unexpected results. Instead of a monolithic Midwestern source, the Northeast is now seen to have a rich variety of sources and transport, a complexity that was totally unanticipated: the Sudbury plume can be detected after transport across the entire Northeast; the Southeast pollutes New England; the East Coast pollutes itself considerably. Ironically, the (Midwestern) source that we had expected to find the most easily has proven the hardest to detect.

Mr. Heckman noted that the report on which Mr. Rahn was commenting was made November 23, 1981, well ahead of the CBS broadcast. He interpreted the Rahn study as a basic challenge "to the original premise of the causes of acid rain deposition."

*CBS responded,* "Our story was about acid rain over the Adirondacks, not the Northeast as a whole. But for the record, *Science* magazine says in its February 1982 report that Dr. Rahn thinks pollution sources in the Midwest may dominate the air over western New York and the Adirondacks. Further for the record, Dr. Rahn has stated that his research on this matter is not yet complete, as acknowledged by the coalition."

**Staff observation:** Dr. Rahn's comments on the reporting of his work by the coalition in its complaint and by CBS in its response are reported in the staff discussion section of this report.

3. Mr. Heckman complained that the following statement by Charles Kuralt, anchorman for the program, "outlines the misleading theme of the program, that acid rain is caused exclusively by a chemical process in the air, and then transported elsewhere":

> The Parthenon in Athens and the Coliseum in Rome stood there for all those centuries until in our century they began to disintegrate under a corrosive attack from the atmosphere. The smoke stacks of industrial Europe belched sulfur and nitrogen into the air and what came down on the great monuments of the past was rain as acid as vinegar.
>
> If such rain can erode the hard, cold stones of antiquity, you can imagine what it can do to a fragile, living thing like a wildflower or a brook trout. This acid rain is no respecter of state lines or national borders. Jedd Duval reports our cover story, "Deadly Exports."

Commenting on Mr. Kuralt's introduction, Mr. Heckman said that CBS either overlooked a study by Edward C. Krug, assistant soil scientist at the the Connecticut Agricultural Experiment Station, or "concluded it would inhibit the theme of their story." He quoted from a speech by Mr. Krug:

> My research indicates that many of the upland lakes and streams in the Adirondacks, and elsewhere in the Northeast are undergoing acidification because of land-use changes . . . . In summary, the Adirondacks and other remote mountainous areas of the Northeast are *not* pristine environments upon which acid rain is acting. The region has undergone extremes in land use associated with the demographic transition from an agrarian/rural and dispersed society, which cut and burned a wide swath, to a more centralized industrial society which is letting those now remote areas revert back to a more natural state. These regions asserted to be impacted by acid rain are precisely the regions undergoing greatest natural soil acidification.

*CBS responded*, "Dr. Krug's associate at the experimental station, Dr. Charles Frink, says this study has not been officially published, that it is being circulated in Xerox and other forms of duplication. He does add there were news stories about Krug's testimony (before a Connecticut state committee on acid rain). CBS News was not aware of these stories. If we had been, we would have taken note of them."

**Staff observation:** A full reading of Dr. Krug's paper indicates that the excerpt offered by CEEB does not represent his complete thought. Dr. Krug does say that the natural acidification of soils, particularly when a logged-off forest is reestablishing itself, is the major factor in lake acidity. However, he adds, acid rain "adds to this effect to critically acidify lakes and streams."

4. Mr. Heckman complained that CBS did not mention a study by the United States Geological Survey (USGS) saying that the acidity of rainfall in New York State has not changed since 1965 when monitoring began. He quoted the study as saying, "In most areas of the state, chemical contributions from urbanization and farming, as well as the neutralizing effect of carbonate soils, conceal whatever effects acid precipitation may have on the pH of streams."

*CBS responded*: "Our story did not say anything, or quote anyone as saying anything in conflict with this report. It does say there are fears more lakes will die in the coming years because of acid rain and the coalition does not, in its videotape, dispute those who express such fears."

**Staff observation:** Norman E. Peters, an author of the USGS report, said it was strictly correct to say there was little change in the acidity of precipitation and ground water in the state as a whole. However, he said, it was only correct because there was a decrease in the eastern part of the state, which balanced off an increase in the western part. He said the only testing station in the Adirondacks showed an increase in acidity.

428

5. Mr. Heckman complained that Jedd Duval asked a "biased" question of Rep. Clarence Brown of Ohio. Mr. Duval asked, "So it seems that one side says let's go ahead with solutions and research and the other side says let's not. . . ."

At this point Mr. Brown interrupts with, "No, it says, it says let's go ahead with guesses as to what we think the solution may be. That's the distinction. These are not solutions. . . ."

*CBS rejected* as unwarranted the suggestion that the question was asked "in an unprofessional manner."

6. Mr. Heckman complained that CBS ignored a report for the U.S. Department of Energy by PedCo Environmental, Inc., a consulting firm in Cincinnati, OH. The study concluded, "The increased use of fuel oil (especially residual oil) and the concentrated use of gasoline by mobile sources in congested areas appear to be important sources of precursor emissions in the northeastern United States, California and Florida. . . ."

Mr. Heckman interpreted the PedCo report "as strong evidence that much of the acid rain originates in the areas which experience acid rain." He asked, "If CBS was trying to do an in-depth, objective program, why would it ignore the PedCo report?"

*CBS responded* that while it did not mention fuel oil specifically, it did cite automobile exhausts as a suspected contributor to acid rain.

7. Mr. Heckman noted that CBS interviewed Allen Gottleib, Canadian ambassador to the U.S., who said the U.S. has "backed away from a joint scientific research effort" on acid rain. Mr. Heckman cited a 1980 memo from a joint U.S./Canadian work group to indicate that joint research is not being ignored.

*CBS responded* that its program included two interviews involving the joint study project, the Gottleib interview and one with Alan Hill, chairman of the U.S. Council on Environmental Quality. In his interview, Mr. Hill says of the joint effort and the United States' posture, "We want to be assured that there—that the scientific community is in some consensus. I'm not saying a hundred percent consensus, because that's never going to happen. But when a specific control technique is imposed, whatever that may be, that it's going to work, that it's going to provide the benefits."

**Staff observation:** The most recent joint meeting at the diplomatic level in June, 1982, broke up with the sides in disagreement.

8. Mr. Heckman cited a number of illustrations to bolster his argument that the Canadians are not doing their part to reduce acid rain, and he

asked, "Why did CBS listen to the Canadians and ignore the local impact theory?"

*CBS responded* that its report does contain the sentence, "Canada acknowledges that its own industries produce acid rain, that its own deadly exports cross the St. Lawrence River into America."

9. Mr. Heckman charged that CBS failed to report that sulfur emissions in the Midwestern region of the country have declined 16 percent in recent years.

*CBS responded* that it did report that "tall smokestacks were imposed on (Midwest) industry years ago to reduce local air pollution." It noted that some scientists feel that the tall stacks have caused pollutants to drift over other parts of the county.

10. Mr. Heckman complained that CBS failed to report that the New York Department of Environmental Conservation has found a decrease in acidity in Adirondack Lakes since 1975.

*CBS responded* that Robert Cross, a spokesman for the department, said no such report exists. He said some groups are misusing preliminary data "which is not scientific and which does not indicate a trend. It doesn't mean anything; they are grasping for straws." He said the data did show some decline in acid precipitation over some of the Adirondack lakes, but the decline is apparently attributable to a decrease in snowfall in the past two or three winters.

**Staff observation:** Mr. Cross confirmed to Council staff that what CEEB referred to as a study was a collection of preliminary field data on some, not all Adirondack lakes. He said his department will publish a report on all the Adirondack lakes in a few months.

11. Mr. Heckman complained that CBS failed to report that "scientists cannot agree on the causes, travels and ultimate deposition of acid rain."

*CBS responded* that its program included at least five allusions to the disagreement of scientists.

One was Mr. Hill's statement that the United States in its dealings with Canada wanted to "be assured that the scientific community is in some consensus."

Second, was Rep. Henry Waxman's statement accompanying his call for immediate controls: "Certainly we should study the problem further."

Third, Rep. Brown is reported saying that science still has not proven conclusively that the Ohio River valley is the source of the problem.

Fourth, Rep. Brown says directly of the proposals to apply direct controls to the industries in the Midwest, "These are not solutions. Those are guesses about how to address a problem that we don't know the cause of."

Fifth, Correspondent Duval says, "Different regions of America are divided over who's to blame."

*CBS concludes*, "We believe the reporting was fair and balanced. . . . We may not have met the coalition's definition of 'complete information'—that is, we didn't cite all the reports they wanted cited, nor did we cite all the reports on the other side."

**Staff discussion:** Council staff's study of the scientific sources cited by Mr. Heckman does not sustain his group's complaint that the CBS program was unfair or inaccurate. Ironically, however, the same staff work reveals a flaw in the program, a flaw that the Council may well decide is outside its purview, a general journalistic flaw in which CBS News is far from being alone. The program, like other broadcasts and newspaper articles, does not make it clear that there is—independent of any political, regional or economic consideration—a serious gap in the scientific knowledge of the origins and transport of the materials that are precursors of acid rain, in knowledge of the mechanism in which acid rain is formed, and in knowledge of the part acid rain plays in the acidification of lakes and streams.

Consider Dr. Kenneth A. Rahn's comments to Council staff. In support of CEEB's attack on the fairness of the CBS program Mr. Heckman quoted Dr. Rahn as saying, "Instead of a monolithic Midwestern source, the Northeast is now seen to have a rich variety of sources and transport, a complexity that was totally unanticipated."

CBS countered by noting Dr. Rahn's paraphrased comment in *Science* magazine that pollution sources in the Midwest "may dominate" the air over western New York.

When Council staff interviewed Dr. Rahn, he said the *Science* paraphrase was fair "in the most literal sense, because 'may' implies that it may *not* dominate." He noted that he had not studied the movement of pollutants over the Adirondacks. His memo was based on observations of aerosols at stations in High Point, NJ, Watertown, MA, and Narrangansett, RI. (Aerosols are suspensions of insoluble particles in a gas.) Based on those observations, he believes that for the Northeast as a whole, which, he notes, is a large and complex area, other sources than the Midwest are unexpectedly important contributors to the airborne aerosols. Dr. Rahn also said:

> I would also like it to be made plain that my work is on aerosol, *not* precipitation. Many people don't point this out and the results for aerosol may not necessarily hold

431

for the results of precipitation. And that's one of the things we have to look into in the near future. . . .

For the record, my experience with various media representations of what I've done is that they are almost overwhelmingly rather inaccurate. For whatever the reason, I don't know, they're trying to condense something which is a little tricky into just a very few sentences.

And I think we have two examples of that here. CEEB is going to one side and CBS News, maybe, going a little bit in the other direction. Anybody who discusses acid precipitation these days and fails to mention that there are very, very deep uncertainties about all aspects of it, including its origin, is doing the public a disservice. And to fail to mention the serious debate that's going on out here is greatly oversimplifying things. . . .

Our work here is concerned with how air pollution moves. Acid precipitation is concerned with how air pollution moves *and then* how it is deposited. . . . There may be a world of difference between how it moves and how it's deposited. . . .

There are very complex chemical reactions; most of the acidity that is formed that is deposited into the rain is formed within the raindrop itself rather than in the atmosphere at the last minute just before the raindrop falls. . . .

So you have two sets of acidity out there. One, the deposit in the rain, and the other moving around in the atmosphere. It has only been in the past year or two that people have begun to understand the difference between these two types of acidity. . . .

There is a consensus beginning to form on this point: On the order of three quarters of the acidity in the rain is formed in the rain, not in the free atmosphere. This makes life much, much more complex out there. So you see, if you use a calculated air mass trajectory to find out where the air came from, you may know virtually nothing about that acidity that falls in the droplet. And that's why I don't wish to extend my conclusions right now between air and rain. Any report on this subject which does not stress this depth of uncertainty is misleading anybody who reads it.

Even as Council staff was discovering the extent of the scientific uncertainty about acid rain, disputes arose about news media reporting on an Audubon Society study showing that more areas were susceptible to acid rain damage than had previously been realized. Also a dispute arose over the reporting on a compendium of studies by 46 scientists for the Environmental Protection Agency (EPA) on the subject of acid rain. Kathleen M. Bennett, assistant administrator of the agency, felt compelled to issue the following statement November 1: "Press reports of a study prepared for EPA having reached the conclusions that Midwestern power plants and industries are causing acid rain are both incorrect and irresponsible. The Critical Assessment Document under review this week by a scientific review panel does not reach or even support that major assertion."

On November 14 *The New York Times* published interviews with Dr. Michael Oppenheimer of the Environmental Defense Fund and Dr.

Volker A. Mohnen of the State University of New York, Albany, each of them atmospheric scientists and each of them taking diametrically opposite views on the question of whether to apply state-of-the-art controls now or whether to await more scientific clarity. (The interviews are included with Council members' back-up material with this case.) In answer to the question, "Do we know enough to act?" Dr. Oppenheimer said:

> Absolutely. A whole body of research including studies by the National Academy of Science, a joint United States-Canada working group and the Office of Technology Assessment came to similar conclusions:
>
> First, that sulfur deposition needs to be decreased in the Northeast by at least 50 percent to 66 percent. Second, that reductions of sulfur dioxide emissions from utilities are the best way to bring about the decrease. Third, that the reduction of utility sulfur dioxide emissions will reduce total sulfur deposition. That is, the reduction of total sulfur deposition over the eastern United States should be nearly proportional to the decrease in sulfur dioxide emissions from utilities. This is consistent with my own research into the subject.

Dr. Mohnen said in part:

> As a scientist I feel very strongly that the source-receptor relationship has not been established, and I know there can be severe ramifications if we go ahead without sufficient knowledge about it. We could end by not benefitting the very regions we want to protect. . . .
>
> The only strategy available to us under a severe time limit of ten years and less would be to retrofit existing coal-fired power plants. To me, that is counterproductive to our overall objectives regarding air pollution and energy—to provide energy, to preserve energy and also to deal not only with acid rain but with carbon dioxide (a principal factor in the so-called greenhouse effect), and the depletion of ozone. All three issues, global issues, are linked through fossil fuel burning.
>
> Also retrofitting plants to control for sulfur dioxide is not energy conservative, because it will make the conversion of coal or oil into electricity inefficient.
>
> If we have more time, we could optimize our strategy. There are emerging technologies that burn oil and coal cleaner than anything we now know, that emit less pollution and that convert coal to electricity more efficiently than we can today. Given time, we could rectify the acid rain problem while mitigating other atmospheric dangers.

Another evidence of the scientific uncertainty about acid rain is demonstrated by the fact that four states, New York, Pennsylvania, Massachusetts and New Hampshire, have filed multiple lawsuits against EPA seeking to overturn the agency's approval of increased emissions in several Midwestern states. Those states, plus Vermont, Rhode Island, the Sierra Club and the Natural Resources Defense Council, have also sued EPA for allegedly subverting a 1977 Congressional amendment to the

Clean Air Act discouraging the building of tall stacks. David Wooley, assistant attorney general in the New York State Environmental Protection Bureau, told Council staff that EPA's reply to the first group of suits is that it does not have scientifically adequate pollution dispersion models to assess long-range impacts of airborne pollution with any degree of precision. This lack of an adequate model was pointed out by others interviewed by staff on the acid rain issue.

With reference to the scientific uncertainty, CBS notes that there were five allusions to it in the program. However, it elicits the arguments for going slowly from Alan Hill, who, the reporter points out, is a Reagan appointee and, by implication, therefore, a defender of the administration position for partisan reasons, and from Rep. Charles Brown, Republican congressman from Ohio who, by implication, is carrying water for his industrialist supporters. Similarly, CBS elicits the argument for immediate control steps from Canadian Ambassador Allen Gottleib, who has a national interest, and from Rep. Henry Waxman, a California Democrat who attacks the go-slow position on partisan grounds.

CBS maintains that it did not set out to "examine conflicting scientific conclusions; the purpose was to talk with people knowledgeable about the issue and to explain what the issue was about."

The question arises: Can one say adequately what the issue is about without making it clear that a scientific dispute exists independent of any partisan consideration?

Finally, on the question of delay in CBS's answer to the CEEB complaint, CBS has not offered an explanation, but the correspondence record suggests that the initial complaint by CEEB's member organization, the Edison Electric Institute, went to the producer of the program segment. He declined to provide rebuttal time on a "Sunday Morning" program. Instead he suggested that Richard D. Morrissey, spokesman for Edison Electric, try to get on Walter Cronkite's "Universe" program which was then appearing.

CBS responded with confusing directives to Council staff's efforts to help Mr. Heckman make his complaint to the appropriate person in the network. Mr. Heckman ultimately sent his videotaped complaint to Robert Northshield (on the basis of a CBS suggestion to Council staff) on August 19. Mr. Chandler's response is dated September 20.

(Note: Council finding is included with finding for Complaint No. 209.

## COMPLAINT NO. 209     (Filed Aug. 19, 1982)
### COALITION FOR
### ENVIRONMENTAL-ENERGY BALANCE
### v.
### CORPORATION FOR
### PUBLIC BROADCASTING AND
### ROBERT RICHTER PRODUCTIONS

**Complaint:** C. Luther Heckman, a Columbus, Ohio, attorney who is executive director of the Coalition for Environmental-Energy Balance (CEEB), complained that a program in the Public Broadcasting System's "Crisis to Crisis" series was unfair. The program entitled "What Price Clean Air?" was broadcast August 13. It dealt with proposals in Congress to modify the Clean Air Act and emphasized the issue of acid rain.

Mr. Heckman complained in a letter that the program accepted as true the concept that "Midwestern sources, particularly coal-burning power plants, cause 'acid rain.' This thesis is unproven by scientific studies." He charged that the program did not examine completely the facts that are available on the subject. In particular, he specified in his letter and in a more detailed videotaped complaint that the PBS program ignored studies by Dr. Kenneth A. Rahn; PedCo Environmental, Inc., and the New York State Department of Environmental Conservation. He said these studies called into question the commonly accepted view that acid rain was caused by sulfur and nitrous oxide emissions from coal-burning Midwestern industries and, in the case of the New York study, called into question the commonly accepted view that Adirondack lakes are becoming progressively acid.

Mr. Heckman wrote, "The public's need to know both sides of a question is paramount where billions of dollars in unnecessary spending could be mandated on the basis of unproven theories." He referred to the program as a "news segment" and said that fair reporting would have dictated a mention of the studies, and "a desire to provide viewers with complete information would have motivated the researchers to seek interviews with the presenters of these positions."

Mr. Heckman's organization, the Coalition for Environmental-Energy Balance, comprises 400 member organizations, including the electric utilities in five Midwestern states. CEEB literature says the group is committed to "open dialogue" on the acid rain issue "using facts and science as the basis for a solution."

**Response:** Edward J. Pfister, president of the Corporation for Public

435

Broadcasting, responded to Mr. Heckman that the "Crisis to Crisis" segment "made an honest attempt to offer both sides of the issue." However, he noted that air pollution in general and acid rain in particular are complicated and controversial issues. "There are conflicting scientific findings, and there are economic and political considerations as well. Given that perhaps no documentary could satisfy everyone involved in such an issue. . . ."

Mr. Pfister noted that "the mandate for balancing programming is acknowledged to mean that over a period of time, a number of different viewpoints may be broadcast, with the result that balance will be achieved, not within every single program, but by airing several perspectives of the same issue." He said:

> For example, the subject of acid rain and the Clean Air Act has been discussed in several other programs in the past year, including several "MacNeil/Lehrer Report" broadcasts, one of them an interview with EPA (assistant) administrator Anne Gorsuch. Additionally, the subject has been examined on several "Lawmakers" programs and "The Regulators: Our Visible Government," a major documentary dealing with the regulatory enforcement of Clean Air Act provisions. The latter program included coverage of the business point of view.

Robert Richter, the independent producer of the program, responded that he thought Mr. Heckman's position represents the views of a certain segment of industry that was represented on "What Price Clean Air?" He wrote:

> We did include the views of those who essentially agree with his position—including an executive from U.S. Steel, another from Jones & Laughlin Steel, an attorney from Ohio, as well as the EPA administrator, Anne Gorsuch, and EPA Assistant Administrator Kathleen Bennett.
> In reference to the various reports from some scientists, there are hundreds, if not thousands, of studies and reports by various scientists who have studied the subject in question. We included in our program reference to some of them, but naturally could not include all of them. The National Academy of Science report and others noted by Rep. Moffett in the program, represent—according to what Mr. Moffett stated—a cross section of significant scientific opinion. . . .
> My evaluation of Mr. Heckman's complaint is that it is the self-serving position of a paid advocate of a particular point of view, who will not be satisfied with any documentary on the subject unless it only presents his group's view and omits the views of any who may disagree for whatever reason.

**Analysis:** The News Council is familiar with the scientific reports offered by Mr. Heckman in support of the CEEB complaint. They were examined in another CEEB complaint against a CBS News program on acid rain.

436

Applying that examination to this program results in similar conclusions: The studies do not prove any major inaccuracy in the program. The examination does, however, reveal that important scientific questions remain unanswered about the origins, transport and mechanism of acid rain and the part it plays in the acidification of lakes. Consequently, there is a scientific question—independent of any political, regional or economic dispute—over what should be done and when to control acid rain.

The PBS program puts the mantle of respectability on only one answer to that question, the answer that says, "Controls now." Support of the "more research" answer is left to two steel company executives; an attorney for the Ohio electric utilities; and two spokeswomen for what the program calls "the Reagan EPA" and which it describes as unready to "take action" on acid rain "despite the pleas from Canada and the findings by scientists." The EPA spokeswomen speak four times, and three of those times their answers are interrupted either by the program's narrator or by Rep. Toby Moffett, D-Conn., who is pressing for controls now. Rep. Moffett says scientists support his view, and no scientist appears on the program urging more research. Yet there are scientists who do take that position. Dr. Volker A. Mohnen of the Atmospheric Science Research Center at the University of New York at Albany, testified before the U.S Sentate committee on Environment and Public Works May 25 as follows:

> It is my opinion . . . that atmospheric science is not yet in a position to reliably establish this crucial source-receptor relationship for use in regulatory decision-making. What limited research has been done to date indicates that the reduction in sulfur dioxide emissions called for by the pending legislation would most likely *not* result in an equivalent reduction in acidic deposition. This means that control strategy adopted by these bills cannot be defended on the basis of science at this time. . . . Harold Macmillan once observed that politicians have to run hard to catch up with scientists, but in this instance, it is the reverse; politicians better slow down and let scientists catch up with them.

Edward Pfister said the program "made an honest attempt to offer both sides of the issue." True, the journalistic convention is observed, both sides are given a voice, but hardly in the even-handed way that would be required of a news program, which is how the complainant characterizes "What Price Clean Air?"

But it is not a news program. It is a point-of-view program pure and simple. Mr. Pfister points out in his answer to the complaint that the concept of balanced programming does not require balance in every program. Nor has the News Council argued for balance in each program.

Instead, the Council has stood foursquare in support of vigorous opinion journalism in both broadcast and printed news.

The Council has urged that opinion journalism be clearly labeled. In this case, Former Congresswoman Barbara Jordan signals the program's point of view in her introduction to the program. She says that the Reagan administration and industry are urging Congress to relax the standards of the 1970 Clean Air Act, and she says:

> And this presents America with a critical choice. If economic progress is more important, we must learn to live with a certain amount of pollution-related illness. If human health and longer life are more important, then the cost must be considered immaterial.

If any doubt remains about the program's point of view, it is erased by the narrator's final comment:

> It is clear that the American people want clean air. What is not clear today is how many Americans realize what industry and the Reagan administration are trying to do with the Clean Air Act. We all can have a voice in the decision. We all have a stake in the outcome.

**Council finding:** The Council, after exploring the state of scientific knowledge on the causes and possible remedies for "acid rain," is convinced that the evidence supplied by the Coalition for Environmental-Energy Balance is insufficient to support its complaint of unfairness against the two programs. Our examination of these programs also convinces us that they do illustrate two significant shortcomings in contemporary journalism, both print and electronic.

One is the frequent failure of news organizations to label adequately reports that present points of view as distinct from news. The Council wholeheartedly endorses vigorous opinion journalism, provided the reader or viewer is put on clear notice that what is being presented is precisely that. Both of these programs were deficient in that regard.

The other defect lies in the reporting of complex scientific subjects in a manner that presents as fact matters on which scientists remain in sharp disagreement. In both of these programs, heavy reliance is placed on the testimony of politicians, industrialists, environmentalists and others with vested interests. Neither made it clear that there is—independent of any political, regional or economic interest—a significant gap in the scientific knowledge of the origins, transport and mechanisms of acid rain and of the part acid rain plays in the acidification of lakes and streams.

**Concurring:** Abel, Barrett, Bell, Benson, Isaacs, Kennedy, Maynard, van den Haag and Woolf.

438

**Dissenting:** Huston and Scott.

Williams did not participate in the discussion or vote.

**Dissenting opinion by Scott:** The complaint against CBS and PBS was that these programs were unfair. The Council admits this complaint is not supported by the evidence. The complaint of unfairness is unwarranted. Equally unwarranted is the Council's incursion into program concept and presentation. The Council's remarks as to some "defect" or "shortcomings" in both programs are inappropriate and unnecessary. While clearly labeling opinion as such is a virtue, the Council should not advise either CBS or PBS on how to conduct their programs, research or program presentation. This is not the business of the Council.

Finally, the Council's finding suggests that the CBS report was opinion journalism. I find nothing in the CBS program to justify such a suggestion.

**Dissenting opinion by Huston:** The complainant alleged that a short segment of the CBS "Sunday Morning" show on acid rain contained an "incomplete examination of the available facts." Secondly, the complainant asked the Council to ask CBS to interview certain additional people and examine certain additional documents on a future segment of the "Sunday Morning" show.

The Council should forthrightly reject both aspects of the complaint. First, news reports by their very nature, are "incomplete examinations of the available facts." The CBS "Sunday Morning" segment properly presented a wide variety of opposing viewpoints. CBS cannot be faulted for not providing every conceivable piece of information on acid rain.

Secondly, the Council would be wrongly overstepping its watchdog role if it started asking particular networks to include particular pieces of information and particular interviews on particular news shows. Therefore, the Council should not ask CBS to do as the complainant requested.
December 3, 1982

<br>

**COMPLAINT NO. 210**     (Filed Oct. 26, 1982)
ARIZONANS FOR A BILATERAL
NUCLEAR WEAPONS FREEZE
against
THE WALL STREET JOURNAL

**Complaint:** In his capacity as co-chair of Arizonans for a Bilateral Nuclear Weapons Freeze, Phineas Anderson, headmaster of the Green

439

Fields Country Day School in Tuscon, asked the National News Council to find that *The Wall Street Journal* had been unfair and inaccurate in an article dealing with the attitude of corporate executives toward the nuclear freeze movement. The article, published at the top of the front page of Section Two on September 13, 1982, declared that the movement, for all the swift growth in its popularity among other sectors of the body politic, "apparently has flopped with one crucial group: the people who run American business."

Mr. Anderson's specific complaint was that the central objective of the movement had been misrepresented in the article and in the key question of the poll undertaken for *The Journal* by the Gallup Organization, on which the story was based. What upset the complainant was that every reference to the freeze movement—in headline, story and poll question— characterized it as a drive for a "unilateral" freeze on nuclear weapons when in fact the goal, according to Mr. Anderson, "is bilateral, and always has been."

The distinction was crucial, he contended, because every one of the freeze proposals that would be before the voters for approval or rejection in Arizona and eight other states, as well as in 25 cities, within six weeks after the article's publication centered on the idea if a mutual and verifiable halt to nuclear arms production by the United States and the Soviet Union. Mr. Anderson added that he himself would oppose the freeze if its purpose was to induce the U.S. to act unilaterally. Bilateral action had been the keystone of all the nearly 800 endorsements of the freeze already voted by town meetings, city councils and other governmental bodies, he said.

His complaint requested that the Council not stop with a judgment on the fairness and accuracy of *The Journal*'s article but that it go on to investigate the motivation for the paper's choice of "unilateral" as a descriptive for the movement's goal. He noted that a memorandum prepared by pollster Lou Harris, which reported a big surge of popular support for nuclear disarmament, had warned backers of the movements that "any even remote suggestion that the U.S. disarm unilaterally will destroy the movement." In recognition of the damage the drive would sustain if its enemies could identify it with such a one-sided approach, Mr. Anderson said, Senator Goldwater and other Republican opponents of any immediate freeze had uniformly sought in polls they sponsored to spread the mistaken notion that what the movement was seeking was unilateral action by this country. On that basis, the complainant declared, it was important for the Council to determine, as best it could, "whether *The Journal*'s mistake was done innocently or not."

**Response:** Frederick Taylor, executive editor of *The Wall Street Journal*, informed the Council that the paper knew, when it conducted its *WSJ*-Gallup Survey in July and August and when it published its story in September, that the various referenda on the nuclear freeze were asking for a mutual freeze rather than a unilateral one. Nevertheless, he said, it seemed to *The Journal* that the question it put in its poll about the attitude of business leaders toward a unilateral freeze was the right one to ask, "if only because it is the next logical issue if a mutual freeze cannot be obtained."

"In addition," Mr. Taylor explained, "it is our belief that the nuclear freeze movement, if it can be called that, isn't monolithic, and that a fair number of supporters of a freeze in fact want a unilateral freeze. They've been muted in their support of the unilateral freeze, viewing it as not politically viable at this time. In other words, our impression is that some supporters of a freeze would prefer a unilateral one, if it were the only alternative to a continuation of the present situation. That is what we wanted to quantify."

Despite that justification for framing the issue as *The Journal* and Gallup did, Mr. Taylor acknowledged that "in our story we shouldn't have referred to the 'nuclear freeze movement' as if it was on one mind on this. And, as you know, we published several Letters to the Editor in an effort to clarify that."

*The Journal* did carry at the head of its Letters columns on September 27 three letters, all of which indicated that, insofar as it purported to reflect a rejection of the freeze movement by business executives, the poll was misleading because of its failure to make clear that the major proponents of a freeze were united in urging a bilateral halt. One letter writer declared that the implication in the news article that one-sided action was the movement's target made the report "dangerously deceptive." Another observed that, far from supporting the conclusion *The Journal* had drawn from its findings, the relatively large number of executives who recorded themselves in favor of a unilateral freeze (36 percent among officials of small companies, 27 percent in medium-sized and 14 percent in large companies) made the writer suspect that a majority would be for a bilateral freeze if the poll had presented that question. "I doubt that 27 percent of freeze advocates, themselves, would support a unilateral freeze by the U.S.," this letter writer commented.

**Analysis:** The staff ruled out at the outset any attempt to assess the "motivation" of *The Journal*, as requested by Mr. Anderson. Quite apart from the quicksand in which such an endeavor would almost certainly have entrapped the Council, it was felt that nothing in this organization's rules of procedure or by-laws empowered it to inquire into why a newspaper asked a particular question or presented its findings in a particular way. The staff started with the asssumption that *The Journal* or any other publication had an incontrovertible right to conduct a poll on any issue it considered of interest. That right was not challenged by Mr. Anderson. On the contrary, he conceded in his communication to the Council that *"The Journal* certainly has the right to ask businessmen any question they like."

Eliminating any exploration into motivation does not, however, remove the Council's obligation under its rules to deal with the issue of substance raised by Mr. Anderson: whether *The Journal* was correct in its description of the movement and whether, if it was not, that erroneous characterization vitiated the results of the poll as an index of the sentiment of business leaders on an issue that was to come before a quarter of the country's voters on Election Day. An auxiliary question left for Council consideration is whether *The Journal* took adequate steps to inform its readers of any mistake it might have made.

To address that triple-pronged inquiry requires a brief recapitulation of the history of what has come to be known at "the nuclear freeze movement," particularly the manner in which the organizations spearheading the movement sought to transform it into a coordinated political instrument with a unified and defined goal. Prior to 1979, concern about the proliferation of nuclear weapons and the arms race between the superpowers was widespread, but nothing that remotedly resembled a "movement" was discernible to give expression to that concern or to weld it into a political force. The groups and individuals eager to limit the arms race were all over the lot on how to proceed. Some made no secret of their distrust of all diplomats and all governments and argued that there would be no security for anyone until popular pressure forced the destruction of all bombs. Others favored unilateral action by the United States as an example to the Soviet Union and other possessors of nuclear warheads. Still others bemoaned the Senate's unwillingness to ratify the 1979 SALT II Treaty limiting strategic offensive weapons in the arsenals controlled by Washington and Moscow.

The person generally credited with a primary role in evolving a lowest common denominator of consensus aimed at bringing coherence inside this whirlpool of disarmament sentiment is Randall Forsberg, president and executive director of the Institute for Defense and Disarmament Studies, a small research and public education center established in 1980 in Brookline, MA. She was principally responsible for persuading leaders of several of the more substantial peace groups in 1979 and 1980 that they would never make much of a dent unless they fused their efforts in public support of a common goal, and that the best starting point would be pressure for a bilateral nuclear freeze.

This concentration of focus represented something of a switch for Miss Forsberg herself. As a member of the Boston Study Group, made up of Harvard- and M.I.T.-based professors and writers, she had helped complete in January, 1978, a book entitled "The Price of Defense." It was in large degree an expression of despair that genuine progress toward disarmament would ever result from "the tedious diplomacy of arms control" unless this country started the process by taking comprehensive steps on its own initiative to scale down its nuclear arsenal. The book's basic argument was that the United States, as the world's foremost military power, bore a distinctive responsibility to begin winding down the arms race and that it could do so without real risk to America's security even if no other nation followed suit.

However, not long after the book came off the press in March, 1979, under the imprint of New York Times Books, Miss Forsberg became convinced that the arguments required to demonstrate that unilateral initiatives could be taken safely were too comlex and too vulnerable to misrepresentation, and she swung to advocacy of a bilateral freeze as the best starting point for a mass movement that could eventually press for still broader moves toward worldwide disarmament. A statement she wrote entitled "Call to Halt the Nuclear Arms Race: Proposal for a Mutual U.S.-Soviet Nuclear Weapons Freeze" was published in April, 1980, under the joint auspices of the American Friends Service Committee, Clergy and Laity Concerned, the Fellowship of Reconciliation and her own research center. It became the manifesto of what is now termed "the nuclear freeze movement" and is said to have been signed by more than 2 million persons. The call's theme is set forth in the opening paragraph, which became the springboard for the referenda conducted in many states and localities in the last two years. It says: "To improve national and international security, the United States and the Soviet Union should stop the nuclear arms race. Specifically, they should adopt a mutual freeze on the testing, production and deployment of nuclear weapons and of missiles and new aircraft designed primarily to deliver nuclear weapons. This is an essential, verifiable first step toward lessening the risk of nuclear war and reducing the nuclear arsenals."

The founding meeting of a campaign for coordinated political action on a nationwide basis was held in Washington in March, 1981, with many organizations and peace activists, including Miss Forsberg, in attendance. A $5,000 gift to finance the conference had been made by Alan F. Kay, a retired Boston electronics manufacturer, whose interest had been sparked by contact with her. Four months before the Washington gathering, voters in three state senatorial districts in Western Massachusetts had approved a call for a bilateral nuclear moratorium in a referendum on the ballot in their districts. One outgrowth of the meeting in Washington was a decision to substitute the word "freeze" for "moratorium" in future referenda. Another was the hiring of a single staff person at Miss Forsberg's center to conduct an information clearinghouse on freeze activities around the country and to issue periodic newsletters. By December the movement had grown to an extent that prompted the establishment in St. Louis of an independent clearinghouse with an expanded staff. It was headed by Randall Kehler, who as director of the Traprock Peace Center had run the successful campaign in Western Massachusetts. When Senators Kennedy and Hatfield and Representatives Markey, Bingham and Conte announced their joint resolution for a bilateral freeze at a Washington news conference on March 10, 1982, Miss Forsberg was present to endorse the proposal in the name of the national freeze campaign. It lost on the floor of the House by a vote of 204 to 202, but a new effort at passage is likely in both houses of Congress next year.

Arizona was the only state in which the call for a bilateral nuclear freeze was rejected by the voters last Election Day. Sizable affirmative majorities were rolled up in Massachusetts, Michigan, Montana, New Jersey, North Dakota, Oregon and Rhode Island. The margin for approval was narrow in California, where the Reagan Administration had sent speakers out to oppose the appeal as a menace to United States security. The specific wording of the proposition differed in each state, but all called for bilateral action by this country and the Soviet Union. Insistence on verification procedures was also part of the wording in most states.

Despite the specificity of the campaign, as reflected in the propositions put to the electorate, a good deal less clarity of objective marked some of the major events that added momentum to the drive. This was the case, for example, with Jonathan Schell's book, *The Fate of the Earth*, which became something of a bible for many inside and outside the peace movement after its publication as a three-part series in *The New Yorker* last February. The book was in the nature of a *cri de coeur*. It dismissed as too limited any freeze that did not extend to the destruction of all nuclear arms. A new world political system that junked the concept of national sovereignty was envisaged by Mr. Schell as an essential underpinning for any adequate attempt to cleanse the earth of nuclear weapons and thus ward off the threat of mankind's annihilation.

There was a similar amorphousness to many of the themes that emerged at the gigantic rally held by opponents of nuclear arms in Central Park last June 12. An estimated 700,000 persons gathered in what has been termed the largest demonstration ever held in this country on any subject. A news story in *The New York Times* said the groups participating ranged from "radicals seeking immediate unilateral disarmament to moderates asking a resumption of negotiations on arms cutbacks." The diversity was indicated by the line-up in a single block of the marshalling area where units of the Communist Party U.S.A., the Kings County Democratic Coalition and Animators Against Armageddon, a cartoonists' group, formed ranks behind one another. The signs and placards bore such messages as "A Feminist World Is a Nuclear-Free Zone," "Bread Not Bombs" and "U.S. Out of El Salvador."

The talk Randall Forsberg made to the demonstrators as chief strategist for the freeze movement zeroed in on the theme of a bilateral halt but contained overtones of unilateral action if nothing happened on that front. She said:

> The politicians in Washington don't yet believe the campaign for a U.S.-U.S.S.R. nuclear weapons freeze. They will. They think that this is just a fad. It's not. They think that if they simply talk about arms control, we will let them build the next generation of nuclear weapons. We won't. . . . Reagan, Washington: Stop the nuclear arms race. If you do not, we will remember in November."

The *Journal* article was based on a telephone survey taken among 845 business leaders, most of them chief executive officers or owner-proprietors, in the period from July 26 to August 11, 1982. Seven basic questions were asked, the first of which related explicitly to the freeze. It asked: "Do you favor or oppose a unilateral freeze by the United States on the production and deployment of nuclear weapons?" The other questions were designed to elicit the sentiment of the businessmen on various aspects of military spending and the extent, if any, to which their attitude toward nuclear arms reduction had been affected by the freeze movement. One query sought an opinion on which did more to increase the chances of nuclear war: A continuation of the nuclear arms build-up here and in the Soviet Union, or the United States falling behind the Soviet Union in nuclear weaponry. There was no reference to a bilateral freeze anywhere in the questionnaire.

The normal practice in polls conducted for *The Journal* by the Gallup Organization is to collaborate in the preparation of the questions after the paper has sent over a basic list indicating the themes it wants explored. Andrew Kohut, president of the Gallup Organization, told Council staff that there had been "absolutely no departure" from that practice in connection with the freeze survey.

"They send over broad suggestions and we hack out specific questions through joint discussion," Mr. Kohut said. "In this case, when their suggestions came over, I looked at them from the standpoint of what questions would best bring out the sentiment of business leaders and made modifications where I felt they were desirable."

He said the object of the poll was to contrast the attitudes of business-men with those of the general population, but added that he now regretted the failure to include a question on feelings toward a bilateral freeze along with the one on the unilateral freeze.

"It was my mistake," Mr. Kohut said. "I wish I had tested a bilateral proposition. It was bad news judgment on our part."

The response certainly would have been different, in his opinion, though he is convinced that overall the results would have been similar. "Businessmen take a dimmer view than the general population of the nuclear freeze movement," the Gallup chief said. "That's natural; they are more conservative." He cited as confirmation of his comment the business executives' response to the question on whether they thought continuation of the nuclear arms build-up or a falling behind by the United States in the arms race posed the greater risk of nuclear war. Other Gallup surveys indicate that the general public splits fairly evenly on that question, whereas 81 percent of the leaders in large companies said in the *Journal* poll they would be more worried by a U.S. lag.

Roger Ricklefs, the reporter who wrote *The Journal*'s story summariz-ing its poll findings, was quoted in *The Arizona Daily Star* as having made this comment on the survey when questioned by a reporter for the Tucson paper: "We could have done the entire matter differently. It seemed at the time a legitimate question to ask . . . but it probably was not the best way to approach that question. I suppose, in retrospect, we could have phrased it better."

When Mr. Ricklefs was queried by Council staff on the accuracy of the quote, he said it was "inexact" in important respects. What he had sought

446

to convey, he said, was that there might have been other ways to phrase the question on the freeze. However, he expressed his conviction that, in totality, the questionnaire was well-designed to bring out accurately the views of business leaders on disarmament.

The editorial position of *The Wall Street Journal* on the nuclear freeze movement, as set forth in several editorials over the past year, is that it makes little difference whether one speaks of a unilateral or a bilateral freeze, because it is delusive to believe that the Soviet Union can be trusted to live up to its promises on arms control, no matter what mechanism for verification might be agreed upon. One such editorial, published July 22, questions the purpose of any arms limitation talks with Moscow when the Russians are "developing biological weapons and supplying 'yellow rain' to their puppets" in flagrant disregard of existing treaties.

The paper's last pre-election editorial on the freeze appeared on October 25. It said the freeze referenda were a meaningless exercise that could do little harm, though President Reagan was undoubtedly right in saying that many of their supporters did not have U.S. interests at heart. What made the whole exercise a waste of time, in the opinion of *The Journal*'s editors, was that "the precondition for any meaningful and broad nuclear arms treaty is a change in the very nature of the Soviet system." So long as it remained a closed society, the editorial said, any agreement providing ironclad verification procedures was extremely unlikely.

Nothing in the Council's exploration indicated any involvement by *The Journal*'s editorial department in the formulation of the *WSJ*-Gallup Survey questions. That is a function of the news department, in association with Mr. Kohut. The editorial department does not get into the choice of either subject or specific questions, according to Mr. Taylor, *The Journal*'s executive editor. In his letter to the Council, Mr. Taylor said the paper recognized that the issue before the voters was a bilateral freeze but felt it was more pertinent to ask for businessmen's reaction to a unilateral cessation, particularly since *The Journal* believed many freeze advocates really wanted a unilateral freeze but did not consider it politically expedient to campaign for that now. The sole flaw acknowledged by Mr. Taylor was the article's reference to the "nuclear freeze movement" in a manner that implied its members were of one mind on the desirability of a one-sided freeze—a misimpression *The Journal* had sought to clarify by its publication of several Letters to the Editor. There was no correction or explanatory note by *The Journal* itself.

Many polls conducted in the last year have indicated that how people respond to questions about a nuclear arms freeze is determined by how the issue is presented. Thus a poll taken last April by Richard B. Wirthlin, president of Decision Making Information, whose services are often called on by White House aides and other Republican officials, produced seemingly contradictory results when the freeze idea was presented in two versions.

The first proposition said: "A freeze in nuclear weapons should be opposed because it would do nothing to reduce the danger of the thousands of nuclear warheads already in place and would leave the Soviet Union in a position of nuclear superiority." That one-sided formulation was approved by 58 percent of the repondents, Mr. Wirthlin reported.

The second proposition took exactly the opposite approach. It said: "A freeze in nuclear weapons should be favored because it would begin a much-needed process to stop everyone in the world from building nuclear weapons now and reduce the possibility of nuclear war in the future." That statement, presented to the same people several minutes after they had commented on the first one, was approved by 56 percent. Included were 27 percent of the total sample who agreed with both propositions. Mr. Wirthlin told *The New York Times* that the overlap represented "the most singular inconsistency on any question we've ever asked."

In a presentation he made to foundation leaders and peace activists last July, Louis Harris said his polls left him convinced that "an urgent, dedicated hunger for peace in a nuclear era has literally overtaken our people" and that this would not be satisfied "until the last vestiges of nuclear weaponry are wiped off the face of this earth." However, Mr. Harris said these same polls showed a 2-to-1 margin of Americans who believed that the Soviet Union might attach the United States within the next two years. An even larger ratio felt that the Russians would not hesitate to use nuclear arms if they were desperate enough.

These findings spurred Mr. Harris to warn sponsors of the movement that "any even remote suggestion" that this country disarm unilaterally would wreck the movement. He cited one survey taken by his organization in which Americans who had recorded themselves 6-to-1 in favor of a nuclear freeze swung to a negative margin of 82 percent to 15 percent when asked whether they would favor or oppose gradual dismantling of the U.S. nuclear arsenal before this country had an agreement from other countries to do the same.

**Council finding:** *The Wall Street Journal*'s news story of September 13 was inaccurate in implying that "the nuclear freeze movement" advocates "a unilateral nuclear freeze." As *The Journal*'s executive editor acknowledges in his letter to the Council, what has come to be known as the freeze movement is not monolithic and includes advocates of many divergent approaches to disarmament. The editor's letter concedes that "in our story, we shouldn't have referred to the 'nuclear freeze movement' as if it was of one mind on this." While *The Journal* commendably published letters pointing out its error, it owed its readers a corrective statement as forthright as the one it made to the Council. To that extent, the complaint is found warranted.

**Concurring:** Abel, Barrett, Bell, Benson, Huston, Isaacs, Kennedy, Maynard, Scott, van den Haag, Williams and Woolf.

December 2, 1982

**COMPLAINT NO. 211**   (Filed March 15, 1982)
DR. ROBERT M. KOHN, M.D.
against
DR. ROBERT MENDELSOHN and
COLUMBIA FEATURES SYNDICATE

**Complaint:** Dr. Robert M. Kohn, a cardiologist in Buffalo, N.Y., complained March 15, 1982, that medical columns written by Dr. Robert Mendelsohn and distributed by Columbia Features, Inc., were both inaccurate and irresponsible.

Dr. Kohn and a number of other leading Buffalo doctors had complained a month earlier to the *Buffalo Evening News* about Dr. Mendelsohn's columns, and the newspaper quit publishing them. Dr. Kohn followed up with a complaint to the National News Council as the appropriate forum to hear a complaint against a columnist who is distributed nationally by Columbia Features.

In his complaint to the News Council Dr. Kohn wrote:

> I feel uncomfortable in the role of a censor, but I believe that such irresponsibility needs control. We have documented cases where patients have discontinued blood-pressure medication after reading the Mendelsohn column and subsequently developed stroke.

Dr. Kohn said that the National Blood Pressure Detection Follow-up Program, conducted under the auspices of the National Institutes of Health, established scientifically that control of blood pressure by medication cuts down on strokes, heart attacks and kidney disease. Yet, he said, Dr. Mendelsohn "urges patients to avoid medications." Dr. Kohn

449

enclosed a Mendelsohn column in which an optometrist expressed the view that high blood pressure is not a disease but "a symptom of smoking, obesity or perhaps inactivity and is really nature's protection to insure proper distribution of sustenance and the carrying away of waste products."

Dr. Kohn wrote: "Citing . . . an optometrist as an authoritative source for silly misinformation is the height of irresponsibility."

Dr. Kohn also enclosed a column in which Dr. Mendelsohn said that the advertisements in medical journals for the drug, Tagamet, "contain absolutely no information about the drug other than its name and a picture of what it looks like." Dr. Kohn insisted that full information about such a drug is required by the Food and Drug Administration (FDA) and does appear in medical journal advertisements.

Dr. Kohn wrote: "The Mendelsohn columns, far from being an expression of contrary opinion, are full of misinformation and dangerously wrong information. Readers enjoy seeing physicians chastised for wrongdoing. I would have no objection if there were scientific documentation for his statements, but they are purely opinion. He often twists material to support his own therapeutic nihilism. This does not serve the public well."

**Response of the news organization:** Joseph M. Boychuck, president and editor of Columbia Features, refused in a telephone conversation with Council staff (August 17, 1982) to provide a formal answer to Dr. Kohn's charge to Dr. Mendelsohn's columns. He said it is not the syndicate's job to answer what are, in this case, medical questions, but he said, "It's the same with all our columns."

"We are not responsible," Boychuck said. "Contractually we are held harmless, particularly in the medical and gossip fields." Mr. Boychuck described Dr. Mendelsohn as dedicated to the view that medicine today is drug-oriented but that doctors are getting inadequate education in pharmacology. Doctors don't know the side effects and relationships of drugs, and "they make some terrible mistakes," he said.

Mr. Boychuck said Dr. Mendelsohn is urging people to educate themselves about drugs, to obtain and use reference books. "He is in the foreground. What he is saying will be common in 10 years." Mr. Boychuck said.

Dr. Mendelsohn's response to the News Council complaint was a threat to sue Dr. Kohn for bringing the complaint. He said his attorneys gave him the preliminary opinion that he was a public figure and that he would not be successful in a libel suit against Dr. Kohn. Nonetheless, he said he wanted everything "on the record" in the discussion of the case so that he can use the record if he decides to sue.

Dr. Mendelsohn said he would not answer Dr. Kohn in the forum provided by the News Council, because in his view Dr. Kohn "loses nothing if he loses before the Council." By contrast, in court, said Dr. Mendelsohn, "I can get his money or his license."

Dr. Mendelsohn said he had been writing a column about medicine since 1965, first for the Chicago Tribune-Daily News Syndicate and more recently for Columbia. He said he had succeeded where other "medical heretics" had failed because "I treat doctors as hostile enemies." He could not recall details of the cases, but he said that he had challenged critical doctors with the threat of a lawsuit three of four times, and each time his critics had backed down.

Asked if he didn't feel a journalist's obligation to answer a reasonable challenge to the accuracy and responsibility of his column, Dr. Mendelsohn replied, "I'm not a journalist; I'm a doctor, and my ethics are different."

Dr. Mendelsohn did say that if a challenge to his columns was presented to him by "someone I respected," he would ask his publishers for page-one space to display the challenge and his reply.

**Staff discussion:** The complaint raises two journalistic issues: Are the Mendelsohn columns inaccurate? Are they irresponsible?

Since the columns are expressions of opinion, the question arises, How accurate must they be? The Council has declined to consider complaints against expressions of opinion unless important facts are alleged to have been seriously (at times the Council has used the word "willfully") distorted. There is no question here but that the complainant is alleging that important facts have been distorted.

The charge of irresponsibility raises the question, Is it appropriate for the Council to judge whether the writing and publication of material—particularly opinion material—is or is not responsible?

As an example of Dr. Mendelsohn's alleged inaccuracy, the complainant cites a column (February 19, 1982) in which Dr. Mendelsohn wrote: "However, I have several times pointed out in this column that the advertisements in medical journals for Tagamet contain absolutely no information about the drug other than its name and a picture of what it looks like."

In another column October 27, 1981, Dr. Mendelsohn spoke of the advertising campaign for Tagamet as massive and to his knowledge unique. He said:

451

> Full-page ads show Tagamet bottles, Tagamet pills, brilliant stripes of green, purple and blue in the background, the name "Tagamet," the generic name "cimetidine," the company name—SmithKline—and six lines which describe the dosage.
>
> Something is missing from these ads, something that I've seen in every other drug company ad: There is no mention of indications for prescribing this drug! Absolutely not one word about which diseases it should be given for! Not a syllable about which symptoms Tagamet is supposed to relieve!

Dr. Kohn, the complainant, protested that all ads in medical journals contain full information about the advertised medicine, but Council staff found that there are two kinds of medical ads.

One kind tells what a drug is for and how effective it is. The FDA requires that such ads include information about contraindications, precautions and adverse side effects. That information is sometimes published in detail as it appears on information sheets packaged with the medicine. More often it is published in summary form. SmithKline has used both summary and full-disclosure forms in Tagamet ads.

The other kind of medical ad is a "reminder" ad. The FDA does not require that such ads include full information as long as they do not say anything about the product beyond the brand name, generic name, name of the firm, price of the drug, dosage forms (tablets, liquid) and packaging (5-ounce bottles, bottles of 250 mg. tablets etc.). Any other statement, such as what the drug is for, would require disclosure of side effects and other information. The rule is so strict that drug firms have to be careful about picturing their products in reminder ads. If a bottle label, visible in a picture, says how many times a day the medicine should be taken, the ad is no longer a reminder ad.

SmithKline & French has used reminder ads in its Tagamet campaign, and it is apparently those ads that Dr. Mendelsohn refers to when he says they contain little information. But Dr. Mendelsohn is wrong to suggest that all Tagamet ads are of the reminder type. Staff found that the firm used both kinds of advertising extensively in such magazines as *The Journal of the American Medical Association, The New England Journal of Medicine, Medical World News* and *The New Physician.*

Going beyond the specific assertion that Dr. Mendelsohn was inaccurate in the matter of the Tagamet ads, Dr. Kohn charged that Dr. Mendelsohn's columns were "full of misinformation and dangerously wrong information." He pointed specifically to a column that appeared in the *Buffalo Evening News* February 17, 1982.

In that column Dr. Mendelsohn quoted a letter to him from an optometrist who believes that high blood pressure is not a disease but a "symptom of smoking, obesity or perhaps inactivity and is really nature's protection to insure proper distribution of sustenance and the carrying away of waste products."

The optometrist wrote:

> Drug therapy does not prevent strokes and coronary problems. Instead it causes them by bringing about a lack of proper blood supply to the tissues.
>
> Specifically, the all important vascular-system wastes lack proper blood supply, and hence a vascular accident is brought about under duress. If that accident happens to be in the coronary or the brain region—well, that's it.
>
> Perhaps physicians should stop taking blood pressures and should start weighing people and asking them about exercise, diet, smoking and work habits.

Dr. Mendelsohn commented, "Perhaps their professional orientation makes optometrists (like you) see some things more clearly than do physicians."

The column is an example of what Dr. Kohn considers misinformation and of what he referred to when he said that "Dr. Mendelsohn . . . urges patients to avoid medications."

After reading the optometrist column, a 69-year-old Buffalo-area woman told her daughter that she was going to give up the medicine she had been taking for five years for high blood pressure. The incident was related by the patient's granddaughter, Barbara J. Matters of Buffalo, in a letter to the *Buffalo Evening News*. Ms. Matters, who is secretary to another Buffalo cardiologist, Dr. John M. Bozer, wrote, "Fortunately we were able to reeducate her in hypertensive disease and prevent her blood pressure from entering stroke level."

Ms. Matters continued, "There are probably many people in this area who have read such nonsense by Mendelsohn and also discontinued their meds. I certainly hope someone gets to them in time to prevent a stroke or death."

That fear, that patients who need medication for high blood pressure might give up their medication, is a strong motivating factor in Dr. Kohn's complaint to the News Council and in his earlier complaint with his colleagues to the *Buffalo Evening News*. Dr. Kohn gave Council staff a clipping from an undated Mendelsohn column about Dyazide and Inderal—both prescribed for high blood pressure. He said a patient brought the clipping in and asked him, "What kind of dangerous medicine are you giving me?" He was able to reassure that patient, because he did come in. Others may not have. "I don't know how many may have stopped seeing me," Dr. Kohn said.

Dr. Peter F. Goergen of Tonawanda, N.Y., sent the *Buffalo Evening*

*News* the following note, which he received along with a copy of the Mendelsohn column in which the optometrist was quoted:

> Doctor Goergen,
>    How come you never told me about this? So medicine doesn't prevent strokes and coronary problems but *causes* them. Are you trying to do us harm to keep up a good business?
>                                                        An ex-patient.

Dr. Bozer, one of the delegation that called on the *Buffalo Evening News*, said he had three patients who suffered strokes after reading Dr. Mendelsohn and quitting their medications. He submitted to the News Council the case history of the most recent of the three, a 76-year-old woman whose stroke was fatal.

The history describes Dr. Bozer's experimentation, starting in 1978, to arrive at a combination of medications that did bring the woman's blood pressure down from a dangerous level. Her pressure had remained under control for nearly a year, according to the history—

> . . . but when she returned in September 1981 she complained of persistent nocturia (complained of for two years), weak legs, and arthritic pains involving the back and legs (symptoms she had complained of when I first saw her in 1978 and explainable by her osteoarthritis). Her blood pressure was 156/80.
>    At that point she announced that she was going to stop all of her medicine and she specifically quoted Dr. Robert Mendelsohn, whom she had metioned to me on several occasions previously, in attributing all her adverse symptoms to the medication. Despite the fact that I was able to arrange an appointment with a rheumatologist, Dr. Germante Bocaldo, just four days later on September 21st, she stated she could not wait and was going to stop all her medicine. I pleaded for her to wait until after his consultation. She did not keep that appointment on Monday, September 21, 1981, but on Tuesday, September 22, 1981, was found in coma in her apartment by her maid. She was immediately admitted to the Buffalo General Hospital where a CT scan of the head revealed a "large right occipital lobe hemorrhage, which extends throughout the entire length of the corpus callousum. Associated intra-ventricular blood. Etiology is uncertain. Angiography is recommended." Her course was progressively downhill and she expired of a massive cerebral hemorrhage September 24, 1981.

A specific column November 25, 1980, drew a reaction from Dr. Bozer that puts the doctors' objections to Dr. Mendelsohn in clear focus. In the column Dr. Mendelsohn wrote: "Like Inderal, Corgard can precipitate or aggravate heart failure."

Dr. Bozer reacted: "Yes, but you've got to explain it in detail. Aspirin can precipitate hemorrhage too. . . . A normal heart I can give you a 100 percent guarantee won't go into heart failure (with Inderal or Corgard, which is similar but requires less frequent doses)."

"Only with a very bad heart" would that possibility arise, he said. "That's why you have phsycians who can manipulate the medicine and know what they are doing."

Dr. Bozer called Inderal a "magic medicine" that was useful in such conditions as migraine headache, high blood pressure, familial tremor, nervous precipitations and many more. But, he said, "I had patients (at the time of a number of Mendelsohn columns on Inderal) that I could not talk into taking Inderal." Dr. Bozer concluded: "What he says is generally true, but there is a great, big BUT."

That is the nub of the accuracy issue between Dr. Mendelsohn and his critics. There is truth in what he writes but, as they see it, it falls so far short of the whole truth, that it amounts, in their view, to misinformation.

The controversy over drugs for high blood pressure is an example. Dr. Kohn says, and disinterested medical experts confirm to Council staff, that the Hypertension Detection and Follow-up Program, which was reported by the National Institutes of Health in 1979, did establish that the control of high blood pressure with drugs reduces death rates. Subsequent research has produced conflicting results when it comes to drug treatment of mild hypertension, but the basic findings for treatment of higher levels of pressure have been reinforced.

To challenge that finding or to exaggerate the dangers of drugs that might be used to control blood pressure is, in the minds of Dr. Mendelsohn's critics, to supply misinformation.

The staff review shows that Dr. Mendelsohn was not entirely accurate about the Tagamet advertising. But does "not entirely accurate" amount to "unfairness"?

Along the same lines, is it inaccurate and unfair to write only about the dangers of drugs without acknowledging their useful effects?

The answer to both questions is, Yes, in a news report. But Mendelsohn is not reporting news; he is writing a column. And, while it is not on the editorial page and not as clearly labeled as it might be, the column is opinion.

The Council traditionally has not held opinion to the same standards of accuracy and fairness it has required of reporting.

As for the charge that the column is irresponsible, it is based on the fear that patients are influenced by Mendelsohn's columns to abandon useful therapies. Indeed the Council is presented with two cases in which patients were so influenced.

An editor at Columbia Features assured staff that Dr. Mendelsohn always cautioned readers to see their doctors before making any change. Staff did not find any such clear warnings, but neither did it find any column in which Dr. Mendelsohn directly urged readers to give up their medications.

What Dr. Mendelsohn does do is urge his readers to learn about the medications they take, and to challenge their doctors.

Again and again Dr. Mendelsohn expresses his opinion that medicines are dangerous and doctors don't know enough about them. Whether he expresses that opinion responsibly or whether it is journalistically responsible to publish his opinions is not a judgment for the News Council to make. Such judgments can only be made by individuals or organizations that do not define themselves in terms of their own impartiality as the News Council does.

The complaint and the investigation do illustrate precisely what is involved in the exercise of editorial discretion. On the one hand is the syndicate editor who exercised that discretion by distributing the Mendelsohn columns and stating clearly that he takes no responsibility for their content. On the other hand there are the editors of the *Buffalo Evening News* who exercised their editorial discretion by canceling the Mendelsohn column when local doctors persuaded them that patients might endanger themselves.

The staff does not suggest that the Buffalo editors were right to drop the Mendelsohn column. Nothing in this report should be interpreted to support that view.

The staff does point to the fact that the Buffalo editors took in information about the impact of the columns, evaluated that information and made a decision on it. Whatever that decision might have been, it represented, because of the intake and evaluation process, a responsible exercise of editorial discretion.

**Council finding:** The Council finds the complaint only partly warranted.

One column did contain an important inaccuracy in alleging that Tagamet advertisements failed to point out the specific uses and potential side effects. The major ads fully disclose both the uses and the side effects and only the permissible 'reminder' ads in medical journals do not—and may not—include information on either uses or side effects.

More important, to recommend suppression of opinion columns would be a dangerous precedent and an unjustified incursion into the responsibilities of editors. At the same time, the potential importance to health and life of published medical advice makes it important for responsible editors who publish medical columns to consider taking special precautions.

One such precaution might be to publish with the column a disclaimer such as, "No advice offered in a column of medical opinion should take the place of an examination by a physician or physicians."

**Concurring:** Ayers, Barrett, Benson, Hornby, Huston, Kennedy, Pulitzer, Pye, Scott, van den Haag and Woolf.

**Dissenting:** Decter.

March 31, 1983

**COMPLAINT NO. 212**     (Filed: Dec. 18, 1982)

AFL-CIO

against

FORBES MAGAZINE

**Complaint:** Murray Seeger, director of the Department of Information, American Federation of Labor and Congress of Industrial Organizations (AFL-CIO), complained that *Forbes* magazine committed two factual errors in a single sentence in an article published in the August 2, 1982, issue. He described one of the errors as minor, but the other as serious, and having "the effect of perpetuating a canard favored in far-right wing political circles that the AFL-CIO receives or received funds directly from the U.S. Labor Department."

Mr. Seeger charged that "This is not only wrong in fact, it is also illegal since a labor organization cannot commingle federal funds with members' dues."

The article, titled "Argumentum ad hominem," was subheaded "One thing is certain about Secretary of Labor Ray Donovan: By his actions in office he has angered organized labor." The sentence which prompted the complaint appeared as the final one (italicized for emphasis) in a paragraph reading as follows:

> What has Donovan done? A lot. Under Donovan's directions, the Labor Department has stopped or drastically reduced hundreds of millions of dollars in annual grants that went to unions to set up job training programs or produce studies. That money also funded the overhead of organizations that as often as not were tied to the Democratic Party. *Donovan aides say privately that the AFL-CIO has had to raise its annual membership tax $15 million a year to make up for lost government cash.*

"The editors," Mr. Seeger charged, "printed this accusation from an anonymous spokesman without asking the AFL-CIO for confirmation."

457

He also said that the magazine has not published or acknowledged two letters seeking a correction (one, on August 9 to the editor, and another on November 9, to the publisher), and that a telephone conversation with the managing editor produced no results.

"We believe this issue should be explored by the National News Council," Mr. Seeger wrote in his letter to the Council dated December 8, 1982, adding that "it involves issues of journalistic ethics beyond the simple facts of the dispute."

In his letter to the magazine in August, Mr. Seeger said that the $15 million dues increase "voted in open convention and well-publicized in November 1981, at most, could be only 60 percent of the printed figure ($15 million) for the year 1982.

"The uses of the new moneys were also spelled out publicly and include such items as the new George Meany Library, the Labor Institute of Public Affairs and dues for the International Confederation of Free Trade Unions with which the AFL-CIO reaffiliated in 1982.

"The dues increase did not replace any government income since the AFL-CIO does not receive any cash from the government. . . .

"The AFL-CIO went to great effort to cooperate with your reporter on this article. We have made the financial records available to him; they were available before he wrote the story, too."

In a follow-up letter to the Council dated December 22, Mr. Seeger said that the minor error he referred to previously concerned the amount of the dues increase and "was a simple error of fact."

**Response:** James W. Michaels, editor of *Forbes*, in a letter dated February 8, 1983, responded to the Council as follows:

> Regarding the complaint from the AFL-CIO's public relations department: We felt their letter did not respond to the thrust of the article, which was that organization's relentless battle to discredit the current Secretary of Labor.
>
> Furthermore it is a matter of interpretation as to whether the particular fact of which they complained was right or wrong. In short, we felt they were splitting hairs.

**Staff analysis:** The "minor" error referred to in the federation's complaint applied to the estimate by "Donovan aides" of the size of the annual dues increase. The aides were quoted as saying it was $15 million a year. The federation's own figures are not seriously at variance with this estimate. The increase voted by the convention was in two steps. In asserting that *Forbes* had overstated the amount by 40 percent, Mr. Seeger was limiting himself to the first installment—an increase of $9 million in per capita payments for 1982. However, the same convention action called for a further rise of $5.4 million in payments for 1983, bringing to $14.4 million the annual increase that now becomes part of the permanent dues structure of the AFL-CIO. Since all the figures represent rough projections, the rounded-out number used in *Forbes* could certainly be considered close to the mark. In terms of the federation's finances for 1982 and 1983, the cumulative effect of the dues increase was to add an anticipated $23.4 million to the AFL-CIO budgetary resources.

Regarding the "serious" error, an examination by Council staff of the "Proceedings, Fourteenth Constitutional Convention" of the AFL-CIO, held in New York City on November 16-19, 1981, made clear that the dues increases were put before the delegates in open session to finance an expansion of federation activities in "five major areas." Three of these areas had been cited by Mr. Seeger in his letter of August 9 to *Forbes*' managing editor.

The "five major areas" cited in the federation's convention proceedings on Page 293, plus another area cited on Page 39, are listed below, together with the amounts (expressed in millions of dollars) from dues increases (supplied to the Council's staff by the AFL-CIO Washington headquarters) allocated to each area for 1982 and 1983.

| Areas | 1982 | 1983 |
|---|---|---|
| Institute of Public Affairs and related activities | 3 | 3 |
| ICFTU affiliation | 1.7 | 1.7 |
| George Meany Library and Archives | 1 | 1.5 |
| COPE (Committee on Political Education) | 3.5 | 3.5 |
| Frontlash (a youth registration group) | | |
| LCLAA (Labor Council for Latin American Advancement) | | |
| A. Philip Randolph Institute (a coalition of Black trade unionists) | 2 | 2 |
| Houston Organizing Project | .25 | .25 |
| Total | $11.45 | 11.95 |
| Grand Total | $23.40 | |

*The Wall Street Journal*, in a news report on the 1981 convention, published on November 19, said that "The AFL-CIO, signaling its intent to play a more active political role, voted a hefty dues increase to help in the effort . . . .

"A big portion of the increase will help bolster organized labor's political strength and public image through increased funding of the Committee on Political Education, the federation's political arm, and creation of an institute to coordinate its public relations efforts." (Institute of Public Affairs)

The record of the federation's 1981 convention proceedings supports this statement. No reference of any kind was made to relationships, financial or otherwise, with the Labor Department or any other government agency when the dues proposal was submitted by the Committee on Constitution or when the delegates approved it two days later. The need for raising dues was explained solely in terms of the AFL-CIO decision to expand services in the areas listed above.

Looking beyond the public record of the convention, is there evidence to support the assertion in *Forbes* that drastic cuts ordered by Secretary Donovan in grants for job-training and research programs conducted under union auspices had deprived the AFL-CIO of money it formerly relied on to fund its basic operations, thus necessitating higher dues?

Rex Hardesty, assistant director for public relations of the federation, supplied Council staff with information designed to back up Mr. Seeger's statement that the AFL-CIO "does not receive cash from the government" to finance any of its standard activities. Even if there were no legal restraints against such a commingling of funds, he said, the federation would shun the practice because of its strong belief as a matter of policy that free trade unions must maintain a clear line of separation from government. Quite apart from that feeling, Mr. Hardesty adds, any use of Labor Department funds in connection with organizing, political education or other normal budget functions of the AFL-CIO would violate federal procurement regulations governing cost-reimbursement contracts—specifically, FPR 1-30.414.

Through adjunct units the federation and many of its affiliated unions do have contracts with the Labor Department, the bulk of them targeted at the recruitment and training for jobs of minority youth and the hard-core unemployed. In all cases, the Labor Department confirms, grants made under these contracts are earmarked for the specific function designated in the contract and are subject not only to standard accounting procedures but to audit by the department's Inspector General if questions arise.

In the case of the AFL-CIO, Mr. Hardesty emphasizes, the divorcement of the special units administering government contracts from the mainline activities of the federation is underscored by setting them up as incorporated institutes with their own officers and staff. As a case in point, he cited the AFL-CIO Human Resources Development Institute, which serves as the employment and training arm of the federation, working with unions generally to enhance job opportunities for the unemployed and disadvantaged.

The institute is headquartered in the AFL-CIO in Washington but it maintains a network of local area offices throughout the country, staffed by labor experts on employment and training. These experts and their clerical assistants, though not technically federal employees, are hired and paid under civil service grade standards for their categories. Proceedings of the 1981 convention show that in April of that year government funding of HRDI was cut back by 37 percent from the level for 1980. As a result the number of the institute's local offices was reduced from 58 to 33 and the network was reorganized under six rather than seven regional directors. Cuts also were made in the institute's national office staff and several special program offices were closed.

That level of service was maintained through 1982 as a result of a new Labor Department grant of $2 million, but the HRDI feared it would have to scale down again when the original allocation for the first nine months of 1983 was set by the department at $1 million. However, in response to an AFL-CIO protest, Secretary Donovan recently authorized a $400,000 supplement. This, Mr. Hardesty says, will enable the institute to keep functioning on an even keel until its future is determined by grants made pursuant to the federal budget for fiscal 1984.

The only other top-level contract involving an AFL-CIO adjunct, so far as Labor Department records show, is a new one for $2 million covering research and publications to be prepared on a global basis under a Labor Department contract with the AFL-CIO Free Trade Union Institute. That institute, according to Mr. Hardesty, is a spin-off under separate corporate structure of the federation's international affairs department and its councils for promoting unionization and development in Latin America, Asia and Africa. The $2 million grant was made by the Labor Department in compliance with a special act of Congress.

Regional subsidiary bodies of the federation as well as its departments covering workers in the building trades and in the food and beverage industries have received Labor Department grants for projects connected with job training and occupational health and safety. The biggest cutback in the last year involved the Appalachian Council, a special unit set up by four state federations in the mid-sixties as part of President Johnson's "war on poverty." In fiscal 1982 the council administered a $10.7 million grant as nationwide recruitment and screening agent for the Job Corps. In the present fiscal year the sum has been reduced to $560,000, plus an additional $70,000 for occupational safety and health.

Paul S. Williams, chief of the Labor Department's Division of Media and Editorial Services, says he has been unable to find any "Donovan aide" who acknowledges having made the statement quoted in *Forbes;* nor has he found any independent verification or substantiation for it. He echoes Mr. Hardesty's insistence that all grants to the federation or its affiliates are for specific purposes, not for payment of general overhead or regular union services.

**Council finding:** The Council finds the protest about a "minor" error so minor as to be unwarranted, since the figure reported was very close to total dues increases voted.

The only issue of substance requiring consideration by the Council is the relationship, if any, between the AFL-CIO's decision to raise dues and the cutbacks ordered by the Labor Department in job-training and other grants it makes to subsidiary units of the federation set up to perform specific services outside regular union functions. It is clear that the statement—attributed by *Forbes* to unidentified "Donovan aides"—that the AFL-CIO dues increase was put into effect in order to "make up for lost government cash" has no discernible foundation in fact.

The Council finds this section of the AFL-CIO complaint warranted.

The editor of *Forbes,* in his response to the Council, gives as the central reason for taking no cognizance of the AFL-CIO's letter the magazine's belief that the federation was ignoring "the thrust of our article, which was that organization's relentless battle to discredit the current Secretary of Labor."

Even though that judgment on "thrust" can be accepted as within the valid exercise of editorial discretion, it scarcely justifies brushing aside an important factual challenge as "splitting hairs." To the federation, there was nothing trivial about the flat assertion that it had put through its dues increase to make up for lost government cash when both practice and law forbade any use of federal funds to finance standard union activities. Under those circumstances, publication of a letter to the editor by *Forbes* was in order as a minimal act of fairness.

**Concurring:** Ayers, Barrett, Benson, Decter, Hornby, Huston, Kennedy, Pulitzer, Pye, Scott, van den Haag and Woolf.

**Abstaining:** Williams

March 31, 1983

462

## COMPLAINT NO. 213     (Filed: Dec. 14, 1982)
## ATOMIC INDUSTRIAL FORUM
### against
## THE WASHINGTON POST

The Atomic Industrial Forum complained that a news story in *The Washington Post* on November 1, 1982, was "erroneous" and "needlessly terrified many persons over nuclear electricity."

The story appeared under a headline saying, "A-Plant Accident Study Shows 'Worst Case' Could Be Worse Than Old NRC Estimates." The lead said:

> The most detailed government study of potential consequences of accidents at atomic power plants has concluded that the worst-case death toll could exceed 100,000 persons and damage could top $300 billion at certain locations.

The story said that the new estimates greatly surpassed the worst-case estimate of 3,300 early deaths and $14 billion in property damage contained in a Nuclear Regulatory Commission safety study in 1975.

The complaint was made by Donald C. Winston, media relations manager for the Atomic Industrial Forum, which is a trade association of the nuclear power industry.

Mr. Winston complained that *The Post* gave "front page prominence to a worst-case hypothetical accident that has only one chance in one billion of occurring." The *Post* story did not include the one-in-a-billion probability estimate.

Mr. Winston wrote:

> The erroneous story captured the attention of the wire services and newspaper editors across the country; the UPI transmitted *The Washington Post's* inaccurate account nearly verbatim.
>
> To date *The Washington Post* has not seen fit to correct the errors in that story or in its second-day follow-up, or to admit that it had been used by a political figure to back a local issue in the man's home state.

The political figure to whom Mr. Winston referred is Rep. Edward J. Markey (D-Mass.), who supplied some material for the story to *The Post*.

Rep. Markey opposes nuclear power. Mr. Winston suggests that he supplied material to *The Post* to strengthen anti-nuclear sentiment in states like his own where nuclear referendums were scheduled the day after the *Post* story appeared.

Mr. Winston said the *Post* story was wrong in three respects:

First, it said that death and destruction estimates for a "worst case"

463

nuclear accident were *part of* a study by Sandia National Laboratories for the Nuclear Regulatory Commission. Mr. Winston said the estimates were not part of the Sandia study.

Second, the *Post* story said the death and destruction estimates came from a study of possible accidents at existing plants. Actually, they came from a study of possible accidents at a hypothetical plant at the sites of existing plants. In some cases the hypothetical plant was different from the existing plant and, consequently, the damage estimates were not realistic.

Third, Mr. Winston did not say so in his letter of complaint, but an Atomic Industrial Forum briefing paper he distributed to the press said that *The Post* reported incorrectly that there was a 2 percent chance of a worst-case accident before 2000.

Mr. Winston particularly criticized *The Post* for failing to obtain a comment from the NRC or from Sandia in its November 1 story. Such a comment might have prevented the alleged errors in the story and might have provided a correct numerical estimate to show how remote the possibility of a worst-case accident is, Mr. Winston said. The NRC provided the one-in-a-billion estimate at a news conference the day the *Post* story appeared and *The Post* reported that figure the next day.

In that second story, Mr. Winston complained, *The Post* again ignored NRC's assertion that the Sandia study did not deal with existing plants. That is "a key consideration," he said.

Mr. Winston noted that *The Post* did publish an article November 6 on its op-ed page by George Keyworth, presidential science advisor, who criticized the reporting of the death and destruction estimates. Also the *Post's* ombudsman, Robert McCloskey, criticized the *Post's* first story in a column November 17; he said the story "needed better balance, with more than a one-sided congressional view. It was heavy on remote possibilities. Too much accelerator, not enough brake."

"But," Mr. Winston wrote, "There was never any attempt to clear up the errors that appeared in the two news stories, or to alleviate the stress that those stories may have put on members of the public living in the vicinity of power plants."

Mr. Winston included copies of stories by United Press International and stories produced by local newspapers using figures from a *Post* table to report the worst-case damage estimates for nuclear plants near them. Some of those stories included the incorrect estimate that there was a 2 percent chance of such an accident before the year 2000.

Mr. Winston also included copies of a full-page ad attacking the various news reports under a headline, "Most of the Stories Were Wrong." The ad was paid for by The Atomic Industrial Forum and the Edison Electric Institute and published in *The New York Times, Washington Post* and *Wall Street Journal*.

**Response of the news organization:** Benjamin C. Bradlee, executive editor of *The Post*, referred to the complaint as the work of "the flack for the nuclear lobby." Nonetheless, he did provide a reply in the form of a memorandum from Milton R. Benjamin, the reporter who wrote both *Post* stories.

Mr. Benjamin did not address himself in his memo to the complaint that the worst-case estimates were not truly part of the Sandia study. But his stories suggest that he believes the worst-case figures were indeed part of the study and were suppressed. In his first story, November 1, he wrote:

> While the draft report on the two-year Sandia story notes that it examined the possibility of worst-case accidents . . . the version given to *The Washington Post* does not contain the worst-case figures. The NRS is expected to release this version.
>
> Rep. Edward J. Markey (D-Mass.), chairman of the House Interior and Insular Affairs subcommittee on oversight and investigations, obtained the full computer results submitted by Sandia to the NRC and a companion Sandia report on financial consequences of nuclear accidents. Markey made this information available to *The Post*.
>
> "Perhaps the authors of the study thought the high-consequence figures would be misinterpreted, but the NRC is misleading the public when it is not honest about what the worst-case possibility is," Markey said yesterday.

Mr. Benjamin's story the next day reflected the same view. It appeared under the headline, "NRC Issues Report, Withholds Worst-Case Estimates." His lede read:

> The Nuclear Regulatory Commission yesterday issued a new report on the potential consequences of accidents at atomic power plants, but did not release the worst-case death and damage estimates *made by the study* . . .

As for the complaint that the damage figures flowed from the study of a hypothetical plant rather than actual plants, Mr. Benjamin responded as follows: Sandia did assume a standardized reactor at each site in order to reduce the variables in the study. It assumed a 1120-megawatt reactor because many that are currently operating and most under construction are about that size. Mr. Benjamin said, the actual reactor at Salem, N.J., where the heaviest death toll might be expected, is 1115 megawatts. That might reduce the projected death toll from 102,000 to 100,000, Mr. Benjamin said. On the other hand, the reactors are slightly larger than

1120 megawatts at 14 other plants in the study "so the consequences at these sites would in fact be worse than *The Post* reported."

Mr. Benjamin pointed out in his memo that his stories did not say, as the AIF charged, that there was a 2 percent chance of a worst-case accident by the year, 2000. His first story said there was a 2 percent chance of a "Group 1" accident by that year. A Group 1 accident would involve severe core damage, melting of uranium fuel, essential failure of all safety systems and a major breach of the reactor's containment resulting in a large release of radioactivity into the atmosphere. The story said:

> For such an accident to produce the worst-case death and damage toll calculated by the computer study, the draft report said a Group 1 accident generally would have to be followed by a "rainout of the radioactive plume onto a population center." The report termed that combination of events "improbable."

Mr. Benjamin said, "*The Post* had been unable to obtain from NRC sources a numerical estimate of the actual probability at the time of the initial story." He noted that the newspaper did publish the next day the NRC's estimate that the probability of worst-case consequences were one in a billion.

In response to the complaint that the story was a "single source" story from a source with an axe to grind and, therefore, should certainly have included comment from the NRC and Sandia, Mr. Benjamin furnished this background:

> The sequence of events postulated by the AIF is simply wrong. This story was based on a two-inch-thick document, "Technical Guidance for Siting Criteria Development," produced by Sandia, a Department of Energy laboratory, for the Nuclear Regulatory Commission, a government agency.
>
> That document had been circulating within the NRC for months, and the reporter had obtained a copy of this document from an NRC source several weeks before the story was published. From references in the document, he had inferred that there were "worst case" numbers that were missing.
>
> Aware that Markey's subcommittee had oversight over the NRC, he enlisted the aid of Markey's staff, which also had been attempting to obtain these numbers. Markey's staff made them available to *The Post* within 24 hours of obtaining them.
>
> Since the massive study, which was quoted from liberally, was produced by Sandia for the NRC, it is hard to conclude that either organization was slighted in the preparation of the story.

**Staff analysis:** The scientists who produced the figures now being called "worst-case" figures have told the News Council staff that they do not consider them worst-case figures at all. They say the figures are merely the "worst" of a set of numbers produced in a computer run that was not designed to find worst-case figures but something different.

David C. Aldrich, project coordinator of the Sandia study, said it was he, not the Nuclear Regulatory Commission, who decided "many, many months before the report was released" not to include the figures that have been labeled worst-case.

"I have no guarantee that these are worst-case numbers. They weren't purposely calculated as worst-case numbers. They just happen to be the worst numbers that the computer code predicted this time around," Mr. Aldrich said.

"If I wanted to, I could have *more* deaths than 100,000. I could put in some assumptions that could make it higher," said Daniel J. Alpert, one of the authors of the study.

The purpose of the Sandia study was to find the effect on the consequences of a nuclear accident of such characteristics as geography, weather and population distribution and movement that were unique at each reactor site.

Mr. Aldrich said he was interested primarily in the "mean" consequences of an accident, what another scientist called "the consequences that might reasonably be expected." For example, the study report included the consequences of weather sequences that might occur once in a hundred years, but the consequences of weather sequences that would occur only once in 10,000 years were left out.

Mr. Aldrich said many of the assumptions made for arriving at mean figures were inappropriate for predicting peak consequences. He said his staff didn't worry about that, because the peaks have little effect on the mean, but, he said the figures based on the inappropriate assumptions "are in the computer calculations."

As examples of the "absurd" assumptions in some of the calculations that produced what are now being called worst-case consequences, Mr. Aldrich noted that the researchers assumed that nobody beyond 10 miles from the accident would flee or take protective action for 24 hours after the accident; and they did not assume any runoff of the radioactive rainfall or any factor for the shelter from the rain that buildings would provide.

"And the reason we didn't do that is because the mean is relatively insensitive to those; so we didn't worry about it too much. But all would have a drastic, or could have a drastic impact on those peaks," he said.

The *Post* story compares the 102,000 deaths predicted in the Sandia study with a worst-case prediction of 3,300 deaths in the NRC's 1975 report. Daniel J. Alpert, one of the authors of the Sandia report, noted that the probability of the worst-case disaster in both studies was about the same, one in a billion reactor years. However, he said a significant assumption was different: The 1975 study assumed evacuation of people in a 25-mile radius while the new study assumed evacuation in a 10-mile radius. If the evacuation assumption is changed from 10 miles to 25 miles in the Sandia study, Mr. Alpert said, the deaths drop to zero for the weather sequence at the Salem plant that produced the 102,000 deaths. And if the 25-mile radius was applied for all the weather sequences in the study, there would be a new peak for the Salem plant, and it would be lower by a factor of about 10, Mr. Alpert said.

The question arises why *The Post* did not supply some measure more specific than "improbable" of the probabilities of the supposed worst-case accident to its readers. Mr. Benjamin said in his memo that he was "unable to obtain" a numerical estimate of the probabilities from NRC sources. But Robert Bernero, director of the risk analysis division of the NRC, said the risk probability is on the same line of the Sandia computer material as the deaths figures. In the column next to the peak deaths figures is the probability of the weather sequence necessary to produce those deaths. Both figures are in a code explained in the beginning of the printout. In the case of a worst-case consequence at the Salem plant the chances of the weather sequence (1 in 10,000 Group 1 accidents) multiplied by the chances of a Group 1 accident (1 in 100,000 years of reactor operation) produce the chances of the worst-case death toll of 102,000 (1 in a billion reactor years).

However, it turns out that *The Post* did not obtain its worst-case figures directly from the Sandia computer printouts. Instead it obtained figures calculated from those printouts by Richard Udell of Rep. Markey's staff.

Mr. Udell said he did not give *The Post* the probability figures.

He said if he had it to do again, he would "make sure the probability was understood." He also said he would probably reduce the figures by 25 percent, because even then the numbers would be "important."

The Sandia study contains only mean figures for accident deaths. Those are adequate "if you want to know the relative risk of nuclear plants" said Mr. Udell. "But if you want to know what we have been trying to find out since 1967, i.e. the worst-case possibilities, you need the peaks." He said Mr. Benjamin reasoned that if there were means in the report, there must be peak figures somewhere, and he asked Mr. Udell to try to get them. Mr. Udell had received a previous request for the peak figures from the Union of Concerned Scientists, a group that opposes nuclear energy.

468

In response to Mr. Udell's request, the NRC made the microfiche pages, some 50,000 of them, available to him on Wednesday, October 27. He began his calculations that afternoon and supplied Mr. Benjamin with a draft of his figures that evening. On Thursday he supplied Mr. Benjamin with a table of worst-case death and damage figures that appeared in *The Post* much as he had prepared it, he said. Mr. Udell said that he had offered *The Post* scaled-down death figures that reflected the actual size of each plant. He also supplied the Sandia figures, which were based on a hypothetical, standardized plant. Mr. Udell said Mr. Benjamin chose to use the Sandia death figures lest the newspaper be criticized for relying too heavily on material from Rep. Markey's office.

The dollar figures in another column of the *Post* table are scaled down to the size of each plant, but Mr. Aldrich said those figures are not what they are described as in the story. They are described as "property damage" and as "financial consequences of a worst-case accident." Instead they are what Mr. Aldrich called "integrated consequences over the life of the plant." They are designed to provide a basis for comparing the cost of a safety measure with the cost of an accident, and they involve calculations of the probability of an accident and the life of the plant, Mr. Aldrich said. Mr. Alpert said that as measures of the potential damage in a worst-case accident, the numbers could be off by as much as a factor of 10. That is, they could be as much as ten times too high. (At Indian Point, for example, where *The Post* table suggests the cost of an accident would be $300 billion, the expected cost of an accident would actually be $14 to $15 billion, said Mr. Aldrich. That includes loss of plant, replacement of power from other sources, property damage, and deaths.) However, Alpert said:

> My problem is not so much that they're off. I guess it's difficult for me as a scientist to understand. The report gave numbers for a certain purpose, and *The Post* just took those numbers and called them something else."

Mr. Udell acknowledged that Mr. Aldrich—whom he said was a foremost expert in the field—had a valid concern about the cost figures as they appeared in *The Post*, but he said the newspaper should not be faulted. "They reprinted what I gave them," he said. Furthermore, he said, "We think they are wildly *under*stated."

Mr. Udell's recollection indicates that *The Post* had four days after it received his figures to seek comment on those figures from NRC or Sandia. Mr. Benjamin's memo is confusing on this point: On the one hand, he says he was unable to obtain a numerical estimate of the worst-case probabilities from NRC sources. On the other hand, he saw no need for comment from Sandia or NRC since both were involved in the Sandia report, and the report was quoted from liberally in the *Post* story.

However, since *The Post* did publish worst-case figures not in the Sandia report, the question arises whether the newspaper did not incur an obligation to obtain comment on those figures beyond the comment in the report itself that the worst-case scenario was "improbable."

As for Mr. Winston's complaint that the *Post* story did not make clear that the worst-case death consequences might be less at a reactor smaller than the Sandia study's 1120-megawatt plant, it is true that there are smaller plants. However, a footnote to the *Post's* table does indicate that the death figures for each site are based on a hypothetical 1120-megawatt reactor. That left it up to news agencies that used figures from that table to make clear that the figures for any particular site might not represent the consequences of an accident at the plant at that site.

That leads to consideration of how the story spread that there was a 2 percent chance of a worst-case nuclear accident in the United States before the year 2000.

In his complaint Mr. Winston charges that UPI transmitted what he called the *Post's* inaccurate story "nearly verbatim." However, it is not true that the *Post* story was inaccurate on this score. The *Post* story said the chances of a Group 1 accident were 2 percent by the year 2000. But it also said that improbable weather conditions would have to occur to produce the worst-case consequences.

That caution appeared in the continuation of the *Post* story on an inside page. Furthermore, the *Post* story did not contain a numerical probability for a worst-case consequence that would have differentiated clearly between the probabilities of those consequences and the probabilities of a Group 1 accident.

Therefore, it is conceivable that the erroneous stories resulted from an inaccurate rewrite of the *Post* story by a wire service.

Mr. Udell said he saw a UPI story timed at 8 a.m. Monday, November 1, with the incorrect probability figure. That afternoon a professor interrupted a press conference put on by Rep. Markey and the Union of Concerned Scientists in Boston to say that an incorrect wire service story had appeared that day in a New Mexico newspaper. Council staff has a clipping of a November 1 UPI story from *The Chapel Hill Newspaper* in North Carolina, which contains the wrong probability information and attributes it to the Sandia study report as quoted in *The Washington Post*.

UPI stories November 2 continued to carry the wrong probabilities, attributing them in some cases to the report and in others to Rep. Markey. Rep. Markey's press staff assured Council staff that the congressman was not responsible for the wrong information; the staff was sending the Council a copy of the congressman's press release on the subject. UPI stories on November 2 did include Mr. Bernero's denial that there was a 2 percent chance of a worst-case consequence by the year 2000.

The Associated Press stories in the hands of Council staff do not contain the incorrect probability figure, but they are dated November 2. Staff is trying to find out if AP carried wrong stories earlier. AP differs from UPI in that it attributes the worst-case figures not to the Sandia study but to the staff of the House Interior Subcommittee on Oversight of which Rep. Markey is chairman.

Some notes about numbers: Both Mr. Udell and Steven Sholly, technical research associate for the Union of Concerned Scientists in Washington, said the NRC's 1 in 100,000 figure for the chances of a Group 1 accident was too low. For some plants the chances are as high as one in 2500 years, Mr. Sholly said. Mr. Udell said some were even higher. However, despite his criticism of the 1 in 100,000 figure, Mr. Sholly agreed with Mr. Bernero that some figure like 1 in a billion was a correct estimate for the chances of a worst-case accident producing 102,000 deaths.

Also, on the same day (November 2) that Mr. Bernero was telling the press that 1 in a billion was the chance for the worst-case accident that would produce 102,000 deaths, Sandia Labs put out a press release giving those odds as 1 in 10 million reactor years. Mr. Bernero said the two figures were not inconsistent, because his estimate might vary by a factor of 10.

It has become clear to the News Council staff that while this case focuses on a dispute about specific numbers, there is an underlying philosophical dispute about the way numbers are used to assess nuclear risks.

The NRC and Sandia in the recent report rely on a method called "probabilistic risk assessment" to determine those risks. Using that method the Nuclear Regulatory Commission in January gave preliminary approval to a safety goal for commercial reactors that would limit the chance of a catastrophic reactor core meltdown to one in 10,000 years of reactor operation. Rep. Markey said at that time that the action "is another step in institutionalizing probabilistic risk assessment, which has inherent uncertainties and ignores things like sabotage."

Rep. Markey was quoted in wire service stories as saying that the worst-case figures in the Sandia study should prompt the closing of all nuclear power plants in the country as soon as alternative power becomes available.

A note on press attitudes toward nuclear energy: In a study reported in *Public Opinion* last fall, Stanley Rothman and S. Robert Lichter found that "the scientific community is highly supportive of nuclear energy development (and) regards nuclear energy as relatively safe . . ." On the other hand, the study found that journalists, particularly those in major national news media including the television networks, *The New York Times* and the *Washington Post,* are skeptical. Furthermore, the study showed that the journalists' skepticism about nuclear energy correlated with a liberal political ideology.

Earlier studies showed that news coverage of nuclear energy became increasingly negative during the 1970s. During that period the Union of Concerned Scientists was the most frequent source for comment on nuclear energy on network evening news and Ralph Nader was the most frequently quoted single "expert." (Mr. Udell, incidentally, worked for Mr. Nader as an investigator before joining Rep. Markey's staff last year.) Despite the finding that scientists in general and nuclear scientists in particular were supportive of nuclear energy, the only experts among the top 10 quoted as pronuclear sources during the 11 year period before and the month after the Three Mile Island disaster were spokesmen for utility companies and the nuclear industry.

**Council finding:** The Atomic Industrial Forum complains that *The Washington Post* reported incorrectly that there was a 2 percent chance of a worst-case nuclear accident by the year 2000. This is not true. The error was made by a wire service.

The AIF complains that *The Post* did not say the consequences of nuclear accidents were based on hypothetical reactors not necessarily the same size as the reactors at a given site. That is not entirely true. *The Post* did note that fact in a footnote accompanying its chart of accident consequences, but that and other limitations of the modeling techniques should have been in the story.

The AIF complains that *The Post* reported incorrectly that a set of worst-case death estimates were part of a study for the NRC. The figures were indeed developed by the study, but they were not part of the study report. It is important that the source of such data be identified. In the *Post* report there is no indication that the newspaper sought comment from the scientists who had decided not to include those figures in their report or any neutral scientist. As a result the reader was left with the impression

472

that the figures had been suppressed, and the reader had no way of judging whether there might be another, more valid reason for leaving the figures out. The *Post* story quoted the Sandia report as saying the figures were left out because a worst-case disaster was "improbable." The reader deserved to know just how improbable.

The charge that *The Post* created needless terror in readers' minds is not supportable by any evidence before us.

The Council does not find the Atomic Industrial Forum's complaint against *The Post* warranted in full. It does find warranted that element of the complaint relating to the failure of *The Post* to obtain comment from those who had decided not to report worst-case figures when those figures were supplied to *The Post* by an opponent of nuclear energy. This failure resulted in a story that was not fully accurate.

*The Post* also used figures that it said were the dollar consequences of a worst-case nuclear accident. It did not give the researcher who produced those figures a chance to comment on them. Both that researcher and the person who supplied the figures to *The Post* acknowledge that the figures do not and were not intended to represent the costs of such an accident.

**Concurring:** Ayers, Barrett, Benson, Decter, Hornby, Huston, Kennedy, Pulitzer, Pye, Scott, van den Haag and Woolf.

**Abstaining:** Williams

April 1, 1983

### COMPLAINT NO. 214     (Filed: Dec. 27, 1982)
### ROBERT M. SHUBOW
### against
### THE SAN FRANCISCO CHRONICLE

**Complaint:** Robert M. Shubow, managing editor of *India West,* a magazine for East Indians in the western United States, complained that a *San Francisco Chronicle* article "unfairly savaged a large group of people for the actions of a few, based solely on their name and national origin."

Mr. Shubow complained about a feature article by Warren Hinckle that appeared in *The Chronicle* December 14, 1982. The Hinckle article began:

> The Patel clan of the state of Gujarat in India, by dint of hard work and penny-pinching, has cornered the market on the cockroach palaces of the Tenderloin and the South of Market, and of this they can be proud.
>
> They have also, in this the coldest of winters, consistently neglected to provide

heat in many of their hotels, and frequently have not provided hot water to the elderly and the poor and the dazed who live in their crummy rooms, and for this they should be ashamed.

Some people say the Patels are cold hearted. I don't know about that. I understand that they are very religious people.

They own so many hotels it's impossible and doubtlessly unfair to say they're all bad, or even cold. What I do know is that the six typical Patel hotels I visited at random were maybe the coldest hotels in Frisco. I've got the names of a dozen more Patel hotels where people have complained about the heat.

The article then went on to detail Mr. Hinckle's findings in a number of hotels and to challenge the city to do something about the plight of the poor residents he found shivering and without hot water.

Mr. Shubow said in his letter to the News Council:

The story has inflamed local prejudice against a large group of immigrants, most of whom are innocent of wrongdoing. This is not the first time a newspaper in this country has engaged in unfair attacks on these people, for they are a convenient and easy target, and I fear that others will follow in other cities. It is, therefore, of national importance to clarify this matter before further damage is done.

Mr. Shubow wrote that he had called both the news editor and the writer of the article and was refused any "redress, retraction or clarification." And he said the newspaper did not publish "our letters to the editor explaining the other side of the matter." He said:

They felt that a mention in the fourteenth graf of a followup story the next day to the effect that others besides members of this group were also involved in wrongdoing was sufficient clarification, and that a side-bar saying the group was religious was sufficient "balance." I believe that an objective view of the matter will result in a different judgment.

Mr. Shubow charged that immediately after the story *The Chronicle* published a number of letters hostile to the Patels and Indians in general. It did not for several days publish letters defending the group, "although several sober letters that I am aware of had been sent them." He specified a letter from himself, a copy of which he enclosed with his complaint, and a letter from San Francisco Supervisor Carol Ruth Silver. He said further that the *Chronicle* covered but did not report on a press conference in which Ms. Silver criticized the *Chronicle* story.

In his own letter to the editor Mr. Shubow said that Mr. Hinckle's stories had an "unjustified and unconscionable anti-Indian slant." He said the first day's investigation by the authorities after the first story appeared showed, that of 35 hotels cited for violations of the code, only

13 were owned by Patels, and 18 were clearly owned by members of other ethnic groups. He wrote:

> By calling the Tenderloin hotels "typical Patel hotels" and describing the Patels as a "closeknit and secretive group of East Indians" who lie, cheat and "laugh in their tenants' faces when asked to turn on the heat," Hinckle has planted a dangerous seed of racial prejudice in our city.
>
> The first fruits of that seed have already appeared in the form of threatening phone calls to many people named Patel, jeering at Indians in public, and one hotel owner has been beaten up.
>
> The fact is that many Patel hotels are not of the low caliber reported in Hinckle's articles, and many Patels are not hotel owners at all, but engineers, doctors and members of other professions. They are making great and welcome contributions to American society. Yet all will now have to live with the branding delivered by one of your self-righteous reporters . . . .
>
> As it was *The Chronicle* which initiated the unfortunate torrent of racism which has now ensued, it is up to *The Chronicle* to rectify their mistake if you intend to live up to your responsibility as journalists.

Ms. Silver said in her press release:

> A group of people have been slandered in the major papers and on television for the actions of one or two people with a common surname. These people—some related to others by blood—and some not— have fallen victim to that same insidious bigotry that has plagued Black, Hispanic, American Indian and Asian Americans. Categorizing any group by the actions of a few is not fair and is more than a shame— it is a crime.

**The story:** The first story was long, the equivalent of a full newspaper page. It started on page one, Mr. Hinckle is a columnist, and the article bore the label, "Hinckle's Journal." Headlines over the story read "The Hotels Without Heat," and "Aged Tenants Shivering in Their Rooms." A continuation headline said, "Putting the Heat on the Slumlords," and another said, "Plight of the Tenderloin Poor—They Can't Get Warm."

The writer said he "visited the elderly in their sad small rooms in the Patel hotels. I touched more radiators than a scrap metal dealer. Nowhere did I find the heat going in their rooms during the hours city housing codes require it to be on."

The article focused on hotels owned by Patels. The writer said the "clan" owns "the lion's share" of the small hotels in which those who depend on various kinds of welfare are housed. At the end of the article, where the writer talks to city officials, there are two sentences that might remind the reader that there are non-Patel owners. In one the writer says, "Hardly anybody, Patel or not, turns on the heat in the Tenderloin." In the other the writer says the district attorney "hasn't heard bo peep from the housing inspectors about the problems in the Tenderloin hotels." Otherwise the Patel hotels are the issue. The name Patel appears 42 times. References to the Patels include:

> The Patels who own upwards of $25 million in property . . . .
>
> Waiting for the heat to come on (in a Patel hotel) is like waiting for the Second Coming . . . .
>
> Navin Patel was a young man with baggy pants and a smile on a wary face . . . He looked at me with eyes that were like pointed guns.
>
> "If you ask a Patel why the heat isn't on, he will tell you that the heat is on. You could be sitting on an iceberg and he will tell you that the heat is on."
>
> "Most of the Patels live in their hotels and save on expenses while they pile up money to buy more hotels. The Patels are a closeknit and secretive group of East Indians who have retained their native customs in the Diaspora. The women wear saris and cook traditional Indian dishes. There was a curry smell in the office the way there is a tree smell in the redwood grove. Kent Patel was eager to show me the furnace. That made me suspicious."
>
> "The Patels have been called before the state labor commission on complaints of making indentured servants of desk clerks and maids in their hotels by getting them to work for less than half the minimum wage. The Patels have been called before the Rent Stabilization Board by tenants who want a reduction in rent because the Patels aren't providing heat. The manager of the Patels' Elm Hotel on Eddy Street admitted at a rent board hearing last Thursday that he hadn't turned on the heat in six months. He said it wasn't cold out."
>
> "But the Patels haven't yet had their hands slapped by the City and County of San Francisco."
>
> The Department of Social Services has been giving taxpayer cabbage to the Patels without checking to see if they have been providing the basic services.

Along with the first story there appeared a sidebar by Mr. Hinckle saying, "The Patels of India have become to the cheap hotels and motels of America what Italians are to pizza parlors." It said:

> The Patels buy small motels the way drunken sailors buy drinks. They own more than a thousand in California and reportedly have virtually cornered the motel market in Oregon, New Jersey and Texas.

The article drew on Professor William Van Greneau, director of the Asian Studies Program at California State University, Hayward, who was described as the expert on the Patels. It said:

> Patel is the Americanization of Patidar, the name for a wealthy Indian caste, which loosely translates as "village head." It has been taken as the legal name of hundreds of thousands of Indians who have emigrated to the United States from the state of Gujarat, near Bombay.

The article said the Patels are known for their merchant skills. Numbers of them migrated to Britain's African colonies where they took over small businesses "at the expense of native blacks." They were expelled when the colonies achieved independence, and many migrated to the United States "where they began to acquire small hotels catering to pensioners and welfare recipients."

The article said the Patels "pyramided" their numbers by capitalizing on what the writer called loopholes in the immigration laws that allowed a foreigner to invest $40,000 in an American business to gain accelerated immigration status. It said:

> One Patel would put a down-payment on a motel, get a green card as the head of a business and get permanent resident status, which made his relatives eligible for immigration. When the relatives got here, they started the process all over again.
>
> The Justice Department once investigated what was called the "motel scheme" to get around immigration quotas. The laws were eventually changed to close the loopholes.

The day after the first article appeared Mr. Hinckle wrote a second article reporting that Mayor Dianne Feinstein had ordered an immediate inspection of every furnace and every radiator in the "200 small hotels in the Tenderloin and the South of Market."

The story noted as background that "A *Chronicle* investigation of several hotels owned by the Patel clan found numerous people who had lived in rooms for one to two years with no heat." The article quoted Public Works Director Jeff Lee as saying the Patels owned 21 of the hotels. The article said, "They also control numerous other hotels through master leases."

The article quoted Lee as saying the problem of heat is not limited to the Patel hotels. It also quoted Raman Patel, owner of one of the hotels described in the previous story as saying he was losing money because residents were withholding rent in a rent-strike "conspiracy" with poverty lawyers.

On December 29, two weeks after the first story appeared, Mr. Hinckle wrote another "Hinckle's Journal" article saying that the "heat cheats" were only the "tip of the iceberg" of exploitation of the poor in hotels in the Tenderloin and South of Market districts. Under a headline, "A City's Shame—The Way it Treats Its Poor," Mr. Hinckle described "broken bedsprings without mattresses," "dirt inches thick on the floor," "Mice and vermin abounding in fields of rotten rugs," "garbage heaped in lightwells," businessmen "paying their disadvantaged employees a wage that amounts to involuntary servitude," "landlords terrorizing the elderly so they are afraid to complain," "landlords who are tyrannizing confused welfare recipients into giving them their government checks," and "hotel owners who rob alcoholic and mentally deficient unfortunates, take their money for a room, then beat them up and throw them out on the street." He wrote:

> Now people hereabouts are angry at certain landlords named Patel, from India, who own a large number of the hotels cited for heat-cheating. It's always easy to blame foreigners.
>
> I don't think the Patels should take all the blame. I think the fundamental blame lies closer to home—with the Robert Levys who command a small army of building inspectors that can't find people being systematically frozen in their rooms, with the Ed Sarsfields who run welfare departments that shell out city money to warehouse the unfortunate and can't bother to make sure they're warm at night, and with the Dianne Feinsteins, because the mayor's office is where the buck must stop.

In this article Mr. Hinckle addressed himself to people named Patel who had criticized his first article. He wrote:

> The landlords named Patel, from the state of Gujarat, on the west coast of India, are taking a lot of heat over the cold comfort of their hotels these days. Seventeen Patel-owned hotels have been cited for violating the city's heat law. On radio call-in shows and in angry letters to the editor the name Patel, which is as common in India as Smith is elsewhere, is becoming synonymous with slumlord. Some people blame me for this.
>
> "You are discriminating one Patel against the others," said Mokush Patel of San Jose. "Not all Patels are related—and not all are hotel Patels," said Dimish Patel, a fire protection engineer with the U. S. Navy. Arvind Patel of San Francisco, who owns a company in Silicon Valley, points out that there are more doctors and engineers named Patel than landlords and asks why I singled out the Patel hotels, out of all the other Tenderloin hotels, for being heartless and heatless.
>
> There is in these criticisms a suggestion of anti-Indian racism, of selective criticism of East Indian slumlords while exempting other slumlords. For the record, there is a hotel on Ellis and another on Kearny, neither owned by a Patel, that are in my opinion among the worst hell-holes in town.
>
> Certainly, treating old people like used furniture is an un-Christian act and its practice is not limited to Hindus, as I have previously reported. (Readers will recall the stories I wrote in 1980 on the chamber of horrors called the Dalt Hotel, which was owned by Irish Catholic entrepreneurs who had studied the Bible at St. Ignatius and Sacred Heart.)
>
> There is good reason to examine the Patel hotel clan of San Francisco and it has nothing to do with selective criticism of East Indians. Patels have aggressively sought to corner the market in housing for the aged and disabled in San Francisco, buying up the lion's share of the cheap residential hotels over the last 15 years and capturing the master contract with the welfare department to house the poor and the helpless. It is their stewardship in this city-financed area that is being examined.
>
> Entrepreneurs named Patel have purchased or control through master leases almost a third of the some 200 residential hotels where those living off government checks have little choice but to dwell. Skid Row has moved from Third Street to Sixth Street, and Sixth Street is now Patel Row. There are actually two Patel Rows,

one on Sixth, and the other on Eddy, and they are establishing another one in the inner Mission.

If not related by blood, these Patels are related by money. Their style of operating is depressingly similar. The city pays two members of the Patel clan—Charlie Patel (he owns five hotels) and Jay Patel (two hotels)—more than $500,000 a year to house welfare applicants for two-week stretches in their hotels. The city's unprecedented crackdown on hotel heat cheats began when three elderly women living in Charlie Patel's Aranada said they were damn mad and weren't going to take living without heat any more and being harassed by the Patels when they complained. Jay Patel is the son-in-law of D. R. Patel, an elder statesman of the clan who owns properties all over Skid Row, including the Sunnyside Hotel at Sixth and Minna, which was cited by housing inspectors for violating heat laws.

An examination of Patel operations in San Francisco indicates that they are not, despite what an attorney hired by some 60 Patel hotels to plead with city officials says, just little people trying to scrape out a living.

The Patels have been called "The Largest Family in Lodging" by Hotel and Motel Management magazine. Patels reportedly own over 20 percent of the motels and small hotels in the United States, and more than 1000 in California alone. They are not universally loved by other motel owners. An editorial in the November issue of the trade journal defended the clan, saying the Patel stereotype is more racist than reasonable. "The mere mention of the name Patel prompts a lot of disgusted headshaking" in industry circles, where they are criticized for running property into the ground "to make a quick buck," wrote editor Peter Romeo. Romeo said all the Patel-owned properties he'd seen were first-cabin. He said that some "lousy properties" were owned by Patels, "but to condemn every Patel for the sins of a few seems very unfair."

From what I've seen and what I've been told over the past two weeks, I'd say that some of the so-called lousy properties that are giving the name Patel a bad rap are right here in San Francisco.

The style of operating in many Patel hotels ranges from deliberately not providing heat to "bagging out" tenants, locking them out of their rooms and putting their possessions in plastic garbage bags on the street. It is a misdemeanor to throw a tenant out of his room without going through the eviction process. Ramesh Patel, who owns the Allen Hotel on Market Street, recently paid $1500 to a former tenant who sued after being "bagged out," and several other lawsuits have been filed against Patels for illegal evictions . . . .

"They were so cheap they used to throw their garbage out the window of the hotel to beat the garbage man. This went on for a year. The garbage landed on the roof of a printing company next door and made a terrible stink.

"When I went to the head Patel and complained, do you know what he told me? He said: 'Maybe garbage fall out of airplane in sky.'

Al McVeigh was talking. McVeigh leased a Howard Street hotel he owned to a Patel. You ask Al McVeigh about the Patels and he'll talk non-stop:

"They never repaired anything—they didn't even change the sheets on the beds. They didn't do anything they didn't have to. The lock on the front door was broken for two years—they always said they were fixing it but they never did. Bums would come in and crap in the hallways. They didn't pay union wages, they made welfare types work for them for peanuts. There was a new furnace in the building but they never turned it on. They let people sit around in their rooms in blankets and freeze, and when the tenants complained they told them the heat was on—they just lied. I've never encountered any people like them."

McVeigh said he went to court to break the lease to get them out. "The way they treated their tenants was outrageous," he said. "But the big problem is that hardly anybody else wants the business they're making their money off of. Nobody wants that trade."

Others told stories similar to McVeigh's. The adjective people kept using to describe the situations they encountered was "outrageous."

"My clients were treated like beasts, to be frozen, exploited, ripped off and stabled like beasts," said a former woman social worker who worked on Skid Row. Most of her clients were suffering from schizophrenia and/or alcoholism, and most of them stayed in Patel hotels. "Their conditions made them easy prey," she said. She knew of one man to whom the manager refused to give his welfare check "because a few nights earlier he'd barfed on their precious filthy staircase rug.

"During this period, there were several Skid Row hotels with managers who cared about their residents, who were willing to put some energy into cleanliness and comfort, and who even seemed to enjoy being needed and functioned as lay social workers."

But she said she was always on the phone "with various Patels, telling them about American law and due process." This criticism did not seem to faze the Patels, she said. "Several Patels had the sheer gall to phone me and ask for business: 'When you have a client who needs a place, I hope you will remember me, I run a very nice hotel over here.'"

On January 3 *The Chronicle* published a story by another writer, not Mr. Hinckle, who painted a different picture of the Patels from his. The story appeared under headlines, "Hotel Owners' Views of a Rough Business," and "S.F.'s Patel Hotel Owners Tell Their Side."

Prabha Patel, 26, was described as answering "calmly in her sari" the knock of a long-haired man with blood on his face and, "in rapid-fire Hindu, she dispatched a younger brother to defuse the fight her bloodied guest was having with his next-door neighbor. Another Patel went to clean up the mess."

The story said, "A lot of Patel sweat and tears have gone into the rag-tag tenement hotels of the city's Tenderloin and South of Market areas, according to those who share the common name of the Indian family. They also share the shame from public disclosures of abuses of elderly and disadvantaged tenants."

The hotel in which Prabha Patel was interviewed was described as "one of the many—some owned or operated by Patels—that were cited last month for missing and defective heat radiators."

The story described some of the difficulties of operating such hotels, noted that some of the citations were for technical matters—lack of a furnace/timing device, for example, that was not required when the present owner bought his hotel—and quoted a tenant who had plenty of heat.

The story said:

> Assuming that all Patels are alike or even remotely related to one another is like saying the same thing about Kate Smith and Reggie Smith, Patels say.

*The Chronicle* published letters to the editor reacting to the Hinckle stories on four days.

One day immediately after the first article, there were eight letters on the subject. Four of them focused their anger at city officials. The other four mentioned the Patels specifically with varying degrees of animosity. One said, "Isn't it generous of Ed Sarsfield to want to pay a bonus to the Patels, who get rich by feeding on human misery?" Another said:

> Get the Patel clan out of San Francisco. God only knows, we don't need them. There is something terribly wrong when we allow foreigners of this caliber to come to this country, reap in the wealth of our land, and then treat our own citizens like animals . . . . The Patels have apparently turned opportunity into opportunism. Perhaps a list of names, addresses and telephone numbers of all offending Patels, along with city building and welfare inspectors published on the front page of your paper might result in action.

Note that the letter specifies Patel phone numbers, not the phone numbers of other owners of Tenderloin hotels.

On December 21 there were four letters printed. Two expressed disgust for the situation and admiration for the newspaper. The other two, while saying that the article was "effective" said in one case that it had "cast shadows of racism and national chauvinism over this important issue." The letter noted that the problems had existed before the Patels and that Patels are landlords "in only a small percentage of inner city hotels which are in violation of the city housing code." The other said, "Hinckle's diatribe against all members of a community is racist and reeks of ignorance."

Finally on January 3, the newspaper published one more letter on the subject. It said the newspaper was incorrect in placing the blame for the situation on the Patels, the Welfare Department, the police or even the mayor. "The blame rests with every individual who closes his or her eyes to the plight of the poor."

**Response of the news organization:** There are two themes in the complaints against *The Chronicle;* one that the first story should have included something about the difficulties of running a hotel for the very poor, the other that the story unfairly stereotyped an ethnic group. Council staff forwarded Mr. Shubow's letter of complaint and the other letters mentioned in the complaint section of this report to William German, Executive Editor of *The Chronicle*. But in a covering letter staff tried to keep the focus of the complaint on the allegation of ethnic stereotyping. That is the journalistic issue that may justify the Council's hearing a complaint that would otherwise be outside its purview, because it is against a local news medium.

The staff asked Mr. German:

> Did the original story unfairly suggest that all Indians named Patel or even all Indians from Gujarat named Patel are members of a "clan" that exploits the poor?
> Should the paper have published letters challenging the story as racist?
> Was it fair to let the original reporter answer the challenges in a follow-up story—to get the last word?

Mr. German answered in part:

> The original *Chronicle* story was the result of lengthy research into the deplorable conditions in residential hotels catering to the elderly and the disadvantaged in San Francisco. *The Chronicle* hotel articles resulted in legislation by the Board of Supervisors toughening the penalties for health and safety violations in these hotels and giving city inspectors broadened powers to correct outrageous conditions. The first article focused on complaints received by the North of Market Planning Coalition, a community organization, about the lack of heat and hot water in residential hotels owned or managed by East Indians named Patel.
>
> The original story did not, as Mr. Shubow alleges, suggest that all Indians, or all Indians from the state of Gujarat, are exploiting the poor. It in fact explained that the name Patel is the Americanization of an Indian caste name which loosely translates as village head and has been taken as the legal name by many Indians who have migrated to the United States from Gujarat. The story said that Indians with the name of Patel had achieved a virtual corner on the motel and small hotel business in California, Oregon, New Jersey and Texas. It quoted a professor of Asian studies at California State University who said that the Patels were "very well thought of" as businessmen and were "a very religious people" who prided themselves in providing a "family atmosphere" in the small hotels they managed. It further stated that Patel tenants had not in the past been known to have made complaints of mistreatment.
>
> The original story reported on conditions in a half dozen residential hotels run mostly by Patels. *The Chronicle* writer visited these hotels because:
>
> 1. They included hotels under a master contract with two Patel brothers by the San Francisco Welfare Department to provide housing for welfare applicants.
>
> 2. According to information provided *The Chronicle* by the North of Market Planning Coalition, a clearinghouse for housing complaints, these were the hotels most complained about for systematically not providing heat to elderly tenants. The hotels reported on were not selected arbitrarily or, as Mr. Shubow seems to believe, with an eye towards their ethnic ownership. These were simply the hotels about which community organizations were receiving the most complaints for not provid-

ing heat. It should be noted here that this was the coldest and wettest winter San Francisco has endured for many years.

The conditions reported in *The Chronicle* were true. They became the subject of a city investigation and were subsequently corrected. There was no ethnic stereotyping involved; these were simply the facts.

If it had been the intention of *The Chronicle* to "savage," as Mr. Shubow claimed, this group of people, the newspaper could readily have availed itself of peripheral information which came to it in the course of the investigation. This included information from local credit bureaus, the city rent stabilization board, state and federal labor departments, a larger number of court actions filed against Patels and a U.S. Department of Justice investigation of Patel immigration tactics. News stories based on this information would certainly have created a more negative impression of the activities of a number of Patels. It was not printed because the aim of *The Chronicle* was not to "savage" any group but simply to focus on the alarming situation of the lack of heat in a number of residential hotels catering to the elderly, especially hotels under contract to a city department.

It should be noted that the thrust of the second story was on the general conditions in hotels catering to the poor and elderly. Of the many unfortunate practices cited, none was described as being exclusive practices of Patel hotels and the residential hotels in general.

In addition, the article quoted at length a defense of Patels printed in a motel-hotel industry magazine which pointed out that not all Patels should be condemned for the unscrupulous practices of a few Patels.

As to the question in Mr. Cunningham's letter about the writer in the follow-up story supplying his own answer to unpublished "Letters to the Editor" complaining that the original story was racist:

Mr. Shubow seems to be under the impression that the writer was replying to a letter from Mr. Shubow. This is a mistaken impression. The writer was responding to telephone calls and letters—which he quoted in the story—from people named Patel commenting on the original story.

This was fair comment and the writer responded to them directly. We felt this was an open and healthy exchange. Not many newspapers would devote such a portion of its news columns to let readers criticize a story.

Implicit in Mr. Shubow's charges is the curious assumption that the letters to the editor column is a more significant forum for dealing with controversial issues than the front page. So incidentally did another article on January 3, 1983 by another reporter representing the problems of residential hotels from the point of view of the Patels.

As to the question about our letters policy: *The Chronicle* printed more letters on this story than any stories in recent years and among those were letters representing the point of view that the story was racist. The real crux of Mr. Shubow's complaint seems to be only that *The Chronicle* did not print *his* letter . . .

Incidentally, the writer has been told that the largest Indian newspaper in the United States considered Mr. Shubow's charges and did not find sufficient merit in them to give them circulation in a news story. He assumes this can be checked further if it is deemed pertinent.

**Staff discussion:** The journalistic issues are:

Did *The Chronicle* unfairly stereotype people named Patel?

Did the newspaper treat fairly those who charged it with unfair stereotyping?

The alleged stereotyping is done in the first Hinckle article December 14. In it he defines the subject group as "The Patel clan of the state of Gujarat in India."

Later in Mr. Hinckle's article of December 27 he defines the subject group a little more precisely.

First he says, "The landlords named Patel from the state of Gujarat on the west coast of India are taking a lot of heat over the cold comfort of their hotels these days." That definition still includes landlords named Patel outside of San Francisco who may or may not run cold hotels.

In a second reference Mr. Hinckle defines his target group precisely:

"There is good reason to examine *the Patel hotel clan of San Francisco*." (emphasis added). He then says that group is related by money if not blood and he proceeds to level new accusations against San Francisco hotel owners named Patel.

The evidence that a stereotype has been laid down appears in a column by *The Chronicle's* popular Herb Caen in February. Caen wrote:

> The Gray Panthers aren't REALLY passing a petition to make Mayor Dianne take a shower in a Patel hotel. That was a joke, but the GPs don't think it's funny. Ever talked to an angry Gray Panther? Scary.

A number of Patels told Council staff that they suffered public abuse after the first Hinckle article. One was D. R. Patel, whom Mr. Hinckle describes as "an elder statesman of the clan." He said that when he and two other East Indian men went to the city hall to protest to Mayor Feinstein that the article was unfair, two or three passersby who did not know him made insulting remarks or insulting finger gestures. He said he had been in this country for 32 years and had never before experienced such abuse. Mr. Patel said women wearing traditional Hindu saris were accosted on the streets with shouts, "Go back to India."

Dr. Rajendra Prasad, assistant superintendent of schools in San Mateo, said Hindu women in his community were reluctant to go into San Francisco wearing saris after the Hinckle story appeared.

Ramesh Patel, owner of the Jefferson Hotel, said that two days after the first Hinckle story he was attacked by two men whom he did not know outside his hotel. The men made remarks about Indian hotel owners not turning on the heat and mistreating residents. One man took a swing at him, Mr. Patel said, adding: "We had obscene phone calls every day," and some hate mail.

Ramesh Patel said he appeared on Channel 7 (ABC) and urged viewers to come look at his hotel and talk to the residents. He said that in his more than eight years in San Francisco, he had difficulties with people "now and again because you make them leave the hotel," but never before had he been exposed to the kind of generalized hostility he has experienced since the Hinckle articles.

Sahib B. S. Mann of San Jose, California, wrote to the editor of *India West* that he and his father were at the San Francisco City Hall from January 3 to 11 involved in a court trial. One noontime they went out on the main steps of the building to watch a demonstration by senior citizens against the Patels. He wrote:

> Abruptly a man yelled from the crowd and asked me and my father, standing by to see what was going on, if we were representing Patels. My father answered no and that we were there for a trial. Nevertheless he rushed up to me and called me nasty names and spit upon my face. My father was angry but was concerned to return back to court but when this guy did not stop my father warned the old man that another bad name coming out his mouth would cause him to retire prematurely comfortable six feet below the ground. Then the group came after him and took him away. This happened in view of all but was not reported.

Council staff asked Jeff Lee of the San Francisco Public Works Department about the breakdown of violations found in the crackdown following Mr. Hinckle's stories. Mr. Lee referred staff to Chief Housing Inspector Don Chan, but warned against focusing on the Patels. He said, "They operate . . . percentagewise, just as many good ones as bad ones . . . compared with others."

Mr. Chan said his department gave out some 166 heat-related notices in the wake of the Hinckle articles, not all of the notices in Tenderloin and South of Market hotels.

He said six cases were referred to the district attorney and, "To my recollection, only one was a Patel; the other five were not."

Mr. Chan said the Patels do not own a majority of the cheap hotels. He guessed people named Patel owned or operated about a third of some 200 such hotels. He made several comments on the Patel owners.

For one thing, he said, he didn't think more than three or four of them are related. For another, he said, "We find them very cooperative when we've given notices. . . . They're the one group that asked for meetings to discuss these matters. . . . They don't speak the language; they don't always understand what is required in the building codes."

He said they had been "very receptive" to suggestions. "If we issue a notice, they comply. . . . They are certainly no worse than anyone else."

**Council finding:** The complaint that *The San Francisco Chronicle* unfairly stereotyped a large group of people based on the actions of a few members of the group is warranted.

The writer defined his target group incorrectly as "the Patel clan of the state of Gujarat in India." There are two defects in that definition: One, the Patels of the state of Gujarat do not fit even the broad definition of "clan," i.e., "a group united by a common interest or common characteristics." The only characteristics common to the large group defined by the writer are their name and their place of origin. The second defect in the definition is it included hundreds of thousands, perhaps even millions of people, whereas the writer is talking at most about a couple of hundred.

It is not until his second reference in his third article that the writer defines his target group precisely as "the Patel hotel clan of San Francisco." For that narrow group the word "clan" might have some justification because of their common interest in the business. But even in that case, the writer is not adequately precise, because he then proceeds to charge that group with certain sins that are clearly not common to all the people named Patel who own hotels in San Francisco.

As for the second element of the complaint, Did *The Chronicle* treat fairly those people who protested against the unfair stereotyping? The answer is, Not entirely.

A supplementary article by the same writer did provide some counterbalance with information about the diversity of Patels.

The newspaper did publish letters to the editor that did make the point that the initial article was racist. And the newspaper did eventually assign a reporter, different from the columnist who initiated the attack, to write an article based on interviews with Patels about the difficulty of running a low-cost hotel. That article did provide readers with some suggestion of what the San Francisco housing inspector later told Council staff, that the Patels who own cheap hotels are cooperative and are "certainly no worse than anyone else."

But *The Chronicle* left the response to the stereotyping charges in the hands of the columnist who did the stereotyping. In his third article Mr. Hinckle did give voice to the protesters, but he saved the last word for himself and used the protests as the kickoff for a new set of charges against Patel hotel owners as a group.

One of the positive changes in American journalism in the past 20 years has been increased sensitivity and precision of language in dealing with segments of the society whose interests have been damaged by stereotyping. In this case, *The San Francisco Chronicle* marred a commendable job of exposing the exploitation of the poor in the city's cheap hotels by stigmatizing an entire group of people.

**Concurring:** Abel, Ayers, Barrett, Benson, Decter, Hornby, Huston, Kennedy, Pye, Scott, Stanton, Williams and Woolf.

**COMPLAINT NO. 215**     (Filed: Jan.13, 1983)
AMERICAN IRISH UNITY COMMITTEE
against
THE NEW YORK TIMES

**Complaint:** The American Irish Unity Committee complained that *The New York Times* published an inaccurate statement November 6, 1982, in a news report about the acquittal of five men charged with trying to smuggle guns to the IRA.

The report said the jury acquitted the men because it apparently believed their assertion that they thought the man they were buying guns from was a CIA operative. The man's name was George DeMeo, and the defendants said they thought the CIA was cooperating with them in order to monitor the flow of arms to the IRA and to see that the business did not fall into the hands of the Soviet Union.

The statement to which the American Irish Unity Committee objected in the *Times* story was:

"Mr. DeMeo's purported relationship to the CIA was not established during the trial as anything but a boast he had often made."

Ray Quinn, publicity director for the American Irish Unity Committee, complained in a letter to Arthur Ochs Sulzberger, publisher of *The Times*. He listed the following items of testimony or evidence introduced in the trial that seemed to establish Mr. DeMeo's link to the CIA as more than just a boast:

> In 1969, Mr. DeMeo was arrested by the FBI on charges of running guns to Chad. An associate of DeMeo's, ex-U.S. Army intelligence officer Earl Vernon Redick Sr., who was also arrested at the time, testified that DeMeo told him that the "boys in Washington" would see to it that the case never came to trial. The case never came to trial for reasons of "national security."
>
> Mr. Redick testified that DeMeo had shown official State Department documents substantiating his claim that he was acting on their behalf.
>
> Redick further testified that DeMeo approached him concerning the purchase of weapons and ammunition which were to be destined for the Irish Republican Army. Redick stated: "He told me the Company was paying for them and the Company

487

would safely see them on board ship." The Company, he explained, was the term used for the CIA in intelligence circles.

In 1967, an internal FBI memo from J. Edgar Hoover stated that the FBI would continue to run checks on different individuals it felt were CIA agents, although the CIA had advised the Bureau that they were not. George DeMeo was one of the persons on the list. When former U.S. Attorney-General Ramsey Clark was asked if it was customary for the CIA to respond falsely to such queries, he replied: "It was more than customary. It was a uniform practice for the CIA to deny any domestic activity . . . (but) we were always skeptical."

When DeMeo was on the witness stand he took the Fifth Amendment over 80 times. The only time he didn't take it was when he was asked about the CIA. Each CIA question received a denial.

A retired CIA officer, Ralph W. McGehee, when asked if the CIA would want to monitor the arms traffic to Northern Ireland answered: "Yes, that is a characteristic response of the CIA to any country. By monitoring, you can somewhat control the flow." When asked if the CIA might actually provide arms for the traffic it wished to monitor, McGehee responded: "That's a basic concept."

Mr. Quinn wrote to Mr. Sulzberger on November 30. When he had not received a reply by January 13, 1983, he complained to the News Council. In his letter to the Council Mr. Quinn said, "The result of the (*Times*) statement was to give an erroneous summary of the testimony and evidence presented at the trial." He wrote:

> The American Irish Unity Committee believes that this type of false statement is but one instance in a continuing pattern of misinformation by *The New York Times* about Northern Ireland and related events. If the American public does not receive fair and accurate information from the "newspaper of record" concerning these events, then the resolution of that tragic war will be greatly hindered.

**Response of the news organization:** On February 21 Council staff forwarded the complaint to Seymour Topping, managing editor of *The Times*, asking whether, since the *Times* reporter appeared to be expressing an opinion on the evidence, the newspaper did not owe the American Irish Unity Committee an opportunity to disagree with the reporter, perhaps in a letter to the editor. Or, at the very least, did the newspaper not owe the complainant some response?

*The Times*—consistent with its policy as defined by Mr. Topping not to "engage" with the News Council—did not respond formally. However, from sources within *The Times*, Council staff was able to confirm what court officials had said, that *The Times* did not staff the gun-running trial. The *Times* story did bear a byline, but the name was that of a rewrite man who pieced together the *Times* story from Associated Press and United Press International reports. The wire services are not credited in the story.

Council staff also learned that the *Times* writer checked his story for accuracy with the prosecuting attorney.

**Staff discussion:** Staff obtained the AP and UPI reports of the trial verdict and determined that the statement that brought the complaint is derived from the AP report. Louis D. Boccardi, executive editor and vice-president of the AP, acknowledged that the line came from his service, but he said:

> As you look at the whole story, including the lead, the two marked passages, the quotes from the defense attorneys and the quotes from jurors, I think you will come to the conclusion I have come to. That is, that there is nothing wrong with the (AP) story and that the CIA angle is accurate and in context.

Indeed staff did come to that conclusion, and in the process, came to the view that the defect in the *Times* story is not that it is inaccurate, as the complaint alleges, but that it is misleading, because it does not contain the context of the AP report.

The *New York Times* story, for example, said:

> No evidence directly linking the CIA to the operation was offered at the seven-week trial, and denials of involvement by the agency were entered repeatedly by the prosecutor and in direct testimony by a CIA lawyer.

The AP story said:

> No evidence ever was presented during the two-month trial directly tying the CIA to the operation, but constant invocation of the agency and its tradition of secrecy allowed the defense to plant the requisite "reasonable doubt" in the minds of the jurors.

The introduction of the concept of reasonable doubt in the AP story makes the jury's finding seem less contrary to the report of the testimony.

Also, an attorney for the Irish group pointed out that the word "directly" has a legal connotation in the *Times* and the AP news reports. It suggests a differentiation between direct and circumstantial evidence. While there is no direct evidence linking Mr. DeMeo to the CIA, there was a quantity of circumstantial evidence, the attorney said.

Another example is in the sentence that produced the complaint to the News Council. The *New York Times* story said:

> Mr. DeMeo's purported relationship to the CIA was not established as anything but a boast he often made.

The AP story said:

> DeMeo's relationship to the intelligence agency never was established as anything

but a boast he often had made, but that tenuous connection was enough for the defense.

A Council staff member has gone through the testimony in the trial transcript that Mr. Quinn cites to support his view that Mr. DeMeo's connection to the CIA was established as more than a boast.

That perusal of the transcript makes the jury's finding more understandable. The AP report of the trial reflects more accurately the impact of the evidence and testimony than does the *Times* rewrite of the report.

As an aside: David Reed used nearly the same language as *The Times* in a strongly anti-IRA article in the April, 1983, *Reader's Digest*. Speaking of the trial, Reed wrote: "DeMeo's purported CIA relationship was not established as anything more than a frequent boast."

**Council finding:** The complaint that a sentence in a *New York Times* report of a gun-running trial was inaccurate, is unwarranted, but the sentence was misleading.

The statement was that the relationship of a key witness to the Central Intelligence Agency was not established in the trial as anything but a boast the witness often made. Standing alone, the statement leads to the conclusion that the jury could not reasonably have acquitted the defendants of the gun-running charge. A study of the trial transcript shows that the jury's not-guilty finding is not so unreasonable as the *Times* story suggests.

Blame for the misleading statement resides exclusively with *The New York Times*. The Associated Press report on which that particular part of the *Times* story depended provided additional context that made the jury's finding more understandable. *The Times* left out that context.

The complaint points up one of the dangers of a practice that is, unfortunately, widespread: rewriting the wire services without crediting them as the source of information. It is particularly questionable for a newspaper to put a staff member's byline on such a rewrite; that leads the reader to believe that the newspaper's reporter actually covered the trial or gathered the information independently.

**Concurring:** Abel, Ayers, Barrett, Benson, Decter, Hornby, Kennedy, Pye, Scott, Stanton, Williams and Woolf.

**Dissenting:** Huston.

**Dissent by Margo Huston:** The National News Council should refrain from relying on unnamed sources except in cases where there is a compelling reason to make a finding. In this case involving *The New York Times,* the *Times* management refused to cooperate in the Council's inquiry. However, one *Times* employee provided a Council staff member with information. Council members were not told the name or title of the source. Furthermore, this is a marginal case at best, one of several filed by the American Irish Unity Committee.

Generally, a responsible news organization uses unnamed sources only when there is an overriding reason for the public to know the information and then, only when verified by more than one source. The Council, in its own practices, should serve as a model for the ethical practice of journalism. In its handling of this case, the Council fell short of the highest standards it expects from others.

**COMPLAINT NO. 216**    (Filed: March 21, 1983)

AMERICAN IRISH UNITY COMMITTEE

against

NBC NEWS

**Complaint:** The American Irish Unity group complained that Roger Mudd reported incorrectly on the NBC Nightly News February 9, 1983, that the Irish Republican Army used kidnapping as a tactic to raise money.

Specifically, Raymond Quinn, publicity director for the Irish group, complained that Mr. Mudd concluded a news item about the disappearance of the Irish racehorse, Shergar, as follows:

> In the past the Irish Republican Army has used kidnappings for ransom to raise money. But the Irish police tonight are refusing to speculate about this.

In a letter to Mr. Mudd the day after the broadcast Mr. Quinn denied that the IRA had used kidnapping as a fund-raising technique. In support of his denial he sent both Mr. Mudd, and later the News Council, a copy of what he described as an intercepted British Intelligence document. The document is dated December 15, 1978, and bears the signature of Brigadier General J. M. Glover, former commander of British forces in Northern Ireland. The document is an analysis of the strength and tactics of the Provisional Irish Republican Army and an assessment of what its tactics might be over five years.

The passage referring to kidnapping reads as follows:

> Kidnapping for both financial and political bargaining has been favoured by many other terrorist organizations. But it forms no part of traditional IRA tactics. Both the Niedermeyer and Herrema incidents, the only preplanned kidnaps in this campaign, were carried out by maverick groups without the authority or subsequent support of the leadership. Those involved lacked the skill to carry the kidnap through to the

bargaining stage. In Ireland prominent personalities are generally well guarded and PIRA may appreciate that neither Her Majesty's Government nor the government of The Republic would readily submit to this kind of coercion. Kidnap, however, provides excellent publicity and might be attempted by PIRA under special conditions such as an attempt to gain concessions. Opportunity kidnap of Security Forces may continue, but in general the risk is low.

Mr. Quinn asked Mr. Mudd in a letter dated February 10 to broadcast a correction on the air to set the record straight. Mr. Mudd replied with a form note reading:

> Thanks for your letter, which I assure you I have read.
> Unfortunately, my reportorial duties virtually preclude a personal reply, but I appreciate the time and care you took in writing.

Mr. Mudd added in his own hand, "I've passed your material on to the N.Y. editor."

When he had not heard further from NBC by March 21, Mr. Quinn complained to the News Council, noting that there had been no IRA kidnappings for ransom or financial bargaining since the 1978 report of Gen. Glover.

He wrote to the News Council:

> If peace is ever to come to that very tragic part of the world known as Northern Ireland, the American Irish Unity Committee believes that the truth about all facts of the war must first be brought out. Roger Mudd and NBC News chose to make an unfair and inaccurate statement regarding one of the organizations involved in that colonial war. The effect of that false statement was to give aid and comfort to England and other enemies of Irish unification and peace who are engaged in an active media campaign to suppress the truth about the North of Ireland.

**Response of the news organization:** News Council staff forwarded the complaint to Thomas Pettit, Executive Vice-President, NBC News, on May 4. On May 13 Mr. Pettit wrote to Mr. Quinn acknowledging that—

> Our reporter was incorrect, so far as we can tell. You can rest assured that our reporter, Mr. Mudd, will not repeat the error, nor will the rest of our staff.
> Thank you for calling this matter to our attention.

Mr. Pettit sent the News Council a copy of his reply to Mr. Quinn, and the Council staff wrote Mr. Pettit May 18 saying—

> I judge from your response that you are not going to broadcast a correction of the incorrect report. Can you tell us why? What criteria does NBC News use to decide whether or not to broadcast a correction?

On May 20 Mr. Pettit wrote back, "The matter of a correction still is under discussion." On May 24 Tom Brokaw broadcast a correction on the NBC Nightly News program as follows:

> TOM BROKAW: In Belfast today, at least twelve people were injured when a car bomb was set off inside a police station in a Catholic neighborhood. No group thus far has claimed responsibility, but that police station has been the target of other attacks by the Irish Republican Army, which wants Northern Ireland to be independent of Great Britain.
>
> Police in Ireland and Northern Ireland now have abandoned their search for Shergar, that's the race horse, kidnapped more than three months ago, and held for three million dollars ransom. One officer in Norther Ireland said he believed the horse was killed, when that ransom was not paid.
>
> During one of our earlier reports on Shergar, we said that the IRA had used kidnappings in the past to raise money through ransom. Well, a check of the records shows that while the IRA has been involved in kidnapping, it's not used them to raise money.

**Council finding:** The News Council commends NBC News for broadcasting a correction of its erroneous report that the Irish Republican Army has in the past used kidnapping for ransom as a fund-raising tactic.

The Council notes, however, that the error was called to the network's attention immediately after the February 9 broadcast. Yet it was not until May 13, after the News Council had intervened, that the network acknowledged the error, and not until May 24 that the network broadcast a correction.

NBC News' own written and published standards call for a prompt investigation when someone asserts that a significant fact is in error. The same standards call for a prompt correction when the investigation shows that there has indeed been an error. In this case neither the investigation nor the correction was prompt.

NBC News, thus, did not live up to its own standards. Preparation and issuance of written guidelines, policies and standards are often healthy and useful. Their value is undermined, however, if they are merely pious declarations for public purposes, ignored by the news organization which issues them.

At the same time, while we criticize NBC News' lack of promptness in this matter, the News Council is at fault on the same score. The Council received Mr. Quinn's complaint about March 21 and did not forward the complaint to NBC News until May 4—six weeks later. Both NBC News and the Council should have done better.

**Concurring:** Abel, Ayers, Barrett, Benson, Decter, Hornby, Huston, Kennedy, Pye, Scott, Stanton, Williams and Woolf.

## COMPLAINT NO. 217      (Filed: June 3, 1983)
## AMERICAN IRISH UNITY COMMITTEE
### against
## NEW YORK DAILY NEWS

**Complaint:** The American Irish Unity Committee complained that on March 15, 1983, the *Daily News* published over a false name an article that the Irish group suspects may be fraudulent.

The complaint is that the *News* did not exercise appropriate responsibility to determine whether the writer and the article were authentic.

The article appeared on the *News*'s op-ed page over the signature of Don Carroll, who was described in an accompanying editor's note as "a Catholic priest serving in a New York area parish." The article described a visit 65 years ago by the repressive British constabulary, the "Black and Tans," to the priest's ancestral farm and a more recent visit by the pro-Nationalist Provisional Irish Republican Army. In the first case the "Tans' were looking for something. In the second case the IRA wanted to hide something. In both cases family members were roughed up and intimidated, according to the article.

The writer deplored the violence in both cases and concluded that the committee for the New York St. Patrick's Day parade owed an apology to the public for having turned the parade into a "pro-IRA" event, presumably by the election of IRA veteran Michael Flannery as grand marshal.

Supporters of the Irish Unity group searched the list of archdiocesan priests and told the *News* they could not find a priest named Don Carroll. On March 17, St. Patrick's Day, two days after the Carroll article appeared, the *News* published a note on its op-ed page saying:

> An article on Ireland on this page Tuesday carried a by-line of Don Carroll, who was described as a priest serving in the metropolitan area. In fact, "Don Carroll" is not the author's real name. It was a pseudonym adopted to protect the priest-author's relatives still resident in Ireland. At the time the article was published, the *News* was unaware the author was using a pseudonym.

The Irish Unity group said in its letter of complaint:

> The American Irish Unity Committee is of the opinion that this op-ed column may be fraudulent. The Unity Committee is concerned that the *Daily News* chose to print a column without attempting to verify its authenticity beforehand. This in itself raises a number of questions as to the *Daily News'* journalistic practices. Would the *Daily News* have printed this column if they knew that the alleged author did not want to publicly identify himself? Did the *News* not verify the article's authenticity because it spoke out against Irish Nationalists and (against) a democratic election

494

whose outcome the *News* did not like? In the past the *News* has consistently refused to print op-ed columns from individuals representing the Irish human rights side in the Northern Ireland conflict.

The complaint letter asked whether the *News* would have published the letter if it knew that the author did not live in New York—a question flowing from the group's belief that British government sources provide anti-Nationalist letters to American publications. The complaint also asked whether the author of the article would be willing to document specifically that his family members were victims of "beatings." "Or," the letter said, "is this being tossed in in an attempt to add substance to allegations without any basis?" The complainants asked:

> Since it is beyond the purview of the Unity Committee to establish conclusively whether or not this column is totally fraudulent, the Committee would appreciate it if the National News Council would use their good offices to investigate the matter and determine responsibility, if any.

**Response of the news organization:** John J. Smee, associate editor of the *News*, told the News Council staff that he received the suspect letter from the Rev. Edwin F. O'Brien, then head of the Office of Communications of the Archdiocese of New York and now secretary to Cardinal Terence Cooke. Father O'Brien called Mr. Smee and told him a priest had written an article based on his personal experiences, and he asked if Mr. Smee would be interested in it in view of the widespread discussion then underway in New York over Mr. Flannery's selection as grand marshal of the St. Patrick's Day parade.

Mr. Smee said he was interested. Father O'Brien sent the article. Mr. Smee edited it for length and called Father O'Brien to ask how to identify Don Carroll more specifically.

According to the *News* executive, Father O'Brien said the priest would rather not be identified by his location for fear of harassment. So Mr. Smee identified him only as a priest in the New York area.

When the article appeared, Mr. Smee said, he received calls saying there was no such priest in the archdiocese. Mr. Smee called Father O'Brien. Father O'Brien apologized. He explained that he thought Mr. Smee had known the name was a pseudonym and that when the editor called before publication, he had been asking only what parish the priest served.

Mr. Smee told the News Council staff that he has since satisfied himself that the author of the article is a priest and does exist in the New York area. He said he did talk with him.

Asked if he was sure the article was not fiction, Mr. Smee said, "I don't know. How do I know whether any of the material we get is fiction?"

Father O'Brien confirmed Mr. Smee's reconstruction of the business and gave Council staff a copy of a letter of apology he sent to Mr. Smee May 23 when he learned that the Council was looking into the matter. The letter makes clear that the harassment the priest-author feared was against his relatives still in Ireland. Father O'Brien wrote to Mr. Smee:

> As a result of our conversation, I wrongly assumed that you understood Don Carroll to be a pseudonym. It was totally my fault that the misunderstanding occurred, but I meant no deception. The piece was written by a priest of good standing, and the facts were accurately presented.

James G. Wieghart, editor and executive vice-president of the *News*, said, "If we had known (that the name was a pseudonym), we either would not have printed it or would have said right up front, 'This is a priest of the New York archdiocese, and he doesn't want his name used.'"

He noted that it is *News* policy to withhold the name and address of letter writers under some circumstances. He also recalled that the *News* accepted the resignation of columnist Michael Daly two years ago after he used a pseudonym for a quote in a story about the conflict in Northern Ireland.

Mr. Wieghart said he did not believe in using pseudonyms in news stories, columns or on the editorial page unless the use is clearly indicated "up front." Furthermore, he said the decision to use a pseudonym "ought to be reviewed at the highest level."

**Staff discussion:** This complaint grew out of an earlier complaint against the *News* by the Irish Unity group. In the earlier complaint the group charged the *News* with inaccurate and unfair reporting in its publication February 28 of a statement by Cardinal Cooke under the heading, "Guest Editorial."

The statement was the second to last sentence of a 2,500-word position paper by the cardinal on the quest for peace in Northern Ireland. The Irish Unity Committee said it was inaccurate to label the statement "Guest Editorial," since it had not been written as such. Moreover, the committee asserted, it was unfair to edit the position paper down to this single sentence:

> The one course of action which we cannot follow is to support in any way, even by signs and symbols, the continuation of senseless, indiscriminate violence as a means to achieve political effects.

The Irish Unity group said the sentence was pulled out of context and was not representative of the position paper. They said, "What was ignored was the sum and substance of the Cardinal's statement, which focused on human and civil rights violations as the root cause of the violence."

The cardinal's paper also specifies the British occupying forces, the Ulster Defense Association and the Ulster Volunteer Force as forces of violence on the British side of the strife in Northern Ireland. It specifies the Provisional IRA and the Irish National Liberation Army as forces of violence on the Nationalist side. The one sentence of his position paper— quoted by the *News* at a time when the focus of public attention was on Michael Flannery as a symbol of IRA violence—seemed to the Irish Unity Committee to suggest that the cardinal was considering only IRA violence.

On March 11 the *News* published a letter to the editor making the point that the *News* had been selective in editing the cardinal's paper and pointing out not only that the paper focused on injustice but that it recognized both pre-British as well as IRA forces as being responsible for violence.

When it received the Irish Unity complaint, Council staff called Cardinal Cooke's office and found that the office had expressed its own annoyance in a "strong" letter to *News* Editor James G. Wieghart for "shutting us out" on the cardinal's statement. The office did not want to pursue the matter further.

Council staff called the Irish Unity group to tell them that since Cardinal Cooke did not want to press the complaint, we were not going to pursue it. Mr. Quinn of the Irish Unity Committee urged Council staff to reconsider; he said the cardinal's office might be reluctant to press a complaint on the guest-editorial matter lest the *News* reveal that the cardinal's office had supplied the newspaper with a "phony op-ed piece."

Finally, after the staff had looked into the op-ed matter and had received a new complaint focusing on it, Father O'Brien put Council staff in touch with Father "Don Carroll" on the understanding that staff would not reveal the priest's real name.

He is indeed a priest ordained 20 years ago and serving in the New York archdiocese. He has written extensively, and he said he was moved to write the article that appeared in edited form in the *News* when he woke up one night during the Flannery controversy thinking about his Uncle Packy. He got up and wrote the piece without any publication in mind. He showed it to Father O'Brien, with whom he shares an interest in writing. Father O'Brien thought the article would be a good one for *Catholic New*

*York,* a periodical published by the archdiocese. Father "Carroll" said he would remove the names of his relatives and disguise his own if the article were to be printed. Father O'Brien subsequently decided to try the article out on the *News*, where it would reach a wider audience.

Father "Carroll" is the son of immigrant parents and has friends and relatives who support the Provisional IRA.

He said he believes, as Cardinal Cooke does, that the Irish have suffered injustice at the hands of the British for centuries and that Catholics in Northern Ireland are victims of injustice today. He believes deeply that the ultimate solution to the problems of Ireland lie in a united Ireland.

Father "Carroll" said, "I have a great deal of compassion for the frustration of people who resort to means I don't agree with. What hurts me is that people who are struggling for the same things that are dear to me can hurt others."

The priest noted that the builder of St. Patrick's Cathedral, Archbishop "Dagger John" Hughes (so nicknamed for the cross in his signature, which looked like a dagger), often used a pen name to express ideas publicly in the 1850s, a time of hostility against Irish immigrants. His own pen name, he said, was from the Latin, "Carroll" for Charles and "Don" for the word "priest."

Council staff came away with no reason to disbelieve the basic accuracy of Father "Carroll's" article in the *News*.

**Council finding:** This case underscores the importance for news publications of making certain they know who is writing for their pages—particularly on issues where the emotions and suspicions run deep.

Newspapers and broadcasters may, on occasion, consider it necessary to disguise the identity of a contributor, just as a reporter needs sometimes to grant confidentiality to a source. However, the editor must first ascertain the authenticity of the contributor and the validity of his or her need to remain unidentified.

When that is done, a parallel obligation exists to let readers or listeners know that a pseudonym is being used.

In this case suspicion arose about the source of the op-ed page article printed in the *News* March 15, because its message was so similar to Cardinal Terence Cooke's position which had been only partially reported by the newspaper in February. The message was that both sides, not just the IRA, should eschew violence.

Investigation convinces the News Council that the cardinal's office did not make up a priest and a story in order to get the cardinal's full message into the newspaper before the St. Patrick's Day parade.

The Council accepts the explanation that a priest who took the pen name "Don Carroll" did just happen to write the article at a time when it was of public interest. The Council accepts the explanation of the cardinal's office that the office thought the *News* understood that the priest was writing under a pen name. But it also accepts the explanation by the *News* that it had no such understanding.

Since the *News* did call the cardinal's office for a more specific identification of the priest, and after calling did conclude that the only thing that was being hidden was the priest's specific parish, the News Council finds unwarranted the complaint that the newspaper exercised inadequate responsibility in this matter.

**Concurring:** Abel, Ayers, Barrett, Benson, Decter, Hornby, Huston, Kennedy, Pye, Scott, Stanton, Williams and Woolf.

# Part 2

# Defending Press Freedom

Mindful that all of its monitoring activities are rooted in a determination to sustain and strengthen press freedom, the Council has consistently sought to open channels of communication sealed off by government in contravention of the First Amendment, or by private actions which affect a free flow of news. Statements issued by the Council and complaints brought before it relating to its efforts in defense of press freedom are contained in the following pages. They cover the period from January 1, 1979, through July 31, 1983, and range from comments on the link between individual freedom and press freedom in arbitrary governmental search and seizure operations to proposals for further restrictions of the Freedom of Information Act that would seriously inhibit a free flow to the public of information essential to the democratic process.

The press, of course, is aware that not all threats to its freedom emanate from the government. There are many individuals, and many organizations who, in one way or another seek to impose limitations on a free flow of information in order to shape the news to their liking or interests. The Council, for example, confronted such an effort in 1979 when *The Day*, a newspaper published in New London, CT, complained (see *The Day* against Electric Boat) that the Electric Boat Division of General Dynamics Corporation had for more than a year unilaterally blacked out all news information to the paper, the chief newspaper serving its area. The company, which is wholly engaged in building nuclear submarines for the United States Navy, contended that the paper had been unfair in its news coverage and the company took its action in retaliation. While recognizing that Navy regulations did not compel defense contractors to observe the same nondiscriminatory policies on release of information which the Navy itself practices, the Council said, "This absence of official obligation in no way diminishes the arbitrariness of Electric

500

Boat's decision to stop talking to the paper or sending it press releases. What goes right at Electric Boat and what goes wrong are both matters of legitimate public concern, particularly in the area in which the company exercises such a dominant economic role."

The Council renewed an offer it had made before rendering its decision to serve in any mediatory capacity that might prove helpful in breaking down the communication barrier, but the company refused, despite periodic follow-up offers by the Council to be of assistance. Two full years passed before Electric Boat decided to resume talking to *The Day*.

In a letter to the Council, Deane C. Avery, the paper's co-publisher and editor, expressed appreciation for the national attention the Council's acceptance of its complaint had focused on the case.

Another action by the Council in defense of freedom of expression by news organizations came in response to a complaint (see UPI against Synanon) filed by United Press International. It was directed against the Synanon Foundation, Inc., an organization set up to combat drug addiction. UPI accused Synanon of flooding the nation's news media with letters threatening libel suits as part of a systematic pattern of intimidation designed to suppress all stories Synanon considered unfavorable.

An exhaustive investigation by the Council led it to conclude that the chilling effect on editors of the flood of lawyers' letters threatening suit was causing many newspapers, especially those of small circulation and limited resources, to shy away from printing stories of any kind about Synanon. While recognizing that this cutoff in the free flow of information damaged the rights of readers and the cause of truth, the Council noted that publishers had been instrumental in putting on the California statute books what was being cited by Synanon as an excuse for its letters demanding retractions. This law required anyone contemplating a libel suit to demand redress from the paper within two weeks or forfeit any right to sue. The ease with which Synanon had turned this law, intended as a safeguard for the press, into an instrument of harassment was cited by the Council as evidence of the unforeseen dangers that might descend on the media when they turn to lawmakers for special-purpose legislation. In any event, the Council said, the right response for editors when confronted with intimidating tactics from any quarter was to stand up for their freedom, whatever the risks involved. It cited specific publications that had taken that route in the face of Synanon's threats, with constructive results.

Damaging confrontations between the bar and the press in criminal trial proceedings which have led, in many instances, to court orders limiting the free flow of information caused the Council in 1980 to publish a "white paper" entitled "Protecting Two Vital Freedoms: Fair Trial and Free Press." The need for such a study was underscored for the Council by its receipt of a complaint (see "14 Reporters against the *Quad-City Times*) alleging prejudicial pretrial publicity in a murder case in the Quad Cities area of Iowa and Illinois. The Council's white paper appraised the broader issues of journalistic responsibility raised by the Quad Cities case and fitted them into the framework of practical machinery for press-bar cooperation.

The Council's white paper was widely distributed by the American Bar Association. Copies were sent by the ABA to its entire House of Delegates. In addition, as is customary with all Council white papers, copies were sent to members of the American Society of Newspaper Editors, to members of the Radio and Television News Directors Association, and to journalism educators.

A complete listing, covering the years of 1979 to March 31, 1983, of Council statements and complaints relating to press freedom follows:

| *Subject* | *Page* |
|---|---|
| Search and Seizure 3/9/79 | 503 |
| Cameras in the Courtroom 3/9/79 | 505 |
| Reportial Privilege 3/9/79 | 507 |
| *The Progressive* Case 6/12/79 | 509 |
| The Herbert Case 6/12/79 | 513 |
| *The Day* against Electric Boat 6/12/79 | 517 |
| The Seberg Case 9/21/79 | 522 |
| Revised Comment on the Seberg Case 9/19/80 | 523 |
| Prior Restraint 9/21/79 | 523 |
| Closing Courtrooms 9/21/79 | 524 |
| 14 Reporters against the *Quad-City Times* 9/21/79 | 525 |
| Abscam Leaks 3/7/80 | 528 |
| United Press International against Synanon 3/6/80 | 532 |
| CIA Use of Journalists 3/7/80 | 553 |
| Belgrade UNESCO Conference 12/5/80 | 554 |
| Richmond Newspaper Decision, with Addendum 6/19/80 | 556 |
| Amendments to the Freedom of Information Act 12/3/81 | 559 |
| Governmental Secrecy 12/3/82 | 559 |
| National Security Classification Rules 3/31/83 | 560 |
| Responsible Journalism 3/31/83 | 562 |

## STATEMENT ON SEARCH AND SEIZURE

Appraisal of the damage to individual and institutional liberties inherent in the restrictive interpretation given to the Fourth Amendment by the Supreme Court in *Zurcher v. Stanford Daily* (May 31, 1978) has brought widespread recognition at both the Federal and state level of the desirability of corrective action through legislation unless a new presentation of the issue brings a quick reversal by the Court of its unfortunate ruling.

Because the decision in The Stanford Daily case so sweepingly imperiled the media by opening newsroom doors to surprise police raids conducted on an ex parte warrant, much of the initial protest has focused on the urgency of safeguards to prevent a drying up of confidential sources of information and other limitations on the effectiveness of the press and on its independence of governmental coercion or control.

Concerns on this point are valid and imperative, but they may have tended to obscure the degree to which the Court's constricted view of the Fourth Amendment has put in jeopardy the fundamental protection all Americans have a right to expect against arbitrary invasion of their homes or offices. The Court, extending the position it took in *Warden v. Hayden* in 1967, has enunciated the strange doctrine that those who are deemed by law-enforcement officials to be innocent of any direct or indirect involvement in a crime are, by that very fact, more vulnerable to search and seizure via ex parte proceedings than presumed culprits.

The National News Council does not presume to set itself up as a definitive assessor of the niceties of constitutional law, but it does not require a scholar to recognize that the Court's view gravely impairs the utility of the Fourth Amendment as a protector of "the right of the people to be secure in their persons, houses, papers and effects, against unreasonable searches and seizures."

The decision, as the Council noted in its initial statement last June, underscores the degree to which freedom and a free press have been inextricably intertwined through all American history. In recognition of that bond, the wise course for remedial legislation, whether legislative or administrative, lies in the direction of universal protection against arbitrary search or seizure rather than toward distinctive safeguards for the media.

Both approaches have influential sponsors in Congress and in many state legislatures. The Carter Administration, through Attorney General Griffin Bell, plans to back a bill that would prohibit almost all police raids in search of notes, photographs, tapes or other "work product" of

503

reporters, broadcasters, free-lance writers and even academicians writing books or articles. The bill, now in process of White House clearance preparatory to its dispatch to Capitol Hill, represents a welcome departure from the amicus brief the Justice Department filed in the Stanford Daily case, in which it urged the Supreme Court to uphold such raids. Nevertheless, despite the breadth of the definition the Administration now recommends for a press immunity, it stops short of a general exemption for all persons considered innocent of complicity of a crime, except where probable cause is shown that the evidence sought will be destroyed if a subpoena is served or other special circumstances exist.

An exemption of this kind is contained in a measure filed in the United States Senate by Senator Birch Bayh of Indiana. A similar prohibition against "third party" search and seizure, except under extraordinary circumstances, marks a bill filed in the New York State Legislature by the chairman of the Assembly Committee on Codes. Without expressing a judgment on the specifics of either measure, the Council believes that both address themselves to the essential issue: the need for restoring the Fourth Amendment to the scope it had before the Supreme Court began whittling away at its scope in the Hayden decision, a trespass made much worse by its ruling in the Stanford Daily case.

The spirit of freedom will be best preserved by a return to the requirement that, particularly where no suspicion of complicity is involved, a search warrant be an instrument of last resort to be used only where there is compelling proof that reliance on a subpoena will defeat the ends of justice. In the case of the press and the great bulk of the citizenry, that is a line that will almost never have to be crossed.

**Concurring:** Cooney, Ghiglione, Hauser, Huston, Isaacs, McKay, Otwell, Pulitzer and Roberts.

**Dissenting:** Rusher

**Dissenting opinion by Mr. Rusher:** The Council's statement strives mightily to give the impression that the Supreme Court broke new ground in *Zurcher v. Stanford Daily*, by authorizing police to search newspaper offices for evidence of a crime after obtaining a "probable cause" search warrant from a judge. On the contrary, law enforcement authorities have had the right (on those same restricted terms) since our nation's inception. Any doubt that it applies to premises not belonging to the suspected criminal was eliminated in 1967 by the Hayden case. The notion that the student editors of *The Stanford Daily*, or any other journalists, are specially privileged against such searches by virtue of their journalistic status was the only question before the Court in the Zurcher case, and the Court rightly scotched it.

I happen to agree with the Court that a reasonable cause search warrant is an important tool of criminal investigation and prosecution. But if it is to be abandoned, I certainly agree with so much of Council's statement as urges that it be abandoned *in toto*, rather than merely selectively in the special case of the media. The proposition that journalists are rare and precious birds, specially privileged and cloaked in unique immunities, would be simply comical if its consequences weren't so deadly dangerous.

March 9, 1979


## STATEMENT ON CAMERAS IN THE COURTROOM

The rejection by the House of Delegates of the American Bar Association of a recommendation by its own special study committee for television and radio coverage of trials makes it important that the individual states continue experiments aimed at establishing whether there is any genuine conflict between the public interest in openness of judicial proceedings and the right of defendants to a fair trial.

The A.B.A. action comes as a disappointment in the wake of the bar's adoption at its convention last August of a revised canon that barred any limitation on access by the print press to coverage of criminal trials except to the extent that such access posed a "clear and present danger" to fair judgment. The accent which the A.B.A. placed on the importance of open judicial proceedings and on an avoidance of prior restraint or sealing of court records rested even more on what it perceived to be Sixth Amendment values than it did on those guaranteed by the First Amendment. It is a combination of these same values that has made the National News Council believe that cameras and microphones can be admitted to courtrooms under rules that would advance public understanding and respect for the judicial process without impairing or prejudicing the rights of accused persons.

Considerable support for this belief has come from some of the experiments conducted thus far at state court levels, but the evidence is still not conclusive. Some judges involved in televised trials are openly skeptical that fairness can be maintained even where maximum care is taken to guard against disruption of courtroom decorum or distortions in the editing of testimony for presentation on TV or radio.

It is the Council's hope that the Conference of Chief Justices, which voted almost unanimously last year in favor of controlled experiments with televising of criminal trials, will continue to give its support to such experiments and that these will provide a basis for sound judgment on what restrictions, if any, best serve the public interest in an equitable and open system of justice. Current technology clearly permits concealment of equipment in such fashion that it need cause no upset to witnesses or other participants in a trial. Similarly, problems of needed lighting and noise suppression can be overcome without undermining the dignity of the courtroom.

At the appellate level, where proceedings are relatively brief and all the participants are professionals, the perils are minimal or nonexistent. It is at the trial level that more evidence will be helpful in the formulation of sound guidelines. As the Council has previously observed, the electronic press as well as print news photographers will have a determinative role in the assessment of experiments in this field. Only to the extent that they operate responsibly inside the courtroom and in the processes of editing and exploitation will the desired access fulfill its twin mission of advancing public knowledge and keeping the scales of justice fairly balanced.

The bar's refusal to endorse access to the courts even on the most limited of permissive arrangements is particularly disappointing at the time when the House of Representatives has recognized that such access to electronic coverage of its proceedings will benefit the democratic process—through increased public knowledge and through the awareness by legislators that a new element of direct accountability to their constituents now exists. The National News Council welcomes the televising of House debates and votes and hopes that experience with the new system will lead to similar televising of Senate proceedings and to relaxation of the rules that now give the House itself absolute control of TV coverage, shutting news organizations out of an area in which they should be free to operate under the First Amendment guarantees of press freedom.

**Concurring:** Ghiglione, Huston, Isaacs, McKay, Otwell, Pulitzer and Roberts.

**Dissenting:** Cooney, Hauser and Rusher

**Dissenting opinion by Mr. Rusher** (Cooney and Hauser concurring):

The constitutional requirement that most legal proceedings must be open is adequately met by the right of the public and the media to attend them. The further requirement that trials must be fair would, in our opinion, be jeopardized by allowing television cameras to record and selectively broadcast criminal proceedings.

What is served here is primarily the desire of the electronic media to gain admission to the courtroom. The discussion in the Council made it plain, however, that members favoring cameras in the courtroom do expect that this step will affect the proceedings themselves in major ways. Naturally, they hope those ways will be favorable to ends they deem desirable. But there has not been nearly enough consideration of what the consequences may in fact be. We concur in the belief of the majority of the House of Delegates of the American Bar Association that this innovation would be profoundly unwise.

March 9, 1979

## STATEMENT ON REPORTORIAL PRIVILEGE

In the wake of the refusal of the United States Supreme Court to review the contempt of court convictions of *The New York Times* and its reporter, M.A. Farber, questions of fundamental importance to American journalism and American democracy remain unresolved.

There is no need for the National News Council to underscore the vital role of the press as a community watchdog bringing the broadest possible range of information to public attention. Much of that information must be obtained through investigations outside the realm of readily available public sources, often from informants who fear for their personal safety, loss of job and possible criminal prosecution if their identities were disclosed.

It has been an article of faith with reporters, fully supported by their editors and news organizations, that they could assure full protection to confidential sources, and such sources have come to rely on such assurances as being inviolable. The confident assumption of the press has been that the integrity of such pledges is underwritten by the freedom of the press guarantee contained in the First Amendment. The correctness of that view has been brought into grave question by a series of Supreme Court rulings, notably in the 1972 decision in the combined cases of Branzburg, Caldwell and Pappas.

Many states believed that they were acting in conformity with a direct suggestion contained in the majority decision in that ruling when they adopted shield laws aimed at providing legal security for the press in invoking the rights of confidentiality.

In ruling that the New Jersey shield law is valid, but refusing to extend the right of source protection to reporter Farber, the state's Supreme Court limited reportorial privilege under the particular facts pertaining in that case.

Uncertainty over the precise status of journalistic privilege is deepened by a confusion of rulings by subordinate courts in other states. Now, no newspaper, broadcaster, and individual reporter or editor can be sure what protection exists under the Federal Constitution.

It is important, however, for journalists to recognize that the restricted reading given to New Jersey's shield law by the courts of that state is not necessarily an operative limitation in any of the twenty-five other states with such laws. In all of those states shield laws remain intact and even in New Jersey the protections intended by its law are still fully effective where judges do not perceive a conflict with the fair trial guarantees of the Sixth Amendment. To the extent that state shield laws effectively have permitted media to maintain confidentiality, they should be used fully, consistent with their legislative purpose and court rulings.

Media should be reminded that some Federal Courts have taken state shield laws into consideration as a basis for protecting reportorial privilege.

In all cases, the oft-stated, oft-feared "chilling effect" should not become a self-fulfilling prophecy by reporters, editors and publishers. Responsible, aggressive news coverage, using confidential sources when necessary, is the best response to Constitutional ambiguities.

**Concurring:** Cooney, Ghiglione, Hauser, Huston, Isaacs, McKay, Otwell, Pulitzer and Roberts.

**Dissenting:** Rusher.

**Dissenting opinion by Mr. Rusher:** The limits on a reporter's right to conceal his sources "remain unresolved" only in the sense that certain spokesmen for the media decline to take the U.S. Supreme Court's "No" for an answer. The fact that some members of the media have taken this alleged right as an "article of faith" and/or a "confident assumption" suggests ways of amending (or interpreting) the Constitution that would be novel indeed.

But as a matter of fact it isn't even true that "the press" as a whole has held such enlarged and gaudy views as to the profession's privileges and immunities. James W. Carey, Gallup Professor of Journalism at the University of Iowa and president of the Association for Education in Journalism, declared only last August that "the rule," to which there are only "rare and well defined exceptions," is that "a journalist always reveals his sources." Clark Mollenhoff, the veteran Washington correspondent, while not going quite so far, does not believe that reporters' sources ought to receive special legal protection against disclosure. Vermont Royster, the longtime editor of *The Wall Street Journal*, has wondered aloud whether a reporter's private papers ought to be protected more fully than those of a President.

Congress and state legislatures, in passing "shield laws" are engaging in an easy and inexpensive form of demagogy, because they know that any application of any such law that actually deprives anyone of a fair trial will be invalidated by the courts as unconstitutional. Unfortunately we will never know how many criminals have gone or may yet go unprosecuted because of other applications of such "shield" laws. I think it is the height of irresponsibility for this Council to urge journalists to use such laws in an "aggressive" way to promote a right the Constitution did not give them and which they alone will have.

March 9, 1979

## STATEMENT ON THE PROGRESSIVE CASE

Prior restraint represents the most dangerous form of judicial interference with the right to publish. By shutting off communication before it occurs, prior restraint nullifies the role of the press as a conveyor of information and ideas and as a stimulator of debate on public issues. So repugnant is such censorship that the Supreme Court has held consistently, since *Near v. Minnesota* in 1931, that any prior restraint on publication comes into court under a heavy presumption against its constitutional validity.

In criminal cases this presumption has gained such standing that the trial standards promulgated by the American Bar Association now prohibit the issuance by judges of any order barring the news media from broadcasting or publishing any information in their possession relating to a case. Except for those who believe that the right to publish ought to be absolute under any and all circumstances, the issue becomes more complex where claims are made that national security would be injured by publication. It is plain that, even in such cases, the asserted risk must be so clear-cut and immediate as to invite irreparable damage if the material is printed or broadcast. It is also plain that the very act of suppression makes impossible intelligent debate on the merits of the prior restraint.

The National News Council, in common with most other outside commentators, finds itself hampered by lack of knowledge of the contents of the article *The Progressive* wanted to run on "The H-Bomb Secret:

How We Got It, Why We're Telling It." The Department of Justice rejected a request for access by a News Council staff member with "top secret" clearance.

Despite this obstacle to informed assessment of the justification for the Federal District Court's restraining order that has blacked out the projected article for ten weeks, the case has already demonstrated with startling force the weaknesses of the security system on which the United Staes relies to safeguard information the government considers vital to national defense.

Every development in the case has heightened public concern about the quixotic nature of the rules governing classification and the degree to which these rules can be perverted to serve political purposes or to protect the government against embarrassing disclosure of its own errors of misfeasance. The officials in charge of the security system were themselves so confused that they appear to have been genuinely and utterly unaware that they were insisting on the need to suppress data already placed in the public domain with their imprimateur in facilities under their own direct control. The result was to put the Secretaries of State, Defense and Energy, all of whom certified that publication of the article would inflict "serious and irreparable harm" on the national security of the United States and its people, in a position destructive of public confidence in the competence or integrity of governmental decision-making.

*The Progressive*'s editors have proved the point that, by their own statement, was among their chief objectives in wanting to publish the article: A demonstration that the "secret" involved in making the most devastating of thermonuclear weapons is not much of a secret. To this end an article was written by a free-lance writer with only rudimentary knowledge of physics, who said he inspected no classified documents and relied primarily on interviews arranged for him by the administrators of the nuclear arms program, the official overseers of the security system.

The vehemence of the subsequent outcry from these same officials that the fruits of the magazine's research would simplify the task of manufacture for nations that do not now know how to make the H-bomb must be taken as dismaying evidence of the inadequacy of the classification rules or of the mythical character of the secrets they are supposed to shield. Anxiety on both counts is made stronger still by the clumsiness of the government's reaction to the discovery that a researcher for the American Civil Liberties Union, preparing a defense against the prior restraint order in *The Progressive* case, had found in the public shelves at the Los

Alamos Scientific Library a document that for nearly four years had put within reach of anyone interested enough to inquire information comparable to that in the suppressed article. The discovery led the government to declare the declassification of the document erroneous and to close the library's public shelves pending a more extensive review of their contents. but the authorities made no immediate attempt to learn the names of the half-dozen persons to whom the researcher had mailed photo-copies of the document, much less to repossess them or place them under embargo.

In fairness to Judge Robert W. Warren, who signed the original restraining order, the tenuousness of some of the underpinnings of the government's case were not then matters of record. He was appropriately concerned, as all of us must be, by the reality that the survival of this nation and of mankind has been placed in constant peril by the fantastic destructiveness of thermonuclear weapons and that their containment is imperative until such time as the world finds a dependable formula for their abolition or neutralization.

Even in the light of such concern, however, there is basis for question that the test of serious and irreparable danger laid down as a prerequisite for prior restraint in Supreme Court cases is adequately met by a government allegation that publication might reduce the time nations outside the nuclear club would need to develop a production capacity.

The danger that even a judge who grappled as conscientiously as Judge Warren did with the weighty implications of any exercise of prior restraint may stray beyond security considerations into unintended trespass on the right of purely editorial judgment is indicated by statements like this one from the Warren order : ". . . this Court can find no plausible reason why the public needs to know the technical details about hydrogen bomb construction to carry on an informed debate on this issue. Furthermore, the Court believes that the defendants' position in favor of nuclear nonproliferation would be harmed, not aided, by the publication of this article."

Whether the judge is right or wrong in his belief is irrelevant to the appropriateness of a suppression order. That must be predicated exclusively on a finding that a threat of irreparable damage to national security would be created by publication in advance of any assessment on the merits. In this case the possibility that the article might disclose material of too sensitive a nature apparently concerned the editors of *The Progressive* sufficiently to induce them to circulate advance copies among scientists familiar with the intricacies of nuclear weaponry. It was this process of informal clearance that resulted in calling the article to the government's attention and bringing the order not to publish without certain deletions. Even though the magazine says it had not intended to submit the article for direct official review, the alternate procedure the editors initiated on their own represented an implicit acknowledgment that judgment is required in deciding what to publish in the area of national security.

When the Attorney General sought a prior restraint order after the magazine had refused to delete information the government wanted to classify, Judge Warren got sharply conflicting opinions from experts in the scientific community on whether the article did or did not contain previously unpublished material that would imperil national security, if revealed. In the hope of sidestepping confrontation on whether to clear the article or suppress it, the judge proposed non-binding mediation between the government and the magazine by a panel made up of two senior weapons scientists, two representatives of the media and a lawyer or former judge. Had *The Progressive* joined the government in accepting that approach, it is conceivable that voluntary agreement might have been reached on the deletion of a modicum of technical data without detracting from the central purpose the editors hoped the article would serve.

The editors chose, instead, to dig in on the proposition that the decision on what to publish had to be theirs under the First Amendment, with the government free to proceed afterward to whatever damages or criminal penalties might be invokable under the Atomic Energy Act and other statutes. We are left with a prior restraint order of necessary concern to all elements in the press. Subsequent disclosures about the shallowness of the government's case may result in speedy termination of that restraint, but the precedent will remain an ominous one.

The whole case serves as an urgent warning of the need for establishing consistent and credible standards for the government's security system so that sound yardsticks will exist for the responsible exercise of editorial judgment by a free press.

**Concurring:** Cooney, Ghiglione, Huston, Isaacs, McKay, Otwell, Renick and Scott.

**Dissenting:** Brady and Rusher.

**Dissenting opinion by Mr. Rusher** (Brady concurring): If the Council had confined its comments on *The Progressive*'s article to the present last three paragraphs thereof (beginning "When the Attorney General"), I would have no difficulty concurring. But the long, disjointed and obscure preamble to those paragraphs wanders into areas of dubious relevance where this Council is, in any case, quite unqualified to do. I decline to associate myself with that preamble.

For one thing, it is by no means clear to me that the fact that our national security was breached accidentally in one or more places justifies *The Progressive* in breaching it deliberately in another. Still less do I think this Council has any business pontificating on "the inadequacy of the classification rules" or the "mythical character of the secrets," whatever the truth of these difficult matters may be.

June 12, 1979

## STATEMENT OF THE HERBERT CASE

The decision of the United States Supreme Court in the libel suit brought by Colonel Anthony Herbert against CBS has stirred fresh concern among some journalists that the courts are gravely impairing freedom of the press, as guaranteed by the First Amendment.

These fears of a more restrictive judicial attitude toward press freedom are perhaps understandable when one reads in quick succession the Supreme Court's opinion in the Herbert case and the landmark decision from which it derives, *New York Times Co. v. Sullivan*, handed down in March, 1964. The stress in that decision, written by Justice Brennan, was all on the desirability of fostering unfettered criticism of public officials.

The Court was unanimous in the *Sullivan* case in affirming the nations' commitment to the principle that "debate on public issues should be uninhibited, robust and wide open." Penalizing good-faith critics of government for their criticism "strikes at the very center of the constitutionally protected area of free expression," the decision said. Three of the concurring justices—Hugo Black, William O. Douglas and Arthur J. Goldberg, all now gone from the Court—felt so strongly on this point that they demurred at the single reservation the decision imposed on critical comment. This was that a statement could be considered defamatory and thus subject to damage suit only when made with "actual malice," a term the Court defined as meaning with "knowledge that it was false or with reckless disregard of whether it was false or not."

The minority within the majority argued that constitutional requirements would be satisfied by nothing less than an "absolute, unconditional privilege" to the citizen and the press to criticize official conduct, but the full Court's insistence on a rule barring knowing or heedless use of false information in the name of criticism impressed many journalistic commentators as reasonable and the press reaction to the decision was overwhelmingly enthusiastic.

513

The burden of proof in libel actions had been reversed. No longer was it up to the news organization to prove that its statement was true; now the obligation was on the plaintiff to prove that it was false and knowingly so. The effect was precisely the one the Court had endorsed as imperative to the health of American democracy: confidence by the press that it could vigorously expose or excoriate the aberrations of government officials without the self-censorship imposed by fear of harassing litigation.

The emphasis on the Herbert decision is markedly different. Where *New York Times Co. v. Sullivan* put its accent on expanding the boundaries of editorial privilege, the focus in the latest decision was entirely in the opposite direction. Its thrust was to deny editors and reporters any constitutional claim to immunity against the efforts of plaintiffs in libel suits to penetrate the privacy of the editorial process as a means of bolstering their charges of defamation. Taken in conjunction with a lengthening list of adverse rulings recently issued in press cases at various levels of the judiciary, so pronounced a shift in emphasis on the part of the nation's highest tribunal was bound to occasion journalistic apprehension.

But a change in tone does not necessarily mean a comparable change in substance and it is important to examine how far, if at all, the Supreme Court has moved away from the protection supposedly given to news organizations by its 1964 verdict in the Sullivan case. In the absence of such an analysis, the press runs the risk of seeming to argue for a limitless right to lie, free of all accountability, whenever it chooses to undermine or destroy the good name of a person in public life.

Careful study of the majority decision in the Herbert case, the concurring opinion by Justice Powell, the partial dissent by Justice Brennan and the full dissents by Justices Stewart and Marshall provides little warrant for argument that the Court has retreated in any fundamental way from the principles laid down in its ruling fifteen years ago. Even the dissenters acknowledge that the element most troublesome to many in the press— the authorization the Herbert decision provides for inquiring into journalists' state of mind as part of the pre-trial discovery process—was clearly implicit in the Sullivan decision. Not one of the justices suggests that the First Amendment provides an automatic shield against such inquiry or that exploration of this kind can be ruled out unless the "actual malice" yardstick is abandoned.

Opening up for virtually inexhaustible questioning the judgmental processes by which reporters and editors decide what information to credit or to reject has disturbing implications for the press, as the National

News Council warned more than two years ago when the first-round decision in the Herbert case was rendered in New York by Federal Judge Charles S. Haight, Jr.

The most obvious of the potential impediments to robust exercise of the journalistic function are those that flow from the staggering cost in time, money and talent, both editorial and legal, of the pre-trial discovery process.

Abuses in the taking of depositions before trial have become an open scandal in virtually all branches of civil procedure, despite the clear admonition of the Federal court rules that the discovery process be conducted in a manner calculated to secure "the just, speedy and inexpensive determination of every action" and that all the material sought through questioning be relevant. The majority decision in *Herbert v. Lando* is as emphatic as are the dissenting opinions in stressing the duty of trial judges to restrict discovery where the effect is to inflict "annoyance, embarrassment, oppression, or undue burden or expense."

Justice Stewart's dissent, though clearly not controlling as a judicial guidepost, could make a useful contribution toward keeping the discovery process in reasonable bounds if trial judges followed his advice to limit the process to what was published and to recognize that "what was *not* published has nothing to do with the case." A similar effect would be achieved if trial judges take seriously the recommendation of Justice Powell in his separate concurring opinion that they give careful weight to values protected by the First Amendment in passing on the relevance of questions.

Realism compels recognition, however, that nothing short of total reform in the rules governing civil procedure in every type of case is likely to check the escalation of costs resulting from the latitude currently allowed in pre-trial discovery. The National News Council urges that the fresh attention focused on this problem by the Herbert decision be translated into prompt action within the judiciary or in Congress, if necessary, to rewrite the existing rules in all branches of civil justice in a manner that will give substance to the promise of "just, speedy and inexpensive determination of every action."

The Council also applauds the efforts presently under way in professional societies of reporters, editors, publishers and broadcasters to establish a coordinated legal defense program to underwrite the high cost of defense against libel suits in cases where news organizations are too poor to defend themselves adequately.

How mountainous these costs can be in libel actions—including many

515

that may be brought primarily to intimidate the press or to harrass it—is well illustrated by the Herbert case, which is now being remanded to the District Court for more pre-trial questioning of a CBS producer whose deposition already runs to 2,903 pages of transcript, plus 240 exhibits. The original complaint was filed early in 1974 and no one can predict with certainty when the taking of depositions will end and trial on the merits begin, much less how or when a final verdict will be rendered.

That libel actions can involve hazards for plaintiffs as well as news organizations was underscored by a decision issued by Federal District Judge Robert L. Carter in New York on the very day that the Supreme Court was rendering its decision in the Herbert case. He ordered an investor and his law firm to pay $50,000 in legal costs to Barron's weekly for having brought a "baseless lawsuit" against it on the strength of unsupported allegations of misinforming the public.

The plain moral of all this painful experience on both sides is that there are advantages to seeking alternatives to the courts in libel cases. The desirability of developing such alternatives to bring down litigative costs and delays has already been widely recognized in a broad range of civil fields, from tenant-landlord disputes to community relations. The British Press Council, after which this National News Council is patterned, is often called on by Britons concerned with vindicating their reputations, who would otherwise file damage suits under the more permissive libel laws that prevail in that country. On occasion similar complaints of alleged mistreatment by the press have been filed with this Council by individuals who have first signed the required waivers of any intention to go to court on the same issue. It is neither our place nor our purpose to put forward the idea that an instrumentality of this kind is necessarily the best or only alternative open to the press and public.

However, the diversity of this organization's membership divided as it is among members from the media and from broad segments of the body politic, does make it appropriate for the National News Council to propose that it take the initiative in eliciting the suggestions of representative groups in the press, the bar and public life on ways to protect the good names of persons against unfair attack without inhibiting the media in its critical function or exposing everyone involved to the tortures of libel litigation in the courts.

**Concurring:** Brady, Cooney, Ghiglione, Huston, Isaacs, McKay, Otwell, Pulitzer, Renick, Roberts, Rusher and Scott.

June 12, 1979

## FREEDOM OF THE PRESS COMPLAINT
### THE DAY
### against
### ELECTRIC BOAT

**Complaint:** *The Day*, a daily newspaper published in New London, Conn., accuses the Electric Boat Division of General Dynamics Corporation of discriminating against the paper by imposing a news blackout. The company, which is wholly engaged in building submarines for the United States Navy, has its principal shipyard in Groton, just across the Thames River from *The Day*'s newsroom and plant. Electric Boat is the largest employer in Southeastern Connecticut, and the great bulk of its 18,500 Groton employees live in *The Day*'s circulation area.

The newspaper alleges that the company for more than a year has excluded it from access to any information about its activities, contending that *The Day* has been unfair in its news coverage of Electric Boat. This exclusion, according to the complaint, has taken the form of refusal to send news releases to *The Day*, though such releases are sent to other papers and broadcasters. The paper further accuses the company of shutting it out of news conferences open to other publications, of refusing to return phone calls, or answer questions posed by reporters for *The Day* and of halting all advertising in *The Day*, while continuing to run frequent help-wanted ads and occasional large institutional ads in other area newspapers.

The only deviation by the company from this keep-out policy, *The Day* says, has been the issuance of press credentials to *Day* representatives to cover four submarine launchings. The first two of these invitations, the paper adds, were received the day before the actual launchings and both came only after intercession in *The Day*'s behalf by members of Congress. The paper notes that Electric Boat dominates the area's economy and that what happens there is "of vital concern" to every resident. "Although *The Day* has continued to cover Electric Boat in great detail for the past year using outside sources, its readers are being denied the company's views in most cases," complains Deane C. Avery, the paper's co-publisher and editor. He adds that this exclusionist policy has made it impossible for *The Day* to do feature stories on significant engineering accomplishments at the yard—stories that would have reflected considerable credit on management.

Mr. Avery charges that the company and its corporate parent in St.

Louis have rebuffed or ignored repeated requests by the paper for conferences aimed at exploring management's grievances against *The Day* and seeking a harmonious resolution of the controversy. The end effect, Mr. Avery contends, is that a newspaper that goes into almost 80 percent of the occupied households in the nine-town primary area around the shipyard has been unable to give full coverage of an enterprise whose product is paid for exclusively with tax dollars.

**Response of the Company:** Copies of the complaint were sent to David S. Lewis, chairman of General Dynamics, and P. Takis Veliotis, general manager of the Electric Boat Division, along with a request for comment. Neither responded. Telephone calls to Mr. Veliotis's office brought notice from a public relations spokesman that Electric Boat would not reply formally to the Council nor would it enter into informal communication of any kind, even for the purpose of supplying background information. The spokesman said that General Dynamics intended to follow the same course.

The embargo on any communications with the Council was carried to the length of refusing to send this organization copies of two 1978 issues of *EB Topics*, the house organ the company distributes among its employees, in which it had discussed its unhappiness with coverage by *The Day*. A suggestion that the Council attempt to serve as mediator in reopening direct communication between the company and the paper was rejected as unwelcome by the Electric Boat spokesman. "No way," was his response.

The Council staff, reluctant to leave the situation in this posture, invoked the good offices of Michael Pulitzer, the Council member resident in St. Louis, in the hope that his intercession with Mr. Lewis and other executives of General Dynamics would open the door to a mediatory role for the Council. Talks between Mr. Pulitzer and Fred J. Bettinger, director of public affairs and advertising for the parent corporation, produced the first break in management's policy of total noncooperation.

Mr. Bettinger told Mr. Pulitzer that the company was irked at what it considered *The Day*'s settled pattern of taking "cheap shots" at Electric Boat on the basis of irresponsible statements made by disgruntled employees and former employees, often on the basis of what he termed barroom interviews. The company's irritation was heightened, Mr. Bettinger said, by the fact that such stories were appearing at a time when a new management team was beginning what was now proved a successful effort to "turn the shipyard around" by straightening out operational, engineering and labor problems that had resulted in production delays and cost overruns of disturbing magnitude in earlier years. Having come to the conclusion that explanatory statements issued by management were regularly ignored, misrepresented or played down by *The Day*, the company finally decided that its interests would be best served by not talking to the paper at all.

In this connection, Mr. Bettinger pointed out that the company was not deeply involved in public relations in general. He said that it rarely put out more than five press releases a year and that it did not hold press conferences on any regular basis, though company officials did on occasion give interviews to other papers, magazines, and broadcasters and press officers were on duty to answer questions from the media by telephone or letter. He made special mention of the company's receptivity to requests for information from business publications, such as *Business Week* and *Forbes*, where it felt its attempts at management overhaul to increase productivity would get sympathetic treatment. Mr. Bettinger acknowledged that the company had been at fault in dragging its feet about issuance of press credentials to *The Day* for attendance at the first two launchings, but he said this problem would not recur. The company was unhappy that *The Day* had gone to the News Council, Mr. Bettinger said, but he acknowledged that Electric Boat had no present plans for ending its cut-off of communications with the paper.

Mr. Pulitzer stressed that the Council's primary purpose was to serve as an intermediary in re-establishing a line of communications between the company and *The Day*. He relayed to Mr. Bettinger the assurances Mr. Avery had given the Council's staff that his paper had no animus against Electric Boat and that its sole interest was in being able to do the most thorough and objective job it could of covering developments in an enterprise it respected as the economic mainstay of the New London-Groton region. Mr. Bettinger promised to explore with his associates in management the possibility of arranging a joint meeting, with or without direct representation by the Council, to seek an adjustment of the dispute. No affirmative response has been relayed to Mr. Pulitzer up to this date.

Though Mr. Bettinger cited no specific stories in his conversation with Mr. Pulitzer, some idea of the kind of coverage the company deemed offensive is contained in the two issues of *EB Topics*, in which management's grievances against *The Day* were first aired. (*The Day* made copies of the issues available to the Council after the company had declined to do so.)

Electric Boat's initial appraisal of what it termed "biased and unbalanced reporting" by the paper came in a commentary section on January 5, 1978, two months before the cutoff of communication with *The Day*. Three stories were cited as obstacles to building the spirit of teamwork the company felt it needed to maintain production schedules. One was an analysis of "construction errors," gleaned by *The Day* from Navy records it had obtained under the Freedom of Information Act. The company called the story exaggerated and misleading.

The second story quoted a union spokesman as charging that Electric Boat production was at an all-time low. The company termed this a "sour grapes" charge by an employee discharged two months before. The fact that production had increased significantly after his departure was buried in the story, according to the company. The third story was headlined, "No Christmas Cheer at EB this Year." It reported that the Friday before Christmas, which fell on Sunday that year, would be a full workday with none of the usual Christmas parties inside the yard. The company accused the paper of ignoring its comment that Monday would be a holiday for the entire work force and that the scheduling of a full day's work on Friday was consistent with the union contract. Employees were urged by *EB Topics* to write to *The Day* protesting its coverage. They were also urged to avoid becoming "rumor-mongers" or "bad-mouthers" of the company in their own right.

In a second Commentary on January 12, 1978, *EB Topics* focused on two headlines from *The Day*, which it termed "speculative at best, misleading at worst." One related to the possibility that Electric Boat might be shut down for inventory for up to 30 days—a possibility the company said never was contemplated on a plantwide basis. The second headline four days later spoke of the possibility of a 10-day inventory layoff for 4,500 EB workers, roughly a quarter of the work force. The story under the head noted, in its fourth paragraph, that for most of those affected the layoff would be only five days, not ten. *EB Topics* advised its readers to question all headlines in *The Day* and to be especially skeptical of those over stories based on information from unnamed sources.

**Council finding:** The circumstances surrounding this complaint were reverse of those that would normally be expected to prevail in a case before the National News Council involving the fairness or accuracy of news coverage. In ordinary course, it would be the company that would appear as complainant, requesting assessment by the Council of its charges of bias and imbalance in coverage by *The Day*. Electric Boat is, of course, under no compulsion to choose this route. It has elected instead, acting unilaterally, to make a conclusive determination of unfairness against *The Day* and to impose its own sanction—a shutoff to *The Day* of all information within its control on activities in a shipyard engaged solely in the fulfillment of government defense orders.

The scope of legitimate public interest in how well Electric Boat discharges its obligations as one of the country's most important defense contractors is indicated by the fact that at the very time the blackout was imposed by the company it was arguing with the Navy over the merits of a company claim for payment of $544 million in cost overruns on a $1.4 billion submarine contract. The claim was eventually settled with an agreement by the Navy to pay $484 million above the contract price for eighteen submarines, which were an average of three years behind schedule. The company, in turn, agreed to absorb a $359 million loss.

When public funds and the public interest are involved to such an extent in a company that employs a quarter of all the workers in South-eastern Connecticut, the community is ill-served by an arbitrary decision on the company's part to withhold all information from the chief news-paper directly serving the region. The Navy's own policy, as officially stated to the Council, is to give access to Navy information on an equal basis to all news media representatives.

"Under this policy," says R. deF. Cleverly, a director of Congressional and public affairs for the Naval Sea Systems Command, "*The Day*'s requests to the Navy for information, interviews, and the like are treated equally with those of all other news media. Therefore, information which the Navy has in its files concerning its contracts with Electric Boat is available to *The Day* on the same basis as it is available to all other members of the news media. Through this procedure, the equal rights of the news media to information about the Government's operations are protected."

However, Federal directives specify no procedures requiring defense contractors to adhere to the same nondiscriminatory policy on release of information, even where those contractors are employed exclusively on government work. Nor does the Freedom of Information Act give *The Day* any special standing to demand information or records from the company. This absence of official obligation in no way diminishes the arbitrariness of Electric Boat's decision to stop talking to the paper or sending it press releases.

What goes right at Electric Boat and what goes wrong are both matters of legitimate public concern, particularly in the arena in which the company exercises such a dominant economic role. It has a right to expect responsible coverage from the media, but not necessarily invariably favorable coverage.

That *The Day* has made occasional errors in its news coverage of the company's activities is conceded by the paper. From the outset it has expressed eagerness to sit down with management for a frank exploration of the company's grievances. The National News Council fully endorses that position. It continues to stand ready to serve in any mediatory capacity that might prove helpful in breaking down the barrier that currently impedes communication.

**Concurring**: Brady, Cooney, Ghiglione, Huston, Isaacs, McKay, Otwell, Pulitzer, Renick, Roberts, Rusher and Scott.

June 12, 1979

## STATEMENT ON THE SEBERG CASE

Only from disclosures by her former husband at the time of her suicide did the American public learn that Jean Seberg was deliberately and outrageously maligned by the F.B.I. in 1970. In order to discredit Ms. Seberg because of her support for the Black Nationalist movement, the F.B.I. concocted statements concerning the paternity of her child who subsequently was stillborn. The F.B.I. in an internal memorandum said: "It is felt that the possible publication of Seberg's plight could cause her embarrassment and serve to cheapen her image with the general public."

When government agents act to disseminate rumors of this kind, as was done in this case, the entire nation is victimized. And any elements of the press which chose to publish the rumor about Ms. Seberg without verification were guilty of abetting the kind of tactics the F.B.I. employed. The press must maintain the highest standards for checking such information.

The National News Council welcomes the statement of F.B.I. director William H. Webster that "the days when the F.B.I. used derogatory information to combat advocates of unpopular causes have passed forever." However, the Council goes on record as deeply regretting the necessity for that statement and condemns the practice in the past that required it.

**Concurring:** Cooney, Dilliard, Ghiglione, Huston, Isaacs, Lawson, Pulitzer and Salant.

**Dissenting:** Rusher.

**Dissenting opinion by Mr. Rusher:** For the F.B.I. to confect and float a false story about an individual would, of course, be profoundly reprehensible at any time, and if the press through carelessness permitted itself to be used for such a purpose it would deserve sharp criticism by this Council. If the story was true, however (which I understand is unclear in this instance), the problem presented is surely more complex, even for those who would ultimately reach the same conclusion. Where national security is involved (and opinions will differ as to whether the Black Panther connection made that the case here), that important factor must also be taken into account. I believe that a rational conclusion in this matter requires the evaluation of all of these considerations, and ought not to reduce to simply one more sweeping condemnation of J. Edgar Hoover's administration of the F.B.I.

September 21, 1979

## REVISED COMMENT ON THE SEBERG CASE

On September 21, 1979, the National News Council condemned the FBI for allegedly "deliberately and outrageously" maligning Jean Seberg because of her support for the Black Panther Party.

Documents recently released by the FBI show that while the agency contemplated leaking embarrassing personal information about Ms. Seberg, that information was not in fact officially released by the agency.

The action of the Council was unfair to the FBI. With respect to the press, the Council holds that news organizations have an obligation to publish no embarrassing or derogatory information about individuals without independent verification.

**Concurring:** Abel, Bell, Brady, Ghiglione, Huston, Isaacs, Lawson, Maynard, McKay, Pulitzer, Rusher, and Williams.

September 19, 1980

## STATEMENT ON PRIOR RESTRAINT

The dropping by the Department of Justice of its prosecution of *The Progressive* case leaves unresolved important issues of the press's obligation in cases involving, or allegedly involving, national security.

The National News Council recognizes that there are situations in which national security has to be a consideration in deciding whether stories should be printed or broadcast. Proceeding from that recognition, we take as the test to be applied before the Government should even talk about invoking the extreme remedy of prior restraint the standard laid down by the Supreme Court in 1971 that the information under challenge raises the danger of "direct, immediate and irreparable damage to our nation or its people."

**Concurring:** Brady, Cooney, Dilliard, Ghiglione, Huston, Isaacs, Lawson, Pulitzer, Roberts, Rusher, Salant and Scott.

September 21, 1979

## STATEMENT ON CLOSING COURTROOMS

The bond of essentiality that links openness and fairness at every stage of the criminal justice system received clear-cut affirmation from the nation's lawyers and judges last year in the revised canon on fair trial and free press overwhelmingly adopted by the House of Delegates of the American Bar Association

Relying almost exclusively on Sixth Amendment values, as distinct from those guaranteed by the First Amendment, the canon enjoins bench and bar to maintain maximum openness in all criminal trials and pretrial proceedings. Under its terms only such limits on access to courtrooms and records are to be imposed as are demonstrably required to protect the right of accused persons to an unprejudiced trial environment. The canon warns explicitly that public confidence in all criminal justice will be eroded by unduly restrictive information policies, whether in the form of blacking out any part of the trial or pretrial procedure, sealing records or attempting to enforce prior restraint on publication of material in the hands of the media.

Hopes that this formulation of standards by the organized bar would greatly reduce the danger of damaging collisions between the courts and the press in fulfilling their respective responsibilities have, regrettably, been set back by the 5-to-4 decision of the United States Supreme Court in the case of *Gannett Co. v. DePasquale*.

The broad authority which that decision seemingly vested in trial judges to exclude press and public from various phases of criminal proceedings has impelled judges in many parts of the country to draw a curtain over crucial phases in the process of determining a defendant's guilt or innocence. Often such denial of public scrutiny has been ordered without notice, hearing or even the most cursory showing of need.

The speed with which this trend has gathered momentum and the indiscriminate fashion in which the new latitude is being applied make swift corrective action urgent to restore the accent on public trials that has historically been the country's most dependable shield against judicial autocracy, corrupt law-enforcement or undue favoritism in the administration of criminal justice. The prospect for effective action along these lines is enhanced by indications that much of the impetus for closing courtrooms stems from imprecision in the language of the DePasquale

524

ruling and that at least five of the Supreme Court justices are in essential accord with both the spirit and letter of the constructive ABA canon.

On that basis, the National News Council applauds the moves under way by the major societies of publishers, broadcasters, editors and reporters to push for prompt consideration by the Supreme Court of a new case that would give it an opportunity to clarify its views and remove all or most of the current confusion. But the Council recognizes that no redefinition of the high court's position, however protective of the principles of openness, will in and of itself be sufficient to end clashes between the press and the courts over the media's obligation to fulfill their vital information function while respecting the rights of defendants.

There remains, and will remain, need for a resumption of direct communication among press, bar and bench on means to implement the precepts of the ABA canon, thus helping to establish a solid underpinning for maintenance of First and Sixth Amendment guarantees and for avoiding conflicts and adversary relationships injurious to both groups in discharging their indispensable duties to the American people. Initial soundings by this Council a year ago indicated considerable receptivity to such efforts at two-way communication on the part of the bar and judiciary.

The press in many states has tended to shy away from such collaborative efforts since the decision of the Nebraska Supreme Court that turned the voluntary fair trial-free press guidelines in that state into legal mandates devoid of any flexibility. The new canon provides an excellent springboard for a renewed attempt at communication involving bench and bar on one side and the media on the other.

**Concurring:** Cooney, Dilliard, Ghiglione, Huston, Isaacs, Lawson, Pulitzer, Rusher and Salant.

September 21, 1979


## FREEDOM OF THE PRESS COMPLAINT
14 REPORTERS (Rock Island Argus)        (Filed: Aug. 20, 1979)
against
QUAD-CITY TIMES


**Complaint:** Fourteen reporters of the *Rock Island* (Ill.) *Argus* joined as a group to complain that a story in the *Quad-City Times* of Davenport (Iowa) giving the background of a 15-year-old boy charged with murder, should not have been published.

Headlined "Who Failed with Scot Darnell?," the story appeared on August 12, 1979. It offered elaborate detail about the home, psychiatric background and prior record of young Darnell prior to his arrest and being charged with the rape and murder of a 10-year-old girl. "Neither treatment nor punishment has had much effect on him," the article noted.

The complaint said: "We feel the story was uncalled for at this point— before the case has even begun to go to trial. As working journalists, we believe the *Times'* stories do not serve either the public interest, the rights of the accused or the reputation of our profession." The complaint termed the article an "irresponsible throwback to an earlier and unmissed era in journalism."

**Response:** Daniel K. Hayes, managing editor of the *Quad-City Times*, in a letter to the Council said:

"We believe the story speaks for itself. We believe professional newspeople can immediately determine our thinking, our sensitivity and our concern for both individual rights and the public's need to know."

In a phone conversation with the Council staff, Forest Kilmer, editor of the *Quad-City Times*, added this comment:

"We saw this story not as a criminal issue, but as a social issue. We were encouraged and assisted at every step of the way in doing the story by prosecutors, court personnel and institutional representatives. We asked ourselves: 'Is the public being better served through the revelations in the story?' We believe that it is. We weighed all of the factors. We believe that if this case ever comes to trial, the court has other recourse to insure a fair trial: change of venue (it happens often around here), jury sequestration, etc,"

**Council finding:** The type of story which appeared in the *Quad-City Times* about Scott Darnell has long posed a dilemma for the press.

There is the journalistic argument that the public has a right and a need to know about failures in society's systems which can open the way to violence and crime. In that context, the Davenport story can be defended by editors as a sound example of enterprise journalism about a major issue. Such reporting in other instances has sometimes led to reforms in the patterns of criminal justice and institutional or custodial operations. The detail in the *Quad-City Times* story confirms the editor's statement that individuals within the governmental agencies, including the court system itself, served as sources for much of the paper's information.

Those who protest the publication contend that the story inevitably created obstacles to a fair trial for the 15-year-old defendant who has been charged with murder as an adult. The challenge obviously raises the years'-old issue of the seeming conflicts between the guarantees of the First and Sixth Amendments.

This case has come before the Council in the form of a grievance involving a specific matter, but it raises basic issues relating to journalism's responsibility concerning pre-trial publicity. Rather than consider the problems in the context of this specific complaint, the Council believes it should examine the whole question of journalism's responsibility, if any, concerning pre-trial publicity in a broader context, and the Freedom of Press Committee is instructed to proceed with such an examination.

**Concurring:** Brady, Cooney, Dilliard, Ghiglione, Huston, Isaacs, Pulitzer, Roberts and Salant.

**Dissenting:** Lawson.

**Dissenting opinion by Mr. Lawson:** For the following reasons, I do not concur with the majority.

1. We have a specific grievance which demonstrates the issue of press coverage in a tragic and emotional juvenile criminal matter. The Council should treat it as a grievance.

2. The *Quad-City Times* should be criticized for the timing of the article which creates the possibility that this juvenile, who having apparently committed a heinous crime, can mount a defense that could enable him to again be a threat to others.

3. In our grievance process the Council is too lenient with the press and demands too much from those who take the time and make the effort to make a grievance. We admit the article poses a dilemma and raises questions of pre-trial publicity. The Council addressing those issues with a very concrete grievance illuminates the discussion far better than an examination of the whole question.

4. In these very perplexing times when we are shocked by outrageous violence and crimes, how does the press so inform the public that we do not become a meaner society, and instead can create a climate for the changing of our institutions? Such serious social change is the only healthy option for turning down and turning off violence and crime.

September 21, 1979

**NOTE:** The Council study which resulted from this complaint was published in 1980 in a booklet entitled "Protecting Two Vital Freedoms: Fair Trial and Free Press." Copies may be obtained from the Council at $2.50 each to cover the cost of production, mailing and handling.

## STATEMENT ON ABSCAM LEAKS

The leaking to newspapers and broadcasters of detailed information about illegal payments allegedly accepted by members of Congress has raised anew concern about the damage that can be done to individual reputations by prejudicial publicity based on information from unidentified sources. The dangers and dilemmas surrounding publication of such material have long been recognized inside and outside journalism. Questions on these points have never been satisfactorily resolved, as everything about the present case underscores.

It is clear that irreparable damage can be done to individual and institutional reputations through the saturation spread of discriminatory data for which no one stands accountable, especially when the processes of justice have not even progressed to the point of impaneling grand juries, much less passing on guilt or innocence.

In any period stories of this kind about people, whether prominent or obscure, can trample on the Sixth Amendment rights to a fair trial of those allegedly implicated. For law-makers who must stand before the voters, another dimension of potential damage operates with special force when such charges are disseminated in an election years.

Whatever the ultimate disposition of the allegations, the legislators' re-election chances are gravely impaired. The flood tide of publicity inflicts hurt that is often ineradicable, even when acquittal is the end result. In the Abscam cases the damage is made greater by the likelihood that some of the cases will not have come to trial and been decided before Election Day. Indeed, it is by no means certain that indictments will have been returned or decisions made on whether ever to press formal charges of wrongdoing.

On the other side of the balance sheet is the disservice the press would unquestionably have done to the political process if it elected to withhold from the public information of such seriousness bearing on the integrity of high-ranking congressional officials—information which editors and reporters had reason to consider authentic, even though the sources could not be publicly disclosed. Implicit in decisions of this kind, of course, is the existence within each news organization of a chain of responsibility adequate to assess the trustworthiness of the confidential sources. A related question is the degree to which the leak may be calculated to serve ulterior purposes of the informer or others unknown even to the reporters or editors. Inquiry into motives is always a beartrap; even assuming these can be determined accurately, is it appropriate for editors to rule out information they consider of public importance because they suspect their sources may be seeking to use the media as vehicles of political spite or character annihilation?

In the Abscam case, it may be that those who leaked the information were afraid that the whole mess would be covered up by superiors in the Justice Department or the White House unless the scandal they had uncovered (and for which they had concocted a setting) received so much publicity that official action could not be avoided. Yet again these sources may have been aware that elements in the press—whether through journalistic enterprise or deliberate plants—had enough of the story to put the government's entire case in jeopardy if any of it was published before the authorities had time to complete their collection of evidence. The seeming result was that officials in possession of details of the investigation made themselves intermediaries in fixing what amounted to a coordinated release time that caused three newspapers and two television networks to move simultaneously in the story's first dissemination. That clandestine go-ahead signal coincided with the government's initial notice to Congressmen that they were targets.

One network had so much of a headstart in rounding up information on the investigation that its camera crews established a stakeout weeks before the denouement outside the Washington house being used by the FBI as a base of operations; even the process of officially informing Congress members that they were under investigation was put on videotape at the very instant the suspects were getting their first personal notice.

Competitive considerations exerted pressures that seemed to produce a lowest common denominator of judgment on the ethics of using names in advance of any criminal process. Thus, NBC omitted names from its first Abscam broadcast, but introduced them in its next after the first edition of *The New York Times* had appeared with the congressmen identified. Editors argued with considerable logic that printing news of the scandal without specific identification of those allegedly involved would touch off a nationwide guessing game that would unfairly besmirch the entire Congress.

It is easy, of course, to dodge the whole issue of journalistic responsibility by noting that the basic ethical breach was by law-enforcement officials who allowed the material to leak in violation of any concept of due process with respect to those under investigation. The American Bar Association, in promulgating its 1978 standards for safeguarding fair trial and free press, wisely put upon judges and law-enforcement officials the

529

duty for directing court personnel and others engaged in the administration of criminal justice not to release specific information that might be prejudicial in its impact on fairness of trial for accused persons. The bar specifically ruled out any idea that the press could or should be enjoined from publishing any material in its possession, even if court officers had given it out in the face of judicial directive, so long as the material was not obtained by theft, bribery or other illegal means.

By the same yardstick editors and writers were under no legal restraint against using whatever information they had in their possession about the Abscam investigation, however defiant of elementary justice it may have been for their sources to have made the material available to the press. But recognition of that freedom does not erase questions about the ethical propriety of "indictment by press" in a campaign year—questions compounded by the mystery that surrounds the choice of targets as well as the selective flow of information that has poured out of some seemingly unstemmable underground in or linked to the FBI. The possibility is evident that through use of such methods an executive or legislative agency with investigative powers can convert the press into an instrument for discrediting any target.

Nearly a quarter-century ago many inside the media felt obliged to scrutinize their own concepts of news when the late Senator Joseph R. McCarthy of Wisconsin made it a practice to appear at Senate hearings brandishing lists of alleged Communists in government and the military. In the end there was considerable agreement that restraint should be exercised in publishing, without some effort at independent verification or response, charges that could blacken individual reputations.

If there was acceptance then of the idea that accusations publicly made by a United States Senator at a formal hearing did not automatically acquire a degree of verisimilitude, is there not more need for restraint in instances where no accuser stands forth publicly and no start toward due process has been made? In such circumstances can the press shrug off the danger that it may be open to manipulation by informants advancing external political purposes of their own? In this instance the news organizations that were first with the story argue that they carefully checked the validity of their information and adhered to sound journalistic principles throughout. What remains troublesome is the absence of clarity on what these principles are.

It is interesting that, just last year, in the awarding of Pulitzer Prizes for investigative journalism and public service some of newspaperdom's most respected elder statesmen refused to concur in the judges' recommendations for awards because of reservations about the use by news organizations and news gatherers of techniques associated with "sting" operations that bore a surface resemblance to those used by the FBI in the Abscam and related operations. Actually, the parallel is decidely inexact because no element of enticement entered into the journalistic "sting." Those in search of illegal payments took the initiative in demanding bribes from an establishment they had every reason to believe was a conventional bar and grill operating on a regular business basis. There is, however, an element of irony—indicative of the confusion enveloping this area of journalistic ethics—that publications whose editors questioned the propriety of such techniques when used by investigative reporters apparently had fewer qualms when it came to the FBI "sting."

The dangers and dilemmas for journalism could be extended at great length. The National News Council does not pretend it has either the information or wisdom with which to catalogue them, let alone evaluate or prescribe in so tangled a field. It is convinced, however, that the debate over the role of the media in this affair is so intense and the divergence of views within and without the profession so ramified that a failure by journalists to attempt to assess and resolve their differences can only invite further pressure for external controls of a kind the press rightly abhors.

For that reason the Council, as a body dedicated to the concept of a free and responsible press, proposes to explore the feasibility of arranging swiftly a calling together of thoughtful analysts drawn from both press and public to grapple with the issues raised by this episode and to explore principles that might serve in such cases as a basis for greater self-restraint and heightened professionalism.

**Concurring:** Cooney, Ghiglione, Huston, Lawson, McKay, Otwell, Pulitzer, and Roberts.

**Dissenting:** Brady, Miller and Rusher.

**Abstaining:** Isaacs.

**Dissenting opinion by Mr. Miller** (Mr. Brady concurring): It seems to me the Council is trying to define what kinds of leaks should be leaked to the press. I am in favor of leaks to the press. I think they are a great public service. I think the press must accept the responsibility for evaluating the leaks and the motives of the sources.

**Dissenting opinion by Mr. Rusher:** Once again the Council has preceded a basically unobjectionable proposal (in this case for a study of the journalistic issue raised by the Abscam leaks) with a long and rambling disquisition which goes at unnecessary lengths into various bypaths and in at least one case into pure fantasy. (I am not aware that the late Senator Joseph McCarthy "made it a practice to appear at Senate hearings brandishing lists of alleged Communists in government and the military.")

A study of the problem, however, would be useful, as I stated in a recent column:

> Here is a classic example of the fundamental vice of basing news stories on anonymous sources. The likeliest source of the information, of course, is some Deep Throat in the Justice Department or the FBI. It is appalling to think that somebody in one or the other is so indifferent to the rights of the accused under our system as to broadcast such charges against hitherto respected public officials weeks or months before they are even indicted.
>
> But we cannot even be sure that the names were leaked by a law-enforcement official. What if political enemies of those men discovered that they were to be indicted and deliberately jumped the gun, simply to injure them further? It is even possible—so prejudicial has all this publicity been to their hope of fair trial—that the leaks came from one or more of the accused politicians themselves, in a desperate effort to derail the prosecution by disclosing the investigation prematurely.
>
> We will probably never know which (if any) of these speculations is valid, because the reporters will stoutly refuse to identify their informants. And since it is quite possible that at least some of those named in the press won't even be indicted, it may be that they will see their careers destroyed because they were identified publicly, as among those involved, on the basis of information supplied by anonymous informants whose motives we shall never know.

March 7, 1980


## FREEDOM OF THE PRESS COMPLAINT
UNITED PRESS INTERNATIONAL      (Filed: Nov. 21, 1979)
### against
SYNANON FOUNDATION, INC.

**Complaint:** The Council, at a meeting on November 30, 1979, at the University of Miami in Coral Gables, Fla., considered a complaint brought before it by United Press International against the Synanon Foundation, Inc. The complaint was in a letter from UPI dated November 21, 1979.

In its letter, UPI charged that the foundation had made systematic efforts "to threaten UPI's reputation and relationships with subscribers and, generally, object to any news coverage which reflects unfavorably upon Synanon." UPI further charged that Synanon's lawyers have been "flooding the nation's news media with letters threatening libel suits as a part of the systematic pattern of intimidation designed to suppress all stories they considered unfavorable."

Even reports on the Pulitzer Prize awared the *Point Reyes* (California) *Light* for its Synanon expose drew "form" letters demanding retraction on pain of suit, the news agency declared.

Following a discussion at the November meeting, the Council instructed its staff to conduct a thorough examination of the issues posed and report back to the Council at the earliest practicable time.

**Staff investigation:** Following the Council's instructions, the staff, under the direction of William B. Arthur, executive director, undertook a thorough investigation.

In a meeting on January 21 in Synanon's offices at Tomales Bay, Calif., Dan L. Garrett, Jr., the foundation's general counsel, gave Mr. Arthur a report on what the foundation calls the "Retraction Project."

The "Retraction Project" report reveals that the writing of letters by Synanon seeking "correction" and "retraction" of news reports concerning the organization is not limited to UPI and its clients. Hundreds of such letters have been sent to print and broadcast organizations such as The Associated Press, the TV networks, *The Wall Street Journal*, *The New York Times*, *San Francisco Chronicle*, *The Milwaukee Journal*, etc.; to many smaller newspapers, such as *The Billings* (Mont.) *Gazette* and the *Times Herald Record*, Middletown, N.Y., to *Time* magazine and to *Editor & Publisher* magazine.

The Synanon report says that 960 such letters were sent out during 1978 and 1979. Of these, 816 were sent to newspapers and 144 to the three commercial television networks—ABC, CBS, and NBC—to their affiliate stations, and to independents. The "Retraction Project" continues into 1980.

Synanon reported that the organization contracted with a nationwide service to provide clips of articles published relating to Synanon. According to Mr. Garrett's aides, 11,136 such clips were provided during 1978 and 1979. Elizabeth Missakian, administrator, Synanon Law Offices, who prepared the report and who was present at the meeting with Mr. Arthur, stated that "There are *many* more (articles) which may not have been picked up and sent to us."

The Synanon letters, Mr. Garrett said, are sent in accordance with Section 48a (demand and publication or broadcast of correction) of the California Civil Code. Paragraph 1 of the section reads as follows:

> 1. In any action for damages for the publication of a libel in a newspaper, or of a slander by radio broadcast, plaintiff shall recover no more than special damages

unless a correction be demanded and not be published or broadcast, as hereinafter provided. Plaintiff shall serve upon the publisher, at the place of publication or broadcaster at the place of broadcast a written notice specifying the statements claimed to be libelous and demanding that the same be corrected. Said notice and demand must be served within 20 days after knowledge of the publication or broadcast of statements claimed to be libelous.

"This requires us," Mr. Garrett said, "if we are going to maintain a proper legal position and preserve our rights, to file a demand for correction whenever we see material printed which is not the truth. And that's all we are concerned about. We are not concerned about criticism or opinion, or that sort of thing, or unfavorable articles. This is something that has been repeated mindlessly in the media that is simply not true. You can look at the numbers of the articles and the number of retractions we have sent out and that will answer that problem for you."

Mr. Garrett continued:

In addition to that law, which affects what we do and why we do it, there is a strategy which we have to be prepared to handle in the litigation that we do have in which it has been indicated to some considerable degree to be the strategy that will be used against us, which is as follows. As you know, we have sued ABC and Time, Inc., and NBC too, although we have not served them.

So far, it appears to us that one of the defense tactics will be, when we get to the point of trying these cases, to inundate us with stories which are the same, or substantially the same, as these defendants have published. Then they will ask us if we have made any complaint, or demanded any retraction, under Section 48a of the California Code of Civil Procedure. If we have not, then, of course, we are open up to the argument that there were hundreds of stories similar to the ones that we are suing these people about which were printed or aired that we took no exception to, that we filed no retraction demands as the law requires, and so on, thus creating the kind of an argument that this is sort of, or akin to, an admission against injury. So, if we are going to protect ourselves against that sort of argument—and that can be devastating in a libel case—then everytime that we see somebody file a story that is not true we must be able to produce for a jury a letter which says that's not true and puts you on notice that these are the true facts and demands that you correct them. So at least, we have a denial of that.

Mr. Garrett said the "Retraction Project" has cost Synanon "an awful lot of manpower to protect ourselves against this flood of ghastly, hot, unfavorable, defamatory publicity because once something is said it just spreads like wildfire and it's repeated with variations all through the media. We have had to maintain a staff that reads the clipping service and devotes itself to sending these people what we think is a polite letter pointing out to them why this story is wrong, where it is wrong, and what the true facts are.

534

"We are stretched to the point where we're sort of a thin broken line. We really can't cover the bases with all of the inundation of litigation that has hit us since the media started making us their favorite subject.

"If I could discontinue the necessity of sending out these notices of retraction without severely damaging the merits of the cases that we do have to prosecute," Mr. Garrett said, "I would do so because we just don't have the personnel to spare on something that is not of vital importance in the litigation that we have gotten going."

Synanon's Legal Department consists of from 60 to 65 people, Mr. Garrett said. There are seven lawyers, with the reminder paralegals (trained within Synanon) and clerks and typists. Most of the letters sent to the media are signed by Philip C. Bourdette, who is secretary of the Synanon Foundation, and Andrew J. Weill. Both are lawyers. Mr. Bourdette also was present during the interview with Mr. Arthur. The Legal Department operates seven days a week.

"Most of the people," said Mr. Garrett, "are on what we call the 'Cubic Day,' which means that they work half the time—and these are long days—and then they're off half the time. So, at any one time about 60 percent of that (number of people) would be working."

Mr. Garrett said that Synanon's lawyers personally participate in all the cases involving the organization in court appearances in Los Angeles "where we (now) have eight matters pending, plus the major criminal charges against (Synanon founder) Chuck Dederich."

The litigation involving Time, Inc., which Mr. Garrett referred to earlier, was entered into on January 11, 1978, in the Superior Court of California, Alameda County. The suit asked $76,750,000 in damages in connection with a report on Synanon and its founder, Charles Dederich, in the December 26, 1977, issue of *Time* magazine. The suit was dismissed on February 1, 1980, at Synanon's request. A letter signed by Mr. Garrett explained that Synanon was so involved in legal actions that its law staff and finances were overstrained. Taking note of a declaration last September by *Time*'s lawyers that the magazine had spent $1.25 million up to that time in defending itself, Mr. Garrett said this sum was "far greater than the funds available to the Synanon Foundation to handle all its varied legal problems."

But a representative of the New York law firm of Cravath, Swaine & Moore, attorneys for *Time*, expressed to the Council staff a different view of Synanon's reasons for dropping the suit. "We were getting close to material that could have been damaging to them in their criminal trial," he said, referring to the impending criminal trial of two Synanon members and of Mr. Dederich in connection with the rattlesnake attack on Los Angeles attorney Paul Morantz on October 13, 1978. He said *Time* had obtained a court order requiring Synanon to turn over specific tapes, files and records relating to use of "terroristic violence." This material was desired by *Time* to strengthen its plea to the court for dismissal of the libel action. The lawyer added that the California Attorney General's office had already served subpoenas on *Time* requiring that, whenever the desired material was received, copies be made available to the Attorney General for use in various investigations relating to Synanon.

The 1977 *Time* article, headlined "Life at Synanon is Swinging: A Once Respected Program Turns into a Kooky Cult," focused on alleged experiments in new lifestyles fostered by Mr. Dederich and other Synanon leaders, with emphasis on wife-swapping and vasectomies. It said "the people at Synanon are treated much as if they were interchangeable auto parts."

On October 16, 1979, Superior Court Judge Robert H. Kroninger dismissed 41 of 44 allegations made by Synanon in support of its libel suit. He said: "No reasonable person could, in or out of context, construe them as defamatory." The counts kept alive by the judge until Synanon made its own move for dismissal related to two statements in the article and to one "asserted innuendo." One statement charged that all male Synanon members were pressured to have vasectomies and the other that most Synanon members paid $400 a month for room and board. The asserted innuendo of which Synanon complained was to the effect that the organization had abandoned its charitable purposes.

In the course of litigation, *Time* introduced evidence from Synanon files which the magazine's lawyers contended substantiated all the statements in the article. In addition, counsel for *Time* presented evidence— some of it in the form of memoranda and of transcripts from tapes by officials and members of Synanon—intended to support the magazine's claim that the entire litigation was part of a plot to harass the media into silence about abuses within Synanon. One memorandum *Time* filed in court represented an alleged summons by Synanon of its members to a "holy war" against *Time* and its editors and top officials. This "holy war," according to *Time*, was to be waged by a separate Synanon organization operating under the name of S.C.R.A.M. (Synanon Committee for a Responsible American Media). S.C.R.A.M., which for a period of time issued *The S.C.R.A.M. Bulletin*, was described by Synanon in 1978 as having as its stated objective "The elimination of irresponsible and malicious news reporting and investigation of corruption and bureaucratic waste." It was further described as being made up "of citizens and religious, labor, business and political groups who are fed up with the highhanded way certain members of the media feel free to distort the truth for their own ends."

During the course of the litigation, lawyers for *Time* submitted memoranda, transcripts and affidavits in support of the following charges:

- A declaration by Mr. Dederich in a television news interview on December 28, 1977, just after publication of the *Time* article, that Synanon's friends might on their own initiative take punitive action against "the persons or the people responsible, their wives, their children . . . Bombs could be thrown into odd places, into the homes of some of the clowns who occupy high places in the *Time* organization, um, that's too bad, that's too bad."

- In a deposition given under questioning by his own attorneys on March 6, 1978, Synanon's founder said: "The families and friends of those clowns can get hurt through no fault of mine, through no fault of Synanon. . . . If this happens it will be through the irresponsible actions of irresponsible people connected with Time Incorporated." He added that the sons, daughters and grandchildren of *Time* executives could be "plunged into grave danger."

- At a news conference on January 25, 1978, representatives of Synanon announced that they had 235 guns and ammunition worth about $63,000 as part of their preparation for a private security force. The move was linked to the *Time* article.

- Shortly after this announcement hundreds of abusive letters cascaded in on officers and employees of *Time*. These letters in many cases threatened to "destroy" and "kill" *Time* or to "rid the world of" the specific editors or reporters to whom they were addressed. One letter writer vowed: "I dedicate my life to harassing you and your family." A Synanon memorandum acknowledged establishment of a coordinated timetable for the letter-writing campaign.

- Specific acts of intimidation were directed at Andrew Heiskell, *Time*'s chairman, and Hedley Donovan, then its editor-in-chief. Two representatives of Synanon accosted Donovan as he was leaving his home and warned: "We are going to ruin your life." On October 18, 1978, the eve of the editor-in-chief's return from an overseas trip, United States Customs officials received a half-dozen calls from persons alleging that Mr. Donovan would be attempting to enter the country smuggling drugs and jewelry. Because of the specificity of their information about the countries Mr. Donovan had visited and the flight on which he would be arriving, Customs officials subjected his luggage to an extensive search and, Mr. Donovan said, it took considerable persuasion to dissuade them from a body search. After he convinced the agents that Synanon must have been behind the tip, the agents apologized and accompanied Mr. Donovan outside where they found the two Synanon representatives waiting to "interview" him.

- On September 14, 1978, four Synanon members pleaded no contest to criminal charges arising out of the beating in April of Thomas J. Cardineau, a former resident, who told police his assailants had accused him of being a "spy" for *Time*. In actuality, he explained, he had simply been on his honeymoon showing his new wife his former residence at Synanon.

When the suit against *Time* was dropped, the magazine said: "This concludes two years of legal action during which Synanon tried to intimidate Time, Inc., from exercising its constitutional right to report the news. That harassment only determined us to fight harder. Had Synanon succeeded, others might well have been encouraged to undertake similar suits in attempts to chill the actions of the press."

On February 18, 1980, *Time* filed a motion seeking $1.9 million from Synanon as sanctions to cover all of its costs and legal fees in connection with the litigation.

A *Time* lawyer told the Council that this "could be a healthy deterrent to future suits of this kind."

During the interview with Mr. Arthur, Mr. Garrett, speaking of other litigation, said that his legal staff also "is involved in handling the litigation in the Federal Court in Fresno," referring to a Federal Civil Rights action brought by Synanon against the *Visalia Times-Delta*, members of the Tulare County Board of Supervisors and certain other Tulare County officials who, Mr. Garrett charged, "conspired to close down our airport" (in Tulare County).

"We also are personally involved in the court appearances in the current litigation with the Attorney General of the state," Mr. Garrett went on. "That's the action that he brought claiming that we have misappropriated charitable funds, which is totally without merit, but the political climate being what it is it's something that we have to appear in court to contest.

"We also make appearances in Washington, D.C., where we have a major lawsuit pending (involving a property case). In addition to that, the lawyers and the legal department are personally involved in all of the on-going governmental investigations. You may be aware that when the media creates such intense controversy the various bureaucratic agencies of the Federal, state and local governments—I guess because they want to look as good as they can—they start to move. So since this onslaught, we have been investigated, I guess, by every Federal, state and local agency that has investigative powers."

Mr. Bourdette said that there are "about 15 such investigations." "You name it, we've got it," said Mr. Garrett. "We're involved in litigation of every kind—the IRS, Attorney General, HEW, State Education surplus, State Board of Equalization, Department of Health, Social Security, Workmen's Compensation laws—that would be the Labor Department—Unemployment Insurance, zoning authorities, grand juries, on and on. . . "

Asked if the Federal government was investigating Synanon's application for status as a religious organization, Mr. Garrett replied: "I shouldn't use the word 'investigation' because the word, in the case of the IRS, involves an implication that there is some sort of criminal investigation or charges of fraud, and there is no such actually on-going with the Federal government. There is no indication that there's any such investigation pending on the part of the Federal government. They are, however, auditing and we are more or less regularly audited by the IRS and they have completed the most thorough audit that they have ever done, mainly as a result of all these stories."

"Contrary to the popular notion," Mr. Garrett said, "there are thousands and thousands of libelous stories that we have not filed suit on. We've only filed three." He named the *Time* suit and suits against the American Broadcasting Company and its station, KGO, in San Francisco, and against the National Broadcasting Company as the three currently filed. Mr. Bourdette said that the suit against NBC, "although filed, has not been served." In the ABC-KGO suit, currently in litigation, Synanon seeks $42 million in damages.

A News Council check revealed that Synanon has been involved in approximately 144 lawsuits in the 1970's and continuing into 1980, as the plaintiff 55 times, and as the defendant 89 times. Many of these actions involved, and involve, personal injury/motor vehicle cases, child custody and property damage, and generated little, if any, press coverage. But the rattlesnake attack on Mr. Morantz received immediate nationwide Page 1 and television network coverage.

Mr. Morantz, who had been involved in a successful $300,000 default legal action against Synanon, was bitten on the hand by a 4 ½ foot rattlesnake as he reached into the mailbox of his home. He survived the attack.

Two days later, two Synanon members were arrested on suspicion of attempted murder, and on December 2, Mr. Dederich, Synanon's founder, was arrested on a warrant charging conspiracy and solicitation to commit murder in connection with the attack. Following the filing of formal charges, trial of all three has been set for early April.

Synanon's report indicates that the "Retraction Project," as applied to newspapers, got underway during the same month that the Morantz attack occurred—October, 1978. From January 1 through September of that year, 1,063 clippings were received by Synanon's Legal Department, but no retraction letters were sent out during the period to newspapers. In October, 701 clippings were received and eight retraction-demand letters were dispatched. In November and December, 3,511 clippings were received and 82 retraction-demand letters were sent. In January, 1979, 1,691 clippings were received and 54 letters were sent.

Broadcasters received 19 retraction demands during the period January 1, 1978, through July. None were sent during August and September, but 77 were sent from October 1, 1978, through January, 1979.

Typical of the letters sent by Synanon to the news media following publication of reports about the Morantz episode, was one dated December 12, 1978, and addressed to Otis Chandler, publisher of the *Los Angeles Times*. The letter, signed by Mr. Bourdette, began:

> Synanon Foundation, Inc., its officers, directors and residents, and all members of the Synanon religion, demand that you correct and retract that certain article published on November 22, 1978 in the *Los Angeles Times* concerning Synanon Foundation Inc. The story is false, malicious and defamatory in its entirety, and it is clear that you, your reporters, writers and others in your organization responsible for its preparation, editing, research and publication published it with the knowledge that it was false, or with reckless disregard for whether it was false or not. . . .

The letter proceeded to charge the *Times* with intentions to create "a false impression and understanding in the minds of those who read the article that Synanon has abandoned its original charitable tax-exempt purposes, that it no longer takes care of juvenile delinquents, alcoholics or other character-disordered persons, that Synanon is an insane, violent terrorist organization that kills persons, including its critics, that Synanon attempted to murder, by rattlesnake, Paul Morantz, that Synanon brainwashes and tortures people, that Synanon performs other immoral acts, and that this story is based on reliable sources."

The *Los Angeles Times*'s story, headlined "Authorities Raid Synanon Ranch, Seize Recordings," reported that investigators, armed with search warrants, had "swooped down on a Synanon ranch in a remote section of Tulare County" and had seized a "sizable number" of tape recordings at the complex there. The story went on:

> The search warrants authorized seizures of all tapes making reference to Los Angeles attorney Paul Morantz, who was bitten by a rattlesnake allegedly placed in his mailbox by two Synanon members.
> 'It was all very peaceful. There was no crazy Jim Jones stuff. It will be a couple of days before we know what we got up there,' Los Angeles County Dep. Atty. Mike Carroll said.

"Exhibit A" accompanying the Synanon letter included Synanon's interpretation of what the above two paragraphs meant to readers. Regarding the first paragraph, Synanon said:

(Meaning to readers that law enforcement authorities made a surprise raid on Synanon and that imminent physical danger to them from Synanon required that they 'swoop' down on a small community.)

Regarding the second paragraph, Synanon stated:

(Meaning to readers that tape recordings were obtained which substantiate that Synanon attempted to murder Paul Morantz with a rattlesnake.)

The Bourdette letter contains paragraphs which are identical to paragraphs freqently used in other retraction letters sent to the news media. For example:

The truth is that Synanon is a law-abiding, charitable tax-exempt organization which has helped thousands of drug addicts, alcoholics, juvenile delinquents and character-disordered persons who have come to it for help, and that it continues to take care of such persons. Synanon does not direct, encourage or condone illegal activities of any sort. The truth is that Synanon at present cooperates and always has cooperated with law enforcement officials at ever (sic) level of government.

Another commonly used paragraph reads:

The truth is that Synanon is a new and precious religious movement in the United States. The truth is that the philosophical and religious ideals and practices of Synanon are indigenous to the western Judeo-Christian and American traditions, and have evolved from the deepest humanistic strain of those traditions. The truth is that Synanon's models for human and moral behavior come typically from Ralph Waldo Emerson, Martin Luther King and Jesus Christ. The truth is that Synanon bears no resemblance in thought or deed to the language of witchcraft and demonology falsely and maliciously employed by the irresponsible media.

The *Los Angeles Times* has received approximately 15 demands for retraction letters from Synanon through January 28, 1980. According to Harold W. Fuson, Jr., the newspaper's staff counsel, the paper has made no retractions or corrections. "In each instance the situation was investigated with considerable care. Some of the stories were wire service stories and we forwarded the complaints to them. In no instance were we advised by them to retract or correct." The paper does, however, keep a watchful eye on its reports on Synanon, coverage which, along with the *San Francisco Chronicle*, is the most thorough of any daily newspapers published in the nation.

William F. Thomas, the *Time*'s editor, calls the letter-writing campaign "harrassment," but points out that the paper has been harassed before. He mentioned the "Church of Scientology" in this connection. He said he can see where such letters could constitute much more harassment for editors and publishers of small newspapers that cannot afford the expenses involved in maintaining legal staffs or even legal counsel.

William German, managing editor of the *Chronicle*, which has received 23 demand letters through February 7, 1980, and has replied to none, told the Council that "It certainly is within legal propriety for them to take legal steps. We've had ephemeral things before, the letter-writing campaigns, the phone-call campaigns, picketing. But this goes on and on, with all these high legal costs getting higher and all the time spent checking. Sometimes you get to the point where you overreact. You think its not bothering you, but it is. We're not intimidated, Ralph (Ralph Craib, a veteran *Chronicle* reporter) has stayed on top of this. But this thing is something that you can't wrap up and put aside. It festers."

The "Retraction Project" follows a pattern. A news organization that originates a story may expect to receive, within 20 days. a long-form letter demanding retraction. The long-form letter goes into detail, specifying what Synanon objects to, with an "Exhibit A" enclosed giving Synanon's interpretation as to what the specified areas mean to readers.

Wire service stories bring on a somewhat different procedure. If AP and UPI originate a story, or if they rewrite a story supplied by a client newspaper, they get the long-form letter. Subscriber or client newspapers who pick up the wire service story and publish it may get short-form letters, or nothing at all, depending on whether Synanon got a clipping and which papers are chosen to get a letter. The short-form letter advises the editor or publisher that a letter of protest has been sent to the wire service, and encloses a copy of that letter.

The short-form letter also includes a reference to the headline used by the paper on the objected-to-story, the date of publication, and the date the clipping was received by Synanon. "Further," the letter states, "your printing of the aforesaid article constitutes republication." And then, a retraction is demanded under Section 48a.

A long-form letter to UPI's President, Roderick W. Beaton, dated March 18, 1979, protesting a story on a closed child custody hearing held in San Rafael, Calif., resulted in 26 UPI clients getting the short-form letter. Seventeen of the letters went to UPI clients in California, and nine went to clients in nine other states.

To UPI's knowledge, only one subscriber published a retraction, the *Evening Outlook* of Santa Monica, on April 5. The paper, which has received six retraction letters in all, included in its retraction the statement that it "regrets publishing the unsubstantiated allegations of child abuse that appeared in the story."

One paragraph of the UPI story was used as a reference, without attribution to UPI, in a guest column distributed by the Capitol News Service of Sacramento to its client newspapers. The CNS, which services State capital news to about 300 small—mostly weekly—papers in California, issued a retraction after two clients insisted that it be done on the grounds that they couldn't afford a lawsuit. Fred Kline, editor and owner of CNS, told the Council that he estimates that "about 25 percent of my clients simply won't publish any stories about Synanon now. They can't afford lawsuits. Their liability insurance for the most part calls for them to pay the first $7,500, and that's a lot of money for a small paper."

UPI's legal counsel had found the report on the child custody hearing legally unobjectionable.

By far the largest number of letters sent by Synanon during a single month were the 223 dispatched to news organizations in May 1979. That was the month that followed the award of a Pulitzer Prize on April 16 to the *Point Reyes Light*, a California weekly (circulation: 2,700) for its coverage of Synanon.

Among the barrage of letters sent out as a result of the Pulitzer Prize award to the *Point Reyes Light* were long-form letters to both UPI and AP. Identical charges were made by Synanon, that "The story contains allegations that Synanon is responsible for beatings, hoarding of weapons, and revenge attacks."

The statement used in both the UPI and AP stories regarding allegations was taken from a Columbia University press release accompanying the announcement of the Pulitzer Prize awards.

Most of the letters sent to subscribers of the wire services regarding the Pulitzer award were in the short-form. One such letter, regarding the UPI story, was sent to Frank Daniels, Jr., president and publisher of *The Raleigh* (North Carolina) *Times*, who referred it to legal counsel who gave the opinion that no reply to the Synanon letter should be made unless the attorneys for UPI in New York should so recommend.

Mr. Daniels wrote to UPI, enclosing the correspondence. H.L. Stevenson, UPI's editor-in-chief, in his response to Mr. Daniels, declared that "We have chosen not to reply to the original demand Synanon made to Beaton (UPI's president). I see no reason that you should reply to their letter to you."

No one knows how many such exchanges took place between client newspapers and the wire services, especially in view of the fact that many such inquiries were handled by telephone. J. Hart Clinton, editor and publisher of the San Mateo *Times & News Leader* in California, which published a retraction, told the Council that "When this story came in—the UPI story—it had this unattributed statement with reference to the *Point Reyes Light*. I called UPI and got little satisfaction, so I ran the retraction (on June 7). There was another case, and I ran the retraction. I have instructed my newsroom not to publish any more material on Synanon unless it is extremely important and we know it to be accurate. I don't want to be harassed. Running a retraction hasn't hurt our credibility."

"It's my opinion," continued Mr. Clinton, "that Synanon apparently was encouraged by the results of the Hearst case—in which they won a big settlement—to seek retractions as a matter of policy, when the story is in the slightest bit defamatory, whether it's true or false. That's harassment. I am a lawyer. I make the decision at the threshold to run a retraction or correction if it is a routine matter. If it is a big matter, I refer it to the law firm in San Francisco that represents us." Mr. Clinton said his paper has received no letters from Synanon since adopting his policy regarding the publication of stories concerning Synanon. It has been several months now since we have even mentioned the name Synanon," Virgil Wilson, the San Mateo's paper's managing editor said. "We will run a story when it's very important."

The Hearst reference by Mr. Clinton deals with a 1976 settlement of one Synanon suit and a subsequent settlement in 1978 of a second suit.

The first settlement was of a libel suit filed in 1972 following two *San Francisco Examiner* articles about Synanon. In a July 1, 1976 settlement of a $32 million suit, the *Examiner* agreed to pay Synanon $600,000, described at that time as the largest amount ever paid to end such an action. Following this settlement, Synanon pressed a second suit, for conspiracy, against the Hearst Corporation, Randolph A. Hearst, William Randolph Hearst, Jr., their lawyers and others for attempting "to injure plaintiffs financially" while the first suit was being litigated. Mr. Dederich and Synanon charged that the defendants had attempted to dissuade major contributors from assisting the charity, interfered with its ability to earn income, and caused the burglary of Mr. Dederich's office and the theft of 69 confidential tapes as part of a conspiracy to attack Synanon.

This second suit was settled for $2,000,000 in 1978. On January 5, 1979, the State Superior Court granted an order, requested by both parties, closing from public examination certain materials developed during the discovery phase of both suits.

According to Ralph Craib of *The Chronicle*, who has covered Synanon regularly, "Once the *Examiner* folded in response to this litigation, most of the press folded. If there had been a little more courage displayed, these people would never have gotten their start. Some pretty ludicrous things happened. If they had all been laid out over the last 18 months I think there would have been enough heat on the authorities to have stopped it."

Several editors and publishers Mr. Arthur spoke with agreed, in part, with Mr. Craib's analysis. "You think a lot about that suit when you receive one of those Section 48a letters," R.D. Funk, editor of the Santa Monica *Evening Outlook*, said.

Because neither suit received extensive publicity, very little in the way of detail found its way into news columns. Apparently there was an agreed press release following settlement of the first suit. *The New York Times* report on the settlement, published July 3, 1976, consisted of 11 paragraphs, two of which were references to a front-page apology the *Examiner* published. Two paragraphs were devoted to a statement by a Synanon spokesman that the organization would press the second suit. Another paragraph dealt with a statement by Mr. Dederich read at a press conference, and another dealt with the method of payment and a statement by the judge that no pretrial agreement would be possible after July 1, the date of the settlement.

Regarding the first suit, Reg Murphy, who became the *Examiner*'s publisher long after the suits were initiated, said it was a matter of record that the work of the reporter who wrote the two articles, and who has since died, caused his dismissal. He added that the reporter had been sent earlier to the People's Republic of China to do a series of articles for the *Examiner*. It was later learned, said Mr. Murphy, that the reporter never entered China; his experiences within that country were reported solely from Hong Kong.

Closure of the records prevented closer examination of both statements. However, the fact that the burglarly had occurred during litigation of the first suit was published at the time of its settlement.

Mr. Murphy the *Examiner*'s publisher in September, 1975, told Mr. Arthur that those suits "do have a chilling effect" on the press. "The *Examiner* happened to be on the wrong end of things and it couldn't defend itself," he said.

Mr. Murphy said that "Synanon is the only organization in the world about which I have had to give standing orders that every story, every headline, has to be checked by legal counsel. This, of course, takes hundreds of hours of lawyer time."

David Mitchell, co-publisher and editor of the *Point Reyes Light* told Mr. Arthur that "It is amazing how much damage the Hearst settlement has done to the rest of the press." Mr. Mitchell's wife, Catherine, who is co-publisher of the *Light*, said that "Now all the rest of the press is forced to stand fast to prove that what Hearst did that brought about the two suits is not typical of what newspapers will do."

After receiving a retraction demand regarding the AP report on the award of the Pulitzer to the Mitchells, Ted M. Natt, editor and publisher of *The Daily News* of Longview, Washington, wrote Mr. Bourdette as follows:

> The volume of boilerplate coming out of your office is most impressive. . . .
> Furthermore, this newspaper has a very high regard for the accuracy, fairness and competence of The Associated Press. We will not retract the article you refer to unless The Associated Press does so and notifies us that it is taking such a step.
> Maybe you will have better luck with your bullying elsewhere.

When *The Atlanta Journal* published a *Los Angeles Times* story, following announcement of the Pulitzer Prize award, on the celebration that took place in the five-room frame building where the *Point Reyes Light* is published, *The Journal* got a retraction-demand letter. Objectionable to Synanon was this quote from David Mitchell of the *Light*:

> A number of stories dealt with Synanon's finances. While purporting to be a non-profit, charitable organization, Synanon, we discovered, had made millions for the top officers of the corporation and was doing very little to rehabilitate drug addicts.

Synanon interpreted this to mean that it "had abandoned its original charitable nature and purpose of rehabilitation and that top corporate officers have managed to embezzle millions of dollars for their personal use."

*The Journal*'s response, according to James Minter, managing editor, was a "routine letter denying any legal obligation or responsibility."

In late December, 1979, California's Attorney General, George Deukmejian, filled a suit in Marin County Superior Court in San Rafael seeking a full accounting of charity funds raised by the Synanon Foundation. The suit alleged that large sums of money had been used for purposes other than rehabilitation, including a $600,000 award to Mr. Dederich and high salaries for other officers, including Mr. Dederich's brother, son and daughter. It also alleged that "substantial funds" had been spent "for the purchases of airplanes, mobile homes, motorcycles, etc., for the personal use of certain officers and directors of Synanon and unrelated to the non-profit corporation's charitable purposes."

Synanon protested stories growing out of the Attorney General's lawsuit. A retraction-demand letter to UPI, with short-form letters to various UPI clients, said that the allegations (which were taken from court records) meant to readers "that Synanon fradulently gave over half a million dollars to Charles Dederich for his personal use, illegally used charitable funds in order to arm itself and purchase lavish luxury items instead of using the funds for their intended charitable purposes."

UPI did not respond to the demand for a retraction.

When United States Supreme Court Justice William Rehnquist was reported by the *Los Angeles Times* as rejecting on December 28, 1980, a request by Synanon to "head off efforts by California Attorney General George Deukmejian to have a receiver appointed to take control of the organization's finances," Synanon's letter to the *Times* declared that this meant to readers "that Justice Rehnquist approved of a plan to place Synanon under receivership and that as a result of Justice Rehnquist's opinion, Synanon will be placed under receivership." The Synanon letter took no cognizance of the fact that the *Times* report also stated that Synanon "has the right to ask another Supreme Court justice for a stay."

The *Times* did not respond to Synanon's demand for a retraction.

"Synanon is unrelenting in its campaign of legal intimidation," a Midwestern editor wrote the Council in forwarding a copy of another Synanon retraction-demand letter to the Council. He called it "unbridled vigilantism."

"Will they never stop?" a California attorney queried in a note to the Council accompanying another retraction demand.

Peter Hunt, of Hunt and Hunt, a San Francisco law firm representing the *Berkeley Independent and Gazette*, a newspaper which has received approximately 10 retraction-demand letters from Synanon, tried a new approach to the problem. In a letter dated October 26, 1978, in response to a Synanon letter, Mr. Hunt wrote:

> The editorial staff of the *Independent and Gazette* tells us that, before the articles in question were published, considerable effort was made to contact officials of Synanon for an expression of Synanon's point of view. These efforts were not successful. While we do not think that any of the publications to which you make reference are actionable, the newspapers, at this juncture do not have from you a great deal to go on in order to sustain a judgment for or against publication of a Section 48 correction. Although your letters are detailed, articulate and complete, they remain, from an editorial, quite apart from a legal, point of view, unverified.
>
> I have an idea. Synanon wants to have its side of the story heard. The *Independent and Gazette*, for its part, has a continuing interest in broadening the base of its news sources. My idea is simply that your interest and the paper's interest can both be

served by conducting something by way of an informal news conference. Your representatives could come to San Francisco or Richmond or the paper's editorial or reportorial, or both, staffs could go to your offices. Upon reflection, you may determine—and I think you will—that treating the subject matter of your respective letters as a news source will have some benefits for Synanon which are not available through the operation of Section 48. More specifically, putting forth your observations as part of a news-gathering process could be more effective than recourse to the totally sterile and unilluminating operations of a correction.

In summary, we think that what the *Independent and Gazette* has published so far constitutes fair reporting; we are not persuaded on the basis of your submissions that the publication of a Section 48 correction is indicated; we invite you to meet with the *Independent and Gazette* news persons involved in order that you may expound—to whatever extent you may wish—on your views, recognizing that your exposition will be treated by the papers as a news event. Naturally, if a conference is set up, we will want it to be a news-oriented meeting rather than an informal deposition for either side. Thus, while I do not want to attend, if Mr. Bourdette or any other attorney representing Synanon is present, I would like to be there too. If the idea of getting together in the way I suggest strikes you as a good one, the time and the place can be arranged either by a call to me, or better, by a call to Mr. Chip Brown at (telephone number).

Mr. Brown is W.A. Brown, the newspaper's publisher. Mr. Hunt did not receive a reply, either by phone, or by letter, to his proposal. Now, he routinely writes "See my letter of October 26, 1978" in his response to Synanon retraction-demand letters. He has had no response.

Ralph Craib, of *The Chronicle*, who originally proposed the *Point Reyes Light* for the Pulitzer Prize competition, told the Council that he has attempted to talk with the Synanon people "many times over the past few years. You get nothing at all. You talk to a secretary, leave a number, and nothing happens. It's very frustrating. and they profess that they are an open charitable organization."

Eight months after the Pulitzer Prize was awarded to the *Point Reyes Light*, the Mitchells were sued by Synanon (on December 28, 1979). Named as third defendant in the action was Richard Ofshe, instructor of Sociology at the University of California in Berkeley, who assisted the Mitchells in their preparation of stories on Synanon.

This new suit, in which $1,250,000 in alleged damages is sought, did not involve the *Light*'s extensive coverage of Synanon, coverage which had brought no retraction-demand letters. The suit charged that David Mitchell and Dr. Ofshe made several statements during a talk show on television station KQED in San Francisco that were "entirely false, malicious, inflammatory and unprivileged." Although Cathy Mitchell was named as a defendant, she was not alleged by the suit to have made any slanderous statements.

548

An AP report on the filing of the suit quoted Mr. Mitchell as saying "We're not worried in the slightest about Synanon being able to recover any damages." He said that everything discussed in the interview had been published before, and that "what we have published on Synanon is well documented."

One month later, on January 28, Synanon sent a retraction-demand letter to The Associated Press, with copies to four California papers. It should be noted that Synanon claimed in the letter that it "first obtained knowledge" of The AP report on January 8. Thus they indicated they were within the 20-day notification period prescribed by Section 48a.

Letters to other newspapers in the nation, their number unknown, followed with the same adherence to 48a. For example, one sent to the *Chicago Sun-Times* was dated February 5, with Synanon declaring it received the *Sun-Times* story (presumably through a clipping) on January 18.

In the retraction-demand letter to AP, Synanon said that the quotes attributed to Mr. Mitchell meant to readers "that Synanon has abandoned its original charitable purposes and has deteriorated into a bizarre cult that has armed itself and has committed illegal acts and that these allegations are based on a reliable source."

In a Council interview at Point Reyes Station, a tiny community near the Pacific in Marin County, about an hour's drive from San Francisco, Mr. Mitchell said that as a result of the suit "I kind of watch myself when I talk and don't express the kind of stuff I normally express. I try not to be loose in what I say under any circumstance, but it does have that, as they call it, 'chilling effect.' You're not quite as candid as you normally would be, and that's not good for the newspaper business."

Referring to the *Light*'s coverage of Synanon, Mr. Mitchell said "There's something else to be considered. It's a hell of a lot easier for Cathy and me to be gutsy. This paper's worth $125,000, maybe. It's not a lot of risk. What happens if you've got a guy who's in his 60s and he's worked at this thing all of his life. He says, 'My God, I'm going to retire in a couple of years. I don't want to take on anything that will jeopardize my entire retirement plans.' People get more and more conservative, not for political reasons, but trying to start all over again in your 60s is a whole lot different than trying to start over at our age." Mr. Mitchel is 36; his wife is 35.

Cathy Mitchell said:

> First of all, we got into it step by step. You just don't do it. When we first got into this, a man was badly beaten on Synanon property. It was possible that we'd be sued,

but we decided that if we couldn't cover a beating in our paper then we didn't want to publish a newspaper. So we decided we'd cover it. And then, having made that decision, we had our lawyer read the libel insurance.

David Mitchell added:

You're just not going to feel right about being in the newspaper business seeing news that you recognize as real news and being afraid to cover it because you're afraid you're going to get sued. If you think that way, you don't belong in the business.

Michael Dorais, general counsel for the California Newspaper Publishers Association, in commenting on the suit, said he felt the Mitchells and Dr. Ofshe "are on a kamikaze mission. They get some personal satisfaction for having done something significant, but get busted in the process."

Mr. Dorais said that it seems that the Mitchells and Dr. Ofshe are getting pro bono legal assistance arranged for by the Reporters Committee for Freedom of the Press and that the defendants are protected under California Evidence Code Section 1070 from identifying confidential sources and from supplying unpublished information.

Mr. Dorais told Mr. Arthur in his office in Sacramento that the CNPA "doesn't help anybody legally. Our philosophy has always been that you are responsible for your own backyard, whether it's in an open meeting violation, an open record violation, or a libel suit. Particularly a libel suit. If you go on appeal, and there's liable to be some precedent set which will affect all of us, then we come in as a friend of the court brief. From a practical standpoint, that doesn't do anybody else any good at all. That means that they're on their own cash, their mortgages and what have you, up until the appellate level. And then all they get is someone with an arm around their shoulder. They don't get any money in their pocket. With the cost of legal protection what it is, if they (Synanon) wanted to pursue the Mitchells, or anybody else, they could put them under."

Regarding Synanon itself, Mr. Dorais said that some people think Synanon is through. "I'm not sure that's true. I think they may be a very viable organization still. His (Dederich's) daughter apparently has a reasonable set of brains. There must be some other people up there in the hierarchy who aren't going to let a multi-million dollar operation like that go under. There must be other people up there who want to keep it going because it was doing some good; who want to recapture its original purpose, which was helping addicts, junkies. I think it's too big and too strong just to say, well, they're out of it, they've been destroyed."

Asked about the "Retraction Project," Mr. Dorais said, "If anybody hits them hard, financially, with a suit, I have the impression that they will continue to use this group of lawyers who, as I understand it, are Synanon members, just to continue to slap people around and scare them. They (the letters) are frightening to that extent."

It is possible, Mr. Dorais said, that the letters will "cause people to draw in their horns. It would change the reporting of information in this country if UPI got hit with a big suit, UPI and the people who publish their material.

"I haven't seen anything UPI has run which I think is particularly libelous, considering *New York Times v. Sullivan* and extension thereof, and all sorts of public interest stories that have been published."

Mr. Dorais added: "And other groups are doing this."

Charles Just, Deputy Attorney General of California, told Mr. Arthur in Sacramento that it is his belief that Synanon is "being hurt financially because of all of these lawsuits, and the resulting publicity. These things dry up not only their funds, and donations, but apparently their membership as well."

Mr. Just said that the Attorney General's office has amassed stacks of material in its own investigation of Synanon, including about 600 tapes, files and records which were subpoenaed from Time, Inc. This material previously had been obtained by the company from Synanon during the course of litigation of Synanon's now dismissed suit against Time, Inc. Among material obtained by a special criminal investigative unit set up in the Attorney General's office is a report compiled by a number of former Synanon members detailing alleged acts of violence by Synanon. Mr. Just said that his office is engaged now in the "monumental job" of computerizing all of this material, after which "we will determine if further action on our part is called for, either in the civil or criminal areas."

**Council finding:** The fact that Synanon, by its own admission, is engaged in a sweeping campaign seeking retraction of news reports which it deems unfair to its reputation and conduct has been confirmed through the Council's investigation. The Council's investigation also has confirmed that Synanon's "Retraction Project" has resulted in creating an atmosphere of apprehension among many of the nation's news executives and reporters because of the flood of retraction-demand letters and the public record of litigation.

It is clear that Synanon is using a law presumably passed to protect publishers and broadcasters—Section 48a of the California Civil Code—

as a weapon for coercing the press into silence about Synanon and its affairs. It is also clear that, as a result of this legal harassment, many editors and news directors, especially those associated with small news organizations of limited resources, are refraining from publishing or broadcasting news they deem legitimate affecting Synanon.

Much as the Council may deplore this result, it is obliged to recognize the First Amendment and other legal rights are at issue on both sides of this controversy. Unquestionably, Synanon is acting in conformity with the law in sending out its demands for retraction, whether or not it has any serious intent of following up with libel suits if no retraction is forthcoming. Yet the practical effect of its policy is to cut off the free flow of information in many places, a condition in which the ultimate victims will be the public and truth itself.

What is the right response of editors and broadcasters who believe the letters' sole purpose is intimidation? The history of press freedom makes it plain that there is no substitute for courage in such cases. The Council recognizes the genuineness of the pocketbook worries that operate in enterprises without legal staffs or substantial treasuries—the fear that combating even a frivolous claim may entail prohibitive cost. But the record in this case indicates that disaster has not befallen those who refused to surrender to harassment, who fulfilled their journalistic obligation to disseminate news they considered of public interest about Synanon. The Council noted particularly the tack taken by the Berkeley *Independent and Gazette*, a newspaper of 50,000 circulation. It has received ten retraction letters from Synanon, to which it routinely replies by inviting the organization to come out from behind its self-erected secrecy shield and to join with the paper's staff in a news-oriented meeting for a full exploration of Synanon's views and activities. Not once has Synanon taken up this invitation.

The Council's investigation leaves no room for doubt that the public in many areas is getting less news about Synanon than it otherwise would because of the chilling effect on editors of the organization's suit-threatening campaign. To the extent that this deplorable condition is invited by the requirements of a law that publishers in California and several other states helped to lobby through as a safeguard against just such misuse of libel litigation, a partial remedy may lie in legislative reconsideration of the law's merit. The more basic answer must lie in the press having the courage to stand up for its freedom.

**Concurring:** Brady, Cooney, Ghiglione, Huston, Isaacs, Lawson,

552

McKay, Miller, Otwell, Pulitzer, Roberts and Rusher.
March 6, 1980

## STATEMENT OF CIA USE OF JOURNALISTS

The National News Council is deeply disturbed by the official disclosure that the Central Intelligence Agency has repudiated its commitment to prohibit use of journalists affiliated with American news organizations in any of its espionage or intelligence activities.

Assurance that no news personnel employed by American press agencies, newspapers, broadcasters or other media groups would be hired by the CIA for any purpose was first given to a delegation from this Council by George Bush, then Director of Central Intelligence, at a meeting in CIA headquarters on June 24, 1976.

A policy directive issued on November 30, 1977, by the current CIA director, Admiral Stansfield Turner, made this assurance formal by declaring that the CIA would not enter into any relationship with journalists "for the purpose of conducting any intelligence activities." The same directive forbade the agency from using "the name or facilities of any U.S. news media organization to provide cover" for its agents or actions.

Now, in testimony before the Senate Select Committee on Intelligence, Admiral Turner has disclosed the authorization since 1977 of what he terms a "very limited" number of waivers breaching the general ban that supposedly rules out employment of journalists among others. Admiral Turner has declined to specify publicly how many, if any, of these waivers have directly affected the press and the CIA has asserted in subsequent "clarification" of this testimony that none of the waivers was actually used. But the Carter Administration has joined the CIA in resisting inclusion in a new Congressional charter for the intelligence agency of a statutory ban embodying the prohibition now theoretically in effect by administrative order.

The National News Council has always recognized this country's need for an effective Central Intelligence Agency. But that need must not be met through practices that make inescapable a destruction of public confidence in the integrity of the press as an independent instrument of public information free from governmental manipulation. A revival of the possibility that the CIA is using journalists as gatherers of intelligence or purveyors of propaganda would not only expose all reporters in many parts of the world to personal peril but also would undermine the credibility of news in ways subversive of democracy. The CIA was right to recognize that danger in its policy directive, but it has shown itself a slack guardian in a field where no slightest deviation from strict separation of journalism and intelligence functions is thinkable. The Council urges Congress to write an unequivocal prohibition into the law establishing a projected charter for the CIA.

**Concurring:** Ghiglione, Huston, Lawson, McKay, Otwell, and Pulitzer
**Dissenting:** Brady, Isaacs, Miller, and Rusher.
**Abstaining:** Cooney, and Roberts.

**Dissenting opinion by Mr. Miller** (Mr. Isaacs concurring): I do not want to encourage the CIA to recruit reporters or encourage reporters to be recruited by the CIA. But I am opposed to extending my invitation to any legislative body to enact any legislation affecting the press.

**Dissenting opinion by Mr. Rusher** (Mr. Brady concurring): I dissent. My reasons are the same as those given June 31, 1978, when the Council last discussed the CIA. I quote:

> The past deeds and/or misdeeds of the CIA are irrelevant here. If it has transgressed, it ought of course to be corrected. The principle question before us is whether the dissemination of false information is an impermissible activity *per se* for an agency of the United States Government. The argument that it is rests on the contention that America is obliged to its own principles to forswear such activities, regardless of any possible deleterious consequences of doing so. The argument to the contrary rests upon the proposition, to which I adhere, that until and unless this country can persuade the rest of the world to subscribe to its principles, it cannot possibly afford to commit itself to their blind observance abroad in all cases whatsoever. In many desperate situations around the world, freedom and even life itself, daily depend upon opposing foreign tyrants by means not permissible here at home.

March 7, 1980

## STATEMENT ON THE BELGRADE UNESCO CONFERENCE

It has been evident since 1976 when UNESCO began at Nairobi its attempt to evolve a global consensus on a "new world information and communications order" that basic conflicts in approach, philosophy, values and governmental structure between East and West, North and South, made a meeting of minds difficult, if not impossible.

Efforts to reach agreement on these issues failed once again at the recent UNESCO conference in Belgrade, which wound up in a decision to defer action for three years, with no certainty that even that much additional study will lead to an accord. Some American and British observers left Belgrade so disquieted by two general resolutions adopted there that they are urging their countries to pull out of further discussions of communications questions and perhaps even out of UNESCO itself. They argue that Third World delegations, with aid from the Soviet bloc, will in the end use their voting control to ram through declarations that will fatally damage freedom of the press.

The National News Council finds basis for concern in the potentialities for governmental manipulation and management of the news and for outright censorship that are embodied in some of the Belgrade solutions. But the Council believes that the least effective way to guard against giving these destructive doctrines official standing as instruments for abridging the freedom of worldwide news agencies would be for the champions of a genuinely free press to withdraw from the battlefield.

The Council has repeatedly set forth its recognition of the warrant that regrettably exists for many Third World complaints about the quality and quantity of news disseminated to the rest of the world on developments in their countries and for their charges of cultural bias on the part of many reporters. With equal regularity, the Council has stressed its conviction that those countries, so recently established in freedom from colonial rule, will be the chief sufferers if the search for improvements turns to governmental monitoring, licensing and other restrictions on the writing, editing and movement of news out of and into their nations. No matter whether the motivation for suppressing press freedom is that of a *totalitarian* government to regiment thought or of a fragile, still ill-established government to avert anarchy, the practice is perilous to all liberty.

The Council remains convinced that the right road to overcoming existing inadequacies and moderating the sense of grievance widespread in the developing countries, especially those in Africa, lies in vastly expanded programs for new journalistic training programs, access to satellites and other new technology and a general strengthening of the communications infrastructure in the Third World.

There was general agreement at UNESCO that two-thirds of humanity is deprived of anything that we in the developed countries would recognize as a functioning communications system. What the world needs is more and wider channels of communication, not a blockage of the few channels that exist today.

The Council has no wish to minimize the hurdles that stand in the way of any possible reconciliation of views on the still decidedly amorphous concept of a new international information order. But we repeat our observation, made before the Paris UNESCO conference two years ago, that it is time for all the developed nations—particularly those involved in the dissemination of news—to recognize a distinction between the power

555

and propaganda drives that animate dictatorial countries on this issue and the much more deep-rooted dissatisfactions that underlie much of the pressure from within the Third World.

The debates and floor actions at both Paris and Belgrade underscored not only the basic diversions in motivation and approach between the Eastern European delegations and the Third World but also the degree to which differences exist inside the Third World. It is not monolithic in either politics or policy. Many journalists in the developing countries yearn for Western encouragement, in the realm of deed even more than preachment, to help them institute freedom of the press in countries that have traded external repression for internal repression.

The important thing for the United States is to press energetically in UNESCO and every other forum the lesson that all history has taught, in every country and every time, that the free flow of information is an indispensable building block of all liberty and that no corrective for perceived distortions or misinterpretations will be found in censorship, suppression or other government-mandated restraint on the press.

**Concurring:** Bell, Benson, Brady, Ghiglione, Huston, Isaacs, Lawson, Maynard, Miller, Roberts, Scott and Williams.

**Abstaining (because of his participation in the Belgrade meeting as a member of the United States delegation):** Abel.

December 5, 1980

## STATEMENT ON RICHMOND NEWSPAPER DECISION

The Supreme Court's decision in *Richmond Newspaper v. Virginia* affirms the principle of openness as both a safeguard and a vitalizing element in American democracy. For the first time the court has given judicial recognition to the force of the First Amendment—and not just the Sixth—as a constitutional underpinning for access to trials by the public and the press. This important extension in the accountability of the courts is wedded to a broadened avenue for public access, via the media, to knowledge about the operations of government in all its phases.

Though the multiplicity of separate concurring opinions makes speculative any forecast of the specific boundaries that may be set in future Court rulings, a majority of the justices now seems ready to subscribe to what in the past has always been a minority view: That the societal value of the First Amendment has as one of its prime ingredients the guaranteeing to the citizenry of access to the information they need for resolving their destiny through free and open debate.

In its application to the criminal justice system, the basic decision by

Chief Justice Burger is eloquent in explaining how indispensable a foundation of openness is to public respect. He traces back to English common law even before the Norman Conquest an awareness that fairness is bulwarked by public attendance at trials. Unless the people perceive the judicial process to be fair, the Chief Justice observes, confidence in the integrity of the process wanes. This invites vigilantism and other forms of vengeful mob action, especially where a particularly shocking crime is involved. "The crucial prophylactic aspects of the administration of justice cannot function in the dark," the Burger decision in behalf of the Court says.

These strictures by the Chief Justice are just as relevant to pretrial moves to close courtrooms or to seal records as they are to trials themselves, the more so since nine out of every ten criminal cases are now disposed of without formal trial. Nevertheless, the predominant tone of the concurring opinions in the Richmond case still sharply differentiates between rights of access to trials as against pretrial proceedings. The hope must be that the illogic of such a distinction will ultimately persuade a clear majority of the Court to set aside the restrictive approach it applied to pretrial proceedings in *Gannett Co. v. De Pasquale* last year. Certainly, public scrutiny is just as essential to public trust in preliminary hearings as it is in trials.

In any event the accent the Court has put on the importance of openness is bound to have a constructive influence on the thinking of trial judges everywhere and thus stop the rash of courtroom closings that came in the wake of the Gannett Co. decision. Beneficial as such a development is sure to be in providing the public with more information about the judicial process, it will not remove all sources of possible confrontation between press and bench nor will it reduce the desirability of continued cooperation between both groups to assure that openness will reinforce, not obstruct, observance of the constitutional mandate for protecting the right of accused persons to a fair trial. That occasional disagreements will arise is made certain by the Court's reminder that the right of press access to courtrooms is not absolute and by the absence from all the decisions of specific criteria on when the requirements of justice may make closure appropriate.

Past studies by the National News Council have underscored how helpful more effective conduits for joint action at state and local levels can be in making secure the freedoms guaranteed by the First and Sixth Amendments without sacrificing one in defense of the other. The Supreme Court's acknowledgement that the Constitution makes the press surrogate for the people in gathering and disseminating the information required for intelligent citizenship provides an ideal launching pad for extending the initiatives along this line already taken by the media and the bar—initiatives that have succeeded best when they are rooted not in prohibitions but rather in the voluntary exercise of responsibility and understanding to resolve differences that may arise.

**Concurring:** Abel, Bell, Brady, Ghiglione, Huston, Isaacs, Lawson, Maynard, McKay, Pulitzer, Rusher and Williams.

September 19, 1980

## ADDENDUM TO COUNCIL STATEMENT
## ON
## RICHMOND NEWSPAPERS, INC.

Gannett Co., Inc. v. Daniel A. DePasquale - 443 U.S. 368 (1979) Richmond Newspapers, Inc., et al. v. Commonwealth of Virginia - 65 L. Ed. 2d 973 (1980)

The several opinions in the two Supreme Court cases cited above and referred to in the National News Council statement merit careful attention by the American public and the media, both of whose vital interests are involved. Together these cases also are a graphic demonstration of how the Supreme Court works.

The Gannett Co. case was argued November 7, 1978, but not decided until July 2, 1979. This is evidence that these important issues were under consideration by our highest tribunal for more than half of its 1979 term. The Richmond Newspapers, Inc., case was argued February 19, 1980, and decided July 2, another long interval for discussion among the judges. Those who read the text of both cases will be rewarded by becoming parties to what amounts to a development in Supreme Court thinking and appraisal of this informed public–free press issue. The dates and citations are listed as an aid in obtaining the texts for the study and discussion they well deserve.

Regrettably, the supply of Gannett Co. decisions in the Government Printing Office has been exhausted and there are no present plans to print more. The Richmond Newspapers decision can be obtained by writing to the Superintendant of Documents, U.S. Government Printing Office, Washington, D.C. 20402. The order number is 028-001-91313-0 and the cost is $3. Most public libraries and many law offices have the decision on file.

558

## STATEMENT ON AMENDMENTS TO THE FREEDOM OF INFORMATION ACT

In its fifteen years on the statute books the Freedom of Information Act has helped to break down walls of secrecy that have limited the access of the American people to knowledge needed for a fuller understanding of the ways their government works or fails to work. The extensive modifications in that act now being sought by the Administration would, if adopted by Congress, represent a serious retreat from the principles of governmental openness to public scrutiny.

The law was put on the statute books with strong bipartisan support. In signing it in 1966, President Johnson said: "This legislation springs from one of our most essential principles: A democracy works best when the people have all the information that the security of the nation permits. No one should be able to put up curtains of secrecy around decisions which can be revealed without injury to the public interest."

That is the yardstick Congress should apply to deciding whether the exemptions the law already gives the F.B.I. against having to disclose certain types of confidential information need broadening or whether additional safeguards ought be included to prevent the release to commercial competitors of information supplied to Federal agencies by business enterprises. Steps unquestionably can be taken to cut down the cost of government of making information available under the law and also to prevent abuse of the law by the 90 percent of applicants for data who are not journalists, historians or others intent on sharing their findings with a broad public.

The important consideration is that whatever changes are eventually approved do not undermine the statute's effectiveness in letting people know more about how their government operates and about its lapses. A free society is strengthened by maximum openness of information about all the activities of government.

**Concurring:** Abel, J. Bell, Ghiglione, Isaacs, Maynard, Miller, Pulitzer, and Williams.
**Abstaining:** Decter.
December 3, 1981

## STATEMENT ON GOVERNMENTAL SECRECY

The incoming Congress will almost certainly have before it a long list of proposals, some initiated by the Administration and others by its own members, for a mandated tightening-up of information made available by the government to press and public. As a strong believer in the principle that maximum openness to public scrutiny is a hallmark of democratic government, the National News Council hopes that Congress will follow the standard articulated by President Johnson in signing the Freedom of Information Act in 1966: "A democracy works best when the people have all the information that the security of the nation permits. No one should be able to put up curtains of secrecy around decisions which can be revealed without injury to the public interest."

**Concurring:** Abel, Barrett, Bell, Benson, Huston, Isaacs, Kennedy, Maynard, Scott, van den Haag, Williams and Woolf.

December 3, 1982

## STATEMENT OF CHANGES IN NATIONAL SECURITY CLASSIFICATION RULES

Reconciling the requirements of secrecy for purposes of national security with the bedrock democratic principle that a free society is strongest when its people have maximum access to information about all the activities of government has been a troublesome problem in every Administration since World War II. The devastating force of modern weaponry and the disordered state of world relationships make indisputable the need for an effective classification system. It is unrealistic in a free society to believe that any machinery will ever totally eliminate leaks, but whatever can be done to stop them must be done within government through rules affecting its own employees. Seeking to get at the source of illegal disclosure by tapping reporters' phones or other tactics targeted at journalists is offensive in concept, ineffective in practice, and generally unacceptable.

Given these realities, the causes of both democracy and law-enforcement are best protected when government restricts to the minimum necessary for safeguarding the nation the volume of material put under classification and holds down with equal rigor the number of people with access to classified data, especially in the most sensitive categories.

In the 1960s and 1970s passage of the Freedom of Information Act and a number of constructive developments in the Executive Branch and the courts helped move the country toward substantially expanded availability of information. Notable among these developments was a 1978 executive order calling for restraint in the security classification of government material. The order established "identifiable" potential harm to the national interest as a yardstick, with doubts to be resolved in favor of the lowest level of security clearance or none at all.

In the last two years the balance has swung sharply in the opposite direction, out of a feeling inside government that security was being inadequately protected. A 1982 executive order undid key features of the 1978 order, including the requirement that classification be based on identifiable potential damage to security. Now the President has signed a new order aimed at reducing "the frequency and seriousness of unlawful disclosure of classified information."

Whenever changes are contemplated in rules aimed at meeting the imperatives of national security without unduly limiting the dissemination of information needed by an alert citizenry, the process ought to include full discussion with the media and all other interested parties to insure that adequate weight will be given to all the competing values important in a democracy. Since such exploration was absent in the preparation of this executive order, the National News Council views it with concern and urges its reconsideration with a view to arriving at a sounder accommodation between the justifiable objective of protecting national security and the dissemination of information useful to a free society.

The order extends to all the tens of thousands of federal employees with access to classified material a mandate that they sign non-disclosure agreements and make themselves subject to lie-detector tests, on pain of possible dismissal if they refuse.

In the case of employees with the highest level of security clearance, the order imposes a lifetime obligation—even long after they have left office—to obtain pre-publication review of any books, reports, studies, articles, lecture notes, even novels that they prepare if they "contain data which may be based upon information classified pursuant to law or executive order." This is an extremely broad specification. It could have blocked or impeded notable books by Dean Acheson, Robert McNamara, Henry Kissinger and others. At worst, despite assurances to the contrary, experience over the years indicates that it almost certainly would result in suppression of material for purely political reasons or for avoidance of embarrassment to persons in power. Instances abound of the misuse of classification as a political device, with information bottled up or abruptly declassified to serve the purposes of those in command. From the standpoint of history, to say nothing of governmental accountability or public understanding of the decision-making process, the perils in so extending the potentialities for secrecy and censorship are too apparent

561

for acceptance without a better explanation than the White House or Justice Department has yet given of why they are deemed necessary.

In the firm belief that an informed citizenry is indispensable to the determination of intelligent public policy, the National News Council urges that, in the absence of such an explanation, the policy be revised along lines less susceptible to abuse of the classification system and more consonant with democratic society. The Council has instructed its own staff to undertake a broad independent study of this whole complex field March 31, 1983

## STATEMENT ON RESPONSIBLE JOURNALISM

The failure of many news organizations to acknowledge adequately their errors has long been a major source of public dissatisfaction with the press. The frequency with which complaints to the National News Council arise out of such media reluctance to correct even glaring instances of inaccuracy or unfairness makes it a pleasure for the Council to commend recent steps taken by several leading news organizations toward greater public accountability in the redress of errors.

A notable advance in print journalism is the institution by *The New York Times* of a feature called, "Editors' Note," which is to be run in the news index whenever the editors deem appropriate over and beyond the routine corrections which regularly appear there. Under this heading *The Times* will amplify or rectify what its editors consider significant lapses of fairness, balance or perspective in news articles, even where specific factual inaccuracies are not involved.

In television, two network developments merit Council commendation. One is the appointment, now nearly two years old, of George Watson, vice president of ABC News, as an unofficial ombudsman for the network's news broadcasts and the establishment of Viewpoint, a late-night program for discussion and debate among people of widely divergent opinions on controversial aspects of news coverage in such fields as terrorism or invasion of privacy.

Also noteworthy in television is the more recent assignment by CBS News of Gene P. Mater, a senior vice president, and Emerson Stone, a vice president, to oversee news practices, including the investigation of complaints and the initiation on their own of measures to enhance the accuracy and fairness of news reports and documentaries.

The National News Council salutes *The New York Times*, ABC News

and CBS News for these independently taken, constructive steps toward more responsible journalism. They are reflective of a growing recognition in the media of the need for increased accountability.
March 31, 1983

# Part 3

# Contributors to the Council

The following are current contributors to the Council:

## FOUNDATIONS

The John & Mary R. Markle Foundation
The Twentieth Century Fund
The Edna McConnell Clark Foundation
Van Loben Sels Charitable Foundation
The Norman and Rosita Winston Foundation, Inc.
W. H. Brady Foundation

## MEDIA

Allentown Call-Chronicle
Anniston Star
Bellevue Daily Journal-American, WA
Bennington Banner, VT
Bergen Record
Berkshire Eagle
Bingham Enterprises of Kentucky
Brattleboro Reformer, VT
Capital Cities Communications, Inc.
CBS
The Charleston Gazette, WV
Chicago Sun-Times
Copley Press
Cowles Charitable Trust
Dallas Morning News
Denver Post
Free Lance-Star, Fredericksburg, VA
Gannett Foundation, Inc.
Harte-Hanks Communications, Inc.
Home News, New Brunswick, NJ

Honolulu Advertiser
Longmont Times-Call, CO
Longview Daily News, WA
Loveland Reporter-Herald, CO
Manhattan Mercury, KS
Milwaukee Journal & Sentinel
Minneapolis Star and Tribune
Northern Virginia Sun
Philip L. Graham Fund
Port Angeles Daily News, WA
Press-Enterprise Co., Riverside, CA
Readers Digest Foundation
Stauffer Communications
St. Louis Post-Dispatch Foundation
St. Petersburg Times
Torrington Register, CT
The News, Southbridge, MA
Western Communications, Inc.

## CORPORATIONS

Alcoa Foundation
American Telephone & Telegraph Co.
Bechtel Foundation
Bethlehem Steel Corp.
Champion International
Continental Group, Inc.
Exxon Corp.
General Electric Co.
General Mills Foundation
General Motors Foundation
Grumman Corp.
IBM
Johnson & Johnson
Monsanto Fund
Pfizer, Inc.
Philip Morris, Inc.
Procter & Gamble Fund
Shell Companies Foundation
Union Camp, Inc.
Union Carbide Corp.
The Xerox Foundation

## INDIVIDUALS

Edward W. Barrett

# Part 4

# The Council's Rules of Procedure

I. Introduction
   1. The National News Council, Inc. is concerned primarily with the freedom, fairness, and accuracy of news reporting by the national print and electronic news organizations, namely, the nationwide wire services as well as supplemental wire services, syndicates, the national news magazines, broadcast networks and newspapers significantly national in character. The Council will, however, concern itself with the freedom, fairness, and accuracy of news reporting in all media, whether national or local in initial circulation, if the matter in question is of national significance as news or for journalism and the Council has available to it the necessary resources. Expressions of opinion in editorials, commentaries and opinion columns are beyond the purview of the Council. The Council concerns itself with editorials, commentaries and opinion columns only in respect to significant facts that are alleged to be false. There may be cases in which there are legitimate differences concerning whether an expression is an opinion or statement of fact. Such cases must be decided as they arise.
   2. In all proceedings, the Council shall respect confidentiality of news sources and of confidential material acquired in gathering news.

II. Filing a Complaint
   3. Any person or organization, private or public, including the Council's Executive Director, may bring a complaint to the Council concerning the accuracy and fairness of news reporting against any national news organization, but not against any employee thereof.

4. Any news organization or any owner, director, manager, officer, or employee of a news organization, and the Council's Executive Director, may bring a complaint to the Council against any person, or organization, public or private, believed to be acting to restrict the freedom of any national news organization to gather and disseminate news.

5. A complaint must be filed in writing, stating the name and address of the complainant, the precise grounds of the complaint and the facts relating to it.

6. A complaint must be filed within 90 days following the conduct, action, or publication of material complained about. In his discretion, the Executive Director may extend the 90-day period for filing a complaint.

III. Further Proceedings

7. Upon receipt of a complaint that appears meritorious, the Council's staff shall send a copy of it to the news organization or to the person or organization complained against.

8. If a complaint is resolved by agreement between the parties at this stage or at any other stage while the complaint is under consideration by the Council, the Council shall take no further action.

9. If a complaint that appears meritorious is not resolved by the parties, a factual inquiry concerning the complaint shall be conducted by the Council's staff.

10. If the Council's staff decides not to forward a complaint to the party complained against or to the Council because the complaint is not filed timely or because the complaint is outside of the Council's purview or because of other reasons, the staff shall so inform the complainant and the Council and give its reason. A party dissatisfied with the staff's decision may ask the Council to review the decision.

11. The Council may in its discretion refuse to consider a complaint (1) if court or administrative action or arbitration based on the same subject matter is pending, or (2) if it requests and a party refuses to sign a waiver, satisfactory to the Council, of his or her right to bring such action in the event that the Council considers the complaint and issues a written decision on it, or (3) if it requests and a party refuses to sign a waiver, satisfactory to the Council of libel and slander claims against anyone

for providing The National News Council with information concerning the complaint, against the Council, its members and staff, and against the media for publication of information acquired by the Council concerning the complaint or included in the Council's report.

IV. Referral to The Council

12. The complaint and other materials gathered during the factual inquiry shall be forwarded by staff to the Council for consideration. The parties shall be informed of the time and place of the Council consideration.

13. If the Council decides that a hearing would be useful to the proper consideration of a case, it shall so inform the parties and notify them of the time and place of the hearing.

14. All parties may present evidence at a hearing, either in person or through a representative.

15. The Council shall have discretion to call witnesses not called by the parties, to request the parties to provide additional evidence, and to receive and consider written evidence.

16. The Council shall receive only such information as is voluntarily disclosed to it, and shall have no power to compel the production of evidence by any party or witness. The Council shall not request or receive in confidence information which is relevant to the consideration of a complaint.

17. The Council shall keep its proceedings as informal and flexible as possible consonant with fairness to all parties. Legal rules of evidence shall not be controlling.

18. Meetings of the Council, including hearings of complaints at which parties or witnesses give testimony, shall be open to the public and to coverage by both print and electronic media. Internal staff and committee papers shall not be public.

19. The Council shall decide each case on the basis of the evidence before it and will be free to decide a case despite the fact that the person or organization complained against refuses to reply to a complaint or participate in a hearing or because information is withheld on the grounds of confidentiality.

20. The Council shall decide each case by a majority of its members voting on the question at a meeting at which a quorum is present at the time of the vote.

21. The Council shall transmit a written report of its final action to

the parties and at the same time shall make public the report.
22. Within thirty days of the day the Council mails notice of its decision to the parties, a party may ask the Council to reopen the case for further consideration except that a party who has declined to participate in a public hearing shall not be permitted to ask for reopening of a Council decision. The Council shall consider the request at its next regular meeting. The request shall be granted if it is favored by a majority of the Council members voting on the question at a meeting at which a quorum is present at the time of the vote.

# Part 5

# The Council's By-Laws

**THE COUNCIL**

*Section 1.* The business and affairs of the corporation shall be managed by its board of directors, referred to here as the Council. The number of Council members constituting the entire Council shall be eighteen. Council members shall be divided into two classes of members, as follows: The first (public members) class shall consist of ten persons chosen from the general public whose work or reputation are in fields other than the news media. The second class (media members) shall consist of eight persons who are associated with the news media. Individuals whose careers were spent in media work, but who no longer have any direct association in the field, may be considered eligible as media members. Both print and broadcast media shall be represented in this second class. The normal terms of office of all members shall be for three years, except when members are elected to fill unexpired vacant terms.

*Section 2.* No person shall be eligible to serve as a member for more than two consecutive terms, excluding any term of less than three years.

*Section 3.* Any member may resign by notice in writing to the president or secretary. A member shall be deemed to have resigned, effective at the pleasure of the Council, (a) by leaving the vocational class (either public or media) from which selected, (b) by becoming a full-time government official or employee, or (c) by being absent from three consecutive meetings of the Council or from all meetings of the Council held during any period of six calendar months, and the Council may by resolution accept the resignation and fix its effective date.

*Section 4.* Upon the expiration of the term of a member, or when a vacancy occurs in the place of a member through death, resignation, or otherwise, a successor shall be elected by the vote of two-thirds of the entire Council. A member elected to fill a vacancy shall serve for the

571

remainder of the term in which the vacancy existed. In the nomination and election of members and officers the Council shall consider the nominees recommended by the nominating committee provided for below but shall not be limited to such nominees.

## MEMBERS

*Section 5.* The corporation shall have no members as defined in Section 601 of the Not-for-Profit Corporation law.

*Section 6.* Annual meetings of the Council shall be held within six months after the close of the fiscal year of the corporation, on a date and at a time determined by the Council, or in the absence of such determination, by the president. All other meetings of the Council shall be called by the president individually or at the request of any five members.

*Section 7.* The secretary shall give to each member not less than ten days written notice of the time, place and purpose of each meeting of the Council.

*Section 8.* All meetings of the Council shall be held at such place as shall be determined by the Council, or by the president.

*Section 9.* At the annual meeting of the Council the president and treasurer shall present a report, dated as of the end of the fiscal year terminating not more than six months prior to the annual meeting, verified by them or certified by an independent public or certified public accountant or a firm of such accountants selected by the Council, showing in appropriate detail the following:

1. the assets and liabilities, including any trust funds, of the corporation as of the end of said fiscal year;
2. the principal changes in assets and liabilities, including any trust funds, of the corporation during said year;
3. the receipts of the corporation, both unrestricted and restricted to particular purposes (if any), during said year; and
4. the expenses and disbursements of the corporation, for both general and restricted purposes, during said year.

The report shall be filed with the records of the corporation and either a copy or an abstract of the report entered in the minutes of the annual meeting of the Council.

*Section 10.* Seven members present in person shall constitute a quorum for the transaction of business at meetings of the Council. The vote of the majority of the members present at the time of the vote, if a quorum is present at such time, shall be the act of the Council.

*Section 11.* In the absence of a quorum at the time and place set for a meeting of the Council, those present may adjourn the meeting until a quorum is present.

## OFFICERS
*Section 12.* The officers of the corporation shall be a chairman, a president, a vice-chairman, an executive director, a secretary, and a treasurer, all of whom shall be elected by the Council; and such other officers as the Council may by resolution appoint.

*Section 13.* The annual election of officers shall take place at the annual meeting of the Council. The appointment of officers by resolution may take place at any meeting of the Council.

*Section 14.* All officers shall hold office at the pleasure of the Council or until their respective successors have been elected or appointed and have qualified.

*Section 15.* A vacancy in any office may be filled by the Council at any meeting.

*Section 16.* Officers shall receive such compensation as the Council may by resolution provide.

## CHAIRMAN
*Section 17.* The chairman shall be chosen from among any of the members of the Council, and when present shall preside at all meetings of the Council; and shall also serve as chief adviser to the staff when requested to do so.

## PRESIDENT
*Section 18.* The president shall be the chief executive officer of the corporation and shall exercise general supervision over the administration of its affairs. The president shall be chosen from among any of the members of the Council. The president shall serve as the Council's representative in consulting with the executive director regarding the implementation of policies formulated by the Council. Except as otherwise provided in these by-laws or by resolution adopted by the Council, the president shall have the power to execute all legal instruments on behalf of the corporation.

## VICE-CHAIRMAN
*Section 19.* The vice-chairman shall be chosen from among the members of the corporation. In the absence or disability of the chairman, the vice-chairman shall assume the duties of the chairman. The vice-chair-

man shall also have such other duties as may be assigned by the Council, the chairman, or the president.

## EXECUTIVE DIRECTOR
*Section 20.* The executive director shall be the chief administrative officer of the corporation, responsible to the Council for the administration of the corporation's operations and affairs in accordance with policies formulated by the Council. The executive director shall have power to execute on behalf of the corporation such legal instruments as the Council shall authorize by resolution. As soon as practicable after the close of each fiscal year the executive director shall submit the Council a report of the operations of the corporation for that year and a statement of its affairs. The executive director shall have such other duties as the Council or the president shall assign.

## SECRETARY
*Section 21.* The secretary shall give notice, as provided in these by-laws, of all meetings of the Council and executive committee; shall prepare, under the direction of the executive director, dockets of the business to be transacted at these meetings; and shall keep the minutes of these meetings. The secretary shall have custody of the corporate seal, and shall perform administrative duties under the general direction of the executive director. In the absence or disability of the secretary, such duties shall be performed by an assistant secretary designated by the Council or the president. No member of the Council shall serve as secretary.

## TREASURER AND ASSISTANT TREASURER
*Section 22.* The treasurer, subject to these by-laws and resolutions of the Council, shall have the oversight responsibility for the custody of the funds and securities of the corporation, and may delegate to the executive director the responsibility for the disbursement of its money.
*Section 23.* The funds of the corporation shall be deposited in such banks, trust companies, or other depositories as may be designated by the Council. Funds so deposited shall be subject to withdrawal only upon checks signed by one or more officers or other persons designated by the Council.
*Section 24.* No indebtedness shall be incurred, except pursuant to a resolution of the Council.
*Section 25.* Payments shall be made only in accordance with pro-

574

cedures established by the Council.

*Section 26.* The treasurer shall authorize the deposit of the securities of the corporation in such deposit vaults or with such banks or trust companies as may be designated by the Council. They may be withdrawn only by the treasurer or other persons designated for such purpose.

*Section 27.* The treasurer and executive director shall oversee the keeping of proper books of account, and other books showing at all times the character, value, and amount of the property and funds of the corporation, and such books shall be at all times open to the inspection of the members of the Council.

*Section 28.* At each annual meeting of the Council the treasurer and/or executive director shall make a report of the accounts for the past fiscal year. At the request of the Council at any regular meeting the treasurer and/or the executive director shall present a recent balance sheet and an account showing the receipts and disbursements of the corporation since the last report.

*Section 29.* The accounts of the treasurer shall be audited annually by an auditor or auditors not connected with the corporation, who shall be chosen by the Council.

*Section 30.* The president, executive director, treasurer, each assistant treasurer, and each other person authorized to withdraw funds or securities of the corporation shall be bonded for the faithful performance of their duties in such sum as may be fixed by the Council. The expense of such bonds shall be paid by the corporation.

## OTHER OFFICERS

*Section 31.* Any officer whose powers and duties are not described in these by-laws shall have such powers and duties as the Council shall determine.

## FINANCIAL SUPPORT

*Section 32.* The financial support required to carry on the operations of the corporation shall be derived from contributions made by private organizations and institutions and members of the general public. No contributions shall be accepted from any government or governmental agency. The Council may impose such limitations upon the amount and sources of contributions as it shall deem desirable in order to insure the independence of the corporation.

575

## ATTENDANCE AT COMMITTEE MEETINGS

*Section 33.* All members of the Council may attend and participate in all committee meetings. Only the members of a committee shall be entitled to vote at meetings of that committee.

## RULES OF PROCEDURE

*Section 34.* The Council, by a vote of the majority of the members present at the time of the vote, if a quorum is present at such time, shall adopt Rules of Procedure for dealing with complaints filed with the Council concerning the accuracy and fairness of news reports, and with issues concerning freedom of the press.

## EXECUTIVE COMMITTEE

*Section 35.* The Council may by resolution adopted by a majority of the entire Council designate an executive committee, consisting of three or more members of the Council, to serve at the pleasure of the Council. A vacancy in the membership of the executive committee may be filled by the Council at any meeting.

*Section 36.* Except as otherwise provided by law or in these by-laws or by the Council, the executive committee, between meetings of The Council, shall have all the powers and duties of the Council, and may adopt rules to govern its procedure.

## FINANCE COMMITTEE

*Section 37.* The Council may by resolution adopted by a majority of the entire Council designate a finance committee consisting of three members of the Council. The finance committee shall serve at the pleasure of the Council. A vacancy on the finance committee may be filled by the Council at any meeting.

*Section 38.* The Council may by resolution provide that the finance committee shall have general supervision of the funds and assets of the corporation and of the investment and reinvestment thereof, including the power to:

1. make and to change investments, and to sell any part of the securities of the corporation or any rights or privileges appurtenant thereto;
2. employ one or more qualified investment counsel or managers and set the fees for their services and to delegate to any such manager the power to make and to change investments and to buy and sell securities in behalf of the corporation subject to such investment policies and procedures as the finance committee may determine;

576

3. participate in the reorganization of any corporation, and to deposit any securities held by this corporation with such protective or reorganization committee and on such terms as the finance committee may determine;
4. authorize one or more officers of the corporation or other persons to execute and deliver in behalf of the corporation, or to rescind, proxies to vote on stock owned by the corporation.

*Section 39.* The chairman of the finance committee shall be designated by the Council. Except as otherwise provided in these by-laws or by the Council, the finance committee may adopt rules to govern its procedure.

## NOMINATING COMMITTEE

*Section 40.* The Council may by resolution adopted by a majority of the members present at a legal meeting designate a nominating committee consisting of an equal number of public members and media members. The nominating committee shall make recommendations to the Council regarding the members to be elected at any meeting of the Council. The nominating committee shall also make recommendations to the Council regarding officers to be elected. Except as otherwise provided in these by-laws or by the Council, the nominating committee may adopt rules to govern its procedure.

*Section 41.* The nominating committee may solicit suggestions for new members of the Council from an advisory panel designated by the Council. The advisory panel may consist of former members of the Council, representatives of funding organizations, and representatives of the media and the public.

## ADVISERS

*Section 42.* The Council may, on recommendation made by the nominating committee, designate by a majority vote at any legal meeting, up to six advisers to the Council to assist in specialized areas of expertise. Such advisers shall be eligible to serve in this capacity for a term of three years. Advisers may resign in writing to the president. An adviser shall be deemed to have resigned upon becoming a government official or employee. When a specific matter arises calling for such special assistance, the president shall invite the adviser or advisers to attend the Council's sessions. In such instances, the advisers shall serve in a non-voting capacity and shall be reimbursed for expenses.

## SPECIAL COMMITTEES
*Section 43.* The Council may by resolution adopted by a majority present at any legal meeting designate from time to time special committees, consisting of three or more members of the Council to serve at the pleasure of the Council. Such committees shall have only the powers specifically granted to them by the Council.

## CONFLICT OF INTEREST
*Section 44.* Whenever a Council member has a conflict of interest or the potential of a conflict of interest by participating in Council or committee consideration of a complaint or any other matter, the member shall abstain from such participation.

## FISCAL YEAR
*Section 45.* The fiscal year of the corporation shall end on July 31.

## REPORTS OF FINAL ACTIONS
*Section 46.* The Council shall provide reports of all its final actions in an annual report.

## INDEMNIFICATION
*Section 47.* The corporation shall indemnify, to the extent permitted and upon the conditions prescribed by law, any person or persons made a party to an action by or in the right of the corporation to procure a judgment in its favor by reason of the fact that they, their testator or intestate, are or were members of the Council or officers or employees of the corporation, against reasonable expenses, including attorney's fees, actually and necessarily incurred by them (and to the extent not covered by their own insurance) in connection with the defense of such action, or in connection with an appeal therein, except in relation to matters as to which such members of the Council, officers, or employees were adjudged to have breached their duties to the corporation under applicable law. The corporation shall also indemnify, to the extent permitted and upon the conditions prescribed by law, any person made, or threatened to be made, a party to an action or proceeding (other than one by or in the right of the corporation to procure a judgment in its favor), whether civil or criminal, by reason of the fact that they, their testator or intestate, were members of the Council or officers or employees of the corporation, against judgments, fines, amounts paid in settlement and reasonable expenses, including attorney's fees, actually and necessarily incurred as a

result of such action or proceeding or any appeal therein, if such members of the Council, officers, or employees acted in good faith for a purpose which they reasonably believed to be in the best interests of the corporation and, in criminal actions or proceedings, in addition, had no reasonable cause to believe that their conduct was unlawful. The foregoing rights of indemnification shall not be exclusive of any other rights to which any such members of the Council, officers, or employees may be entitled as a matter of law, or which may be lawfully granted to them; and the indemnification hereby granted by the corporation shall be in addition to and not in limitation of any other privilege or power which the corporation may lawfully exercise with respect to indemnification or reimbursement of its Council members, officers, and employees.

**AMENDMENTS**
*Section 48.*    These by-laws may be amended by a vote of two-thirds of the Council members at any legal meeting provided notice of the proposed amendment of the by-laws is given in the notice of the meeting.

# Part 6

# How to Complain to the Council

Any individual or organization can file a complaint with the Council.

The Council prefers that the complaint first be taken up with the news organization involved. If this effort fails to bring redress, the Council is in a position to consider the complaint.

In writing to the Council include supporting information that is specific. If the complaint concerns a printed news report, include a copy of the report plus the name and date of the publication.

If the complaint concerns a radio or television news report, include the name of the station and the name of the network (if any), and date and time of the airing.

Those complaining to the Council are required to sign a waiver stipulating that no legal action is under way or contemplated. The reason for this is that the Council is an alternative form of settling disputes—totally apart from courts or administrative bodies such as the Federal Communications Commission. As such, it is not willing to have its research or findings used in legal or governmental actions.

Complaints to the Council should be addressed to:

The National News Council
805 Third Avenue
New York, N.Y. 10022

# Part 7

# Subject Index

The following is an index of Council complaints No. 1 through 217 by subject matter of news reports in question and of the texts and findings in those complaints.

Statements by the Council relating to press freedom, and reports on complaints relating to press freedom are in Part 2 of this volume, p. 500-563; p. 23-48 of Volume I; p. 316-414 of Volume II.

A numerical listing of complaints is on p. 7-30 of this volume; p. 12-27 of Volume II.

A table of complaints by type of news organization may be found on p. 6 of this volume; p. 12 of Volume I; p. 11 of Volume II.

**Key to abbreviations:**
e.g. abortion, #1: I, 57-58 . . .

**#1** denotes complaint number; **I** denotes volume of *In the Public Interest;* **57-58** denotes page number.


abortion, #1: I, 57-58; #15: I, 73-74; #44: I, 107-110; #95: II, 114-117; #109: II, 162-164; #110: II, 164-167; #131-136: II, 249-266; #146: II, 292-294; #151: II, 315-318; #152: II, 318-320
access, media to information and sources, *see* information, classified; sources, availability of; *Freedom of Press statements and complaints.*
access, public to media, *see* letters to editor; reply and rebuttal
accountability of news organizations, *see* corrections; letters to the editor; ombudsmen; reply and response of news organizations to inquiries and complaints
accuracy

*Note: Nearly all complaints involve some factual dispute. See the journalistic issue at stake (i.e., corrections; sources; verification; etc.); or subject matter of report in question or of specific factual dispute (i.e., abortion; etc.).*

acid rain, #208: III, 424-434; #209: III, 435-439

advertising, editorial, #82: II, 81-83; #83: II, 83; #109: II, 162-164; #142: II, 275-277; #158: III, 38, 39, 40, 41; #184: III, 213; #213: III, 464-465

advertising, general, #16: I, 74; #114: II, 178-179; #122, 123: II, 214, 220

advocacy journalism, *see* opinion in reporting, viewpoint j.

AFL-CIO, #18: I, 75-76

Agnew, Spiro, #3: I, 59; #4: I, 60-61; #5: I, 61-63; #19: I, 76-77

agriculture, #192, III, 305-314

analysis, "instant," #20, I, 78; #58: I, 132-135

analysis, general, #26: I, 86-87; #27: I, 89-90; #58: I, 132-135; #69: II, 49-50; #95: II, 114-117; #120: II, 209; #176: III, 126; #177: III, 143, 150, 165; #182: III, 198, 204

    *see also* op-ed page; opinion in reporting

AP, The, #215: III, 489, 490

Arab/Israel conflict, *see* Israel/Arab conflict

Army, U.S., #73: II, 58; #91: II, 106

Asians, #139: II, 269-270

Associated Press, The, #215: III, 489, 490

attribution, *see* sources, attribution of

automobile repairs, #79: II, 72-76

balance, *see* fairness; opinion in reporting

Baptists, American, #182: III, 193-204

Better Government Association, #184: III, 212, 213

bias, *see* fairness; opinion in reporting

Blacks, #6: I, 63-66; #12: I, 70-72; #188: III, 244, 270, 274

Boston University, #145: II, 287-291

business/financial reporting, #163: III, 55-64; #168: III, 87-88; #175: III, 120-124; #205: III, 404-411

busing, court-mandated school, #70: II, 50-52

bylines and credits, #150: II, 313

    *see also* sources, attribution of

cancer, *see* medical/health reporting, cancer

Carter, Jimmy, #95: II, 114-117

cartoons, editorial, #38: I, 101; #105: II, 146; #108: II, 161-162;

#124: II, 220-223

*see also* illustrations

Castro, Fidel, #64: II, 33-35

Catholics, #1: I, 57; #15: I, 73-74; #44: I, 107-110; #131, 132: II, 249-258; #134: II, 260-262; #136: II, 264, 266; #151: II, 318-320; #175: III, 120-124

Central Intelligence Agency, #215: III, 487-490

checkbook journalism, #99: II, 124-130; #187: III, 235, 236, 238-240, 241, 242, 243

chemical warfare, #194: III, 320-323

Chicanos, *see* Hispanics

child care agencies, New York, #167: III, 81-86

Chile, #7: I, 66-67

chiropracty, #69: II, 48-50; #96: II, 117-119

CIA, #215: III, 487-490

cigarette smoking, #114: II, 178-179; #181: III, 192

classified information, #34: I, 95-97

*see also Freedom of the Press statements and complaints*

columnists, *see* op-ed page; opinion; opinion in reporting

commentary, *see* analysis; cartoons; op-ed page; opinion

competition in newsroom, #188: III, 42-45, 58, 60, 271-273, 281, 282-283

confidentiality of sources, *see* sources, attribution of, confidentiality

conflict of interest for news organizations (charges of), #114: II, 178-179; #125: II, 224-226; #145: II, 287-291; #158: III, 38-41; #163: III, 61-62; #183: III, 206; #206: III, 411-421

context, *see* interviews, editing of; quotations, context of; omissions, specific; scope, of a given story

Cooke, Janet, #188: III, 244-283

corrections, #18: I, 76; #99: II, 124-129; #101: II, 133-140; #115: II, 180-183; #116: II, 183-184, 187-188; #154: II, 322-323; #155: III, 34; #156: III, 35, 36; #161: III, 48, 49; #182: III, 198, 203-204; #186: III, 201, 202; #192: III, 313-14; #194: III, 324; #203: III, 396, 397, 398; #205: III, 409; #206: III, 420; #210: III, 442, 447, 449; #213: III, 463; #216: III, 492-493; #217: III, 494;

*see also* follow-up

corroboration, *see* sources, reliability, selection of; verification

credits, #150: II, 313

crime reporting, #188: III, 255-256, 264, 267, 281-282; #195: III,

325-326

*see also* rape

Cronkite, Walter, #111: II, 167-171

crowd estimates, #54: I, 123; #109: II, 163; #136: II, 264, 266; #153: II, 320-321

Cuba, #64: II, 33-35

deadline pressures, #109: II, 163-164

Dean, John, #99: II, 124-130

decency, *see* taste, questionable

defense, national, #34: I, 95-97; #50: I, 119

*see also,* Army, U.S.; classified information; State Department

denials, *see* reply and rebuttal, before publication or broadcast

dentists, #88: II, 98-101

detachment, reportorial, *see* humanitarian concerns v. journalistic detachment

docudramas, #68: II, 46-48

Douglas, William O., #40: I, 102-103

drug abuse, #130: II, 241-249; #188: III, 244-283

economic reporting, *see* business/financial r.

editing, *see* interviews, editing of; omissions, specific; newsworthiness; scope of a given story

editorial opinion, *see* opinion

editorial oversight, #188: III, 244-245, 247-248, 249-250, 251-253, 255, 260-264, 275, 276-277, 277-279, 280, 281, 282-283; #195: III, 328

editorial page, *see* opinion

Editorial Writers, National Conference of, #85: II, 88; #101: II, 139

"Editor's Notebook," NBC Evening News, #18: I, 76

Eisenhower, Dwight, #74: II, 60-62

elderly, the #78: II, 70

election coverage, #8: I, 67; #14: I, 73; #92: III, 108-110; #177: III, 142-170; #186: III, 234

*see also* political reporting

El Salvador, #197: III, 346-351

energy, general, #40: I, 102-103; #172: II, 112; #205: III, 404-411; #208: III, 424-434; #209: III, 435-439

*see also* nuclear power; oil

environmental reporting, #21: I, 78-80; #48: I, 116; #49: I, 117-118; #108: II, 161-162; #117: II, 189-200; #118: II, 200-205; #122, 123:

II, 213-220; #124: II, 220-223; #160: III, 44-46; #179: III, 181-185; #208: III, 424-434; #209: III, 435-439

"equal time," *see* letters to the editor; reply and rebuttal, after publication or broadcast

*see also* corrections; follow-up

ethics, *see* conflict of interest for news organizations; humanitarian concerns v. journalistic detachment; impact of the act of reporting; impact of news reports; lawbreaking by reporters in pursuit of a story; masquerading reporters; privacy, right of; staging of news events; subterfuge

ethnic groups, *see individual groups*

euthanasia, #106: II, 151-153

fact-checking, *see* verification

factual disputes, *see* accuracy

fairness, *Note: Nearly all complaints involve some question of fairness. See the journalistic issue at state* (i.e., analysis; letters to the editor; opinion in reporting, *etc.); or subject matter of report or specific dispute* (i.e., abortion, *etc.*).

Fairness and Accuracy, Bureau of, *Chicago Sun-Times* and *Chicago Daily News,* #69: II, 50

Fairness Doctrine, #6: I, 63-64, 65; #25: I, 85

fair trail/free press, #103: II, 141-143

*see also* crime reporting; legal issues, reporting of

film footage, #155: III, 31, 33; #184: III, 212, 215, 216, 217, 220, 221, 222; #193: III, 316, 317, 318, 319

firing of reporters for political views (charges of), #4: I, 60-61

flu, *see* influenza

fluoridation, #77: II, 67-69; #119-121: II, 205-213

Flynt, Larry, #103: II, 141-142

follow-up (to news stories), #21: I, 79-80; #26: I, 87; #27: I, 90; #61: I, 142; #79: II, 75; #86: II, 88-90; #104: II, 143-145; #115: II, 181; #122, 123: II, 215-216, 220; #139: II, 270; #143: II, 278, 279; #165: III, 70; #184: III, 213, 219-220; #197: III, 349, 352; #208: III, 426; #214: III, 480, 486

*see also* corrections; "Editor's Notebook"; letters to the editor; reply and rebuttal, after publication or broadcast

Food and Drug Administration, #113: II, 174-177; #128: II, 236-238

Ford, Gerald R.

vacated congressional seat, #14: I, 73

April 10, 1975 address to Congress, #58: I, 132-135

foreign affairs, *see* defense, national; State Department; *specific nations*

Freedom of Information Act, #162: III, 50, 53

*see also Freedom of Information statements and complaints*

Gallup Organization, #210: III, 440, 441, 446, 447

gays and lesbians, #153: II, 320-321; #177: III, 142-171; #189: III, 286, 288, 289-292

Grace, Princess of Monaco, #65: II, 35-38

Gravel, Mike, #23: I, 81

gun control, #29: I, 91-92

Haig, Alexander, #194: III, 320, 322, 323, 324

Halberstam, Dr. Michael, #187: III, 235-243

Haldeman, H.R., #187: III, 242

harassment, press (charges of), #56: II, 52; #163: III, 56

Harris, Louis, #30: I, 92-93; #106: II, 151-153; #210: III, 440, 448

headlines, #78: II, 70, 71-72; #163: III, 64; #167: III, 87; #171: III, 102-103; #176: III, 126; #187: III, 235-236, 240-241; #194: III, 320-323

health reporting, *see* medical/health reporting

Hennicker-Heaton, Sir Perrigine, death of, #42: I, 104-105

herbicidal spraying, #21: 78-80; #160: III, 44-46

hiring practices of news organizations, #188: III, 247, 252, 269-271, 277, 279, 281, 282

Hispanics, #16: I, 74; #161: III, 46-47; #176: III, 125

hoaxes, #188: III, 244-283

homosexuals, *see* gays and lesbians

Hughes, Paula, #163: III, 59

humanitarian concerns v. journalistic detachment, #188: III, 249, 255-256, 257, 257-258, 264, 267, 281-282; #201: III, 383-388

illustrations, #188: III, 274

*see also* photographs

impact of the act of reporting, #202: III, 388-395

impact of news reports, #188: III, 244, 249, 264, 267-269, 280, 281; #204: III, 399-404; #213: III, 463, 473

*see also* humanitarian concerns v. journalistic detachment; interviews, safety or welfare of inteviewees; medical/health reporting; rape; security, national; terrorism

independent producers and networks, #165: III, 69, 70, 71, 73

Indians, American, #13: I, 72

586

Indians, East, #214: III, 473-486
Indochina, *see* Southeast Asia
influenza, #113: II, 174-177; #190: III, 298-301
information, availability of, *see* classified information; sources, attribution of, confidentiality; sources, availability of; *Freedom of the Press statements and complaints*
information, freedom of, *see* sources, availability of; *Freedom of the Press statements and complaints*
"instant" analysis, *see* analysis, "instant"
intelligence quotient, #60: I, 137-139
international news, *see individual countries*
International Police Academy, #46: I, 111-113
interpretation, *see* analysis; opinion in reporting; translations
interviews
    editing of, #184: III, 7; #200: III, 1-2, 2, 5, 6, 18-19
    manner of questioning, #60: I, 137, 138; #90: II, 104-105; #93: 110-112; #121: II, 211-213; #150: II, 300; #177: III, 153, 158-159, 162, 163-164; #200: III, 2, 6, 11-15, 21; #208: III, 7-8
    "never took place," #39: I, 101-102; #111: II, 168; #189: III, 285, 291, 292, 296-297
    off the record, #186: III, 229-234
    paid, *see* checkbook journalism
    refusal of, #26: I, 86-88; #99: II, 124-130; #184: III, 222
    safety or welfare of interviewees, #61: I, 140; #200: III, 369, 377, 380-381
    *see also* quotations; sources, attribution of, confidentiality
Ireland, Northern, #73: II, 59-60; #76: II, 66-67; #80: II, 76-79; #91: II, 106-107; #94: II, 112-114; #97: II, 120-122; #203: III, 395-398; #215: III, 487-490; #216: III, 491-493; #217: III, 494-499
Irish Republican Army, *see* Ireland, Northern
Israel/Arab conflict, #24: I, 82; #42: I, 104-105; #61: I, 140-142, II, 58; #84: II, 84; #86: II, 88-90; #155: III, 31-34; #174: III, 117-119; #193: III, 315-319
    *see also* Palestine Liberation Organization
Jews, Syrian, #61: I, 140-142, II, 58; #86: II, 88-90
Johnson, Lyndon B., #163: III, 59-60
Kawaida Towers, Newark, NJ, #6: I, 63-66
Kelly, Grace, #65: II, 35-38
Kent State incident aftermath, #115: II, 179-183
Kissinger, Henry, #24: I, 82

labeling, of individuals, groups, causes, etc. in news stories, #1: I, 57;
#15: I, 73-74; #44: I, 107-110; #76: II, 66-67; #94: II, 112-114;
#131: II, 250, 254; #132: II, 255, 257, 258; #134: II, 260-262;
#136: II, 264; #146: II, 293-294; #150: II, 314-315; #151: II, 316;
#152: II, 318-320; #214: III, 473, 475, 476, 478-479, 482, 484, 486
labeling, of reports and articles (i.e., "opinion," "analysis"), #25: I,
83-85; #26: I, 87; #60: I, 139; #69: II, 50; #78: II, 71; #127: II,
233-235; #144: II, 286; #127: II, 233-235; #131: II, 252; #144: II,
286; #149: II, 298-300; #150: II, 314-315; #190: III, 301; #201: III,
387; #209: III, 438, 439
labor, organized, #125: II, 223-226; #125: II, 227-231; #137: II,
266-267; #142: II, 275-277; #144: II, 279-286; #148: II, 296-298;
#158: III, 38; #197: III, 346-351; #206: III, 411, 412, 415, 417, 420;
#212: III, 457-462
laetrile, see medical/health reporting, cancer
Lance, Bert, #163: III, 55, 56
language, questionable use of, #1: I, 57-58; #4: I, 60; #26: I, 88-89;
#30: I, 92-93; #35: I, 97-98; #57: I, 126, 129, 130-131, 132; #71: II,
55-57; #98: II, 123; #106: II, 151-153; #117: II, 191; #126: II, 230;
#155: III, 31, 33; #161: III, 47-48; #164: III, 66, 67, 68; #166: III,
76, 78, 79; #169: III, 93; #184: III, 216-217, 220, 221; #189: III,
292-293, 297; #191: III, 305; #194: III, 320-323; #214: III, 486
see also translations; labeling of individuals, groups, causes, etc. in
news stories
Laotian immigrants, #182: III, 193-204
lawbreaking by reporters in pursuit of story (charges of), #105: II, 146,
150; #129: II, 245; #202: III, 389
Law Enforcement Assistance Administration, #37: I, 99
leaks, #21: I, 78
see also sources, attribution of, confidentiality
legal issues, reporting of, #11: I, 69-70; #19: I, 76-77; #133: II,
258-260; #156: III, 34-36; #215: III, 487-490
letters to the editor
broadcast news, #201: III, 387-388
complainant failed to write letter when offered opportunity, #66: II,
39; #69: II, 48; #186: III, 229, 230, 233
editing of letters, #2: I, 58; #112: I, 172, 173
letters page, #214: III, 18
non-publication policy for all letters, #182: III, 199, 203, 204
non-publication of critical letters, #21: I, 78, 79-80; #107: II, 155,

588

156; #112: II, 172, 173-174; #114: II, 178-179; #132: II, 256, 257-258; #147: II, 295, 296; #192: III, 307-308, 309, 313-314; #194: III, 324; #196: III, 333-334, 341, 346; #203: III, 396, 398; #212: III, 457-458, 462; #214: 474, 482

publication of critical letters, #105: II, 147-148; #122-123: II, 216, 220; #128: II, 237, 238; #130: II, 242-243, 248; #158: III, 39, 40, 42; #167: III, 81; #176: III, 126; #192: III, 307-308, 314; #198: III, 356, 362; #210: III, 441, 447, 449; #214: III, 474, 481, 482, 483, 486; #217: III, 497

publication of critical letters with editor's comment: #112: II, 171, 172, 173; #130: II, 243; #176: III, 140-141; #186: III, 231; #204: III, 399, 400

publication of letters containing unsubstantiated allegations, #170: III, 100-101

publication of uncritical letters, #192: III, 307-308, 314; #214: III, 481

routing of critical letters in news organization, #203: III, 398

syndicated stories, #69: II, 48

Tornillo v. *Miami Herald,* #186: III, 231

Love Canal, NY, #179: III, 181-185

Lowenstein, Allard, #189: III, 284-297

MacArthur, General Douglas, #74: II, 60-62

management involvement in news judgment, #12: I, 70-72; #158: III, 40-42

    *see also* conflict of interest

Mansion House, St. Louis, #56: I, 125-126, II, 52-55

Marin County, CA, #150: II, 300-315

masquerading reporters, #100: II, 131; #105: II, 146, 150; #130: II, 241, 243-245

Meany, George, #18: I, 75-76

medical/health reporting

    cancer, #85: II, 85-88; #129: II, 238-241; #198: III, 356-368

    other, #21: I, 78-80; #22: I, 80-81; #32: I, 94; #33: I, 94-95; #62: II, 28-31; #69: II, 48-50; #77: II, 67-69; #96: II, 117-119; #113: II, 174-177; #114: II, 178-179; #116: II, 183-189; #119, 120, 121: II, 205-213; #128: II, 236-238; #141: II, 273-275; #147: II, 294-296; #154: II, 321-325; #157: III, 36, 37; #164: III, 65-67; #173: III, 113-116; #178: III, 171-180; #180: III, 186-191; #185: III, 223-228; #191: III, 302-304; #211: III, 449-456

mental illness, #9: I, 68

Middle East, *see* Israel/Arab conflict; Jews, Syrian

"milk fund," #36: I, 98-99

minorities, *see* stereotyping, racial; *individual groups* (e.g. Blacks)

misrepresentation, by reporters of identity or intention, *see* subterfuge; masquerading reporters

Monaco, #65: II, 35-38

Morris, Dr. J. Anthony (reputed "whistle blower"), #113: II, 174-177; #128: II, 236-238; #190: III, 298-301

"New Journalism," #188: III, 272, 282; #189: III, 292

newsworthiness, #9: I, 68; #15: I, 73-74; #19: I, 77; #28: I, 90-91; #29: I, 91-92; #36: I, 98-99; #42: I, 105; #42: I, 105; #43: I, 106; #49: I, 117-118; #52: I, 120-121; #53: I, 121-122; #56: II, 53; #59: I, 135-137; #67: II, 45; #72: II, 57-58; #73: II, 58-60; #78: II, 71; #83: II, 83; #91: II, 106-108; #92: II, 108-110; #110: II, 164-167; #135: II, 262-264; #136: II, 264, 265; #137: II, 266-267; #145: II, 287-291; #154: II, 321-322, 324; #162: III, 52; #177: III, 166
*see also* omissions, specific; scope of given news story

Nicaragua, #87: II, 91-98; #101: II, 133-140; #107: II, 153-161

Nixon Administration, #4: I, 60; #10: I, 68-69; #14: I, 73; #24: I, 82; #34: I, 95-97; #36: I, 98-99; #37: I, 99-100
*see also* Watergate

Nixon, Richard, #10: I, 68-69; #14: I, 73; #17: I, 75; #18: I, 75-76; #19: I, 77; #24: I, 52; #34: I, 95-97; #35: I, 97-98; #36: I, 98-99; #37: I, 99-100; #162: III, 50
*see also* Nixon Administration

Northern Ireland, *see* Ireland, Northern

nuclear power, #117: II, 189-200; #159: III, 42-44; #199: III, 364-368; #213: III, 463-472

nuclear weapons, #210: III, 439-448

oil, #25: I, 83-84; #40: I, 102-103; #48: I, 116; #82: II, 81; #98: II, 122-123; #102: II, 140-141; #169: III, 89-99; #172: III, 103-112

ombudsmen, #186: III, 230, 232; #188: III, 245, 246-253, 256, 258-259, 264, 265-266, 267, 280, 282; #207: III, 422; #213: III, 464

omissions

    specific and found by Council to be misleading or significant, #41: I, 103-104; #46: I, 112; #74: II, 62; #113: II, 177; #128: II, 237; #150: II, 302; #184: III, 218; #198: III, 361, 362, 363

    other, *see* newsworthiness; quotations, context of; scope of given news story

"op-ed" page, #17: I, 75; #82: II, 81-82; #114: II, 178; #132: II, 256, 257; #217: III, 494-499

opinion (editorials, commentary, columnists), #10: I, 68-69; #17: I, 75; #20: I, 78; #29: I, 91-92; #35: I, 97-98; #38: I, 101; #58: I, 133-135; #63: II, 31-33; #77: II, 67-69; #80: II, 76-77, 79; #85: II, 85-88; #105: II, 146; #120: II, 208, 209; #132: II, 256, 257-258; #142: II, 276-277; #156: III, 34-36; #188: III, 266-267; #190: III, 301, 302; #197: III, 346-352

*see also* analysis; cartoons; "op-ed" page, opinion in reporting; reviews

opinion in reporting

viewpoint journalism, #25: I, 84-85; #34: I, 95-97; #47: I, 115-116; #56: II, 53-55; #60: I, 139; #66: II, 38-42; #69: II, 49-50; #96: II, 119; #100: II, 132-133; #113: II, 177; #117: II, 194-195, 200; #119: II, 207; #120: II, 208-211; #122, 123: II, 215, 219-220; #126: II, 230; #130: II, 245-249; #144: II, 279-286; #147: II, 295-296; #150: II, 300-315; #158: III, 39-40; #165: III, 72; #167: III, 86-87; #169: III, 89-99; #172: III, 103-112; #177: III, 143, 152, 159-160, 166, 170; #184: III, 214, 216, 222; #190: III, 299, 301-302; #198: III, 352-363; #201: III, 386-387; #209: III, 435, 437, 438; #211: III, 449

other, #90: II, 105

*see also* analysis

opinion polls, *see* polls, opinion

*Pacific Sun*, #150: II, 300-312

Palestine Liberation Organization, #155: III, 31-34

Panama Canal, #71: II, 55-57

"paranormal" phenomena, #127: II, 231-235

participatory journalism, *see* humanitarian concerns v. journalistic detachment; impact of the act of reporting; staging of news events

Passwater, Richard, #185: III, 223-228

payments by news organizations to news sources, *see* checkbook journalism

photographs, #139: II, 269-270; #140: II, 271-273; #187: III, 235, 238-240, 241; #192: III, 306, 312

placement of stories and features (in relation to other news items), #14: I, 73; #15: I, 73-74; #18: I, 75-76; #38: I, 101; #49: I, 117; #82: II, 82; #105: II, 148; #214: III, 483

*see also* timing of publication or broadcast (in relation to news events)

PLO, #155: III, 31-34

police, Riverside, CA, #161: III, 46-50

Police Academy, International, #46: I, 111-113

Political Action Committees, #201: III, 383-387

political reporting, #166: III, 73, 80; #177: III, 142-170; #210: III, 439-448
*see also* elections

polls, opinion, #23: I, 81; #30: I, 92-93; #106: II, 151-153; #210: III, 439-448

polyurethane furniture, inflammable, #181: III, 162-63

poverty, #214: III, 473-487

presentation of news stories, *see* headlines; labeling of reports and articles; opinion in reporting; placement of news stories, production techniques

privacy, right of, #19: I, 77; #195: III, 324-332; #204: III, 399-403
*see also* harassment

production techniques, disputed broadcast, #117: II, 191, 193, 199-200; #155: III, 32-33; #161: III, 47; #166: III, 73, 80; #177: III, 145, 159, 164, 169; #184: III, 221-222; #200: III, 379-380
*see also* film footage

promotional items, #98: II, 122-124; #129: II, 238, 240-241; #131: II, 252; #150: II, 307-308; #191: III, 303; #200: III, 369-370, 475

pseudonyms, #217: III, 494-499

Pulitzer Prize, #188: III, 244-45, 250-251, 273-274, 276, 282; #189: III, 284, 285, 288, 296

quotations
context of, #19: I, 77; #39: I, 101-102; #43: I, 106; #46: I, 111-112; #57: I, 126, 128; #64: II, 33-35; #66: II, 39; #75: II, 62-65; #95: II, 115, 116-117; #100: II, 131; #150: II, 302-304; 306-307; #163: III, 56, 49, 64; #168: III, 88; #182: III, 195-196, 201; #196: III, 333-345; #203: III, 395-397
*see also* interviews, editing of
disputed, #40: I, 102-103; #39: I, 101-102; #57: I, 126, 128, 130; #111: II, 167-171; #151: II, 316, 318; #163: III, 56, 64; #186: III, 229-233; #196: III, 339-340, 343-344, 345; #203: III, 395-397

Rainier, Prince of Monaco, #65: II, 35-38

rape, #195: III, 324-332; #204: III, 399-403

Reagan Administration, #207: III, 422-423

Reagan, Ronald, #19: I, 77

real estate fraud, #104: II, 143-145

rebuttal, *see* reply and rebuttal; *see also* corrections; follow-up; letters to the editor

reply and rebuttal

after publication or broadcast (editorial issue), #28: I, 90-91; #45: I, 110-111; #29: I, 91; #56: II, 54-55; #65: II, 36, 38; #66: II, 39; #77: II, 68-69; #120: II, 209; #139: II, 270; #142: II, 276-277; #156: III, 35; #158: III, 38; #162: III, 51, 52, 53, 54; #165: III, 70; #166: III, 73-74, 75, 76, 80-81; #182: III, 193, 196, 199, 201, 203, 204; #186: III, 231, 232, 233; #201: III, 387-388; #205: III, 408, 409, 410; #212: III, 457-458, 462

*see also* corrections; follow-up; letters to the editor

before publication or broadcast (reporting issue), #24: I, 82; #28: I, 90-91; #45: I, 110-111; #72: II, 57-58; #120: II, 209-210, 211; #131: II, 250; #157: III, 38; #162: III, 53, 54; #163: III, 56, 59, 61; #176: III, 136; #183: III, 206, 207, 211, 211-212, 212; #184: III, 216; #187: III, 241-242; #205: III, 405, 406, 407, 408, 409, 410; #212: III, 457-458; #213: III, 464, 466, 470, 472-473

reply and response of news organizations to inquiries and complaints, #66: II, 39; #87: II, 92-94, 98; #98: II, 123; #118: II, 202-205; #138: II, 267-269; #176: III, 140-141; #182: III, 196-197, 204; #184: III, 213, 221; #185: III, 224; #186: III, 231-232; #188: III, 245-246, 280; #192: III, 307-308, 313-314; #196: III, 335, 336, 338, 339; #199: III, 365, 367, 368; #208: III, 425, 434; #214: III, 482, 483, 486-487; #216: III, 492-493

reporter involvement in news events, *see* humanitarian concerns v. journalistic detachment; impact of act of reporting; staging of news events

reporting, *see* crime r.; environmental r.; impact of act of r.; interviews; lawbreaking by reporters; legal issues, r. of; masquerading reporters; medical/health r.; opinion in r.; reply and rebuttal, before publication or broadcast; rumor, r. of; science r.; speculation, r. of; subterfuge, by reporters

retractions, *see* corrections

reviews, #68: II, 46-48; #151: II, 316-317, 318

"Right to Life" movement, *see* abortion

Roman Catholicism, *see* Catholics

Roosevelt, Franklin Delano, #74: II, 60

rumor, reporting of, #42: I, 104-105; #189: III, 285, 286, 288, 290, 297

*see also* sources, reliability, selection of; speculation, reporting of

Samoa, American, #47: I, 113-116

Santarelli, Donald (resignation from Law Enforcement Assistance Administration), #37: I, 99-100

scheduling of news broadcasts, *see* analysis, "instant;" placement of stories, features (in relation to other news items); newsworthiness; timing of publication or broadcast (in relation to news events)

science reporting, #57: I, 126-132; #119: II, 207-208; #159: III, 42, 43; #208: III, 424-434; #209: III, 435-439

  *see also* environmental r.; medical/health r.; nuclear energy

scope, of a given story, #3: I, 59; #13: I, 72; #36: I, 98-99; #41: I, 103-104; #57: I, 126, 127; #70: II, 51-52; #79: II, 74; #84: II, 84; #97: II, 122; #102: II, 141; #131: II, 252; #136: II, 265; #148: II, 297-298; #154: II, 324-325; #155: III, 32, 34; #160: III, 46; #165: III, 71-72, 73; #177: III, 169, 170, 171; #181: III, 193; #185: III, 224, 227; #192: III, 308-309; #193: III, 316; #201: III, 385; #208: III, 426-427, 434; #209: III, 436, 439; #212: III, 462

secrecy, *see* classified information; sources, availability of; *Freedom of the Press statements and complaints*

security, national, *see* classified information; defense, national

selection of approach, sources, or subject matter for news reports, *see* newsworthiness; opinion journalism; sources, reliability, selection of; omissions, specific; scope of a given story

senior citizens, #78: II, 70

"sensationalism" (charges of), #33: I, 94; #171: III, 102-103; #176: III, 140; #178: III, 172, 181; #194: III, 320-323; #195: III, 325, 328, 331, 332; #198: III, 362

sex crimes, *see* rape; sexuality

sexuality, #196: III, 333-345

  *see also* gays and lesbians

shielding of sources, *see* sources, attribution of, confidentiality

smoking cigarettes, *see* cigarette smoking

Somoza Garcia, Anastasio, #87: II, 91-98; #101: II, 133-140; #107: II, 154

sources, attribution of

  confidentiality, #4: I, 60-61; #7: I, 66-67; #24: I, 82-83; #56: II, 54-55; #65: II, 37-38; #78: II, 70-71; #80: II, 76-79; #89: II, 102, 104; #100: II, 132; #107: II, 154-155; #166: III, 75-79, 80-81; #175: III, 121; #176: III, 129, 135, 140; #188: III, 244, 247-249, 253, 255-264, 277, 280, 282; #212: III, 457-458, 462; #217: III, 494-499

  *see also* leaks

other cases of incomplete or incorrect identification, #55: I, 124-125; #57: I, 130-131, 132; #67: II, 42, 44; #140: II, 271-273; #143: II, 277-279; #153: II, 320; #162: III, 55; #169: III, 100; #174: III, 117-119; #182: III, 194; #183: III, 209; #185: III, 223-229; #189: III, 285, 286-287, 293, 296, 297; #193: III, 316-317, 318, 319, 320; #207: III, 421-422, 423-424; #208: III, 426-427; #213: III, 468-469, 472; #215: III, 488, 490; #217: III, 494-499

sources, availability of, #21: I, 79-80; #26: I, 86-88; #28: I, 90-91; #37: I, 100; #40: I, 102-103; #45: I, 110-111; #53: I, 121-122; #72: II, 57-58; #122, 123: II, 215, 219; #140: II, 272; #176: III, 129; #208: III, 427, 428, 430; #213: III, 468

*see also* classified information; interviews, refusal of

sources, reliability, selection of, #7: I, 66; #21: I, 78-80; #30: I, 92-93; #31: I, 93; #42: I, 105; #56: II, 55; #58: I, 132-134; #59: I, 136-137; #60: I, 137, 138, 139; #62: II, 28-31; #63: II, 32-33; #67: II, 42-45; #79: II, 72-76; #87: II, 91, 94-98; #89: II, 102-103; #100: II, 131, 132; #115: II, 182: #120: II, 210; #122, 123: II, 217-218; #126: II, 228; #150: II, 304-306, 311-312; #158: III, 38, 40; #160: III, 44, 45; #162: III, 51; #164: III, 66; #167: III, 82; #173: III, 114; #175: III, 121, 124; #177: III, 155, 157; #178: III, 174, 180; #179: III, 182, 183, 184-185, 185; #180: III, 186-192; #184: III, 217; #185: III, 223-229; #189: III, 289, 290; #205: III, 404-405, 406, 407, 409-410; #208: III, 426-427, 427-428, 429, 434; #211: III, 450; #213: III, 463, 466, 468-469, 472

*see also* leaks; rumor, reporting of; speculation, reporting of

South Vietnam, *see* Vietnam

Southeast Asia, #26: I, 89; #59: I, 135-137; #194: III, 320-323

*see also* Laotian immigrants; Vietnam

Soviet Union, #52: I, 120

Soviet-U.S. conflict, #194: III, 320; #200: III, 368-383; #210: III, 439-449

speculation, reporting of, #10: I, 68-69; #42: I, 104-105; #78: II, 70, 71; #87: II, 97; #127: II, 231-235; #182: III, 198, 199-200, 204; #189: III, 285, 286, 288, 290, 297; #205: III, 409-410

*see also* rumor, reporting of

spies, #200: III, 368-383

staging of news events, #117: II, 199-200; #150: II, 300, 301-302, 309; #177: III, 165; #184: III, 219; #201: III, 383-388

State Department, #46: I, 111

statistics, #184: III, 220-221, 222; #198: III, 361-362; #213: III, 463-466, 466-472, 473

stereotyping, racial, #214: III, 473-487

subterfuge by reporters (charges of), #165: III, 69, 71-72; #184: III, 213, 214, 216; #187: III, 236-238, 241; #200: III, 369, 371-372, 372-376, 376-379, 381

    *see also* masquerading

suppression of information

    by news organizations (charges of), *see* newsworthiness

    by others, *see* classified information; sources, availability of; *Freedom of the Press statements and complaints*

Sweaney, Dennis (convicted murderer of Allard Lowenstein), #189: III, 284-297

Syrian Jews, *see* Jews, Syrian

talk shows, #32: I, 94

taste, questionable, #187: III, 235, 236, 240, 241, 243; #195: III, 324-332; #204: III, 399,403, 404

terrorism, #73: II, 58-60; #76: II, 66-67; #94: II, 112-114; #97: II, 120, 121, 122; #155: III, 31-34

theater, #207: III, 421-424

timing of publication or broadcast (in relation to news events), #103: II, 141-143

    *see also* analysis, "instant;" placement of stories, features (in relation to other news items)

torture, #46: I, 111, 113

training of news personnel, #188: III, 278-279, 282

translations, #63: II, 31-33; #176: III, 127, 140

trial, fair, v. free press, *see* fair trial/free press

Udall, Morris, #102: II, 140-141

UFOs, #111: II, 167-171

unidentified flying objects, #111: II, 167-171

United Press International *see* UPI

UPI, #176: III, 125-141; #213: III, 464, 465; #215: III, 488

vegetarians, #154: II, 321-325

verification, corroboration, fact-checking, #56: II, 55; #62: II, 28-31; #67: II, 42-45; #160: III, 45; #163: III, 15; #173: III, 114, 115, 117; #176: III, 141; #178: III, 173, 181; #182: III, 196, 197, 200, 201; #183: III, 211; #184: III, 222; #185: III, 223, 227, 228; #189: III, 296, 296-297; #196: III, 333, 340, 343; #205: III, 409, 409-410; #212: III, 457 *see also* leaks, rumor, reporting of; sources, reliability, selection of; speculation, reporting of

veterinary medicine, #81: II, 79-81

victims of crime, publishing names and/or addresses of, #195: III, 328-331; #204: III, 399-404

Vietnam, #21: I, 78-80; #26: I, 85-89; #51: I, 120; #58: I, 132; #63: II, 31-33; #67: II, 42-45; #140: II, 271-273

    *see also* Southeast Asia

viewpoint, editorial, *see* opinion

viewpoint journalism, *see* opinion in reporting, viewpoint j.

Welch, Bernard (convicted murderer of Dr. Michael Halberstam), #187: III, 235-243

Watergate

    subject matter of a story in question, #14: I, 73; #36: I, 98-99; #99: II, 124-130; #162: III, 51-53

    impact on journalism, #188: III, 250, 262, 274

"whistle blowers," #113: II, 174-177; #128: II, 236-238; #190: III, 298-301

women, #66: II, 38-42; #75: II, 62-66

"yellow rain," #184: III, 212-223

Yom Kippur War (U.S. Military Alert during), #10: I, 68-69; #34: I, 95-97

# Part 7 (Continued)

# Participants' Index

The following is an index of Council complaints No. 1 through 217 by complainants and news organizations.

**Key to abbreviations:**
  **e.g. ABC-TV**
  **affiliates, #136: II, 264-266 (WJLA, Washington, DC) . . .**
**#136** denotes complaint number; **II** denotes volume of *In the Public Interest;* **264-266** denotes page number; **(WJLA, Washington, DC)** denotes call letters and location of affiliate.

ABC-TV
    affiliates, #98: II, 122-124 (WABC, New York); #136: II, 264-266 (WJLA, Washington, DC); #138: II, 267-269 (WABC, New York)
    network
        news, #8: I, 67; #20: I, 77-78; #43: I, 105-106; #63: II, 31-33; #76: II, 66-67; #102: II, 140-141; #146: II, 292-294; #193: III, 315-320
        special reports, #25: I, 83-85; #58: I, 132-135; #155: III, 31-34
        "20/20," #159: III, 42-44; #160: III, 44-46; #164: III, 65-68; #184: III, 212-223; #198: III, 352-364; #200: III, 368-383
Accuracy in Media, #7: I, 66-67; #21: I, 78-80; #46: I, 111-113; #59: I, 135-137; #64: II, 33-35
ACLU, *see* American Civil Liberties Union
AFL-CIO
    national office, #212: III, 457-462

598

Public Employee Department, #144: II, 279-286

Task Force on Labor Law Reform, #142: II, 275-277

Agence France-Press, #22: I, 80-81

Aguilar, Andrew, #16: I, 74

AIM, *see* Accuracy in Media

Alfred, Randy, #177: III, 142-171

Allan, Rupert, #186: III, 229-234

American-Arab Anti-Discrimination Committee, #193: III, 315-320

American-Arab Relations Committee, #174: III, 117-120

American Civil Liberties Union, #156: III, 34-36

American Dental Association, #188: II, 98-101

American Electric Power Service Corporation, Columbus, OH, #205: III, 409-410

American Irish Unity Committee, #203: III, 395-398; #215: III, 487-491; #216: III, 491-493; #217: III, 494-499

American Jewish Congress, #61: I, 140-142, II, 58-60

American Postal Workers Union, #125: II, 223-226

Amory, Cleveland, #81: II, 79-81

Anderson, Bryce, #125: II, 223-226

Anderson, Carl E., #8: I, 67

Anderson, Jack, #46: I, 111-113; #87: II, 91-98; #101: II, 133-136; #190: III, 298-302

AP, The, *see* Associated Press, The

Arizonans for a Bilateral Weapons Freeze, #210: III, 439-449

Ashbrook, John M. #26: I, 85-89

Associated Press, The, #30: I, 92-93; #39: I, 101-102; #40: I, 102-103; #41: I, 103-104; #42: I, 104-105; #49: I, 117-118; #52: I, 120-121; #53: I, 121-122; #59: II, 57-58; #78: II, 70-72; #94: II, 112-114; #95: II, 114-117; #115: II, 179-183

Atomic Industrial Forum, #213: III, 463-473

Baker, Marshall E., #112: II, 171-174

Barrett, Dr. Stephen, #69: II, 48-50; #77: II, 67-69; #85: II, 85-88; #113: II, 174-177; #128: II, 236-238; #180: III, 156-162; #190: III, 298-302; #191: III, 302-305

Bartlett, Charles, #5: I, 61-63

Basset, Gene, #124: II, 220-223

*Bay City Times, The,* #170: III, 100-102

Beaudin, Chris, #170: III, 100-102

Behr, Joseph, #24: I, 82-83

Belden, Joseph, #140: II, 271-273

Bender, Henry J., #78: II, 70-72

Bergfalk, The Rev. Lynn, #182: III, 193-205

Bergman, Dr. Abraham B., #33: I, 94-95; #62: II, 28-31

"Black Journal" (Corporation for Public Broadcasting), #6: I, 63-66

Blair, Earl R., #83: II, 83-84

Blonigen, Julie, #146: II, 292-294

Blum, Dr. Alan, #114: II, 178-179; #181: III, 192-193

Boise Cascade Corporation, #168: III, 87-89

Boriskin, Dr. Joel M., #119: II, 205-208

*Boston Globe, The,* #145: II, 287-290, 290-292

*Boston Herald American, The,* #123: II, 213-220

Bouman, Jim, #206: III, 411-421

Boxer, Barbara, #150: II, 300-315

Braden, Tom, #4: I, 60-61

Brainard, G. R., Jr., #40: I, 102-103

Bryant High School, New York, NY, #165: III, 68-73

Budny, C. T., #22: I, 80-81

*bu exposure,* #145: II, 287-290, 290-292

*Camden Courier-Post,* #175: III, 120-124

Cameron, Bruce, #197: III, 346-352

Cape Cod Chamber of Commerce, #122, 123: II, 213-220

Capitol Hill News Service, #23: I, 81

Carpenter, Teresa, #189: III, 284-297

Carter, John F., #28: I, 90-91; #45: I, 110-111

Catholic Defense League, #151: II, 315-318; #153: II, 320-321

Catholic League for Religious and Civil Rights, #175: III, 120-124

CBS Radio

  network, #174: III, 117-120

  WCBS, New York, #156: III, 34-36

CBS-TV

  affiliates, #121: II, 205-206, 211-213 (KSLA, Shreveport, LA); #129: II, 238-241 (WBBM, Chicago); #153: II, 320-321 (WCBS, New York); #166: III, 73-81 (KDKA, Pittsburgh); #202: III, 388-394 (WTVJ, Miami)

  network

    news, #10: I, 68-69; #13: I, 72; #29: I, 91-92; #35: I, 97-98; #36: I, 98-99; #37: I, 99-100; #50: I, 119; #54: I, 122-123; #67: II, 42-45; #70: II, 50-52; #71: II, 55-57; #79: II, 72-76; #84: II, 84; #97: II, 120-122; #131: II, 249-255; #133: II, 258-260;

#135: II, 262-264; #149: II, 298-300; #154: II, 321-325; #201: III, 383-388

"60 Minutes," #61: I, 140-142, II, 58-60; #86: II, 88-90; #100: II, 130-133; #103: II, 141-143; #104: II, 143-145; #141: II, 273-275; #161: III, 46-49, reconsideration, III, 49-50; #179: III, 181-186

special reports, #34: I, 95-97; #58: I, 132-135; #60: I, 137-139; #64: II, 33-35; #74: II, 60-62; #177: III, 142-171

"Sunday Morning," #208: III, 424-434

Central Conference of American Rabbis, #155: III, 31-34

Central States Southeast and Southwest Areas Health and Welfare Pension Funds (Teamsters Union), #126: II, 227-231

Champagne, Alphonse E., #19: I, 76-77

*Charlotte* (NC) *News*, #2: I, 58

*Chicago Daily News*, #69: II, 48-50

*Chicago Sun-Times*, #69: II, 48-50

*Chicago Tribune*, #83: II, 83-84; #106: II, 151-153

Chicago Tribune-New York News Syndicate, #183: III, 205-212; #205: III, 404-411

Child Care Agencies, New York Council of Voluntary, #167: III, 81-87

Children Before Dogs, #81: II, 79-81

Chiropractors Association, International, #96: II, 117-119

Clark, Judy, #70: II, 50-52

Coalition for Environmental-Energy Balance, #208: III, 424-434; #209: III, 435-439

Cohen, Dr. Bernard L., #117: II, 189-200; #159: III, 42-44

Columbia Broadcasting System, *see* CBS

Columbia Features Syndicate, #211: III, 449-457

*Columbia Journalism Review*, #176: III, 125-141

Connor, Harry, #57: I, 126-132

*Conservative Digest*, #140: II, 271-273

Constantine, Larry L., #196: III, 333-345

Consul of Monaco, #65: II, 35-38

*Consumer Reports*, #96: II, 117-119

Cook, Richard, #99: II, 124-130

Copley News Service, #1: I, 57-58; #27: I, 89-90; #77: II, 67-69

Corporation for Public Broadcasting, *see* Public Broadcasting, Corporation for

Cote, Tom G., #4: I, 60-61; #5: I, 61-63

Cott, Lawrence V., #31: I, 93

*Country Journal* Magazine, #122: II, 213-220

CPB, *see* Public Broadcasting, Corporation for

Cresci, Francis, #65: II, 35-38

*Daily Hampshire Gazette* (Northampton, MA), #143: II, 277-279

*Daily News*, New York, #217: III, 494-499

Daniels, Albert G., #199: III, 364-368

Denny, Virginia P., #135: II, 262-264

*Des Moines Register & Tribune*, #110: II, 164-167

De Toledano, Ralph, #77: II, 67-69

De Vault, Walter, #27: I, 89-90

De Vaux, Gene, #17: I, 74-75

Doctors Ought to Care (DOC), #181: III, 192-193

Dole, Vincent P., #130: II, 241-247, reconsideration, 247-249

Donovan, Mrs. Thomas J., #1: I, 57-58

Dorfman, Dan, #183: III, 205-212; #205: III, 404-410

Driscoll, The Rev. Paul, #131: II, 249-255; #132: II, 255-258

Duffy, Thomas, #76: II, 66-67

Duggan, D. C., #95: II, 114-117

Durand, Enrique, #176: III, 125-141

Edwards, Robert A., #12: I, 70-72

*Esquire* magazine, #163: III, 55-65

Evans and Novak (syndicated columnists), #51: I, 120

Evans, Rowland Jr., #51: I, 120

Exxon Corporation, #172: III, 103-113

Fala, Eleanor M., #157: III, 36-38

Felker, Clay, #55: I, 123-125

Fetterman, Dr. Henry, #72: II, 57-58

Field Newspaper Syndicate, #108: II, 161-162

Fisher, Dr. Hettie Hughes, #30: I, 92-93

Florida Real Estate Commission, #104: II, 143-145

*Forbes* magazine, #112: II, 171-174; #212: III, 457-462

Frank, Maurice B., #56: I, 125-126, II, 52-55

Frucci, Michael J., #122-123: II, 213-220

Fund for Animals, The, #118: II, 200-205

Gannett News Service, #62: II, 28-31; #175: III, 120-124

Garvin, Joseph, #167: III, 81-87

Gaumond, Mary, #14: I, 73

Gavin, William F., #44: I, 107-110; #134: II, 260-262; #152: II, 318-320

Gay Task Force, National, #177: III, 142-171
Geran, Juliana, #34: I, 95-97; #54: I, 122-123
Gibson, Judy, #195: III, 324-332
Giddens, Earle A., #50: I, 119
Glaser, Rabbi Joseph B., #155: III, 31-34
Glasser, Ira, #156: III, 34-36
Gomez, Leonel, #197: III, 346-352
Gran, Guy, #51: I, 120
Griffin, Merv, #32: I, 94
Griffin Productions, #32: I, 94
Gulack, Robert, #194: III, 320-324
Haggerty, Timothy, #109: II, 162-164
Halberstam, Dr. Michael J., #141: II, 273-275
Hansen, Judith, #66: II, 38-42
Harari, Rabbi Joseph, #86: II, 88-90
Hardin, A. Wood, #10: I, 68-69
Harris, Louis, #106: II, 151-153
Haydon, John, #47: I, 113-116
Hayes, Robert B., #168: III, 87-89
Heeger, Jack J., #192: III, 305-314
Hennelly, Edmund P., #98: II, 122-124
Herbert, Dr. Victor, #180: III, 186-192; #185: III, 223-229
Hogge, Dr. Gary A., #173: III, 113-117
Holt, William J., #35: I, 97-98; #36: I, 98-99; #37: I, 99-100; #58: I,
    132-135; #149: II, 298-300
*Hospital Physician* magazine, #147: II, 294-296
Howard University Journalism Faculty, #188: III, 244-284
Howe, Dr. William G., #15: I, 73-74; #60: I, 137-139
Howes, Billie M., #143: II, 277-279
*Huntsville* (AL) *Times*, #38: I, 101
Illivicky, Martin, #165: III, 68-73
Indochina Resource Center, #51: I, 120; #63: II, 31-33; #67: II, 42-45
Institute for American Strategy, #50: I, 119
Instructional Development, Center for (Amherst, MA), #143: II,
    277-279
Iowans for Life, Inc., #110: II, 164-167
Irish Americans, National Council of, #80: II, 76-79; #94: II, 112-114
Irish News Service, #76: II, 66-67
Janeway, Eliot, #163: III, 55-65
Jewish Community Federation of Louisville, KY, The, #84: II, 84

Jewish Congress, American, #61: I, 140-142, II, 58-60

Johnson, Theordore W., #23: I, 81

Juergens, Mary Ellen, #106: II, 151-153

Kalis, William #202: III, 388-394

Kamber, Victor, #142: II, 275-277

Karim, Ruth, #133: II, 258-260

KDKA-TV, Pittsburgh, #166: III, 73-81

Kelley, Warren F., #9: I, 68

Kerman, Herbert D., #198: III, 356-368

Khatami, James A. #89: II, 101-104

Kheel, Theodore, #158: III, 38-42

Kilpatrick, James J., #85: II, 85-88

Kirk, Carter W., #39: I, 101-102

Knight News Service, #33: I, 94-95

Koch, Hugo C., #151: II, 315-318; #153: II, 320-321

Koenigsberg, Lee, #130: II, 241-247, reconsideration, II, 247-249

Kohn, Dr. Robert M., #211: III, 449-457

Kohn, Stephen, #145: II, 287-292

Kral, Elmer, #111: II, 167-171

Kramer, Morris H., #82: II, 81-83

Krause, Arthur, #115: II, 179-183

KSLA-TV (Shreveport, LA), #121: II, 205-206, 211-213

Landsburg Productions, Inc., #127: II, 231-235

Lang, Dr. Anton, #21: I, 78-80

Leahigh, Alan, #88: II, 98-101

Lee, Fran, #81: II, 79-81

Lehigh Valley (PA) Committee Against Health Fraud, Inc., #69: II,
    48-50; #77: II, 67-69; #85: II, 85-88; #113: II, 174-177; #128: II,
    236-238; #190: III, 298-302; #191: III, 302-305

Liberty Lobby, #53: I, 121-122

*Life* magazine, #187: III, 235-243

Longshoremen's Association, International, #148: II, 296-298

Litman, Roslyn M., #166: III, 73-81

Lorea, Leo T., #161: III, 49-50, reconsideration, III, 50-55

*Los Angeles Herald Examiner*, #186: III, 229-234

Los Angeles Times Syndicate, #4: I, 60-61; #191: III, 302-305

*Louisville Courier-Journal*, #173: III, 113-117

Lowenstein, Larry, #189: III, 284-297

McAndrews, J. F., #96: II, 117-119

McClennan, W. Howard, #144: II, 279-286

MacKenzie, Ian R., #87: II, 91-98; #101: II, 133-140; #107: II, 153-161

Maloney, Mrs. Paul, #103: II, 141-143

Maloney, Thomas C. (Mayor of Wilmington, DE), #92: II, 108-110

Mansion House, #56: II, 52-55

Marin County, CA, Board of Supervisors, #150: II, 300-315

Martin, Graham (U.S. Ambassador to South Vietnam), #26: I, 85-89

Mauldin, Bill, #108: II, 161-162

"Media, The" (at large), #9: I, 68; #11: I, 69-70; #19: I, 76-77 (see also Network Television News)

Media Alliance, The, #139: II, 269-270

Medical Society, State of Wisconsin, #105: II, 146-150

Mehdi, Dr. H. T., #174: III, 117-120

Mendelsohn, Dr. Robert, #211: III, 449-457

Mendelson, Charles, #204: III, 399-404

Meyer, Karl E., #138: II, 267-269

*Miami Herald, The*, #114: II, 178-179

Miles, Audrey, #73: II, 58-60; #91: II, 106-108

Miller, Michael P., #139: II, 269-270

Miller, Dr. Robert W., #179: III, 181-185

*Milwaukee Journal, The*, #105: II, 146-150; #206: III, 411-421

*Milwaukee Sentinel, The*, #206: III, 411-421

Mobil Oil Corporation, #25: I, 83-85

Mohr, Charles, #187: III, 235-243

Montanari, Adelio J., #100: II, 130-133

Montanari Residential Treatment Center, #100: II, 130-133

*Morning News, The* (Wilmington, DE), #207: III, 421-424

Morris, W. K., #102: II, 140-141

*Mother Jones*, #198: III, 352-353, 362

Moyers, Bill, #201: III, 383-388

Moyers, Judith, *et al.*, #75: II, 62-65

Mutual Broadcasting System, #12: I, 70-72

National Broadcasting Corporation, *see* NBC

*National Enquirer, The*, #111: II, 167-171; #119: II, 205-208; #178: III, 171-181

National Foundation for Sudden Infant Death, #33: I, 94-95

*National Observer, The*, #66: II, 38-42

*National Star*, #65: II, 35-38

NBC-TV
    News, #3: I, 59; #15: I, 73-74; #18: I, 75-76; #19: I, 76-77; #24: I,

82-83; #90: II, 104-106; #93: II, 110-112; #135: II, 262-264; #148: II, 296-298; #169: III, 89-100; #172: III, 103-113; #181: III, 192-193; #216: III, 491-493

Special reports, #117: II, 189-200; #150: II, 300-315

"Today Show," #90: II, 104-106; #99: II, 124-130

"Weekend," #47: I, 113-116

Entertainment, #118: II, 200-204; #127: II, 231-235

Nelson, Lyle M., #200: III, 368-383

Network Television News (at large), #8: I, 67; #19: I, 76-77; #20: I, 77-78. (*See also specific networks.*)

Neustadt, Carolyn, #84: II, 84

*New Times*, #139: II, 269-270; #147: II, 294-296

*New York Daily News*, #194: III, 320-324

*New York* magazine, #130: II, 241-247, reconsideration, 247-249; #158: III, 38-42; #167: III, 81-87

*New York Post*, #171: III, 102-103; #204: III, 399-404

*New York Times*, #16: I, 74; #17: I, 74-75; #21: I, 78-80; #26: I, 85-89; #44: I, 107-110; #48: I, 116-117; #49: I, 117-118; #55: I, 123-125; #59: I, 135-137; #68: II, 46-48; #80: II, 76-79; #82: II, 81-83; #89: II, 101-104; #109: II, 162-164; #128: II, 236-238; #132: II, 255-258; #134: II, 260-262; #151: II, 315-318; #152: II, 318-320; #192: III, 305-314; #203: III, 395-398; #215: III, 487-491

New York Times News Service, #17: I, 74-75; #21: I, 78-80

*New Yorker, The*, #182: III, 193-205

Newhouse News Service, #56: I, 125-126, II, 52-55

Newman, Marian, #118: II, 200-205

News-Journal Company (Wilmington, DE), #92: II, 108-110

Newspaper Enterprise Association, #162: III, 50-55

*Newsweek*, #7: I, 66-67

Newton, Jane, #160: III, 44-46

Nicaragua Government Information Service, #87: II, 91-98; #101: II, 133-140; #107: II, 153-161

Nilan, Patrick J. #125: II, 223-226

Nordeen, Donald L., #79: II, 72-76

Norevil, Thomas, #42: I, 104-105

Novak, Robert, #51: I, 120

Novotny Furs, Inc., #108: II, 161-162; #124: II, 220-223

Nuclear Society, American, #117: II, 189-200

Oregon Women for Timber, #160: III, 44-46

*Parade* magazine, #113: II, 174-177; #190: III, 298-302

Pennsylvania Program for Women and Girl Offenders, #66: II, 38-42
*People* magazine, #185: III, 223-229
Pharmaceutical Manufacturers Association, #164: III, 65-68
*Philadelphia Bulletin*, #157: III, 36-38
*Philadelphia Inquirer*, #22: I, 80-81
Pilon, Roger, #34: I, 95-97; #54: I, 122-123; #71: II, 55-57
Porter, Gareth, #63: II, 31-33; #67: II, 42-45
Porter, Sue, #49: I, 117-118
"Press, The" (at large), *see* "Media, The"
Public Affairs Council, #201: III, 383-388
Public Affairs Press, #11: I, 69-70
Public Broadcasting, Corporation for
    "Black Journal," #6: I, 63-66
    "Soul," #6: I, 63-66
    "Crisis to Crisis," #209: III, 435-439
    WNET, New York, #165: III, 68-73
Publishers Hall Syndicate, #5: I, 61-63
Putnam, Robert R., #178: III, 171-181
Rabbis, Central Conference of American, #155: III, 31-34
Railroads, Association of American, #184: III, 212-223
*Reader's Digest*, #88: II, 98-101; #199: III, 364-368
Reichenberg, Peter, #97: 120-122
Remsco Management, Inc., #56: I, 125-126
Reuters News Service, #73: II, 58-60; #91: II, 106-108
Reynolds, Jan, #195: III, 324-332
Right to Life Organization
    South Dakota, #133: II, 258-260
    Longview, TX, #135: II, 262-264
    Prince Georges, MD, #136: II, 264-266
Robert Richter Productions, #209: III, 435-439
Robertson, Nan, #187: III, 235-243
Rockville Centre (N.Y.) Diocese, #131: II, 249-255; #132: II, 255-258
Rossman, Kenneth L, #18: I, 75-76; #38: I, 101
Rowley, Horace P., III, #6: I, 63-66
Ruff, Howard, #183: III, 205-212
Ryan, Michael, #137: II, 266-267
Ryba, Debra, #171: III, 102-103
San Francisco Board of Supervisors, #177: III, 142-171
San Francisco Human Rights Commission, #177: III, 142-171
*San Francisco Chronicle, The*, #91: II, 106-108; #214: III, 473-487

*St. Louis Globe-Democrat*, #56: I, 125-126; II, 52-55

Scanlon, John P., #148: II, 296-298

Schnapper, M. B., #11: I, 69-70

Select Western Lands, Inc., #39: I, 101-102

Senior Citizens, Legislative Council on, of St. Paul, MN, #78: II, 70-72

Sheaffer, Robert, #127: II, 231-235

Shell Oil Company, #169: III, 89-100

Sheridan, Robert, #57: I, 126-132

Shneour, Dr. Elie, #32: I, 94

*Shreveport* (LA) *Times, The*, #120: II, 205-206, 208-211

Shubow, Robert M., #214: III, 473-487

Siefert, Rick, #49: I, 117-118

"60 Minutes" (*see* CBS-TV, "60 Minutes")

Slagle, Edward S., #90: II, 104-106; #93: II, 110-112

Smith, Florence D., #136: II, 264-266

Smith, Mrs. Robert H., #43: I, 105-106

Snow, Howard, #2: I, 58

"Soul" (Corporation for Public Broadcasting), #6: I, 63-66

Spencer, William L., #116: II, 183-189

Standard Oil Company of California, #102: II, 140-141

Stans, Maurice, #162: III, 50-55

Stetler, C. Joseph, #164: III, 65-68

Strategy, Institute for American, #50: I, 119

Strentz, Herbert, #111: II, 167-171

Sudden Infant Death, National Foundation for, #33: I, 94-95; #62: II, 28-31

Sunkist Growers, Inc., #192: III, 305-314

Survival Anglia, Ltd., #118: II, 200-205

Swartz, Elizabeth, #80: II, 76-79; #94: 112-114

Swift, James, #48: I, 116-117

Syntex Corporation, #116: II, 183-189

Syrian Jewry, Committee for Rescue of, #86: II, 88-90

Taylor, Dr. Samuel G., #129: II, 238-241

Teamsters Union, #126: II, 227-231

Teter, Elizabeth, #20: I, 77-78

Thayer, Earl R., #105: II, 146-150

Thayer, Richard N., #13: I, 72

Theater Communications Group, #207: III, 421-424

*Time*, #31: I, 93; #107: II, 153-161; #126: II, 227-231; #144: II, 279-286; #192: III, 305-314; #196: III, 333-346

Traband, Roy, #29: I, 91-92; #74: 60-62

Trillin, Calvin, #182: III, 193-205

United Features Syndicate, #46: I, 111-113; #87: II, 91-98; #101: II, 133-136; #124: II, 220-223

United Press International (UPI), #52: I, 120-121; #53: I, 121-122; #62: II, 28-31; #115: II, 179-183; #116: II, 183-189; #137: II, 266-267; #168: III, 87-89; #176: III, 125-141

*Us* Magazine, #180: III, 156-162

Van Liew, Virginia, #3: I, 59

*Vegetarian Times*, #154: II, 321-325

Veterans Administration, #178: III, 171-181

*Village Voice*, #55: I, 123-125; #189: III, 284-297

VIVA (Voice for Innocent Victims of Abortion), #109: II, 162-164

WABC-TV News (New York City), #98: II, 122-124; #138: II, 267-269

*Wall Street Journal*, #28: I, 90-91; #45: I, 110-111; #197: III, 346-352; #210: III, 439-449

Walters, Barbara, #102: II, 140

*Washington Observer Newsletter*, #52: I, 120-121

*Washington Post*, #51: I, 120; #57: I, 126-132; #75: II, 62-65; #188: III, 244-284; #198: III, 356-368; #213: III, 463-473

*Washington Star-News*, #14: I, 73

Washington Star Syndicate, Inc., #85: II, 85-88

WBBM-TV, Chicago, #129: II, 238-241

WCBS-TV, New York, #153: II, 320-321

WCBS Newsradio, New York, #156: III, 34-36

Wechsler, James A., #189: III, 284-297

"Weekend" (NBC-TV), #47: I, 113-116

WGN (Channel 9, Chicago), #83: II, 83-84

*Winfield* (KS) *Daily Courier*, #195: III, 324-332

"Wire Services" (in general), #52: I, 120-121; #53: I, 121-122

Wischmann, Lesley, #115: II, 179-183

WJLA-TV, Washington, D.C., #136: II, 264-266

WNET (Channel 13), New York, #165: III, 68-73

Wolper Organization, Inc., The, #68: II, 46-48

Wolper, David L., #68: II, 46-48

Wood, John R., #104: II, 143-145

*Woonsocket* (R.I.) *Call, The*, #142: II, 275-277

Wooten, James, #187: III, 235-243

WTVJ-Miami, #202: III, 388-394

Yiamouyiannis, Dr. John, #120: II, 205-206, 208-211; #121: II, 205-206, 211-213
Zeisler, Peter, #207: III, 421-424
Zevenberger, William #41: I, 103-104
Zogby, James J. #193: III, 315-320

| | | DATE DUE | |
|---|---|---|---|
| | | | |
| | | | |
| | | | |
| | | | |
| | | | |
| | | | |
| | | | |
| | | | |
| | | | |
| | | | |
| | | | |